BRITISH FILM INSTITUTE

bfi

FILM AND TELEVISION HANDBOOK 1991

Editor: David Leafe
Deputy Editor: Susan Oates
Consultant Editor: Wayne Drew
Research: Sue George
Additional research/editorial assistance:
Allen Eyles, Simon Faithfull, Lira
Fernandes, Jane Ivey, Mark Mason, Pat
Perilli, Brian Robinson, Linda Wood
Cover: Alec S Hitchins,
designer/illustrator, 081 460 8610
Design: Bobbett Design & Advertising Ltd,
Penshurst, Kent
Production: Landmark Production
Consultants Ltd
Advertisement Managers: Marot & Co

**With a special thanks for their assistance
and advice to BFI staff**

Many thanks also to all those who assisted
with illustrations: Amber, Anglia Films,
Artificial Eye Film Co, Arts Council, BBC
Photographic Library, BBC Picture
Publicity, BBC Scotland, BBC Wales, Black
Audio Film Collective, British Satellite
Broadcasting (BSB), Buena Vista Home
Video, Cannon Cinemas, Castle Target
International, Central Independent
Television, Channel Four Television,
Columbia Tri-Star Films (UK), Complete
Communications Corporation, Rupert
Conant, Contemporary Films, Corbett and
Keene, Marie Curie Memorial Foundation,
DDA, Richard Driscoll, East End Films,
Electric Pictures, Enterprise Pictures,
Entertainment Film Distributors, Allen
Eyles, Film Network, Frontline Public
Relations, Fugitive Features, Gala Film
Distributors, The Grade Co, Granada
Television, Guild, HTV, HandMade Films,
Hobo Film Enterprises, Home Office, House
of Commons, ICA, Jam Jar Films, LWT,
Lambeth Productions, Lorimar Film
Entertainment, Majestic Films
International, Medusa Pictures, Metro
Pictures, National Amusements (UK),
Oasis, Odeon Cinemas, Palace Pictures,
Pas Paschali, Quantel-Link Systems
Group, The Sales Co, Sands Films, Sky
Television, Stone Hallinan McDonald, TVS
Television, Thames Television
(International), Twentieth Century Fox,
Tyne Tees Television, UCI (United
Cinemas International (UK)), Umbrella
Films, United International Pictures,
United Media Film Sales, Vestron UK,
Videographics, Virgin Vision UK, Warner
Bros, Warner Bros Theatres (UK), Warner
Home Video, Winsor Beck Public Relations,
Yorkshire Television, Zenith Productions

The articles in this book are an expression
of the authors' views, and do not necessarily
reflect BFI policy in any given area

All reasonable measures have been taken
to ensure the accuracy of the information in
this handbook, but the publisher cannot
accept any responsibility for any errors or
omissions or any liability resulting from
the use or misuse of any such information

© British Film Institute 1990
21 Stephen Street, London W1P 1PL
Tel: 071 255 1444
Fax: 071 436 7950

Typeset by Florencetype Ltd, Kewstoke,
Avon

Made and printed in Great Britain by
Butler & Tanner Ltd, Frome, Somerset

Colour separation by Fotographics Ltd,
Hong Kong

British Library
Cataloguing in Publication Data
    BFI film and television handbook 1991
    1. Great Britain. Cinema Industries.
    Serials. 2. Great Britain. Television
    Services. Serials. I. British Film
    Institute. 348'.8'0941

ISBN 0 85170 277 5

Price £14.95

CONTENTS

Foreword by Sir Richard Attenborough *4*
About the BFI *5*

REVIEW

Cinema 1989-90 – Production 12
Terry Ilott examines the year in British filmmaking

Cinema 1989-90 – Production Focus 25
John Woodward highlights key events for independent producers

Cinema 1989-90 – Distribution 30
Julian Petley on developments in film distribution

Cinema 1989-90 – Exhibition 36
Allen Eyles reports on the continuing growth of the multiplexes

Cinema 1989-90 – British Films 46
Sheila Johnston reviews British film releases

Television 1989-90 – Background 50
Bob Woffinden on an eventful year in broadcasting

Television 1989-90 – Programmes 60
Alkarim Jivani reviews the TV companies' output as they prepare
for the broadcasting revolution

DIRECTORY

68   Archives and Libraries
70   Awards
80   Bookshops
82   Cable and Satellite
94   Cinemas
110   Courses
126   Distributors (Non-Theatrical)
132   Distributors (Theatrical)
136   Facilities
148   Festivals
156   Film Societies
166   International Sales
173   Laboratories
174   Legislation
178   Organisations

PR Companies   192
Press Contacts   194
Preview Theatres   204
Production Companies   206
Production Starts   224
Publications   238
Releases   248
Specialised Goods and
  Services   268
Studios   270
Television Companies   272
Video Labels   286
Workshops   290
List of Abbreviations   298

300   Index
Index to Advertisers   304

Foreword

By BFI Chairman Sir Richard Attenborough CBE

THE British Film Institute strives to ensure that its accumulated knowledge and expertise is made fully accessible to the public. This 'Film and Television Handbook', which is published annually, fulfils a major element of that commitment.

The introductory section provides a unique reference guide to the year past, combining reviews, analysis and comment with useful statistics and other information.

On a day-to-day basis the BFI is, of course, concerned with all aspects of cinema and television including archiving, production, distribution, exhibition, education,

publishing, information provision and funding. The complete range of these activities is reflected in the Handbook's comprehensive and up-to-date directory which contains thousands of invaluable contacts, facts and addresses covering every sector of the relevant industries.

For anyone working in film or television these listings should prove absolutely invaluable. I feel sure that all those who simply enjoy, and want to find out more about, the moving image will also find within this Handbook reading matter that is both fascinating and illuminating.

Photo: Terry O'Neill

About the BFI

By BFI Director Wilf Stevenson

THIS Handbook is published by the British Film Institute whose task is to promote the 20th century's major new art form, the moving image. In response to questions about how we do this, I sometimes answer that our primary product is influence. Certainly we are responsible for more tangible activities. However, these all contribute to our main purpose, to exert a powerful influence over the development, study and appreciation of the culture of the moving image, be it film or television.

We are in the forefront of discussions about the new broadcasting environment; we are actively campaigning to establish a national television archive to preserve this long-neglected part of our heritage; our innovative programmes at the National Film Theatre and the Regional Film Theatres continue to discover new aspects of moving image culture; our publications aim to keep enthusiasts abreast of the latest developments in film scholarship, while our education programmes bring to a wider public the delights and challenges of a study of the moving image. Crowning a series of successful initiatives in recent years, we have in the Museum of the Moving Image an institution combining education and entertainment which has already been visited by more than a million people.

So our role is to influence as many people as possible, to encourage the development of the culture and to foster a wider and deeper appreciation and awareness of it. We do this at a national level and with many partners at a regional level. We do it through discussion and debate as well as through the films, books, and other products which we create. Every division participates in achieving this overall goal, as described on the pages which follow.

Below: BFI headquarters at Stephen Street

BFI South Bank

Museum of the Moving Image (MOMI)

THE Museum of the Moving Image explores the unique and magical history of cinema and television, beginning in 2,000 BC with the Javanese shadow puppets which were among the earliest experiments with light, shadow and movement. Moving on through a range of early Victorian pre-cinema toys, visitors reach the Temple of the Gods which transports them through the silent era and beyond, the golden age of Hollywood, the birth of television, international cinema and the more recent story of satellite and cable TV. MOMI's award-winning design and exciting interactive exhibits embody its aims to entertain and inform. Amongst others, awards have come from the British Tourist Authority, the Museums Association and BAFTA.

National Film Theatre

The National Film Theatre aims to bring audiences the widest possible range of film and television from all over the world, screened in the best possible conditions and supported by background notes, lectures and other activities designed to stimulate debate and inform as well as entertain. More than 2,000 films and television programmes are screened annually at the NFT, arranged in seasons centred round a particular director, star, period, genre, idea or issue. A series of live interviews and debates has been sponsored by 'The Guardian' newspaper since 1981. The NFT is also home to the London Film Festival which presents the best of new world cinema and has built up a considerable reputation for introducing directors previously unknown to British audiences.

The Museum of the Moving Image

BFI STILLS, POSTERS AND DESIGNS

THE BFI's unique collection of illustrations and photographs from cinema and television is developed, preserved and made accessible by BFI Stills, Posters, and Designs. Images from more than 60,000 films and television programmes are held in the collection on some 5 million black and white prints and 500,000 colour transparencies. A fascinating visual account of the development of world cinema and television, these capture the action both on-screen and off. A further 20,000 files contain portraits of film and television personalities and the collection also holds around 15,000 posters and 2,000 set and costume designs including the original work of production designers and art directors.

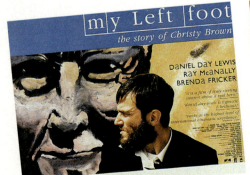

Publicity posters from the BFI's unique Stills, Posters and Designs collection

BFI LIBRARY AND INFORMATION SERVICES

THE world's largest collection of information on film and television is held by BFI Library and Information Services which holds both published and unpublished material including books, periodicals, newspaper cuttings, press releases, scripts and theses, as well as special collections of private papers from major figures such as Carol Reed, Michael Balcon and Joseph Losey. BFI Library and Information Services has moved into the computer age with the arrival of the Summary of Information on Film and Television (SIFT), an on-line database which makes sophisticated information searches possible on more than 400,000 films, television programmes and videos, 280,000 personalities, 115,000 organisations and 5,000 events. Each year, information on a further 11,000 titles is added.

BFI Distribution

BFI Distribution aims to increase the availability of film, television and video by distributing copies of historic, innovative and newly discovered material for screening and study. The Division also provides programming advice and publicity services to a wide variety of clients, including the BFI-supported network of Regional Film Theatres. Originally concerned with supplying 16mm prints of 'classics' to mainly education and film society users, and with nurturing the early Regional Film Theatre movement, the Division has expanded to become a major holder of rights and prints on an international scale. The staff of the Film Society Unit, a part of BFI Distribution, service some three hundred film societies throughout the UK which belong to the British Federation of Film Societies. The FSU gives practical advice on starting, developing and running film societies and offers a range of other services and events.

National Film Archive

THE National Film Archive was founded in 1935 "to maintain a national repository of films of permanent value". Its moving image collection now comprises 150,000 titles dating from 1895 to the present day, covering features and shorts, documentaries, newsreels, television programmes, amateur films and videos, on a comprehensive range of gauges and formats. The NFA began, in the mid-fifties, to acquire television, the recording and preservation of which is now a major part of the Archive's work, aided by substantial annual grants from ITV and Channel 4. Business and private sponsors also contribute to the nitrate film preservation and restoration programmes. There is as yet no law of statutory deposit for film and video production in the UK (as there is for books, for example) and acquisition is mostly by donation.

The J Paul Getty Jnr Conservation Centre, opened in June 1987 at Berkhamsted, Herts, and named after its generous sponsor, is the Archive's storage site for safety film and video, and the location for all preservation and restoration work. Approximately 140 million feet of flammable nitrate film is kept at a specially equipped site a further 50 miles away in Warwickshire; this material, which shrinks and decomposes with age, is systematically copied on to modern safety film as part of the preservation process.

The Cataloguing section, based in London, provides information, in the form of indexing, descriptive cataloguing and subject analysis on titles held in the collection, and answers personal, telephone and postal enquiries. The Viewing Service organises viewings on the premises for bona fide researchers and arranges loans of material to the National Film Theatre and the BFI-supported network of cinemas and educational venues. It also promotes retrospectives of British cinema at home and abroad. Donor Access handles enquiries specifically from donors and copyright owners, while the Production Library supplies film-makers and TV producers with extracts for use in compilation films and documentary programmes.

Singin' in the Rain: part of the NFA's 360 classic feature film project

Planning

ALTHOUGH based in London, the BFI is very much a regional body and the Planning Unit co-ordinates the regional policies within which other departments carry out their work. The Planning Unit is also responsible for enhancing the BFI's input and influence in development of the regional exhibition and production infrastructure and for helping implement the Institute's Corporate Plan through the co-ordination of pan-Institute activity, for example cultural issues relating to equal opportunities, Europe, etc. The Planning Unit also co-ordinates the Institute's involvement in the increasingly important area of training. For example, the Training Co-ordinator provides short training courses for Regional Film Theatre staff, produces a guide to short production courses, and represents the BFI on a number of national training initiatives, including the Independent Media Training Federation.

Research

Communications Group

The Communications Group co-ordinates various projects which further the BFI's cultural objectives in film and television. It includes the TV and Projects Unit whose work has recently included the massive 'One Day in the Life of Television' project which pooled the experiences, via more

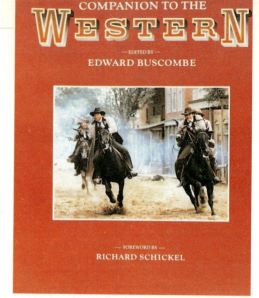

than 18,000 diaries, of both viewers and those working in the television industry on 1 November 1988. This culminated in the screening of a network ITV documentary in 1989 and the publication of a book, containing 800 of the diaries, edited by Sean Day-Lewis. The Unit's Race and Ethnicity project is an important research initiative, exploring the history of black people in British television since 1936. The TV and Projects Unit also organises other events such as the Script-to-Screen events at the NFT which bring together audiences and television professionals to discuss programmes, and debates on issues such as the future of broadcasting. In many cases, the work of the TV and Projects Unit is supported by books and documentation produced by the publishing arm of the Communications Group.

BFI Education

BFI Education aims to develop knowledge and ideas about the media – film, television and video in particular. By working with people in formal education, from primary to university level, in the community at large, and in many other institutions, the Department tries to ensure that such knowledge and ideas are spread as widely as possible. Its work includes research, teaching, materials production and lobbying, and in all these areas it aims to set agendas and provoke debate. BFI Education strives to enable as many people as possible to discover new ways of thinking about, producing and enjoying these media.

BFI Publishing Services

BFI Publishing Services produces a range

Early cinema techniques featured at MOMI

of books on film and television on behalf of the various departments within the Research Division, for a readership which ranges from scholars and teachers through to the film and broadcasting communities and the general public at large. Its aims are to assist the spread of new ideas and knowledge, to raise the level of public awareness of film and television, and to provide a platform for debate on issues of public concern.

BFI Periodicals

BFI Periodicals produces the 'Monthly Film Bulletin' and the quarterly 'Sight and Sound'. The 'Monthly Film Bulletin' covers all new feature films released in the UK, while 'Sight and Sound' aims to stimulate public interest in films and television and to comment, chronicle, and speculate on their past, present and future.

BFI Production

BFI Production produces a range of projects from short films and videos to feature-length films, acting as producer and co-investor. Focusing on work which is innovative both in theme and style, it aims to encourage challenging and different approaches to cinema in Britain and to foster a film culture which represents the lives and concerns of those people generally under-represented on both sides of the camera. As well as producing, it also funds some independent film and videomakers on a grant basis. Channel 4 has supported the Production Board since 1985 with an annual subvention (currently £450,000) and the Board is also supported by the

Award-winning BFI production **Silent Scream** *(1990)*

Independent Television Association (£50,000). In a given year, BFI Production would also hope to raise extra funding in the form of co-finance and pre-sales tied to individual projects. BFI Production undertakes its own distribution and sales, and its releases over the last few years include *Distant Voices Still Lives*, *Play Me Something*, *Fellow Traveller* and *Silent Scream*.

Contacts at the BFI

British Film Institute
21 Stephen Street
London W1P 1PL
Tel: 071 255 1444
Telex: 27624 BFILDNG
General fax: 071 436 7950
Fax for BFI Stills, Posters and Designs:
071 323 9260
Director: Wilf Stevenson
Assistant Director: Michael Prescott

Corporate Press Contacts

Head of Press and Promotions: Wayne Drew
Press Officer: Brian Robinson

Planning Division

Head: Barrie Ellis-Jones
Deputy Head: Irene Whitehead

National Film Archive

(At Stephen Street)
Curator: Clyde Jeavons
Deputy Curator: Anne Fleming
(At the J Paul Getty Jnr Conservation Centre, Kings Hill Way, Berkhamsted, Hertfordshire HP4 3TP. Tel: 04428 76301 Fax: 04428 75607)
Head of Conservation: Rex Belgrove

BFI Distribution Division

Head of Distribution: Ian Christie
Deputy Head and Head of Programming Service: Jayne Pilling
Head of Acquisitions and Contracts: Barry Edson
Head of Sales and Marketing: Nigel Algar
Head of Film Society Unit: Tom Brownlie
Film Society Unit Information Officer: Peter Cargin

BFI Stills, Posters and Designs

Head: Bridget Kinally

BFI Library and Information Services

Head: Gillian Hartnoll

BFI Research Division

Head of Research: Colin MacCabe
Senior Research Fellow: Geoffrey
Nowell-Smith
Head of Education: Manuel Alvarado
Head of Publishing Services:
Caroline Moore
(Sales enquiries 29 Rathbone Street,
London W1P 1AG Tel: 071 636 3289)
Head of Communications Group: Richard
Paterson
Head of Trade Publishing: Ed Buscombe
Head of TV and Projects Unit: Tana Wollen

BFI Production

29 Rathbone Street
London W1P 1AG
Tel: 071 636 5587/4736
Fax: 071 580 9456
Head: Ben Gibson
Deputy Head: Angela Topping
Sales: Sue Bruce-Smith
Press and Publicity: Liz Reddish

BFI South Bank

National Film Theatre and Museum of the
Moving Image
South Bank London SE1 8XT
Tel: 071 928 3535
Fax: 071 633 9323
Telex: 929229 NATFIL G
Controller: Leslie Hardcastle
Deputy Controller: Paul Collard
Head of Programming: Deac Rossell
London Film Festival Director:
Sheila Whitaker
Head of Marketing: Helen MacKintosh
Press Officer: Susan Santini

Facilities for people with disabilities:
The British Film Institute is working to improve
access to its buildings for visitors with disabilities. Facilities include:

21 Stephen Street: unisex toilet on ground floor,
car parking at rear of building (please contact
security staff beforehand to check availability,
and on arrival to gain access via ramp into rear
ground floor corridor). There is no access for
wheelchairs to the nitrate viewing area on the
roof. Otherwise access to all floors is possible
using lifts. Lifts are located in the main reception

area and in the rear of the ground floor corridor.
There are no steps into the main reception area
from the street. Assistance may be necessary for
unaccompanied wheelchair users since there are
several heavy fire doors.

Museum of the Moving Image: reduced
admission charge, and group rate, for registered
disabled people. Unaccompanied wheelchair
users are welcome. There are several heavy fire
doors in MOMI which may be difficult to use but
there is always assistance available.

There are three parking spaces for people with
disabilities on the Royal Festival Hall access
road and two on the access road leading to
MOMI. Visitors may also use Euro car parks at
the Hayward Gallery and National Theatre.
There is a ramp from the Hayward Gallery car
park to MOMI.

There are no steps into the main foyer of the
building where a central telephone call point can
be used to gain help with buying tickets and
entry to MOMI.

Most areas of the museum are accessible to
wheelchair users although in a slightly different
order from the usual route. Two scissor lifts and
one stair lift operate between the ground and
first floor and there is one stair lift between the
first and second floor. There are help points
placed at each of these lifts to enable visitors
with disabilities to call for assistance.

MOMI's cinema, the Image Workshop, has
three wheelchair positions at the front of the
auditorium and an induction loop system for
those wearing hearing aids incorporating a
T switch. There are disabled toilet facilities in
the toilets in the first exhibition area.

National Film Theatre: NFT1 has 6 wheelchair
positions at the rear of the auditorium which
must be booked in advance. A disabled person
may occupy seat N1 in NFT2 if accompanied by
an able-bodied person who will occupy the adjacent seat. A wheelchair may only be used when
the general lighting is on and it must be stored
out of the way at the rear of NFT2. There is a
unisex disabled toilet situated at the far end of
the corridor to the right of the restaurant
entrance, near NFT1, and in the black and white
passageway off the main NFT/MOMI foyer.
NFT1 and NFT2 both have an induction loop
system for those with hearing aids incorporating
a T switch, and also certain seats with a special
earphone facility. Please ask for this service
when booking.

29 Rathbone Street: lift access to the first floor
offices and ramp access to the technical facilities.
Three parking spaces, please contact reception
(071 636 5587) before arrival to check availability.

National Film Archive, Berkhamsted: ramps
into J Paul Getty Jnr Conservation Centre,
electronically operated doors, unisex disabled
toilet, lift access to all areas.

1991 – AND BEYOND

TOTAL RECALL · THE DOORS

DANCES WITH WOLVES

AIR AMERICA · TEXASVILLE

GALE FORCE · TERMINATOR II

NARROW MARGIN

AWOL · DEAD RECKONING

EVE OF DESTRUCTION

HAMLET · JACOB'S LADDER

A RIVER RUNS THROUGH IT

REPOSSESSED · THE LA STORY

UNIVERSAL SOLDIER

THE TAKING OF BEVERLEY HILLS

GUILD

GUILD FILM DISTRIBUTION LIMITED
KENT HOUSE, 14/17 MARKET PLACE, GT. TITCHFIELD STREET, LONDON W1N 8AR
TEL: 071-323 5151 TELEX: 924390 FAX: 071-631 3568

Cinema 1989-90 – Production

1989-90 was a dismal year for UK film production. However, says Terry Ilott, the news was not all bad

THE year witnessed the lowest level of theatrical feature film production in the UK since 1981. However, this downturn in production coincided with a period of unprecedented change in the screen entertainment industries which presented a number of reasons for optimism in the long term.

For example, as cinema admissions rose (see page 37) and the broadcasting revolution got underway, the signs were that the demand for feature films – in the cinemas, on satellite and cable television, free television and video – would continue to increase. While a large part of this increased demand will be met by Hollywood-produced movies, there is every reason to believe that the rest will be made up of an eclectic selection of films from many sources, including the British film production sector.

The approach of 1992 and the single European Community market made the UK increasingly attractive to Japan and the USA as a way into Europe, both as a market for their products (hardware in the case of the Japanese and software in the case of the Americans) and as a source of talent to generate more product.

Despite the imminent franchise auction, the existing TV broadcasters continued to invest in UK theatrical films. Anxious to protect their investments, they increasingly took the front seat in creative decision-making.

And the British film industry continued to survive. Not because it makes any kind of economic sense but because people still wanted to make films and found all manner of ingenious financial arrangements to allow them to do so.

British filmmakers are nevertheless anxious. Their fear is not that the opportunities are lacking but that the British film industry is ill-prepared to take advantage of them. Before the British film industry can prosper, it must first achieve a critical mass from which can emerge companies of such size that they will be able to make mistakes without placing their own existence in jeopardy. Such a critical mass could be achieved, possibly as an adjunct to some kind of pan-European private television network, but there was no sign of it during the year.

The year started on an optimistic note, following a significant increase in feature film production in the first quarter of 1989 compared to the same period in 1988. Between January and March 1989, ten feature films had been shot by British companies or crews, at a total cost of

Nuns on the Run

£55 million. As the first quarter is usually the quietest period for film production, one could look forward to a significant improvement in the overall level of production for the year. This expectation seemed all the more justified in that in the whole of 1988 only £198 million had been invested in 56 features – not a difficult target to beat.

During April, a comedy starring Richard E Grant, Julie Walters and Denholm Elliott, *Killing Dad*, and a new Peter Greenaway picture, *The Cook, The Thief, His Wife and Her Lover*, finished principal photography. In the USA, the Karel Reisz/Jeremy Thomas picture *Everybody Wins* was still shooting while, in the UK, *Black-eyes*, *Nuns on the Run*, *Nightbreed* and *Wilt* started production. This assortment of titles demonstrated two of the leading characteristics of UK film production: its varied output in terms of scale, subject-matter and style, and its equally varied financial arrangements embracing, in the case of these films in particular, Japanese and Dutch equity investment, pre-sales to foreign theatrical and video distributors, television deals, and pick-ups by major distributors in the USA.

Perhaps the most significant new players in film finance were British Satellite Broadcasting, which had recently announced its decision to invest in film production, and the drama department of the BBC which, under the leadership of former film producer Mark Shivas, had undertaken to invest up to £3 million in six theatrical feature films a year. These new sources, along with the continued commitment to production on the part of Channel 4 and a handful of ITV companies, underlined a third characteristic of British film production, especially at the lower end of the budget scale: its dependence on money from television.

Meanwhile, the mainstay of low-budget British filmmaking was fighting for survival. British Screen, the government aided film financier, had only one more instalment of its annual £1.5 million government grant to come and it faced the prospect of its private shareholders – Rank, Cannon, Channel 4, and Granada – asking, as they were entitled to, for their original investments back. Should the government grant not be extended and should the private investors recall their funds, British Screen would almost certainly have had to close down. The company had no hope of standing on its own feet and there was no new source of funding in sight. In May, British Screen's Chief Executive Simon Relph launched a vigorous campaign to get the Government to extend its support for a further five years, to 1995. At the same time, he set about looking for new investors.

Relph's arguments were not helped by the fact that no British film was selected for the official competition at the May 1989 Cannes Film Festival which in recent years has become an important showcase for new British films. Cannes' recognition of British films was limited to the selection of the BFI

Play Me Something, a BFI production

productions *Venus Peter* and *Melancholia* for the Un Certain Regard section and the Director's Fortnight respectively, and Palace Pictures' *Scandal* as a non-competitive film within the official selection. There were, however, 38 new British feature films, ranging from the $14 million (approximately £8 million) *The Return of the Musketeers* to BFI Production's ultra low-budget (£0.3 million) *Play Me Something*, screening in the Cannes market. Nearly a third of these films had been supported by British Screen. Relph could also point to British Screen's involvement in three new pictures, *1871*, *December Bride* and *The Bearskin*, which were due to start shooting that month.

AVERAGE FEATURE FILM PRODUCTION COSTS, INCLUDING CO-PRODUCTIONS (£ million)

	1984	1985	1986	1987	1988	1989
UK	4.2	4.7	4.1	3.6	2.8	4.4
France	1.0	1.3	1.3	1.4	1.8	—
Italy	0.6	0.7	0.9	1.0	1.3	1.2
US	9.3	10.8	11.2	12.9	11.7	—

Compiled by BFI Library and Information Services from the following sources: 1 'Screen International''s annual production review (includes some American-financed films shot in Britain) 2 CNC (Centre Nationale de Cinématographie) Paris 3 'Cinema d'Oggi' 4 'International Motion Picture Almanac'
Note: the average budgets for solely UK-financed films were £2.12m in 1989 (£2.07 million in 1988)

Almost as hard-pressed as Relph was Charles Denton, Chief Executive of Zenith Productions, formerly the industry's favourite company and heir apparent to Goldcrest. Zenith, which started life as a subsidiary of Central Television, had had little luck in the film production arena, and had found itself thwarted in its attempts to move into the higher-budget bracket where it could compete with the output of the major studios. Nevertheless, in May, Denton announced that Zenith was to get back into feature production with three new films, *Exile, After You've Gone* and *The Sparrow*.

"There is a conviction," Denton observed at the time, "that the brief but quite sparky era of British cinema – which might have begun with *My Beautiful Laundrette* and ran through films like *Wish You Were Here* and *Personal Services* – has perhaps come to a close." His note of pessimism was to have an unlooked for resonance; none of the three Zenith films was to come to fruition.

On 4 May 1989, MEDIA 92, the pan-European initiative for the promotion of European film and television, unveiled seven projects, providing assistance in film production, distribution, dubbing, subtitling and script-writing, to representatives of the British industry at the National Film Theatre. Scepticism about the bureaucratic nature of such interventions quickly gave way to enthusiasm when MEDIA 92 revealed that 500,000 ECUs (approximately £350,000) had already been spent by the European SCRIPT Fund on 30 projects from nine countries. British writers and producers figured prominently in the lists.

Nightbreed

For all the talk about Europe, however, the British film industry continued to look first to America. In June, one of the UK's most energetic production companies, Working Title, signed a theatrical output deal with New Line Cinema which was to distribute all Working Title's films in the USA. This arrangement gave Working Title longed for stability in the all important US market. A few weeks later, Working Title unveiled Manifesto Film Sales, a joint centre with LA-based Propaganda Films. Manifesto would give Working Title direct access to foreign distributors. Before the year was out, Working Title unveiled a third distribution link, this time with International Video Enterprises, which was to handle the US home video release of Working Title pictures. Other British production companies, including Palace, Zenith and HandMade, began looking for similar ongoing relationships in the USA to give them security in the longer term.

Coincidentally, at about the time of the New Line announcement, Working Title's *For Queen and Country*, starring Denzel Washington, opened weakly in the US, taking $62,000 from 33 screens for an opening weekend-per-screen average of $1,902. A much better performance was achieved by Palace Pictures' *Scandal*, distributed in the USA by Miramax, which was to take more than $8 million, making it Palace's most successful US release to date.

Fools of Fortune

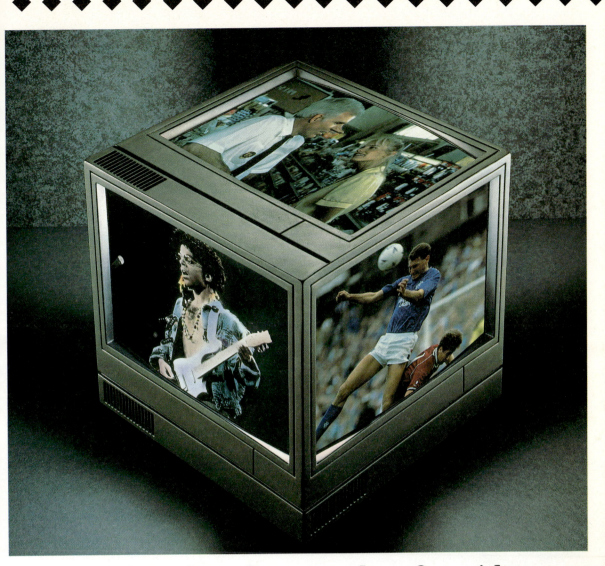

Now the box has another five sides.

Just what we need, we hear you say, even more television.

And we'd agree, except that British Satellite Broadcasting isn't offering more of the same.

BSB has five themed channels.

The Movie Channel screens full-length feature films at 6.00, 8.00, 10.00 and 12.00 every night.

On our Sports Channel at around 8.00 every evening, often live, you'll see tennis, FA Cup and Scottish football, golf, rugby league or boxing.

Now – The Channel for Living – offers practical advice on everything from food to fashion, travel to health care, as well as a healthy dose of music and arts programmes at the weekend.

Music of a different (and louder) kind forms the basis of The Power Station, our youth channel.

While Galaxy Channel has soaps, drama, game shows and classic British comedy.

All you need to receive BSB is a compact dish or Squarial™ and a receiver box.

Tens of thousands of you answered our request to tell us what you'd like to see on TV, and we're now trying to reflect your views in the types of programmes you'll find on BSB.

Suffice it to say, already BSB's reception has been excellent.

If you would like the opportunity to give your views or you simply want more information, telephone free on **0800 800 200**.

5 CHANNEL TV

The Reflecting Skin

Another US independent with strong British links, Atlantic Releasing, collapsed in June, thereby throwing a host of British pictures, among them David Hare's *Strapless*, into a limbo of litigation. Atlantic's demise was the latest in a series of collapses in the US independent distribution sector. It was quickly followed by a decision by Island Pictures – also an important distributor of British films – to withdraw from distribution altogether. Prices paid for

Memphis Belle

British films by the handful of distributors still active in the US market-place fell dramatically. According to British Screen's Simon Relph, where an average UK-produced picture might have secured as much as 60% of its budget from a US distributor two or three years ago, it might now only achieve 15-20% if it sold at all.

By July, it was apparent that the hoped-for recovery in film production had failed to materialise. In the first six months of 1989, 22 British theatrical films had been shot at a cost of £92 million. This compared with 27 features, worth £88 million, in the same period in 1988. Of the 22 productions, five had been shot at Pinewood, three at Shepperton and two each at Elstree and Twickenham. At the height of the summer, traditionally the busiest time for film production, there were several weeks during which there was no feature film shooting in any of the major British studios. They got by on a diet of television drama and commercials.

The British Screen Advisory Council warned that independent television companies were preparing to cut back their spending on production in anticipation of the Government's Broadcasting Bill, which was expected to put the independent television franchises up for auction to the highest bidders. One consequence of this, said the BSAC, was that the ITV companies – specifically Anglia, Central, Euston, Granada, HTV, Scottish Television and LWT – would withdraw from feature film finance. The BSAC report sent a shiver down the spine of British film producers – 11 of the 22 films made in the first half of 1989 relied on funding from ITV companies.

Memphis Belle, David Puttnam's first film since his return to the UK from Columbia Pictures, started shooting on 17 July 1989. In the same week, the Cable Authority reported that the cable industry was at last beginning to find its feet, thus holding out the promise of a new source of film production funds. Another new source came in the form of video distributor Parkfield Entertainment, which put up the bulk of the money for *The Krays*, a first feature from Fugitive Films that was to start production in August.

On 25 July, the First Film Foundation was set up. The Foundation's aim is to "create opportunities in film and television for new talented filmmakers, writers and technicians". Patrons of the Foundation are

Chicago Joe and the Showgirl

Tyne Tees Television, Ffilm Cymru and European Film and Television Year. First-year funding for the Foundation came from the Department of Trade and Industry, Channel 4 and the Rank Organisation. Under the chairmanship of producer Tim Burrill and with a board that includes Karin Bamborough (Channel 4), film producer Tim Bevan (Working Title), independent television producer Steve Walsh, and Sir John Read, the Foundation has invested in new work by filmmakers in the UK, France, Italy and the Soviet Union.

Rounding off the good news in July was the announcement, on 29 July, that the Government had agreed to extend its funding of British Screen, albeit for three years rather than the five years Simon Relph had asked for. Relph also secured undertakings from his private shareholders that, while they might not put new money in, they would not press for the repayment of their original investments.

Little noticed at the beginning of August was the opening of *My Left Foot*, which did respectable business at the Curzon Mayfair and at art-houses round the country but which failed to cross over to mainstream cinemas. The film was later to provide Irish/British film production with its biggest boost of the year.

Paper Mask, *The Reflecting Skin*, *The Sheltering Sky*, *The Krays*, *Fools of Fortune* and *Chicago Joe and the Showgirl* started production. Again, the list reflected the eclectic nature of British film production. *Paper Mask* teamed a television company, Granada, with an experienced filmmaker Christopher Morahan. *The Reflecting Skin*, the debut of 28-year-old Philip Ridley, was part-funded by the BBC. Ridley also wrote *The Krays*. *Fools of Fortune* and *Chicago Joe and the Showgirl* both came from Working Title, which was now backed by record giant PolyGram while *The Sheltering Sky* came from the same team – producer Jeremy Thomas and director Bernardo Bertolucci – that made the Oscar-winning *The Last Emperor*.

In the same month, BSB signed an agreement with Equity, the actors union, whereby a straight 12½% residual payment would be paid to artists appearing in programmes that had already been shown on BBC and which were now to be shown on BSB. This agreement opened the door to the development of a secondary television market which many independent producers

Only one place in Britain can boast 16mm, 35mm, 70mm and Imax film facilities. Piccadilly? Leicester Square? No, Bradford. For further details

see as an important step towards recouping a larger proportion of production costs from the UK.

Overshadowing everything in August, however, was Sony's purchase of Columbia Pictures. It was a reminder, if one was needed, that the levers of power in the film industry are accessible only to those with real financial muscle. Increasingly, such muscle is to be found in Japan. Japanese investors underpin the output of the UK's two most senior producers, David Puttnam (Fujisankei) and Jeremy Thomas (Shochiku-Fuji).

By October, the UK film production scene looked dismal. Only 30 theatrical features, costing £127 million, had gone into production in the first nine months of the year, compared to 46, costing £155 million, in the first nine months of 1988. Of the 30 film starts, 18 had been the beneficiaries of investment by ITV companies. British Screen had invested in six productions while the BBC, BFI and BSB had invested in two each. Seven of the productions had been shot at Pinewood, five at Shepperton, and three each at Elstree and Twickenham.

Henry V, Shirley Valentine and *The Cook, The Thief, His Wife and Her Lover* opened well in London. *The Big Man* (Palace) and *The Field* (Granada) started production.

In November, Paramount grabbed the headlines by buying a 49% stake in Zenith. The return of the US studio to UK production was widely welcomed, though there were those who preferred to reserve judgement on the deal until something concrete had come of it. Paramount made no secret of the fact that its motive in buying into Zenith was to circumvent EC quota restrictions and to position itself to take best advantage of the single European market in 1992. Zenith chief

Shirley Valentine

Charles Denton disappointed many by saying that the deal was all about television production and would have "no effect" on the company's stalled feature film plans. Once the hullabaloo had settled down, Zenith's Director of Production Margaret Matheson quietly resigned from the company, leaving the way for Zenith's Head of Creative Affairs Scott Meek to take over. The ebullient Meek said that his tastes might well be "more vulgar" than Matheson's and that Zenith's output could take a more commercial turn.

Hard on the heels of the Paramount deal was the announcement that Francesca Barra, formerly Head of International Acquisitions for CBS/Fox Video, was to become London-based Vice-President of International Production for Twentieth Century Fox. Barra's mission was to bring new international talent to the attention of Fox production chief Joe Roth. This development, which promised to give British filmmakers direct access to Fox's production funds, was also widely welcomed in the British film community.

Shortly before Christmas, the Broadcasting Bill was published (see pp52 ff) and provoked immediate controversy. It

Top: Charles Denton
Above: Scott Meek
Right: Francesca Barra

Tees, and HTV each invested in one completed feature film. 47% of the films made were in the low-budget category (up to £2 million), 37% in the medium-budget category (up to £5 million) and 16% in the high-budget category (over £5 million). The average budget for those films financed solely from UK sources was £2.12 million while for those which had secured investment from elsewhere the average budget was £9.2 million. The number of films made in 1989 was the lowest for a decade.

The new year started on a high note, with Paramount installing Ileen Maisel to do the same job for them as Barra was to do for Fox. CBS bought 15% of Renaissance Films, the company that made *Henry V*. And, in February 1990, the Association of Independent Producers and the British Film and Television Producers Association joined forces to form the Producers Association.

But a report from the Institute of Manpower Studies warned that the film industry faced a crippling skills shortage. The report said that there should be agreed standards laid down for each job and grade, that freelancers should have access to training and that a supervisory body should be set up to monitor skill standards and training throughout the industry. The report was received with an ominous silence.

In March, the finishing touches were put to the British Film Partnership, a bold plan to cut the costs of small British films to the

appeared to make money the sole criterion for the ownership of an independent television franchise in the UK. Since there was to be no bar on foreign ownership, this conjured up the spectacle of Britain's airwaves being controlled by Japanese, Australian, American, Italian or Arab investors. The relevant paragraphs in the Bill were soon to be amended to include a 'quality' threshold and the existing ITV companies – and, one suspects, most of the film community – breathed a sigh of relief.

Henry V and *My Left Foot* opened in the USA. Both received rave reviews and were immediately tipped for major awards.

The production tally at the end of 1989 showed a significant decline on the previous year: 38 feature films were completed (at a cost of £165 million) compared with 56 films (at a cost of £198 million) in 1988. Of the 38 films, 26 were financed solely from UK sources. Investment by television companies fell slightly – 19 theatrical features were television-backed in 1989 as opposed to 20 in 1988. American companies were notable mainly by their absence, investing in only nine films. European investors put money into four films, Channel 4 invested in eight, British Screen in seven and Central, the BBC, the BFI, Granada, and Radio Telefis Eirann in two each. LWT, Tyne

NUMBER OF FEATURE FILMS PRODUCED (INCLUDING CO-PRODUCTIONS)

	1984	1985	1986	1987	1988	1989
UK	53	55	39	51	56	38
France	161	151	134	133	137	—
West Germany	75	64	60	65	57	—
Italy	103	89	114	116	124	117
Japan	333	319	311	286	265	255
Spain	75	76	60	69	63	47

Compiled by BFI Library and Information Services from the following sources: 1 'Screen International''s annual production review (includes some American-financed films shot in Britain) 2 CNC (Centre Nationale de Cinématographie) Paris 3 'Filmstatistisches Taschenbuch', published by Spitzenorganisation der Filmwirtschaft EV, Wiesbaden 4 'Cinema d'Oggi' 5 'Japanese Film', published by UniJapan, Tokyo 6 'Cineinforme' 7 'International Motion Picture Almanac'

Henry V, *Academy Award winner*

point where their entire budgets could be covered from the UK alone. The plan calls for technicians to work for basic rates of pay and with a flexible attitude towards job demarcation. This combination allows the producer to schedule the film over standard eight-hour days and five-day weeks with no need to budget for overtime payments. At the same time, suppliers and facilities houses which agree to join the scheme will offer their services at special rates.

By these means, it is hoped that the direct costs of making a film can be cut by as much as 30%. The UK end-users, theatrical and video distributors as well as free- and pay- television broadcasters, will be expected to put up more than the normal level of advances to ensure that the entire (though much-reduced) cost of the film is covered from the UK market. All income that is earned over and above the level of those advances will be divided between cast, crew, facilities houses, financiers and end-users according to an agreed formula. In effect, the scheme makes everyone involved in the film an 'investor'. The British

Film Partnership scheme got off the ground with *Dakota Road*, a Working Title production that started shooting in April under the direction of Nick Ward. If the experiment proves to be a success, it could open the doors to a much higher level of production of low-budget pictures in the UK.

A further boost came at the end of March when the British production *Henry V* and the British-financed, Irish-produced *My Left Foot* both won Academy Awards. These accolades were small comfort however when 'Screen International's' production figures for the first quarter of 1990 revealed a further drop in feature film activity. Only eight theatrical features were shot by UK companies or crews during this period, on estimated budgets of £27.8 million – a drop of 55% in investment from the first quarter of 1989.

TOTAL INVESTMENT IN NATIONAL PRODUCT, INCLUDING CO-PRODUCTIONS (£ million)

	1984	1985	1986	1987	1988	1989
UK	220	259.5	160.01	182.09	155.34	165.58
France	187.9	194.0	171.4	181.2	243.0	—
Italy	57.0	65.7	100.3	117.7	159.9	143.9

Source: BFI Library and Information Services

Terry Ilott is Co-Editor of the 'Financial Times' newsletter, 'Screen Finance', and Co-Author of 'My Indecision is Final: the Rise and Fall of Goldcrest Films'
For an updated list of UK production companies, see under the Production Companies section of the Directory. Films which went into production during the year are listed in the Production Starts section. For feature films released during the period, see under Releases

The Sheltering Sky, *from the team which made* **The Last Emperor**

23

Cinema 1989-90 – Production Focus

John Woodward examines a "watershed" year for independent film and television producers

IT is a matter of fact that the triple blow brought about by the abolition of the Eady Levy in 1985, the abolition of capital allowances for British films in 1986 and the adjustments made to the ITV Exchequer Levy in 1989 have effectively brought the UK film and TV production industry to its knees.

The USA remains the only country with a large enough population audience to recover production costs in its domestic market. UK producers must currently find, on average, 70% production finance from outside the UK. However, unlike the majority of European countries, there is no financial assistance or incentive available to make film investment in the UK attractive.

Therefore it is perhaps unsurprising that, as outlined on pp12–13, UK feature film production fell to its lowest level for a decade during 1989, a fall which continued during the first quarter of 1990.

However, 1989-90 was also a watershed year for independent producers. Amongst various other positive developments outlined below, there were signs, towards the end of the year reviewed by this Handbook, that the Government is attaching increasing importance to the UK film and television industry. For the first time, politicians are recognising that Britain occupies a key position at the crossroads between Europe and the USA. As an English speaking country with access to a potential US market of 245 million and a European market of 325 million people, the opportunity exists for Britain to become a major film and television production base.

(This was to result in June 1990, in a half day seminar at Downing Street, chaired by the Prime Minister, at which a group of senior representatives of the British film industry examined the current state of feature film production. One outcome of the

Independent production: Chatsworth Television's Beyond the Groove (for Channel 4)

meeting was the setting up of two industry working parties to examine potential structural, fiscal and tax incentives to encourage both investment in UK features and UK based features production. The working parties will have reported back to Government by the beginning of 1991.)

There were other reasons for optimism during the year. The major Hollywood studios' renewed interest in Britain continues. As UK box office receipts look set to hit the £100 million mark in 1991, aided by the opening of more multiplex cinemas (see p 36), Britain becomes more attractive to Hollywood both as a foreign market as well as a gateway into Europe. 1991 will undoubtedly see an upswing in the number of features shot in British studios.

There were also positive developments as regards independent production with Europe. The MEDIA 92 initiative (see pp 14, 24, 33) made funds available to producers through 11 projects including distribution and script development, and these have been fully utilised by British producers. Of the 1,450 applications received over the past year, 476 have been British and of these 26 have received funding. The future expansion of MEDIA 92 into MEDIA 95, with an expanded brief to cover training will, however, require UK government endorsement.

More generally, the independent sector has, with the honourable exception of JOB-FIT (the film based technicians training scheme now being expanded to cover video-taped productions), in recent years been concentrating on its own survival rather than training for its future. However, the past year has seen the beginning of a coherent positive attitude towards training due almost entirely to the efforts of producer David Puttnam who, in addition to his central role as Chairman of the Board of Governors of the National Film and Television School, lobbied for a mandatory training provision to be included in the 1990 Broadcasting Bill, and continues to lobby for the establishment of a European Film School. In addition, an all industry group has established a body to set standards and procedure for film and TV industry national vocational qualifications. In an increasingly fragmented labour market, a unitary, recognisable and validated set of professional qualifications will become increasingly important.

1989-90 also saw some important success in influencing the content of the Broadcasting Bill which began its passage through Parliament four years after the publication of the Peacock Report. After heavy lobbying, the Government has included a provision to ensure that a minimum of 25% of all new programming shown on the BBC, ITV, and Channel 5 will, after 1992 when the Act comes into force, be supplied by independent producers. Channel 4 continues to be the sector's largest customer, taking approximately half of its new programming from independents. However, the 25% quota will provide independents with access to an additional minimum of 5,000 hours of programming per annum. In addition, the 25% target is also expressed in terms of the broadcasters' programme expenditure and guarantees that a range of programming is offered to independents.

It is estimated that by 1992 the independent sector will be producing some 7,000 hours of TV programming as opposed to the current 3,000 hours. This rate of growth is extraordinary by any standards but it must be seen in the context of an emerging multi-channel environment in which a limited pool of revenue drawn from advertising sales, licence fees and subscription will be spread across an increasing number of TV channels. The net effect for producers will be a decreasing amount of money available to any one TV system to finance programming. More and more the onus will be placed upon producers to reduce costs and effect economies of scale.

It seems unlikely that this new environment will be able to support the existing 1,000, mainly small, production companies. It is more probable that the next few years will see a smaller number of larger companies emerge as key programme suppliers to the broadcasters. Effective control of co-production sources, programme distribution and operating overheads will become increasingly important. As the independent sector matures, takeovers, mergers and bankruptcies will become as common as they are in any other industry. With the exception of companies occupying niche positions supplying 'boutique' or highly specialised programming, the immediate challenge for the independent TV sector is to attract investment into production companies to enable the rapid growth necessary for survival in the harsher climate of the 1990s.

Screen
INTERNATIONAL
YEARBOOK

This year's Yearbook covers 52 territories, contains more listings than ever, with expanded and improved coverage. Order your yearbook(s) now.

For this reason, the current argument between the independent sector and the broadcasters over the issue of ownership of programme rights is central to the future of the sector. Until independents own or control the exploitable rights arising from their programmes (programme distribution rights, book rights etc), production companies have no asset base to make them attractive to external investors. The last year has seen some independents begin to claw valuable rights back off broadcasters but only positive Government action can redress the imbalance of power crippling

visual industry. The future laid out by the Broadcasting Bill irrevocably binds 'quality' programming to 'money'. The TV producers are now entering the marketplace that feature film makers have occupied for years. It is no longer enough to be a good programme-maker. The quality of future TV output will now also be determined by the financial acumen of producers. If Channel 4's track record and the early flowering of independent programmes on the BBC are anything to go by, the future of British television is in safe hands.

Independent production: Zenith's **The Paradise Club**

production companies currently attempting to strike a reasonable deal with British broadcasters.

To end on a more optimistic note, it is heartening to see that the independent production companies now make up the fastest growing sector in the UK audio-

John Woodward is Chief Executive of the Producers Association which represents film, television and video producers

For an updated list of UK production companies, see under Production Companies in the Directory. Films which went into production during the year are listed in the Production Starts section. For feature films released during the period, see under Releases

GPO

THE PAST

and present...

▶ The Post Office Film & Video Library has a wealth of archive footage available for sale. Ideal for television researchers, it is a record of the lifestyles of the British people since the Thirties.

From trawling fish on Viking Bank (1934) to living and working in the Yorkshire Dales (1990), the collection is a view of society as seen through the eyes of some of the most famous drama and documentary makers, employing cinematic styles from the avant garde to animation and the drama documentary.

For further information please contact
The Post Office Film & Video Library
PO Box 145, Sittingbourne, Kent ME10 1NH
Telephone 0795 426465.

THE POST OFFICE

Cinema 1989-90 – Distribution

Concern about the British cinema often focuses on the problems besetting our film producers. Julian Petley discusses the difficulties facing an equally important link in the chain – the distributors

FEW subjects illustrate so clearly the British passion for secrecy and mystery than the distribution and exhibition of feature films. There has never been any kind of statutory onus on distributors to make public their films' takings and, since the 1985 Films Act, new releases no longer have to be registered with the Department of Trade and Industry. Anyone who has ever tried to probe the relationship between distributors and exhibitors in the UK, and especially the vexed and officially frowned-upon question of 'barring' (the system by which major distributors and exhibitors enter into exclusivity agreements which effectively bar independent cinemas access to new releases till they are largely played

A Cry in the Dark

out), comes up against either a wall of silence or a frustratingly large number of 'off the record' conversations.

Given the lack of official statistics, the best guide to the numbers of new films released each year is either the 'Monthly Film Bulletin' (published by the British Film Institute) or the lists published by the British Board of Film Classification. According to the former, 276 features were released between 1 April 1989 and 31 March 1990. This compares to 254 in the previous year. As tables 1 and 2 show, this rise in number of films released, and the increase in cinema admissions over the year which is outlined in detail on p36, mainly benefited the Americans since their films dominated the UK box-office both in terms of number of releases and revenue.

For example, of the Top 70 box-office films for 1989, as listed by 'Screen International', 55 films were wholly US-financed. The UK was involved in only 12, including *Batman* and *Licence to Kill* which were US/UK co-productions, two were Australian, *Young Einstein* and *A Cry in the Dark*, and one French, *The Bear*. However if, following the 'Monthly Film Bulletin', one counts *Shirley Valentine*, *Batman*, and *Licence to Kill* as American productions, then the British share becomes smaller still. (This neatly illustrates the difficulties in defining what is in fact a 'British' film).

The highest-ranking UK films in the 'Screen International' Top 70 for 1989 were *A Fish Called Wanda* (though this was in fact released in October 1988) at no 12 and Palace's *Scandal* at no 16 (released 3 March 1989 and grossing £3.7 million), which is also the first release from an independent distributor in the chart. *Shirley Valentine* at no 13, though British in many respects, was produced by Paramount, an American company. The first British film,

Dead Poets Society

released in the financial year covered by this Handbook (1 April 1989 to 31 March 1990), to appear in the chart was *Wilt* at no 27 (released 3 November 1989 by Rank and grossing £2.1 million).

Thanks to the strong UK box-office presence of films made by the American majors during the year, the five companies responsible for distributing their product here continued to dominate UK distribution. They are UIP (which distributes films from Paramount, Universal, and MGM/UA), Warner Bros, Twentieth Century Fox, Columbia Tri-Star and Rank. Between them they distributed 118 (ie 43%) of the 276 films released between April 1989 and March 1990, 56 of which were among 'Screen International's' Top 70 box-office earners for 1989. Table 3 shows their relative shares of the market during 1989.

Apart from these five major distributors, UK theatrical distribution is also made up of independent companies, ranging from small traditional 'art house' companies like Contemporary Films through to much larger and more diverse operations such as

Palace Pictures, Oasis and Virgin Vision. Several of the independents also have their own cinemas. These include Artificial Eye, Pathé, Electric Pictures, the ICA, Mainline, Metro Pictures (formerly The Other Cinema), and Oasis (formerly Recorded Releasing) who between them account for a total of 23 London screens. In terms of box-office takings during the year, Palace led with four films in the 'Screen International' Top 70, Virgin and Entertainment had two each and Guild, Vestron, Medusa, Pathé, Premier Releasing and Curzon all had one each.

With the release of *Batman*, marketing hype reached quite unprecedented levels although one would have thought that some kind of limit had been reached with *Who Framed Roger Rabbit?*. Clearly the blockbuster phenomenon is still very much with us as a comparison of the takings of the top and bottom films in the Top 10 makes very obvious. It is also interesting to note that *Licence to Kill* failed, unlike most Bond films, to make the Top 3 – presumably as a result of the BBFC's insistence on the higher than usual '15' certificate (which, incidentally, still did not prevent the Board from trimming some of the more violent scenes).

During the year, some of the independents began to go in for bigger releases and more heavyweight marketing, for example Virgin with *sex, lies, and videotape*, and Palace with *Scandal* and *When Harry Met Sally . . .* . The presence of *sex, lies, and videotape* at no 39, *Dead Poets Society* at no 9 (Touchstone/Warner) and *Dangerous Liaisons* (Warner) at no 23 in the 'Screen International' Top 70 chart shows that it is possible for more specialised releases to prosper.

When Harry Met Sally . . .

Women on the Verge of a Nervous Breakdown

quarter of 1990, 961. Many of these, of course, had cinema releases first, but those which did not included David Lynch's *Twin Peaks*, James Toback's *Pick Up Artist*, Robert Altman's *The Caine Mutiny Court Martial*, and Larry Cohen's *It's Alive III* and *Return to Salem's Lot*.

One of the most striking features of the past year has been the speed at which certain cinema releases have re-appeared on video, the most notable example being *Rain Man*'s rapid transition to 'sell thru'. However, the suspicion has been growing that a number of films are being dumped in small and often obscure cinemas for the briefest periods of time simply in order to generate publicity and audience awareness for the video release. And it is certainly a fact of life that whilst films attract critical attention, videos do not. This undoubtedly has something to do with the sheer numbers of videos released but also snobbery

The trend for sequels also showed no sign of petering out in 1989. However, with the exception of *Lethal Weapon 2* and *Indiana Jones and the Last Crusade*, which made the Top 10, the majority of the sequels did less well than their predecessors and the *Police Academy* and *Elm Street* films slipped out of the Top 20 for the first time.

It is interesting to note that the majors distributed a few 'specialised' European films during 1989-90. These were Scola's *Splendor* (Warner), Szabó's *Hanussen*, Carlos Vanziana's *I Miei Primi 40 Anni (My First Forty Years)* and Pasquale Squitieri's *Russicum* (all Columbia Tri-Star) and cult favourite Almodóvar's *Mujeres al borde de un ataque de nervios (Women on the Verge of a Nervous Breakdown)* (Rank).

It's also noteworthy that three Finnish films are amongst the releases of the period, signalling the discovery of Aki Kaurismäki by UK audiences. The gradual awakening of interest in African cinema can be glimpsed in the welcome appearance of *La vie est belle* (Burkino Faso/France/Switzerland) and *Camp de Thiaroye* (Senegal/Algeria/Tunisia). This, undoubtedly, is an area to watch. It will also be worth keeping an eye out on the restoration front which, during the year, saw reconstituted versions of *Lawrence of Arabia* (Columbia Tri-Star) and *Pat Garrett and Billy the Kid* (BFI/UIP), and brand new prints of *8½* courtesy of the BFI.

Of course, many interesting films never make it into the cinemas at all in the UK and go straight onto video. In 1989, there were 3,347 features released on video according to the BBFC, and in the first

Batman

and the lack of any magazine à la 'Monthly Film Bulletin' which would seriously review at least those films on video which had not had any kind of cinema life in this country.

Consideration of the small screen brings us on to the role played by television companies in feature film distribution, especially in the independent and 'art house' sectors. In recent years, first Channel 4 and now BBC2 have renewed television's role as buyers and exhibitors of foreign films. Paradoxically, perhaps, this increases our chances of seeing those films in cinemas, since independent distributors today are usually insistent on having both television and theatrical rights to their films.

According to Kenneth Rive of Gala: "I would never buy a film today unless I could buy all the rights. I buy most of my films in conjunction with the BBC and it's a very happy relationship," a remark echoed by Blue Dolphin's Joe d'Morais: "Television rights are absolutely vital. I wouldn't be interested in taking on a film without them. What you get from selling the film to TV goes a little way towards covering you if the film doesn't do anything theatrically". Of course, most distributors would argue that the TV companies are not paying enough for the rights and there's also the interesting point raised by film critic Derek Malcolm: "If people will now show foreign films only if TV is interested in them, then the real arbiters of what we see on our

Above: **The Bear**
Below: **Lawrence of Arabia**

cinema screens are the people in charge of film buying at Channel 4 and BBC2. And they, of course, are thinking more about their audience ratings than about the state of specialised exhibition."

The major difficulties facing this 'specialised' part of the sector can be summarised as: rising costs (ranging from rents, rates and other overheads to the prices being asked by producers); audiences' unadventurous tastes; the depressing state of much of what passes for film criticism in the papers and magazines; and, for those distributors not fortunate enough to have their own cinemas, the difficulty of finding cinemas that will both take their films and treat them with the care they deserve.[1]

One of the most interesting and rewarding developments on the independent distribution front has undoubtedly been MEDIA 92's EFDO scheme. MEDIA 92 is an initiative of the Commission of the European Communities, formed to provide support for the European film and television industries with a particular eye to helping

TABLE ONE: COUNTRY OF ORIGIN OF FEATURE FILMS EXHIBITED IN THE UK BETWEEN 1 APRIL 1989 AND 31 MARCH 1990

Country of origin*	Number of films
USA	154
UK	52
Western Europe	35
Eastern Europe	6
Australia	10
Others	19
Total	276

* includes co-productions with European partners
Source: 'Monthly Film Bulletin', published by the British Film Institute

their country of origin. Therefore, the main problems facing low-budget productions are not simply finding the money to make the films in the first place (serious enough in itself) but lack of financial backing for distribution in other countries and an adequate cinema release.

EFDO's form of aid consists of an interest-free loan which will cover up to 50% of the distribution pre-costs of a low budget film. To be eligible, the film must be taken by at least three different distributors from three different EC countries. The loan amounts to a maximum of 70,000 ECUs (£49,000) per film and per country, and the repayment of the loan is conditional on the distributor's expenditures and revenues. Since the start of EFDO's activities in November 1988, 25 films have been thus supported and the

American Stories them to profit from the single market. Its aim is to act as a catalyst, injecting seed money into projects in an attempt to attract additional capital from both public and private sources. The purpose of the EFDO project is to channel distribution aid to low budget films of EC origin, though in the form of investment rather than subsidy.

EFDO's genesis lay in a study which revealed that 80% of all films produced in EC countries have budgets of up to 2.25 million ECUs (£1.6 million) and are therefore, in European terms, low budget films. Significantly, 80% of these never leave

Resurrected

fund has paid out over 2½ million ECUs (£1.75 million). It is estimated that nearly five million people have seen the films in

Reefer and the Model

TABLE TWO: TOP TEN BOX OFFICE FILMS FOR 1989

Rank	Film	Total gross (£m)	Distributor
1	Indiana Jones and the Last Crusade	15.9	20th Century Fox
2	Who Framed Roger Rabbit?	15.6	Warner Bros
3	Batman	12.0	UIP
4	Rain Man	9.7	UIP
5	The Naked Gun	7.7	UIP
6	Licence to Kill	7.5	UIP
7	Lethal Weapon 2	6.7	Warner Bros
8	Twins	6.5	UIP
9	Dead Poets Society	5.9	Warner Bros
10	Cocktail	5.7	Warner Bros

Source: 'Screen International'

Life is a Long Quiet River

TABLE THREE: UK MARKET SHARE OF THE FIVE MAJOR UK DISTRIBUTORS IN 1989

Company	No of films	Approx gross box-office revenue (£m)
UIP	22	£79,224,084
Warner	18	£69,471,745
Columbia Tri-Star	7	£14,900,000
20th Century Fox	5	£9,256,000
Rank	4	£7,382,140

Source: 'Screen International'

question. EFDO has helped more than 100 European distributors, some of whom have already begun to repay their loans, thus enabling EFDO to re-invest the money in other productions.

Up until the end of 1989, EFDO had supported three UK films – *Distant Voices Still Lives, Drowning by Numbers* and *Resurrected* – to the tune of nearly 260,000 ECUs (£181,000). UK distributors involved in EFDO projects included Electric Pictures (*Georgette Meunier* and *La vie est un long fleuve tranquille (Life is a Long Quiet River)*), Metro Pictures (*Histoires d'Amérique: Food, Family and Philosophy (American Stories)* and *Reefer and the Model*), Mainline (*Der Philosoph*), ICA (*La Senyora*) and Artificial Eye (*Tempos difíceis este tempo*).

In March 1990, EFDO decided its next allocations of distribution aid. Over 1 million ECUs (£0.7 million) were to be lent to be distributed in 13 countries by a total of 48 distribution companies. The UK films involved are *The Dressmaker, Queen of Hearts*, and the co-productions with UK participation *Berlin Jerusalem* and *Melancholia*.

During the 1990 MIP-TV event, it was announced that over the next five years 250 million ECUs (£175 million) would be made available for MEDIA 92 projects of which £100 million would be allocated to the dis-

tribution of films. As MEDIA 92's indefatigable Holde Lhoest put it: "distribution is the first instrument in the creation of the European market". So far, the UK government's response to the whole MEDIA programme has been polite but hardly wildly enthusiastic, and one can only hope for a more positive approach to what is undoubtedly an extremely important initiative. Anyone who has ever looked into the fate of 'foreign' films in this country will realise the precariousness of their position, and see the difficulties of independent distribution and exhibition writ painfully large. Given the growing seriousness of the problems facing the production sector it's all too easy to forget the next stage in the chain – actually getting the films shown. This is clearly an area worthy of greater attention though one which, as noted at the start of this piece, is all too shrouded in secrecy. The majors may argue that this is necessary on commercial grounds, but it could also be said that such secrecy simply serves to conceal restrictive practices which discourage fresh entrepreneurial development within the exhibition sector, inhibit flexibility and limit the choices on offer to producer, distributor, exhibitor and spectator alike.

Julian Petley is a freelance broadcaster and writer
Details of UK theatrical and non-theatrical distributors are in the Distributors sections of the Directory. For a list of feature films released in the UK during the period, see under Releases

1 For a more detailed consideration of this subject see Julian Petley's article 'Where have all the foreign films gone?' in 'Sight & Sound' Autumn 1989 (published by the British Film Institute)

Cinema 1989-90 – Exhibition

Allen Eyles reports on the multiplex boom and the outlook for traditional cinemas

THE year in cinema exhibition was dominated by the continuing spread of multiplexes in the UK, as signalled by the opening of a seven-screen Cannon at Parkhead Forge, Glasgow, in April 1989. By the end of March 1990, the number of multiplexes had more than doubled with a further 16 sites opened, bringing the total to 31, with 307 screens (approximately 20% of total UK screens). Their place as part of the British cinema scene was further confirmed by a report from CAVIAR (Cinema and Video Industry Audience Research)[1] in February 1990, which estimated that as many as 25% of all British cinema visits are made to these multi-screen complexes.

The multiplex boom has been a major contributor to the growth in number of cinema screens and seating capacity in the UK since 1984. This continued during the year in review, as shown by the Policy Studies Institute's annual survey of cinema trends[2] which estimated that there were 1,561 cinema screens in Great Britain in May 1990, an increase of 277 from August 1988. The influence of the multiplexes was demonstrated by the fact that, while the PSI's figures show an overall increase of 283 screens in complexes with six screens or more, there was a net loss of six screens overall for those with five screens or less. Similarly, the increase in seating capacity from 440,000 in August 1988 to 469,000 in May 1990 can largely be attributed to the proliferation of the multiplexes.

While the multiplexes have brought pressure on traditional picture houses, they have undoubtedly helped to make

Warner's Bury multiplex

TABLE ONE: CINEMA ADMISSIONS 1984 – 1988 (MILLIONS)

	1984	1985	1986	1987	1988	1989
UK	52.7	72.5	75.8	78.7	84.2	96.4
France	190.8	175.0	167.8	136.7	122.4	—
West Germany	112.1	104.2	105.2	108.1	108.9	—
Italy	131.6	123.0	125.0	109.0	95.0	—
Japan	150.5	155.1	160.7	143.9	144.8	143.6
Spain	119.0	101.0	87.0	86.0	70.0	44.5
USA	1176.0	1056.0	1017.0	—	1085.0	—

Sources: 1 The UK figure for 1984 is from the Department of Trade and Industry and does not include Northern Ireland. In the absence of official statistics, UK figures from 1985 onwards are estimates compiled from several sources and do include figures for Northern Ireland. 2 CNC (Centre Nationale de Cinématographie) Paris 3 'Filmstatistisches Taschenbuch', published by Spitzenorganisation der Filmwirtschaeft EV, Wiesbaden 4 'Cinema d'Oggi' 5 'Japanese Film', published by UniJapan, Tokyo 6 'Cineinforme' 7 'International Motion Picture Almanac'

cinema-going a popular leisure activity again and reverse the decline in cinema attendances in the 1980s (see table 1). From a low of only 52.7 million admissions in 1984, the national total climbed to around 96.4 million in 1989 – 12 million more than 1988 and the highest figure since 1980.

Cinema-goers have doubled the frequency of their visits over the past five years according to CAVIAR's February 1990 report which suggests that approximately 5.1 million people visit the cinema at least once a month, compared to 2.6 million in 1984 (admittedly a nadir year for cinema-going). The biggest volume of admissions is to be found in the 15-24 age group, with the biggest increase in 1989 being in the 11-14 age group and the C2 (skilled working class) category (see table 2). The CAVIAR research also suggests that multiplexes are successfully appealing to older people – 27% of their audiences are aged 35 and over compared to 19% in non-multiplex cinemas. This is an important target market since the fall in the birthrate since 1965 means that the number of the most frequent cinema-goers in the population, the 15-24 year olds, is set to decrease until the middle of the 1990s.

The attraction of the multiplexes lies in the new cinema-going environment which they have created. With as many as 14 screens, they give cinema-goers a wide choice of films at one location (although critics argue that the choice has not been extended much beyond the mainstream commercial films which simply enjoy longer runs).

They also offer clean pleasant surroundings, convenient parking, and are often part of larger developments which include other attractions such as eating-places and shops. Visiting a multiplex can be part of a whole day or evening out; for example, among the attractions surrounding the multiplexes which opened this year were bowling alleys, souvenir shops, and indoor 'water-worlds'.

Above: Traditional chains such as CAC Leisure are meeting the multiplex competition in various ways

TABLE TWO: ANNUAL TRENDS IN CINEMA-GOING, BY AGE GROUP (%)

	1985	1986	1987	1988	1989
All ever go to cinema (age 7+)	49	53	54	56	60
Ever go (7–14)	86	87	88	84	85
Ever go (15–24)	76	82	82	81	86
Ever go (25–34)	62	65	65	64	72
Ever go (35+)	28	33	49	41	44
Go once a month or more (15–24)	23	25	26	27	30

Source: Cinema and Video Audience Research (CAVIAR)

The multiplex revolution brought American companies into British exhibition on a large scale for the first time and two American companies continued to dominate this style of exhibition in the UK this year. UCI (UK) is owned by Paramount Communications and MCA (via various intermediary companies), while National Amusements runs its Showcase chain of UK multiplexes direct from its Massachusetts headquarters. The year also saw the entry of another American company, Warner Bros, into the UK multiplex business.

UCI (UK) was formed to take over existing cinemas and sites under development from Britain's first multiplex operator, American Multi-Cinema which, beset by financial problems back in the United States, withdrew from this country in December 1988. This year, UCI (UK) completed several AMC projects (see table 3), including the Parc Tawe 10 at Swansea (the first multiplex in Wales).

Among the new UCI (UK) sites was the Whiteleys 8, an interesting departure from the out-of-town locations (mainly accessible by car) favoured so far by the multiplex operators. This eight-screen multiplex, which opened in November 1989, is housed well within the Whiteleys shopping centre in Bayswater, central London, an elegantly

UCI's Whiteleys 8

TABLE THREE: UK MULTIPLEXES OPENED BETWEEN APRIL 1989 AND MARCH 1990

Town/City	Screens	Operator
Glasgow	7	Cannon
Southampton	5	Cannon
West Thurrock	10	UCI
Swansea	10	UCI (AMC)
East Kilbride	9	UCI (AMC)
Poole	10	UCI (AMC)
Preston	10	UCI (AMC)
Solihull	8	UCI (CIC)
Bayswater, London	8	UCI (CIC)
Walsall	12	National Amusements
Manchester	14	National Amusements
West Derby	12	National Amusements
Birstall	12	National Amusements
Bury	12	Warners
Newcastle	9	Warners
York	12	Warners
Stoke-on-Trent	8	Rank

converted former department store. This kind of location has proved successful in North America, in highly profitable cinemas like the Water Tower complex in Chicago. As part of the central London first-run scene, the UCI Whiteleys multiplex is able to charge £4.75 for evening performances compared to £2.95 at UCI's new Preston multiplex.

There are drawbacks. For example late night shows are not possible since the main shopping centre closes at midnight. However, according to Ian Riches, Managing Director of UCI (UK), the Whiteleys 8 will have achieved 1 million admissions by the end of its first year. This is despite being allowed only limited advertising on the outside of the centre (a listed building) which means the Whiteleys 8 is nowhere near as conspicuous as the former Cannon triple cinema in Bayswater which stands derelict nearby.

By March 1990, UCI was operating 150 screens on 16 sites. Whereas AMC had followed the general American practice of banning screen advertising, UCI decided to permit a maximum of four minutes, believing this a tolerable amount for British

Rank's new 8-screen Hull multiplex

audiences. (There was considerable income to be derived from cinema advertising; revenues rose from £27 million in 1988 to £31 million in 1989).

National Amusements is the only large UK circuit to refuse to accept screen advertising. It opened four new multiplexes during the year (see table 3) which brought its total to seven, with 85 screens. The Showcase in Manchester has more screens, 14, than any British multiplex to date. National Amusements has a number of other sites in mind but is now "proceeding cautiously" according to President, Ira A Korff. "We have opened in areas with catchment populations of 500-600,000 and that policy has proved right. There are now fewer areas left uncovered and the UK is fairly well-screened already. In five or ten years, when per capita cinema-going in the UK has increased, it may be possible to operate in areas with catchment populations of 200-300,000. But, until then, those who build more run the risk of over-screening."

By far the largest multiplexes, in terms of overall seating, were those opened by Warner Bros. Their multiplex operations began in June 1989 with a £9 million development at Bury, Manchester. The Bury scheme was much larger than rivals with 3,996 seats in 12 cinemas – a pattern followed by the subsequent Warner multiplexes which opened at Newcastle in December 1989 (only nine screens but a

massive 3,384 seats) and York in March 1990 (12 screens, 3,066 seats).

The amount invested in the multiplexes varies; UCI and National Amusements have spent approximately £6 million at each location while the latter says its larger Showcases in Liverpool and Manchester cost more than £8 million each. The multiplex operators are guarded about releasing admissions figures. National Amusements does not release figures for individual sites but Ira Korff says each of the Showcases achieves around one million admissions each year. According to UCI (UK), its Metro 10 in Gateshead, widely acknowledged as the most successful of the UK multiplexes, enjoys annual audiences of around 1.5 million. UCI (UK) also releases favourable statistics such as those for the arrival of *Batman* at its ten sites in the week ending 17 August 1989 which pushed total attendances to 313,000.

However, the multiplexes are clearly not having things all their own way. In the spring of 1989, National Amusements were quoted in 'Variety' as being concerned at the low attendances for some films during the hot weather. And, with only so many sites to exploit, the inevitable problems of overlap between rival multiplexes in the same area became apparent during the year. Competition for sites, and higher interest rates, have helped push up starting costs.

Multiplexes also affected each other when built too close together. In Derby, for example, the 11-screen Showcase multiplex is in direct competition with UCI's 10 screens at the Meteor Centre. Cinema-going has increased nearly ten-fold over the time when Derby had only one city-centre screen offering mainstream films. But, with a total of approximately one million admissions shared annually between them, there have clearly not been sufficient attendances to justify two multiplexes in the area.

Despite the multiplex competition, Rank and Cannon, the two companies who dominate the traditional cinema exhibition scene, reported rising attendances and profits. Rank reported a 15% rise in admissions and a 30% increase in profits, for its financial year ending October 1989, while Cannon also registered healthy upturns with an 11% increase in attendance for the twelve months until December 1989.

However, the multiplexes were clearly causing Rank and Cannon to rethink their business strategies. During the year,

Warner Bros. — A Time Warner Company

Cannon conceded to the multiplex competition in several areas, for example closing cinemas at Peterborough in November 1989 and Newcastle in January 1990, with other affected locations reportedly for sale. Cannon also put up for sale 18 cinemas, mostly single screen or twins, that had become marginal to its operations, and some were taken over by the smaller Apollo circuit (Crosby, Dewsbury) and local concerns (Birkenhead, Hoylake).

Rank claimed that a new multiplex within three miles of one of its Odeons hit business by 30-50%, and that one between three and ten miles distant made a 10-25% difference, although one further away had no effect. With most to lose from the proliferation of multiplexes by other groups, Rank painted a grim scenario for the new multiplexes. According to a computer model developed by Rank, in conjunction with accountants Coopers & Lybrand, a multiplex needs to achieve 250,000 to 300,000 admissions annually for each £1 million spent on it to yield a healthy 20% return on investment. This, suggested Rank, meant that many multiplexes would never show an adequate return on their investment and would eventually have to close, but only after they have forced older cinemas in the area to close down as well. But Rank has yet to close a cinema because of a multiplex (except in the special case of its own multiplex at Stoke-on-Trent).

By March 1990, Cannon were operating 381 screens on 138 sites while Rank's Odeon chain had 256 screens on 75 sites. They, and other operators of traditional cinemas, have reacted to the multiplex competition in part by refurbishing and adding further screens. But whereas these are often awkward subdivisions of old auditoria, the multiplexes are purpose-built, offering good sight-lines, large screens and state-of-the-art sound. Therefore, it was perhaps inevitable that the traditional cinema operators would fight the multiplex competition by joining it.

Cannon had already ventured into the multiplex business in 1986, when it opened the UK's second multiplex at Salford Quays, Manchester, a scheme inherited from EMI, the previous owners of the ABC chain. However, the Parkhead Forge multiplex was the first Cannon had developed on its own. Apart from this and its five-screen Ocean Village, Southampton (see table 3), which opened in July 1989, Cannon also began work during the year on several seven-screen multiplexes. It abandoned its long-held plans for a 17-screen complex in London's West End, based on extending the Moulin cinemas in Great Windmill Street (which have been closed), but began considering a number of 'megaplexes' with as many as 25 screens on the edge of London, within and close to the M25. In addition, Cannon took over, at a reported cost of

A universal stock for all situations.

In critical scenes from bright to low light, with filters and long lenses, in ample or confined space on location or in the studio, AGFA XT 320 outperforms any combination of multiple stocks.

AGFA XT 320's high speed and extra wide latitude ensures consistent image quality throughout your entire production.

AGFA XT : a universal colour negative pushing forward the creative border for today's cinematographers.

Agfa-Gevaert Ltd.
Motion Picture Division
27, Great West Road
Brentford
Middlesex TW8 9AX
Tel. : 081-560 2131

AGFA XT 125 & XT 320
COLOUR NEGATIVE FILMS

They reflect the best of you.

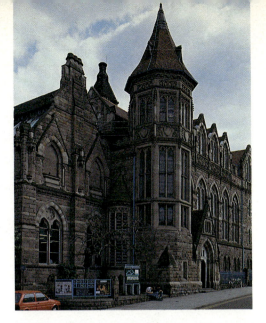

£22.5 million, the Gallery multiplex at Slough and 12 schemes for further Gallery multiplexes at various stages of development, after this British subsidiary of the huge Canadian Cineplex Odeon concern was put up for sale to relieve financial pressures on the parent company.

Rank concentrated on increasing the number of screens at existing Odeons, frequently by creating new auditoria in disused front stalls areas, as well as by opening its cinemas much earlier in the day to allow extra screenings of the feature attractions. However, the year also saw the opening of Rank's first multiplex, at Stoke-on-Trent (eight screens with a total of 1,804 seats) replacing the nearby three-screen Odeon at Hanley. Some indication of how far the multiplexes had reversed Rank's

Pioneering: Film Network's Greenwich cinema

thinking could also be seen in two new Odeon schemes. Only a few years ago, Rank had felt it adequate to replace its old three-screen Gaumont Sheffield, seating 2,015, with a two-screen Odeon seating only 824. At that time, Rank seemed only interested in creaming off the major attractions. But the company announced plans in September 1989 for a Sheffield multiplex with eight to ten screens on the site of a multi-storey car park, after acquiring two existing mini-cinemas already established there. And at Hemel Hempstead where films had been reduced to sharing time with bingo at the town's single-auditorium Odeon, Rank also began planning a new multiplex.

Multiplexes weren't the only flavour of the year. At Greenwich, in south-east London, a brand-new three-screen cinema (with a total of 782 seats) pioneered the concept of smaller borough-financed cinema development. The Greenwich cinema is a free-standing building in an excellent central location, and makes a striking impression externally. The operators, Film Network, were selected in a contest with two rival independent exhibitors. It was hoped that other councils would follow suit by providing a shell for similar centres which can concentrate on a blend of mainstream and specialised films, ignoring the lower end of the market.

The multiplexes left some room for other cinemas. The BFI-supported Regional Film Theatres in places like Derby, Newcastle and Manchester found themselves affected initially as audiences sampled the novelty of a multiplex but they soon returned. Multiplexes found themselves unable to develop a regular audience for foreign-language and specialised films, or to provide the same kind of atmosphere as the better RFTs, while RFTs found that they could no longer mix in recent mainstream films as their appeal had been exhausted in long runs at the multiplexes. The chain of RFTs as a whole was able to show a slight increase in admissions in 1989.

Many areas do not have sufficient population to support a multiplex and some independent cinemas were encouraged to invest in modernisation and expansion. Extra screens were opened by cinemas at Cromer, Grantham, Hollinwood and Port Talbot for instance. In Coventry, a leading independent operator put forward plans for his own multiplex.

Outside London's West End, the old-

The Derby Metro, a BFI-supported Regional Film Theatre

fashioned single-screen cinema became more and more an anomaly. The huge State at Grays surrendered to the impact of the West Thurrock multiplex. But the much-loved Parkway at Camden Town, London, re-opened after two years, again with one large auditorium and a 'mini' attached even though redevelopment of its site is likely. An even more welcome appearance was made by one of Britain's oldest cinemas after the failure of attempts to turn it into an antiques market: London's Electric Cinema in Portobello Road, Notting Hill, opened its doors for the first time in two and a half years in January 1990, beautifully restored with its original proscenium arch brought back into view. An imaginative mix of live shows (on the slackest nights of the week) and repertory double-bills deserves to succeed.

Inside Cannon's Parkhead Forge multiplex Other historic single-screen cinemas were newly 'listed' for their special architectural or historical interest. This helped

London's Electric Cinema before re-opening
Photo: Rupert Conant

the Coronet Notting Hill Gate (originally a late Victorian live theatre) to survive a proposal for conversion to a McDonald's and gave new heart to the fight to retain the Dome at Worthing. The long-closed Rialto, a gem dating from 1913 in London's West End, was belatedly listed but its future became no clearer. Another listed building was the still active and beautifully maintained Picture House at Stafford. The two-screen Coronet Well Hall in south-east London (a former Odeon), also received a preservation notice, as did surviving Odeons at Barnet and Chester along with the closed Odeon at Hanley (all three adapted to three screens, but preserving the most important original features). While listing has failed to prevent changes of use and harmful alterations at many other cinemas, it continued to aid the conservation battle by organisations like the Cinema Theatre Association to keep some vestiges of the traditional cinema building and picture-going atmosphere.

Allen Eyles is a freelance writer and film historian, and editor of 'Picture House', the magazine of the Cinema Theatre Association

For an up-to-date list of UK cinemas, see the Cinemas section of the Directory

1 'Cinema and Video Industries Audience Research 7'. Published February 1990. For further details contact the Cinema Advertising Association, 127 Wardour Street, London W1V 4AD.
2 'Cultural Trends 1990, no 6, Cinema, Film and Home Video'. Published by the Policy Studies Institute, 100 Park Village East, London NW1 3SR.

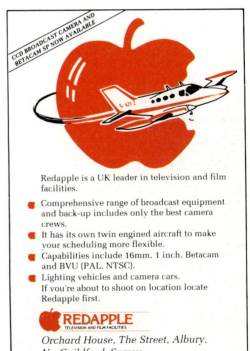

Cinema 1989-90 – British Films

The British cinema lacks identity argues Sheila Johnston in her review of British films released during the year

AS a lighthearted stunt, *The Media Show* asked advertising agencies to devise a concept for improving the image – and self-image – of British cinema. One of them came up with a mascot, a little animated man in a bowler hat. That the stereotype was quaint, outdated and generally risible was only part of the problem though; the product itself seemed to have even less of a coherent identity than ever.

The roots of the trouble lay in the demise of the quality low-budget picture; the films which surveyed distinctive British-scapes across the spectrum from Rooms with Views to Beautiful Laundrettes. Money was tighter, with the continued lack of support for funding bodies like British Screen, and the sharpening conservatism of television companies mindful of deregulation looming on the horizon. And the erosion of the American independent distribution network had made it much more difficult for this kind of film to attract a sale

– or pre-sale – in the US market.

A rethink was indicated, towards a more commercial approach, but the contemporary British cinema had never been strong on genre, or what Hollywood calls high-concept, filmmaking. The odd comedy or horror movie was about the closest it got. Certainly, comedies were made, but often they were chasing the tail of *A Fish Called Wanda* (a big success on both sides of the Atlantic) with less than hilarious consequences. Terry Jones' *Erik the Viking* might have been expected to tap into the Python's considerable following in America but foundered, there and here, on the infelicities of a flabby script.

Killing Dad was a burlesque Oedipus Rex, in which Richard E Grant journeyed to Southend to bump off his reprobate father. It tried for Ortonian viciousness but wound up closer to coarse end-of-the-pier slapstick. Although Tom Sharpe's novels had been adapted before for television, with some

Dancin' thru the Dark

Queen of Hearts

success, *Wilt* demonstrated the pitfalls and pratfalls that awaited his absurdist comedy on screen. Even Bruce Robinson's bilious *How to Get Ahead in Advertising*, a media satire bracingly full of spit and vinegar, baffled audiences tuned in to the mellower tones of his first film, *Withnail and I*.

They preferred *Shirley Valentine*, (produced by the American major Paramount but British in almost every other respect) from the pen of the prolific Willy Russell, who also wrote the original screenplay for *Dancin' thru the Dark*. This, cleverly adapted from the original one-woman play, was another of his cosy, faintly patronising, pop-feminist fables with a pungent, extremely likeable performance from Pauline

Dealers

Collins as a Liverpool housewife who goes to Greece and finds female liberation in the doubtful form of sun, fun, self-respect and the perfect orgasm.

In a bid to court the vanishing transatlantic market, token Americans continued to people the British cinema. Rebecca De Mornay played a Wall Street high flyer cutting a swathe through the City in *Dealers*, a trot along the familiar territory of the yuppie fast lane. It was too toothless to draw much blood and (lacking the zest and exuberance of *Wall Street* or *Serious Money*) too po-faced to be entertaining even if, released in the wake of the stock market crash, it had not so patently missed its moment.

Jeff Goldblum played the main character in Mel Smith's *The Tall Guy*, a clumping

affair whose title itself was 'Americanised' from the original, more parochial, *Camden Town Boy*. Most glaringly, *The Rachel Papers* cast Ione Skye as the love interest, a British character in Martin Amis's original novel and, further, excised the book's dark vicious elements to make a perky comedy about getting laid. None of these three pictures was likely to play in Peoria (that iconic bastion of Middle-American tastes) or even to do particularly well in the UK market.

It all went to prove yet again that this kind of casting works best when the characters' nationality is an integral part of the story, as in the previous year's *A Fish Called Wanda*, or in one of the best films of 1989-90, Philip Saville's *Fellow Traveller*. It took the figure of a blacklisted Hollywood screenwriter (Ron Silver) living in London to dramatise the background to the House un-American Activities Committee hearings. But it also, since the Silver character assisted at the birth of the ITV network writing episodes for *Robin Hood*, reflected fruitfully and wittily on the differences between American and British cultures – and popular cultures – in the fifties, when there was still a discernible difference between them.

Also moving over from television, Jon Amiel came up with a strong feature debut. *Queen of Hearts* was a charming and fantastical portrait of an Italian family living in London after the war, visually as atmospheric and imaginative as one expected from the director of *The Singing Detective* and thematically an intriguing excursion into one of Britain's immigrant communities.

As 1992 approached, the talk was of looking to Europe – West and, increasingly, East. Andi Engel, the German-born British-based distributor and exhibitor, made a promising first feature, *Melancholia*, which took a cool, ironic, look at the contemporary London cultural scene and the flagging political ideals of a German radical from the 1968 generation. David Hare made two Euro-thrillers almost back to back, *Paris by Night*, and *Strapless*, both centred, as seems to be his preference, on the deceptions and self-deceptions of contemporary independent women and weaving words and images of a mysterious elegance around annoyingly implausible plots.

Hotel du Paradis, from the Czech-born Jana Boková, one of Britain's very few women directors, followed a cluster of expatriates in languid orbit around a Paris hotel and was characteristically vague and evanescent. And João Botelho's unusual relocation of Charles Dickens' 'Hard Times' to contemporary Portugal in *Tempos difíceis este tempo* was a reminder that the Euro-connection meant promoting projects and directors abroad as well as soliciting European funding for British features.

Peter Greenaway, of course, has always had close ties with Europe. Not only can he attract co-production finance there, but his regular collaborators, who include the great French director of photography Sacha Vierny and a superb Dutch art direction team, must take a large chunk of credit for the films' pictorial beauty. Inspired by Flemish art, in particular Franz Hals, *The Cook, the Thief, His Wife and Her Lover*, revisited all Greenaway's familiar obsessions – murder, betrayal, and fleshly pleasures – through the figures of a vulgar, nouveau-riche gangster and his faithless wife.

The ruthless cruelty and amoralism were, as ever, hard to stomach. But it was also, apart from the stylised use of colour, relatively free from the modernist elements – the play with narrative and the obsessive lists and taxonomies – that have made Greenaway seem a difficult director; this was one of his more accessible films yet. For all his enthusiastic following in Europe, especially France, he has had trouble being distributed in America, but *The Cook, the Thief, His Wife and Her Lover* did open

Strapless

there, albeit with an X rating.

The British (or, more correctly, the Irish) did hearteningly well at the Oscars. There were the usual laurels for the excellence of UK technicians employed on American projects (Freddie Francis was named Best Cinematographer for *Glory*, and Anton Furst Best Art Director for his remarkable designs for *Batman*). *Henry V* attracted several major nominations, including Best Direction and Best Film, and though it only bagged an award for costume design, Kenneth Branagh, the director-star, could console himself with very respectable box-office and respectful reviews.

It was *My Left Foot* which carried the day, winning two Oscars with real box-office clout – Best Actor (Daniel Day Lewis) and Best Supporting Actress (Brenda Fricker). It was not without irony, since this story of the disabled Irish writer and painter Christy Brown was precisely the kind of film that had fallen so steeply from favour; low-budget, television co-produced (by Granada), apparently un-commercial. Besides the excellence of the performances, *My Left Foot* appealed to audiences for its simplicity and integrity. On the minus side, it was not the most visually exciting of films, although it should also be said that Jim Sheridan received a Best Director nomination and was acknowledged by his peers in several other award ceremonies.

There were signs of life elsewhere on the Celtic fringe, with Gillies MacKinnon's shoestring film of Manfred Karge's play *Conquest of the South Pole*. One admired its spunk and energy, even if in the end the central conceit (the characters' flight from the doldrums of unemployment by re-enacting Roald Amundsen's heroic Antarctic expedition) was far harder to

The Cook, the Thief, His Wife and Her Lover

believe in when wrested from a theatrical space into the real locations of Edinburgh's Leith Docks.

Venus Peter, meanwhile (whose makers raised the development finance by selling shares to their friends) took refuge in the past. Centred on a small boy growing up, surrounded by adult secrets and cabals, in the Orkneys after the war, it celebrated a colourful island fishing community whose way of life would soon be lost forever. Based on Christopher Rush's autobiographical book 'A Twelvemonth and A Day', it is a film of which one remembers principally the glowing images and the costumes, a fine array of Fair Isle sweaters; for the co-writer/director Ian Sellar did not equip his study of innocence tested and miraculously retained with enough teeth to take it – like the much tougher work of Terence Davies or Bill Douglas – beyond the realm of heavily-filtered, gorgeously-lit, nostalgia.

British cinema has often been taxed with

Venus Peter, a BFI production

The workshop and collective movements soldiered on and, while their films will never prime the pump of the industry, the survival of groups like Black Audio (*Testament*) and Amber (*In Fading Light*) must be welcomed and encouraged. Then there was the wealth of short films being produced under the auspices of television, and the BFI's New Directors programme. Indeed it was a British short, *Work Experience*, which won the Oscar in that category.

So the diagnosis must be that the patient's

My Left Foot

an over-fondness for bland costume drama, but last year there were conspicuously few literary adaptations of the sort which has traditionally formed its backbone and none of real distinction. Of the older generation of filmmakers, Ken Russell was one of the few still (after a brief excursion to America) firmly to be based in his beloved England. With *The Rainbow*, he sought to repeat the success of *Women in Love*, two decades on. If *The Rainbow* – unusually restrained for Russell – failed to strike the same chord, it might be that it was perhaps too well-mannered or else that D H Lawrence, so compatible with the wayward spirit of the seventies, has since fallen deeply out of fashion.

condition remained serious but not yet desperate. Even in a year offering little that might lay claim to long-term classic status, one was struck by the number of first-time directors and the range and vigour of ideas. But that diversity could also be seen as the symptom of a cinema in transition and uncertain where to go. The solution, not easy to achieve, was probably to slough off the bowler-hatted view of British culture and to embrace a cinema that would be both wholly cosmopolitan and confident in its own national identity.

Sheila Johnston is film critic for 'The Independent'
For a full list of films released during 1989 and the first quarter of 1990, see the Releases section of the Directory.

Television 1989-90 – Background

Bob Woffinden surveys a television industry on the verge of transformation

ON 21 April 1989, BBC2 celebrated its twenty-fifth anniversary. Viewers were reminded both of examples of its magnificent output over the past quarter-century and also of the time when a third channel had seemed scarcely imaginable largesse. Now, in 1990, British television stations are beginning to seem two a penny, although with Rupert Murdoch's patronage of Sky Television costing him an estimated £2 million per week, the metaphor is hardly an apt one. Perhaps the most reassuring broadcasting news of the year was that the Government had decided not to press ahead with plans to launch a sixth national television channel.

Nevertheless, this was the start of the era of proliferation. Ideas began to be exchanged about the identity and location of the fifth national channel (about which the initial news was less than encouraging). The Department of Trade and Industry revealed that it would be unavailable throughout large areas of the country, and would also necessitate the re-tuning of all video recorders. From February 1989, Sky Television had begun broadcasting four channels from the Luxembourg-registered Astra satellite and the holding company which owned Astra announced that it was bringing forward to October 1990 plans to launch a second satellite, which would make available a further 16 channels. Meanwhile, Britain's own official DBS service, British Satellite Broadcasting, was awarded two more channels by the IBA, thereby giving it five altogether and a monopoly on home DBS services.

All this happened at a time when there was some evidence that people were watching less television anyway. The BBC's own research, for example, indicated that those in social groups A and B had devoted progressively fewer of their leisure hours to watching television. The existing stations searched for an audience in the knowledge that they had merely to persuade potential viewers to press the appropriate switch. The satellite companies had first to persuade them to disfigure their property. Invariably, the unsightly receiver dishes could never be discreetly sited; they required prominent positioning in order to pick up the satellite signal. Throughout 1989-90 the press (or, at least, those parts of it not owned by Rupert Murdoch), intermittently carried reports of objections to satellite dishes by those living in architecturally sensitive parts of the country, like historic villages, and although the government had waived existing regulations with regard to a single satellite dish, the installation of two (ie for Sky and BSB) would require planning permission. To anyone taking a train journey throughout the country in 1989, the lack of penetration of satellite TV was immediately apparent.

Against a background of poll findings[1] which indicated that 80% of the populace displayed no interest at all in satellite television – and that only a small percentage of the rest would genuinely consider installing it – Rupert Murdoch's News International organisation embarked on a typically vigorous promotional campaign. There were several special all-in subscription offers of £4.49 per week and decoders were given away. Additional viewers were indeed wooed. Murdoch himself turned up in Bedford to make a special presentation to the millionth satellite subscriber. It seemed a rather old-fashioned promotional gambit (and, after all, actual sales had by then reached only 352,000), but it was covered enthusiastically by 'The Times', 'Today' and 'The Sun'. Sky's management had originally anticipated that sales of satellite dishes would reach 2.5 million by the end of the first year on air. This aim was subsequently halved, to 1.25 million, and then slashed again to 500,000. That target, at least, was met, with the 'Financial Times' monthly satellite television monitor reporting at the end of February 1990, total sales of 629,000.

There were other setbacks for Sky – the Walt Disney company pulled out of its agreement to supply films and programming for two channels – but at least it was up and running. BSB twice postponed its launch and suffered further embarrassment when the Australian Broadcasting Tribunal ruled that entrepreneur Alan Bond, who held a 35% stake in BSB, was unfit to control broadcasting interests. (The ruling was subsequently reversed at appeal). In January 1990, however, BSB announced that it had secured an extra £900 million in funding, and then went on air in March with a service that, for the first month, was available to cable subscribers only.

Despite the evident pioneering enthusiasm of staff working in satellite TV,

Rupert Murdoch, vigorously promoting Sky

despite the almost reckless use of vast sums of money, a widespread feeling persisted that the terrestrial broadcasting structure was so well-entrenched and enjoyed such popularity and prestige, that only if it were significantly weakened would satellite television be able to make its mark. This, according to many of its critics, was precisely the aim of the Broadcasting Bill; to destabilise the existing networks. While ministers argued that fundamental change was inevitable because of the range of new technological possibilities, critics insisted that the object of the exercise was to impose free-market conditions and allow naked commercial interests to flourish.

The focal point of the argument thus became the proposed auction for the allocation of franchises for ITV (or Channel 3, as this prosaic bill re-designated the network). The government's notion that franchises must be awarded to the highest bidder, other than in exceptional circumstances, was fiercely contested. Both before and after publication of the bill, dissenting voices had sought to amend this critical provision. There had, however, been one significant background change during the period of the debate. In the government reshuffle made necessary by Nigel Lawson's resignation, Timothy Renton became Chief Whip and David Mellor replaced him as the Home Office Minister responsible for broadcasting. There were many who suspected that Mellor's personal views on this matter were more sympathetic to the broadcasting establishment than he would ever publicly admit. Hence, the traditionalists were able to take fresh heart from his appointment.

With the bill under close scrutiny in committee, the rampant commercial principles underlying it were finally made subject to some qualification. Mellor acceded to industry opinion in general, and the lobbying of the Campaign for Quality Television (originally set up by a caucus within Granada TV) in particular. The allocation of franchises would not, after all, be determined on the sole criterion of who had submitted the highest bid. Programming requirements would be introduced and these, by a combination of obligations and illustrations, seemed to be both profitable and workable. Franchise-bidders would need to outline programming proposals and in particular be required to show a range of programmes – which would maintain the kind of diverse service that ITV has hitherto provided – and also indi-

Above: Mike Tyson, a popular draw for Sky
Below: Sir Alastair Burnet, resigned from ITN board

cate what sums they would allocate to programme-making. In the final analysis, the 'exceptional circumstances' clause could be invoked, so that a bidder's programme proposals could still come up trumps. Mellor introduced the notion of 'illustrative guidelines' very deftly so that they did not appear to undermine the original thrust of the legislation – that TV stations should not be told what to show – but at the same time the guidelines did lay down minimum programming standards. The indications were that the ITC would be able to ensure that C3 franchise-holders met standards that, if not as robust as previously, would still be reasonably exacting.

The government's acceptance of that argument took the heat out of the debate and ITV broadcasters also drew comfort from the appointment of David Glencross, the IBA's Director of Television, as Chief Executive-Designate of the ITC. A number of potential problems did remain. Most obviously, the bill made no provision for any kind of moratorium on take-overs of successful bidders. Previously, the IBA had been able to prevent take-overs of contract-holders, notably when it stopped the Rank

Organisation from taking over Granada, and when it required Carlton to enter into an agreed deal with Thorn and BET in order to acquire an interest in Thames TV. Under the Broadcasting Bill, the ITC would have no equivalent powers.

A successful applicant might well overbid, for fear of under-bidding and losing out, and thereby suffer a short-term lack of profitability which would threaten its survival. An unsuccessful applicant, on the other hand, would be able to become an immediate predator. Without a moratorium on take-overs, the whole auction process would inject instability into the system, with corporate energies perhaps being directed into fighting take-overs rather than ensuring the successful launch of the new franchise-holder.

For satellite operators trying to attract viewers, the bill did offer some satisfaction. It proposed to end the listing of some sporting events (the FA Cup Final, Wimbledon and the Boat Race, for example), as of such national importance that they must be nationally available. Satellite companies were keen to buy exclusive rights to major sporting occasions, particularly as the first Sky Television transmissions to capture widespread interest were those of the Mike Tyson v James 'Buster' Douglas world heavyweight contest and the test matches from the West Indies. However, for all the BBC's fretting about forfeiting the principle of unrestricted national access, it must be doubtful whether any sporting body would yield to satellite TV exclusive rights in a major event, thereby depriving it of essential promotion.

The positions of Channel 4 and ITN were also altered under the Broadcasting Bill. Channel 4 was left to fend for itself, cut adrift from ITV, but with appointments to its restructured board subject to government veto. There was considerable consternation about this – Chairman Sir Richard Attenborough threatened to resign – until a fresh form of words was drawn up, which seemed to leave honour satisfied on all sides.

Notwithstanding the award of a knighthood to its Chairman David Nicholas, the year was altogether less happy for ITN, beset by a number of problems, not least the apparent determination of the Government to ensure that one or even two other companies offered a competitive news service to the independent radio and television companies. ITN faced other difficulties too; falling ratings, which were probably attributable to effective programme scheduling on BBC1 (especially at 9.30pm) and disagreements at board level over provisions in the Broadcasting Bill and whether to make the organisation more profit-oriented. These culminated in the resignation (from the board) of Sir Alastair Burnet, the doyen of ITV news.

The BBC had a torrid and turbulent year that, in comparison with all the other torrid and turbulent years it had endured during the '80s, was almost serene. There was, though, the delicate matter of serious industrial unrest. The overt reason for this was a grievance over pay, the underlying cause was probably the strained loyalty of staff over what they perceived to be the market-oriented approach of management which seemed to conflict with the BBC's cherished historic role. The outcome was a series of twelve lightning strikes called by the unions over a three-month period from April to July. The CIA monitored the strikes (they were concerned about interruptions in the BBC's monitoring of Soviet broadcasts) but in Britain viewers probably just enjoyed the repeats.

Although it was evident almost from the outset that Michael Checkland, BBC Director-General, had underestimated the genuine grievances of staff, he adopted a

David Nicholas, ITN Chairman

MUSIC · ARTS · DOCUMENTARIES · DRAMA · SHORT FILMS · FEATURES

Production, Co-Production, Acquisitions, Distribution (Video, T.V.)
Development and Investment Finance . . .

ISLAND
VISUAL ARTS

More than meets the eye

Island Visual Arts Limited, 22 St Peter's Square, London W6 9NW.
Tel: 081-741 1511, Telex: 934541, Fax: 081-748 0841.

tough and not unsuccessful negotiating stance. When the dispute reached one of its more bitter points, in early July 1989, he suggested that it could be resolved by a re-packaging of the existing offer. But having hinted that the answer could lie in creative accounting he, though an accountant himself, disdained to look for it. When it was finally re-packaged, the staff accepted what was broadly an 8.8% increase. Even then, Checkland, who had already ordered programme cuts to fund the original (rejected) offer, had two further tricks up his sleeve. He appointed the Phillips committee to find ways of funding the revised pay award. The answer, when it came, was inevitable; further job losses. Moreover, the Peat Marwick McLintock review of the BBC salary structure concluded that BBC salaries were not noticeably out of line with those elsewhere (which the unions had alleged) although it did nevertheless recommend that the BBC should adopt a more market-orientated approach. Union members would point to the recruitment of Peter Sissons from ITN, at the height of

Blackeyes: *tabloid target*

Peter Sissons: *controversial move to BBC*

the industrial dispute, for a particularly inflated salary, as evidence that the BBC had already adopted such policies.

There was some good news for the unions in April 1989 however, with the publication of the Monopolies and Mergers Commission report on restrictive practices in the entertainment industry. This found that either the supposed restrictions did not exist or, if they did, they might "realistically be expected to disappear".

Inevitably, given the predilections of many newspapers, the BBC had to endure the usual incessant adverse publicity, much of which concentrated on Dennis Potter's serial, *Blackeyes*; surely no programme of less intrinsic interest to its readership has ever generated such sustained coverage from the tabloid press.

There were a number of political rows, though none of any real consequence or lasting effect. For example, the criticism of the Radio 4 *Today* programme, conjured up by the 'Daily Express' and the self-appointed Media Monitoring Unit, flared up briefly but, there being insufficient kindling for this fire, quickly died down.

Today

Produced in association with

POWERGEN

Ground-breaking: weather from Powergen

However, the BBC did re-assess its interviewing techniques as a result but, overall, hostile attacks on the BBC's editorial stance became more perceptibly gratuitous. After all, Michael Checkland had significantly said, in an interview on Radio 4, that the BBC had for some time failed to reflect the country's move to the Right during the '80s, but "I think we reflect that move now".

In relation to the Broadcasting Bill, Checkland's primary concerns seemed to be with the potential loss of 'listed' sporting events and with 'listings' copyright (though this would probably affect 'Radio Times' and 'TV Times' far less than has been suggested) and also with the apparent inhibitions it imposed on the BBC's business activities, at the very time when, in response to government pressures, he was trying to maximise the BBC's commercial opportunities.

Another problematic provision of the Broadcasting Bill, allowing the police to seize tapes and scripts in advance of programme transmission, was also signifi-cantly diluted after overtures from broadcasters. During the year, however, the police consistently won orders from magistrates, allowing them to take tapes and untransmitted material of programmes or newsreel which had been broadcast.

Michael Checkland: tough negotiating stance

Script conference for **What the Papers Say**

the onward rush of market forces. In April 1989, the IBA informed ITV contractors of a relaxation in its sponsorship code. The first deal of its kind in British TV ensued when Powergen agreed to sponsor ITV weather forecasts (the first being transmitted on 11 September 1989). A somewhat more dubious development occurred in February 1990 when Lloyds Bank agreed to sponsor the BBC's *Young Musician of the Year*. This would have infringed even the IBA's relaxed rules and it was a moot point whether it also infringed the BBC's own guidelines. This was not an outside event which television was covering but an event specially created by the BBC itself. It will be the Proms next, murmured disenchanted voices, and indeed the 'Sunday Times' reported that the BBC was poised to offer the Proms to a commercial sponsor.

At a time of less than buoyant advertising sales, ITV also relaxed the rules regarding charities although it advised agencies to avoid 'emotional overkill'. On 8 September 1989, Marie Curie Cancer Care (promoting its community nursing service) became the first charity to advertise on ITV.

Altogether, ITV too acquiesced in government initiatives to facilitate the implementation of market forces. The one prob-

Marie Curie Cancer Care became the first charity to advertise on ITV

The BBC Governors chafed at the erosion of their responsibilities in two respects. It was felt that Lord Rees-Mogg's Broadcasting Standards Council might compromise their function of adjudicating on matters of taste and decency in BBC programmes. (The Broadcasting Complaints Commission was even more alarmed by the emergence of the BSC, but lobbied successfully to remain independent of it.) Further, the governors were concerned about a legislative provision to allow the Office of Fair Trading to measure the extent of the BBC's output which it ceded to independent producers – again, something which seemed to the Governors to be a matter for them.

In fact, the most intriguing development in this direction was BBC2's imaginative acquisition of two prestigious programmes from Granada TV – the long-running *What the Papers Say*, and *Hypotheticals*. Would these count towards the quota of independent productions?

This transaction was just a solitary extraordinary demonstration of changing times in British television which, however reluctantly, was having to accommodate

Yellowthread
Street

lem with a commercial orientation, of course, is that it can't guarantee commerciality. During the year three big-budget ITV series, designed to attract large audiences and free-spending advertisers, all failed spectacularly: *Saracen, Yellowthread Street,* and *TECX.*

The most successful innovation of the year was perhaps the least anticipated. On 21 November 1989, the televising of the House of Commons began. The notion had been widely derided in advance, not least because the timorous Commons had insisted initially on such restrictions on camera shots that, for example, Channel 4 decided to drop plans to transmit a regular programme. Some independent observers even believed that the experiment was being designed to fail. In the event, broadcasters and politicians alike behaved with restraint and good sense, so that even the sceptics were won over to the principle of televising the Commons. By 1 February 1990, progress had been such that the Commons committee monitoring TV coverage relaxed its rules to permit more general shots of the Chamber and some reaction shots of MPs.

Clearly, the House of Commons had successfully entered the second half of the twentieth century and, at the same time, sanctioned a fundamental extension of the democratic process. Moreover, even before this had been confirmed, another group of reputedly conservative professionals, the Bar, accepted a recommendation of its own advisory committee, to permit the televising of all trials and court proceedings. One way and another, there is clearly going to be much more to watch on television in the '90s.

Bob Woffinden is a regular contributor to 'The Listener'
For further information on UK television companies and programmes, see the Television Companies section of the Directory

1 'Financial Times' monthly satellite TV monitor 8 May 1989

every question we have the answer.

THAMES TELEVISION

Thames Television Studios Division represents the resources available from Britain's major independent television company.

For details contact Peter Kew:

☎ 071-387 9494

mes Television PLC 306 Euston Road London NW1 3BB

THAMES A TALENT FOR TELEVISION

Television 1989-90 – the Programmes

Alkarim Jivani reviews the programmes produced against a background of change in the television industry

TELEVISION has rarely been regarded as a tool of revolution but 1989-90 gave the lie to that. One of the eye-openers of the year in review has been the way a medium which the Western intelligentsia finds trivial and trivialising became an instrument of change everywhere east of Berlin. The process began with Glasnost which allowed Soviet programme-makers to produce pieces on previously forbidden subjects and reached its apogee last Christmas when the Romanians made their television station the seat of their provisional government.

Whereas in the previous decade it was writers and artists who had been at the cutting edge of change in Eastern Europe, programme-makers suddenly found themselves coming into their own, notably the amateurs with their camcorders who recorded and transmitted historic footage of the changes which have taken place. For the first time the samizdat video had replaced the samizdat newspaper.

But while the winds of change were whooshing through Eastern European edit suites, Britain also saw its own revolution, albeit a less dramatic one: the arrival of the third age of broadcasting. Although Rupert Murdoch's Sky Television had actually been launched at the beginning of February 1989, it wasn't until the spring that the first material signs of change were seen. Astra dishes (or 'wall woks' as Liverpudlians with their linguistic facility dubbed them) began to go up and a new form of urban blight was born. Astra dishes (unavailable at the time of launch) were given away in competitions in 'The Sun' and became impossible to avoid.

Despite all the fancy rhetoric about choice and change, what the dishes actually received was largely no different from what viewers were all too familiar with. Sky's main entertainment channel carried dozens of Australian soaps with the odd American mini-series thrown in to relieve the tedium. The sense of déjà vu was compounded by the presence of *The Price is Right* and *Sale of the Century* in Sky's schedules. Sky Movies was stumped by the fact that if it beamed films out for free it couldn't show the best ones and if it made people pay they might not bother to subscribe to Sky. Murdoch decided to hook people by showing the channel free for an experimental period with the inevitable corollary that good movies were few and far between. And the few decent films being shown (notably *Aliens* and *The Fly*) were repeated ad infinitum. Where there did seem to be some

Eurosport draws on footage from the EBU

genuine innovation was in *Sky News* which provided a round the clock service with fresh bulletins every half hour. There was silence from those who, in anticipation of *Sky News*, had sniggered that it would be full of News International's hack pack producing a version of 'The Sun' for those

*Familiar formats: Sky's **The Price is Right***

without reading skills. Although the channel's news values are closer to ITN than BBC News, and though it is singularly lacking in analysis, it provides a perfectly decent service and the only one which will give news junkies a fix in the middle of the night.

Of the non-Murdoch owned channels on Astra, W H Smith's Screensport provides what might be most politely termed minority-interest sport. Eurosport (given financial backing and marketed by Sky but owned by a consortium of members of the European Broadcasting Union), can draw on footage culled by members of the EBU and has come up with events which have rather more mainstream appeal than Thai boxing. Lifestyle (also owned by W H Smith) is a daytime channel 'aimed at women' which makes ketchup bottle blurb look intellectually challenging. The final English-language channel on Astra is MTV (in which Robert Maxwell has a substantial stake) which provides wall to wall music. Although it is rather more adventurous than its American counterpart in the way it selects and packages record companies' promotional videos, the station has an in-built fatigue factor for anyone past pubescence.

In response to all this competition raining down from the sky, terrestrial broadcasters have been remarkably sanguine. No doubt this is partly because they were preoccupied with politicking and power-broking as the Broadcasting Bill was drafted, debated and enacted. Nonetheless, if you are arguing that you produce the best television in the world it is politic to put your money where your mouth is. The best defence against attack would have been a continuous stream of excellent programmes which proved the broadcasters' point for them. Alas this did not happen.

That is not to say that there weren't any fresh or interesting or innovative programmes made over this period. There were plenty. The problem was that there was nothing that created the kind of stir caused by programmes like *Brideshead Revisited* or *The Edge of Darkness*. The pieces which did break new televisual territory were largely small-scale programmes. The first of these, last spring, was Channel 4's *Hard News* which finally devised an approach to the press which worked on television. Despite the long reign of *What the Papers Say,* television has always had difficulty when it comes to dealing with newspapers. The BBC alone made several attempts to produce such a programme but each time the result was stifled at birth. The obvious idea, hit upon by *Hard News,* was to provide a platform for those who had been done over by Fleet Street (as was). This makes compelling viewing and almost compensates for Michael Grade's decision to dump *What the Papers Say*. Had the BBC not decided to offer it a home, the programme (the longest running in Britain) might have disappeared without a trace.

*Hard News: **breaking new territory***

News from the past

In April, Channel 4 launched its early morning programming which, it was claimed, would be as different from TV-am and *Breakfast Time* as croissants are from cornflakes. The mix included: *Business Daily,* aimed at the City; Carol Barnes move from ITN to present world news; an arts and entertainment strand called *Box Office*; an opinions slot for sport enthusiasts and a consumer programme. The publicity blurb issued at the time compared *Channel Four Daily* to a grapefruit 'whose segments can be chosen individually'. In the event viewers found these segments too sour to swallow and stayed away in their droves. Before the year was out it was announced that *Channel Four Daily* would introduce specially produced children's programming. Pundits noted that TV-am had been pulled out of the mire by similar means when Roland Rat was introduced, the only instance when a rat saved a sinking ship.

To mark BBC2's 25th anniversary, in April 1989, the BBC decided to run an archive evening which included episodes of *Yes Minister* and *Not the Nine O'Clock News*. While both of these turned out to be disappointing, the third offering *Talking to a Stranger* proved its potency even though it had lain in the vaults since 1964 when it was first transmitted. The irony was that the BBC had not intended to show it at all. The original plan was to show *Boys from the Blackstuff* but Alan Bleasdale declined and suggested that the quartet of plays by John Hopkins be shown instead. The piece told the story of the Stephens family from the point of view of each of its members (played by Maurice Denham, Margery Mason, Judi Dench, and Michael Bryant).

A few days later *Club X* (Channel 4's abortive arts series) came clanging onto the air amid much smirking from *The Late Show*. The two series provided a perfect antithesis to each other. Whereas one was staid the other was irreverent to the point of irrelevance; where one was calm and considered, the other was frenzied; where one was watchable, the other was not. Programme-makers were aghast that the bulk of Channel 4's youth budget had been frittered away.

Summer (usually the point when television hits its low point) was unusually lively in 1989. This was helped no end by the large number of anniversaries that fell in the traditionally dead period. The tenth anniversary of Margaret Thatcher's arrival at Number 10 kicked it off in May with endless analyses about the effect of the woman and the political creed named after her. Then there was the bicentennial of the French Revolution which gave both the BBC and Channel 4 a chance to pull out the stops. Channel 4 decided to concentrate its fire power on the day itself with nearly 24

A Sense of Guilt

hours given over to the event. Gallic-flavoured films and programmes were then peppered through Channel 4 schedules for a few months afterwards. The BBC devoted a whole week to the event with documentaries and dramas plus special editions of *Newsnight, Question Time* and *Building Sights*. Given this deluge, viewers were quickly saturated. The other problem was that when so many related programmes are shown at once the best are tarnished by the taint of the worst. ITV joined the anniversary game in July with LWT's celebration of its 21st year with such edifying programmes as *The Best of Blind Date* and a trawl through of Michael Aspel's greatest interviews. No doubt more than one parliamentarian began to wonder if it wasn't time to inject some new blood into the London franchise.

The biggest bash of them all came just as the summer ended with the BBC launching a blitzkrieg of programmes to mark the start of the Second World War. Palates jaded by the eight months of anniversary stodge of one sort or another should have recoiled at this but it turned out to be surprisingly toothsome. Ironically the most interesting was also the cheapest and simplest to make. In *News '39*, Sue Lawley provided a daily 15 minute bulletin which delivered the news from the corresponding day half a century earlier.

In the autumn the debate on the Broadcasting Bill began in earnest and British broadcasting should have been showing the stuff it was made of. Instead it seemed like nobody had bothered to tell the schedulers that this was the time to show their strength. ITV, which stands to lose most from the Broadcasting Bill, also happened to have the weakest schedule. The only memorable series it put forward for the autumn season was *Capital City* and even that looked better than it really was for lack of competition. The BBC did rather better with a splendid adaptation of David Lodge's *Nice Work* and John Gielgud hamming it up in *Summer's Lease* for the highbrows, and the very last series of *Blackadder* although there were rumours that yet another 'very last' series is now in the offing with the ophidian oaf transported to the '60s as a John Lennon figure.

By October the long predicted shower of soft porn floating down from satellites like so many discarded silk stockings had begun. Radio Tele Veronique, a channel from Luxembourg, most of whose output was entirely blameless not to say bland, began to run a programme called *Verotique* in which various women put on clothes merely to take them off again for the cameras. RTV had been given a licence to broadcast by the government of Luxembourg and therefore there was much political buck-passing. The Home Office said it was a matter for the Broadcasting Standards Council which said it would consider it and, if necessary, take action. What action could it take? Refer the matter to the Home Office. Eventually RTV quietly dropped the programme. In November we had an example of a senior British broad-

Thames Television's **Capital City**

caster mentioning the unmentionable on the air. The results of the BFI's massive archive project conducted the previous year, 'One Day in the Life of Television', were published in book and programme version. The latter proved to be particularly piquant not least because we heard Leslie Megahey, Head of BBC TV Music and Arts, and Jonathan Powell, Controller of BBC1, discuss the acceptability of "four fucks and a cunt" in an edition of *Omnibus*.

On 21 November 1989, Westminster joined most of the rest of the Western world and allowed us to watch our politicians at work. The cameras went into the Houses of Parliament and the world did not come to an end. Indeed, within weeks parliamentary coverage seemed as natural a part of our televisual output as weather forecasts. As the experimental period draws to a close

Controversial: DV8

it seems unthinkable for the cameras to be withdrawn from the chamber. Viewers like it with afternoon coverage now accruing more viewers than some soaps and the politicians love it even though it does mean

The New Year began dramatically in both senses of the word with *Oranges Are Not the Only Fruit* with its explosive mixture of sex and religion. Jeanette Winterson's adaptation of her own novel about a young girl's growing awareness of her lesbianism and her lack of faith set down a benchmark. The new year was barely a week old and it seemed that we were already seeing the best drama of 1990. At the other extreme was Andrea

Outrageous cabaret star Regina Fong (left) was part of Club X's *irreverent approach which contrasted sharply with that of* The Late Show *(below)*

a crush in the cloakrooms before Prime Minister's question time as coiffures are adjusted ready for the cameras. In the same week Dennis Potter was knocked off his pedestal by a self-inflicted blow as *Black-eyes,* the series with which he made his directorial debut, began transmission. Potter, whose intention was to capture the subtlety of thought and nuance of feeling, ended up with a crude and confused concoction which pleased no-one.

Newman's *A Sense of Guilt* which had the chattering classes chirruping away in a way they hadn't done since the first episode of *Blackeyes*. Of course, nobody actually admitted to liking it without endless qualification. Dennis Potter returned as a conversational topic with the first repeat of *Pennies from Heaven* which the BBC had finally managed to buy back from Hollywood. The series seemed as fresh as when it first went out in 1978 and went some way towards restoring the dent caused by *Blackeyes*.

Those who wish to wield an electronic censor over our airwaves got their first rant of the decade over *The South Bank Show* in early March which gave its slot over to the dance group, *DV8*, and its piece on Dennis Nilson. The LWT switchboard began receiving calls of protest even before the programme had begun transmission. One of the MPs to complain was David Blunkett who, even if representing the views of his constituents, is blind and so would not have been able to fully appreciate a piece which was wordless.

The end of March saw BSB begin test transmissions and the BBC lost no time in panning them. Ludovic Kennedy was wheeled in to host a one-off edition of *Did You See . . . ?* for *The Late Show* which found an ingenious way of getting round the BSB embargo. A hotel room was hired in Windsor where BSB's transmissions were being previewed by cable subscribers. Tapes were made off-air and these were then transmitted on *Did You See . . . ?* BSB executives considered slapping on an injunction but demurred after visions of headlines screaming 'BSB Doesn't Want its Programmes Seen' began to float in front of their eyes. The programmes did not get a favourable review from Kennedy and the clip of Selina Scott in a set which seemed to be dismantling around her didn't help.

However BSB's five channels (movies, general entertainment, sport, music and finally a channel devoted to the arts and factual programming) turned out to have a higher sprinkling of goodies than Sky. There were cheap badly-made soaps like *The Bold and the Beautiful* and expensive, badly-made soaps like *Jupiter Moon*. However there was a higher quotient of interesting programmes than on Sky. These included *La Triviata*, a kitschy look at the little things in life and *Nina Against the Rest* in which the self-styled bitch on the box gave as good as she got to an invited panel; both of which bent a few formats. There were others which copied existing formats for music programming and stand-up comedy but were no less good for that. The problem of course was that at launch only a handful of people had BSB dishes. The chortling of Sky executives could be heard across London, the irony of which was that they had been in exactly the same position the previous year.

Alkarim Jivani is Broadcast Editor of 'Time Out'
For further information on UK television companies and programmes, see the Television Companies section of the Directory

THE TOP 20 DIFFERENT PROGRAMMES OF 1989

No	Programme	Transmission date	Channel	Viewing audience
1	Coronation Street	Wed 15, Sun 19 Mar	ITV	26.93
2	Eastenders	Thu 23, Sun 26 Feb	BBC1	24.08
3	Crocodile Dundee	Mon 25 Dec	BBC1	21.77
4	Neighbours (1331/1736)	Tue 4 Apr	BBC1	20.92
5	Only Fools and Horses	Mon 25 Dec	BBC1	20.12
6	Blind Date	Sat 18 Nov	ITV	16.86
7	Bread	Mon 25 Dec	BBC	16.51
8	Forever Green	Sun 12 Mar	ITV	15.75
9	Inspector Morse	Wed 25 Jan	ITV	15.49
10	Man With the Golden Gun	Mon 27 Mar	ITV	15.48
11	Royal Variety Performance	Sat 25 Nov	ITV	15.47
12	Beadle's About	Sat 18 Nov	ITV	15.39
13	The Heroes	Sun 2 Apr	ITV	15.10
14	This Is Your Life	Wed 22 Feb	ITV	15.08
15	Russ Abbott Xmas Show	25 Dec	BBC1	15.01
16	The Bill	Tue 25/ Fri 28 Apr	ITV	14.90
17	A Bit of a Do	Fri 17 Feb	ITV	14.78
18	'Allo, 'Allo	Sat 25 Feb	BBC1	14.73
19	The Good Life	Tue 4 Apr	BBC1	14.73
20	Minder	Mon 2 Jan	ITV	14.54

Source: BARB/AGB

DIRECTORY

CONTENTS

68   Archives and Libraries
70   Awards
80   Bookshops
82   Cable and Satellite
94   Cinemas
110   Courses
126   Distributors (Non-Theatrical)
132   Distributors (Theatrical)
136   Facilities
148   Festivals
156   Film Societies
166   International Sales
173   Laboratories
174   Legislation
178   Organisations

300   Index

PR Companies   192
Press Contacts   194
Preview Theatres   204
Production Companies   206
Production Starts   224
Publications   238
Releases   248
Specialised Goods and
   Services   268
Studios   270
Television Companies   272
Video Labels   286
Workshops   290
List of Abbreviations   298

Index to Advertisers   304

Reflecting
the
South West

TSW–Television South West

ARCHIVES AND LIBRARIES

International Federation of Film Archives (FIAF)
Coudenberg 70
1000 Brussels
Belgium
Tel: 511 13 90
Fax: (32-2) 514 58 10
Though not itself an archive, FIAF, which has over 50 member archives and many observers from 58 countries, exists to develop and maintain the highest standards of film preservation and access. It also publishes handbooks on film archiving practice which can be obtained from the above address

International Federation of Television Archives (FIAT)
c/o Vittorio Sette
FIAT/IFTA General Secretary
RAI Radiotelevisione Italiana
Direzione Amministrativa/GSA
Via Cernaia 33
10121 Torino
Italy
Tel: 11 88 00 x2626
Fax: 11 535885

NATIONAL ARCHIVES

There are two national archives in the UK that are recognised by FIAF:

Imperial War Museum
Department of Film
Lambeth Road
London SE1 6HZ
Tel: 071 416 5000
Fax: 071 416 5379

National Film Archive
21 Stephen Street
London W1P 1PL
Tel: 071 255 1444
Fax: 071 436 7950
See also p 7

REGIONAL COLLECTIONS

East Anglian Film Archive
Centre of East Anglian Studies
University of East Anglia
Norwich
Norfolk NR4 7TJ
Tel: 0603 56161 x2664
David Cleveland
Cathryn Terry

North West Film Archive
Manchester Polytechnic
Minshull House
47-49 Chorlton Street
Manchester M1 3EU
Tel: 061 228 6171 x2590
Maryann Gomes
Marion Hewitt

Northern Film and Television Archive
36 Bottle Bank
Gateshead
Tyne and Wear NE8 2AR
Tel: 091 477 3601
Fax: 091 478 3681
Bob Davis

Scottish Film Archive
Dowanhill
74 Victoria Crescent Road
Glasgow G12 9JN
Scotland
Tel: 041 334 4445
Fax: 041 334 8132
Janet McBain

Wessex Film and Sound Archive
Hampshire Archives Trust
20 Southgate Street
Winchester SO23 9EF
Tel: 0962 847742
David Lee

NEWSREEL, PRODUCTION AND STOCK SHOT LIBRARIES

These are film and television libraries which specialise in locating material on a particular subject. For other, sometimes more specialised, film libraries consult the 'Researcher's Guide to British Film and Television Collections' and the 'Researcher's Guide to British Newsreels', published by the BUFVC

Archive Film Agency
21 Lidgett Park Avenue
Roundhay
Leeds LS8 1EU
Tel: 0532 662454
Agnese Geoghegan
Film and stills archive. 16mm and 35mm newsreel, documentary and feature material from 1900

Boulton-Hawker Films
Hadleigh
Ipswich
Suffolk IP7 5BG
Tel: 0473 822235
Fax: 0473 823187
Peter Boulton
Educational films produced over 44 years. Subjects include: health, biology, botany, geography, history, archaeology, and the arts

British Movietone News Film Library
North Orbital Road
Denham
Uxbridge
Middx UB9 5HQ
Tel: 0895 833071
Fax: 0895 834893
London Office
71 Dean Street
London W1V 6DE
Tel: 071 437 7766 x206
Newsreel (1929-1979), b/w, some colour, 35mm

British Pathé News Library
Pinewood Studios
Iver Heath
Bucks SL0 0NH
Tel: 0753 630361
Fax: 0753 655365
George Marshall
35mm newsreel from 1896 to 1970, b/w and colour. Index on text search computer

Chameleon Film and Stockshot Library
The Magistretti Building
Harcourt Place
Leeds LS1 4RB
Tel: 0532 434017
Helen Osman

16mm material from 1970s onwards includes climbing and caving films for use as stockshots. Also output from Trident Television, including *Whicker's World* and Channel 4 programme trims

Educational and Television Films (ETV)
247a Upper Street
London N1 1RU
Tel: 071 226 2298
Documentaries on Eastern Europe, USSR, China, British Labour movement, b/w and colour, 16mm and 35mm, 1896 to present day

Film Research and Production Services
25-27 Heddon Street
London W1R 7LG
Tel: 071 734 1525
Amanda Dunne
David Collier
Gerard Wilkinson
James Clarkson-Webb
Film holdings, with comprehensive film research and copyright clearance facilities

GB Associates
80 Montalt Road
Woodford Green
Essex IG8 9SS
Tel: 081 505 1850
Malcolm Billingsley
An extensive collection of fact and fiction film from 1896 onwards, 35mm and 16mm

Fred Goodland Collection
81 Farmilo Road
Leyton
London E17 8JN
Tel: 081 539 4412
16mm documentaries, shorts and extracts, colour and b/w, from 1896 to the present day. Specialist collections in the coming of sound and early sound material, music from the 1920s to the 1960s, and entertainment

Huntley Film Archives
22 Islington Green
The Angel
London N1 8DU
Tel: 071 226 9260

Fax: 071 704 0847
John Huntley
Amanda Huntley
Documentary and newsreel film, 16mm/35mm specialist collections in transport, street scenes, industrial history, music etc from 1895

ITN Film, Stills and Information Library
ITN House
48 Wells Street
London W1P 4DE
Tel: 071 637 2424
Fax: 071 636 6531
David Warner
Newsreel and TV news coverage worldwide. Colour and b/w, 1956 to present day. Variety of formats including 16mm, ¾" video, and Beta SP. Copy facility to any format available. Library also offers stills collection and information service

Index Stock Shots
12 Charlotte Mews
London W1P 1LN
Tel: 071 631 0134
Fax: 071 436 8737
Stock footage on film and video, including international locations, aircraft, and wildlife

Kobal Archive Films
28-32 Shelton Street
London WC2H 9HP
Tel: 071 240 9565
Fax: 071 836 3381
Footage and stills from silent films, features, newsreels, industrial films, documentaries; b/w and colour

Oxford Scientific Films
Long Hanborough
Oxford OX7 2LD
Tel: 0993 881881
Fax: 0993 882808
Stock footage and stills library; 16mm, 35mm film and transparencies covering wide range of wildlife and special effects subjects

RSPB Film and Video Unit
The Lodge
Sandy
Beds SG19 2DL
Tel: 0767 680551
Fax: 0767 692365
Pauline Miller

Over one million feet of 16mm film covering a wide variety of wildlife subjects and their habitats, particularly European birds. Viewing facilities and tape duplication are available on request. See also under Distributors (Non-Theatrical) and Production Companies

Visnews Library
Cumberland Avenue
London NW10 7EH
Tel: 081 965 7733
Fax: 081 965 0620
Pam Turner
Newsreel, TV news, special collections. Colour and b/w, 16mm, 35mm, 1896 to present day and all material pre 1951 and post July 1981 on 1" video

WTN (Worldwide Television News)
WTN House
31–36 Foley Street
London W1P 7LB
Tel: 071 872 9349
Fax: 071 872 9521
David Simmons
David Muddyman
Jane Dickenson
Collection of videotape, film and stills covering world events from the turn of the century. Computerised retrieval system (for all stories from 1980). Libraries in London and New York

Weintraub Feature Film Library
Pinewood Studios
Pinewood Road
Iver
Bucks SL0 0NH
Tel: 0753 631111
Fax: 0753 655813
John Herron
Feature films and stock shot, b/w and colour, 35mm, 1925 to present day

World Backgrounds Film Production Library
Imperial Studios
Maxwell Road
Borehamwood
Herts
Tel: 081 207 4747
Fax: 081 207 4276
Ralph Rogers
Ron Saunders
Worldwide establishing

shots, colour, 35mm and back projection plates, 1964 to present day, supplied to TV series, commercials, features, documentaries and sports programmes

AWARDS

BAFTA AWARDS – BRITISH ACADEMY OF FILM AND TELEVISION ARTS

Awarded March 1990 for 1989 films/ programmes

BAFTA special award 1990: Dame Peggy Ashcroft
Academy fellowship: Paul Fox CBE
Michael Balcon award for outstanding British contribution to cinema: Lewis Gilbert
Academy award: Leslie Halliwell
Desmond Davis award for outstanding creative contribution to television: John Lloyd (BBC)
Writer's award: Andrew Davis for *Mother Love* (BBC)
Richard Dimbleby award: Kate Adie (BBC)

Film

Best film: *Dead Poets Society* (USA) Dir Peter Weir
Best achievement in direction: Kenneth Branagh for *Henry V* (UK)
Best actress: Pauline Collins for *Shirley Valentine* (USA)
Best actor: Daniel Day Lewis for *My Left Foot* (Eire/UK)
Best supporting actress: Michelle Pfeiffer for *Dangerous Liaisons* (USA)
Best supporting actor: Ray McAnally for *My Left Foot*
Best original screenplay: Nora Ephron for *When Harry Met Sally* (USA)
Best adapted screenplay: Christopher Hampton for *Dangerous Liaisons*
Best film score: Maurice Jarre for *Dead Poets Society*
Best foreign language film: *La vie et rien d'autre (Life and Nothing But)* (France) Dir Bertrand Tavernier

Best short film: *The Candy Show* (National Film and Television School) Peter Hewitt, David Freeman, Damian Jones
Best short animated film: *A Grand Day Out* (National Film and Television School) Nicholas Park

Television

Best single drama: *The Accountant* (BBC) Prod Paul Knight Dir Les Blair
Best drama series/serial: *Traffik* (Channel 4) Prod Brian Eastman Dir Alastair Reid
Best factual series: *Forty Minutes* (BBC) Prod Edward Mirzoeff
Best light entertainment programme: *Clive James on the '80s* (BBC) Prod Elaine Bedell Ed Richard Drewett
Best comedy series: *Blackadder Goes Forth* (BBC) Prod John Lloyd
Best news/OB coverage: *Tiananmen Square Massacre (BBC News)* Steve Selman

Dead Poets Society

Blackadder Goes Forth

Fabrizio Szforza, Pam Meager for *The Adventures of Baron Munchausen*
Costume design: Gabriella Pescucci for *The Adventures of Baron Munchausen*

Television
Video lighting: Clive Thomas for *The Ginger Tree* (BBC)
Design: Hans Zillman and Martin Herbert for *Traffik* (Channel 4)
Film cameraman: Clive Tickner for *Traffik*
Sound supervisor: Graham Haines for *Love for Three Oranges* (BBC)
Film sound: David

Hildyard, David Old, Kim Weston for *Traffik*
Film editor: Howard Billingham for *Around the World in 80 Days* (BBC)
Graphics: Pat Gavin for *Agatha Christie's Poirot* (LWT)
VTR editor: John Baldwin for *Spitting Image* (Central)
Make-up: Hilary Martin, Christine Cant, Roseann Samuel for *Agatha Christie's Poirot*
Costume design: Linda Mattock for *Agatha Christie's Poirot*
Video cameraman: Ron Green for *The Ginger Tree*

BAFTA CRAFT AWARDS

Awarded March 1990 for 1989 films/ programmes

Film
Cinematography: Peter Bizou for *Mississippi Burning* (USA)
Production design: Dante Ferretti for *The Adventures of Baron Munchausen* (UK/W Germany)
Editing: Gerry Hambling for *Mississippi Burning*
Sound: Bill Phillips, Danny Michael, Robert Litt, Elliot Tyson, Richard C. Kline for *Mississippi Burning*
Achievement in special visual effects: Ken Ralston, Michael Lantieri,
John Bell, Steve Gawley for *Back to the Future II* (USA)
Make-up: Maggie Weston,

Best actress: Diana Rigg for *Mother Love* (BBC)
Best actor: John Thaw for *Inspector Morse* (Thames TV)
Best light entertainment performance: Rowan Atkinson for *Blackadder Goes Forth* (BBC)
Best original music: Christopher Gunning for *Agatha Christie's Poirot* (LWT)
Best children's programme (entertainment/drama): *Maid Marian and Her Merry Men* (BBC)
Best children's programme (documentary/educational): *The Really Wild Show* (BBC) Prod Paul Appleby
Flaherty documentary award: *First Tuesday: Four Hours In Mai Lai* (Yorkshire TV) Prod/Dir Kevin Sim
Huw Wheldon award (best arts programme): *Omnibus: Art in the Third Reich* (BBC) Prod/Scr Peter Adam
Best foreign television programme: *Hotel Terminus: The Life and Times of Klaus Barbie* (France) Dir Marcel Ophuls

Agatha Christie's Poirot

BFI Fellows Gérard Depardieu (left) and Dame Peggy Ashcroft with Larry Chrisfield of Ernst & Young (second left) and Sir Richard Attenborough

BFI AWARDS 1989

Awarded October 1989 in association with Ernst & Young

BFI fellowship: Dame Peggy Ashcroft and Gérard Depardieu
Grierson award: John Morgan, Adam Alexander for *Concerning Cancer* (Channel 4)
Film award: British Screen Finance
Independent achievement: Amber Side Workshop
Archival achievement: Christine Whitaker, film researcher for *Out of the Doll's House* (BBC 2)
Technical achievement: *The Adventures of Baron Munchausen* (UK/W Germany) Dir Terry Gilliam
Career in the industry: Annette Caulkin, senior script editor at British Screen Finance
Television award: Peter Kosminsky for *Afghantsi* and *First Tuesday: Murder in Ostankino Precinct* (Yorkshire TV)
Book award: Joel Finler for 'The Hollywood Story' (Octopus)
British book award: James C Robertson for 'Hidden Cinema' (Routledge)
Anthony Asquith film music award: Andrew Dickson for *High Hopes* (Channel 4)
Anthony Asquith young composer award: Philip Appleby
Kodak newcomer of the year: Bob Hartley for *. . . And I Was Such a Lovely Baby* (National Film and Television School)
Mari Kuttna award: Erica Russell for *Feet of Song* (Malinka Films)
Sutherland trophy: Nils Gaup, Dir *Ofelas (Pathfinder)* (Norway)

BERLIN FESTIVAL

Awarded February 1990

GOLDEN BEARS
Grand prix: *Music Box* (USA) Dir Costa Gavras
40th anniversary special prize: Oliver Stone for *Born on the Fourth of July* (USA)
Short film: *Mistertao* (Italy) Dir Bruno Bozetto
SILVER BEARS
Special jury prize: *Asteničeskij Sindrom (The Asthenic Syndrome)* (USSR) Dir Kira Muratova
Best director: Michael Verhoeven for *Das Schreckliche Mädchen (The Nasty Girl)* (W Germany)
Best actor: Iain Glen for *Silent Scream* (UK) Dir David Hayman
Best joint performance: Jessica Tandy and Morgan Freeman for *Driving Miss Daisy* (USA)
Short film: *Ilha das Flores (Island of Flowers)* (Brazil) Dir Jorge Furtado
Best film for sensitive handling of minorities: *Coming Out* (W Germany) Dir Heiner Carow
Outstanding single achievement: Xie Fie for *Ben Min Niam (Black Snow)* (China)
FIPRESCI prize: *Karaul (The Guard)* (USSR) Dir Aleksandr Rogoschkin
Alfred Bauer prize (to a film which opens new perspectives in cinematographic art): *Karaul*
OCIC (Catholic) prize: *Silent Scream*
Interfilm (Protestant) prize: *Das Schreckliche Mädchen*
GDF (German Art Film Theatre Association) prize: *Driving Miss Daisy*
Berliner Morgenpost (audience) prize: *Das Schreckliche Mädchen*
CIAE (International Confederation of Arts Cinemas) prize: *Rikyu* (Japan) Dir Hiroshi Teshigahara
UNICEF prize: *Mahi (The Fish)* (Iran) Dir Kambuzia Partovi
Best short film: *In and Out* (Canada) Dirs David Fine, Alison Snowden
CIFEJ (International Centre of Films for Children and Young People) prize: *Kunst und Vliegwerk (At Stalling Speed)* (Netherlands) Dir Karst van der Meulen

BFI production **Silent Scream**

BROADCASTING PRESS GUILD AWARDS 1989

Presented March 1990

Best single drama: *The Accountant* (BBC)
Best drama series: *Traffik* (Channel 4)
Best single documentary: *First Tuesday: Four Hours in Mai Lai* (Yorkshire TV)
Best documentary series: *Around the World in 80 Days* (BBC)
Best entertainment programme: *A Bit of a Do* (Yorkshire TV)
Best children's programme: *The Chronicles of Narnia* (BBC)
Best imported programme: *Cheers* (Channel 4) (USA – Paramount TV)
Best performance by an actor: Alfred Molina for *The Accountant*
Best performance by an actress: Diana Rigg for *Mother Love* (BBC)
Outstanding contribution to broadcasting: Kate Adie (BBC)

CANNES FESTIVAL 1989

Golden Palm: *sex, lies, and videotape* (USA) Dir Steven Soderbergh
Special jury prize: *Trop belle pour toi!* (France) Dir Bertrand Blier and *Nuovo Cinema Paradiso (Cinema Paradiso)* (Italy) Dir Giuseppe Tornatore
Jury prize: *Jésus de Montreal* (Canada) Dir Denys Arcand
Best director: Emir Kusturica for *Dom za Vesanje (Time of the Gypsies)* (Yugoslavia)
Best actor: James Spader for *sex, lies, and videotape*
Best actress: Meryl Streep for *A Cry in the Dark* (Australia)
Best artistic contribution: *Mystery Train* (USA) Dir Jim Jarmusch
Golden camera (best first film): *Az En XX. Szazdom (My 20th Century)* (Hungary) Dir Ildíko Enyedi
Grand prize for superior technical achievement: *Kuroi Ame (Black Rain)*

sex, lies, and videotape

(Japan) Dir Shohei Immamura
Short film Golden Palm: *Cinquante ans* (Canada) Dir Gilles Carle
Short film prize (animation): *Yes We Can* (USA) Dir Faith Hubley
Short film prize (fiction): *Performance Pieces* (USA) Dir Tom Abrams
Special career award: Gregory Peck
FIPRESCI (international critics' award): *sex, lies, and videotape* (in competition) and *Yaaba* (Burkina Faso) Dir Idrissa Ouedraogo (out of competition)
Prix jeunesse: *Erreur de jeunesse (Youthful Indiscretion)* (France) Dir Radovan Tadic
Roberto Rossellini award for special contribution to cinematic achievement: Emir Kusturica
Ecumenical prize: *Jésus de Montreal*

CESARS

Awarded March 1990

Best actor: Philippe Noiret for *La vie et rien d'autre (Life and Nothing But)*
Best actress: Carole Bouquet for *Trop belle pour toi!*
Best supporting actor:

Robert Hirsch for *Hiver 54, l'Abbé Pierre (Winter of '54)*
Best supporting actress: Suzanne Flon for *La vouivre*
Most promising young actor: Yvan Attal for *Un monde sans pitié (A World without Pity)*
Most promising young actress: Vanessa Paradis for *Noce blanche (White Wedding)*
Best director: Bertrand Blier for *Trop belle pour toi!*
Best French film: *Trop belle pour toi!*
Best foreign film: *Dangerous Liaisons* (USA)
Best first feature: *Un monde sans pitié* Dir Eric Rochant
Best screen adaptation: Bertrand Blier for *Trop belle pour toi!*
Best music: Oswald d'Andrea for *La vie et rien d'autre*
Best poster design: Jouineau-Bourduge and Gilles Jouin for *Nuovo Cinema Paradiso (Cinema Paradiso)* (Italy)
Best short feature: *Lune froide* Dir Patrick Bouchitey
Best documentary short: *Chanson pour un marin* Dir Bernard Aubouy
Best animated short: *Le porte-plume* Dir Marie-Christine Perrodin

Carole Bouquet in Trop belle pour toi!

Best cinematography: Yves Angelo for *Nocturne indien*
Best set design: Pierre Guffroy for *Valmont* (France/UK)
Best sound: Pierre Lenoir and Dominique Hennequin for *Monsieur Hire*
Best editing: Claudine Merlin for *Trop belle pour toi!*
Best costume: Theodor Pistek for *Valmont*

41ST PRIMETIME EMMY AWARDS FOR TELEVISION – NATIONAL ACADEMY FOR TELEVISION ARTS AND SCIENCES

Awarded September 1989
DRAMA
Lead actor: Carroll O'Connor for *In the Heat of the Night* (NBC)
Lead actress: Dana Delaney for *China Beach* (ABC)
Supporting actor: Larry Drake for *L A Law* (NBC)
Supporting actress: Melanie Mayron for *thirtysomething* (ABC)
Director: Robert Altman for *Tanner '88* (HBO)
Outstanding series: *L A Law*
Writing: Joseph Dougherty for *thirtysomething*
Outstanding special (drama/comedy): *Day One* (AT&T Presents) (CBS) and *Roe vs Wade* (NBC)
COMEDY
Lead actor: Richard Mulligan for *Empty Nest* (NBC)
Lead actress: Candice Bergen for *Murphy Brown* (CBS)
Supporting actor: Woody Harrelson for *Cheers* (NBC)
Supporting actress: Rhea Perlman for *Cheers*
Outstanding series: *Cheers*
Director: Peter Baldwin for *The Wonder Years* (ABC)
Writing: Diane English

LA Law

for *Murphy Brown*
Outstanding programme (variety/music/comedy): *The Tracey Ullman Show* (Twentieth Century Fox)
MINI-SERIES/SPECIALS
Lead actor: James Woods for *My Name is Bill W* (Hallmark Hall of Fame) (ABC)
Lead actress: Holly Hunter for *Roe vs Wade*
Supporting actor: Derek Jacobi for *The Tenth Man* (Hallmark Hall of Fame) (CBS)
Supporting actress: Colleen Dewhurst for *Those She Left Behind* (NBC)
Outstanding mini-series: *War and Remembrance* (ABC)
Director: Simon Wincer for *Lonesome Dove* (CBS)
Writing: Abby Mann, Robin Vote, Ron Hutchinson for *Murderers Among Us: The Simon Wiesenthal Story* (HBO)
Individual performance: Linda Ronstadt for *Canciones de mi Padre* (Great Performances) (ABC)

Directing: Jim Henson for *The Jim Henson Hour* (ABC)
Informational series: *Nature* (PBS)
Informational special: *Lillian Gish: The Actor's Life for Me* (American Masters) (PBS)
Animated programme: *Garfield: Babes and Bullets* (CBS)
Children's programme: *Free to be . . . a Family* (ABC)
INDIVIDUAL ACHIEVEMENT SPECIAL EVENTS
Directing: Dwight Hemion for *The 11th Annual Kennedy Center Honors: A Celebration of the Performing Arts* (CBS)
Performance: Billy Crystal for *The 31st Annual Grammy Awards* (CBS)
Writing: Jeffrey Lane for *The 42nd Annual Tony Awards* (CBS)
Governors award: Lucille Ball

INTERNATIONAL EMMYS 1989

Awarded November 1989
Best drama: *Traffik* (UK-Channel 4) Dir Alastair Reid
Best documentary: *First Tuesday: Four Hours in Mai Lai* (UK-Yorkshire TV)
Best arts documentary: *Omnibus: Gwen – A Juliet Remembered* (UK-BBC)
Best performing arts programme: *La Boheme* (Australia-ABC)
Best popular arts programme: *Alexei Sayle's Stuff* (UK-BBC)
Children's and young people award: *My Secret Identity* (Canada) Dir Don McBrearty

EUROPEAN FILM AWARDS 1989

Awarded November 1989
Best film: *Topio Stin Omichli (Landscape in the Mist)* (Greece/France/Italy) Dir Theo Angelopoulos
Best young film: *300 Mil do Nieba (300 Miles to Heaven)* (Poland/Denmark) Dir Maciej Dejczer
Best director: Géza Bereményi for *Eldorado (The Midas Touch)* (Hungary)
Best actor: Philippe Noiret for *La vie et rien d'autre (Life and Nothing But)* and *Nuovo Cinema Paradiso (Cinema Paradiso)* (Italy)
Best actress: Ruth Sheen for *High Hopes* (UK)
Best supporting actress: Edna Doré for *High Hopes*
Best script: Maria Khmlik for *Malenkaya Vera (Little Vera)* (USSR) Dir Vasily Pichul
Special jury award: Joris Ivens
Special awards: Bertrand Tavernier for *La vie et rien d'autre* and Giuseppe Tornatore for *Nuovo Cinema Paradiso*

Best composer: Andrew Dickson for *High Hopes*
Best cinematography: Ulf Brantas and Jorgen Persson for *Kvinnorna pa Taket (Women on the Roof)* (Sweden)
Best documentary: *Recsk 1950-53: Egy Titkos Kenszermunkatabor Tortenete (Recsk 1950-53: The Story of a Secret Forced Labour Camp* (Hungary) Dir Géza Böszömenyi, Livia Gyarmathy

High Hopes

47TH GOLDEN GLOBE AWARDS

Awarded January 1990

Film

Best drama: *Born on the Fourth of July* (USA) Dir Oliver Stone
Best comedy/musical: *Driving Miss Daisy* (USA) Dir Bruce Beresford
Best foreign language film: *Nuovo Cinema Paradiso (Cinema Paradiso)* (Italy) Dir

Giuseppe Tornatore
Best actor (drama): Tom Cruise for *Born on the Fourth of July*
Best actor (comedy/musical): Morgan Freeman for *Driving Miss Daisy*
Best supporting actor: Denzel Washington for *Glory* (USA)
Best actress (drama): Michelle Pfeiffer for *The Fabulous Baker Boys* (USA)
Best actress (comedy/musical): Jessica Tandy for *Driving Miss Daisy*
Best supporting actress: Julia Roberts for *Steel*

Topio Stin Omichli (Landscape in the Mist)

Magnolias (USA)
Best director: Oliver Stone for *Born on the Fourth of July*
Best screenplay: Oliver Stone and Ron Kovic for *Born on the Fourth of July*
Best original score: Alan Menken for *The Little Mermaid* (USA)
Best original song: 'Under the Sea' from *The Little Mermaid* (Music Alan Menken, Lyrics Howard Ashman)

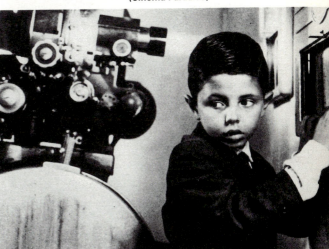

Nuovo Cinema Paradiso (Cinema Paradiso)

Television

DRAMA
Best series: *China Beach* (ABC)
Best actress: Angela Lansbury for *Murder She Wrote* (Universal TV)
Best actor: Ken Wahl for *Wiseguy* (USA)
COMEDY/MUSICAL
Best series: *Murphy Brown* (CBS)
Best actress: Jamie Lee Curtis for *Anything But Love* (USA)
Best actor: Ted Danson for *Cheers*
MINI-SERIES OR FILMS MADE FOR TV
Best series: *Lonesome Dove* (CBS)
Best actress: Christine Lahti for *No Place Like Home* (CBS)
Best actor: Robert Duvall for *Lonesome Dove*
Best supporting actress: Amy Madigan for *Roe vs Wade* (NBC)

Best supporting actor: Dean Stockwell for *Quantum Leap* (NBC)
Special award (Cecil B DeMille): Audrey Hepburn

LOCARNO FILM FESTIVAL 1989
Awarded August 1989

Gold Leopard: *Dharmaga Tongjoguro Kan Kkadalgun? (Why did Bodhi-Dharma Leave for the Orient?)* (South Korea) Dir Bae Yong-Kyun

Silver Leopard: *Piravi (The Birth)* (India) Dir Shaji

Bronze Leopard: *Khaneh-je Doost Kojast? (Where is My Friend's House?)* (Iran) Dir Abbas Kiarostami

Best actor: Adam Kamien for *Kornblumenblau* (Poland)

FIPRESCI (international critics') prize: *Dharmaga Tongjoguro Kan Kkadalgun?*

FIPRESCI special mention: *Khaneh-je Doost Kojast?*

Ecumenical jury prize: *Khaneh-je Doost Kojast?*

Art cinemas jury prize (CICAE): *Khaneh-je Doost Kojast?*

Leopard of Honour: Ennio Morricone

Ernest Artaria prize for best technical achievement: Michael Haneke, Dir *Der Siebente Kontinent (The Seventh Continent)* (Austria)

Ecumenical jury prize: *Piravi* and *Khaneh-je Doost Kojast?*

Barclay jury prizes for promoting distribution: *Dharmaga Tongjoguro Kan Kkadalgun?* and *Khaneh-je Doost Kojast?*

MONTE CARLO TV FESTIVAL 1989

Awarded February 1990

NEWS (DOCUMENTARY)
Gold nymph: *Tiananmen Square* (UK-BBC)
Silver nymph: *Panama* (W Germany-ZDF)
Special jury mention: *Panama* (France-TF1)

The Shell Seekers

NEWS (MAGAZINE)
Gold nymph: *The Black City with the White House* (Sweden-STV)
Silver nymph: *Sous le regard de Lenine* (France-A2)
Special jury mention: *Les enfants de felgueiras* (Belgium-RTBF)
FICTION
Mini-Series
Gold nymph: *Les grandes familles* (France-A2)
Silver nymph (best director): Marianna Ahrne for *Dandelion Child* (Sweden-STV)
Silver nymph (best script): David Lodge for *Nice Work* (UK-BBC)
Special jury mention: Jean-Pierre Marielle and Jean Carmet for *Bouvard et Pécuchet* (France-FR3)
FILMS FOR TV
Gold nymph: *One Way Out* (UK-BBC)
Silver nymph (best director): Peter Deutsch for *Der Weg nach Lourdes* (W Germany-ARD/SR)
Silver nymph (best script): Alison Cross for *Roe vs Wade* (USA-NBC)
Silver nymph (best actor): Frankie Sakai for *Santoka* (Japan-NHK)
Silver nymph (best actress): Holly Hunter for *Roe vs Wade*
Special jury mention for cinematography: *Quartier Nègre* (Switzerland-TSR)

PRIX UNDA
Documentary: *Soudan: Children of Darkness: Rivers of Blood* (Canada-CBC)
Fiction: *The Shell Seekers* (UK/USA-Central TV/Marian Rees Associates)
PRIX DE LA CRITIQUE INTERNATIONALE DES MAGAZINES
Documentary: *Si Pol Pot Revenait* (Switzerland-TR)
Fiction: *Le prix du silence* (France-TF1)
PRIX URTI
International Grand Prix for documentary: *L'agneau mystique d'Anton Stevens* (Belgium-BRT)
Youth television prize: *Hilacha de Pedro Neira* (Peru-Videoteca Alternativa)
Silver medal: *Africa Blues* (France-FR3) Dir Jean-Francois Delassus
Bronze medal: *Coupe a blanc* (W Germany-ARD) Dir Joachim Faulstch
Special mention: *La ruelle* (Egypt-URTE) Dir Naguib Mahfouz de Samiha el Ghoneimi
PRIX DE CROIX ROUGE MONEGASQUE
Fiction: *A Path Across the Danube* (Czechoslovakia-CST)
Prix du public: *Quartier Nègre*
Prix amade: *Der Weg nach Lourdes*

Piravi (The Birth)

MONTREUX FESTIVAL OF LIGHT ENTERTAINMENT 1989

Golden Rose: *Hale & Pace* (UK-LWT)
Silver Rose: *La pucelle de Rouen ou boule de suif* (USSR-Televidenie Sovietskovo Soiuza)
Bronze Rose: *Gagman* (Czechoslovakia-CTC)
Golden Rose for independent producers: *Le cirque de soleil: le cirque reinventé* (Canada-les Productions Telemagik)
City of Montreux prize for funniest programme: *Kurt Olsson Television* (Sweden-SVT2)

Hale & Pace

City of Montreux prize for independent producers: *The Tracey Ullman Show* (USA-Twentieth Century Fox)
Special mention: *El cabrero, le chant de la sierra* (France-Production Realisation Video)
Press prize: *Hale & Pace*

MOSCOW FILM FESTIVAL 1989

Alternates with Karlovy Vary
Golden prize of St George: *Ladri di Saponette (The Icicle Thief)* (Italy) Dir Maurizio Nichetti

Silver prize of St George: *Posetitel Muzeia (Visitor to a Museum)* (USSR) Dir Konstantin Lopushanski
Bronze St George (Best actor): Turo Pajala for *Ariel* (Finland)
Bronze St George (Best actress): Kang Soo-yeon for *Aje Aje Bara Aje (Come, Come, Come Upward)* (South Korea)
UNIATEC prize: Nikolai Pokoptsev for *Posetitel Muzeia*
Tapestry of life prize (Instituted by the African Culture Centre Foundation/African Film Company Egbakoku Cinema): Zhang Jun Zhao for *Huguan (Shining Arc)* (China)
Silver prize for contribution to cinema: Joris Ivens

Ecumenical prize: *Posetitel Muzeia*
FIPRESCI critics' prize: *Ariel*
Special prize: *The Unknown Soviet Cinema* compiled by Naum Kleiman

OSCARS – ACADEMY OF MOTION PICTURE ARTS AND SCIENCES

Awarded March 1990 for 1989 Films
Best film: *Driving Miss Daisy* (USA) Dir Bruce Beresford

Best foreign language film: *Nuovo Cinema Paradiso (Cinema Paradiso)* (Italy) Dir Giuseppe Tornatore
Best director: Oliver Stone for *Born on the Fourth of July*
Best actor: Daniel Day Lewis for *My Left Foot* (Eire/UK)
Best actress: Jessica Tandy for *Driving Miss Daisy*
Best supporting actor: Denzel Washington for *Glory* (USA)
Best supporting actress: Brenda Fricker for *My Left Foot*

Best original screenplay: Tom Schulman for *Dead Poets Society* (USA)
Best screenplay adaptation: Alfred Uhry for *Driving Miss Daisy*
Best cinematography: Freddie Francis for *Glory*
Best editing: David Brenner, Joe Hutsing for *Born on the Fourth of July*
Best original song: 'Under the Sea' Music Alan Menken Lyrics Howard Ashman from *The Little Mermaid* (USA-Walt Disney)
Best original music score: Alan Menken for *The Little Mermaid*

Driving Miss Daisy

Ariel

Best art direction: Anton Furst for *Batman* (USA)
Best set direction: Peter Young for *Batman*
Best costume design: Phyllis Dalton for *Henry V* (UK)
Best make-up: Manlio Rocchetti, Lyn Barber, Kevin Haney for *Driving Miss Daisy*
Best visual effects: John Bruno, Dennis Muren, Hoyt Yeatman, Dennis Skotak for *The Abyss* (USA)
Best sound: Donald O Mitchell, Greg C Rudloff, Elliot Tyson, Russell Williams II for *Glory*
Best sound effects editing: Ben Burtt, Richard Hymns for *Indiana Jones and the Last Crusade* (USA)
Best short film (animated): *Balance* (USA) Prods Christopher Lauenstein, Wolfgang Lauenstein
Best short film (live action): *Work Experience* (UK) Dir James Hendrie
Best documentary feature: *Common Threads: Stories from the Quilt* (USA) Prod Bill Couturie Dir Robert Epstein
Best documentary short: *The Johnstown Flood* (USA) Prod Charles Guggenheim
Academy honorary award: Akira Kurosawa

Ian Hersholt humanitarian award: Howard W Koch
Gordon E Sayer award: Pierre Angenieux

ROYAL TELEVISION SOCIETY AWARDS 1989

Programme and Performance Awards May 1989
Light entertainment:

Alexei Sayle's Stuff (BBC)
Situation comedy: *The Comic Strip...The Strike* (Channel 4)
Single drama: *Tumbledown* (BBC)
Drama series: *Blind Justice* (BBC)
Drama serial: *A Very British Coup* (Channel 4)
Single documentary: *Afghantsi* (Yorkshire TV)
Documentary series: *Armada* (BBC South & East)

Colin Firth in Tumbledown

Arts: *Omnibus: Whale Nation* (BBC)
Outside broadcasts:

Scrumdown (Yorkshire TV)
Regional award: *The Calendar Fashion Show* (Yorkshire TV)

Beiqing Chengshi (City of Sadness)

She's Been Away

Technique award: Steve Seddon (VTR editor) for *How to be Cool* (Granada)
Performance awards: Maggie Smith for *Talking Heads: Bed among the Lentils* (BBC) and Colin Firth for *Tumbledown*
Gold medal: Owen Edwards
Cyril Bennett award: David Plowright
Judges' award: John Lloyd

Television Journalism Awards February 1990

Regional daily news magazine: *Coast to Coast* (TVS)
Regional current affairs: *Friday Report: Condition Critical* (BBC South & East)
News, home: *Kegworth Air Crash* (ITN)
Current affairs, home: *Families at War: The Volunteer* (BBC)
News, topical feature: *Hard News* (Channel 4)
Current affairs, international: Charles Wheeler for *Panorama: Tbilisi – Bloody Sunday* (BBC)
News, international: ITN for *Bucharest* and BBC for *Tiananmen Square*
Television news cameraman of the year: Ian Young (BBC)
Television journalist of the year: Paul Davies (ITN)
Judges' award: Kate Adie (BBC)

VENICE FESTIVAL 1989

Golden Lion: *Beiqing Chengshi (City of Sadness)* (Taiwan) Dir Hou Hsiao-hsien
Special grand prix: *Et la lumière fut (And There Was Light)* (France/Germany/Italy) Dir Otar Yoseliani
Silver Lion: *Recordações da Casa Amarela (Memories from the Yellow House)* (Portugal) Dir João César Monteiro and *Sen No Rikyu (Death of a Tea Master)* (Japan) Dir Kei Kumai
Volpi Cup for best actor: Marcello Mastroianni and Massimo Troisi for *Che Ora È (What Time is it?)* (Italy)
Volpi Cup for best actress: Peggy Ashcroft and Geraldine James for *She's Been Away* (UK)
Osella for cinematography: Yorgos Arvanitis for *Australia* (Belgium/France/Switzerland)
Osella for screenplay: Jules Feiffer for *I Want to Go Home* (France)
Osella for musical talent: The young cast of *Scugnizzi* (Italy)
Italian senate prize: *Scugnizzi* Dir Nanni Loy
Italian critics' prize: *Un monde sans pitié (A World Without Pity)* (France) Dir Eric Rochant
FIPRESCI (International critics') prize: *Dekalog* (Poland) Dir Krzysztof Kieslowski and *Un monde sans pitié*
OCIC (Catholic) prize: *Che Ora È*
Special lifetime achievement award: Robert Bresson

BOOKSHOPS

Most bookshops stock film and cinema books and, if they don't have the book you want, they are usually happy to order it for you direct from the publisher. However, if the book you are looking for proves elusive or if you are looking for magazines, posters or memorabilia, you might try the specialist mail order services offered by the following bookshops

Arnolfini Bookshop
First Floor
16 Narrow Quay
Bristol BS1 4QA
Tel: 0272 299191
Fax: 0272 253876
Stock: A, B, C, E, F
Opening hours: 10.00-19.00 Monday-Saturday, 12.30-18.30 Sunday
Based in the Arnolfini Gallery. No catalogues are issued. Send requests for specific material with SAE

B H Blackwell
50 Broad Street
Oxford OX1 3BQ
Tel: 0865 792792
Stock: A
Opening hours: 09.00-18.00 Monday-Saturday
There is a section of cinema books in Blackwell's monthly catalogue, all of which are available by mail order. Contact the Marketing Department for further details

Blackwell's Art & Poster Shop
27 Broad Street
Oxford OX1 2AS
Tel: 0865 792792
Stock: A, B, C, F
Opening hours: 09.00-18.00 Monday-Saturday
A wide selection of art books, posters, cards, calendars and gift items, all available by mail order

The Cinema Bookshop
13-14 Great Russell Street
London WC1B 3NH
Tel: 071 637 0206
Stock: A, B, C, D
Opening hours: 10.30-17.30 Monday-Saturday

No catalogues are issued. Send requests for specific material with SAE

The Cinema Shop
45 Summer Row
Birmingham B3 1JJ
Tel: 021 236 9879
Stock: A, B, C, D, E, F
Opening hours: 11.30-17.30 Tuesday-Saturday, closed Sunday, Monday
Shop rather than mail order service, but will accept telephone queries

Geoffrey Clifton
Performing Arts Bookshop
44 Brazennose Street
Manchester M2 5EA
Tel: 061 831 7118
Stock: A, B, C, D, F
Opening hours: 10.00-17.30 Monday-Saturday
Stock mainly new books but a search service is available for out-of-print titles. Send SAE for details

Cornerhouse Books
70 Oxford Street
Manchester M1 5NH
Tel: 061 228 7621
Stock: A, B, C, E, F
Opening hours: 10.30-20.30 daily (Monday-Sunday)
No catalogues are issued. Send requests for specific material with SAE

A E Cox
21 Cecil Road
Itchen
Southampton SO2 7HX
Tel: 0703 447989
Stock: A, B, C, D
Telephone enquiries and orders are accepted at any time. Mail order only. A catalogue, including scarce items, is published

at least six times yearly. Send two first-class stamps or three international reply vouchers overseas to receive the current issue

Richard Dalby
4 Westbourne Park
Scarborough
North Yorks YO12 4AT
Tel: 0723 377049
Stock: A, B
Mail order only. Send SAE for specific rare, out-of-print and secondhand cinema books. Free search service for titles not in stock. Lists issued

Dress Circle
57-59 Monmouth Street
Upper St Martin's Lane
London WC2H 9DG
Tel: 071 240 2227
Stock: A, B, C, D, E, F
Opening hours: 10.00-19.00 Monday-Saturday
Specialists in music and soundtracks. A catalogue of the entire stock is issued annually. Send SAE for details

58 Dean Street Records
58 Dean Street
London W1V 5HH
Tel: 071 437 4500/734 8777
Stock: E
Opening hours: 10.00-18.30 Monday-Thursday, 10.00-19.00 Friday, Saturday
Retail shop with recorded mail order service. Over 7,000 titles including soundtracks, original cast shows, musicals and nostalgia. Telephone for information

Film Magic
18 Garsmouth Way
Watford
Herts
Stock: A, B, C, D, E, F
Mail order only.
Comprehensive catalogue
costing £1.00 available on
request

Filmworld
De Courcy's Arcade
5 Cresswell Lane
Glasgow G12 8AA
Tel: 041 339 5373
Fax: 041 334 8422
Stock: A, B, C, D, F
Opening hours: 10.00-
17.30 Monday-Saturday,
12.00-17.00 Sunday
Catalogues of posters and
postcards are issued free
of charge. Send SAE for
details

Anne FitzSimons
62 Scotby Road
Scotby
Carlisle
Cumbria CA4 8BD
Tel: 0228 513815
Stock: A, B, C, D, F
Mail order only.
Antiquarian and out-of-
print titles on cinema,
broadcasting and
performing arts. A
catalogue is issued three
times a year. Send three
first-class postage stamps
for current issue

Flashbacks
6 Silver Place
Beak Street
London W1R 3LJ
Tel: 071 437 8562
Stock: C, D
Opening hours: 10.30-
19.00 Monday-Saturday
Shop and mail order
service. Send SAE and
'wanted' list for stock
details

Forbidden Planet
71 New Oxford Street
London WC1A 1DG
Tel: 071 836 4179/379
6042
Stock: A, B, C, D, E, F
Opening hours: 10.00-
18.00 Monday-
Wednesday, Saturday
10.00-20.00 Thursday,
Friday
Science fiction, horror,
fantasy and comics
specialists

Heffers Booksellers
20 Trinity Street

Cambridge CB2 3NG
Tel: 0223 358351
Stock: A
Opening hours: 09.00-
17.30 Monday-Saturday
A cinema and theatre
catalogue is issued.
Copies are available free
on request

David Henry
36 Meon Road
London W3 8AN
Tel: 081 993 2859
Stock: A, B
Mail order only. A
catalogue of out-of-print
and secondhand books is
issued two or three times
a year and there is a
search service for titles
not in stock. New books
can also be obtained to
order, including those
published in the USA

MOMI Bookshop
South Bank
London SE1 8XT
Tel: 071 928 3535
Stock: A, B, C, D, F
Opening hours: 10.30-
20.30 Tuesday-Saturday,
10.30-19.00 Sunday,
12.00-19.00 Monday
Based in the Museum of
the Moving Image. Mail
order available with
special orders on request

**The Media
Bookshop**
Book Base
PO Box 1057
Quinton
Birmingham B17 8EZ
Tel: 021 429 2606
Stock: A
Mail order only. A
complete catalogue of
books is produced once
a year. Send request for
catalogue with A4 SAE

Movie Finds
Shop: Units 1/2/3
The Village Arcade
George Street
Old Town
Hastings
East Sussex
Mail order: 2 Laurel Walk
Juniper Close
St Leonards on Sea
East Sussex TN38 9RH
Stock: C, D
Two catalogues are
available: one for posters,
one for portraits. Both
cost £1.00 and are
updated every three
months

**National Museum
of Photography,
Film and Television**
Princes View
Bradford BD5 0TR
Tel: 0274 727488
Fax: 0274 723155
Stock: A, B, C, F
Opening hours: 10.30-
18.00 Tuesday-Sunday
Mail order available.
Send SAE with requests
for information

**Offstage Theatre &
Cinema Bookshop**
37 Chalk Farm Road
London NW1 8AJ
Tel: 071 485 4996
Stock: A, B, D, F
Opening hours: 10.00-
18.30 Monday, 10.00-
17.30 Tuesday-Saturday,
11.00-18.00 Sunday
Cinema and television
catalogue available. Send
SAE for details

**Tyneside Cinema
Bookshop**
10 Pilgrim Street
Newcastle upon Tyne NE1
6QG
Tel: 091 232 5592
Fax: 091 221 0535
Stock: A, B, C, D, F
Opening hours: 11.30-
19.00 Monday-Saturday
Based in Tyneside
Cinema. Send requests for
specific material with
SAE

**Vintage Magazine
Co**
39-41 Brewer Street
London W1R 3FD
Tel: 071 439 8525
Stock: B, C, D, F
Opening hours: 10.00-
20.00 Monday–Saturday,
12.00-19.00 Sunday
247 Camden High Street
London NW1
Tel: 071 482 0587
Opening hours: 10.00-
18.00 Monday-Friday,
10.00-19.00 Saturday,
Sunday
Picture library and
research service
Tel: 081 533 7588
No catalogues are issued.
Send requests for specific
material with SAE

Peter Wood
20 Stonehill Road
Great Shelford
Cambridge CB2 5JL
Tel: 0223 842419

Stock: A, D, F
Mail order, monthly
PBFA Hotel Russell
London book fair and
others in provinces.
Visitors are welcome by
appointment. A free
catalogue is available of
all books in stock

A Zwemmer
80 Charing Cross Road
London WC2H 9NJ
Tel: 071 836 4710 x21/379
7886
Stock: A, B
Opening hours: 09.30-
18.00 Monday-Friday,
10.00-18.00 Saturday
A catalogue of new and
forthcoming cinema,
television and video titles
is issued as well as a
catalogue of out-of-print
titles still available. All
books are available by
mail order. Contact John
Nichol for more
information

A – Books
B – Magazines
C – Posters
**D – Memorabilia (eg
stills)**
**E – Records, cassettes
and compact discs**
**F – Postcards and
greetings cards**

CABLE AND SATELLITE

Cable networks in the UK are divided into two categories: the new full-franchise operations currently under construction or in the process of allocation (listed below by franchise area), and the older systems which have been upgraded to carry satellite programme channels (listed according to ownership). The operators and their ownership are detailed separately to show group franchise holdings, followed by information on the English-language satellite channels available in Europe. Unless otherwise stated, services have not yet begun on full franchise networks

UK FULL CABLE FRANCHISE AREAS

Franchises which have been granted or offered by the Cable Authority (including 11 previously granted by the Department of Trade and Industry) are arranged in alphabetical order of area. Where appropriate the principal towns in the area are identified under the area name

Aberdeen
franchise holder: Aberdeen Cable Services
homes in area: 96,000 (build complete)
homes passed: 92,000
date awarded: Nov 1983
service start date: May 1985
service:
  basic: 23 channels
  à la carte: 4 additional channels

Amersham/ Aylesbury/ Chesham
franchise to be awarded
homes in area: 62,000

Andover
franchise holder: Andover

Cablevision
homes in area: 11,500
homes passed: 1,000 (Jan 1990)
date awarded: Apr 1988
service start date: Mar 1990
service: 'all available satellite channels'

Avon
Bristol, Bath, Weston-super-Mare, Frome, Melksham, etc
franchise holder: United Artists Communications (Avon)
homes in area: 300,000
date awarded: Nov 1988
service start date: June 1990
service:
  basic: 31 channels
  Premium: à la carte channels – HVC, Indra Dhnush, Sky Movies, BSB Movies

Barnsley
franchise to be awarded
homes in area: 82,000

Bearsden/ Milngavie
franchise to be awarded
homes in area: 16,000

Bedford
franchise to be awarded
homes in area: 55,000

Belfast
franchise holder: Ulster

Cablevision
homes in area: 136,000
date awarded: Nov 1983
service start date: to be announced
service:
  basic: 12 channels
  Premium: range of additional channels

Birmingham/ Solihull
franchise holder: Birmingham Cable
homes in area: 465,000
homes passed: 29,000
date awarded: Oct 1988
service start date: Mar 1990
service: under revision

Black Country
Dudley, Sandwell, Walsall, Wolverhampton, urban parts of Bromsgrove, Cannock, Kidderminster
franchise holder: West Midlands Cable Communications
homes in area: 470,000
date awarded: July 1989

Bolton
franchise holder: Bolton Telecable
homes in area: 135,000
date awarded: Aug 1985

Bournemouth/ Poole/Christchurch
franchise holder: Bay Cable

The Cable and Satellite section has been compiled by the editors of Screen Digest (see entry under Publications): John Chittock, David Fisher, Ben Keen, Susan Barrett. We gratefully acknowledge their continuing support in providing this information

homes in area: 130,000
date awarded: Apr 1990

Bradford
franchise to be awarded
homes in area: 175,000

Brighton/Hove/ Worthing
franchise holder:
Southdown Cablevision
homes in area: 135,000
date awarded: Oct 1989

Bromley, London Borough of
franchise holder:
Telecommunications
Network
homes in area: 117,000
date awarded: Mar 1990

Burton-on-Trent/ Swadlincote/ Ashby
franchise to be awarded
homes in area: 40,000

Bury/Rochdale
franchise holder:
Comment Cablevision
Bury and Rochdale
homes in area: 143,000
date awarded: May 1990

Cambridge and district
Cambridge, Newmarket,
Ely, Saffron Walden,
Huntingdon, St Ives, St
Neots, Royston, etc
franchise holder:
Cambridge Cable
homes in area: 134,000
date awarded: June 1989

Camden, London Borough of
franchise holder: Cable
Camden
homes in area: 70,000
homes passed: 4,500
date awarded: Feb 1986
service start date: Dec
1989
service:
    Darwin: 9 channels – 4
broadcast, Lifestyle,
MTV, SC, Sky, SS,
teletext
    Darwin Plus: 11
channels
    Additional à la carte
channels: CNN, CC
Service will include
option of direct Mercury
telephone connections

Cardiff/Penarth
franchise holder: British
Cable Services

homes in area: 103,000
date awarded: Feb 1986

Carlisle
franchise to be awarded
homes in area: 30,000

Cheltenham/ Gloucester
franchise holder: United
Artists Communications
(Cotswolds)
homes in area: 90,000
date awarded: Aug 1985
service start date: to be
announced
service:
    basic: 31 channels
including 5 broadcast
    Premium: additional à
la carte channels – HVC,
Indra Dhnush, Sky
Movies, BSB Movies

Cheshire, North
Chester, Ellesmere Port,
Warrington, Widnes,
Runcorn
franchise holder:
Cheshire Cable
homes in area: 175,000
date awarded: Jan 1990

Colchester/Ipswich
franchise holder: East
Coast Cable
homes in area: 126,000
date awarded: July 1989

Corby/Kettering/ Market Harborough/etc
franchise to be awarded
homes in area: 90,000

Coventry
franchise holder:
Coventry Cable
Television
homes in area: 119,000
homes passed: 116,000
(build complete)
date awarded: Nov 1983
service start date: Sept
1985
service: First Choice
(basic) plus optional
channels

Crawley/Horley/ Gatwick
franchise holder: Mid
Downs Cable
homes in area: 40,000
date awarded: Apr 1989

Croydon, Merton and Sutton/ Kingston and Richmond, London Boroughs of
franchise holder: United

Artists Communications
(London South)
homes in area: 373,000
homes passed: 100,000
date awarded: Croydon
Nov 1983, others May
1989
service start date:
Croydon Sept 1985, others
to be announced
service:
    basic: 31 channels
including 5 broadcast
    Premium: additional à
la carte channels – HVC,
Indra Dhnush, Sky
Movies, BSB Movies

Cumbernauld/ Kilsyth/Airdrie/ Coatbridge
franchise holder: Cable
North
homes in area: 55,000
service start date: to be
announced

Darlington
franchise to be awarded
homes in area: 34,000

Dartford/Swanley
franchise holder: East
London
Telecommunications
homes in area: 35,000
date awarded: Mar 1990
service start date: to be
announced
service:
    basic: 21 channels
    DeLuxe: basic + Bravo,
SS, CNN, MTV
further 3 channels
available à la carte –
HVC, Sky Movies, BSB
Movies

Derby/Spondon
franchise holder:
Derbyshire Cablevision
homes in area: 85,000
date awarded: Feb 1990

Devon, South Exeter, Plymouth, Torbay
franchise holder: Devon
Cablevision
homes in area: 236,000
date awarded: Dec 1989

Doncaster/ Rotherham
franchise holder: South
Yorkshire Cablevision
homes in area: 192,000
date awarded: May 1990

Dorset, West
Dorchester, Weymouth,
Portland

franchise holder: Coastal
Cablevision
homes in area: 35,000
date awarded: Feb 1990

Dumbarton/Vale of Leven
franchise holder: Cable
North
homes in area: 18,000
date awarded: Apr 1989

Dundee/Perth
franchise holder: Tayside
Cable Systems
homes in area: 99,000
date awarded: Jan 1990

Ealing, London Borough of
franchise holder:
Westside Cable
homes in area: 105,000
homes passed (Jan 1990):
20,000
date awarded: Nov 1983
service start date: Nov
1986
service:
    basic: four broadcast,
Bravo, Cable Jukebox,
CNN, Discovery,
Lifestyle, MTV, SC, Sky,
TV5, WN, community
channel, multiplex
channel guide, teletext
    additional channels:
CC, HVC, Indra Dhnush,
SS

Edinburgh
franchise holder:
Cablevision (Scotland)
homes in area: 183,000
homes passed: 4,500
date awarded: Feb 1986

Enfield
franchise to be awarded
homes in area: 105,000

Epping Forest
franchise holder: East
London
Telecommunications
homes in area: 45,000
date awarded: May 1990
service start date: to be
announced
service:
    basic: 21 channels
    DeLuxe: basic + Bravo,
SS, CNN, MTV
further 3 channels
available à la carte –
HVC, Sky Movies, BSB
Movies

Epsom/Mole Valley/Reigate/ Redhill
franchise to be awarded

homes in area: 98,000

Falkirk/West Lothian
franchise to be awarded
homes in area: 30,000

Glamorgan, West Swansea, Neath, Port Talbot
franchise holder:
Starvision Network
homes in area: 110,000
homes passed: 2,000
date awarded: Nov 1989
service start date: to be
announced

Glasgow, Central/ Clydebank, North West
franchise holder: Clyde
Cablevision
homes in area: 112,000
homes passed (Jan 1990)
54,000
date awarded: Nov 1983
service start date: Oct
1985
service:
Tier 1 (Basic): 8
channels – 4 broadcast,
SC, Sky, local, teletext
classified
Tier 2 (Bronze): 16
channels – tier 1 + CC,
Lifestyle, MB, Premiere,
RAI, SS, WN, teletext
channels
Tier 3 (Silver): 19
channels – tier 2 + Arts,
Bravo, TV5
Tier 4 (Gold): 18
channels – tier 2 +
Bravo, HVC
Tier 5 (Platinum): 20
channels – tier 2 + Arts,
Bravo, HVC, TV5
Senior Citizen special
package: 12 channels
including Lifestyle, SS
and choice of Bravo/HVC

Glasgow, Greater
franchise to be awarded
homes in area: 274,000

Glenrothes/ Kirkcaldy/Leven
franchise to be awarded
homes in area: 60,000

Grantham
franchise holder:
Diamond Cable
homes in area: 14,000
date awarded: Apr 1990

Great Yarmouth/ Lowestoft/Caister
franchise to be awarded
homes in area: 64,000

Greater London East
Boroughs of Barking/
Dagenham, Bexley,
Redbridge
franchise holder: East
London
Telecommunications
homes in area: 229,000
homes passed: 6,000
date awarded: Dec 1988
service start date: to be
announced
service:
basic: 21 channels
DeLuxe: basic + Bravo,
SS, CNN, MTV
Further 3 channels
available à la carte –
HVC, Sky Movies, BSB
Movies

Greenock/Port Glasgow/Gourock
franchise to be awarded
homes in area: 32,000

Greenwich/ Lewisham, London Boroughs of
franchise holder:
Videotron London
homes in area: 175,000
date awarded: Apr 1989

Grimsby/ Cleethorpes
franchise to be awarded
homes in area: 63,000

Guildford/West Surrey
franchise holder: British
Cable Services
homes in area: 22,000 +
115,000
date awarded: Nov 1983
+ Aug 1985
service start date: July
1987
service:
Welcome: broadcast
channels, Sky1, CC,
MTV, SC, Eurosport, Sky
News
Variety: Welcome +
RAI, TV5, WN, HVC
Premiere: Tiers 1 and 2
+ Sky Movies

Hackney/Islington, London Boroughs of
franchise holder: Cable
Hackney and Islington
homes in area: 150,000
date awarded: Apr 1990
service start date: to be
announced
service: to include Sky,
BSB, TV5, Sat Eins,
alternative telephone
service

Halifax/Brighouse
franchise to be awarded
homes in area: 75,000

Haringey, London Borough of
franchise holder: Cable
Haringey
homes in area: 80,000
date awarded: Sept 1989

Harlow/Bishops Stortford/Stansted Airport
franchise holder: Stort
Valley Cable
homes in area: 43,000
date awarded: Mar 1990

Harrogate/ Knaresborough
franchise holder:
Harrogate
Telecommunications
Complex
homes in area: 27,000
homes passed: 3,925
(jointly with York
franchise)
date awarded: Mar 1990
service start date: to be
announced
service:
basic: 16 channels
extended: basic + 8
channels à la carte: 4
additional channels

Harrow
franchise to be awarded
homes in area: 79,000

Havering, London Borough of
franchise holder: East
London
Telecommunications
homes in area: 90,000
date awarded: Apr 1990
service start date: to be
announced
service:
basic: 21 channels
DeLuxe: basic + Bravo,
SS, CNN, MTV
à la carte: further 3
channels – HVC, Sky
Movies, BSB Movies

Haywards Heath/ Burgess Hill
franchise to be awarded
homes in area: 25,000

Hertford/Cheshunt /Ware
franchise to be awarded
homes in area: 60,000

Hertfordshire, Central
Stevenage, Welwyn,
Hatfield, Hitchin,
Baldock, Letchworth
franchise holder:
Cablevision
Communications
Company
homes in area: 100,000
homes passed: 2,000
date awarded: Nov 1989
service start date: to be
announced

Hertfordshire, South
Watford, Chorleywood,
Rickmansworth, Bushey,
Radlett, Elstree,
Borehamwood, Potters
Bar
franchise holder: Jones
Cable Group
homes in area: 95,000
date awarded: Nov 1989
service start date: to be
announced
service: to be confirmed –
most of available satellite
channels plus local
channels

Hertfordshire, West
Harpenden, Hemel
Hempstead, St Albans,
Berkhamsted, Tring,
Redbourne
franchise holder: Herts
Cable
homes in area: 100,000
homes passed: 6,000
date awarded: Nov 1989
service start date: Oct
1990
service: to be decided

Hillingdon
franchise to be awarded
homes in area: 92,000

Hinckley
franchise holder: N-Com
Cablevision of Hinckley
homes in area: 20,000
date awarded: Apr 1990

Hounslow
franchise to be awarded
homes in area: 79,000

Huddersfield/ Dewsbury
franchise to be awarded
homes in area: 148,000

Isle of Thanet see Thanet, Isle of

Kenilworth/ Leamington Spa/ Stratford-upon-

Avon/Warwick
franchise holder:
Heartland Cablevision
homes in area: 50,000
date awarded: Mar 1990

Kensington/Chelsea
franchise holder:
Westside Cable
homes in area: 68,000
homes passed: 7,000
date awarded: Feb 1988
service start date: Sept
1989
service:
   basic: 14 channels
   à la carte: full menu

Kent, South East
franchise holder: North
Downs Cable
homes in area; 77,000
date awarded: May 1990

Lambeth/Southwark, London Boroughs of
franchise holder:
Videotron London
homes in area: 191,000
date awarded: July 1989

Lancashire, Central
Preston, Chorley, Leyland
franchise holder:
Lancashire Cable
Television
homes in area: 114,000
date awarded: Feb 1986

Lancashire, East
Blackburn, Accrington,
Nelson, Colne,
Rossendale Valley
franchise holder: East
Lancashire Cablevision
homes in area: 168,000
homes passed: 33,500
date awarded: May 1988
service start date: Nov
1989
service:
   basic: 27 channels
Further 3 premium
channels – Sky Movies,
BSB Movies, HVC

Lancaster/Morecambe
franchise to be awarded
homes in area: 40,000

Leeds
franchise holder: Jones
Cable Group
homes in area: 289,000
date awarded: Mar 1990
service start date: to be
confirmed
service: to be confirmed –

most of available satellite
channels, plus local
channels

Leicester
franchise holder:
Leicester
Communications
homes in area: 147,000
date awarded: Apr 1989
service start date: Sept
1990
service: all currently
available UK satellite
channels + some
European language
channels, video delivered
services and 2 community
channels. A la carte
choice also available

Lincoln
franchise to be awarded
homes in area: 30,000

Liverpool, North/Bootle/Crosby
franchise to be awarded
homes in area: 100,000

Liverpool, South
franchise holder:
Merseyside Cablevision
homes in area: 125,000
date awarded: Nov 1983

London, North West
Boroughs of Barnet,
Brent, Hammersmith and
Fulham
franchise holder:
Westside Cable
homes in area: 280,000
date awarded: Jan 1989

London see also Greater London, East and individual boroughs

Loughborough/Shepshed
franchise holder:
Leicester
Communications
homes in area: 30,000
date awarded: Mar 1990
service start date: to be
announced
service: all currently
available UK satellite
channels, some European
language channels, video
delivered services, 2
community channels; plus
à la carte choice

Luton/Dunstable/Leighton Buzzard
franchise holder:
Cablevision Bedfordshire

homes in area: 104,000
homes passed: 10,000
date awarded: July 1986
service start date: Mar
1990
service:
   basic package: 24
channels
   Premium service
available

Macclesfield/Wilmslow
franchise to be awarded
homes in area: 45,000

Manchester/Salford
franchise holder: Greater
Manchester Cablevision
homes in area: 363,000
date awarded: May 1990

Mansfield/Sutton/Kirkby-in-Ashfield
franchise holder:
Diamond Cable
(Mansfield)
homes in area: 58,000
date awarded: Mar 1990
service start date: to be
announced
service:
   Tier 1: Primary – 10
channels including 4
broadcast
   Tier 2: Primary + 15
channels and 4 free
foreign language
channels
   Tier 3: Premium –
Tiers 1 and 2 + 4
channels

Melton Mowbray
franchise holder:
Diamond Cable (Melton
Mowbray)
homes in area: 30,000
date awarded: Apr 1990

Middlesbrough/Stockton/Hartlepool
franchise to be awarded
homes in area: 170,000

Motherwell/East Kilbride/Hamilton/Wishaw/Lanark
franchise holder: Cable
North
homes in area: 125,000
date awarded: Apr 1989

Newark on Trent
franchise holder:
Diamond Cable (Newark)
homes in area: 18,000
date awarded: Apr 1990

Newham/Tower Hamlets, London Boroughs of
franchise holder: East
London
Telecommunications
homes in area: 127,000
homes passed: 50,000
date awarded: Aug 1986
service start date: Apr
1987
service:
   basic: 21 channels
   DeLuxe: basic + Bravo,
SS, CNN, MTV
   à la carte: further 3
channels – HVC, Sky
Movies, BSB Movies

Newport/Cwmbran/Pontypool
franchise to be awarded
homes in area: 85,000

Northampton
franchise holder: Cable
Television
homes in area: 72,000
date awarded: Jan 1989

Norwich
franchise holder: Norwich
Cablevision
homes in area: 83,000
date awarded: July 1989
service start date: May
1990

Nottingham
franchise holder:
Diamond Cable
(Nottingham)
homes in area: 160,000
homes passed: 25,000
date awarded: Sept 1989
service start date: July
1990
service:
   Tier 1: Primary – 10
channels including 4
broadcast
   Tier 2: Primary + 15
channels and 4 free
foreign language
channels
   Tier 3: Premium –
Tiers 1 and 2 + 4
channels

Nuneaton/Bedworth/Rugby
franchise holder:
Heartland Cablevision
homes in area: 67,000
date awarded: Apr 1990

Oldham/Tameside
franchise holder:
Comment Cablevision
Oldham and Tameside
homes in area: 170,000
date awarded: May 1990

Oxford/Abingdon
franchise to be awarded
homes in area: 55,000

Paisley/Renfrew
franchise to be awarded
homes in area: 67,000

Peterborough
franchise holder:
Peterborough Cablevision
homes in area: 58,000
date awarded: July 1989
service start date: May
1990

Portsmouth/Fareham/Gosport/Havant
franchise holder:
Britannia Cable Systems
homes in area: 150,000
date awarded: Feb 1990

St Helens/Knowsley
franchise to be awarded
homes in area: 100,000

Salisbury
franchise holder: Wessex
Cable
homes in area: 15,000
date awarded: Apr 1990

Sheffield
franchise to be awarded
homes in area: 210,000

Southampton/Eastleigh
franchise holder:
Videotron Corporation
homes in area: 97,000
date awarded: Sept 1986
service start date: Oct
1989

Stafford/Stone
franchise holder: Stafford
Communications
homes in area: 24,000
date awarded: Dec 1989

Stockport
franchise holder:
TeleCable of Stockport
homes in area: 113,000
date awarded: May 1990

Stoke-on-Trent/Newcastle-under-Lyne
franchise holder:
Staffordshire Cable
homes in area: 140,000
date awarded: Dec 1989

Sunderland/Durham/Washington
franchise to be awarded
homes in area: 200,000

Surrey, North
Elmbridge, Runnymede
franchise to be awarded
homes in area: 71,000

Swindon
franchise holder: Swindon
Cable
homes in area: 75,000
homes passed: 65,000
date awarded: Nov 1983
service start date: Sept
1984
service:
    basic: 14 channels – 6
broadcast, SAT1, SC, Sky,
TCC, TV5, local, cabletext
    Additional channels:
MTV, HVC, Bravo, Sky
Movies

Tamworth
franchise holder: N-Com
Cablevision of Tamworth
homes in area: 25,000
date awarded: Apr 1990

Telford
franchise holder: Telford
Telecommunications
homes in area: 50,000
date awarded: Apr 1990

Thames Estuary North
Southend, Basildon,
Brentwood, Chelmsford,
etc
franchise holder: United
Artists Communications
homes in area: 300,000
date awarded: 16 Nov
1988
service start date: to be
announced
service:
    basic: 31 channels
including 5 broadcast
    Premium: additional à
la carte channels – HVC,
Indra Dhnush, Sky
Movies, BSB Movies

Thames Estuary South
Gravesend, Chatham,
Rochester, Gillingham,
Maidstone, Sittingbourne
franchise holder: United
Artists Communications
homes in area: 145,000
date awarded: Nov 1988
service start date: to be
announced
service:
    basic: 31 channels

including 5 broadcast
    Premium: additional à
la carte channels – HVC,
Indra Dhnush, Sky
Movies, BSB Movies

Thames Valley
Reading, Twyford,
Henley-on-Thames,
Wokingham, High
Wycombe, Marlow,
Bracknell, Basingstoke,
Newbury, Thatcham
franchise holder: Cable
Thames Valley
homes in area: 215,000
date awarded: Dec 1988

Thamesmead
franchise to be awarded
homes in area: 11,000

Thanet, Isle of
Margate, Ramsgate,
Broadstairs
franchise holder: Coastal
Cablevision
homes in area: 51,000
date awarded: Feb 1990

Tyneside
Newcastle upon Tyne,
Gateshead, North and
South Tyneside
franchise holder:
Comment Cablevision
homes in area: 325,000
date awarded: Dec 89

Wakefield/Pontefract/Castleford
franchise holder:
Wakefield Cable
homes in area: 94,000
date awarded: Mar 1990

Waltham Forest, London Borough of
franchise holder: East
London
Telecommunications
homes in area: 83,000
date awarded: Sept 1989
service start date: to be
announced
service:
    basic: 21 channels
    DeLuxe: basic + Bravo,
SS, CNN, MTV
Further 3 channels
available à la carte –
HVC, Sky Movies, BSB
Movies

Wandsworth, London Borough of
franchise holder:
Videotron London
homes in area: 100,000
date awarded: Aug 1985

Westminster, London Borough of
franchise holder:
Westminster Cable
Television
homes in area: 107,000
homes passed: 80,000
(build complete)
date awarded: Nov 1983
service start date: Sept
1985
service:
    Sat 1 Welcome
Package: 9 channels – 4
broadcast, SC, Westscan
(13-image multiplex),
Discovery, Galaxy, Now;
plus Text Services,
Broadcast
    Radio Services, FM
Radio
    Sky Package: Sky One,
Sky News, Eurosport
    à la carte programmes:
SS, MRV, European
Channel, CC, CNN, HVC,
Bravo, Sky Movies,
Arabic Channel, The
Movie Channel, Power
Station, SC

Wigan
franchise holder: Cable
Communications (Wigan)
homes in area: 110,000
date awarded: May 1990

Winchester
franchise holder:
Videotron South
homes in area: 33,000
date awarded: Apr 1990

Windsor/Slough/Maidenhead/Ashford/Staines/Stanwell/Heathrow
franchise holder: Windsor
Television
homes in area: 110,000
homes passed (Jan 1990):
80,000
date awarded: Nov 1983
service start date: Dec
1985
service:
    basic: Cablescene – 18
channels including 5
broadcast, Bravo, Cable
Jukebox, Discovery,
Eurosport, Landscape,
Lifestyle, SC, Sky, Sky
Arts, Sky News, Arcade
    Cable Choice:
additional channels –
SAT1/TV5, RAI, CC,
Disney Channel, Indra
Dhnush, MTV, SS, Sky
Movies

Wirral, The
franchise to be awarded
homes in area: 120,000

Wisbech/March/Whittlesey
franchise to be awarded
homes in area: 21,000

Worcester/Redditch/Droitwich
franchise to be awarded
homes in area: 70,000

York
franchise holder: York
Telecommunications
Complex
homes in area: 47,500
homes passed: 3,925
(jointly with Harrogate
franchise)
date awarded: Mar 1990
service start date: to be
announced
service:
   basic: 16 channels
   extended: basic + 8
channels
   à la carte: 4 channels

UPGRADE CABLE SYSTEMS

*Cable networks which
pre-existed the franchise
era and usually operate
on a limited basis on old
installations. These
services are gradually
being phased out as full
franchise network
construction proceeds.
Because a number are in
groups, systems are
listed in alphabetical
order of ownership*

British Cable Services
(trading as Maxwell
Cable Television)
areas:
Barrow-in-Furness

	HP 11,200
Burnley	HP 18,360
Hull	HP 73,040
Lancaster	HP 6,936
Leicester	HP 7,654
Mansfield	HP 19,603
Nottingham	HP 71,976
Rotherham	HP 18,102

Stoke-on-Trent/
Newcastle-under-
Lyne   HP 46,400
Teeside: Hartlepool/
Stockton/Billingham/
Middlesborough

	HP 25,032
Tyneside	HP 23,427
Wirral MBC (Birkenhead)	HP 23,000
Worcester	HP 9,964
Ashford	HP 11,000
Basildon	HP 26,100
Brighton/Hove	HP 20,000
Bristol	HP 47,000
Canterbury	HP 11,000
Deal/Dover/Folkestone	HP 23,000
Eastbourne	HP 20,250
Exeter	HP 16,087
Guildford	HP 2,236
Hastings	HP 30,000
Heads of Valley	HP 3,500
Maidstone	HP 15,000
Merthyr Tydfil	HP 13,000
Newbridge/Bargoed	HP 42,900
Norwich	HP 7,120
Oxford	HP 8,100
Reading	HP 14,600
Plymouth	HP 21,000
Rhondda	HP 35,000
Southampton	HP 21,000
Swansea	HP 16,140
Thanet	HP 30,000
Welwyn Garden City/ Hatfield	HP 13,100
West Wales	HP 9,200

service:
   Tier 1: 4 channels –
CC, SS, MTV, Sky
   Optional channels
available

British Telecom Visual Communication
areas (HP 71,360):
Barbican
Bracknell
Irvine/Milton Keynes
Washington
service: basic plus options

Broadcast Satellite Television
areas:
Barrow in Furness
          HP 18,360
Billingham/Teesside/
Hartlepool   HP 27,752
Birkenhead and Wirral
          HP 24,025
Brighton   HP 21,705

Cable and Satellite Television Holdings
area: Neath/Port Talbot
(HP 28,000)
service:
   Bronze: 10 channels – 5
broadcast, Sky, Sky Sport,
CC, Discovery, BSB
Galaxy
   Gold: 13 channels –
bronze + Sky movies,
BSB Sport, BSB Now,
BSB Power

Cablevision (Wellingborough)
area: Wellingborough
(HP 7,000)
service: 4 broadcast, SC,
Sky One, Sky Movies, CC,
SS

Greenwich Cablescene
area: Plumstead,
Woolwich, Abbey Wood,
Belvedere and Charlton
(HP 20,000)
service:
   Tier 1 (basic): 13
channels including 4
broadcast
   Tier 2: basic + choice of
additional channels

Gwent Cablevision
area: Tredegar (HP 5,200)
service: 9 broadcast, CC,
SC

Harris of Saltcoats
area: Saltcoats and Largs
(HP 6,975)

Jersey Cable
area: Jersey (HP 8,000)

Maxwell Cable Television see British Cable Services

Medway Cablevision/ Sittingbourne Cablevision
area: Sittingbourne
service: broadcast
channels, 5 BSB
channels, SC

Perth Cable Television
area: Perth (HP 9,500)
service: broadcast
channels + Eurosport,
CC, Discovery, Lifestyle

Salford Cable Television
area: Salford
service: broadcast
channels + Galaxy, Now,
Sports Channel, Power
Station, SC

Teleline
area: Princes Risborough
(HP 1,000)
service:
   basic: 7 channels – 5
broadcast, Sky One, Sky
Movies

West Wales Aerials
area: Llandeilo and
district (HP 1,500)
service: 4 broadcast
channels + Sky, Sky
Movies, Sky News, SS

ADDRESSES

Aberdeen Cable Services
303 King Street
Aberdeen AB2 3AP
Scotland
Tel: 0224 649444
Contact: John Miller
Ownership: British
Telecom, Legal & General
Assurance, Time Life
International, Standard
Life Assurance, Investors
In Industry, North of
Scotland Investment
Company, Clydesdale
Bank and others
Area: Aberdeen

Andover Cablevision
PO Box 77
Andover
Hampshire SP10 1YB
Tel: 0264 332300
Fax: 0264 332071
Contact: Peter Funk,
Chairman
Ownership: IVS Cable
Services
Area: Andover
See also Jersey Cable,
Stafford
Communications, Stort
Valley Cable, Wessex
Cable

Bay Cable
1-9 Cotlands Road
Bournemouth
Dorset BH1 3RP
Tel: 0202 294346
Contact: Martin Colvey
Ownership: Cross
Country Cable, NYNEX
Area: Bournemouth,
Poole and Christchurch

Birmingham Cable
154 Great Charles Street
Birmingham
Tel: 021 233 9696
Fax: 021 233 0125
Contact: Russell Griffiths,
Sales and Marketing
Director
Ownership: private
company
Area: Birmingham and

Solihull

Bolton Telecable
27-28 Queensbrook
Bolton Technology
Exchange
Spa Road
Bolton BL1 4AY
Tel: 0204 365440
Fax: 0204 365417
Contact: Peter Collins,
Managing Director
Ownership: Masada UK,
Pacific Telesis UK
Area: Bolton

Britannia Cable Systems
Capitol House
2-4 Church Street
Epsom
Surrey KT17 4NY
Tel: 0372 744050
Fax: 0372 744059
Contact: Peter Lynch,
Chief Executive
Ownership: Falcon Cable
TV, Mearing-Lynch
Cable, Camelot Cable,
First Carolina
Communications
Area: Portsmouth,
Fareham, Gosport and
Havant

British Cable Services
c/o Maxwell
Entertainment Group
(Welsh Region)
Partridge Road
Llywnpia, Rhondda
Mid Glamorgan CF40
2SH
Tel: 0443 441382
Fax: 0443 435700
Contact: Jeff James,
Regional Manager
Ownership: wholly owned
subsidiary of Metromode
(Pergamon Press 50%,
Robert Maxwell 50%)
Area: Cardiff and Penarth

British Cable Services
170 Walnut Tree Close
Guildford
Surrey GU1 4RX
Tel: 0483 505200
Contact: Tony Weeden,
Manager
Ownership: wholly owned
subsidiary of Metromode
(Pergamon Press 50%,
Robert Maxwell 50%)
Area: Guildford and West
Surrey

British Cable Services
c/o Maxwell Cable

Television
Maxwell Entertainment
Group
3 Plough Place
London EC4A 1PD
Tel: 071 822 3681
Fax: 071 583 3135
Ownership: wholly owned
subsidiary of Metromode
(Pergamon Press 50%,
Robert Maxwell 50%)
Areas: 37 upgrade
systems within UK
See also Clyde
Cablevision

British Telecom Visual Communication
New Towns System
51 Alston Drive
Bradwell Abbey
Milton Keynes MK13
9HB
Tel: 0908 322522
Fax: 0908 321896
Contact: David Hunter,
General Manager
Ownership: British
Telecom
Areas: upgrade systems
in Barbican, Bracknell,
Irvine, Milton Keynes
and Washington
See also Aberdeen Cable,
Cable Thames Valley,
Coventry Cable, Swindon
Cable, Ulster
Cablevision, Westminster
Cable

Broadcast Satellite Television
303 King Street
Aberdeen AB2 3AP
Tel: 0224 646644
Fax: 0224 644601
Contact: Graham
Duncan, Chairman
Ownership: private
company
Areas: upgrade systems
in Barrow in Furness,
Billingham/Teesside/
Hartlepool, Birkenhead/
Wirral and Brighton
See also Gwent
Cablevision, Medway
Cablevision/
Sittingbourne
Cablevision, Salford
Cable Television, Tayside
Cable Systems

Cable and Satellite Television Holdings
Newcome Drive
Hawkesworth Estate
Swindon
Wiltshire SN2 1TU
Tel: 0793 611176
Fax: 0793 542512

Contact: Michael O'Brien
Ownership: private
company
Area: upgrade system in
Neath/Port Talbot

Cable Camden
23 Mandela Street
London NW1
Tel: 071 528 5333
Contact: Jan Tilling
Ownership: wholly owned
subsidiary of Cable
London – Logica UK
(18.3%), Investors In
Industry (14.6%), D R
Djanogly (14.6%), Sound
& Vision Technology
(9.5%), McNicholas
Construction (5.8%),
Research Recordings
(5.8%), Mercury (5.3%)
Area: London Borough of
Camden

Cable Communications (Wigan)
c/o Oyston Cable
Communications Group
Oyston Mill (2nd Floor)
Strand Road
Preston PR1 8UR
Tel: 0772 721505
Fax: 0772 734640
Contact: David Whitaker,
Managing Director
Ownership: Southwestern
Bell, Oyston Cable
Communications
Area: Wigan
See also Lancashire
Cablevision, Merseyside
Cablevision

Cable Hackney and Islington
Cable Haringey
c/o Cable London
Centro House
20-23 Mandela Street
London NW1 0DU
Tel: 071 911 0911
Fax: 071 911 0111
Contact: Sally Davis,
Managing Director
Ownership: Cable London
(see Cable Camden)
Area: London Boroughs of
Hackney and Islington,
Haringey

Cable North
5 Woodlands Terrace
Glasgow G3 6DD
Tel: 041 333 9292
Fax: 041 331 1230
Contact: W D Stewart
Ownership: W D Stewart,
Cable (UK)
Areas:
Cumbernauld, Kilsyth,

Airdrie and Coatbridge
Dumbarton and Vale of
Leven
Motherwell, East
Kilbride, Hamilton,
Wishaw and Lanark

Cable Television
Forsyth Road
Sheerwater
Woking
Surrey
Tel: 0486 761861
Fax: 0483 766275
Contact: Ron Dean,
Managing Director
Main shareholders: CUC
Broadcasting, Dean

Cable Thames Valley
c/o British Telecom
Visual Communication
Room 26/20
Euston Tower
London NW1 3DG
Tel: 071 728 3798
Contact: Roger Wilson,
Managing Director
Ownership: British
Telecom Visual
Communication (qv)
Area: Thames Valley

Cablevision Bedfordshire
Cablevision House
20 Cosgrove Way
Luton
Bedfordshire LU1 1XL
Tel: 0582 401044
Fax: 0582 401055
Contact: George Carr
Ownership: private
company
Area: Luton, Dunstable
and Leighton Buzzard

Cablevision Communications Company
Cablevision House
20 Cosgrove Way
Luton
Bedfordshire LU1 1SL
Tel: 0582 401044
Fax: 0582 401055
Contact: A J Minta, Joint
Chairman
Ownership: private
company
Area: Hertfordshire,
Central

Cablevision (Scotland)
4 Melville Street
Edinburgh EH3 7NZ
Tel: 031 243 8322
Fax: 031 243 8324
Contact: Charles Young
Ownership: British Linen

Bank, Christian Salvesen, Cox Cable, Ferranti, Grampian Television, Johnston Press, Radio Forth, Radio Rentals, D C Thomson (10.47% each), Press Construction (5.77%)
Area: Edinburgh

Cablevision (Wellingborough)
c/o Mobile Radio Services
Central Hall Buildings
Wellingborough
Northants NN8 4HT
Tel: 0933 222078
Contact: P W Elson
Ownership: private company
Area: upgrade system in Wellingborough

Cambridge Cable
24 Thompson's Lane
Cambridge CB5 8AQ
Tel: 0223 464201
Fax: 0223 467347
Contact: Chris Curry, Chairman
Main shareholder: Telecable
Area: Cambridge and district

Cheshire Cable Wakefield Cable
41 Gloucester Place
London W1H 3PD
Tel: 071 935 5809
Contact: Bill McDougal
Ownership: Maclean Hunter Cablevision, Kingston Communications (Hull)
Areas:
 Cheshire, North Wakefield, Pontefract and Castleford
See also East Coast Cable, Staffordshire Cable

Clyde Cablevision
40 Anderston Quay
Glasgow G3 8DA
Tel: 041 221 7040
Fax: 041 248 2921
Contact: Sir Ian MacGregor, Chairman
Ownership: Insight Communications, GEC, Cable and Wireless, Maxwell Communications
Area: Glasgow (Central) and Clydebank (NW)

Coastal Cablevision
7-11 Kensington High Street
London W8 5NP
Tel: 071 937 4610

Contact: Tom Engel, Managing Director
Ownership: Leonard Communications International
Areas:
 Dorset, West Thanet, Isle of

Comment Cablevision
c/o BIS Applied Systems
Maybrook House
40 Blackfriars Street
Manchester M3 2EG
Tel: 061 831 7031
Contact: Nick Perryman
Ownership: US Cable Corporation, Nynex Corporation
Areas:
 Bury and Rochdale Oldham and Tameside

Comment Cablevision
20 Leazes Park Road
Newcastle upon Tyne
NE1 4PG
Tel: 091 281 8623
Contact: Mike McGraw
Main shareholders: US Cable Corporation, US West
Area: Tyneside

Coventry Cable Television
London Road
Coventry
West Midlands CV3 4HL
Tel: 0203 505345
Fax: 0203 505445
Contact: Roy Emerson
Ownership: British Telecom (75.5%), CUC Broadcasting (13.5%), Equity & Law (11%)
Area: Coventry

Derbyshire Cablevision see Greater Manchester Cablevision

Devon Cablevision
Southernhay House
36 Southernhay East
Exeter EX1 1LA
Tel: 0392 211185
Contact: Roger Acock
Ownership: Maclean Hunter Cablevision
Area: Devon, South
See also Cheshire Cable, East Coast Cable, Staffordshire Cable

Diamond Cable
Suite 1D, Advanced Business Centre

59 Maid Marian Way
Nottingham NG1 6BH
Tel: 0602 503021
Fax: 0602 413772
Contact: Gary Davis, Managing Director
Ownership: Robert Wall and Allan J McDonald
Areas:
 Grantham
 Melton Mowbray
 Newark

Diamond Cable (Mansfield/ Nottingham)
PO Box 39
Nottingham NG1 6BZ
Tel: 0602 503021
Fax: 0602 413772
Contact: Gary Davis, Managing Director
Ownership: Diamond Cable UK (qv)
Areas:
 Mansfield, Sutton and Kirkby-in-Ashfield
 Nottingham

East Coast Cable Staffordshire Cable
41 Gloucester Place
London W1H 3PD
Tel: 071 935 5809
Contact: Bill McDougall, Director
Ownership: Maclean Hunter Cablevision
Areas:
 Colchester and Ipswich
 Stoke-on-Trent and Newcastle-under-Lyne
See also Cheshire Cable, Devon Cable

East Lancashire Cablevision
Glenfield Park Site 2
Northrop Avenue
Blackburn
Lancashire BB1 5QG
Tel: 0254 680094
Fax: 0254 679236
Contact: Edward Hadden, Managing Director
Ownership: Maclean Hunter, Cablevision
Area: Lancashire (East)

East London Telecommunications
ELT House
2 Millharbour
London E14 9TE
Tel: 071 895 9910
Fax: 071 895 9755
Contact: B Turner-Smith, Director
Ownership: Jones Intercable (45%), Pacific Telesis International (45%), others

Areas:
 Dartford and Swanley
 Epping Forest Local Authority
 London Borough of Havering
 Greater London East
 London Boroughs of Newham and Tower Hamlets
 London Borough of Waltham Forest

Greater Manchester Cablevision Derbyshire Cablevision
Regency Court
62-66 Deansgate
Manchester M3 2EN
Tel: 061 832 5182
Contact: Peter Collins
Ownership: Masada UK Cable Partners, Pacific Telesis UK
Area: Derby and Spondon
See also Norwich Cablevision, Peterborough Cablevision

Greenwich Cablescene
62-64 Beresford Street
London SE18 6BG
Tel: 081 316 1200
Contact: Richard Tripp
Ownership: Videotron Group
Area: upgrade system in Plumstead, Woolwich, Abbey Wood, Belvedere and Charlton

Gwent Cablevision
88 Commercial Street
Tredegar
Gwent NP2 3DN
Tel: 0495 252600
Fax: 0495 717892
Contact: Gordon Sleigh, Managing Director
Ownership: Broadcast Satellite Television (qv)
Area: upgrade system in Tredegar

Harris of Saltcoats
104-106 Dockhead Street
Saltcoats
Strathclyde KA21 5EL
Scotland
Tel: 0294 64330
Contact: Hugh Mackay
Ownership: private company
Area: Saltcoats and Largs

Harrogate Telecommunications Complex see York Telecommunications

Complex

Herts Cable
17 Marlowes
Hemel Hempstead
Hertfordshire HP1 1LA
Tel: 0442 65599
Contact: Adam Haas,
Managing Director
Ownership: CUC
Broadcasting (90%),
Rondean (10%)
Area: Hertfordshire, West

Heartland Cablevision
c/o CUC Cablevision (UK)
3-6 The Colonnade
High Street
Maidenhead
Berkshire SL6 1QL
Tel: 0628 777611
Fax: 0628 32558
Contact: Vernon Achber
Ownership: CUC
Cablevision (UK)
Areas:
  Kenilworth,
Leamington Spa,
Stratford-upon-Avon and
Warwick
  Nuneaton, Bedworth
and Rugby

Jersey Cable
PO Box 233
St Helier
Jersey
Channel Islands
Tel: 0534 33789
Fax: 0534 65019
Contact: Peter Funk,
Chairman
Ownership: private
company
Area: upgrade system in
Jersey
See also Andover
Cablevision, Stafford
Communications, Stort
Valley Cable, Wessex
Cable

Jones Cable Group
PO Box 448
Kings Langley
Herts WD4 8TD
Tel: 0923 270177
Fax: 0923 270207
Contact: A C Bates,
Managing Director
Ownership: Jones
International
Areas:
  Hertfordshire, South
Leeds

Lancashire Cable Television
c/o Oyston Cable
Communications Group
Ribble View

Frenchwood Avenue
Preston
Lancashire PR1 4QF
Tel: 0772 202888
Contact: David Whitaker,
Managing Director
Ownership: Southwestern
Bell, Oyston Cable
Communications
Area: Lancashire, Central
See also Cable
Communications
(Wigan), Merseyside
Cablevision

Leicester Communications
12 Elstree Way
Borehamwood
Hertfordshire WD6 1NF
Tel: 081 207 5232
Fax: 081 207 5910
Contact: Alan Poole,
Commercial Director
Ownership: Community
Communications (46%),
Kingston
Communications (18%),
Leicester cc (7%), Radio
Trent (8%), Q Studios
(8%), Morgan Grenfell
(8%), Alliance & Leicester
Building Society (5%)
Areas:
  Leicester
  Loughborough and
Shepshed

Medway Cablevision/ Sittingbourne Cablevision
2-4 William Street
Sittingbourne
Kent ME10 1HR
Tel: 0795 429711
Fax: 0795 422807
Contact: Chris Homfray,
General Manager
Ownership: Broadcast
Satellite Television (qv)
Area: Sittingbourne

Merseyside Cablevision
c/o Oyston Cable
Communications Group
Oyston Mill (2nd Floor)
Strand Road
Preston PR1 8UR
Tel: 0772 721505
Fax: 0772 734640
Contact: David Whitaker,
Managing Director
Ownership: Southwestern
Bell, Oyston Cable
Communications
Area: Liverpool, South
See also Cable
Communications
(Wigan), Lancashire
Cablevision

Mid Downs Cable
Simpson House
Cherry Orchard Road
Croydon
Surrey CRO 6BA
Tel: 081 686 6823
Fax: 081 680 3473
Contact: Alan Boyd,
Chairman
Ownership: Swedtel, HTV
Group, Goldcrest
Communications
Area: Crawley, Horley
and Gatwick

N-Com Cablevision of Hinckley
c/o Malarkey Taylor
International
150 Regent Street
London W1R 5FA
Tel: 071 439 7117
Fax: 071 734 4166
Contact: Nicolas Mellersh
Ownership: N-Com
Limited Partnership
Area: Hinckley

N-Com Cablevision of Tamworth
c/o Swedtel
Simpson House
6 Cherry Orchard Road
Croydon CRO 6BA
Tel: 081 686 6823
Fax: 081 680 3473
Contact: Alan Boyd
Ownership: N-Com
Limited Partnership
Area: Tamworth

North Downs Cable
c/o Starside Network
6 Prince Albert Road
Regents Park
London NW1 7SR
Tel: 071 284 0432
Contact: Dean Hazen
Ownership: wholly owned
subsidiary of Starstream
Europe
Area: Kent, South East

Norwich Cablevision
Unit D1, Wensum Point
32A Whiffler Road
Norwich NR3 2AZ
Tel: 0603 787892
Fax: 0603 787851
Contact: Keith Davis,
Director of UK
Operations
Ownership: Masada UK,
Pacific Telesis UK
Area: Norwich
See also Derbyshire
Cablevision,
Peterborough Cablevision

Perth Cable Television
North Muirton
Perth PH1 3DZ
Tel: 0738 38794
Contact: Archie Alston,
General Manager
Ownership: Broadcast
Satellite Television (qv)
Area: upgrade system in
Perth

Peterborough Cablevision South Yorkshire Cablevision
2 Mancetter Square
Werrington
Peterborough PE4 6BX
Tel: 0733 320434
Fax: 0733 320535
Contact: Keith Davis,
Director of UK
Operations
Ownership: Masada UK,
Pacific Telesis UK
Areas:
  Peterborough
  Doncaster/Rotherham
See also Derbyshire
Cablevision, Norwich
Cablevision

Salford Cable Television
102 Mather Way
Salford M6 5JA
Tel: 061 737 9313
Contact: Graham Sleigh
Ownership: Broadcast
Satellite Television (qv)
Area: upgrade system in
Salford

South Yorkshire Cablevision see Peterborough Cablevision

Southdown Cable
Skycom House
4 Cavendish Street
Brighton
East Sussex
Tel: 0273 679071
Fax: 0273 674084
Contact: Brian Thornton,
Managing Director
Ownership: Cross
Country Cable, Electra
Investment Trust
Area: Brighton, Hove and
Worthing

Stafford Communications Stort Valley Cable Wessex Cable
c/o IVS Cable Holdings
54 Warwick Square
London SW1V 2AJ

Tel: 071 834 6012
Fax: 071 630 6270
Contact: Peter Funk,
Managing Director
Ownership: IVS Cable
Holdings
Areas:
Stafford and Stone
Harlow, Bishops
Stortford and Stansted
Airport
Salisbury
See also Andover
Cablevision

Starvision Network
Network House
Baglan Industrial Park
Baglan
Port Talbot SA12 7DJ
Tel: 0639 899999
Contact: Mike Graves
Ownership: Cable &
Satellite Television
Holdings, Starvision
Network and others
Area: Glamorgan, West

Swindon Cable
Newcome Drive
Hawkesworth Estate
Swindon
Wiltshire SN2 1TU
Tel: 0793 615601
Fax: 0793 619535
Contact: Roger Wilson
Ownership: British
Telecom
Area: Swindon

Tayside Cable Systems
303 King Street
Aberdeen AB2 3AP
Tel: 0224 644600
Fax: 0224 644601
Contact: Graham
Duncan, Chairman
Ownership: Broadcast
Satellite Television (qv),
Vento Cable
Management, Malarkey
Taylor Associates
Area: Dundee and Perth

Telecable of Stockport
Sun Alliance House
9 Bond Court
Leeds LS1 2SN
Tel: 0800 777421
Contact: Page Lea
Ownership: Telecable
Corporation
Area: Stockport

Telecommunications Network
98 St James Street
Brighton
East Sussex BN2 1TP
Tel: 0273 606702

Fax: 0273 674084
Contact: Brian Thornton,
Managing Director
Ownership: Cross
Country Cable
Area: London Borough of
Bromley
See also South Down
Cable

Teleline
3-5 High Street
Princes Risborough
Buckinghamshire HP17
0AE
Tel: 0844 43196
Contact: Roy Boughton
Ownership: private
company
Area: upgrade system in
Princes Risborough

Telford Telecommunications
see West Midlands
Cable
Communications

Ulster Cablevision
40 Victoria Square
Belfast BT1 4QB
Tel: 0232 249141
Contact: George F Alton,
Executive Vice-Chairman
Ownership: British
Telecom Visual
Communication
Area: Belfast

United Artists Communications
United Artists International
Unit 1, Genesis Business
Park
Albert Drive, Woking
Surrey GU21 5RW
Tel: 0483 750900
Fax: 0483 750901
Contact: Ms Terry
Collins, VP Business
Development
Ownership: United
Artists International
Areas:
Avon
Cheltenham and
Gloucester
Croydon, Merton/
Sutton and Kingston
Richmond, London
Boroughs of
Thames Estuary North
Thames Estuary South

Videotron Corporation
Ocean House Business
Centre
West Quay Road
Southampton SO1 OGY
Tel: 0703 333020

Fax: 0703 335237
Contact: Peter Alden,
Managing Director
Ownership: private
company
Area: Southampton and
Eastleigh

Videotron London
Belmont House
11-29 Belmont Hill
London SE13 5AU
Tel: 081 852 0123
Contact: Ross Jepson,
Managing Director
Ownership: Videotron,
Bell Canada
Areas:
London Boroughs of
Greenwich and Lewisham
London Boroughs of
Lambeth and Southwark
London Borough of
Wandsworth
See also Greenwich
Cablescene

Videotron South
Ocean House Business
Centre
West Quay Road
Southampton SO1 0XL
Tel: 0703 333020
Fax: 0703 335237
Contact: Richard Tripp,
Director
Ownership: Videotron,
Bell Canada
Area: Winchester

Wakefield Cable see Cheshire Cable

West Midlands Cable Communications
Telford Telecommunications
Ye Big House
44 Church Street
Oldbury
Warley
West Midlands B69 3AE
Tel: 021 544 8244
Fax: 021 544 4057
Contact: Alan Robinson,
Managing Director
Main shareholder:
Goldcrest
Areas:
Black Country
Telford

West Wales Aerials
97 Rhosnan Street
Llandeilo
Dyfed SA19 6HA
Wales
Tel: 0558 823278
Contact: A J E Jones
Ownership: private
company

Area: upgrade system in
Llandeilo

Westminster Cable Company
87-89 Baker Street
London W1M 1AH
Tel: 071 935 6699
Fax: 071 486 9447
Contact: Samantha Gates
Ownership: British
Telecom, City Centre
Cable, Lapari, Sanoma
Area: London Borough of
Westminster

Westside Cable
Parkways
179-181 The Vale
London W3 7QS
Tel: 081 740 4848
Fax: 081 740 0817
Contact: Sir George
Jefferson, Chairman
Ownership: Videotron
Corporation (80%), BRIT
(20%)
Areas:
London Borough of
Ealing
London Borough of
Kensington and Chelsea
London, North West

Windsor Television
Cable House
Waterside Drive
Langley
Berkshire Sl3 6EZ
Tel: 0753 44144
Fax: 0753 46310
Contact: Tim Halfhead,
Managing Director
Ownership: Compagnie
Générale des Eaux
(30.1%), Standard Life
Assurance (25.5%), US
West (6%), McNicholas
Construction (5.3%),
others (33.1%)
Area: Windsor, Slough,
Maidenhead, Ashford,
Staines, Stanwell and
Heathrow

York Telecommunications Complex
Harrogate Telecommunications Complex
c/o YorCan
Communications
Westgate Point
Westgate
Leeds LS1 2AX
Tel: 0532 424511
Fax: 0532 420905
Contact: Laurie Craigen,
General Manager
Ownership: Harrogate:
YorCan Communications

(91%), Harrogate Telecommunications (9%); York: YorCan Communications (91%), York Telecommunications (9%)
Areas:
Harrogate and Knaresborough
York

ENGLISH-LANGUAGE SATELLITE-DELIVERED TELEVISION CHANNELS IN EUROPE

All channels transmitting via satellite in Europe, wholly or partly in the English language. The television standard and encrypting system used are indicated after the name of the satellite. Not all channels are intended for reception in the UK

AFRTS Germany
HQ USAFE/PAI
6720 Flugplatz Ramstein
German Fed Rep
Ownership: US Government
Satellite: Intelsat F15 (B-MAC/clear)
Programming: entertainment

BBC Europe
Woodlands
80 Wood Lane
London W12 0TT
Tel: 081 576 2248
Ownership: BBC
Satellite: Intelsat F11 (PAL/Save)
Programming: entertainment

British Satellite Broadcasting (BSB)
The Marcopolo Building
Chelsea Bridge
Queenstown Road
London SW8 4NG
Tel: 071 978 2222
Ownership: BSB (Bond Corp) (36.6%), Granada (15.1%), Pearson (14.1%), Chargeurs (12.1%), Reed (10.1%), Next (4.4%), London Merchant Securities (2.9%), Anglia TV (2.6%), Invest Int'l (1.4%), Trinity Int'l (0.7%)

See Galaxy, Movie Channel, Now, Power Station, Sports Channel

CNN (Cable News International)
19-22 Rathbone Place
London W1P 1DF
Tel 071 637 6800
Fax 071 637 6868
Ownership: Turner Broadcasting System
Satellite: Intelsat F11 (PAL)
Programming: news

Channel E
European Institute for the Media
The University
Manchester M13 9PL
Tel: 061 273 2754
Ownership: VNU, EIM, SES, European Commission, IFCBEBF
Satellite: Astra 1A (PAL/clear)
Programming: education

Children's Channel
9-13 Grape Street
London WC2H 8DR
Tel: 071 240 3422
Ownership: Central TV (25%), Thames TV (25%), D C Thomson (25%), British Telecom (25%)
Satellite: Intelsat F11 (PAL/clear)
Programming: children's

Discovery Channel
Twyman House
16 Bonny Street
London NW1 9PG
Tel: 071 482 4824
Ownership: United Artists International
Satellite: Intelsat F11 (PAL/clear)
Programming: documentaries

Enterprise Channel
Woodlands
80 Wood Lane
London W12 0TT
Tel: 081 576 0563
Ownership: BBC
Satellite: Olympus 1A F1 (D2-MAC)
Programming: entertainment

European Business Channel
Wagistrasse 4
Schlieren/Zürich
Switzerland
Ownership: AWF (62.5%), Blackbox (15%), Jean Frey (10%), CLT (6.5%),

Telekurs (4.5%), Thames TV (1%)
Satellite: Astra 1A, Kopernikus 1, Eutelsat F4 (PAL/clear)
Programming: news

Eurosport
6 Centaurs Business Park
Grant Way
Isleworth
Middlesex TW7 5QD
Tel: 081 782 3000
Ownership: Sky Television (qv), in association with 14 EBU members
Satellite: Astra 1A, Eutelsat F4 (PAL/clear)
Programming: sport

Eurostep
Rapenburg 63
2311 GJ Leiden
Netherlands
Ownership: educational institutions in several countries
Satellite: Olympus 1 (D2-MAC/clear)
Programming: education

Galaxy
Ownership: British Satellite Broadcasting (qv)
Satellite: BSB-1 (D-MAC/clear)
Programming: entertainment

Lifestyle
180 Wardour Street
London W1V 8AA
Tel: 071 439 1177
Ownership: W H Smith (74%), D C Thomson (15%), TVS (5%), Yorkshire TV (6%)
Satellite: Astra 1A (PAL/clear)
Programming: women's

MTV Europe
20-23 Mandela Street
London NW1 0DU
Tel: 071 383 4250
Ownership: Maxwell Communications (50%), Viacom (50%)
Satellite: Astra 1A (PAL/clear)
Programming: music

Movie Channel
Ownership: British Satellite Broadcasting (qv)
Satellite: BSB-1 (D-MAC/Eurocypher)
Programming: films

Now
Ownership: British Satellite Broadcasting (qv)
Satellite: BSB-1 (D-MAC/clear)
Programming: information

One World Channel
93 Wardour Street
London W1V 3TE
Tel: 071 494 2083
Ownership: All Europe Satellite TV
Satellite: Eutelsat F4 (PAL/clear)
Programming: religion

Power Station
Ownership: British Satellite Broadcasting (qv)
Satellite: BSB-1 (D-MAC/clear)
Programming: music

SIS
17 Corsham Street
London N1 6DR
Tel: 071 253 2232
Ownership: Racal (20%), Ladbroke (18%), Brent Walker (15%), Sears (13%), Bass (12%), RAL (10%), MAI (7%), Tote (5%)
Satellite: Intelsat F11 (B-MAC)
Programming: horse racing

Screensport
180 Wardour Street
London W1V 8AA
Tel: 071 439 1177
Ownership: W H Smith (75%), ESPN (25%)
Satellite: Astra 1A (PAL/clear)
Programming: sport

Shopping Channel
Baltic Centre
1-7 Great West Road
Brentford
Middlesex TW8 9BV
Tel: 0328 738447
Ownership: Next/Grattan (50%), E-Sat Communications (50%)
Satellite: Astra 1A (PAL/clear)
Programming: home shopping

Sky Movies
Ownership: Sky Television (qv)
Satellite: Astra 1A (PAL/Videocrypt)
Programming: films

Sky News
Ownership: Sky
Television (qv)
Satellite: Astra 1A (PAL/
clear)
Programming: news

Sky One
Ownership: Sky
Television (qv)
Satellite: Astra 1A (PAL/
clear)
Programming:
entertainment

Sky Television
6 Centaurs Business Park
Grant Way
Syon Lane
Isleworth
Middlesex TW7 5QD
Tel: 071 782 3000
Ownership: News
International (89%)
See Eurosport, Sky
Movies, Sky News, Sky
One

Sports Channel
Ownership: British
Satellite Broadcasting
(qv)
Satellite: BSB-1 (D-MAC/
clear)
Programming: sport

Super Channel
Melrose House
14 Lanark Square
Limeharbour
London E14 9QD
Tel: 071 418 9418
Ownership: Beta
Television (55%), Virgin
(45%)
Satellite: Eutelsat F4
(PAL/clear)
Programming:
entertainment

Worldnet
US Information Agency
American Embassy
24 Grosvenor Square
London W1A 1AE
Tel: 071 499 9000
Ownership: US
government
Satellite: Eutelsat F4
(PAL/clear)
Programming: news

Abbreviations
BSB – British Satellite
Broadcasting
CC – Children's
Channel
CNN – Cable News
Network
HP – homes passed
HVC – Home Video
Channel
SC – Super Channel
SS – Screensport
WN – Worldnet

CINEMAS

Listed below are the companies which control the major chains of cinemas and multiplexes in the UK, followed by the cinemas themselves listed by area, with seating capacities. Disabled access information has been included for the first time (see key), covering in this edition the London area and BFI-supported cinemas around the country only. In future editions, we hope to extend this information to the rest of the UK. The assistance of Artsline, London's information and advice centre on arts and entertainment for disabled people, is gratefully acknowledged

CINEMA CIRCUITS

Apollo Cinemas
Apollo Leisure (UK)
11 Arkwright Office Suite
Mill Lane
Coppull
Lancs PR7 5AN
Tel: 0257 471012
Now includes the Unit Four circuit and operates 49 screens on 16 sites. Apollo's Theatre Division operates the Dominion, London, and Futurist, Scarborough, which occasionally show films

CAC Leisure
PO Box 21
23-25 Huntly Street
Inverness IV1 1LA
Tel: 0463 237611
Operates 19 screens on 9 sites, all in Scotland

Cannon Cinemas
Pathé House
76 Hammersmith Road
London W14 8YR
Tel: 071 603 4555
Operated 381 screens on 138 sites in April 1990

National Amusements (UK)
200 Elm Street
Dedham
Massachusetts 02026-9126
USA
Tel: 0101 617 461 1600
Operators of seven Showcase multiplexes with 83 screens. Further UK sites are under consideration

Panton Films
Coronet Cinema
Notting Hill Gate
London W11
Tel: 071 221 0123
Operates the Coronet circuit of 11 screens on 5 sites, comprising former circuit cinemas of Rank and Cannon

Rank Theatres
439-445 Godstone Road
Whyteleafe
Surrey CR3 0YG
Tel: 0883 623355
Operates the Odeon chain totalling 256 screens on 75 sites at the end of March 1990, with many additional screens under construction

Tatton Group
Davenport Theatre
Buxton Road
Stockport
Greater Manchester
Tel: 061 483 3801
Operates 8 screens on 4 sites in the Manchester area

UCI (UK)
Parkside House
51-53 Brick Street
London W1Y 7DU
Tel: 071 409 1346
Formerly CIC/UA. Operators of 16 purpose-built multiplexes with 151 screens in spring 1990, with 7 more scheduled to open shortly

Warner Bros Theatres (UK)
135 Wardour Street
London W1V 4AP
Tel: 071 437 5600
In addition to the 5-screen Warner West End in Leicester Square, operated 3 multiplexes with 33 screens at Bury, Newcastle and York in spring 1990, with at least 8 more to follow

LONDON WEST END – PREMIERE RUN

Astral
Brewer Street
Tel: 071 734 6387
Seats: 1:89, 2:159

Barbican ♿
Silk Street
Tel: 071 628 8795/638 8891
Seats: 1:280, 2:255*, 3:153*

Camden Parkway
Parkway
Tel: 071 267 7034
Seats: Kings:946, Regency:90

Camden Plaza ♿
Camden High Street
Tel: 071 485 2443
Seats: 340

Cannon Baker Street
Marylebone Road
Tel: 071 935 9772
Seats: 1:171, 2:169

Cannon Chelsea
King's Road

Tel: 071 352 5096/351
1026
Seats: 1:233, 2:264, 3:151,
4:119

**Cannon Fulham
Road**
Tel: 071 370 0265/2636/
2110
Seats: 1:416⧓, 2:374⧓,
3:223⑤, 4:223⑤, 5:222

Cannon Haymarket
Tel: 071 839 1527/1528
Seats: 1:448, 2:200, 3:201

**Cannon Oxford
Street**
Tel: 071 636 0310/3851
Seats: 1:334, 2:227, 3:195,
4:225, 5:47

**Cannon Panton
Street**
Tel: 071 930 0631/2
Seats: 1:127⑤, 2:144⑤,
3:138, 4:136 ·

**Cannon Piccadilly
Circus**
Tel: 071 437 3561
Seats: 1:124, 2:118

Cannon Premiere
Swiss Centre
Tel: 071 439 4470/437
2096
Seats: 1:97, 2:101, 3:93,
4:108

**Cannon
Shaftesbury
Avenue**
Tel: 071 836 6279/379
7025
Seats: 1:616, 2:581

**Cannon Tottenham
Court Road**
Tel: 071 636 6148/6749
Seats: 1:328, 2:145, 3:137

**Centre Charles
Peguy** ⑤*
Leicester Square
Tel: 071 437 8339
Seats: 100

Chelsea Cinema
King's Road
Tel: 071 351 3742
Seats: 713

Coronet
Notting Hill Gate
Tel: 071 727 6705
Seats: 396

Curzon Mayfair
Curzon Street
Tel: 071 499 3737/465

8865
Seats: 542

Curzon Phoenix
Phoenix Street
Tel: 071 240 9661
Seats: 212

Curzon West End
Shaftesbury Avenue
Tel: 071 439 4805
Seats: 624

Design Museum ⑤*
Butler's Wharf, Shad
Thames
Tel: 071 403 6933
Seats: 70

Dominion ⑤*
Tottenham Court Road
Tel: 071 580 9562/3
Seats: 2000

Electric ⑤*
Portobello Road
Tel: 071 792 2020
Seats: 437

**Empire Leicester
Square**
Tel: 071 497 9999/437
1234
Seats: 1:1330⑤, 2:353,
3:80

French Institute*
Queensberry Place SW7
Tel: 071 589 6211
Seats: 350

Gate ⑤
Notting Hill Gate
Tel: 071 727 4043
Seats: 241

Goethe Institute*
Princes Gate SW7
Tel: 071 581 3344
Seats: 170

ICA Cinema ⑤
The Mall
Tel: 071 930 0493
Seats: 208, C'thèque: 50

**Imperial War
Museum** ⑤*
Lambeth Road
Tel: 071 735 8922
Seats: 216

**London Film
Makers'
Co-op***
Gloucester Avenue NW1
Tel: 071 586 8516
Seats: 100

Lumière ⑤
St Martin's Lane
Tel: 071 836 0691/379

3014
Seats: 737

Metro ⑤
Rupert Street
Tel: 071 437 0757
Seats: 1:195, 2:85

Minema
Knightsbridge
Tel: 071 235 4225
Seats: 68

**Museum of
London** ⑤*
London Wall EC2
Tel: 071 600 3699/1058
Seats: 270

**National Film
Theatre/
Museum of the
Moving Image** ⑤☑
South Bank, Waterloo
Tel: 071 928 3232
Seats: 1:466, 2:162,
MOMI:130

**Odeon
Haymarket** ⑤☑
Tel: 071 839 7697
Seats: 600

**Odeon High Street
Kensington**
Tel: 071 602 6644/5
Seats: 1:657, 2:301⑤,
3:193⑤, 4:234⑤

**Odeon Leicester
Square**
Tel: 071 930 6111/4250/
4259
Seats: 1983⑤;
Mezzanine: 291
(5 screens)

**Odeon Marble
Arch** ☑
Tel: 071 723 2011
Seats: 1360

**Odeon Swiss
Cottage**
Finchley Road
Tel: 071 586 3057
Seats: 1:736, 2:152⑤,
3:155⑤

Odeon West End
Leicester Square
Tel: 071 930 5252/3
Seats: 1402

**Plaza Piccadilly
Circus**
Lower Regent Street
Tel: 071 497 9999/437
1234
Seats: 1:732, 2:367⑤,
3:161, 4:187

Prince Charles ⑤
Leicester Square
Tel: 071 437 8181
Seats: 487

**Queen Elizabeth
Hall** ⑤*
South Bank, Waterloo
Tel: 071 928 3002
Seats: 906

Renoir
Brunswick Square
Tel: 071 837 8402
Seats: 1:251, 2:251

**Royal Festival
Hall** ⑤*
South Bank, Waterloo
Tel: 071 928 3002
Seats: 2419

Scala Kings Cross
Pentonville Road
Tel: 071 278 8052/0051
Seats: 350

**Screen on Baker
Street**
Tel: 071 935 2772
Seats: 1:95, 2:100

**Screen on Islington
Green** ⑤
Upper Street
Tel: 071 226 3520
Seats: 300

Screen on the Hill
Haverstock Hill
Tel: 071 435 3366/9787
Seats: 339

UCI Whiteleys 8 ⑤
Queensway, Bayswater
Tel: 071 792 3332/3303
Seats: 1:333, 2:281, 3:196,
4:178, 5:154, 6:138, 7:147,
8:125

Warner West End
Leicester Square
Tel: 071 439 0791
Seats: 1:150, 2:900, 3:272,
4:434, 5:108

OUTER
LONDON

Acton
Acton Screen High
Street
Tel: 081 993 2558
Seats: 100(V)

Barking
Odeon Longbridge
Road
Tel: 081 594 2900
Seats: 1:806, 2:83,

3:131ⓗ, 4:130, 5:132, 6:162

Barnet
Odeon Great North Road
Tel: 081 449 4147
Seats: 1:543, 2:140ⓗ, 3:140ⓗ

Battersea
Arts Centre Old Town Hallⓗ*
Lavender Hill
Tel: 071 223 2223
Seats: 180

Beckenham
Cannon High Street
Tel: 081 650 1171/658 7114
Seats: 1:478, 2:228, 3:127ⓗ

Borehamwood
Hertsmere Hall*
Elstree Way
Tel: 081 953 9872
Seats: 664

Brentford
Watermans Arts Centreⓗ
High Street
Tel: 081 568 1176
Seats: 240

Brixton
Ritzy Brixton Oval
Tel: 071 737 2121
Seats: 420

Bromley
Odeon High Street
Tel: 081 460 4425
Seats: 1:402, 2:125ⓗ, 3:98ⓗ, 4:273

Catford
Cannon Central Parade
Tel: 081 698 3306/697 6579
Seats: 1:519ⓗ, 2:259

Croydon
Cannon London Road
Tel: 081 688 0486/5775
Seats: 1:650, 2:399, 3:187
Fairfield Hall/Ashcroft Theatre, Park Lane*
Tel: 081 688 9291
Seats: Fairfield: 1552ⓗ, Ashcroft: 750ⓗ ☑

Dalston
Rio Kingsland High Streetⓗ ☑
Tel: 071 254 6677/249 2722
Seats: 400

Ealing
Cannon Northfields Avenue
Tel: 081 567 1075
Seats: 1:155, 2:149
Cannon Uxbridge Road
Tel: 081 567 1333/579 4851
Seats: 1:764, 2:414ⓗ, 3:210

East Finchley
Phoenix High Roadⓗ
Tel: 081 883 2233
Seats: 300

Edgware
Cannon Station Road
Tel: 081 952 2164/951 0299
Seats: 1:705, 2:207ⓗ, 3:146ⓗ

Elephant & Castle
Coronet Film Centre
New Kent Road
Tel: 071 703 4968/708 0066
Seats: 1:546, 2:271ⓗ, 3:211ⓗ

Enfield
Cannon Southbury Road
Tel: 081 363 4411/367 4909
Seats: 1:700, 2:356, 3:217ⓗ, 4:140ⓗ

Ewell Surrey
Cannon Kingston Road
Tel: 081 393 2211/0760
Seats: 1:606, 2:152ⓗ

Golders Green
Cannon Ionic
Finchley Road
Tel: 081 455 1724/4134

Greenwich
Cinema High Roadⓗ ☑
Tel: 0426 927799
Seats: 1:350, 2:288, 3:144

Hammersmith
Cannon King Street
Tel: 081 748 0557/2388
Seats: 1:955, 2:455, 3:326
Odeon Queen Caroline Streetⓗ*
Tel: 081 748 4081/2
Seats: 3485
Riverside Studios
Crisp Road
Tel: 081 748 3354
Seats: 200

Hampstead
Cannon Pond Street
Tel: 071 794 4000/435 3307
Seats: 1:474, 2:197ⓗ,

3:191ⓗ
Everymanⓗ
Holly Bush Vale
Tel: 071 435 1525
Seats: 285

Harrow
Cannon Station Road
Tel: 081 427 1743/863 4137
Seats: 1:612, 2:133
Cannon Sheepcote Road
Tel: 081 863 7261
Seats: 1:628, 2:207ⓗ, 3:204ⓗ

Hayes
Beck Theatreⓗ ☑*
Grange Road
Tel: 081 561 8371
Seats: 536

Hendon
Cannon Central Circus
Tel: 081 202 7137/4644
Seats: 1:572, 2:346ⓗ, 3:320ⓗ

Holloway
Odeon Holloway Road
Tel: 071 272 6331
Seats: 1:388, 2:198, 3:270, 4:391, 5:361

Ilford
Odeon Gants Hill
Tel: 081 554 2500
Seats: 1:768, 2:225ⓗ, 3:315ⓗ, 4:180

Kingston
Options Richmond Road
Tel: 081 546 0404
Seats: 1:303, 2:287, 3:208

Muswell Hill
Odeon Fortis Green Road
Tel: 081 883 1001
Seats: 1:610, 2:134ⓗ, 3:130ⓗ

Purley
Cannon High Street
Tel: 081 660 1212/668 5592
Seats: 1:438, 2:135ⓗ, 3:120ⓗ

Putney
Cannon High Street
Tel: 081 788 2263/3003
Seats: 1:434, 2:312ⓗ, 3:147

Richmond
Odeon Hill Street
Tel: 081 940 5759
Seats: 1:478, 2:201ⓗ, 3:201ⓗ

Filmhouse Water Laneⓗ
Tel: 081 332 0146
Seats: 150

Romford
Cannon South Street
Tel: 0708 43848/47671
Seats: 1:652, 2:494ⓗ, 3:246ⓗ
Odeon Mercury Gardens
Tel: 0708 729040
Seats: 1:410, 2:255, 3:150, 4:181, 5:181, 6:150, 7:335, 8:253

Sidcup
Cannon High Street
Tel: 081 300 2539/309 0770
Seats: 1:516ⓗ, 2:303

Streatham
Cannon High Road
Tel: 081 769 1928/6262
Seats: 1:630, 2:432ⓗ, 3:231ⓗ
Odeon High Road
Tel: 081 769 3346
Seats: 1:1095, 2:267ⓗ, 3:267ⓗ

Sutton
Cannon Cheam Road
Tel: 081 642 8927/0855
Seats: 1:260ⓗ, 2:120, 3:120
Secombe Centre Cheam Roadⓗ ☑*
Tel: 081 642 2218
Seats: 330

Turnpike Lane
Coronet Turnpike Parade
Tel: 081 888 2519/3734
Seats: 1:624, 2:417ⓗ, 3:269ⓗ

Walthamstow
Cannon Hoe Street
Tel: 081 520 7092
Seats: 1:960, 2:181ⓗ, 3:181ⓗ

Well Hall
Coronet Well Hall Road
Tel: 081 850 3351
Seats: 1:450, 2:131ⓗ

Wimbledon
Odeon The Broadway
Tel: 081 542 2277
Seats: 1:702, 2:218ⓗ, 3:190ⓗ

Woodford
Cannon High Road
Tel: 081 989 3463/4066
Seats: 1:562, 2:199ⓒ, 3:131ⓗ

Woolwich
Coronet John Wilson
Street
Tel: 081 854 2255
Seats: 1:678, 2:370©

ENGLAND

Aldeburgh Suffolk
Aldeburgh Cinema
High Street
Tel: 072 885 2996
Seats: 286

Aldershot Hants
Cannon High Street
Tel: 0252 317223/20355
Seats: 1:313, 2:187, 3:150

Alton Hants
Palace Normandy
Street
Tel: 0420 82303
Seats: 654

Ambleside Cumbria
Zeffirelli's Compston
Road
Tel: 0966 33845
Seats: 180

Andover Hants
Savoy London Street
Tel: 0264 52624

Seats: 350

Ardwick Greater
Manchester
Apollo Ardwick Green*
Tel: 061 273 6921
Seats: 2641

Ashford Kent
Picture House Beaver
Road
Tel: 0233 620124
Three screens

Ashton-under-Lyne
Greater Manchester
Metro Old Street
Tel: 061 330 1993
Seats: 987

Aylesbury Bucks
Odeon Cambridge
Street
Tel: 0296 82660
Seats: 1:450, 2:108, 3:113

Banbury Oxon
Cannon The Horsefair
Tel: 0295 62071
Seats: 1:432, 2:225

Barnsley South Yorks
Odeon Eldon Street
Tel: 0226 205494
Seats: 1:419, 2:636

Barnstaple Devon
Astor Boutport Street
Tel: 0271 42550
Seats: 360

Barrow Cumbria
Astra Abbey Road
Tel: 0229 825354
Seats: 1:640, 2:260, 3:260

Basildon Essex
Cannon Great Oaks
Tel: 0268 27421/27431
Seats: 1:644, 2:435,
3:101(V)
Towngate*
Tel: 0268 23953
Seats: 459

Basingstoke Hants
Cannon Wote Street
Tel: 0256 22257/59446
Seats: 1:407, 2:218

Bath Avon
Cannon
Westgate Street
Tel: 0225 61730/62959
Seats: 733
Gemini St John's Place
Tel: 0225 61506
Seats: 1:126, 2:151, 3:49
Little Theatre
St Michaels Place
Tel: 0225 66822
Seats: 1:222, 2:78

Bedford Beds
Civic Theatre*
Tel: 0234 44813
Seats: 266
Cannon St Peter Street
Tel: 0234 53848
Seats: 1:1476, 2:209

Belper Derbys
Ritz
Tel: 0773 827284
Two screens

Berwick
Northumberland
Playhouse Sandgate
Tel: 0289 307769
Seats: 650

Beverley East Yorks
Playhouse
The Market Place
Tel: 0482 881315
Seats: 310

Bexhill-on-Sea East
Sussex
Curzon Western Road
Tel: 0424 210078
Seats: 200

Billingham Cleveland
Forum Theatre*
Town Centre
Tel: 0642 552663
Seats: 494

Birkenhead
Merseyside
Empire Conway Street
Tel: 051 647 6509
Seats: 528

Birmingham West Mids
Cannon John Bright Street
Tel: 021 643 0292/2128
Seats: 1:699, 2:242
Capitol Alum Rock Road
Ward End
Tel: 021 327 0528
Seats: 1:340, 2:250, 3:130
Midlands Arts Centre
Cannon Hill Park
Tel: 021 440 3838
Seats: 1:202, 2:144
Odeon New Street
Tel: 021 643 6101
Seats: 1:330, 2:387, 3:308, 4:239, 5:210, 6:190
Tivoli Station Street
Tel: 021 643 1556
Two screens
🅑 **Triangle**
Gosta GreenⓈ
Tel: 021 359 4192/2403
Seats: 180
Warwick Westley Road
Acocks Green
Tel: 021 706 0766
Seats: 462

Blackburn Lancs
Unit Four King William Street
Tel: 0254 51779
Seats: 1:315, 2:256, 3:186

Blackpool Lancs
Cannon Church Street
Tel: 0253 27207/24233
Seats: 1:717, 2:330, 3:231
Odeon Dickson Road
Tel: 0253 23565
Seats: 1:1404, 2:190, 3:190
Royal Pavilion
Rigby Road
Tel: 0253 25313
Seats: 347

Blyth Northumberland
Wallaw Union Street
Tel: 0670 352504
Seats: 1:850, 2:150, 3:80

Bognor Regis West Sussex
Cannon Canada Grove
Tel: 0243 823138
Seats: 1:391, 2:96

Bolton Greater Manchester
Cannon Bradshawgate
Tel: 0204 25597
Seats: 1:275, 2:329, 3:100

Boston Lincs
Regal West Street
Tel: 0205 50553
Seats: 182

Bourne Lincs
Film Theatre North Street
Seats: 55

Bournemouth Dorset
Cannon Westover Road
Tel: 0202 28433/290345
Seats: 1:652, 2:585, 3:223
Odeon Westover Road
Tel: 0202 22402
Seats: 1:757, 2:359, 3:267, 4:119, 5:121

Bovington Dorset
Globe Bovington Camp
Wool
Tel: 0929 462666
Seats: 396

Bowness-on-Windermere
Cumbria
Royalty Lake Road
Tel: 09662 3364
Seats: 399

Bracknell Berks
South Hill Park Arts CentreⓈ
Tel: 03444 27272
Seats: 1:60, 2:200*
UCI The Point
Ten screens

Bradford West Yorks
🅑 **National Museum of Photography, Film and TV**Ⓢ
Prince's View
Tel: 0274 732277/727488
Seats: 340
Odeon Prince's Way
Tel: 0274 726716
Seats: 1:467, 2:1190, 3:244
🅑 **Playhouse and Film Theatre**Ⓢ☒
Chapel Street
Tel: 0274 720329
Seats: 1:295, 2:45

Braintree Essex
Studio Fairfield Road
Tel: 0376 20378
Seats: 812

Brentwood Essex
Cannon Chapel High
Tel: 0277 212931/227574
Seats: 1:300, 2:196

Bridgnorth Salop
Majestic Whitburn Street
Tel: 0746 761815/761866
Seats: 1:500, 2:200

Bridgwater Somerset
Film Centre Penel Orlieu
Tel: 0278 422383
Seats: 1:230, 2:240

Bridport Dorset
Palace South Street
Tel: 0308 22167
Seats: 420

Brierfield Lancs
Unit Four Burnley Road
Tel: 0282 698030
Seats: 1:70, 2:70, 3:61, 4:66

Brierley Hill West Mids
UCI Merry Hill 10
Tel: 0384 78244/78282
Seats: 1:175, 2:254, 3:226, 4:254, 5:350, 6:350, 7:254, 8:226, 9:254, 10:175

Brighton East Sussex
Cannon East Street
Tel: 0273 27010/202095
Seats: 1:835, 2:345, 3:271, 4:194
Duke of York's
Preston Circus
Tel: 0273 602503
Seats: 359
Odeon West Street
Tel: 0273 25890
Seats: 1:388, 2:883, 3:504, 4:275/5:242, 6:103

Bristol Avon
ArnolfiniⓈ☒
Narrow Quay
Tel: 0272 299191
Seats: 176
Arts Centre CinemaⓈ
Tel: 0272 422110
Seats: 124
Cannon Frogmore Street
Tel: 0272 262848/9
Seats: 1:411, 2:301
Cannon Northumbria Drive
Henleaze
Tel: 0272 621644
Seats: 1:186, 2:124, 3:129
Cannon Whiteladies Road
Tel: 0272 730679/733640
Seats: 1:372, 2:253, 3:135
Concorde Stapleton Road
Tel: 0272 510377
Seats: 1:166, 2:183
Gaiety Wells Road
Tel: 0272 776224
Seats: 650
Odeon Union Street
Tel: 0272 290882
Seats: 1:399, 2:224, 3:215
🅑 **Watershed**Ⓢ☒
Tel: 0272 276444
Seats: 1:200, 2:50

Bridgwater Somerset

Broadstairs Kent
Windsor Harbour Street†
Seats: 100

Bungay Suffolk
Mayfair Broad Street
Tel: 0986 2397
Seats: 400

Burgess Hill West Sussex
Robin's Take Two
Cyprus Road
Tel: 0444 232137
Seats: 1:130, 2:100

Burnham-on-Crouch Essex
Rio Station Road
Tel: 0621 782027
Seats: 200

Burnham-on-Sea
Somerset
Ritz Victoria Street
Tel: 0278 782871
Seats: 260

Burton-on-Trent
Staffs
Odeon Guild Street
Tel: 0283 63200
Seats: 1:502, 2:110, 3:110

Bury Greater Manchester
Warner 12
Tel: 061 766 2440/1121
Seats: 1:559, 2:322, 3:278, 4:434, 5:208, 6:166, 7:166, 8:208, 9:434, 10:278, 11:322, 12:573

Bury St Edmunds
Suffolk
Cannon Halter Street
Tel: 0284 754477
Seats: 1:196, 2:117

Camberley Surrey
Cannon London Road
Tel: 0276 63909/26768
Seats: 1:441, 2:114, 3:94
Globe Hawley*
Tel: 0252 876769
Seats: 200

Camborne Cornwall
Palace Roskear
Tel: 0209 712020
Seats: 212

Cambridge Cambs
🅑 **Arts Market Passage**Ⓢ☒
Tel: 0223 352001/462666
Seats: 275
Cannon St Andrews Street
Tel: 0223 354572/645378
Seats: 1:736, 2:452

Cannock Staffs
Cannon Walsall Road
Tel: 05435 2226
Seats: 1:363, 2:178

Canterbury Kent
Cannon St Georges Place
Tel: 0227 462022/453577
Seats: 1:536, 2:404
bfi **Cinema 3**&*
University of Kent
Tel: 0227 764000
Seats: 300

Carlisle Cumbria
Lonsdale Warwick Road
Tel: 0228 25586
Seats: 1:410, 2:220, 3:50

Chatham Kent
Cannon High Street
Tel: 0634 42522/46756
Seats: 1:520, 2:360, 3:170

Chelmsford Essex
Select
New Whittle Street
Tel: 0245 352724
Seats: 400

Cheltenham Glos
Odeon Winchcombe Street
Tel: 0242 524081
Seats: 1:756, 2:129, 3:104, 4:90, 5:204

Chester Cheshire
Cannon Foregate Street
Tel: 0224 22931
Seats: 1:468, 2:248
Odeon Northgate Street
Tel: 0224 24930
Seats: 1:798, 2:122, 3:122

Chesterfield Derbys
Regal Cavendish Street
Tel: 0246 73333
Seats: 484

Chippenham Wilts
Cannon Marshfield Road
Tel: 0249 652498
Seats: 1:215, 2:215

Chipping Norton Oxon
The Theatre Spring Street*
Tel: 0608 2349/2350
Seats: 195

Christchurch Hants
Regent Centre*
High Street
Tel: 0202 499148
Seats: 370

Cirencester Glos
Regal Lewis Lane
Tel: 0285 658755

Seats: 1:100, 2:100

Clacton Essex
Coronet Century Pier Avenue
Tel: 0255 429627
Seats: 1:600, 2:187

Clevedon Avon
Curzon Old Church Road
Tel: 0272 872158
Seats: 425

Clitheroe Lancs
Civic Hall York Street
Tel: 0200 23278
Seats: 400

Colchester Essex
Odeon Crouch Street
Tel: 0206 572294
Seats: 1:482, 2:208, 3:120, 4:135

Coleford Glos
Studio High Street
Tel: 0594 333331
Seats: 1:200, 2:80

Corby Northants
Forum Queens Square
Tel: 0536 203974
Seats: 1:339, 2:339

Cosford Staffs
Astra RAF Cosford*
Tel: 090 722 2393
Seats: 460

Cosham Hants
Cannon High Street
Tel: 0705 376635
Seats: 1:441, 2:118, 3:107

Coventry West Mids
bfi **Arts Centre**&
University of Warwick
Tel: 0203 417417/417314
Seats: 1:250
Odeon Jordan Well
Tel: 0203 22042
Seats: 1:712, 2:155, 3:172, 4:390, 5:121
Theatre One Ford Street
Tel: 0203 224301
Seats: 1:230, 2:140, 3:135

Cranleigh Surrey
Regal High Street
Tel: 0483 272373
Seats: 268

Crawley West Sussex
Cannon High Street
Tel: 0293 27497/541296
Seats: 1:297, 2:214, 3:110

Crewe Cheshire
Apollo High Street
Tel: 0270 255708
Seats: 1:110, 2:110, 3:95
Lyceum Theatre*

Heath Street
Tel: 0270 215523
Seats: 750
Victoria Film Theatre†
West Street
Tel: 0270 211422
Seats: 180

Cromer Norfolk
Regal Hans Place
Tel: 0263 513311
Seats: 1:129, 2:136

Crookham Hants
Globe
Queen Elizabeth Barracks
Tel: 0252 876769
Seats: 340

Crosby Merseyside
Apollo
Crosby Road North
Tel: 051 928 2108
Seats: 1:671, 2:103, 3:103

Darlington Co Durham
Arts Centre Vane Terrace*
Tel: 0325 483168/483271
Seats: 100
Cannon Northgate
Tel: 0325 62745/484994
Seats: 1:590, 2:218, 3:148

Dartington Devon
bfi **Barn Theatre**&*
Tel: 0803 862224
Seats: 203

Deal Kent
Flicks Queen Street
Tel: 0304 361165
Seats: 173

Derby Derbys
Assembly Rooms*
Market Place
Tel: 0332 255800
Seats: 998
bfi **Metro Green Lane**& ☑
Tel: 0332 40170
Seats: 126
Showcase Cinemas
Outer Ring Road
Osmarton Park Road at Sinfin Lane
Tel: 0332 270300
Seats: 2600 (11 screens)
UCI Meteor Centre 10
Mansfield Road
Tel: 0332 295010/296000
Seats: 1:192, 2:189, 3:189, 4:192, 5:278, 6:278, 7:192, 8:189, 9:189, 10:192

Dereham Norfolk
CBA Dereham Entertainment Centre
Market Place
Tel: 0362 3261
Seats: 210

Devizes Wilts
Palace Market Place
Tel: 0380 2971
Seats: 253

Dewsbury West Yorks
Apollo Market Place
Tel: 0924 464949
Seats: 1:315, 2:151

Didcot Oxon
New Coronet The Broadway*
Tel: 0235 812038
Seats: 490

Doncaster South Yorks
Cannon Cleveland Street
Tel: 0302 67934/66241
Seats: 1:477, 2:201, 3:135
Civic Theatre Waterdale*
Tel: 0302 62349
Seats: 547
Odeon Hallgate
Tel: 0302 344626
Seats: 1:1003, 2:155, 3:155

Dorchester Dorset
Plaza Trinity Street
Tel: 0305 3488
Seats: 1:100, 2:320

Dorking Surrey
Grand Hall*
Dorking Halls
Tel: 0306 889694
Seats: 851

Dudley West Mids
Odeon Castle Hill
Tel: 0384 55518
Seats: 1:540, 2:215

Durham Co Durham
Cannon North Road
Tel: 091 384 8184
Seats: 1:420, 2:199

Eastbourne East Sussex
Cannon Pevensey Road
Tel: 0323 23612/642443
Seats: 1:585, 2:160
Curzon Langley Road
Tel: 0323 31441
Seats: 1:530, 2:236, 3:236

Elland Yorks
Rex
Tel: 0422 372140

Ely Cambs
The Maltings*
Tel: 0353 666388
Seats: 212

Epsom Surrey
Playhouse*
Tel: 03727 42555/6

99

Esher Surrey
Cannon High Street
Tel: 0372 65639/63362
Seats: 1:918, 2:117

Evesham Hereford &
Worcs
Regal Port Street
Tel: 0386 6002
Seats: 540

Exeter Devon
Northcott Theatre*
Stocker Road
Tel: 0392 54853
Seats: 433
Odeon Sidwell Street
Tel: 0392 54057
Seats: 1:744, 2:119, 3:105,
4:344

Exmouth Devon
Savoy Market Street
Tel: 0395 268220
Seats: 1:230, 2:110

Fawley Hants
Waterside Long Lane
Tel: 0703 891335
Seats: 355

Felixstowe Suffolk
**Top Rank Crescent
Road**
Tel: 0394 282787
Seats: 1:150, 2:90

Filey Yorks
Grand Union Street†
Tel: 0723 512129

Folkestone Kent
**Silver Screen Guildhall
Street**
Tel: 0303 221230
Seats: 1:459, 2:110

Frome Somerset
Westway Cork Street
Tel: 0373 65685
Seats: 304

Gainsborough Lincs
Trinity Arts Centre*
Trinity Street
Tel: 0427 617 242
Seats: 210

Gateshead Tyne &
Wear
**UCI Metro 10
Metro Centre**
Tel: 091 493 2022/3
Seats: 1:196, 2:196, 3:227,
4:252, 5:364, 6:364, 7:252,
8:227, 9:196, 10:196

Gatley Greater
Manchester
Tatton Gatley Road
Tel: 061 491 0711
Seats: 1:648, 2:247, 3:111

Gerrards Cross
Bucks

**Cannon Ethorpe
Crescent**
Tel: 0753 882516/883024
Seats: 1:350, 2:212

Gloucester Glos
**Cannon St Aldate
Street**
Tel: 0452 22399/415215
Seats: 1:658, 2:348, 3:294
Guildhall Arts Centre*
Eastgate Street
Seats: 125

Godalming Surrey
Borough Hall*
Tel: 0483 861111
Seats: 250

Gosport Hants
Ritz Walpole Road
Tel: 0705 501231
Seats: 1136

Grantham Lincs
**Paragon St Catherine's
Road**
Tel: 0476 70046
Seats: 1:270, 2:160

Gravesend Kent
Cannon King Street
Tel: 0474 356947/352470
Seats: 1:576, 2:320, 3:107

Grays Essex
**Thameside Orsett
Road***
Tel: 0375 382555
Seats: 303

Great Yarmouth
Norfolk
**Cinema Royal
Aquarium**
Tel: 0493 842043/842707
Seats: 1:1180, 2:264
**Empire Marine
Parade*†**
Tel: 0493 843147
Seats: 967
**Windmill Theatre
Marine Parade*†**
Tel: 0493 843504
Seats: 892

Grimsby Humberside
**Cannon Freeman
Street**
Tel: 0472 42878/49368
Seats: 1:419, 2:251, 3:130
(bfi) **Whitgift Crosland
Road⑥***
Tel: 0472 887117
Seats: 206

Guildford Surrey
Odeon Epsom Road
Tel: 0483 504990
Seats: 1:452, 2:135, 3:144,
4:250

Halifax West Yorks
Cannon Ward's End
Tel: 0422 52000/46429
Seats: 1:670, 2:199, 3:172

Halstead Essex
Empire Butler Road
Tel: 078 7477001
Seats: 320

Halton Bucks
Astra RAF Halton
Tel: 0296 623535
Seats: 570

Hanley Staffs
Cannon Broad Street
Tel: 0782 22320/268970
Seats: 1:573, 2:233, 3:162

Harlow Essex
Odeon The High
Tel: 0279 26989
Seats: 1:450, 2:243, 3:201
Playhouse The High*
Tel: 0279 24391
Seats: 435

Harrogate North
Yorks
Odeon East Parade
Tel: 0423 503626
Seats: 1:532, 2:108, 3:75,
4:259

Harwich Essex
Electric Palace*
King's Quay Street
Tel: 0255 553333
Seats: 204

Haslemere Surrey
**Haslemere Hall Bridge
Road***
Tel: 0428 2161
Seats: 350

Hastings East Sussex
Cannon Queens Road
Tel: 0424 420517
Seats: 1:376, 2:176, 3:128

Hatfield Herts
Forum*
Tel: 07072 71217
Seats: 210

Haywards Heath
Sussex
Clair Hall*
Perrymount Road
Tel: 0444 455440/454394
Seats: 350

Heaton Moor Greater
Manchester
**Savoy
Heaton Manor Road**
Tel: 061 432 2114
Seats: 496

Hebden Bridge West
Yorks
Cinema New Road
Tel: 0422 842807
Seats: 498

Hemel Hempstead
Herts
Odeon Marlowes*

Tel: 0442 64013
Seats: 785

Henley-on-Thames
Oxon
Kenton Theatre*
Tel: 0491 575698

Hereford Hereford &
Worcs
**Cannon Commercial
Road**
Tel: 0432 272554
Seats: 378

Hexham
Northumberland
Forum Market Place
Tel: 0434 602896
Seats: 207

High Wycombe
Bucks
**UCI Wycombe 6 Crest
Road
Cressex**
Tel: 0494 463333/464309/
465565
Seats: 1:390, 2:390, 3:285,
4:285, 5:200, 6:200

Hinckley Leics
Cannon Trinity Lane
Tel: 0455 637523
Seats: 1:350, 2:206, 3:224

Hoddesdon Herts
Broxbourne Civic Hall*
High Road
Tel: 0992 441946/31
Seats: 564

Holbury Hants
Waterside Long Lane
Tel: 0703 891335
Seats: 355

Hollinwood Greater
Manchester
Roxy Hollins Road
Tel: 061 681 1441
Seats: 1:470, 2:130, 3:260,
4:260, 5:320

Hordern Co Durham
**Fairworld Sunderland
Road**
Tel: 0783 864344
Seats: 1:156, 2:96

Horsham Sussex
**Arts Centre (Ritz
Cinema and Capitol
Theatre)**
North Street
Tel: 0403 68689
Seats: 1:126, 2:450*

Horwich Lancs
**Leisure Centre Victoria
Road***
Tel: 0204 692211
Seats: 400

Hoylake Merseyside
Cinema Alderley Road
Tel: 051 632 1345

Hucknall Notts
Byron High Street
Tel: 0602 636377
Seats: 430

Huddersfield West
Yorks
**Cannon Queensgate
Zetland Street**
Tel: 0484 530874
Seats: 1:495, 2:214

Hull Humberside
Cannon Anlaby Road
Tel: 0482 224981
Seats: 1:308, 2:308, 3:165

bfi **Film Theatre**Ⓖ*
Central Library
Albion Street
Tel: 0482 224040 x30
Seats: 247
Odeon Kingston Street
Tel: 0482 586420
Seats: 1:170, 2:170, 3:150,
4:172, 5:418, 6:206, 7:132,
8:150

Hulme Greater
Manchester
**Aaben Jackson
Crescent**
Tel: 061 226 5749
Seats: 1:100, 2:100, 3:100

Huntingdon Cambs
**Cromwell Cinema
Centre
Princes Street**
Tel: 0480 411575
Seats: 300

Hyde Greater
Manchester
**Royal Corporation
Street**
Tel: 061 368 2206
Seats: 1:800, 2:224

Ilfracombe Devon
**Pendle Stairway
High Street**
Tel: 0271 63484
Seats: 460

Ilkeston Derbys
Scala Market Place
Tel: 0602 324612
Seats: 500

Ipswich Suffolk
bfi **Film Theatre Corn
Exchange**Ⓖ
Tel: 0473 55851
Seats: 1:221, 2:40
Odeon St Helens Street
Tel: 0473 53641
Seats: *1:1813, 2:186

Keighley West
Yorkshire
**Picture House North
Street**
Tel: 0535 602561
Seats: 1:376, 2:95

Kendal Cumbria
Brewery Arts Centre
Highgate
Tel: 0539 725133
Seats: 148

Keswick Cumbria
**Alhambra St John
Street**†
Tel: 0596 72195
Seats: 313

Kettering Northants
Ohio Russell Street
Tel: 0536 515130
Seats: 1:145, 2:206

King's Lynn Norfolk
**Fermoy Centre King
Street***
Tel: 0553 4725/3578
Seats: 359
Majestic Tower Street
Tel: 0553 2603
Seats: 1:847, 2:136

Kirkby-in-Ashfield
Notts
Regent
Tel: 0623 753866

Kirkham Lancs
Empire Birley Street
Tel: 07722 684817
Seats: 256

Knutsford Cheshire
Civic Hall Toft Road*
Tel: 0565 3005
Seats: 400

Lake Isle of Wight
**Screen De Luxe
Sandown Road**
Tel: 0983 406056
Seats: 150

Lancaster Lancs
Cannon King Street
Tel: 0524 64141/841149
Seats: 1:250, 2:250
bfi **Duke's
Playhouse**Ⓖ✉*
Moor Lane
Tel: 0524 66645/67461
Seats: 307

Leamington Spa
Warks
Regal Portland Place
Tel: 0926 26106/27448
Seats: 904
Royal Spa Centre*
Newbold Terrace
Tel: 0926 34418
Seats: 1:799, 2:208

Leatherhead Surrey
Thorndike Theatre*
Church Street

Tel: 0372 376211/377677
Seats: 526

Leeds West Yorks
Cannon Vicar Lane
Tel: 0532 45101⅓/452665
Seats: 1:670, 2:483, 3:227
Cottage Road Cinema
Headingley
Tel: 0532 751606
Seats: 468
**Hyde Park Brudenell
Road**
Tel: 0532 752045
Seats: 360
Lounge North Lane
Headingley
Tel: 0532 751061/58932
Seats: 691
Odeon The Headrow
Tel: 0532 430031
Seats: 1:982, 2:441, 3:200,
4:174, 5:126
**Showcase Gelderd
Road Birstall**
Tel: 0924 420071
Seats: 3400 (12 screens)

Leicester Leics
Cannon Belgrave Gate
Tel: 0533 24346/24903
Seats: 1:616, 2:408, 3:232
Odeon Queen Street
Tel: 0533 22892
Seats: 1:872, 2:401, 3:111,
4:142
bfi **Phoenix Arts
Newarke
Street**Ⓖ✉*
Tel: 0533 559711/555627
Seats: 270

Leiston Suffolk
**Film Theatre High
Street**
Tel: 0728 830 549
Seats: 350

Letchworth Herts
Broadway Eastcheap
Tel: 0462 684721
Seats: 1410

Lichfield Staffs
Civic Hall Castle Dyke*
Tel: 054 32 54021
Seats: 278

Lincoln Lincs
Ritz High Street
Tel: 0522 46313
Seats: 1400

Littlehampton West
Sussex
**Windmill Church
Street***
Tel: 09064 6644
Seats: 252

Liverpool Merseyside
Bluecoat Arts Centre*
**(Merseyside Film
Institute)**
Tel: 051 709 4260

Cannon Allerton Road
Tel: 051 709 6277/708
7629
Seats: 493
Cannon Lime Street
Tel: 051 709 6277/708
7629
Seats: 1:697, 2:274, 3:217
Odeon London Road
Tel: 051 709 0717
Seats: 1:976, 2:597, 3:167,
4:148, 5:148
Showcase West Derby
Tel: 051 549 2021
Seats: 3400 (12 screens)
Woolton Mason Street
Tel: 051 428 1919
Seats: 256

Long Eaton Notts
Screen Market Place
Tel: 060 732185
Seats: 253

Longridge Lancs
Palace Market Place
Tel: 07747 85600
Seats: 212

Looe East Cornwall
**Cinema Higher Market
Street**
Tel: 05036 2709
Seats: 95

Loughborough Leics
Curzon Cattle Market
Tel: 0509 212261
Seats: 1:407, 2:199, 3:185,
4:135, 5:80

Louth Lincs
**Playhouse Cannon
Street**
Tel: 0507 603333
Seats: 218

Lowestoft Suffolk
**Hollywood London
Road South**
Tel: 0502 564567
Seats: 460
**Marina Theatre The
Marina**
Tel: 0502 573318/514274
Seats: 751

Ludlow Shropshire
**Picture House Castle
Square***
Tel: 0584 875363

Luton Beds
Cannon George Street
Tel: 0582 27311/22537
Seats: 1:615, 2:458, 3:272
St George's Theatre*
Central Library
Tel: 0582 21628
Seats: 238

Lyme Regis Dorset
Regent Broad Street
Tel: 0297 42053
Seats: 400

Lymington Hants
Community Centre*
New Street
Tel: 05907 2337
Seats: 110

Mablethorpe Lincs
Bijou Quebec Road
Tel: 0521 77040
Seats: 264

Macclesfield Ches
Majestic Mill Street
Tel: 0625 22412
Seats: 687

Maghull Merseyside
Astra Northway
Tel: 051 526 1943
Seats: 1:200, 2:200, 3:300,
4:300

Maidstone Kent
**Cannon Lower Stone
Street**
Tel: 0622 52628
Seats: 1:260, 2:90, 3:260

Malton Yorks
Palace Yorkersgate*
Seats: 140

Malvern Hereford &
Worcs
Cinema Grange Road
Tel: 0684 892279/892710
Seats: 407

Manchester Greater
Manchester
**Cannon 1 and 2
Deansgate**
Tel: 061 832 5252/2112
Seats: 1:639, 2:167
🅑🅕🅘 **Cornerhouse
Oxford Street**🅐 ☑
Tel: 061 228 7621
Seats: 1:300, 2:170, 3:58
Odeon Oxford Street
Tel: 061 236 8264
Seats: 1:629, 2:737, 3:203
**Showcase Hyde Road
Belle Vue**
Tel: 061 220 8765
Seats: 3400 (14 screens)

Mansfield Notts
Cannon Leeming Street
Tel: 0623 23138/652236
Seats: 1:367, 2:359, 3:171
Studio Leeming Street
Tel: 0623 653309
Seats: 75

March Cambs
**Hippodrome Dartford
Road***
Tel: 0354 53178
Seats: 150

Margate Kent
**Dreamland
Marine Parade**
Tel: 0843 227822
Seats: 1:378, 2:376,
3:66(V)

Marple Greater
Manchester
Regent Stockport Road
Tel: 061 427 5951
Seats: 285

Matlock Derbys
Ritz Causeway Lane
Tel: 0629 2121
Seats: 1:176, 2:100

Melton Mowbray
Leics
Regal King Street
Tel: 0664 62251
Seats: 226

Middlesbrough
Cleveland
**Odeon Corporation
Road**
Tel: 0642 242888
Seats: 1:616, 2:98, 3:122,
4:246

Middleton Greater
Manchester
**Palace Manchester
Middleton Gardens**
Tel: 061 643 2852
Seats: 234

Midsomer Norton
Somerset
Palladium High Street
Tel: 0761 413266
Seats: 482

Millom Cumbria
Palladium Horn Hill†
Tel: 0657 2441
Seats: 400

Milton Keynes Bucks
**UCI The Point 10
Midsummer Boulevard**
Tel: 0908 661662
Seats: 1:156, 2:169, 3:248,
4:220, 5:220, 6:220, 7:220,
8:248, 9:169, 10:156

Minehead Somerset
Regal The Avenue
Tel: 0683 2439

Mirfield West Yorks
**Vale Centre
Huddersfield Road**
Tel: 0924 493240
Seats: 1:98, 2:96

Monkseaton Tyne &
Wear
Cannon Caldwell Lane
Tel: 091 252 5540
Seats: 1:351, 2:116

Monton Greater
Manchester
Princess Monton Road
Tel: 061 789 3426
Seats: 580

Morpeth
Northumberland

**New Coliseum
New Market**
Tel: 0670 516834
Seats: 1:132, 2:132

Nantwich Cheshire
**Civic Hall Market
Street***
Tel: 0270 628633
Seats: 300

Nelson Lancs
Grand Market Street
Tel: 0282 692860
Seats: 391

Newark Notts
**Palace Theatre
Appleton Gate***
Tel: 0636 71636
Seats: 351

Newbury Berks
Cannon Park Way
Tel: 0635 41291/49913
Seats: 484

**Newcastle-under-
Lyme** Staffs
Savoy High Street
Tel: 0782 616565
Seats: 200

**Newcastle upon
Tyne**
Tyne & Wear
**Jesmond Cinema
Lyndhurst Avenue**
Tel: 091 281 0526/2248
Seats: 626
Odeon Pilgrim Street
Tel: 091 232 3248
Seats: 1:1228, 2:159,
3:250, 4:361
🅑🅕🅘 **Tyneside Pilgrim
Street**🅐 ☑
Tel: 091 232 8289/5592
Seats: 1:400, 2:155
Warner Manors
Tel: 091 221 0202/0545
Seats: 1:404, 2:398, 3:236,
4:244, 5:290, 6:657, 7:509,
8:398, 9:248

Newport Isle of Wight
Cannon High Street
Tel: 0983 527169
Seats: 377

Newport Pagnell
Bucks
Electra St John Street
Tel: 0908 611146
Seats: 400

Newquay Cornwall
Camelot The Crescent
Tel: 063 73 874222
Seats: 812

Newton Abbot
Devon
**Alexandra Market
Street**
Tel: 0626 65368
Seats: 360

Northallerton North
Yorks
Lyric Northend
Tel: 0609 2019
Seats: 305

Northampton
Northants
**Cannon Abingdon
Square**
Tel: 0604 35839/32862
Seats: 1:1018, 2:275,
3:210
🅑🅕🅘 **Forum, Weston
Favell Centre***
Tel: 0604 401006/407544
Seats: 250

Northwich Ches
Regal London Road
Tel: 0606 3130
Seats: 1:797, 2:200

Norwich Norfolk
**Cannon Prince of
Wales Road**
Tel: 0603 624677/623312
Seats: 1:524, 2:343, 3:186,
4:105
🅑🅕🅘 **Cinema City**🅐
St Andrews Street
Tel: 0603 625145
Seats: 230
Noverre Theatre Street
Tel: 0603 626402
Seats: 272
Odeon Anglia Square
Tel: 0603 621903
Seats: 1016

Nottingham Notts
Cannon Chapel Bar
Tel: 0602 45260/418483
Seats: 1:764, 2:437, 3:280
🅑🅕🅘 **Broadway,
Nottingham
Media Centre
Broad Street**
Tel: 0602 410053
Seats: 450 (to be
converted to 3 screens)
Odeon Angel Row
Tel: 0602 417766
Seats: 1:924, 2:581, 3:141,
4:153, 5:114, 6:96
Savoy Derby Road
Tel: 0602 472580
Seats: 1:386, 2:128, 3:168
Showcase Redfield Way
Lenton
Tel: 0602 866766
Seats: 3200 (13 screens)

Nuneaton Warwicks
**Nuneaton Arts Centre
Abbey Theatre Pool
Bank Street**
Tel: 0203 382706

Okehampton Devon
Carlton St James Street
Tel: 0822 2425
Seats: 380

Oswestry Salop
Regal Salop Road
Tel: 0691 654043
Seats: 1:261, 2:261, 3:66

Oxford Oxon
Cannon George Street
Tel: 0865 244607/723911
Seats: 1:626, 2:326, 3:140
Cannon Magdalen Street
Tel: 0865 243067
Seats: 866
Not the Moulin Rouge New High Street Headington
Tel: 0865 63666
Seats: 350
Penultimate Picture Palace Jeune Street
Tel: 0865 723837
Seats: 185
Phoenix Walton Street
Tel: 0865 54909/512526
Seats: 1:200, 2:95

Oxted Surrey
Plaza Station Road West
Tel: 0883 712567
Seats: 442

Padstow Cornwall
Capitol Lanadwell Street†
Tel: 0841 532344
Seats: 210

Paignton Devon
Torbay, Torbay Road
Tel: 0803 559544
Seats: 484

Penistone South Yorkshire
Town Hall
Tel: 0226 767532/205128
Seats: 450

Penrith Cumbria
Alhambra Middlegate
Tel: 0768 62400
Seats: 202

Penzance Cornwall
Savoy Causeway Head
Tel: 0736 3330
Seats: 450

Peterborough Cambs
Odeon Broadway
Tel: 0733 43319
Seats: 1:544, 2:110, 3:110
Showcase Mallory Road
Boongate
Tel: 0733 558498
Seats: 2600 (11 screens)

Pickering North Yorks
Castle Burgate
Tel: 0751 72622
Seats: 386

Plymouth Devon
bfi **Arts Centre Looe Street**⊕
Tel: 0752 660060
Seats: 73
Cannon Derry's Cross
Tel: 0752 63300/25553
Seats: 1:583, 2:340, 3:115
Odeon Derry's Cross
Tel: 0752 668825/227074
Seats: 1:946, 2:168, 3:168

Pocklington East Yorks
Ritz Market Place
Tel: 0759 303420
Seats: 250

Pontefract West Yorks
Crescent Ropergate
Tel: 0977 703788
Seats: 412

Poole Dorset
Ashley Arts Centre*
Kingsland Road
Seats: 143
UCI Tower Park 10
Tel: 0202 715010
Seats: 1:192, 2:186, 3:186, 4:192, 5:270, 6:270, 7:192, 8:186, 9:186, 10:192

Portsmouth Hants
Cannon Commercial Road
Tel: 0705 823538/839719
Seats: 1:542, 2:255, 3:203
Odeon London Road
Tel: 0705 661539
Seats: 1:640, 2:225, 3:225
Rendezvous†
The Hornpipe Kingston Road
Tel: 0705 833854
Seats: 90

Potters Bar Herts
Oakmere House*
Tel: 0707 45005
Seats: 165

Preston Lancs
Odeon Church Street
Tel: 0722 23298
Seats: 1:1166, 2:112
UCI Riversway 10⊕
Tel: 0772 728888/722322
Seats: 290 (2 screens), 180 (8 screens)

Quinton West Midlands
Cannon Hagley Road West
Tel: 021 422 2562/2252
Seats: 1:300, 2:236, 3:232, 4:121

Ramsgate Kent
Granville Victoria Parade*
Tel: 0843 591750
Seats: 861

Rawtenstall Lancs
Picture House
Tel: 0706 226774
Seats: 120
Unit Four Bacup Road
Tel: 070 62 3123
Seats: 1:121, 2:118, 3:165, 4:118

Reading Berks
Cannon Friar Street
Tel: 0734 573907
Seats: 1:532, 2:226, 3:118
Film Theatre Whiteknights*
Tel: 0734 868497/875123
Seats: 409
Odeon Cheapside
Tel: 0734 507887
Seats: 1:410, 2:221, 3:221

Redcar Cleveland
Regent The Esplanade
Tel: 0642 482094
Seats: 381

Redditch Hereford & Worcs
Cannon Unicorn Hill
Tel: 0527 62572
Seats: 1:208, 2:155, 3:155

Redruth Cornwall
Regal Film Centre Fore Street
Tel: 0209 216278
Seats: 1:200, 2:128, 3:600, 4:95

Reigate Surrey
Screen Bancroft Road
Tel: 0737 223213
Seats: 1:139, 2:142

Retford Notts
Majestic Coronation Street
Tel: 0777 709405
Seats: 1:444, 2:136

Rickmansworth Herts
Watersmeet Theatre*
High Street
Tel: 0923 771542
Seats: 390

Ripley Derbys
Hippodrome High Street
Tel: 0773 746559
Seats: 350

Rochdale Greater Manchester
Cannon The Butts
Tel: 0706 524362/45954
Seats: 1:538, 2:276, 3:197

Royston Herts
Priory, Priory Lane
Tel: 0763 43133
Seats: 305

Rugeley Staffs
Plaza Horsefair

Tel: 08894 2099
Seats: 621

Rushden Northants
Ritz College Street
Tel: 0933 312468
Seats: 822

St Albans Herts
City Hall Civic Centre*
Tel: 0727 44488
Seats: 800
Odeon London Road
Tel: 0727 53888
Seats: 1:452, 2:115, 3:128, 4:145

St Austell Cornwall
Film Centre Chandos Place
Tel: 0726 73750
Seats: 1:605, 2:125, 3:138

St Helens Merseyside
Cannon Bridge Street
Tel: 0744 51947/23392
Seats: 1:494, 2:284, 3:179

St Ives Cornwall
Royal, Royal Square
Tel: 0736 796843
Seats: 682

Salford Quays Lancs
Cannon Quebec Drive Trafford Road
Tel: 061 873 7155/7279
Seats: 1:265, 2:265, 3:249, 4:249, 5:213, 6:213, 7:177, 8:177

Salisbury Wilts
Odeon New Canal
Tel: 0722 22080
Seats: 1:471, 2:120, 3:120

Scarborough North Yorks
Futurist Forshaw Road*
Tel: 0723 365789
Seats: 2155
Hollywood Plaza†
North Marine Road
Tel: 0723 365119
Seats: 275
Opera House*
St Thomas Street
Tel: 0723 369999
Seats: 225

Scunthorpe Humberside
Majestic Oswald Road
Tel: 0724 842352
Seats: 1:177, 2:162, 3:193
bfi **Film Theatre**⊕***
Central Library Carlton Street
Tel: 0724 860161 x30
Seats: 249

Sevenoaks Kent
Stag Theatre London Road

Tel: 0732 450175/451548
Seats: 1:455*, 2:102, 3:102

Sheffield South Yorks
Fiesta Flat Street
Tel: 0742 723981
Seats: 1:141, 2:189
Odeon Barker's Pool
Tel: 0742 767962
Seats: 1:500, 2:324
**UCI Crystal Peaks 10
Eckington Way Sothall**
Tel: 0742 480064/470095
Seats: 1:200, 2:200, 3:228,
4:224, 5:312, 6:312, 7:224,
8:228, 9:200, 10:200

Sheringham Norfolk
**Little Theatre†
Station Road**
Tel: 0263 822347
Seats: 198

Shipley West Yorks
**Unit Four Bradford
Road**
Tel: 0274 583429
Seats: 1:89, 2:72, 3:121,
4:94

Shrewsbury Shrops
Cannon Empire Mardal
Tel: 0743 62257
Seats: 573
**The Cinema in the
Square Music Hall**
Tel: 0743 50763
Seats: 100

Sidmouth Devon
Radway, Radway Place
Tel: 039 55 3085
Seats: 400

Sittingbourne Kent
Cannon High Street
Tel: 0795 23984
Seats: 1:300, 2:110

Skegness Lincs
Tower Lumley Road
Tel: 0754 3938
Seats: 401

Skelmersdale Lancs
Premiere Film Centre
Tel: 0695 25041
Seats: 1:230, 2:248

Skipton North Yorks
Plaza Sackville Street
Tel: 0756 3417
Seats: 320

Sleaford Lincs
**Sleaford Cinema
Southgate**
Tel: 0529 30 3187
Seats: 60

Slough Berks
Gallery High Street
Tel: 0753 692233/692492
Seats: 2058 (10 screens)

Solihull West Mids
Cinema High Street
Tel: 021 705 0398
Seats: 650
**Metropole Hotel*
National Exhibition
Centre**
Tel: 021 780 4242
Seats: 200
UCI 8 Stratford Road
Tel: 021 733 3696
Seats: 286 (2 screens), 250
(2 screens), 210 (2
screens), 180 (2 screens)

Southampton Hants
**Cannon Above Bar
Street**
Tel: 0703 223536/221026
Seats: 1:688, 2:433
Cannon Ocean Village
Tel: 0703 330666
Seats: 1:421, 2:346, 3:346,
4:258, 5:258
**The Gantry⊛
Off Blechynden
Terrace**
Tel: 0703 229319/330729
Seats: 194
**Mountbatten Theatre*
East Park Terrace**
Tel: 0703 221991
Seats: 515
**Odeon Above Bar
Street**
Tel: 0703 333243
Seats: 1:476, 2:756, 3:127

Southend Essex
**Cannon Alexandra
Street**
Tel: 0702 344580
Seats: 1:665, 2:498
Odeon Elmer Approach
Tel: 0702 344434
Seats: 1:455, 2:1235

Southport Merseyside
**Arts Centre Lord
Street***
Tel: 0704 40004/40011
Seats: 400
Cannon Lord Street
Tel: 0704 30627
Seats: 1:494, 2:385

Spilsby Lincs
**Phoenix Reynard
Street**
Tel: 0790 53675/53621
Seats: 264

Stafford Staffs
Apollo New Port Road
Tel: 0785 51277
Seats: 1:305, 2:170, 3:168
**Picture House Bridge
Street**
Tel: 0785 58291
Seats: 483

Staines Surrey
**Cannon Clarence
Street**
Tel: 0784 53316/59140
Seats: 1:586, 2:361, 3:173

Stalybridge Greater
Manchester
**New Palace Market
Street**
Tel: 061 338 2156
Seats: 414

Stanley Co Durham
Civic Hall*
Tel: 0207 32164
Seats: 632

Stevenage Herts
**Cannon St Georges
Way**
Tel: 0438 313267/316396
Seats: 1:340, 2:182
**Gordon Craig Theatre*
Lytton Way**
Tel: 0438 354568/316291
Seats: 507

Stockport
Greater Manchester
**Cannon
Wellington Road South**
Tel: 061 480 0779/2244
Seats: 1:520, 2:325
**Davenport Buxton
Road**
Tel: 061 483 3801/2
Seats: 1:1794†, 2:170

Stockton Cleveland
Cannon Dovecot Street
Tel: 0642 676048
Seats: 1:242, 2:110, 3:125
**Dovecot Film Centre
Bishop Street**
Tel: 0642 605506/611626
Seats: 100

Stoke-on-Trent
Staffs
🅱🅵🅸 **Film Theatre
College Road**
Tel: 0782 411188
Seats: 212
Odeon 8 Etruria Road
Tel: 0782 215311
Seats: 1:177, 2:177, 3:309,
4:150, 5:160, 6:160, 7:521,
8:150

Stowmarket Suffolk
**Movieland Church
Walk**
Tel: 0449 672890
Seats: 234
Regal Ipswich Street*
Tel: 0449 612825
Seats: 234

**Stratford-upon-
Avon** Warks
Waterside
Tel: 0789 69285
Seats: 140

Street Somerset
🅱🅵🅸 **Strode Theatre
Church Road⊛☑***
Tel: 0458 42846
Seats: 400

Sudbury Suffolk
**The Quay Theatre
Quay Lane**
Tel: 0787 74745
Seats: 129

Sunderland Tyne &
Wear
Cannon Holmeside
Tel: 091 567 4148
Seats: 1:550, 2:209
**Empire High Street
West***
Tel: 0783 42517
Seats: 1000
Studio High Street West
Tel: 0783 42517
Seats: 150

Sunninghill Berks
**Novello Theatre*
High Street**
Tel: 0990 20881
Seats: 160

Sutton Coldfield
West Mids
**Odeon Birmingham
Road**
Tel: 021 354 2714
Seats: 1:598, 2:132, 3:118,
4:307

Swanage Dorset
Mowlem Shore Road
Tel: 0929 422229
Seats: 400

Swindon Wilts
Cannon Regent Street
Tel: 0793 22838/40733
Seats: 1:604, 2:402, 3:151
**Wyvern Theatre
Square***
Tel: 0793 24481
Seats: 617

Tadley Hants
**Cinema Royal*
Boundary Road**
Tel: 073 56 4617
Seats: 296

Tamworth Staffs
Palace Lower Gungate
Tel: 0827 57100
Seats: 325

Taunton Somerset
Cannon Station Road
Tel: 0823 72291
Seats: 1:502, 2:71

Telford Shrops
**UCI Telford Centre 10
Forgegate**
Tel: 0952 290606/290126
Seats: 1:192, 2:189, 3:189,
4:192, 5:278, 6:278, 7:192,
8:189, 9:189, 10:192

Tenbury Wells
Hereford & Worcs
Regal Teme Street
Tel: 0584 810235
Seats: 260

Tewkesbury Glos
Roses Theatre
Tel: 0684 295074
Seats: 375

Thirsk North Yorks
Studio One
Tel: 0845 24559
Seats: 238

Tiverton Devon
Tivoli Fore Street
Tel: 0884 252157
Seats: 364

Toftwood Norfolk
CBA Shipham Road
Tel: 0362 3261
Seats: 30

Tonbridge Kent
**Angel Centre Angel
Lane***
Tel: 0732 359588
Seats: 306

Torquay Devon
Odeon Abbey Road
Tel: 0803 22324
Seats: 1:309, 2:346

Torrington Devon
Plough Fore Street
Tel: 0805 22552/3
Seats: 108

Truro Cornwall
Plaza Lemon Street
Tel: 0872 72894
Seats: 1:849, 2:102, 3:160

Tunbridge Wells
Kent
**Cannon Mount
Pleasant**
Tel: 0892 41141/23135
Seats: 1:450, 2:402, 3:124

Uckfield East Sussex
**Picture House High
Street**
Tel: 0825 763822
Seats: 1:150, 2:100

Ulverston Cumbria
**Laurel & Hardy
Museum***†
Upper Brook Street
Tel: 0229 52292/86614
Seats: 50 (free)
Roxy Brogdon Street
Tel: 0229 52340
Seats: 310

Urmston Greater
Manchester
Curzon Princess Road
Tel: 061 748 2929
Seats: 1:400, 2:134

Uttoxeter Staffs
Elite High Street
Tel: 08893 3348
Seats: 120

Uxbridge Middx
Odeon High Street
Tel: 0895 813139
Seats: 1:230, 2:439

Wadebridge Cornwall
Regal The Platt
Tel: 020 881 2791
Seats: 1:250, 2:120

Wakefield West Yorks
Cannon Kirkgate
Tel: 0924 373400/365236
Seats: 1:532, 2:233, 3:181

Walkden Greater
Manchester
Unit Four Bolton Road
Tel: 061 790 9432
Seats: 1:118, 2:108, 3:86,
4:94

Wallasey Merseyside
Unit Four Egremont
Tel: 051 639 2833
Seats: 1:181, 2:127, 3:177,
4:105, 5:91, 6:92

Wallingford Oxon
Corn Exchange*
Tel: 0491 39336
Seats: 187

Walsall West Mids
Cannon Townend Bank
Tel: 0922 22444/644330
Seats: 1:506, 2:247, 3:143
**Showcase Bentley Mill
Lane, Darlaston**
Tel: 0922 22123
Seats: 2800 (12 screens)

Waltham Cross
Herts
Cannon High Street
Tel: 092 761160
Seats: 1:460, 2:284, 3:103,
4:83

Wantage Oxon
Regent Newbury Street
Tel: 02357 67878
Seats: 228

Wareham Dorset
Rex West Street
Tel: 092 95 2778
Seats: 239

Warrington Ches
**Odeon Buttermarket
Street**
Tel: 0925 32825
Seats: 1:576, 2:291, 3:196
**UCI Westbrook 10
Westbrook Centre
Cromwell Avenue**
Tel: 0925 416677
Seats: 1:192, 2:189, 3:189,
4:192, 5:278, 6:278, 7:192,
8:189, 9:189, 10:192

Washington Tyne &
Wear

**Fairworld Victoria
Road**
Tel: 091 416 2711
Seats: 1:227, 2:177

Watford Herts
Cannon Merton Road
Tel: 0923 24088/33259
Seats: 1:356, 2:195

Wellingborough
Northants
**Palace Gloucester
Place**
Tel: 0933 222184
Seats: 200

Wellington Somerset
Wellesley Mantle Street
Tel: 0823 272291
Seats: 429

Wells Somerset
Regal Priory Road*
Tel: 0749 73195
Seats: 498

**Welwyn Garden
City** Herts
Campus West*
Tel: 0707 332880
Seats: 365

West Bromwich
West Midlands
Kings Paradise Street
Tel: 021 553 7605/0030
Seats: 1:326, 2:287, 3:462

West Thurrock Essex
**UCI Lakeside 10
Waterglade Park
Centre**
Tel: 0708 869920
Seats: 270 (2 screens), 192
(4 screens), 186 (4
screens)

Westcliff-on-Sea
Essex
Cannon London Road
Tel: 0702 332436/342773
Seats: 1:350, 2:300

Westgate-on-Sea
Kent
**Carlton St Mildreds
Road**
Tel: 0843 32019
Seats: 303

**Weston-super-
Mare** Avon
Odeon The Centre
Tel: 0934 21784
Seats: 1:875, 2:110, 3:133
Playhouse High Street*
Tel: 0934 23521/31701
Seats: 658

Weymouth Dorset
**Cannon Gloucester
Street**
Tel: 0305 785847
Seats: 412

Whitby North Yorks
**Coliseum Victoria
Square***
Tel: 0947 604641
Seats: 226

Whitefield Lancs
Mayfair Bury Old Road
Tel: 061 766 2369
Seats: 1:578, 2:232

Whitehaven Cumbria
Gaiety Tangier Street
Tel: 0946 3012
Seats: 330

Whitley Bay Tyne &
Wear
Playhouse Park Road
Tel: 0632 523505
Seats: 860

Wigan Greater
Manchester
Ritz Station Road
Tel: 0942 323632
Seats: 1:485, 2:321, 3:106
**Unit Four Ormskirk
Road**
Tel: 0942 214336
Seats: 1:99, 2:117, 3:88

Wilmslow Ches
Rex Alderley Road*
Tel: 0625 522145
Seats: 838

Wincanton Som
Plaza South Street*
Seats: 346

Winchester Hants
**Theatre Royal Jewry
Street***
Tel: 0962 843434
Seats: 405

Withington Greater
Manchester
**Cine-City Wilmslow
Road**
Tel: 061 445 3301
Seats: 1:150, 2:150, 3:150

Woking Surrey
QEII Cinema*
Tel: 0483 755855

Wokingham Berks
**Ritz Easthampstead
Road**
Tel: 0734 781888
Seats: 1:200, 2:200

Wolverhampton
West Midlands
Cannon Garrick Street
Tel: 0902 22917/11244
Seats: 1:590, 2:127, 3:94
**Light House Lichfield
Street**
Tel: 0902 312033
Seats: 120

Woodbridge Suffolk
Riverside Theatre
Quay Street
Tel: 039 43 2174
Seats: 280

Woodhall Spa Lincs
Kinema in the Woods
Coronation Road
Tel: 0526 52166
Seats: 365

Worcester Hereford &
Worcs
Odeon Foregate Street
Tel: 0905 24733
Seats: 1:650, 2:205, 3:109,
4:109, 5:66

Worksop Notts
Regal Carlton Road
Tel: 0909 482896
Seats: 1:326*, 2:154

Worsley Greater
Manchester
Unit Four Bolton Road
Tel: 061 790 9432
Seats: 1:118, 2:108, 3:86,
4:94

Worthing West Sussex
Connaught Theatre
Union Place*
Tel: 0903 31799/35333
Seats: 400
Dome Marine Parade
Tel: 0903 200461
Seats: 650

Wymondham
Norfolk
Regal Friarscroft Lane
Tel: 0953 602025
Seats: 300

Yeovil Somerset
Cannon Court Ash
Terrace
Tel: 0935 23663
Seats: 1:575, 2:239, 3:247

York North Yorks
 City Screen
Tempest
Anderson Hall&*
Yorkshire Museum
Tel: 0904 612940
Seats: 300

bfi **Film Theatre**&*
Central Hall, York
University
Tel: 0904 612940
Seats: 750
Odeon Blossom Street
Tel: 0904 23040
Seats: 1:834, 2:111, 3:111
Warner Clifton Moor&
Tel: 0904 691199/691094
Seats: 1:128, 2:212, 3:316,
4:441, 5:185, 6:251, 7:251,
8:185, 9:441, 10:316,
11:212, 12:128

CHANNEL ISLANDS AND ISLE OF MAN

Douglas Isle of Man
Palace Cinema
Tel: 0624 76814
Seats: 1:319, 2:120
Summerland Cinema
Tel: 0624 25511
Seats: 200

St Helier Jersey
Odeon Bath Street
Tel: 0534 24166
Seats: 1:719, 2:171, 3:213

St Peter Port
Guernsey
Beau Sejour Centre
Tel: 0481 26964
Seats: 398

St Saviour Jersey
Cine de France
St Saviour's Road
Tel: 0534 71611
Seats: 291

SCOTLAND

A number of BFI-supported cinemas in Scotland also receive substantial central funding and programming/ management support via the Scottish Film Council

Aberdeen Grampian
Cannon Union Street
Tel: 0224 591477/587458
Seats: 1:566, 2:153, 3:146
Capitol Union Street
Tel: 0224 583141
Seats: 2010
Odeon Justice Mill
Lane
Tel: 0224 586050
Seats: 1:793, 2:123, 3:123

Annan Dumfries & Gall
Ladystreet, Lady
Street†
Tel: 046 12 2796
Seats: 450

Arbroath Tayside
Palace James Street
Tel: 0241 73069
Seats: 900

Aviemore Highland
Speyside Aviemore
Centre
Tel: 0479 810627
Seats: 721

Ayr Strathclyde
Odeon Burns Statue
Square
Tel: 0292 264049
Seats: 1:433, 2:138, 3:138

Bathgate Lothian
Regal North Bridge
Street
Tel: 0506 630869
Seats: 467

Brechin Tayside
Kings High Street
Tel: 035 62 2140
Seats: 754

Campbeltown
Strathclyde
Picture House Hall
Street
Tel: 0586 2264
Seats: 430

Castle Douglas
Dumfries & Gall
Palace St Andrews
Street†
Tel: 0556 2141
Seats: 400

Clydebank
Strathclyde
UCI Clydebank 10
Clyde Regional Centre
Britannia Way
Tel: 041 951 1949/2022
Seats: 1:200, 2:200, 3:228,
4:252, 5:385, 6:385, 7:252,
8:228, 9:200, 10:200

Cumnock Strathclyde
Picture House
Glaisnock Street
Tel: 0290 20160
Seats: 652

Dumfries Dumfries &
Gall
Cannon Shakespeare
Street
Tel: 0387 53578
Seats: 532
Robert Burns Centre
Film Theatre*
Mill Road
Tel: 0387 64808
Seats: 67

Dundee Tayside
Cannon Seagate
Tel: 0382 26865/25247
Seats: 1:618, 2:319
bfi **Steps Theatre**&*
The Wellgate
Tel: 0382 24938/23141
Seats: 250
Victoria, Victoria Road
Tel: 0382 26186
Seats: 350

Dunfermline Fife
Orient Express East
Port
Tel: 0383 721934
Seats: 1:212, 2:157,
3:97(V)

Dunoon Strathclyde
Studio John Street
Tel: 0369 4545
Seats: 1:188, 2:70

East Kilbride
Lanarkshire
UCI Olympia Mall 9
Town Centre
Tel: 03552 49022
Seats: 319, 217 (3
screens), 209, 206 (4
screens)

Edinburgh Lothian
Cameo Home Street
Tollcross
Tel: 031 228 4141
Seats: 398
Cannon Lothian Road
Tel: 031 228 1638/299
3030
Seats: 1:868, 2:738, 3:318
Dominion Newbattle
Terrace
Tel: 031 447 2660
Seats: 1:584, 2:296, 3:50
bfi **Filmhouse**
Lothian Road◻
Tel: 031 228 2688/6382
Seats: 1:285, 2:90↻
Odeon Clerk Street
Tel: 031 667 7331/2
Seats: 1:695, 2:293, 3:201,
4:259, 5:182
Playhouse Leith Walk*
Tel: 031 557 2692
Seats: 3131
UCI Craig Park
Seats: 2400 (12 screens)

Elgin Grampian
Moray Playhouse High
Street
Tel: 0343 542680
Seats: 1:330, 2:220

Eyemouth Berwicks
Cinema Church Street
Tel: 0390 50490
Seats: 220

Falkirk Central
Cannon Princess Street
Tel: 0324 31713/23805
Seats: 1:704, 2:128, 3:128

Fort William
Highlands
Studios 1 and 2
Tel: 0397 5095

Galashiels Borders
Kingsway Market
Street
Tel: 0896 2767
Seats: 395

Girvan Strathclyde
Vogue Dalrymple
Street†
Tel: 0465 2101
Seats: 500

Glasgow Strathclyde
Cannon Clarkston Road
Muirend
Tel: 041 637 2641
Seats: 1:482, 2:208
Cannon Grand Jamaica Street
Tel: 041 248 4620
Seats: 326
Cannon Parkhead Forge
Tel: 041 556 4343
Seats: 1:434, 2:434, 3:322, 4:262, 5:208, 6:144, 7:132
Cannon Sauchiehall Street
Tel: 041 332 1592/9513
Seats: 1:970, 2:872, 3:384, 4:206, 5:194
bfi **Film Theatre Rose Street**&♿ ☑
Tel: 041 332 6535
Seats: 404
Grosvenor Ashton Lane
Hillhead
Tel: 041 339 4298
Seats: 1:277, 2:253
Odeon Renfield Street
Tel: 041 332 8701/3413
Seats: 1:1138, 2:208, 3:227, 4:240, 5:288, 6:222
Salon Vinicombe Street
Hillhead
Tel: 041 339 4256
Seats: 406

Glenrothes Fife
Kingsway Church Street
Tel: 0592 750980
Seats: 1:294, 2:223

Hamilton Strathclyde
Odeon Townhead Street
Tel: 0698 283802/422384
Seats: 1:466, 2:224, 3:310

Inverness Highland
Eden Court Bishops Road
Tel: 0463 221718/239841
Seats: 1:797, 2:70
La Scala Strothers Lane
Tel: 0463 233302
Seats: 1:438, 2:255

Inverurie Grampian
Victoria West High Street
Tel: 0467 21436
Seats: 473

Irvine Strathclyde
Magnum Harbour Street
Tel: 0294 78381
Seats: 323
WMR Film Centre Bank Street
Tel: 0294 79900/76817
Seats: 252

Kelso Borders
Roxy
Tel: 0573 24609
Seats: 260

Kilmarnock Strathclyde
Cannon Titchfield Street
Tel: 0563 25234/37288
Seats: 1:602, 2:193, 3:149

Kirkcaldy Fife
bfi **Adam Smith Theatre**&♿ ☑*
Bennochy Road
Tel: 0592 260498/202855
Seats: 475
Cannon High Street
Tel: 0592 260143/201520
Seats: 1:547, 2:287, 3:235

Kirkwall Orkney
Phoenix Junction Road
Tel: 0856 4407
Seats: 500

Lerwick Shetland
North Star Harbour Street
Tel: 0595 3501
Seats: 200

Livingston Lothian
The Cinema Almondvale Centre
Tel: 0506 33163
Seats: 1:168, 2:165

Lockerbie Dumfries & Gall
Rex Bridge Street†
Tel: 05762 2547
Seats: 195

Millport Strathclyde
The Cinema (Town Hall)†
Clifton Street
Tel: 0475 530741
Seats: 250

Motherwell Lanarkshire
Civic Theatre*
Tel: 0698 66166

Newton Stewart Dumfries & Gall
Cinema Victoria Street
Tel: 0671 2058
Seats: 412

Oban Strathclyde
Highland Theatre George Street*
Tel: 0631 62444
Seats: 420

Paisley Strathclyde
Kelburne Glasgow Road
Tel: 041 889 3612
Seats: 1:249, 2:248

Perth Tayside
Playhouse Murray Street
Tel: 0738 23126
Seats: 1:590, 2:227, 3:196

Peterhead Grampian
Playhouse Queen Street
Tel: 0779 71052
Seats: 731

Pitlochry Tayside
Regal Athal Road†
Tel: 0796 2560
Seats: 400

St Andrews Fife
New Picture House North Street
Tel: 0334 73509
Seats: 1:739, 2:94

Saltcoats Strathclyde
La Scala Hamilton Street
Tel: 0294 63345/68999
Seats: 1:301, 2:142

Stirling Central
Allanpark, Allanpark Road
Tel: 0786 74137
Seats: 1:321, 2:287
bfi **MacRobert Centre**&♿ ☑*
University of Stirling
Tel: 0786 73171
Seats: 500

WALES

Aberaman Aberdare
Grand Theatre*
Cardiff Road
Tel: 0685 872310
Seats: 950

Aberystwyth Dyfed
Commodore Bath Street
Tel: 0970 612421
Seats: 410

Bala Gwynedd
Neuadd Buddig*
Tel: 0678 520 800
Seats: 372

Bangor Gwynedd
Plaza High Street
Tel: 0248 362059
Seats: 1:306, 2:163
Theatr Gwynedd Deiniol Road
Tel: 0248 351707/351708
Seats: 343

Bargoed Mid Glam
Cameo High Street
Tel: 0443 831172
Seats: 302

Barry South Glam
Theatre Royal Broad Street
Tel: 0446 735019
Seats: 496

Brecon Powys
Coliseum Film Centre Wheat Street
Tel: 0874 2501
Seats: 1:164, 2:164

Brynamman Dyfed
Public Hall Station Road
Tel: 0269 823232
Seats: 838

Brynmawr Gwent
Market Hall Market Square
Tel: 0495 310576
Seats: 320

Builth Wells Powys
Wyeside Arts Centre Castle Street
Tel: 0982 552555
Seats: 210

Cardiff South Glam
Cannon Queen Street
Tel: 0222 31715
Seats: 1:616, 2:313, 3:152
bfi **Chapter Market Road**&
Tel: 0222 396061
Seats: 1:195, 2:78
Monico Pantbach Road
Tel: 0222 691505
Seats: 1:500, 2:156
Monroe, Globe Centre
Albany Road
Seats: 216
Odeon Queen Street
Tel: 0222 27058
Seats: 1:448, 2:643
bfi **Sherman Theatre**&♿ ☑*
Senghennydd Road
Tel: 0222 30451/396844
Seats: 474
St David's Hall*
The Hayes
Tel: 0222 371236/42611
Seats: 1600

Carmarthen Dyfed
Lyric King's Street*
Tel: 0267 232632
Seats: 800

Cwmbran Gwent
Scene The Mall
Tel: 063 33 66621
Seats: 1:115, 2:78, 3:130

Denbigh Powys
Futura
Tel: 0745 715210
Seats: 112

Fishguard Dyfed
Studio West Street

Tel: 0348 873421/874051
Seats: 252

Gilfach Goch Mid Glam
Workmen's Hall
Glenarvon Terrace
Tel: 044 386 231
Seats: 400

Haverfordwest Dyfed
Palace Upper Market Street
Tel: 0437 2426
Seats: 538

Holyhead Gwynedd
Empire Stanley Street
Tel: 0407 2093
Seats: 1:350, 2:159

Llandudno Gwynedd
Palladium Gloddaeth Street
Tel: 0492 76244
Seats: 355

Llanelli Dyfed
Entertainment Centre
Station Road
Tel: 0554 774057/752659
Seats: 1:516, 2:310, 3:122

Merthyr Tydfil Mid Glam
Studio Castle Street
Tel: 0685 3877
Seats: 1:98, 2:198

Milford Haven Dyfed
Torch Theatre
St Peters Road
Tel: 064 62 4192/5267
Seats: 297

Mold Clwyd
bfi Theatr Clwyd&
Civic Centre
Tel: 0352 56331
Seats: 1:530, 2:129

Monmouth Gwent
Magic Lantern
Church Street
Tel: 0600 3146
Seats: 124

Newport Gwent
Cannon Bridge Street
Tel: 0633 54326
Seats: 1:572, 2:190, 3:126

Newtown Powys
Regent Broad Street
Tel: 0686 25917
Seats: 210

Pontypool Gwent
Scala Osborne Road
Tel: 049 55 56038
Seats: 197

Pontypridd Mid Glam

bfi Muni Screen& ✉*
Municipal Hall
Gelliwasted Road
Tel: 0443 485934
Seats: 400

Porthcawl Mid Glam
Regent Trecco Bay†
Tel: 065 671 2103
Seats: 168

Portmadoc Gwynedd
Coliseum Avenue Road
Tel: 0766 2108
Seats: 582

Port Talbot West Glam
Plaza Theatre Talbot Road
Tel: 0639 882856
Seats: 1:846, 2:196, 3:111

Prestatyn Clwyd
Scala High Street
Tel: 07456 4365
Seats: 314

Pwllheli Gwynedd
Town Hall Cinema
Tel: 0758 613371
Seats: 450

Resolven West Glam
Welfare Hall
Tel: 063 710410
Seats: 541

Rhyl Clwyd
Apollo High Street
Tel: 0745 353856
Seats: 1:250, 2:225

St Athan South Glam
Astra Llantwit Major
RAF St Athan
Tel: 04465 3131 x4124
Seats: 350

Swansea West Glam
Filmcenta Worcester Place
Tel: 0792 53433
Seats: 650
Odeon Kingsway
Tel: 0792 52351
Seats: 1:708, 2:242, 3:172
UCI Parc Tawe 10
Tel: 0792 644980
Seats: 277 (2 screens), 174 (4 screens), 156 (4 screens)

Taibach West Glam
Entertainment Taibach
Seats: 200

Tenby Dyfed
Royal Playhouse
White Lion Street
Tel: 0834 4809
Seats: 479

Treorchy Mid Glam
Parc and Dare Hall

Station Road
Tel: 0443 773112
Seats: 794

Tywyn Gwynedd
The Cinema
Tel: 0654 710260
Seats: 368

Welshpool Powys
Pola Berriew Street*
Tel: 0938 2145
Seats: 500

Wrexham Clwyd
Hippodrome Henblas Street
Tel: 0978 364479
Seats: 613

NORTHERN IRELAND

Antrim Antrim
Cinema Castle Street
Tel: 084 94 3136
Seats: 400
Coltworthy House
Arts Centre
Louth Road

Ballymena Antrim
State Ballymoney Road
Tel: 0266 2306
Seats: 1:215, 2:166

Banbridge Down
Iveagh Huntley Road
Tel: 082 06 22423
Seats: 930

Belfast Antrim
Cannon Fisherwick Place
Tel: 0223 222484/248110
Seats: 1:551, 2:444, 3:281, 4:215
Curzon 300 Ormeau Road
Tel: 0232 491071/641373
Seats: 1:453, 2:360, 3:200
bfi Queen's Film Theatre&
University Square Mews
Tel: 0232 244857/667687
Seats: 1:250, 2:150
The Strand Hollywood Road
Tel: 0232 673500
Four screens

Coleraine
Londonderry
Palladium Society Street
Tel: 0265 2948
Seats: 538

Cookstown Tyrone
Ritz Studio Burn Road
Tel: 06487 65182

Seats: 1:192, 2:128

Downpatrick Down
Grand Market Street
Tel: 0396 2104
Seats: 450

Dungannon Tyrone
Astor George's Street
Tel: 08687 23662

Dungiven Derry
St Canice Hall
Main Street

Enniskillen
Fermanagh
Ritz Forthill Street
Tel: 0365 22096
Seats: 450
Ardhowen Centre
Dublin Road
Tel: 0365 23233
Seats: 296

Keady Armagh
Scala Cinema
Granemore Road
Tel: 0861 531547
Seats: 200

Kilkeel Down
Vogue Newry Street
Seats: 413

Londonderry
Londonderry
Strand, Strand Road
Tel: 0504 262084
Seats: 1:293, 2:178

Magherafelt
Londonderry
Cinema Queen Street
Tel: 0648 33172
Seats: 230

Newry Down
Savoy 2 Merchant's Quay
Tel: 0693 67549
Seats: 1:197, 2:58

Portrush Antrim
Playhouse
Tel: 0265 823917

& – Accessible to people with disabilities (advance arrangements sometimes necessary – please phone cinemas to check)
✉ – Induction loop for the hard of hearing
bfi – Supported by the BFI through finance, programming assistance or occasional programming/ publicity services
* – Part-time or occasional screenings
† – Cinema open seasonally
V – Video

109

COURSES

Film and TV study courses generally fall into two categories: academic and practical. Listed here are the educational establishments which offer film and television as part of a course or courses. Where a course is mainly practical, this is indicated with a **P** *next to the course title. In the remaining courses, the emphasis is usually on theoretical study; some of these courses include a minor practical component as described. The information here is drawn from two BFI education booklets – 'Film and television training: A guide to courses' and 'Studying film and tv: A list of courses in higher education'. More information about listed courses can be found in these booklets, along with information on certain further education courses not included here*

Barking College of Technology
General Education Department
Dagenham Road
Romford RM7 0XU
Tel: 0708 766841
P **B/TEC National Diploma in Media**
Two year full-time course in video, radio and print. Facilities include 3 camera colour television studio, S-VHS and VHS editing facilities, sound recording studios and full desktop publishing and print workshops

University of Bath
School of Modern Languages and International Studies
Claverton Down
Bath BA2 7AY
Tel: 0225 826826
BA (Hons) Modern Languages and European Studies
First year lectures and seminars on the language and theory of film, whilst the second and fourth years offer a wide range of options on French films between the wars, the films of the Nouvelle Vague, film and television in German speaking countries and film in Italy and the Soviet Union. There is a final year

option dealing with European cinema in the 70s and 80s. No practical component
MPhil and PhD
Part-time or full-time research degrees in French cinema

Bedford College of Higher Education
Polhill Avenue
Bedford
Tel: 0234 51671
BA (Hons) Combined Studies
Two-year option, (2 hours per week), involving critical work on image formation, television drama and film. Taught as part of a course in the Contemporary Stage and including practical and theoretical work in Twentieth Century drama. Facilities include 3-camera TV studio and 200 seater Community Theatre
Modular BA/BSc Programme (Arts Pathway) Dance and Drama in Contemporary Culture
Two modules in Year: Film, Television and Realism. Each module 3 hours per week for 15 weeks. One and a half hours theory in Dance and Drama; one and a

half hours practical video production focussing on either Dance or Drama

University of Birmingham
Department of Cultural Studies
Faculty of Commerce and Social Sciences
PO Box 363
Birmingham B15 2TT
Tel: 021 414 6060/6061
BSocSc (Hons) Media and Cultural Studies
A wide-ranging analytic degree concerned with contemporary social and cultural issues, of which media are a part. Course (brochure available) includes media history; year's course on contemporary media, particularly press and TV; option of specialist dissertation on media; some practical SLR photography (Year 1), video (Year 2), plus short period of placement in local media organisations.
BA (Combined Hons) Media and Cultural Studies
A half degree, either combined with another Arts subject or as base for a General degree. Because the department is small, the single

honours degree includes courses outside the department. In practice the half degree omits little of the full degree. All modes of entry are heavily oversubscribed: standard offer BBC. Mature/access candidates especially welcome.

Department of French Language and Literature
BA (Hons) French
Four-year course which includes options on French cinema (Year 1), documentary film (Year 2) and the practice of transposing works of fiction to the screen (Year 4)

Bournemouth and Poole College of Art and Design
School of Film, Television and Audio Visual Production
Wallisdown Road
Poole
Dorset BH12 5HH
Tel: 0202 595281
P BTEC ND in Audio Visual Production
A new course, offering initial experience of tape slide, video production and audio recording at a practical level. Facilities include 9 projector Multivision rig, 4 track and 8 track music studios, VHS cameras and edit suite and full photographic rostrum. Supported by design studies, creative writing, music and word processing
P B/TEC Higher National Diploma in Design (Film and Television)
An extensive two-year course based on the production process. All areas of film and television production are covered, with an emphasis on drama and documentary. The majority of work is student originated, with an equal emphasis on film and tape. The course has a substantial input from, and contact with, working professionals within the industry
The course has full ACTT

accreditation. Facilities include: Arriflex SR and BL Film cameras, Nagra 4.2 recorders, Steenbeck, pic-syncs, PAG dubbing suite, 2 TV studios, 2 Hitachi FP60 cameras, 2 FP21 and 1 FP40 cameras, Sony 4800 recorders, Sony 5 series edit suites, Quantel paintbox, video and film rostra, 4 and 8 track music studios etc
P Advanced Diploma in Media Production
Film/television option. One-year production opportunity for post B/TEC, postgraduate and mid-career students. Application through personal statement of intent and interview. Equipment as HND, above

University of Bristol
Department of Drama
29 Park Row
Bristol BS1 5LT
Tel: 0272 303030
BA Drama
Three-year course, includes introduction to critical and theoretical approaches to film and television in year one; core seminar courses in film history, with additional academic and practical options in year two, and a number of optional extras in film and television in year 3. Practical courses extend the critical and practical work using multi-camera studio and single camera OB video resulting in the production of original works in the most appropriate format
P Postgraduate Certificate in Radio, Film and Television
One-year practical course. It offers a grounding in practical skills in film and tv production, centering on group exercises in studio television, location and studio film and video projects, and fiction and non-fiction productions for public exhibition and/ or broadcast. Production equipment includes a broadcast-standard

television studio, U-Matic video production and post-production facilities, 16mm Arriflex/Nagra production outfits, and 4 film cutting rooms with Steenbeck and Prevost tables. Additional video, sound and photographic facilities are available for students' preparatory work. In addition the Drama department has a fully equipped professional theatre whose resources and technical support are available to students. The course is ACTT accredited

Brunel University
Department of Human Sciences
Uxbridge
Middx UB8 3PH
Tel: 0895 56461
BSc Communication and Information Studies
Four-year interdisciplinary course which aims to give an understanding of the social, intellectual and practical dimensions of the new technologies. Includes practical courses in computing and in video production and technology. All students undertake three periods (five months) of work placement
MA in Communications and Technology
Offers an advanced training in the social study of new technology in relation to issues of communications and cultural policy and technological and social change. It is structured around a programme of formal lectures, directed reading and participation in seminars and class discussion. Students take a core course in Communications and Technology, a research course resulting in a dissertation and two optional courses. The course is completed in one year (full-time) or two years (part-time)

College of Cardiff
University of Wales
PO Box 908
French Section
EUROS

Cardiff
Tel: 0222 875000
BA French
Study of French cinema included as part of optional courses. Small practical component
BA German
Study of contemporary German cinema forms part of both compulsory and optional courses

Polytechnic of Central London
Faculty of Communication
18-22 Riding House Street
London W1P 7PD
Tel: 071 486 5811
P BA (Hons) Film, Video and Photographic Arts
Gives equal emphasis to filmmaking and to film theory and criticism. After a general introductory year, students choose either a Film Option or a Photography Option. Film Option students combine theoretical study with filmmaking in years 2 and 3. The film course is ACTT-accredited. Facilities include a photographic studio suite, a film studio and television studio with all the associated control rooms, changing rooms and stores, a 24-seat dubbing theatre, transfer room, editing rooms, animation room, radio and recording studios, design studio, black and white and colour processing and printing areas, loading rooms, silk screen room, tape/slide room, workshops and labs. Film equipment includes self-blimped and non-synchronous film cameras (all film-making is done on 16mm), tape-recorders, 12 motorised editing machines, 7-track 'rock and roll' dubbing system, 10-channel mixing desk, animation stand, 3 U-matic ENG systems, VHS portapack systems and 3 U-Matic/ VHS edit suites
P BA (Hons) Media Studies
This degree studies the social context in which the institutions of mass

communications operate, including film and television, and teaches the practice of print and broadcasting journalism and television production

Linked MA and Postgraduate Diploma in Film and Television Studies
Advanced level part-time course (evenings and study weekends) concerned with theoretical aspects of film and TV. Modular credit and accumulation scheme, with exemption for work previously done. Postgraduate Diploma normally awarded after two years (70 credits), MA after three years (120 credits). Modules offered in 1990/91: Authorship, Structuralism, Realism and Anti-Realism, the Film and TV Audience, Problems of Method, Hollywood, Psychoanalysis, Third World Cinema, Issues in British Film Culture, Public Service Broadcasting, TV Genres and Gender, the Documentary Tradition, British TV Drama, Soviet Cinema, Production Studies. No practical component

MPhil and PhD Film and Television Studies (CNAA)
Research degrees in film and television history, theory and criticism. Applicants should have the Postgraduate Diploma and the MA in Film and Television Studies or equivalent qualifications and be able to submit a detailed research proposal

Polytechnic of Central London
Centre for Communication and Information Studies
235 High Holborn
London WC1V 7DN
Tel: 071 404 5353
MPhil and PhD research degrees in Communication and Information studies

Central Manchester College
East Manchester Centre
Taylor Street

Gorton
Manchester M18 8DF
Tel: 061 223 8282 x476

P **B/TEC National Diploma in Audio Visual Design**
Multi-disciplinary integrated, group-based course working between graphics, video, film/animation, sound recording, photography and tape/slide production. Assessment is continuous, based on practical projects linked to theoretical studies. Equipment includes 4 VHS portapacks and cameras, VHS Camcorder, 2 JVC KY1900 cameras, VHS and low-band U-Matic edit suites, 16mm Bolex camera, VHS effects generator plus supporting studio/portable sound, lighting equipment and computer graphics

Central Saint Martin's College of Art and Design
Film and Video
27-29 Long Acre
London WC2E 9LA
Tel: 071 753 9090
x 426/428

P **BA (Hons) Fine Art**
Three years full-time. After a first year during which students undertake a number of projects related to film and video (with one project carried out in another area of Fine Art), the second and third years can be spent exclusively in film and video. 80% practical; 20% theoretical. Equipment includes 16mm facilities: (Arriflex, Bolex, Aaton cameras; 5 Steenbecks; 5 pic syncs); U-Matic video recorders, cameras and 3 edit suites; 2 sound rooms; 3 16mm animation rostra; computerised tape/slide equipment; lighting studio and 2 viewing rooms/ seminar spaces

P **MA Independent Film and Video**
Two years part-time. Aimed at students working (or who intend to work) in the independent sector of film and video production. It offers a lecture/seminar-based directed study programme and a

Workshop Attachment Scheme. Students should have access to production facilities outside St Martin's

Christ Church College
North Holmes Road
Canterbury
Kent CT1 1QU
Tel: 0227 762444

P **BA (Hons)/ BSc (Hons) Combined Studies**
Radio, film and television can be studied along with one other subject. Course introduces students to an understanding of radio, film and TV as media of communication and creative expression, and the practice of production skills in each of the three media. Where possible, industrial attachments are arranged. Production facilities include: Super 8mm and 16mm film equipment; fully colourised 3-camera TV studio with two editing suites, portapacks and supporting sound and lighting equipment

MA in Media Production
A taught MA in Media Production for graduate students wishing to develop or extend expertise in practical production in Radio, Film and Television. The course lasts for a year and assessment is based upon a major production and an extended essay. Though largely practical (75%) the Course includes a theoretical component and integrates theory and practice. BA and MA degrees are validated by the University of Kent

City of London Polytechnic
Department of Fine and Applied Art
Sir John Cass Faculty
31 Jewry Street
London EC3N 2EY
Tel: 071 283 1030

BA (Hons) Art, Design and Visual Communication
This new part-time degree is designed to meet the needs and aspirations of mature students (twenty-one and over). It

provides an opportunity to work with a variety of media across three related fields of study: Fine Art, Design and Communications media

Coventry Polytechnic
Faculty of Art and Design
Department of Graphic Design and Communication
Gosford Street
Coventry CV1 5RZ
Tel: 0203 224166

BA (Hons) Communication Studies
Three-year course which includes optional modules in Film Studies, Video-making and Media Policy. Students must undertake an extended essay and are encouraged to include practical/field work in this project. This has included making video pieces

P **BA (Hons) Fine Art**
BA (Hons) Graphic Design
Students may specialise in film and video within the Fine Art and Graphic Design degrees

P **MA/PhD Electronic Graphics**
The course offers full-time students the choice of a three-term postgraduate diploma, or four-term MA. All students register initially for the postgraduate diploma and may, on successful completion, progress to the MA. The course is essentially a practical one and the majority of students' time is spent using the computing equipment for the generation of electronic images. There is a significant theoretical component which is integrated with the practical activities. The faculty has four purpose built computer studios which are interfaced to the video post-production facilities. There are also video studio facilities, film and mainframe computing

Derbyshire College of Higher Education

Faculty of Art and Design
Kedleston Road
Derby DE3 1GB
Tel: 0332 47181

P BA (Hons) Photographic Studies

Three-year course divided into two parts of five and four terms. The course offers students the ability to specialise in film/video practice in addition to the normal photographic and academic routes. Part 1 concentrates on development of ideas and investigation of ways they may be carried out. In Part 2 students are expected to assume considerable responsibility for their own work programmes. Academic studies form 30% of the course. Creative and inventive use of the media is encouraged from conception to projection. Facilities include: Super 8mm sound and silent cameras, editing and projection; 16mm Bolex, Pathe, Auricon, Beaulieu, Eclair NPR, time lapse and rostrum cameras; Uhers, Nagra, Revox and 40-track Teac recorders; 6-plate flat-bed and pic sync editing; animation stand for 16mm and QAR video animation; VHS and U-Matic portable video recorders; U-Matic edit suite; studio; cinema with 35mm, 16mm and video projection

Linked Postgraduate Diploma/MA in Film Studies

Part-time evening course over three years with the intermediate award of the Postgraduate Diploma at the end of year two. An academic course with the study of film and the institution of cinema as its principal concerns. No practical component. Thesis supervision offered in the areas of American, British, European, and Third cinema. Exemption from certain course requirements can be made for students with a background in Film Studies at undergraduate level. Opportunity exists for students to register for MPhil or PhD

Dewsbury College

School of Art and Design
Cambridge Street
Batley
West Yorkshire
WF17 5JB
Tel: 0924 474401
Fax: 0924 457047

P B/TEC National Diploma in Design (Communications) Video Production and Related Studies

Two-year course in video production in which some role specialisation is possible in the second year. Students are placed in industry for a minimum of four weeks during Year 2. Facilities include: VHS and U-Matic Portapacs; 2 U-Matic low-band edit suites with TBCs and FX generator; 2-camera studio with full mixing and Chromakey; computer graphics with animation, frame grab and video interface; computer tapeslide production; 16mm cameras; animation rostrum; still photography studios and darkrooms. Yearly intake: 16 students

Dorset Institute of Higher Education

Department of Communication and Media
Wallisdown Road
Poole
Dorset BH1 5BB
Tel: 0202 524111

P BA (Hons) Production

A three-year course covering the academic, practical, aesthetic, technical and professional aspects of work in the media. The course is equally divided between practical and theoretical studies. After Year 1 students can specialise in audio, video or computer graphics, leading to a major production project in Year 3. In addition students complete a piece of individual research in the area of Communication Processes. Facilities include 4-colour CCTV studio with DVE

equipment, 6 U-Matic edit suites, 6 U-Matic O/B units, 5 sound studios (including a radio studio linked directly to BBC Radio Solent), 21 computer graphics workstations including Iris 2400 Turbo, DG MV400 and 3 Sony SMC 70s

P Postgraduate Diploma/MA in Video Production

A one-year full-time course starting in October 1990 for graduates wishing to acquire the skills of producing and directing television and video. It is based on practical project work in the studio and on television

Ealing College of Higher Education

School of Humanities
St Mary's Road
Ealing
London W5 5RF
Tel: 081 579 4111

BA (Hons) Humanities

Students take 10 units as part of degree, of which six may be in media studies, including one practical video unit

MA Cultural Studies

Part-time taught evening course of six units plus dissertation. Topics include film and television, popular culture. No practical component

University of East Anglia

School of English and American Studies
Norwich NR4 7TJ
Tel: 0603 56161

BA (Hons) Film and English Studies

A Joint Major programme which integrates Film and Television study with Literature, History and Cultural Studies. Course includes either a practical project on film or video or an independent dissertation on a film or television topic

BA (Hons) in Literature, History, Linguistics, Drama or American Studies

Film can be taken as a substantial Minor programme (up to 40% of degree work) in combination with any of these Major subjects

There is no formal practical element in these programmes, but students have access to instruction in the use of 8mm, 16mm and video equipment

MA Film Studies

One-year full-time taught programme. MA is awarded 50% on coursework, 50% on individual dissertation. Courses include: Early Cinema, Film Industry/Film History, Structuralist and Post-structuralist Film Theory, British Cinema. There is scope for work on television as well as on other aspects of cinema. This MA includes a new specialist option, offering training in the operations and use of film archives

MPhil and PhD

Students are accepted for research degrees

Polytechnic of East London

School of Art and Design
Greengate Street
London E13
Tel: 081 590 7722
Fax: 081 519 3740

P BA (Hons) Fine Art

During the first year of the course students can experiment with each of the disciplines that are available but can also specialise in film and video throughout the three years. Facilities include studio, U-Matic colour cameras and edit suite, Sony portapacks, 16mm and Super 8mm film cameras, Revox and Teac tape-recorders

Department of Cultural Studies
Livingstone House
Livingstone Road
London E15 2LL

BA (Hons) Cultural Studies

Three-year course offering options on media, film and photography in Years 2 and 3. Also includes a practical component (20%) in video, tape-slide and photography over all three years

BSc (Hons) New Technology (Interdisciplinary Studies)
This new degree examines the development, applications and implications of new technologies. Options will involve the study and practice of video, computer graphics and newspaper production

Edinburgh College of Art
Visual Communications Department
School of Design and Crafts
Lauriston Place
Edinburgh EH3 9DF
Tel: 031 229 9311
P BA (Hons) in Design
Film/TV students enter the Visual Communications Dept at second year level following a foundation year in Art and Design at ECA or elsewhere) or other relevant course or experience. Applications close on 15th March annually. Some interest in a related discipline (Illustration, Animation, Photography, Graphic Design) is expected, as the first part of the course is general. After this, Film/TV students do a combination of individual projects (eg animated sequences, TV graphics, music videos, small scale documentary) and group projects (eg live-action drama). Postgraduate applications are also welcome for the Diploma in Design (three terms) or the MDes (four terms). Facilities include: 16mm rostrum camera, 16mm sync-sound shooting facilities, 16mm editing, super 8 equipment, video animation rostrum, computer graphics facilities, three camera TV studio, eight track sound mixing, and video portable VCRs and edit suites in VHS, S-VHS, Lo-Band and Hi-Band SP formats

University of Exeter
American and Commonwealth Arts
School of English

Queen's Building
The Queen's Drive
Exeter EX4 4QH
Tel: 0392 264263
Fax: 0392 263108
BA (Hons) American and Commonwealth Arts
BA (Combined Hons) American and Commonwealth Arts and English
BA (Combined Hons) American and Commonwealth Arts and Music
BA (Combined Hons) American and Commonwealth Arts and Italian
Students can take up to a third of their degree in Film Studies, with the emphasis on American film. Combined Hons with Italian also include a course on Italian cinema and culture. No practical component
MA, MPhil and PhD
Students wishing to take an MA degree by coursework and dissertation or an MPhil or PhD by thesis alone can be accommodated and candidates with proposals in any aspect of American or Commonwealth cinema will be considered. Applications for postgraduate study in American Film History will be particularly welcome

School of Modern Languages
Italian Department
BA (Combined Hons) Italian
Italian combined with another subject. One of the six courses that students take is Italian cinema and culture. In general, Neo-realism to the present day

School of Education
St Luke's
Exeter EX1 2LU
Tel: 0392 76311
Includes a subsidiary unit of media studies. Some practical work

Farnborough College of Technology
Boundary Road
Farnborough
Hampshire GU14 6SB

Tel: 0252 515511
P HND Media Production and Business Studies
Two year full-time course to study media production techniques with business studies. Course includes TV and video production, video and audio systems and finance in the media

Glasgow College
Department of Communication
Cowcaddens Road
Glasgow G4 0BA
Tel: 041 331 3000
Fax: 041 331 3005
BA Communication Studies
Three-year course examining the place of mass communication in contemporary society. Includes practical studies in print, television, advertising and public relations

University of Glasgow
Department of Theatre, Film and TV Studies
Glasgow G12 8QQ
Tel: 041 339 8855
Fax: 041 330 4808
MA Joint Honours in Film and Television Studies
Four-year undergraduate course. Film/TV Studies represents 50% of an Honours degree or 30% of an Ordinary degree. Year 1 is concerned with Film and TV as 'languages', the institutional structures of British TV, and the implications of recent developments in technology and programming. Year 2 is structured under two headings: Genre in Film and Television and Film, Television and British National Culture. Years 3 and 4 consist of a range of Honours courses, four to be taken in each year. There is also a compulsory practical course, involving the production of a video

Department of French
Glasgow G12 8QQ
Tel: 041 339 8855
MA (Hons) French
Study of French Cinema is a one-year special subject comprising one

two-hour seminar per fortnight plus weekly screenings. No practical component

Goldsmiths' College, University of London
Lewisham Way
London SE14 6NW
Tel: 081 692 7171
P BA Communications
This new course brings together theoretical analyses in social sciences and cultural studies with practical work in TV, film, photography, journalism, radio and electronic graphics. The practical element constitutes 50% of the total degree course. The theoretical element includes media history and sociology, textual and cultural studies, personal and interpersonal contexts of communication and media management
BA Anthropology and Communication Studies
Half of this course constitutes Communication Studies and is split equally between practice and theory. Practical options include TV, film, journalism, photography, radio and electronic graphics. The theory component of the Communications is concerned with media history, sociology, psychology, textual and cultural studies
BA Communication Studies/Sociology
Communication studies constitutes half of this course and is split equally between theoretical studies and practice. Practical options include TV, film, photography, journalism, radio and electronic graphics. The theory component of communications is concerned with psychology, media sociology, cultural studies, semiotics and media history
P Diploma in Communications
One-year full-time course with practical work in one

of the following: TV and video, film, radio, photography, electronic graphics and creative writing. Students complete 10,000-word dissertation (or three 3,000-word essays) which counts for 30% at final assessment. Equipment includes 8mm, 16mm, VHS and U-Matic editing facilities, multi-camera TV studio, Paintbox, computer graphics laboratory and video animator, photographic studio, colour and black and white darkrooms

Department of Continuing and Community Education A programme of evening courses are offered which include video production and editing

Gwent College of Higher Education
Faculty of Art and Design
Clarence Place
Newport
Gwent NP9 0UW
Tel: 0633 259984

P **B/TEC Higher National Diploma in Film and Video Production: Live Action and Animation**
Two-year intensive vocational course. Two strands: Live Action: lighting camera operating, sound recording, film and video editing, scriptwriting, directing and art directing and producing; and Animation: scripting and storyboarding, 2 and 3D animation techniques and theory, and post production skills. All students go on placement with BBC, ITV or other production companies. Facilities include: Arriflex, Eclair and Bolex cameras, Nagra tape recorders, Steenbeck editors, Neilson Hordell rostrum camera, and VHS and lo-band U-matic production and editing

Harrogate College of Arts and Technology
Hornbeam Park
Hookstone Road
Harrogate HG1 8QT
Tel: 0423 879466

P **B/TEC Diploma in Design (Communications)**
Two-year course providing training in a range of high tech arts subjects. Options include video production, TV graphics, computer imaging and animation, DTP, basic design, animation and model-making, sound creation, radio and tape/slide. Research and scripting are included in all areas. Course is 80% practical and vocationally based. Entry requirements: four GCSE or equivalent plus folder of relevant work. Equipment includes: 3 U-Matic edit benches, 3 portable edit packs, TV studio with 6 colour cameras, TV graphics, Chromakey and SEG/TBC computer graphics, 19 Amigas/Macs with laser and colour printers, purpose-built sound, radio and TV rooms and portable recorders. Also available for course use: 16mm film and darkrooms

Harrow College of the Polytechnic of Central London
School of Design and Media Communication
Northwick Park
Harrow
Middlesex HA1 3TP
Tel: 081 864 5422

P **BA (Hons) in Photography, Film and Video**
A practical course with integrated theoretical, historical and critical studies. After a first year which is both fundamental and experimental, students may specialise or continue using a variety of media. 60% practical, 40% theoretical. Equipment includes Arriflex, Eclair and Bolex 16mm cameras; Bolex, Nalcom, Canon and Eumig Super 8mm cameras; three studio colour video cameras; colour portapacks; Nagra, Uher, Philips, Revox, Tanberg, Ferrograph and Teac tape-recorders; 8mm, 16mm, VHS and U-Matic editing facilities; specialist AV facility;

computer image generators with video interface

Hatfield Polytechnic
School of Humanities and Education
Wall Hall Campus
Aldenham
Watford
Herts WD2 8AT
Tel: 0923 852511

BA (Hons) Contemporary Studies
Full-time and part-time course for mature students. Media Studies is a one-year optional course for second year students and introduces study of media practices and institutions/apparatuses. No practical component

Havering College of Further and Higher Education
Department of Art and Design
Ardleigh Green Road
Hornchurch
Essex RM11 2LL
Tel: 04024 55011

P **Media Production Course**
(B/TEC applied for)
A two year, full-time programme. The core studies are City and Guilds course 279 Television and Video Production, which covers programming production, vision operations, audio production, TV graphics and media related electronics, and Film and Communication Studies A levels. Facilities include: (cameras) Super-8, VHS Camcorders, S-VHS, Video 8, C-format video, Sony eng, still cameras; Low band U-matic and VHS edit suites, digital vision mixer Rostrum camera set up, 8 track audio studio with range of FX

University of Hull
Department of Drama
Cottingham Road
Hull HU6 7RX
Tel: 0482 46311

BA Joint and Special Honours
Introduction to film and TV studies in Year 1. Honours students may opt for practical courses in TV and radio in subsequent

years. Special Honours students may also opt for practical course in filmmaking. Equipment includes 16mm cameras, TV and radio studios, film and U-Matic editing

Humberside College of Higher Education
School of Art and Design
Queens Gardens
Hull HU1 3DH
Tel: 0482 224121
Fax: 0482 586721

P **BA (Hons) Graphic Design**
Students may specialise in film/video, photography, graphic design or illustration. After a common first term, film primers are introduced in the second term, and specialisation may begin at the start of term 3. The course is essentially practical, with a strong theoretical/critical back-up and a programme of visiting animators and filmmakers. Most work is in documentary, animation and public information film, but an increasing amount of work is being carried out using video formats. Computer graphics is a new major component. Equipment includes Bolex and Eclair cameras, Uher, Nagra and Tandberg recorders, VHS and U-Matic video portapacks; 16mm editing tables and U-Matic editing suites; film/video studio; three animation stands (16mm); video line-test rostrum; optical printer; computer animation systems including Picasso; post-production/dubbing sound rooms; TV and sound studios

P **BA (Hons) Fine Art**
Time-based media: 8mm and 16mm film; VHS and U-Matic video; sound photography; and related live work. Course is essentially practical (80%), projects being student-initiated following the first general introductory term. Work frequently crosses disciplines including

COURSES

printmaking, painting and sculpture. Supported by a programme of visiting tutors, artists, film/videomakers, screenings and critical/theoretical studies (20%). Equipment as for BA (Hons) Graphic Design

P BA (Hons) Documentary Communication
This is a mixed mode honours degree with three production pathways: still photography/text; sound/radio; and video. The course will provide the educational content within which individuals will acquire the knowledge and skills pertinent to communicating in documentary forms, their understanding and interpretation of the nature and variety of human society. The course will seek to produce graduates who are able to operate professionally in a variety of contexts, and who will have developed the interpersonal skills necessary to working with others in a co-operative manner. The minimum and maximum periods of study are normally 3 and 6 years respectively for the full and part-time modes of attendance. Equipment as for the other courses plus additional camcorders and PCs

Institute of Education, University of London
Joint Department of English and Media Studies
20 Bedford Way
London WC1H 0AL
Tel: 071 636 1500
Fax: 071 436 2186
PGCE English and Media Studies
One-year full-time teacher training course, including practical component. Additional PGCE Further Professional Option in Film, TV and Media Studies available within general PGCE framework (equivalent to approx 20% of qualification)

MA Film and TV Studies for Education
One-year full-time or two-year part-time. Three elements: 1) Mandatory module in The Theory and Practice of Media Education, assessed by final examination; 2) Optional module, assessed by course work, from the following: Childhood, Youth and Popular Culture; Media Education, Race and Gender; The Theory and Practice of Media Education; Ideology and the Media; British and European Media; Hollywood Cinema: Text and Context; Television and its Audiences; 3) Dissertation
MA Media Studies/MA Media Education
One year full-time, two years part-time, with three elements: 1) Mandatory Model in Ideology and the Media (assessed by final examination); 2) Optional module, assessed by course-work, drawn from those listed under MA Media Education above; 3) Dissertation
MPhil and PhD
Supervision of research theses in the area of Film Studies, TV Studies, Media Studies and Media Education
Institute Associateship
Individualised one-year courses for mature educationalists wishing to study pedagogic and intellectual developments in the field of Media Education and Media Studies

Kent Institute of Art and Design
Rochester upon Medway College
(formerly Medway College of Design)
Fort Pitt
Rochester
Kent ME1 1DZ
Tel: 0634 830022
P B/TEC Higher National Diploma in Advertising and Editorial Photography
Two-year course which includes the possibility of specialising in film and video

Kent Institute of Art and Design at Maidstone (formerly Maidstone College of Art)
Oakwood Park
Oakwood Road
Maidstone
Kent ME16 8AG
Tel: 0622 757286
Fax: 0622 692003
P BA (Hons) Communication Media Pathway in Time-Based Studies
Full-time production and theory centred and mainly video based, seeking to explore new creative developments in moving imagery as well as linking to other pathways through such areas as animation and computer generated imagery

University of Kent
Rutherford College
Canterbury
Kent CT2 7NX
Tel: 0227 764000
BA Combined Hons
A Part 1 course on Narrative Cinema is available to all Humanities students in Year 1. The Part 2 component in Film Studies in Years 2 and 3 can vary from 25% to 75% of a student's programme. Courses include Film Theory, British Cinema, Early Film Form, and Sexual Difference and Cinema. The rest of a student's programme consists of courses from any other Humanities subject. No practical component
MA and PhD
There are no courses at postgraduate level but students are accepted for MA or PhD by thesis

King Alfred's College of Higher Education
Sparkford Road
Winchester SO22 4NR
Tel: 0962 841515 x231
Fax: 0962 842280
P BA (Hons) (CNAA) in Drama, Theatre and TV
Three-year practical course that relates theories of contemporary television and drama to practical work in both media. The course looks

at both the institutions and the practices of the two media from the perspectives of psychology and critical ideologies. Facilities include: 2 & 3-machine editing facilities for S-VHS or U-matic, 10 portable cameras recording onto Super VHS, TV studio with 3 Sony M3 cameras, control room with broadcast-standard vision mixer and 8-channel audio-sound mixer. Access to 3 camera outside broadcast unit

Kingston Polytechnic
School of Three Dimensional Design
Knights Park
Kingston-upon-Thames
Surrey KT1 2QJ
Tel: 081 549 6151
CNAA Post-Graduate Diploma in Design for Film and Television
One-year course in scenic design tailored to the needs of those who wish to enter the industry with the eventual aim of becoming production designers or art directors. The course is constructed as a series of design projects to cover different types of film and television production Department of History of Art and Design and Contextual Studies
BA (Hons) Architecture
Options in History of Film. No practical component
BA (Hons) Fine Art
Two-year Complementary Studies course. First year is an 18-week introductory course. Second year is a 12-week course on Modernism in the cinema. No practical component
BA (Hons) Three Dimensional Design
Second year Complementary Studies: one-term option on scenography
BA (Hons) Graphic Design
First year Complementary Studies: History of Animation and History of Documentary. No practical component

116

School of Graphic Design

P BA (Hons) Graphic Design
Includes some practical filmmaking (animation)

School of Languages
Penrhyn Road
Kingston-upon-Thames
Surrey KT1 2EE
BA (Hons) Modern Arts
Two-term option course in Year 2 on French Cinema since 1930. No practical component

Kingsway College
Grays Inn Centre
Sidmouth Street
Grays Inn Road
London WC1H 8JB
Tel: 071 837 8185
P B/TEC National Diploma in Design Communications (Media Studies)
Two-year full-time course for those interested in pursuing a career in the media industry. The course covers an integrated programme of practical training in photography, video, film and computer technology, and theoretical studies relating to the analysis of media texts.
Facilities include: VHS video studio/cameras/recorders etc, VHS two machine edit with Time Base Correction, Super-8 film equipment (cameras and editors), rostrum camera for animation, computer graphics facilities and studios, photographic workshops, cinema, sound recording facilities

Leicester Polytechnic
Department of Art History
PO Box 143
Leicester LE1 9BH
Tel: 0533 551551 x2119
P BA (Hons) Arts and Humanities: Media Studies (Single, Joint or Combined Studies Degrees)
As a Single Honours degree, Media Studies offers a range of courses which focus specifically on Film, Television/Video, Photography and Media institutions. It offers courses in both theoretical and practical

work which provide students with the opportunity to develop their skills and learning through detailed analysis of media texts, through understanding the social and political processes of media industries and institutions and through practical work in video, photography and time-based arts. As Joint Honours, it is possible to take Media Studies in conjunction with one other arts discipine; for Combined Honours, with two other disciplines

University of Leicester
Centre for Mass Communication Research
104 Regent Road
Leicester LE1 7LT
Tel: 0533 523863
Fax: 0533 523874
MA Mass Communications
One-year taught course studying the organisation and impact of the mass media both nationally and internationally and providing practical training in research methods

Liverpool Polytechnic
School of Art, Media and Design
Hope Street
Liverpool L1 9HW
Tel: 051 207 3581
Fax: 051 709 0172
P BA (Hons) Graphic Design
Film/Animation is a specialised option within the Graphic Design degree. After a general first year a number of students may specialise in Film/Animation in their second and third years
BA (Hons) Media and Cultural Studies
Some practical components within this degree are integrated into a theoretical study of television, film, videos and radio. First year courses in reading and producing the media lead to specialist options in film studies, video, photography and broadcast journalism

University of Liverpool
Department of Communication Studies
Chatham Street
Liverpool L69 3BX
Tel: 051 794 2653/6
BA Combined Hons (Arts)
BA Combined Hons (Social Studies)
BA Joint Hons (English and Communication Studies)
Film and television studies form a substantial component within the above degrees. In Year 1 there is an introductory course on Communication, involving work on photography and television; in Year 2, courses on Broadcasting, Film Studies and Drama; and in Year 3, a course on Documentary and a course on Persuasion which includes an element of media analysis. No practical component

London College of Printing
School of Media
Division Film, Video and Animation
Back Hill
Clerkenwell Road
London EC1R 5EN
Tel: 071 278 7445
P BA (Hons) Film Video and Animation
The first autonomous course in Film and Video leading to the award of BA (Hons) degree. Main concerns are Women's Cinema, Third World Cinema, Popular Culture and Film. Stress on experimentation and innovation, education, independent filmmakers rather than specialised technicians. Practice/Theory ratio is 70:30. Course stresses integration of theory and practice. As from 1988 the course includes an option in Animation. Facilities include 8mm, 16mm film and VHS, U-Matic Lo and Hi band video, production and postproduction facilities. This course is accredited by ACTT

London International Film School
Department F15
24 Shelton Street
London WC2H 9HP
Tel: 071 836 9642
P Two-year Diploma course in the Art and Technique of Filmmaking
A practical course teaching skills necessary for professional employment in the industry, recognised by LEAs and the ACTT. Courses commence in January, April and September. Each student works on one or more films in every term. Approximately half of each term is spent in filmmaking, half in practical tuition, lectures, tutorials, film analysis and scriptwriting. Facilities include two viewing theatres, two fully-equipped studios, a video rehearsal studio, and comprehensive editing and sound departments. Equipment includes 35mm Mitchell, 16mm and 35mm Arriflex cameras, Nagra sound recorders and Steenbeck and Hollywood Magnasync editing tables

University College London
Department of Spanish and Latin American Studies
Gower Street
London WC1 6BT
Tel: 071 380 7121
BA (Hons) Spanish
Two courses are available on Images of Women in Latin American Film and Narrative: one at MA level, the other at undergraduate level. No practical component

Manchester Polytechnic
Department of Communication Arts and Design
Capitol Building
School Lane
Didsbury
Manchester M20 0HT
Tel: 061 434 3331
P BA (Hons) Design for Communication Media
Television Production and

Design is a main area of study offering a three year full-time course of a largely practical nature. The two elements, Production and Design, represent separate options within the area. The Production option aims to develop a range of programme-making skills (research, scripting, direction, camera-work, editing etc). The Design option is divided into two areas of work, TV Production Design (concentrating on set design but including costumes and graphics) and animation (including puppetry). Production and Design students collaborate on some projects. Facilities include a colour TV studio, a sound studio, JVC Portable cameras. Hi-Band and VHS recording and editing, 16mm rostrum and scenic workshop. Video animation facilities expected for 1990/91

Department of Interdisciplinary Studies
Aytoun Street
Manchester M1
Tel: 061 228 6171
BA (Hons) Modern Studies
Film/TV small component. A mixed course of English, Film and Current TV News
BA (Hons) English Studies/Historical Studies
Film/TV small component. A mixed course including documentary film, TV soap opera and TV news. No practical component

Department of General Studies
Chester Street
Manchester M1 5GD
Tel: 061 228 6171
BA (Hons) General Arts
One-year course for students with Dip HE or equivalent. Mass Media: a multi-disciplinary course which applies the methodologies of the social sciences and the humanities to the mass media. No practical component

Dip HE
Two-year course which includes an introduction to film and film theory in Year 1 and a course on film as propaganda in Year 2. No practical component

University of Manchester
Department of Drama
Oxford Road
Manchester M13 9PL
Tel: 061 273 3333
Fax: 061 275 5584
BA Single and Joint Honours in Drama
Normally an optional course in film studies in Year 3 with a compulsory course for Single Honours in Year 2 (optional for Joint). No practical component
MLitt
Possibility for research theses on aspects of film and TV drama
Department of Education
Oxford Road
Manchester M13 9PL
Tel: 061 275 3463
MEd in Education and the Mass Media
Course offered on a full or part-time basis, which enables teachers and youth and community workers to explore effective communication techniques within their fields of work. Some practical work. Visits to media organisations and contributions from media specialists are arranged
Diploma in Advanced Study in Education and the Mass Media
Designed for educators from the UK and overseas, this full or part-time course provides an introduction to the study of mass media systems and the use of audiovisual material for teaching and learning

Middlesex Polytechnic
Modular Scheme
Combined Studies
Trent Park
Cockfosters Road
Barnet
Herts EN4 0PT
Tel: 081 368 1299
BA (Hons) Combined Studies
Modular system degree. In years 2 and 3 students

take twelve modules. From the range on offer a student may take four on film or TV
BA (Hons) History of Art, Design and Film
Modular system degree. First two years as combined studies. Third year allows greater specialisation and includes dissertation which could be in film or TV studies. The modules are: British Cinema and TV; History of the Cinema; Hollywood, Authorship and Genre; Art and the Mass Media; Realisms; Independent Film. No practical component

Faculty of Art and Design
Cat Hill
Barnet
Herts EN4 8HT
Tel: 081 368 1299
BA (Hons) Contemporary Cultural Studies
One-year course (or 2/3 years part-time) designed for students who possess a Dip HE or equivalent (2 years full-time degree-level work). Film and television are studied as aspects of cultural practice. No practical component

P MA in Video
A one year full-time course (48 weeks) emphasising the creative aspects of professional video production in the independent sector. Intended for graduate students with considerable low-band video experience. The course covers all aspects of the production cycle, with an emphasis on scriptwriting. 50% practical; 50% theoretical.

Napier Polytechnic
Photography Department
61 Marchmont Road
Marchmont
Edinburgh EH9 1HU
Tel: 031 444 2266
Fax: 031 452 8532
BA Photographic Studies
Three years full-time with option of specialising in film and television production in third year

HNC (Scottish Vocational Educational Council) Audio Visual Techniques
One year full-time or two years part-time. Students should have previously done an ONC or similar course

National Film and Television School
Beaconsfield Studios
Station Road
Beaconsfield
Bucks HP9 1LG
Tel: 0494 671234
P The School offers a three-year, full-time professional course leading to an Associateship (ANFTS) with specialisation in the training of producers, directors, writers, directors of photography, editors, animators, art directors, sound recordists, documentary and film composers. Students are encouraged to interchange roles in any practical activity at the same time as developing their specialisation. Approximately 35 students are admitted annually, with six or seven places reserved for overseas students. Average age is 27 years. Previous experience in film or a related field is expected. Facilities include three studios, fully equipped to professional standards, hi-band and low-band U-Matic video editing suites, 20 film editing rooms, professional cameras and tape recorders, lighting equipment for studio and location work, 35mm/16mm Oxberry rostrum camera with 3-D facility, viewing facilities. The school is funded by a partnership of Government and industry (film and TV). Its graduates occupy leading roles in all aspects of film and TV production. It is a full member of CILECT (Centre International de Liaison des Ecoles de Cinéma et de Télévision) and actively co-operates with professional bodies in the UK and abroad

Newcastle upon Tyne Polytechnic

Faculty of Art and Design
Squires Building
Sandyford Road
Newcastle upon Tyne
NE1 8ST
Tel: 091 232 6002

P BA (Hons) Media Production
Three-year course, started in September 1986. Practical course with fully integrated theoretical and critical components in which students are offered the opportunity to specialise in individual programmes of work. Organised into three stages with the Media Theory programme continuing throughout. Facilities include nine computer workstations, a sound studio, U-Matic 3-camera studio with mixing and effects facility, edit suite, U-Matic portapack, Super 8mm and 16mm cameras and Rostra

BA (Hons) History of Modern Art, Design and Film
Offered as a three-year full-time course or as a five-year part-time course (over two evenings a week). Film Studies is given equal weighting with painting and architecture/design in the first two years of both the full and part-time courses. Thereafter a student can spend up to 75% of his or her time involved with the study of film

MPhil
There are possibilities for research degrees in either film theory or practice

University of Newcastle upon Tyne

School of English
Newcastle upon Tyne
NE1 7RU
Tel: 091 222 6000

BA (Hons) English Literature
Third year optional course: theoretical introduction and special areas of study (mainly Hollywood interests). No practical component

MA in Twentieth Century Studies:

English and American Literature and Film
Modules in film and television are available in one-year, full-time course

Combined Honours Centre
Newcastle upon Tyne
NE1 7RU
Tel: 091 222 6000

BA (Hons) Combined Studies
Two-year course, available in the second year of the degree. Year 1 covers British and American film, and Theory and History of Film; Year 2 Studies in European Film and a dissertation

School of Modern Languages
Newcastle upon Tyne
NE1 7RU
Tel: 091 232 8511

BA (Hons) Modern Languages
Optional final year course: studies in European film

Department of Spanish and Latin-American Studies
Claremont Bridge
Newcastle upon Tyne
NE1 8ST
Tel: 091 222 6000

BA (Hons) Spanish
Undergraduate special subject Hispanic Drama and Film

MA Hispanic Drama and Film
MA in film is in two parts: Bunuel and post-50s Spanish Film. No practical component

Northbrook College

Littlehampton Road
Goring-by-Sea
Worthing
West Sussex BN122 6NU
Tel: 0903 830057

P B/TEC HND Design (Audio Visual)
Two year, full-time course. A video-based production course which also includes audio, computer graphics, business and technical studies, visual studies and some film and animation work. Work experience is also a feature of the course. In the second year, students

may specialise in pre-production, production or post-production. Equipment includes: high band and low-band U-matic, VHS and Video 8 camera and editing equipment, rostrum camera, computer graphics equipment, sound equipment

North Cheshire College

Padgate Campus
Fearnhead Lane
Fearnhead
Warrington WA2 0DB
Tel: 0925 814343

P BA (Joint Hons) Media with Business Management and Information Technology
A modular system degree. The media component combines practical production work in video, sound recording, photography, graphics and print media, with academic analysis of the media through modules on Forms, Representations, Institutions and Audiences. The course structure enables students to relate their business and information technology studies to their work in media. Year 3 calls for specialisation in one medium of production, combined with a choice of options in the theory course. The programme includes one term in Year 2 devoted to work experience in the media industry and institutions. Facilities include well-equipped graphics and photography studios, multi-track sound studio and desk-top publishing. There is a three colour-camera TV studio with extensive post-production facilities, chromakey, U-Matic and VHS edit suites, U-Matic and VHS location cameras and equipment

BA (Hons) Mature Student Programme
A modular system degree, designed specifically for mature student entry. A broad range of modules is available, and students can choose some or all of the media modules,

theoretical and practical **Diploma in Media Education**
A part-time postgraduate Diploma designed for serving teachers in the primary, secondary and further education sectors who are, or who wish to be, involved in teaching some aspect of media education. The course calls for analysis of key theoretical issues, consideration of issues of curriculum and pedagogy, together with practical work in video, sound and photography. Attendance is either one evening a week over two years or day release over one year

Northern School of Film and Television

This is a joint venture between Leeds Polytechnic, Sheffield City Polytechnic and Yorkshire Television providing postgraduate level professional training in practical film production. At present two courses are offered

NSFTV
Leeds Polytechnic
Calverley Street
Leeds LS1 3HE
Tel: 0532 832600

P MA/Postgraduate Diploma in Scriptwriting for Film and Television (Fiction)
This is an intensive one-year practical course running from January to January, based at Leeds Polytechnic. Staffed largely by working professional writers, it covers the various forms of fiction scriptwriting for film and TV – short film, feature film, TV drama, soap opera, series etc. The course has a strong emphasis of professional presentation, and aims to help graduates to set up a credible freelance practice. After a first term of instruction and short projects, the course proceeds to a short film script in term two and a TV script in term three. The major project, in the third term and over the summer, is a 10,000 word script, either feature film or TV drama

NSFTV
Sheffield City Polytechnic
School of Cultural Studies
Psalter Lane
Sheffield S11 8UZ
Tel: 0742 556101

P MA/Postgraduate Diploma in Film Production (Fiction)
This is an intensive one-year practical course running from October to October, and is based at Sheffield City Polytechnic. Students are admitted into specialist areas: Direction (6 students per year), Production (3), Camera (3), Art-Direction (3), Editing (3) and Sound (3). Students work in teams to produce six short films, in two batches of three. The resulting films may be broadcast on Yorkshire Television, who provide the base production funding and some facilities. Scripts are normally drawn from the product of the Scriptwriting Course at NSFTV and the emphasis is on team working and joint creativity under pressure. It is not a course for 'author' filmmakers There is also a theatrical studies component. Full professional equipment is available, and each film has its own cutting room for the length of production

Polytechnic of North London
School of Literary and Media Studies
Prince of Wales Road
London NW5 3LB
Tel: 071 607 2789
Humanities Scheme
Three-year full-time course. Six-year part-time course by day or evening study. Film Studies is one of 13 subject components and may be taken as a Major, Joint or Minor. One practical component
MA Modern Drama Studies
Two-year part-time evening course with optional one-year Film Studies unit in Year 2. No practical component

Nottingham University
School of Education

Nottingham
Tel: 0602 506101
BEd/BPhil/Diploma/ Certificate Specialist Options in Mass Media Communication
Particular emphasis on TV and media studies in schools. Opportunities are provided for a good deal of practical work, though the major emphasis is upon analysis and criticism
PGCE
Second area option in media studies
MPhil and PhD
Research can be supervised for higher degrees by thesis

Plymouth College of Art and Design
Department of Photography, Film and Television
Plymouth College of Art and Design
Tavistock Place
Plymouth
Devon PL4 8AT
Tel: 0752 221312
B/TEC Higher National Diploma in Photography
Students can specialise in photography, film and video or follow a multi-media option including video, multi-vision, digital imaging and related photographic studies. Underwater photography is an additional specialist option

Portsmouth Polytechnic
School of Social and Historical Studies/School of Languages and Area Studies
Kings Rooms
Bellevue Terrace
Southsea PO5 3AT
Tel: 0705 827681
BA (Hons) Cultural Studies
Year 1: 10 one-hour introductory lectures, five seminars. Year 2 options: Power Politics and Television, Gender, Genre I and II. Year 3 options: British Cinema 1939-49; British Cinema 1950-65; Feminist Film and the Avant-Garde; British TV Plays; Audience Responses

Department of Fine Art

Lion Terrace
Portsmouth PO1 3HF
Tel: 0705 827681
P BA (Hons) in Multi-Area Design
Three-year course. In the first year students experience working in four main resource areas, one of which is film and video. By the second year, students concentrate on two areas, so film may become a major preoccupation. Equipment includes 16mm and 8mm sound cameras, editing facilities, animation rostrum, U-Matic portapack and edit suite, VHS portapack and edit suite

Ravensbourne College of Design and Communication
School of Television
Walden Road
Chislehurst
Bromley
Kent BR7 5SN
Tel: 081 464 3090
P B/TEC Higher National Diploma in Engineering Communications (for Television and Broadcasting)
Two-year full-time vocational course designed in consultation with the TV broadcasting industry leading to employment opportunities as technician-engineers
B/TEC Higher National Diploma in Design Communication (Television Programme Operations)
Two-year full-time vocational course designed in consultation with the TV broadcasting industry leading to employment opportunities as programme operators in lighting, camera operators, sound, video recording and editing, vision-mixing, telecine, and audio-recording. Facilities include two TV studios each with production, lighting and sound control rooms. Each studio has its own vision apparatus room and shares a central

apparatus room, telecine and video recording and editing facilities

University of Reading
Faculty of Letters and Social Sciences
Whiteknights
Reading RG6 2AA
Tel: 0734 875123
BA Film and Drama (Single Subject)
After the first two terms in which three subjects are studied, students work wholly in film and drama. The course is critical but with significant practical elements which are designed to extend critical understanding. It does not provide professional training
BA Film and Drama with English, French, German, Italian or Sociology
Students in general share the same teaching as Single Subject students but the course does not include practical work

Department of English
BA (Hons) English
Third year optional course in media semiotics
PhD
Research can be supervised on the history of the British Broadcasting Corporation

Department of German
BA (Hons) German
Two-term Finals option: The German Mass Media. Involves study of mass media in East and West Germany. No practical component. Two-year core course: German Literature and Civilisation 1900 to the Present

Department of Italian Studies
BA (Hons) Italian/ French and Italian with Film Studies
First year introductory course: Post-War Italian Cinema (one half-term). Second year course: Italian Cinema (three terms). Final year course: European Cinema (two terms). Dissertation on an aspect of Italian cinema. These courses are

available to students reading other subjects in the Faculty. No practical component

MA Italian Cinema
One-year full-time or two-year part-time course on Italian Cinema: compulsory theory course, options on film and literature, Bertolucci, Italian industry and genre – the Spaghetti Western. No practical component

MPhil and PhD
Research can be supervised on Italian cinema for degree by thesis

Graduate School of European and International Studies
MA European Media Studies
One year full-time or two years part-time. The course covers the mass media of Great Britain, France, Italy, East and West Germany. Two compulsory courses: Theory, Institutions and Forms of the Mass Media; and The European Media. Two options to be chosen from: Press and Broadcasting in the Two Germanies; The Sociology of Popular Culture; Representations of Women in the Mass Media; French Film; Genre and Industry in the Italian Cinema; and Literature and Film

Richmond upon Thames College
Egerton Road
Twickenham TW2 7SJ
Tel: 081 892 6656
P B/TEC Diploma in Communication Design Media Studies
This two year full-time course offers an introduction to media studies and production skills in photography, video and desk top publishing, with specialisation in the second year

College of Ripon and York St John
Lord Mayor's Walk
York YO3 7EX
Tel: 0904 56771
BA Combined Hons
Honours degree students

take 16 courses in four years. Of these, five may be film/TV courses including three practical TV courses. The practical component includes some off-campus work and experience in related industries

Roehampton Institute
Department of Drama
Digby Stuart College
Roehampton Lane
London SW15 5PU
Tel: 081 876 8273
BA (Joint Honours) Drama
The Drama programme (Major, Equal, Minor) is combined with one other subject. Year One includes a one term module in Film Analysis and a study of television drama within the Popular Drama module, with some practical work in portable video. Year Two includes Shakespeare on Screen. An optional module in Contemporary Television Drama, including a practical studio production component, is offered in Year Three. Students may also specialise in areas of film and television for dissertations. Facilities include multi-camera colour TV studio, VHS and U-matic editing suites and VHS portable cameras

Royal College of Art
School of Film and Television
Kensington Gore
London SW7 2EU
Tel: 071 584 5020
Fax: 071 225 1487
P MA in Film
Two-year course. Three postgraduate courses offered:
1 Filmmaking – Year 1 advertising and pop promos, Year 2 narrative and documentary making;
2 Production – a training in the business and entrepreneurial skills of low budget film production;
3 3D design for the moving image – concentrates on art direction and design for film and television.

Course units include costume, set design, location dressing. Entries to the filmmaking course must submit up to 30 minutes of film or video. Entries to design course must submit a relevant portfolio of design material. Entries to the production course should demonstrate some knowledge of film production methods. Equipment includes 16mm cameras and editing equipment, studio and cutting rooms

Department of Animation
P MA in Animation
Two-year full-time course with work divided roughly into 80% practical and 20% theoretical. Equipment includes 2 16mm cameras, 2 video scanners and video edit suite. Also 16mm Steenbeck, editing and sound recording equipment

Royal Holloway and Bedford College, University of London
Department of Drama and Theatre Studies
Egham Hill
Egham
Surrey TW20 0EX
Tel: 0784 34455
BA (Hons) Drama and Theatre Studies
History of Film: a two-year course for second and third-year students, constituting one paper at Finals. Principally a historical and critical account of the development of cinema and the use of film for entertainment and art. Film – mainly film theory – is also taught as a special subject. Examination includes a dissertation. No practical component
P Television Drama
A two-year studio production course for second and third-year students. Largely practical with some critical analysis of television and television drama. By the end of the course all students direct their own short production

St Helens College
Faculty of General and Community Education
Brook Street
St Helens
Merseyside WA10 1PZ
Tel: 0744 33766 x221
P B/TEC National Certificate/ Diploma in Media
Two years full-time, the course aims to provide a foundation of basic skills relevant to many areas of the media industry and the opportunity, through option selection, to examine one or more sectors in detail

University of Salford
Department of Modern Languages
Salford M5 4WT
Tel: 061 736 5843
BA (Hons) Modern Languages
One of three Final Year options is in French Cinema. One hour per week out of a total of 15 hours of language work. No practical component
MA Modern Languages
Includes three modules on French Cinema

Sandwell College of Further and Higher Education
High Street Campus
High Street
West Bromwich
West Midlands B70 8DW
Tel: 021 556 6000 x8736/ 8001
P B/TEC National Diploma in Electronics and Television Studio Operations
Two-year course for those seeking a career in the broadcast media and associated industries. Offers a sound foundation in electronics and computer awareness. Course consists of the following components: vision and sound principles and operations; micro-electronics systems; computer graphics and assignments; transmission principles; radio and TV systems; programme production; communications and media studies; electrical and electronic principles;

electronics; mathematics; industry and society

Sheffield City Polytechnic

Department of Communication Studies
36 Collegiate Crescent
Sheffield S10 2BP
Tel: 0742 665274

BA (Hons) Communication Studies

Course covers all aspects of communications, one area being Mass Communication. Option course in TV Fictions and Applied Media Studies in Year 3. Some practical work

Totley Hall Lane
Sheffield S17 4AB
Tel: 0742 369941

MA Communication Studies

Part-time course over six terms, followed by the completion of a dissertation by the end of term eight. Aims to develop theoretical understandings and analytical skills in relation to the processes and practices of communication in modern society. Students attend for two sessions of 2+ hours each week
Faculty of Cultural Studies
Psalter Lane
Sheffield S11 8UZ
Tel: 0742 556101

BA (Hons) History of Art, Design and Film

Film studies is a major component of this course.
Year 1: introduction to film analysis and history.
Year 2: special study on Hollywood. Year 3: critical and theoretical studies in Art, Design and Film and Contemporary Film Theory and Practice.
No practical component

MA Film Studies

Two-year part-time course; two evenings per week, plus dissertation to be written over two terms in a third year. Main areas of study: Problems of Method; The Classical Narrative Tradition; British Cinema 1927-45; British Independent Cinema 1966-84. No practical component

Faculty of Art and Design
Psalter Lane

Sheffield S11 8UZ
Tel: 0742 556101

P BA (Hons) Fine Art (Combined and Media Arts)

After initial work with a range of media, students can specialise in film and/or video. Film productions can range from short 8mm films, through 16mm documentaries or widescreen features, to small 35mm productions. There are professional facilities for shooting, processing, editing, recording and dubbing 16mm films, and good animation equipment. Also well-equipped video and sound studios, with studio cameras, portable units, automatic colour edit suite, multi-track sound recording and mixing, disc tape-cassette transfer and synthesisers

University of Sheffield

Department of English Literature
Shearwood Mount
Shearwood Road
Sheffield S10 2TD
Tel: 0742 768555 x6043/6276

BA (Hons) English Literature

Students may study one or two Special Subjects in Film in their second or third years

MA Theatre and Film

One-year course on elements of both theatre and film studies. Work on all topics is assessed at the conclusion of the course

South Thames College

Wandsworth High Street
London SW18 2PP
Tel: 081 870 2241
Fax: 081 874 6163

P B/TEC Higher National Certificate in Design (Communication) – Television Production

Two-year part-time course aimed to equip students with the knowledge, skills and experience required for work in the professional or corporate field of TV production. Students make both single camera and studio television programmes. Facilities

include: 3-colour studio with telecine, caption camera, caption generator, source and record VCRs and a microprocessor controlled lighting rig, plus 8-channel sound mixing with usual sources. Further facilities are bookable by arrangement including Nimbus computers with Pluto graphics packages and an audio laboratory with 16 into 4 into 2 audio mixer, and 4-track recording

University of Southampton

Faculty of Educational Studies
Southampton SO9 5NH
Tel: 0703 595000

Postgraduate Certificate in Education

This one-year initial training course for secondary/6th form teachers offers specialist work in Media Studies as an integral part of English Drama and Media Studies

MA (Ed) Media Education

The MA in Education is run on a modular basis in this full- or part-time taught course. The course as a whole requires the completion of six modules and a supervised dissertation. Included are television studies, media and communication, video in education, and others

MPhil and PhD

Research degrees in any area of Media Education, Media Studies, Educational Broadcasting and Educational Technology are available
School of Modern Languages
Southampton SO9 5NH
Tel: 0703 595000 x2389/2256
Fax: 0703 593939

MA Culture and Society in Contemporary Europe

A core course of weekly lectures and seminars examines a series of issues in contemporary European culture and society. Accompanied by an option course chosen from three topics including Contemporary European Cinema

Staffordshire Polytechnic

Department of History of Art and Design and Complementary Studies
College Road
Stoke on Trent ST4 2DE
Tel: 0782 744531

BA (Hons) History of Design and the Visual Arts

An introductory course in film studies is compulsory in Year 1. Other film studies courses are optional in Years 2 and 3. There is a practical element in Year 2. Dissertation in Year 3
Department of Design

P BA (Hons) Multi-disciplinary Design

Audiovisual Communication is a major design specialisation within a broad-based design course. Students are introduced to techniques and equipment through a series of projects, workshops and short courses. Many final year projects are for clients external to the Polytechnic. Facilities include two U-Matic edit suites, two colour video rostrum-animation suites, full 16mm production facilities, an 8-track sound recording studio, 3 sound editing suites, multi-screen slide-tape production facility, computer graphics, still photography facilities, full location sound recording facilities, 4 ENG/EFP video kits

University of Stirling

Stirling FK9 4LA
Scotland
Tel: 0786 73171
Fax: 0786 51335

BA (Hons) in Film and Media Studies (Single and Joint Honours)

Four-year degree in which students follow courses in the theory and analysis of all the principal media. All students take courses on the theory of mass communication and on problems of textual analysis and then select from a range of options, including practical courses in the problems of news reporting in radio and TV. As a joint honours degree Film and Media Studies can be combined with a variety of other subjects

BA General Degree
Students can build a component of their degree in film and media studies ranging from as much as eight units (approximately 50% of their degree) if they take a major in the subject, down to as little as three if they wish merely to complete a Part 1 major. For the most part students follow the same units as do Film and Media Studies Honours students

MLitt and PhD
Applications are considered for research in a number of areas of film and media studies

Suffolk College of Higher and Further Education
School of Art and Design
Rope Walk
Ipswich
Suffolk IP4 1LT
Tel: 0473 55885

P B/TEC Higher National Diploma in Design Communication
A two-year course with options in film/TV graphics, animation and art direction. Students complete a period of work experience with employers in film and TV companies. Facilities include two colour TV studios, post-production facilities for film and video, and a film animation unit

P CNAA BA (Hons) in Design Studies
A one year follow on from the above B/Tec in Design Communications. Options in Advanced TV Graphic Design, Animation, TV Set Design

Sunderland Polytechnic
School of Humanities
Forster Building
Chester Road
Sunderland SR1 3R
Tel: 091 515 2188/9
Fax: 091 515 2105
BA (Hons) Communication Studies
Study of linguistics,

psychology and sociology in relation to interpersonal communications and mass communication. The course is primarily academic, but includes practical study of radio, video and computing. Options include: Perspectives on Visual Communications, The Languages of Film and Representations of Women in Painting and Film

MA/Postgraduate Diploma in Film and Television Studies
Two-year part-time course. Sociologically based, with the main emphasis on the British context. One evening a week, with a second evening for screenings. MA by thesis in year 3. Next intake September 1990

MA/Postgraduate Diploma in Communication Studies
Two-years part-time. Year 1 concentrates on interpersonal communication (linguistics, social psychology, sociology); Year 2 deals with mass communication (with units on new communications technologies and the representation of history in film and television). One evening per week for two years; followed by a year-long research project. Next intake September 1991. These two MAs are being revised to incorporate full-time/part-time mode

University of Sussex
Arts Building
Brighton BN1 9QN
Tel: 0273 606755
BA English with Media Studies
A three-year full-time degree course which includes analysis of television, film and the press, together with some opportunity (unassessed) to be involved in practical television and video production

Educational Development Building

Brighton BN1 9RG
Tel: 0273 606755
MA Language, the Arts and Education
Full-time and two-year part-time course, primarily for teachers in schools, FE and HE. Though work on film/TV forms only a small part of the taught seminar courses, students can specialise in the film/TV area for all written and practical work

Trent Polytechnic
School of Art & Design
Department of Fine Art
Burton Street
Nottingham NG1 4BU
Tel: 0602 418418
P BA (Hons) Fine Art
Filmmaking and video are available as options within the Fine Art degree. These options, separately or in combination, can be taken as the main area of study. At present up to eight students in each year do this. Equipment includes Arriflex, Bolex and Beaulieu cameras, Oxberry Animation Rostrum, Nagra, Revox and Bauer tape-recorders, sound desk and 16mm editing facilities

Trinity and All Saints College
Faculty of Academic Studies
Brownberrie Lane
Horsforth
Leeds LS18 5HD
Tel: 0532 584341
BA (Hons) Communications and Cultural Studies
Three-year course in combination with a professional study in either Public Media or Business Management and Administration. Film and TV Studies is a major component within the course, which includes some practical work

University of Ulster
Coleraine
Co Londonderry
Northern Ireland BT52 1SA
Tel: 0265 44141
BA (Hons) Media Studies
Three-year course

integrating theoretical, critical and practical approaches to film, TV, radio and the press. Film and TV Studies constitutes over 60% of the course. Important practical component. Facilities include: colour TV studio; portable VHS and S-VHS, Hi-band and low-band; post-production COX 58, Gemini 2; Hi-band video animation suite; 16mm Frezzolini; 4-plate Steenbeck; Super 8; professional 8-track sound studio; Uher and Marantz portables; Apple Mac computer lab; Amiga graphics generator

Faculty of Art and Design
BA (Hons) Fine Art
BA (Hons) Design
BA (Hons) Combined Studies in Art and Design
B/TEC Higher National Diploma in Design Communication
Minor component units in theoretical and some practical elements of film, video and media studies as part of the core studies of all BA courses. Combined Studies students undertake a greater Media Studies input. Fine Art students may specialise in Fine Art video as part of their final studio work. Design students may take video production as part of their graphic design studio work. Design Communication students all take video production project work in Year 1

University of Warwick
Joint School of Film and Literature
Faculty of Arts
Coventry CV4 7AL
Tel: 0203 523523
BA Joint Degree in Film and Literature
Four courses offered each year, two in film and two in literature. Mainly film studies but some TV included. No practical component

BA French or Italian with Film Studies
This degree puts a particular emphasis on film within and alongside its studies of French or

Italian language, literature and society. No practical component
Various Degrees
Options in film studies can be taken as part of undergraduate degrees in other departments. No practical component
MA in Film and Television Studies
Taught courses on Textual Analysis, methods in Film History, Modernity and Innovation, and Issues of Representation
MA, MPhil and PhD
Students are accepted for research degrees

West Glamorgan Institute of Higher Education
Townhill Road
Swansea SA2 0UT
Tel: 0792 203482
P BA (Hons) Combined Studies
Three year degree with several options. The Art in Society option includes a substantial amount of practical work, of which video and tape-slide form a major element. Facilities include: a Sony Series 5 animation unit, a sound studio based on a Tascam Portastudio, a Fairlight Computer Video Instrument. U-Matic editing suite and portable U-Matic unit dedicated to the course. Additional facilities include U-Matic and VHS editing suites and 3-camera studio. The Modern English Studies option includes Film and TV Studies (no practical component)
BEd Primary
This course includes a Literature and Media Studies main subject option.

West Surrey College of Art and Design
Department of Fine Art and Audio-Visual Studies
Falkner Road
The Hart
Farnham
Surrey GU9 7DS
Tel: 0252 722441
P BA (Hons) Photography
BA (Hons) Film

and Video
BA (Hons) Animation
The approach in each Course is essentially practical, structured to encourage a direct and fundamental appraisal of photography, film, video and animation through practice and by theoretical study. 70% practical, 30% theoretical. Equipment includes 16mm Arriflex, Bolex, Canon Scopic and CP16 cameras; sound studio with Neve 12 channel mixer; 10 edit rooms; 4-camera TV studio; Ikegami 3-tube camera; portable 3-tube video camera; U-Matic record and edit suites; range of VHS equipment; three animation rostra; aerial image faculty; NAC quick action recorder; Image Artist and Picasso computer graphics systems; 3 photographic studios; full range of flash and tungsten lighting, all camera formats, B & W and colour processing and printing. Courses are ACTT accredited

Weymouth College
Cranford Avenue
Weymouth
Dorset DT4 7LQ
Tel: 0305 208856
P B/TEC National Diploma in Media
Two year full-time course designed as a solid foundation in a range of media skills but which allows for some specialisation in either television and video or sound and radio. Facilities available are VHS and Super VHS camcorders, Low-band U-matic camera and full edit suite

Wimbledon School of Art
Merton Hall Road
London SW19 3QA
Tel: 081 540 0231
P BA (Hons) Fine Art
Students enrol in either Painting or Sculpture. It is more usual for Painting students to study Film and/or Video. Equipment includes Super 8mm sync sound and editing facilities; 16mm Bolex

with post-sync sound; ½" b/w video and colour U-Matic with editing
P BA (Hons) Theatre Design
There are substantial opportunities for Super 8 filmmaking within the course of Theatre Design. Equipment include Beaulieu and Nizo cameras; Schmidt 4-plate sound mixing/editing suite; Uher, Revox, Teac, Soundcraft, MXR, Lexicon, Greengate and Casio sound facilities

The Polytechnic, Wolverhampton
School of Humanities and Cultural Studies
Wulfruna Street
Wolverhampton WV1 1DT
Tel: 0902 313001
Diploma in Higher Education
Two-year course for formally unqualified students. Work on film and television is situated within a cultural studies perspective, and students are offered four modules over two years in combination with other study areas
BA (Hons) Theme Studies
One-year degree programme open to those who have completed a DipHE. Film and TV emphasis dependent upon subject of the Independent Study paper (50% of the final assessment)
A three-year modular degree programme offering a Cultural Studies theme in Years 2 and 3. Film and TV are also components of complementary modules in History, French and Drama. No practical component
BA and BA (Hons) Combined Studies
TV and film components as for BA Humanities

Working Men's College
Crowndale Road
London NW1 1TR
Tel: 071 387 2037/8208
In association with the Charitable Trust for the Advancement of Film Education

P Part-time course in practical 16mm filmmaking
a) One year Beginners course, leading through a series of mute group exercises to a short (colour) film with added (not shot-synchronous) sound, made by each student individually. All stages are in 16mm
b) One year Intermediate course, incorporating sync-sound, leading through stages to a completed sync-sound film, made not individually, owing to cost, but with roles assigned
Both courses based on attendance of two half-days/eves per week for three twelve-week terms

DISTRIBUTORS (NON-THEATRICAL)

Companies here control UK rights for non-theatrical distribution (for domestic and group viewing in schools, hospitals, airlines and so on). For an extensive list of titles available non-theatrically with relevant distributors' addresses, see the 'British National Film & Video Catalogue', available for reference from BFI Library Services and major public reference libraries. Other sources of film and video are listed under Archives and Libraries (p68) and Workshops (p290)

ABC Films
via Glenbuck Films

Air India
Publicity Dept
17-18 New Bond Street
London W1Y 0BD
Tel: 071 493 4050

Albany Video Distribution
Battersea Studios
Television Centre
Thackeray Road
London SW8 3TW
Tel: 071 498 6811
Fax: 071 498 1494
Val Martin
Julia Knight
Education videos

Amber Films
5 Side
Newcastle upon Tyne
NE1 3JE
Tel: 091 232 2000
Fax: 091 261 5509

Argus Film Library
15 Beaconsfield Road
London NW10 2LE
Tel: 081 451 1127

Arthritis Research Film Library
via Guild Sound and Vision

Artificial Eye Film Co
via Glenbuck Films

Arts Council of Great Britain
via Concord Video and Film Council

Association of British Insurers
via Multilink Film Library

Audience Planners
4 Beadles Lane
Oxted
Surrey RH8 9JJ
Tel: 0883 717194
Fax: 0883 714480

Australia Tourist Commission
and
Austrian Tourist Office
via Audience Planners

Avon Distributors
Everyman Cinema
Holly Bush Vale
London NW3 6TX
Tel: 071 485 4326

BBC Enterprises Video Sales
Woodlands
80 Wood Lane
London W12 0TT
Tel: 081 743 5588/576 2000
Fax: 081 749 0538

BFI Film + Video Library
21 Stephen Street
London W1P 1PL
Tel: 071 255 1444
Fax: 071 436 7950

BFI Production
via BFI Film + Video Library

BP Film Library
15 Beaconsfield Road
London NW10 2LE
Tel: 081 451 1129

Banking Information Service
and
Barclays Bank Film Library
via Multilink Film Library

Belgian National Tourist Office
via Audience Planners

Big Bear Records
PO Box 944
Birmingham B16 8UT
Tel: 021 454 7020/8100

Birmingham Film and Video Workshop
2nd Floor
Pitman Buildings
161 Corporation Street
Birmingham B4 6PH
Tel: 021 233 3423

Black Audio Film Collective
89 Ridley Road
London E8 2NH
Tel: 071 254 9527/9536
Lina Gopaul
Avril Johnson
David Lawson
Black independent films

Blue Dolphin Films
via Glenbuck Films

Boulton Hawker Films
Brett Works
Pound Lane
Hadleigh
near Ipswich
Suffolk IP7 5BG
Tel: 0473 822235
Fax: 0473 823187
Educational films and videos, specialising in health education, biology, and social welfare

Brent Walker Films
via Glenbuck Films

British Gas Film Library
and
British Steel Films
via Viscom

British Telecom Film Library
via Random Film Library

British Transport Films
via CFL Vision, Film Archive Management and Entertainment, and SCFVL

British Universities Film and Video Council
via SCFVL

Bryanston Films
via Filmbank

Bulgarian Tourist Office
via Audience Planners

John Burder Films
7 Saltcoats Road
London W4 1AR
Tel: 081 995 0547
Fax: 081 995 3376
Training and safety programmes

CBS Broadcast
via Glenbuck Films

CFL Vision
PO Box 35
Wetherby
Yorks LS23 7EX
Tel: 0937 541010
Fax: 0937 541083

CSIRO Australia
via Darvill Associates

CTVC Video
Beeson's Yard
Bury Lane
Rickmansworth
Herts WD3 1DS
Tel: 0923 777933
Fax: 0923 896368
Christian, moral and social programmes. Free catalogue available

Canada House Film and Video Library
Canada House
Trafalgar Square
London SW1Y 5BJ
Tel: 071 629 9492 x2284
Fax: 071 321 0025
Features, animation, wildlife and documentaries from Canada on free loan to film societies, educational institutions, etc

Castrol Film and Video Library
Athena Avenue
Swindon

Wiltshire SN2 6EQ
Tel: 0793 693402
Fax: 0793 511479
Motorsport films

Central Independent Television
Video Resource Unit
Broad Street
Birmingham B1 2JP
Tel: 021 643 9898

Central Office of Information
See CFL Vision

Channel Four Television
via Guild Sound and Vision

Children's Film and Television Foundation
via Glenbuck Films. For further details, see under Organisations

Cinema Action
27 Winchester Road
London NW3 3NR
Tel: 071 586 2762
Fax: 071 722 5781
Features and documentaries "provoking the bourgeoisie"

Cinema of Women
Unit 313
31 Clerkenwell Close
London EC1R 0AT
Tel: 071 251 4978
Fax: 071 490 0063
Distribute a wide selection of films and videos for sale and hire, made by and about women, such as *Women of South Lebanon*. For programming advice, contact Jenny Wallace or Abina Manning. Book through Glenbuck Films

Circles (Women's Film and Video Distribution)
113 Roman Road
London E2 0HU
Tel: 081 981 6828
Over 35 new films and videos are now available by women filmmakers from around the world including *Love, Women and Flowers, Serpent River, Moodeitj Yorgas (Solid Women)* and *Sari Red*

Columbia Tri-Star Films (UK)
via Filmbank

Concord Video and Film Council
201 Felixstowe Road
Ipswich
Suffolk IP3 9BJ
Tel: 0473 715754/726012
Videos and films for hire/sale on domestic and international social issues for training and discussion

Connoisseur Films
and
Contemporary Films
via Glenbuck Films

Danish Embassy
55 Sloane Street
London SW1X 9SR
Tel: 071 235 1255

Darvill Associates
280 Chartridge Lane
Chesham
Bucks HP5 2SG
Tel: 0494 783643
Fax: 0494 784873
Available through Glenbuck Films

Derann Film Services
99 High Street
Dudley
W Midlands DY1 1QP
Tel: 0384 233191
8mm package movie distributors
16mm via Glenbuck Films

The Walt Disney Co
via Filmbank

Walt Disney Educational Media
via Viewtech Audio Visual Media

Duke of Edinburgh Awards
via Glenbuck Films

Dutch Embassy Films
via National Audio Visual Aids Library (NAVAL)

Eastern Arts Association
Cherry Hinton Hall
Cherry Hinton Road
Cambridge CB1 4DW
Tel: 0223 215355

Educational and Television Films
247a Upper Street
London N1 1RU
Tel: 071 226 2298
Documentary films from USSR and Eastern Europe. Archive film library

Educational Media International
235 Imperial Drive
Rayners Lane
Harrow
Middx HA2 7HE
Tel: 081 868 1908
Health and educational material

Electric Pictures
via Glenbuck Films and BFI Film + Video Library

Electricity Council Film Library
30 Millbank
London SW1P 4RD
Tel: 071 834 2333 x5456
Fax: 071 931 0356

Enterprise Pictures
via Glenbuck Films

Entertainment Films
via Filmbank

Essential (16mm) Films
via Concord Video and Film Council

Esso Film & Video Library
via Viscom

Film Archive Management and Entertainment (FAME)
Imperial Studios
Maxwell Road
Borehamwood
Herts WD6 1WE
Tel: 081 207 6446

Filmbank Distributors
Grayton House
498-504 Fulham Road
London SW6 5NH
Tel: 071 386 9909/5411
Fax: 071 381 2405
Handles 16mm film on behalf of major, and some other, UK distributors

Films of Israel
via Viscom

Films of Poland
Polish Cultural Institute
34 Portland Place
London W1N 4HQ
Tel: 071 636 6032/3/4
Fax: 071 637 2190

Films of Scotland
via SCFVL

Finnish Embassy
via Audience Planners

Ford Film and Video Library
via Guild Sound and Vision

French Scientific Film Library
via SCFVL

David Furnham Films
39 Hove Park Road
Hove
Sussex BN3 6LH
Tel: 0273 559731

GTO
and
Gala Film Library
via Glenbuck Films

Gas Council
see British Gas Film Library

German Film and Video Library
via Viscom

Glenbuck Films
Glenbuck House
Glenbuck Road
Surbiton
Surrey KT6 6BT
Tel: 081 399 0022/5266
Fax: 081 399 6651
Handles non-theatrical 16mm and video

Gower/TFI
Gower House
Croft Road
Aldershot
Hants GU11 3HR
Tel: 0252 331551
Fax: 0252 317446

Sheila Graber Animation
50 Meldon Avenue
South Shields
Tyne and Wear NE34 0EL
Tel: 091 455 4985

Granada Television Film Library
via Concord Video and Film Council

Greater London Arts
Coriander Building
20 Gainsford Street
London SE1 2NE
Tel: 071 403 9013
Fax: 071 403 9072

Greek National Tourist Office
via Audience Planners

Colin Gregg Films
via BFI Film + Video Library

Guild Sound and Vision
6 Royce Road
Peterborough PE1 5YB
Tel: 0733 315315
Fax: 0733 315395
Produce and market video packages for training, education, PR, and informational use

HandMade Films
and
Hobo Films Enterprises
via Glenbuck Films

IAC (Institute of Amateur Cinematographers)
63 Woodfield Lane
Ashstead
Surrey KT21 2BT
Tel: 03722 76358

ICA Video
Institute of Contemporary Arts
Nash House
The Mall
London SW1Y 5AH
Tel: 071 930 0493
Fax: 071 873 0051

India Government Tourist Office
via Audience Planners

India House Information Service
India House
Aldwych
London WC2B 4NA
Tel: 071 836 8484 x147
Video documentaries

Institut Français du Royaume-Uni
17 Queensberry Place
London SW7 2DT
Tel: 071 589 6211
Fax: 071 581 5127

Intercontinental Films
via Glenbuck Films

International Defence and Aid Fund for Southern Africa
Canon Collins House
64 Essex Road
London N1 8LR
Tel: 071 359 9181

Irish Tourist Board
via Viscom

Jamaica Tourist Board
via Audience Planners

Japan Tourist Organisation
and
Japanese Embassy Films
via Viscom

Robert Kingston Films
via Glenbuck Films

Leeds Animation Workshop
(A Women's Collective)
45 Bayswater Row
Leeds LS8 5LF
Tel: 0532 484997
Producers and distributors of animated films on social issues

London Film Makers' Co-op
42 Gloucester Avenue
London NW1 8JD
Tel: 071 586 4806
Experimental/art-based films: 2,000 classic and recent titles for hire from 1920s to current work

Luxembourg National Tourist Office
via Audience Planners

MTV Finland
via Darvill Associates

Mainline Pictures
via Glenbuck Films and BFI Film + Video Library

Melrose Film Productions
16 Bromells Road
Clapham Common
London SW4 0BL
Tel: 071 627 8404

Mercedes Benz Film Library
via Viscom

Multilink Film Library
12 The Square

Vicarage Farm Road
Peterborough PE1 5TS
Tel: 0733 67622/3
Distributors of films/videos to the education sector

National Audio Visual Aids Library (NAVAL)
(DS Information Systems)
George Building
Normal College
Bangor
Gwynedd LL57 2PZ
Tel: 0248 370144
Fax: 0248 351415
Educational audio visual aids consisting of videotapes, 16mm films, slides and overhead projector transparencies available for hire or purchase

National Film and Television School
Beaconsfield Studios
Beaconsfield
Bucks HP9 1LG
Tel: 0494 671234
Fax: 0494 674042

National Society for the Prevention of Cruelty to Children
67 Saffron Hill
London EC1N 8RS
Tel: 071 242 1626
Fax: 071 831 9562

National Westminster Bank Film Library
via Viscom

Netherlands Information Service
and
Netherlands PD Films
via Darvill Associates

Northern Arts
via Amber Films

Norwegian Embassy Films
via National Audio Visual Aids Library (NAVAL)

Oasis (UK) Films
(formerly Recorded Releasing)
via Filmbank and Glenbuck Films

Open University
via Guild Sound and Vision

FRAGILE

Handle with care

"A Stake in the Soil" joins the catalogue of Shell films and videos
caring for our planet, people and prosperity.
For further details, please contact your local Shell company or
Shell International Petroleum Company Limited, PAC/231,
Shell Centre, London SE1 7NA.

Shell Film & Video Unit

Palace Pictures
and
Palladium Media
via Glenbuck Films

Pathé Cannon
via Filmbank

**Edward Patterson
Associates**
Treetops
Cannongate Road
Hythe
Kent CT21 5PT
Tel: 0303 264195
Fax: 0303 264195

**Pedigree Pet Foods
Film Library**
via Viscom

**Polytechnic of
Central London
(Film Section)**
18-22 Riding House
Street
London W1P 7PD
Tel: 071 486 5811 x2726

**Post Office Film
and Video Library**
PO Box 145
Sittingbourne
Kent ME10 1NH
Tel: 0795 426465
Fax: 071 320 7437

RNLI
via Viscom

RoSPA
Film Library
Head Office
Cannon House
Priory Queensway
Birmingham B4 6BS
Tel: 021 233 2461
Safety films

RSPCA
Causeway
Horsham
West Sussex RH12 1HG
Tel: 0403 64181
Fax: 0403 41048

**Radio Sweden
International**
via Darvill Associates

**Random Film
Library**
Unit 2 Cornwall Works
Cornwall Avenue
Finchley
London N3 1LD
Tel: 081 349 0008

**Rank Film
Distributors**
via Filmbank

Rank Training Films
Cullum House
North Orbital Road
Denham
Uxbridge
Middx
Tel: 0895 834142
Fax: 0895 833616

**Retake Film and
Video Collective**
19 Liddell Road
London NW6 2EW
Tel: 071 328 4676

Royal College of Art
Department of Film
Queensgate
London SW7 5LD
Tel: 071 584 5020 x337
Fax: 071 225 1487

**Royal Society for
the Protection of
Birds**
Film Hire Library
15 Beaconsfield Road
London NW10 2LE
Tel: 081 451 1127

**Scottish Central
Film and Video
Library (SCFVL)**
74 Victoria Crescent Road
Dowanhill
Glasgow G12 9JN
Tel: 041 334 9314
Fax: 041 334 6519
Educational, training and
general interest titles

**Scottish Tourist
Board Films**
via SCFVL

Shell Film Library
via Random Film Library

**South West Arts
Association**
Bradninch Place
Gandy Street
Exeter EX4 3LS
Tel: 0392 218188
Fax: 0392 413554

**Steel Bank Film
Co-op**
Brown Street
Sheffield S1 2BS
Tel: 0742 721235
TV documentaries, drama
features, arts programmes

Supreme Films
via Glenbuck Films

**Swedish Embassy
(Cultural Dept)**
via Darvill Associates

**Swiss National
Tourist Office/
Swiss Federal
Railways**
Swiss Centre
10th Floor
New Coventry Street
London W1V 8EE
Tel: 071 734 1921
Fax: 071 437 4577

**TTT PlayBack
Communications**
69 New Oxford Street
London WC1A 1BG
Tel: 071 497 0710
Fax: 071 497 3374

TV Choice
80-81 St Martin's Lane
London WC2N 4AA
Tel: 071 379 0873

**Team Video
Productions**
Canalot
222 Kensal Road
London W10 5BN
Tel: 081 960 5536

**Television History
Centre**
42 Queen Square
London WC1N 3AJ
Tel: 071 405 6627
Fax: 071 242 1426
Programmes for hire or
purchase about work,
health, women,
community action,
particularly suitable for
educational discussion
groups 16 plus

Texaco Film Library
and
**Thames Television
Video Sales**
via Guild Sound and
Vision

**Touchstone
Pictures**
via Filmbank

Transatlantic Films
Blythe Hall
100 Blythe Road
London W14 0HE
Tel: 071 727 0132
Fax: 071 603 0668

**Twentieth Century
Fox**
and
UIP (UK)
via Filmbank

**UK Atomic Energy
Authority Film
Library**
via Viscom

**United States
Travel and Tourism
Administration**
via Audience Planners

Vestron (UK)
via Glenbuck Films

Video Arts
Dumbarton House
68 Oxford Street
London W1N 9LA
Tel: 071 637 7288
Fax: 071 580 8103
Distributes the John
Cleese training films 'In
Search of Excellence' and
other films from the
Nathan/Tyler Business
Video Library and the
Harvard Business School
Video Series

**Viewtech Audio
Visual Media**
161 Winchester Road
Brislington
Bristol BS4 3NJ
Tel: 0272 773422/717030

Virgin Films
via Glenbuck Films

Viscom
Unit B11
Park Hall Road Trading
Estate
London SE21 8EL
Tel: 081 761 3035
Fax: 081 761 2698

Warner Bros Films
via Filmbank

Welsh Arts Council
Museum Place
Cardiff CF1 3NX
Tel: 0222 394711
Fax: 0222 221447

**Workers Film
Association**
9 Lucy Street
Manchester M15 4BX
Tel: 061 848 9782

Yorkshire Arts
Glyde House
Glydegate
Bradford BD5 0BQ
Tel: 0274 723051
Fax: 0274 394919

**Yorkshire
Television**
Video Sales Department
The Television Centre
Leeds LS3 1JS
Tel: 0532 438283 x4060
Fax: 0532 429522

**Yugoslavian
Tourist Board**
via Audience Planners

INTERNATIONAL VISUAL COMMUNICATIONS ASSOCIATION

THE PROFESSIONAL ASSOCIATION
FOR VISUAL COMMUNICATIONS

Royal Patron: HRH Duke of Gloucester · *Honorary President:* Sir Terence Beckett KBE

IVCA is the professional association representing the interests and needs of the visual communications user or supplier. In particular, the Association represents those organisations involved in the non-broadcast commissioned film, video and av market. The Association strives to advance the standing and recognition of the industry and its practitioners, and markets visual communications to potential users.

IVCA is a non-profit making Association and is the only British association whose membership and interests span film, video, live events and audio-visual communications. The Association offers a professional network, information and advice services, special interest groups, insurance and other membership services, a monthly magazine, national and regional events and produces publications on a wide range of subjects. The Association also organises the UK's premier film and video communications festival and a residential Convention.

MEMBERS OF THE IVCA INCLUDE:

- Production companies providing programmes to meet a wide range of applications
- Businesses and organisations using or commissioning film, video and av programmes to enhance their communications activities
- Suppliers of facilities to the production industry
- In-house production units in both the corporate and institutional sectors
- Suppliers of hardware to the production and visual communications industry

- Live Event and Multi-Image suppliers
- Companies providing miscellaneous services to the production and visual communications industry
- Freelance individuals and sole traders servicing the production and visual communications industry
- Companies and institutions who need to be kept informed about activities and developments within the visual communications industry
- Students in recognised full or part-time courses

For a membership prospectus and application form, please contact
THE MEMBERSHIP SECRETARY
IVCA · BOLSOVER HOUSE · 5/6 CLIPSTONE STREET · LONDON W1P 7EB
Tel 071-580 0962 · Fax 071-436 2606

DISTRIBUTORS (THEATRICAL)

These are companies which acquire the UK rights to films for distribution to cinemas and, in many cases, also for sale to network TV, satellite, cable and video media. Listed is a selection of features certificated by the censor for those companies in 1989 and the first quarter of 1990, and some past releases or re-releases available during this period

Albany Video Distribution
Battersea Studios
Television Centre
Thackeray Road
London SW8 3TW
Tel: 071 498 6811
Fax: 071 498 1494
Films and video art

All American Leisure Group
6 Woodland Way
Petts Wood
Kent BR5 1ND
Tel: 0689 71535
Fax: 0689 71519

Apollo Film Distributors
14 Ensbury Park Road
Bournemouth BH9 2SJ
Tel: 0202 520962

Artificial Eye Film Co
211 Camden High Street
London NW1 7BT
Tel: 071 267 6036/482 3981
Fax: 071 267 6499
L'Atalante
Black Rain
A City of Sadness
Eat a Bowl of Tea
Jesus of Montreal
The Legend of the Holy Drinker
Leningrad Cowboys Go America
Life and Nothing But
A Strange Place to Meet
Trop belle pour toi!

Arts Council of Great Britain
See under Organisations

Atlantic Film Distributors
1st Floor
Paramount House
162 Wardour Street
London W1V 3AT
Tel: 071 437 4415/9513

French Massage Parlour
Luscious
St Tropez Vice

BFI Distribution
21 Stephen Street
London W1P 1PL
Tel: 071 255 1444
Fax: 071 436 7950
See also p 7

BFI Film & Video Library
21 Stephen Street
London W1P 1PL
Tel: 071 255 1444
Fax: 071 436 7950
Captain Johnno
The Intruder
James Baldwin: The Price of the Ticket
The Magic Flute
The Naked Kiss
Shock Corridor

BFI Production
29 Rathbone Street
London W1P 1AG
Tel: 071 636 5587
Fax: 071 580 9456
See also p 9
Caravaggio
Distant Voices, Still Lives
Draughtsman's Contract
Fellow Traveller
Melancholia
New Directors Shorts
On the Black Hill
Play Me Something
Silent Scream
Young Soul Rebels

Black Audio Film Collective
89 Ridley Road
London E8 2NH
Tel: 071 254 9527/9536
Testament
Twilight City
See under Distributors (Non-Theatrical) for further details

Blue Dolphin Films
15-17 Old Compton Street

London W1V 6JR
Tel: 071 439 9511
Fax: 071 287 0370
Backlash
Cactus
Explorers
The Fantasist
The Holy Innocents
The Hustler
Kamikaze
The Last of England
McCabe and Mrs Miller
PI Private Investigations
La vie est belle
What Happened to Kerouac?

Bordeaux Films International
22 Soho Square
London W1V 5FJ
Tel: 081 959 8556
See under Production Companies for list of films

BratPack Programme Distribution Co
Canalot Studios
222 Kensal Road
London W10 5BN
Tel: 081 969 7609
Fax: 081 969 2284
Bump
Puppydog Tales
Tiko's Adventures in Kash Koosh

Brent Walker Film Distributors
36-44 Brewer Street
London W1R 3HP
Tel: 071 437 8696
Fax: 071 437 4448

John Burder Films
7 Saltcoats Road
London W4 1AR
Tel: 081 995 0547
Fax: 081 995 3376
Broadcast TV programmes
See also under Distributors (Non-Theatrical)

Castle Premier Releasing
(formerly Premier Releasing)
360 Oxford Street
London W1N 9HA
Tel: 071 493 0440
Fax: 071 491 9040
Bill and Ted's Excellent Adventure
Da
Encounter at Raven's Gate
Fistfighter
Heathers
Hellbound: Hellraiser II
Patti Rocks
Phantom of the Opera
The Punisher
That Summer of White Roses

Cavalcade Films
Regent House
235-241 Regent Street
London W1R 8JU
Tel: 071 734 3147
Fax: 071 734 2403

Chain Production
11 Hornton Street
London W8 7NP
Tel: 071 937 1981
Fax: 071 376 0556
Specialist in Italian films: library of 1,000 titles available for UK exploitation. Releasing *Mignon is Missing* theatrically through Metro Pictures

Cinema of Women
Unit 313
31 Clerkenwell Close
London EC1R 0AT
Tel: 071 251 4978
Fax: 071 490 0063 (mark for the attention of Cinema of Women, Unit 313)
See under Distributors (Non-Theatrical) for information on product. Book through Glenbuck Films

Circles (Women's Film and Video Distribution)
113 Roman Road
London E2 0HU
Tel: 081 981 6828
Castles of Sand
Cover Up: Behind the Iran Contra Affair
Nice Coloured Girls
Rabbit on the Moon
Shadow Panic
A Song of Ceylon
Surname Viet Given Name Nam
See also under

Distributors (Non-Theatrical)

Columbia Tri-Star Films (UK)
19-23 Wells Street
London W1P 3FP
Tel: 071 580 2090
Fax: 071 528 8980
Feature releases from the Columbia and Tri-Star companies, and Weintraub Screen Entertainment
The Bear
Casualties of War
Ghostbusters II
Glory
Look Who's Talking
Old Gringo
See No Evil Hear No Evil
Slaves of New York
Steel Magnolias

Consolidated Distribution
5 Jubilee Place
London SW3 3TD
Tel: 071 376 5151/8
Fax: 071 225 2890
See also under International Sales and Production Companies

Contemporary Films
24 Southwood Lawn Road
Highgate
London N6 5SF
Tel: 081 340 5715
Fax: 081 348 1238
Piravi
Suddenly One Day
Also co-distribute product with Electric Pictures
Celia
C'est la vie
I Hired a Contract Killer
Match Factory Girl
Max Mon Amour
Plot against Harry
Sweetie
The Unbelievable Truth
Please contact Contemporary Films for bookings, and Electric Pictures for publicity material

Crawford Films
15-17 Old Compton Street
London W1V 6JR
Tel: 071 734 5298
Fax: 071 287 0370

Curzon Film Distributors
38 Curzon Street
London W1Y 8EY
Tel: 071 465 0565
Fax: 071 499 2018
Au Revoir Les Enfants

Dark Eyes
Henry V
La Lectrice
Pelle the Conqueror
Torrents of Spring

Darvill Associates
280 Chartridge Lane
Chesham
Bucks HP5 2SG
Tel: 0494 783643
Fax: 0494 784873

Dee and Co
Suite 204
Canalot
222 Kensal Road
London W10 5BN
Tel: 081 960 2712
Fax: 081 960 2728
See under International Sales

The Walt Disney Co
31-32 Soho Square
London W1V 6AP
Tel: 071 734 8111
Fax: 071 734 5619
Television distribution arm of US production company.
See under Warner Bros for theatrical release information

Electric Pictures
22 Carol Street
London NW1 0HU
Tel: 071 267 8418/284 0524/0583
Georgette Meunier
Hamlet Goes Business
Pierrot Le Fou
Also co-distribute product with Contemporary Films (for a list of jointly-owned titles, see under Contemporary). Please contact Contemporary Films for bookings of these titles, and Electric Pictures for publicity material

Elephant Entertainments
Tivoli Cinema
Station Street
Birmingham B5 4DY
Tel: 021 616 1021
Fax: 021 616 1019
City of the Living Dead
House by the Cemetary
The Last Hunter

English Film Co
6 Woodland Way
Petts Wood
Kent BR5 1ND
Tel: 0689 71535
Fax: 0689 71519

Enterprise Pictures
113 Wardour Street
London W1V 3TD
Tel: 071 734 3372
Fax: 071 734 7626
Heart Condition
House Party
Loser Takes All
A Nightmare on Elm Street 5: The Dream Child
Queen of Hearts
Time of the Gypsies

Entertainment Film Distributors
27 Soho Square
London W1V 5FL
Tel: 071 439 1606
Fax: 071 734 2483
Cat Chaser
Cop
Full Moon in Blue Water
Kansas
Kickboxer
Near Dark
Patty Hearst
The Return of the Musketeers
Slipstream
The Wolves of Willoughby Chase

Film and Video Umbrella
Top Floor, Chelsea Reach
79-89 Lots Road
London SW10 0RN
Tel: 071 376 3171
Fax: 071 351 6479
Programming and touring agency for artists' film, video and television

Gala Films
26 Danbury Street
Islington
London N1
Tel: 071 226 5085
Fax: 071 226 5897
The House of Bernarda Alba
The Revolving Doors
A Short Film about Killing
A Short Film about Love
Sur

Glenbuck Films
Glenbuck House
Glenbuck Road
Surbiton
Surrey KT6 6BT
Tel: 081 399 0022/5266
Fax: 081 399 6651

The Samuel Goldwyn Company
St George's House
14-17 Wells Street
London W1P 3FP
Tel: 071 436 5105

Fax: 071 580 6520
Breaking In
Drugstore Cowboy
Longtime Companion
The Object of Beauty
Stella

Guild Film Distribution
Kent House
14-17 Market Place
Great Titchfield Street
London W1N 8AR
Tel: 071 323 5151
Fax: 071 631 3568
Field of Dreams
Fourth War
Johnny Handsome
Last Exit to Brooklyn
Lock Up
Mountains of the Moon
Music Box
Shocker
Total Recall
Triumph of the Spirit

HandMade Films (Distributors)
26 Cadogan Square
London SW1X 0JP
Tel: 071 584 8345
Fax: 071 584 7338

Hobo Film Enterprises
9 St Martin's Court
London WC2N 4AJ
Tel: 071 895 0328
Fax: 071 895 0329
A Chorus of Disapproval
Henry V
I Bought a Vampire Motorcycle

ICA Projects
12 Carlton House Terrace
London SW1Y 5AH
Tel: 071 930 0493
Fax: 071 873 0051
Alice
The Big Parade
Comic Book Confidential
Dust in the Wind
Horse Thief
King of the Children
Rouge
Summer Vacation 1999
The Terroriser

Ideal Communications Films and Television
26 Soho Square
London W1V 5FJ
Tel: 071 494 0011
Fax: 071 287 8337
See under Production
Companies for list of titles

Ideal-Opyx Sales
26 Soho Square

London W1V 5FJ
Tel: 071 494 0011
Fax: 071 287 8337
Television programming.
For further details, see
under International Sales

Kruger Leisure Organisation
PO Box 130
Hove
East Sussex BN3 6QU
Tel: 0273 550088
Fax: 0273 540969
Adventures of Scaramouche
Blood Kill
Gallavants
The Mark of Zorro

MGM/UA
See United International
Pictures (UK)

Mainline Pictures
37 Museum Street
London WC1A 1LP
Tel: 071 242 5523
Fax: 071 430 0170
Apartment Zero
Bagdad Cafe
Let's Get Lost
The Music Teacher
The Nasty Girl
Rosalie Goes Shopping
Salaam Bombay
Santa Sangre
3 Women in Love

Medusa Pictures
41-42 Berners Street
London W1P 3AA
Tel: 071 255 2200
Fax: 071 637 4318
The Fugitive
Grand Tour
Lemon Sisters
Shock to the System
Spaced Invaders
Wings of the Apache
See also Medusa
Communications under
Video Labels

Metro Pictures
(formerly The Other
Cinema)
79 Wardour Street
London W1V 3TH
Tel: 071 734 8508/9
Fax: 071 287 2112
Citadel
Icicle Thief
Kamikaze Hearts
Mignon is Missing
Plaff
The Vanishing
What Have I Done to Deserve This?

Miracle Communications
69 New Oxford Street

London WC1A 1DG
Tel: 071 379 5006

New Realm Entertainments
Hammer House
113-117 Wardour Street
London W1V 3TD
Tel: 071 437 9143
Fax: 0372 69816

New World/Trans Atlantic Pictures
27 Soho Square
London W1V 5FL
Tel: 071 434 0497
Fax: 071 434 0490
The Applegates
Brenda Starr
Da
Felix the Cat
Heathers
Hellbound: Hellraiser II
Patti Rocks
The Punisher
Spike of Bensonhurst
Stealing Heaven

Oasis (UK) Films
(formerly Recorded
Releasing)
66-68 Margaret Street
London W1N 7FL
Tel: 071 734 7477
Fax: 071 734 7470
A Bout de Souffle
Drowning by Numbers
Manhunter
Speaking Parts
Venus Peter
We Think the World of You
Wings of Desire
Withnail and I
Yaaba

Orbit Films
14 Campden Hill Gardens
London W8 7AY
Tel: 071 221 5548
Fax: 071 727 0515
The Adventures of Buckaroo Banzai
The Golden Years of Television: vintage
product from the first
decade of American
TV, including
features and serials

Palace Pictures
16-17 Wardour Mews
London W1V 3FF
Tel: 071 734 7060
Fax: 071 437 3248
Cinema Paradiso
The Cook, The Thief, His Wife and Her Lover
Dancin' thru the Dark
Family Business
Fools of Fortune
Monsieur Hire

My Left Foot
Mystery Train
Nuns on the Run
When Harry Met Sally...

Paramount
See United International
Pictures (UK)

Parkfield Entertainment
Unit 12 Brunswick
Industrial Estate
Brunswick Way
New Southgate
London N11 1HX
Tel: 081 368 7788/2233
Fax: 081 361 8877
Best of Times
Halloween V
Highlander II
The Krays
Lonesome Dove
Moontrap
The Stick
Tales from the Darkside
Tank Malling

Poseidon Film Distributors
Hammer House
113 Wardour Street
London W1V 3TD
Tel: 071 734 4441
Fax: 071 437 0638
Ashik Kerib
The Asthenic Syndrome
The Fountain
Little Vera
Paper Eyes

Rank Film Distributors
127 Wardour Street
London W1V 4AD
Tel: 071 437 9020
All Dogs Go to Heaven
Another Woman
Great Balls of Fire
Millennium
Monkey Shines
Physical Evidence
Scenes from the Class Struggle in Beverly Hills
Weekend at Bernie's
Welcome Home
Wilt

Recorded Releasing
See **Oasis (UK) Films**

Respectable Films
6 Silver Place
Beak Street
London W1R 3LJ
Tel: 071 437 8562
Bleak Moments
Last Night at the Alamo
Mala Noche

Supreme Film Distributors
Paramount House
162 Wardour Street
London W1V 3AT
Tel: 071 437 4415/9513

TCB Releasing
Stone House
Rudge
Frome
Somerset BA11 2QQ
Tel: 0373 830769
Fax: 0373 831028
Theatrical features and
television programming

Touchstone Pictures
See Warner Bros

Twentieth Century Fox Film Co
20th Century House
31-32 Soho Square
London W1V 6AP
Tel: 071 437 7766
Fax: 071 437 1625
The Abyss
Alien Nation
Cocoon The Return
Earth Girls are Easy
Enemies A Love Story
Major League
Rooftops

Talk Radio
War of the Roses
When the Whales Came

UA (United Artists)
See United International
Pictures (UK)

United International Pictures (UK)
Mortimer House
37-41 Mortimer Street
London W1A 2JL
Tel: 071 636 1655
Fax: 071 636 4118
Releases product from
Paramount, Universal,
and MGM/UA
Back to the Future part II
Black Rain
Born on the Fourth of July
A Dry White Season
The Hunt for Red October
*Indiana Jones and the
   Last Crusade*
Licence to Kill
Parenthood
Sea of Love
Shirley Valentine

Vestron UK
69 New Oxford Street
London WC1A 1DG
Tel: 071 379 0406
Fax: 071 528 7772
Backtrack
Blue Steel
Cannonball Fever
Communion
Enid is Sleeping
Fear
Love Hurts
Upworld

Virgin Vision
1 Rockley Road
Shepherds Bush
London W12
Tel: 071 494 3756
(number changing Sept
1990. New number not
available at time of going
to press)
Crusoe
Drugstore Cowboy
*How to Get Ahead in
   Advertising*
The Lady in White
Mystic Pizza
The Rachel Papers
Renegades
sex, lies, and videotape
Strapless
The Tall Guy

Warner Bros Distributors
135 Wardour Street
London W1V 4AP
Tel: 071 734 8400
Fax: 071 437 5521
Feature releases from
Warner Bros and Disney/
Touchstone
Batman
Dead Calm
Dead Poets Society
Driving Miss Daisy
Honey, I Shrunk the Kids
Lethal Weapon 2
Oliver & Company
Tango and Cash
Turner and Hooch
Young Einstein

Weintraub Screen Entertainment
Distributed through
Columbia Tri-Star Films
and Hobo Film
Enterprises

Winstone Film Distributors
84 Wardour Street
London W1V 3LF
Tel: 071 439 4525
Sub-distributors for
Palace and Oasis

TWENTIETH CENTURY FOX
CENTURY HOUSE 31 SOHO SQUARE LONDON W1V 6AP TELEPHONE 071 - 437 7766 FAX 071 - 437 1625

FACILITIES

AIRtv Facilities

Hawley Crescent
London NW1 8NP
Tel: 071 485 4121
Fax: 071 485 3667
Video formats: C, BVU,
Betacam
Editing: Paltex Esprit
controller in two suites,
Paltex ES1 controller in
third suite
Vision effects: ADO,
2-channel Quantel with
rotate, Aston 3, colour
caption cameras
Graphics: 5 workstations
Super Nova/Matisse
Telecine: Rank Cintel
Mk3

AKA

Film and Television
Services
60 Farringdon Road
London EC1R 3BP
Tel: 071 251 3885
Fax: 071 253 2045
Editing: Three machine
Betacam SP Component
with 1″, Zeno, Aston 3,
Nagra T¼″, and colour
caption camera,
Charisma, Matisse
computer graphics; off-
line editing, 16mm film
cutting room; sound
transfer; equipment hire
incl. Aaton 16mm,
Betacam SP
Studios: 2 sound proofed
stages, 180° cyc, overhead
rigging
Full crewing and
production management

Abbey Road Studios

3 Abbey Road
London NW8 9AY
Tel: 071 286 1161
Fax: 071 289 7527
Four studios; music to
picture; film sound
transfer facilities; audio
post-production; audio
sweetening for video and
TV; Sonic Solutions
computer sound
enhancement system
Residential
accommodation,
restaurant and bar

Abbey Video

Five Lamps Studio
West Avenue
Derby DE1 3HR
Tel: 0332 40693
Fax: 0332 291268
Editing: three-machine
BVU SP edit suite
Vision effects: Grass

Valley and X-calibre DVE
Camera: ENG camera
crew
Sound: voiceover studio
Drive-in studio with cyc

Acricius

86 Albert Street
London NW1 7NR
Tel: 071 387 2183
Special effects
cinematography
Live action, stop-motion,
time-lapse and
programmable camera
equipment
Matte and process

Advision Studios

Montague Place
Kemptown
Brighton BN2 1JE
Tel: 0273 677375
Fax: 0273 672597
Digital/analogue 24/48-
track studio; Sony 3000-
based digital editing
suite; wide range of
outboard gear; fully
residential
Two state-of-the-art
mobile studios for location
recording, post-
production and audio for
video; Lexicon Opus
Digital Post-Production
System

After Image Facilities

32 Acre Lane
London SW2 5SG
Tel: 071 737 7300
Fax: 071 326 1850
Cameras: Sony 330P, M3
Studios: broadcast studio
A: 2000 sq ft
Ultimatte/packshot
studio B: 27 x 27 x 11ft
with cyc
Editing: Grass Valley
200, Sony BVE 5000,
Charisma DVE,
Ultimatte and
Chromakey
Video formats: 1″C, Beta
SP and BVU

Air Recording Studios

214 Oxford Street
London W1N 9DF
Tel: 071 637 2758
Fax: 071 636 5001
Studio 1: 65 musicians,
72Ch Neve/Focusrite;
Studio 2: 30 musicians,
56Ch SSL, G series
computer; Studio 3: O/D
Booth, 48Ch Neve V
series, GML automation;
Studio 4: O/D Booth, 48Ch

SSL, G series Computer
Sony 48tk and 24tk,
Mitsubishi 32tk, Studer;
A800 24tk/48tk, U-Matic
on site available in any
room

Angel Recording Studios

311 Upper Street
London N1 2TU
Tel: 071 354 2525
Fax: 071 226 9624
2 x 100-musician studio
complex with mixing to
35mm and 16mm film
Customised Neve desks

Anner Communications

Stillorgan Industrial
Park
Blackrock
Co Dublin
Tel: 0001 952221
Fax: 0001 952193
Studio: 3,000 sq ft drive-
in studio with Ultimatte
Four Betacam SP ENG
crews
Film: Rank Cintel MkIII
Telecine with 'Colour
Grade' Film post-
production
Editing: CMX 3600, GVG
200, Dual Channel
Abekas A53 with Key-
channels, Aston
3 Character Generator
Ampex VPR-3 1″ C-
formats and Bosch 1″
B-format Betacam SP and
Nagra T; CMX 3600,
GVG 100 component,
Dual Channel Abekas
A53 with key-channels,
Aston 3 Character
Generator, Betacam SP
and Nagra T
Duplication: 250 VHS
PAL Slaves

Anvil Film and Recording Group

Denham Studios
North Orbital Road
Denham
Uxbridge
Middx UB9 5HH
Tel: 0895 833522
Fax: 0895 835006
35/16mm film and video
production; studio re-
recording, ADR, post-sync
FX recording, transfers,
foreign version dubbing;
cutting rooms, neg
cutting

Ariada Film Productions

Goldcrest Elstree Studios

Shenley Road
Borehamwood
Herts
Tel: 081 953 1600
Fax: 081 207 5658
Post-production facilities

Aspen Spafax Television
6 Portland Place
Pritchard Street
Bristol BS2 8RH
Tel: 0272 232880
Fax: 0272 429545
Graphics, Quantel
Paintbox, editing formats,
BVU SP, Betacam SP,
1″C, ADO Digital Effects,
Sony 9000 Edit
Controller, GBG 200
Vision Mixer, sound
dubbing, AMS Audio File

Avolites Production Co
184 Park Avenue
London NW10 7XL
Tel: 081 965 8522
Fax: 081 965 0290
Manufacture, sale and
hire of dimming systems,
memory and manual
lighting control consoles
and chain hoist control
systems
Sales of relevant cabling
and connectors
Distributors for SL series
Socapex connectors in UK

Geoff Axtell Associates
16a Newman Street
London W1P 3HD
Tel: 071 637 9321
Fax: 071 637 2850
Harry/Paintbox/Encore
digital suite, Cypher XL,
film opticals, titles and
effects, computerised
motion control, film and
video rostrum cameras

BBRK
Shepperton Studio Centre
Studios Road
Shepperton
Middx TW17 0QB
Tel: 0932 564922
Fax: 0932 560598
Art direction and
construction, building
services, prop hire,
catering services, three
stages

BTS Television
115 Portland Street
Manchester M1 6DW
Tel: 061 236 6911
Fax: 061 236 6914
Transfers 1″, Beta SP,

BVU SP, VHS, Betamax,
standards conversions,
off-line editing, A/V to
video transfers

BUFVC
55 Greek Street
London W1V 5LR
Tel: 071 734 3687
Fax: 071 287 3914
16mm cutting room and
viewing facilities

Jim Bambrick and Associates
10 Frith Street
London W1V 5TZ
Tel: 071 434 2351
Fax: 071 734 6362
16mm, 35mm cutting
rooms, off-line video edit
suite

Barcud
Cibyn
Caernarfon
Gwynedd
Tel: 0286 3458
Fax: 0286 5330
Video formats: 1″C, Beta
SP
2-7 camera OB unit,
Betacam units
6500 sq ft studio with
audience seating and
comprehensive lighting
rig, 1500 sq ft studio with
vision/lighting control
gallery and sound gallery
Editing: Sony 9000 full-
effects suite with GVG
200; Sony 5000 full-effects
suite with GVG 100, Sony
900 cut suite
Graphics: Paintbox,
Rank-Cintel Artfile,
Chyron Infinite etc
DVE: 3 channels
Charisma, 2 channels
Cleo
Sound: 2 suites each with
AMS Audiofile, V/O booth
and CD fx and music
library
BT lines
VHS off-line

CTS Studios
The Music Centre
Engineers Way
Wembley
Middlesex HA9 0DR
Tel: 081 903 4611
Largest of 4 studios holds
130 musicians with three
alternatives between 10
and 40
Synchronised film
projection available with
Telecine or video facilities
for recording music to
picture
Digital or analog

available, restaurant,
large car park

CTV
PO Box 1098
Gerrards Cross
Bucks SL9 8DY
Tel: 02407 71513
Fax: 02407 71086
Video production cassette
duplication; standards
conversions; film to video
transfers; edit suite hire

Capital Group Studios
(formerly Ewart
Television)
13 Wandsworth Plain
London SW18 1ET
Tel: 081 874 0131
Fax: 081 871 9737
Studios: 3000 sq ft, 2000
sq ft; separate galleries,
8 cameras, 2 x Ampex
mixers each with 3 ME
decks; Charisma digital
effects; Aston caption
Video formats: D2, C,
Quad, Beta SP
Editing: Ampex Ace,
Grass Valley, Cox mixers,
Charisma digital effects,
Aston 3
Sound: 24(with SR)/4/2
track to picture, Calrec 48
input/Trident 32 input
desks, CD effects
Telecine with TOPSY,
caption camera, canteens,
car park

Capital Television Facilities
22 Newman Street
London W1P 4AJ
Tel: 071 636 3663
Fax: 071 436 3989
Video formats: Quad, 1″C,
BVU, Betacam, U-Matic,
Betacam SP
Cameras: Ikegami
Editing: Datatron, 3
machine lo-band U-Matic
off-line
Vision effects: Ampex
ADO, Gemini 3
Graphics: Quantel
Paintbox
Standards conversion;
cassette duplication

Carlton Television
St Johns Wood Studios
St Johns Wood Terrace
London NW8
Tel: 071 722 8111/9255
Fax: 071 483 4264
ENG/Multi Camera OB
Units: 4-10 camera OB
unit, 1-4 camera OB unit,
3-8 VTR/editing truck, 2-
4 VTR recording truck,

single and multi-camera
units
Post production: two 4x1″
edit suites with Abekas
A64, ADO and Abekas
A53 digital effects, colour
caption camera, Aston 4
and Aston 3 character
generator, Beta and BVU
play-in machines, vertical
interval time code and
disc conform editing; 1x4
Beta SP component edit
suite with A53,
VistaVision mixer, Aston
3 and colour correctors

Cell Animation
See under Tele-Cine

Chamberlain Film Studio
16-20 Wharfdale Road
London N1 9RY
Tel: 071 837 3855
Stage: 80 sq metres
Construction facilities

Chatsworth Television
97-99 Dean Street
London W1V 5RA
Tel: 071 734 4302/3/4
Fax: 071 437 3301
Transportable Sony edit
suite with RM440
controller

Roger Cherrill
65-66 Dean Street
London W1V 6PL
Tel: 071 437 7972
Fax: 071 437 6411
25 cutting rooms for
35mm and 16mm; ADR
(Automatic Dialogue
Replacement); 16mm,
35mm dubbing theatre;
effects recording; Dolby
'A' and SR; Telecine; film
opticals and titles;
trailers

Cherry Video
65-66 Dean Street
London W1V 6PL
Tel: 071 437 7972
Fax: 071 437 6411
Video formats: 1″C, PAL
and NTSC, Beta SP,
BVU, lo-band and VHS
Telecine: Rank Cintel
MkIIIC, in PAL and
NTSC with computerised
colour grading.
35mm, 16mm and 8mm
with autoshot, varispeed
and XYZoom
ADAC digital standards
conversion

Chess Valley Films and Video
Film House
Little Chalfont
Bucks HP7 9PY
Tel: 0494 76 2222
Fax: 0494 76 3333
Video formats: Betacam SP, BVU SP, 1″; 35mm, 16mm film; all equipment/lighting/viewing; off-line edit facilities; corporate TV and films for marketing/sales/promos/training etc
Established 1961

Chromacolour
16 Grangemills
Weir Road
London SW12
Tel: 081 675 8422
Fax: 081 675 8499
Animation supplies and equipment

Cinecontact
175 Wardour Street
London W1V 3AB
Tel: 071 434 1745
Fax: 071 494 0405
3x16mm film cutting rooms, each fitted with 1901s; 2xVHS off-line suites; 16mm film gear and Sony Betacam for hire

Cine-Europe
7 Silver Road
Wood Lane
London W12 7SG
Tel: 081 743 6762
Fax: 081 749 3501
16mm, 35mm and full range of grip equipment hire

Cinefocus
1 Pavilion Parade
Wood Lane
London W12 0HQ
Tel: 081 743 2552
Fax: 081 743 0822
Unit 9, Orchard Street
Industrial Estate
Salford
Manchester M6 6FL
Tel: 061 745 8146
Film, video, grip; Arriflex 16/35mm, Sony SP, Chapman, cranes, full equipment rental service

Cine-Lingual Sound Studios
27-29 Berwick Street
London W1V 3RF
Tel: 071 437 0136
Fax: 071 439 2012
3 sound studios
35mm and 16mm high speed ADR; Dolby Stereo

4-track recording; 2x16mm, 35mm sound transfer bays

Cinequip Lighting Co
Units 6-8 Orchard Street
Industrial Estate
Salford
Manchester M6 6FL
Tel: 061 736 8034
Fax: 061 745 8023
Lighting equipment hire

Cinevideo
Broadcast Television Equipment Hire
7 Silver Road
White City Industrial Park
Wood Lane
London W12 7SG
Tel: 081 743 3839
Fax: 081 743 8417
Video formats: 1″, Beta SP, MII
Cameras: Ikegami HL355, HL-55, Sony range, PAL and NTSC

Colosseum Production Centre
Portland Gate
Leeds LS2 3AW
Tel: 0532 461311
Fax: 0532 422547
6,000 sq ft television studio theatre. Full broadcast production and technical facilities, technical and workshop crews, British Telecom sound and vision links; 250 permanent audience seating; licensed catering facilities

Colour Film Services
10 Wadsworth Road
Perivale
Greenford
Middx UB6 7JX
Tel: 081 998 2731
Fax: 081 997 8738
Videotape to film transfer specialists, direct from broadcast video to 35mm and 16mm negative; Telecine mastering and tape dubbing all formats; Betacam SP component edit suite and 'Alphabet' video assembly from A+B cut neg; 16mm sound dubbing studios; bulk cassette duplication; full film laboratory services; equipment hire; conference centre; media management

Compass Production Associates
3rd Floor
18-19 Warwick Street
London W1R 5RB
Tel: 071 439 2581
Fax: 071 439 1865
Production offices; 16mm cutting rooms; U-Matic off-line edit suite

Complete Video Facilities
Slingsby Place
London WC2E 9AB
Tel: 071 379 7739
Fax: 071 497 9305
Telecom lines
Video formats: 1″C, D1, D2, BVU, U-Matic, SP Betacam
Editing: Sony BVE 9000, Grass Valley 200 Vision Mixer, Harry, Abekas A64, Aston 3
Vision effects: Grass Valley DVE, ADO 100, Quantel Mirage, Encore, Paintbox, Abekas A60, Symbolics 3D Computer Graphics System
Sound: SSL 32 channel and DDA 16 channel consoles, voiceover and sound library
Telecine: 35mm/16mm 4:2:2 telecine, Steadifilm, Colourist colour corrector, pin registration gate

Corinthian and Synchro-Sonics
5 Richmond Mews
Richmond Buildings
London W1V 5AG
Tel: 071 734 3325
Fax: 071 437 3502
16mm cutting rooms; sound transfer, video transfer; equipment hire; 16mm or video commentary to picture studio; rough dubs

Crow Film and Television Services
12 Wendell Road
London W12 9RT
Tel: 081 749 6017
Fax: 081 740 0795
Video formats: 1″, Betacam SP, Betacam, BVU
Cameras: Sony BVP 50/7 P, Arriflex SR2
Editing: 1″ to 1″/Betacam SP; multiformat editing; 2 channel Charisma; Questech; Aston caption camera; Grass Valley 200 vision mixer

Crystal Film and Video
50 Church Road
London NW10 9PY
Tel: 081 965 0769
Fax: 081 965 7975
Aatons, Arriflex, Nagras Radio mics, lights and transport; Sony Beta SP; studio 50′ x 30′; crews

Cygnet
The Studios
Communication Business Centre
14 Blenheim Road
High Wycombe
Bucks HP12 3RS
Tel: 0494 450541
Fax: 0494 462154
Full production facilities for 16mm and video; editing suites; sound department

DATS Video
Nicholford Hall
Norland Lane
Widness WA8 9AX
Tel: 051 423 4040
Video format: U-Matic
Cameras: Ikegami 2400, Sony DXC M3A
Editing: Cox vision mixer with Chromakey, downstream keyer, IVC time base corrector, 3M character generator
Studio: 500 sq metres

DBA Television
21 Ormeau Avenue
Belfast BT2 8HD
Tel: 0232 231197
Fax: 0232 333302
Crew hire and 16mm edit facilities, off-line and sound transfers; Aaton, Steenbeck
Studio: 600 sq ft

Dateline Productions
79 Dean Street
London W1V 5HA
Tel: 071 437 4510
Fax: 071 287 6544
16mm, 35mm film editing, off-line editing, negative cutting

De Lane Lea Sound Centre
75 Dean Street
London W1V 5HA
Tel: 071 439 1721
Fax: 071 437 0913
2 high speed 35mm Dolby stereo dubbing theatres (inc 1 x 16/35mm) with Dolby SR; high speed ADR and FX theatre (16/

35mm and video);
Synclavier digital FX
suite; digital sound FX
suite with audition room
inc video; sound rushes
and transfers; video
transfers to VHS and
U-Matic; 13x35mm
cutting rooms

Dean Street Studio
75 Dean Street
London W1V 5HA
Tel: 071 494 0735
Fax: 071 734 2519

Delta Sound Services
Lee Shepperton Studios
Centre
Squires Bridge Road
Shepperton
Middx
Tel: 0932 568989
Fax: 0932 568989
16mm, 35mm and video
dubbing theatre; post-
sync and footsteps; effects
work; in-house sound
transfers

Denman Productions
60 Mallard Place
Strawberry Vale
Twickenham TW1 4SR
Tel: 081 891 3461
Fax: 081 908 6262
Video and film
production, ENG crews
and equipment

Diverse Production
6 Gorleston Street
London W14 8SX
Tel: 071 603 4567
VHS, lo-band, hi-band,
Beta and 1″ editing,
Abekas DVE, image
processing and computer
graphics

Document Films
8-12 Broadwick Street
London W1V 1FH
Tel: 071 437 4526
Film and video cutting
rooms; 16mm Aaton/
Nagra and video crews,
16mm, 35mm sound
transfer bay, mono and
stereo
Production offices

Dolby Laboratories
346 Clapham Road
London SW9 9AP
Tel: 071 720 1111
Fax: 071 720 4118
Cinema processors for
replay of Dolby Stereo
and Dolby Stereo SR

encoded soundtracks
Audio noise reduction
equipment

Dubbs
25-26 Poland Street
London W1V 3DB
Tel: 071 629 0055
Fax: 071 287 8796
Videotape duplication
Standards conversion

Joe Dunton Cameras
Wycombe Road
Wembley
Middx HA0 1QN
Tel: 081 903 7933
Fax: 081 902 3273
Camera equipment hire;
services many major
feature productions

ECO
The Exchange Building
Mount Stuart Square
Cardiff CF1 6EA
Tel: 0222 493321
Studio 1: 16-track Dolby
U-Matic video sound
dubbing; Studio 2: film
dubbing; Studio 3: Otari
8-track U-Matic with
AMS audiofile; Studio 5:
Otary 8-track U-Matic;
transfer suite

ENG Video
The Facilities Centre
3 Nimrod Way
Elgar Road South
Reading
Berks RG2 0EB
Tel: 0734 751555
Fax: 0734 861482
Video formats: 1″,
Betacam SP, BVU SP
Cameras: Betacam SP
507
Facilities: Fully
component mixed format
broadcast editing facility
with 2 channels DVE
duplication, standards
conversion
Equipment hire, technical
support

EOS Electronics AV
EOS House
Weston Square
Barry CF6 7YF
Tel: 0446 741212
Fax: 0446 746120
Lo- and hi-band editing,
standards conversion;
broadcast video
animation controller;
Neilson Hordell camera;
rostrum and Sony
DXCM7; frame by frame
video recording

Edinburgh Film and Video Productions
Edinburgh Film and TV
Studios
Nine Mile Burn by
Penicuik
Midlothian EH26 9LT
Tel: 0968 72131
Fax: 0968 72685
Stage: 50 sq metres;
16mm, 35mm cutting
rooms; 16mm, 35mm
transfer facilities;
preview theatre; sound
transfer; edge numbering;
lighting grip equipment
hire; scenery workshops

Edinburgh Film Workshop Trust
29 Albany Street
Edinburgh EH1 3QN
Tel: 031 557 5242
Facilities include lo-band
edit suite, rostrum
camera; VHS off-line
suite; film cutting room
(16mm)

Edit 142
20 St Anne's Court
London W1V 3AW
Tel: 071 439 7934
Fax: 071 287 1814
16mm and 35mm cutting
rooms; video off-line

The Edit Works
Units 1-6, 2nd Floor
Chelsea Garden Market
Chelsea Harbour
London SW10 0XE
Tel: 071 352 5244
Fax: 071 376 8645
Video formats: 1″C, D2 SP
Betacam
Editing: Component –
Sony 5000, Grass Valley
200 vision mixer
Composite: Sony 5000,
Grass Valley 300 vision
mixer; off-line: Sony 5000,
4 x U-Matic
Vision effects: ADO100,
Abekas A72
Sound: voiceover booth
available to all suites

Edric Audiovisual Hire
Unit 3
Chalfont Industrial Park
Chiltern Hill
Chalfont St Peter
Bucks SL9 9UQ
Tel: 0753 884646
Fax: 0753 887163
Audiovisual and video
production facilities

Eye Film and Television
The Guildhall
Church Street
Eye
Suffolk IP23 7BD
Tel: 0379 870083
Fax: 0379 870987
Betacam SP production
crew; component Betacam
SP editing suite

Fantasy Factory Video
42 Theobalds Road
London WC1X 8NW
Tel: 071 405 6862
Video formats: U-Matic,
hi-band SP, hi-band and
lo-band, Hi 8, video 8
Editing: three machine
hi-band SP and lo-band
with listing, automated
vision mixer, EDIS DVE,
with full timecode system
using VITC and LTC and
Quanta Cap Gen
2-machine BVU SP/lo-
band with a caption
camera, CEL DVE, For-A
Cap Gen and timecode
reader/generator,
6-channel audio mixer;
training courses in video
editing on the above
suites

SG Fenner Lighting
Unit 5a
1-5 Standard Road
London NW10 6EX
Tel: 081 961 1935
Fax: 081 961 8595
Lighting equipment hire

Film Clinic
8-14 Meard Street
London W1V 3HR
Tel: 071 734 9235/6
Fax: 071 734 9471
Scratch treatment,
reconditioning and
restoration of 16/35mm
film. Archive specialists

FinePoint Broadcast
The Red Lodge
Brighton Road
Tadworth
Surrey KT20 6UQ
Tel: 0737 833099
Fax: 0737 833743
Broadcast facilities hire
in PAL and NTSC; VTRs
in 1″, Beta SP and BVU
Sony CCD cameras;
Abekas A53, Charisma,
Paintbox, Aston etc;
editing, dubbing,
standards conversion;
6 camera, 4VTR outside
broadcast vehicles

Flintdown – Channel Five Television
339 Clifton Drive South
St Annes on Sea
Lancashire FY8 1LP
Tel: 0253 725499
Fax: 0253 713094
Cintel Telecine 9.5/8/16/35mm
Video formats: C, BVU, U-Matic
Cameras: IVC

Fox Television
10-12 Fitzroy Mews
London W1P 5DQ
Tel: 071 387 3308
Fax: 071 388 6265
Video formats: BVU, 1″C, Beta
Cameras: Ikegami HL79 and HL95
Editing: 3-machine BVU and Beta, Pinnacle DVE with 3-D Prism Unit

Mike Fraser
225 Goldhawk Road
London W12 8ER
Tel: 081 749 6911
Neg cutting, rubber numbering, Profilm EFC logging; videotape recycling

Frontline Television Services
44 Earlham Street
London WC2H 9LA
Tel: 071 836 0411
Fax: 071 379 5210
2 x Betacam/BVU to 1″ and 3-machine computerised editing with Abekas Zeno, Gemini 3 digital FX, Z6000 edit controller and Aston 4 graphics generator; tape duplication, standards conversion, all formats, telecine and studio

Fundamental Films
15 Wardour Mews
D'Arblay Street
London W1V 3FF
Tel: 071 437 9475/7445
Film and video production
Editing: 16mm/35mm, lo-band U-Matic

GBS Film Lighting
169 Talgarth Road
London W14
Tel: 081 748 0316
Fax: 081 563 0679
Lighting equipment hire

General Screen Enterprises
Highbridge House

Oxford Road
Uxbridge
Middx UB8 1LX
Tel: 0895 31931
Fax: 0895 35335
Studio: 100 sq metres
16mm, 35mm opticals including matting, aerial image work, titling; editing, trailers, promos, special effects, graphics, VistaVision; computerised rostrum animation; video suite; preview theatre

Goldcrest Elstree Studios
Borehamwood
Herts
Tel: 081 953 1600
Fax: 081 207 0860
Viewing and dubbing theatres; cutting rooms; complete Dolby installation; post-production department with a re-recording theatre providing 16mm, 35mm and 70mm facilities; transfer suites

Grip House Facilities and Studios
5-11 Taunton Road
Metropolitan Centre
Greenford
Middx UB6 8UQ
Tel: 081 578 2382
Fax: 081 578 1536
Equipment hire

Hall Place Studios
4 Hall Place
Leeds LS9 8JD
Tel: 0532 405553
16mm/U-Matic/VHS production units, lighting, cutting rooms, edit suite with TBC, rostrum camera, film/video studio, 16-track sound studio, 4-track 16mm dubbing, sound transfer, sound effects library
See also under Workshops for information on training courses

Hammonds Audio Visual and Video Services
Presentation Division
60-64a Queens Road
Watford
Herts WD1 2LA
Tel: 0923 39733
ENG crews; Betacam SP, BVU, BVP 7 DXC M7; editing; multiformat,

DVE, computer graphics (animation), audio and studio facilities. S-VHS off-line; duplication and STDS conversion via AVS systems

Hillside Studios
Merry Hill Road
Bushey
Herts WD2 1DR
Tel: 081 950 7919
Fax: 081 950 1437
Production and post-production facilities
Betacam, BVU, 1″C and Betacam SP plus component shooting
Two studios: 1500 sq ft – drive in access and 384 sq ft
On-line and off-line editing suites – composite and component
Audio pre-production and post-production studios
Audience seating for 100, set design, construction, 3 conference rooms and licensed restaurant

Holborn Studios
Herbal House
10 Back Hill
London EC1
Tel: 071 278 4311
Fax: 071 833 1377
Three film stages, set building

Humphries Video Services
Unit 2, The Willows
Business Centre
17 Willow Lane
Mitcham
Surrey CR4 4NX
Tel: 081 648 6111
Fax: 081 648 5261
Evershed House
71 Chiltern Street
London W1M 1HT
Tel: 071 636 3636
Fax: 071 486 3636
Videocassette duplication, standards conversion, mastering, dubbing facilities; full packaging and distribution service

ITN House
48 Wells Street
London W1P 4DE
Tel: 071 580 8333
Video formats: Quad, 1″C, BVU
Cameras: 4 Marconi Mk9
Studio: 45 sq metres
Vision effects: Quantel
Standards conversion via ACE

OB unit three cameras, C format VTR, Grass Valley mixer, Links

In-Video Productions
16 York Place
Edinburgh EH1 3EP
Tel: 031 557 2151
Fax: 031 557 5465
Four Ampex 1″ VTRs, Sony 9000 edit controller, Grass Valley 300 switcher with Kaleidoscope digital effects unit, Quantel digital effects unit, Dubner character generator, Abekas A64 digital recorder
Cameras: Ampex CVC 50 (2), Ampex CVC 7
Off-line edit suite; video studio; voiceover booth

Andre Jacquemin Recording
68a Delancey Street
London NW1 7RY
Tel: 071 485 3733
Fax: 071 284 1020
24 track post-production suite, large screen projection, computer mixing. Large sound effects library, music library, array of keyboards, samplers and special effects

Terry Jones Post Productions
The Hat Factory
16-18 Hollen Street
London W1V 3AD
Tel: 071 434 1173
Fax: 071 494 1893
35mm, 16mm post-production facilities

LTM (UK) Cinebuild
Studio House
Rita Road
London SW8 1JU
Tel: 071 582 8750
Fax: 071 793 0467
Special effects: rain, snow, fog, mist, smoke, fire, explosions; lighting and equipment hire
Studio: 200 sq metres

Ladbroke Films (Dubbing)
4 Kensington Park Gardens
London W11 3HB
Tel: 071 727 3541
Fax: 071 727 3632
16mm/35mm Steenbeck editing; 16mm/35mm dubbing up to 6 tk; 70mm Dolby stereo (12 tk); ADR, footsteps, sound transfer

Lane End Productions
63 Riding House Street
London W1P 7PP
Tel: 071 637 2794
Fax: 071 580 0135
Video formats: 1"C,
Betacam SP, BVU,
U-Matic, VHS
Vision effects: Grass
Valley mixer, colour
camera, Aston 3, Abacus
A53D, off-line
Transfer and standards
conversion

Lazer F.I.L.M.S.
Building No 1
GEC Estate
East Lane
Wembley
Middx
Tel: 081 904 1448
Editing and other post-
production facilities

Lee Lighting
Wycombe Road
Wembley
Middx HA0 1QD
Tel: 081 900 2900
Fax: 081 902 5500
Lighting equipment hire

Lee International Studios
Studios Road
Shepperton
Middx TW17 0QD
Tel: 0932 562611
Fax: 0932 568989
Manchester Road
Kearsley
Bolton BL4 8RL
Tel: 0204 73373
Fax: 0204 795741
Cutting rooms; 16mm,
35mm viewing theatres

Light House Media Centre
Art Gallery
Lichfield Street
Wolverhampton WV1
1DU
Tel: 0902 312033
Fax: 0902 26644
Video production with
3-machine edit, computer
graphics/animation

Lighthouse Film and Video
19 Regent Street
Brighton BN1 1UL
Tel: 0273 686479
Video cameras: Panasonic
F70, F15 and S-VHS
camcorder
Video editing: Series 5
two machine or S-VHS to
U-Matic two machine;

JVC KM-1200 effects
generator, Fostex 8 track
mixer, video typewriter
16mm Film: Arriflex BL,
Nagra III, O'Connor
tripod, 4 plate Steenbeck
and pic-sync
Lights: 4 x 800W kit, 2kW
kit
Dry hire, crews and
training

Limehouse Television
3rd Floor, Trocadero
Centre
19 Rupert Street
London W1
Tel: 071 287 3333
Fax: 071 287 1998
Two studios with post-
production facilities

London Fields Film and Video
10 Martello Street
London E8 3PE
Tel: 071 241 2997
Computer graphics; video
editing; 16mm editing

London Film Makers' Co-op
42 Gloucester Avenue
London NW1 8JD
Tel: 071 722 1728
Houses a wide range of
16mm and Super 8
production equipment
and facilities including B
& W printing and
processing (service or
DIY), optical printer,
rostrum camera,
steenbecks (both 16mm
and Super 8), sound
dubbing and transfer
facilities

London Video Access
23 Frith Street
London W1A 4XD
Tel: 071 734 7410/437
2786
Fax: 071 734 2003
Workshop with
production and editing
facilities up to 3-machine
U-Matic with digital
effects. Training
workshops in all aspects
of video production and
post-production

Lynx Video
Lynx House
7 High Road
Ickenham
Uxbridge
Middx UB10 8LE
Tel: 0895 676221

Fax: 0895 621623
Video formats: 1"C,
Betacam SP, BVU
Cameras: Ikegami
HL79Es, HL95s
Vision effects: Questech,
Charisma and graphics

MAC Sound Hire
1-2 Attenburys Park
Park Road
Altrincham
Cheshire WA14 5QE
Tel: 061 969 8311
Fax: 061 962 9423
Hire of professional sound
equipment

Margaret Street Studio
79-80 Margaret Street
London W1N 7HB
Tel: 071 636 4444
Fax: 071 436 9872
1300 sq ft 3 camera
component broadcast
studio, 3 x Sony BVP7,
Ace T8 component vision
mixer, Aston 3B cap gen;
Editing: component on-
line edit suites, Sony
BVW75, 2 x Sony
BVW65, Grass Valley
100CV vision mixer,
Aston cap gen, Sony 900
edit controller; BT lines;
graphics facilities; video
crews; production offices

Austin Martin Film and Video Services
87 Wardour Street
London W1B 3TS
Tel: 071 439 4397
Editing rooms

Mayflower Sound Studios
3 Audley Square
Mayfair
London W1Y 5DR
Tel: 071 493 0016
Fax: 071 355 4071
High-speed computerised
film and video recording
studio specialising in
Automated Dialogue
Replacement (ADR) and
sound effects including
digital sound effects
library

Media Arts
Town Hall Studios
Regent Circus
Swindon SN1 1QF
Tel: 0793 493454
Video cameras: F10s,
KY1900s, M3
Video editing: VHS
2-machine, Series 5 2/3-
machine, 3-machine lo-/

hi-/SP and effects; sound
studio and effects,
interview studio
8mm/16mm cutting
rooms
B/W and colour
photography; lighting:
Reds and 2000W; dry
hire, crews, training

Mercury Studio Sound
84-88 Wardour Street
London W1
Tel: 071 734 0263
Fax: 071 434 9990
Dubbing and sound
transfer facilities, cutting
rooms, production offices

Merseyside Film and Video Resource
110 Bold Street
Liverpool L1 4HY
Tel: 051 708 5259
Lo-band 3 machine
editing, 2 machine VHS;
Omega 2000 computer
graphics cameras,
microphones etc

Metropolis Video
8-10 Neal's Yard
London WC2H 9DP
Tel: 071 240 8423
Fax: 071 379 6880
Off-line editing: 4 suites
1 x 3 machine
computerised lo-band
giving 8"CMX Disc for
autoconform
2 x 2 machine lo-band
1 x 2 machine VHS
Video duplication: all
formats, large or small
runs
Overnight Betacam
rushes service. Rushes
transferred with BITC,
VITC overnight for off-
line next day

MetroVideo
The Old Bacon Factory
57-59 Great Suffolk
Street
London SE1 0BS
Tel: 071 928 2088
Fax: 071 261 0685
Metro Mansions
6-7 Great Chapel Street
London W1V 3AG
Tel: 071 439 3494
Fax: 071 439 3782
Video formats: Betacam
SP, MII, BVU SP, lo-band
Cameras: BVP5/7/50,
BVW 507/550, DXC-M7,
DXC3000/325
OB unit, standards
conversion, duplication,

Telecine, videowalls, video projectors, large screen monitors

PMPP (Paul Miller Post-Production)
69 Dean Street
London W1V 5HB
Tel: 071 437 0979
Fax: 071 434 0386
Editing: on-line 1", Betacam, Component Betacam SP with Charisma and ADO digital effects with Aston 3
Off-line: 3 machine computerised lo-band, 2 machine lo-band and VHS Matisse 2D and Rodin 3D computer graphics; 24 track sound dubbing studio with Q lock and voiceover; duplication, standards conversion

Molinare
34 Fouberts Place
London W1V 2BH
Tel: 071 439 2244
Fax: 071 734 6813
Video formats: Quad, C, BCN, BVU SP, Beta SP, Beta Component, D2
Video studios: Studio 1 – 33' x 45', broadcast TV studio with drive-in access, soft eye, black drapes on track 'Ultimatte', 4 Ikegami HL79 cameras on Vinten Peds, GVG 300 24-input 3-M/E vision mixer, TV grid, computer-controlled lighting console; 16 Ch audio mixer; Studio 2 – 25' x 15'. 3 Ikegami HL79 cameras, soft eye, black drapes on track
Editing: computer edit suites, Grass Valley vision mixers, 3-channel ADO with options. Aston character generators, colour caption cameras, Abekas A64
Graphics: Quantel Paintbox, Digital Library Store, Abekas A64, Caption Camera
Digital telecine with digigrade 3 and secondary colour correction 35mm/16mm
Dubbing: Ace standards converter 1"C Pal, NTSC, Secam, 1"B Pal/Secam, 2" Quad Pal/Secam Betacam SP, BVU, VHS, U-Matic, Betamax
BT lines, 3.5m satellite downlink, satellite video and audio downlink; 2 multitrack audio dubbing

studios with Eclipse edit controllers and Mastermix; 4 OB units available

Morgan Laboratories
Unit 4.16
Wembley Commercial Centre
East Lane
Wembley
Middx HA9 7XD
Tel: 081 908 3856
Fax: 081 908 4211
Post-production facilities

Tom Morrish Films
171 Wardour Street
London W1V 3TA
Tel: 071 437 2136
Fax: 071 734 5295
16mm, 35mm post-production

Motion Control Studio
Vision House
19-22 Rathbone Place
London W1P 1DF
Tel: 071 436 5544
Fax: 071 436 9534
Studio with overhead motion control rig

The Moving Picture Company
25 Noel Street
London W1V 3RD
Tel: 071 434 3100
Fax: 071 439 3951/734 9150
Video formats: 1"C, D1, D2, MII, Beta SP, Betacam, hi-/lo-band, S-VHS
Cameras: Sony BVP 330 portable and Sony DXC 3000 CCD
Editing: five editing suites (three fully digital), using CMX editors
Vision effects: ADO, Mirage, Abekas A53-D, A64, A84
Telecine: two 4.2.2 Digital Rank Cintel MK3 enhanced 16mm/35mm machines with Digigrade and da Vinci colour correctors, Register Pin and Steadiguide gates. Digital noise reduction, Matchbox, Ultimatte 5
Graphics: 3 x Paintbox/Harrys, with Encore HUD and A53D
2 x Alias 3-D computer animation systems, with 4-D 120 renderers; Aston 3 and 4 character generators, Pierrot Studios: motion control

studio for special effects/model work; main studio: 50' x 35', with a 45' cyc; rostrum camera studio with Steadifilm 16mm/35mm cutting rooms and off-line editing suite

Mr Lighting
2 Dukes Road
Western Avenue
London W3 0SL
Tel: 081 993 9911
Fax: 081 993 9533
Lighting equipment hire

Nant Films
Moreia
Penrallt Isaf
Caernarfon
Gwynedd L55 1NS
Tel: 0286 5722
Fax: 0286 5159
Production company with two 16mm cutting rooms, off-line facilities

National Screen Productions
2nd Floor
2 Wedgwood Mews
12-13 Greek Street
London W1V 5LW
Tel: 071 437 2783
Fax: 071 494 1811
Creative and technical services for production of promos, documentaries, trailers, teasers and TV spots. Logo and main title design and animation. All aspects of on-screen promotion and presentation for feature films, TV, cable and video. In-house film/video editing, design and art studio. Videowall programming

Northern Light
39-41 Assembly Street
Leith
Edinburgh EH6 7RG
Tel: 031 553 2383
Lighting equipment hire

Numo Productions
The Hat Factory
16-18 Hollen Street
London W1V 3AD
Tel: 071 437 2877
Fax: 071 437 8706
Stop-frame, live-action special effects
Mitchell S35R with colour video assist

The OBE Partnership
8-18 Smith's Court
off Great Windmill Street
London W1V 9PF

Tel: 071 734 3028
Fax: 071 734 2830
Film editing

Omnititles
37 Ripplevale Grove
London N1 1HS
Tel: 071 607 9047
Fax: 071 704 9594
Spotting and subtitling services for film, telecine, video, satellite and cable. Subtitling in most world languages and for the deaf

Roger Owen and Associates
8-18 Smith's Court
off Great Windmill Street
London W1V 9PF
Tel: 071 439 3772
Fax: 071 734 2830
Video formats: all cassette formats
Editing: 3-machine lo-band off-line editing suite Mk2 telecine

Oxford Film and Video Makers
The Stables
North Place
Headington
Oxford OX3 9HY
Tel: 0865 60074
Cameras: Sony DXC-325, Panasonic F10, Arriflex 16mm and Super 8
Recorders: Sony 4800, Panasonic NV-180
Editing: Sony lo-band U-Matic, 16mm Steenbecks

The Palace (Video Editing Centre)
8 Poland Street
London W1V 3DG
Tel: 071 439 8241
Fax: 071 287 1741
Video formats: 1", Beta SP, Beta, BVU
Editing: three 5-machine suites
Digital effects: 3 ADO 3000 with infinity and digimatte, Quantel digital effects
Off-line editing: multimachine U-Matic and VHS
Graphics: Spaceward Matisse system

Picardy Television
Picardy House
4 Picardy Place
Edinburgh EH1 3JT
Tel: 031 558 1551
Fax: 031 558 1555
Facilities include: dry/crewed camera hire; multi format editing including

Betacam SP component, DVE and graphics; full broadcast standard studio for single/multi camera shoots and casting; EVS video paint system with 2 and 3D animation

Picture Post-Productions
13 Manette Street
London W1V 5LB
Tel: 071 439 1661
Fax: 071 494 1661
35/16mm film editing; off-line editing

Pinewood Studios
Iver
Bucks SL0 0NH
Tel: 0753 656301
Fax: 0753 656844
Two large high-speed stereo dubbing theatres with automated consoles; small general purpose recording theatre; large ADR and sound effects theatre; preview theatre: 115 seats, 70/35/16mm, all formats stereo sound; four-bay sound transfer area; mono/stereo sound negative transfer; 60 fully-serviced cutting rooms

Prominent Studios
68a Delancey Street
London NW1 7RY
Tel: 071 284 0242
Fax: 071 284 1020
Cutting rooms (film or video); production offices; preview theatre

Q Studios
Queniborough Industrial Estate
1487 Melton Road
Queniborough
Leicester LE7 8FP
Tel: 0533 608813
Fax: 0533 608329
Video formats: Betacam SP, BVU
Component editing with Charisma DVE, off-line edit, 24 track sound, original music production; two drive-in studios (1,350 and 754 sq ft), black and chromakey drapes, computer controlled lighting. Full production services available including crews, set construction, on-line and off-line editing

Rank Video Services
Phoenix Park
Great West Road

Brentford
Middx TW8 9PL
Tel: 081 568 4311
Fax: 081 847 4032
3000 slaves, hi-fi capable; specialist corporate duplication department including standards conversion

Recording and Production Services
3 Chrysalis Way
Langley Bridge
Eastwood
Nottingham NG16 3RY
Tel: 0773 718111
Fax: 0773 716004
OB units 1" and Beta to 10 cameras: composite and component; edit suite: 1" and Beta with DVE and Aston

Redapple
Orchard House
The Street
Albury, Nr Guildford
Surrey GU5 9AG
Tel: 048641 3797
Fax: 048641 3781
Video formats: 1"C, Beta, Beta SP, BVU, NTSC/PAL
Cameras: Sony BVP50, Sony BVP7, ENG/EFP units
Film: 16mm Arriflex unit
Transport: 5 estate cars, pressurised twin engine aircraft
Two lighting vehicles

Richmond Film Services
The Old School
Park Lane
Richmond
Surrey TW9 2RA
Tel: 081 940 6077
Fax: 081 948 8326
Sound equipment available for hire, sales of tape and batteries, and UK agent for Ursta recordists' trolleys and Denecke timecode equipment

Rockall Data Services
320 Western Road
London SW19 2QA
Tel: 081 640 6626
Fax: 081 640 1297
Safe storage of film, video and audio material

Rushes
66 Old Compton Street
London W1V 5PA
Tel: 071 437 8676
Fax: 071 734 2519

Television post-production, graphics, special effects, 1" on-line, Harry, Paintbox, Telecine, CIS suite, FGS 4500, Alias, motion control studio, studio

SVC Television
142 Wardour Street
London W1V 3AU
Tel: 071 734 1600
Fax: 071 437 1854
8 x edit suites including 4 x 1", 2 x Betacam SP, 1 x off-line, 1 fully digital with A84; Mirage, Encore, A53, Harry, Symbolics, Paintbox, motion control rostrum camera, 3 x telecine including Ursa and Mastergrade colour grading facility

Salon Post-Productions
13-14 Archer Street
London W1V 7HG
Tel: 071 437 0516
Fax: 071 437 6197
35/16mm Steenbecks and editing equipment hire; cutting rooms; 35/16mm Steenbeck, telecine, U-Matic and VHS edit suites

Sammy's – Samuelson Film Service London
21 Derby Road
Metropolitan Centre
Greenford
Middx UB6 8UJ
Tel: 081 578 7887
Fax: 081 578 2733
Cameras: Panavision, moviecam, arriflex
Lenses: Canon, Cooke, Nikon, Leitz, Zeiss, Hasselblad
Video assist, sound, editing, stock, consumables and transport. 24hrs

Michael Samuelson Lighting
Pinewood Studios
Iver Heath
Bucks SL0 0NH
Tel: 0753 631133
Fax: 0753 630485
10 Back Hill
Clerkenwell Road
London EC1R 5EN
Tel: 071 833 8719
Fax: 071 833 8721
Milford Place
Lennox Road
Leeds LS4 2BL
Tel: 0532 310770
Lighting equipment hire

Screenworks
Portsmouth Media Trust
The Hornpipe
143 Kingston Road
Portsmouth PO2 7EB
Tel: 0705 861851/833854
Video hire and post-production; 90-seat auditorium with 35mm and 16mm, video and slide projection; VHS edit suite; U-Matic to VHS

Sheffield Independent Film
Avec
Brown Street
Sheffield S1 2BS
Tel: 0742 720304
16mm Aaton LTR, Arriflex BL, Beaulieu R16, 6-plate Steenbeck and Picsyncs, Nagra IS, Nagra 3, Revox B77, Fostex 350 mixer
Sony U-Matic type 5 including TBC mixer and captions, National Panasonic VHS, M5 VHS camcorder, Sony portapaks VO 8800 and VO 6800, Sony DXC 3000 and 3 machine edit suite
Lighting equipment and studio facilities hire

Signal Vision
Park Gate Industrial Estate
Knutsford
Cheshire
Tel: 0565 52871
Fax: 0565 4164
Five-machine edit suite; two-channel Quantel CDL mixer; purpose-built studio

Sound House
14 Livonia Street
London W1V 3TH
Tel: 071 434 2928/437 7105
Fax: 071 287 9110
Sound transfer base, magnetic and DAT as well as a comprehensive sound effects library; recording booth

Brian Stevens Animated Films and Rostrum Cameras
11 Charlotte Mews
off Tottenham Street
London W1P 1LN
Tel: 071 637 0535/7
Fax: 071 323 3892
Rostrum cameras; studio animation facilities

Stockwell Media Productions
Hippodrome Studios
131 High Street
Colchester
Essex CO1 1SP
Tel: 0206 44551/762555
Fax: 0206 572840
Cameras: Sony CCD,
portable U-Matic, hi-band
SP
Editing: 2/3 machine edit
suites
Production personnel;
tape dubbing

Studio Film and Video
Video Facilities
Royalty House
72-73 Dean Street
London W1V 5HB
Tel: 071 734 9471
Fax: 071 437 4161
Video formats: 1"C,
Betacam SP, BVU SP,
BVU, U-Matic, VHS,
Betamax, Video 8
Telecine: 35mm, 16mm
and Super 8, Rank Cintel
MkIII with Digigrade.
Also 8mm and 9.5mm
Editing: U-Matic suite,
standards conversion,
NTSC, PAL, Secam via
ADAC or AVS

Studio Operation SW
The Old Chapel
Abbey Hill
Lelant
Cornwall TR26 3EG
Tel: 0736 753538/071 379
6724
Fax: 0736 756744
1500 sq ft studio with
production office, cam,
lighting, sound, special
effects, pyrotechnics, post
production film/video and
digital sound suite

TSI Video
10 Grape Street
London WC2H 8DY
Tel: 071 379 3435
Fax: 071 379 4589
Video formats: 1" x 9,
Betacam SP plus BVU
Editing: 3 suites Sony
BVE 9000 edit controllers
in component and
composite with any
combination of above,
Grass Valley vision
mixer, 4 channels of
Charisma DVE with key
channels and Cleo,
caption camera, Aston 3 B
character generators
Computer graphics:
Quantel Paintbox with

Pro 4 software and digital
library store, Digipix 3D
software running on
Silicon Graphics Iris 4D
Series. Matisse with
Frame 3D, and
traditional animation
Sound: Q Lock/Eclipse
synchronisers, 24 track
dubbing and voiceover
recording with Opus
Digital Audio post
production facility
Four BT lines (vision and
sound), BT control lines
(2 in, 2 out), colour
caption camera, Sony
BVH 2500 single frame
recorder, Honeywell
Matrix camera

TVi
Film House
142 Wardour Street
London W1V 3AU
Tel: 071 434 2141
Fax: 071 439 3984
Video formats: PAL/625
and NTSC/525: D1, D2,
1"B, 1"C, Betacam SP,
BVU SP, BVU, U-Matic,
VHS, S-VHS with PAL/
625 2" Quad
Editing: six stereo edit
suites with D2, 1"C,
Betacam SP, BVU VTRs
– A53 with warp and
dimension or ADO digital
effects, A64 digital disc
recorder for multi-
layering, colour caption
camera, Aston III or A72
character generator. VHS
and U-Matic off-lines
Sound: Post production
dubbing to picture (D2, 1",
Beta, BVU or U-Matic)
with TS 24 channel
mixer, voiceover booth
and DAR hard disc digital
recorder – PAL/NTSC
operation
Telecine: 16mm/35mm to
625/PAL/SECAM or 525/
NTSC Rank Cintel 4:2:2
telecines with wetgate
Graphics: Matisse and
A72

TWTV
20 Kingly Street
London W1R 5LD
Tel: 071 437 4706
Fax: 071 437 5992
Video editing and post-
production, standards
conversion, video
duplication, computer
graphics based around
Paintbox and Harriet

Tattooist International
3 Centro House
20 Mandela Street
London NW1 0DU
Tel: 071 380 0488
Fax: 071 388 8890
16mm cutting room,
Super 16 and stereo
options, lo-band U-Matic
off-line, Aaton camera
hire specialists,
Steadicam, time lapse
equipment, production
offices

Team Television
The Exchange Buildings
Mount Stuart Square
Cardiff CF1 6EA
Tel: 0222 484080
Fax: 0222 494210
Edit 1 Multiformat: 1"C,
Beta SP, BVU, 2 Channel
Charisma, Quantel DLS;
Edit 2: fully component
Beta SP; Telecine 16mm/
35mm
Quantel V series
Paintbox; duplicating and
standards conversion

Tele-cine & Cell Animation
(Tele-cine Cell Group)
48 Charlotte Street
London W1P 1LX
Tel: 071 637 3253
Fax: 071 631 3993
Three motion control
studios up to 85'x52'x25'
3D Silicon Graphics with
Softimage, Harry,
Paintbox, Encore HUD,
Sony DVTRs, film/video
rostrum, on-line multi-
format and off-line
editing, Telecine with da
Vinci, standards
conversion. All VT
formats from 2" Quad to
D2

Third Eye Productions
Unit 210 Canalot Studios
222 Kensal Road
London W10 5BN
Tel: 081 969 8211
Fax: 081 960 8790
Fully equipped 16mm
cutting room and S-VHS
off-line edit suite

Tiny Epic Video Co
138-140 Wardour Street
London W1V 3AU
Tel: 071 437 2854/434
2377
Fax: 071 434 0211
14 suites of off-line
editing 24 hours a day,

7 days a week. 9 x Sony 5
series U-Matic (and
shotlister); 3 x Panasonic
6500 VHS (and
shotlister); 1 x Panasonic
7500 S-VHS (and
shotlister); 1 x 3 machine
Sony series 9 U-Matic
with GVG100 (with vision
mixer and edit master
controller)
Music and sound effects;
EDL generation; EDL
translation; dubbing;
autoconforming (Beta,
Beta SP)

Transworld TV Productions
Whitecrook Centre
Whitecrook Street
Clydebank
Glasgow G81 1QS
Tel: 041 952 4816
Production facilities;
location camera crews;
3-machine hi- and lo-band
editing

Roy Turk Opticals
57 Rupert Street
London W1V 7HW
Tel: 071 437 8884
Fax: 071 734 6579
Titles and opticals

Twickenham Studios
St Margaret's
Twickenham
Middlesex TW1 2AW
Tel: 081 892 4477
Fax: 081 891 0168
Two dubbing theatres,
ADR effects theatre, 41
cutting rooms, Dolby
installation

Mike Uden Opticals
21a Kingly Court
off Beak Street
London W1R 5LE
Tel: 071 439 1982
Fax: 071 734 0950
Opticals; special effects
and titling

VMTV
1st Floor
34 Fouberts Place
London W1V 2BH
Tel: 071 439 4536
Fax: 071 437 0952
OBs: Four units with 2-12
cameras, 1" or Beta SP
record format, full
complement
ancillary equipment
Studios: Two West End
broadcast studios
Dry hire: Betacam SP and
16mm equipment with/
without crews

The Video Duplicating Co

Barnes City Building
South Way
Wembley
Middx HA9 0EH
Tel: 081 903 6288
Comprehensive video
services in all formats,
tape to tape, bulk cassette
duplication

Video Time

22-24 Greek Street
London W1V 5LG
Tel: 071 439 1211
Fax: 071 439 7336
Video formats: 1″C, 1″B,
BVU, BVU SP, Betacam,
Betacam SP, MII, VHS,
Betamax, V8, S-VHS (all
PAL/NTSC/Secam)
Video disc cutting, audio
layback, full 3M/C edit
suite BVU SP/U-Matic
Standards conversion:
ACE, 2 x ADAC, AVS
Telecine: 2 x Cintel MKIII
Video duplication

Videola

171 Wardour Street
London W1V 3TA
Tel: 071 437 5413
Fax: 071 734 5295
Video formats: 1″, BVU,
U-Matic
Cameras: Sony, Ikegami
Computer rostrum
camera
Editing: hi-band to 1″,
BVU

Videolondon Soundstudios

16-18 Ramillies Street
London W1V 1DL
Tel: 071 734 4811
Fax: 071 494 2553
Sophisticated sound
recording studio with
overhead TV projection
system. 16mm, 35mm and
video post-synch
recording and mixing. All
sound facilities for film or
video post-production
including 1″ PAL and
Betacam SP

Videoscope

Ty-Cattwg Cottage
Llancarfan
Barry
South Glamorgan CF6
9AG
Tel: 0446 710963
Fax: 0446 710023
Video format: hi-band U-
Matic, Betacam, 1″
Cameras: Sony 3000
Timecode transfer, 3-
machine, hi-band editing,
SP editing; copying bank

VisCentre

66-67 Newman Street
London W1P 3LA
Tel: 071 436 5692
Fax: 071 580 9676
Three-camera broadcast
interview studio; ENG
crews worldwide; video
formats: 1″, Betacam,
BVU; 3-machine Betacam
SP PAL; 2-machine
Betacam SPBVU 525/625;
standards conversion:
AVS; telecine: Rank
Cintel enhanced MkIII
4:2:2 digital telecine 35/
16 and 8mm with Da
Vinci colour corrector;
satellite transmissions

Visions

8 Dean Street
London W1V 5RL
Tel: 071 734 5231
Fax: 071 439 0252
Harry, 2 x Paintbox,
Encore HUD, D1, digital
edit suite, 1″ on-line edit
suite, multiformat edit
suite, 4 x A53, 2 x ADO,
A72, 2 x A60, Digital
Rank Cintel Telecine
with Colorist, Steadigate,
Steadigate and Digislate;
8/16/35mm; BT lines; off-
line facilities

Visnews

Cumberland Avenue
London NW10 7EH
Tel: 081 965 7733
Fax: 081 965 0620
Video formats: 1″C, 1″B,
2″, MII, Betacam SP, BVU
SP, Betacam, BVU, Video
8, U-Matic, VHS,
Betamax
Standards conversion:
Ace, Quantel and AVS
Transcoding: PAL-
SECAM-PAL
Post production: BVE
3000, Grass Valley,
Quantel 5001, Aston 3
Telecine: Rank Cintel
Enhanced MkIIIC 4:2:2
digital telecine, 35/16 and
8mm with da Vinci colour
corrector
Satellite transmissions

Warwick Dubbing Theatre

WFS (Film Holdings)
151-153 Wardour Street
London W1V 3TB
Tel: 071 437 5532
Sound transfer
Sound mixing and
dubbing
Edge numbering

Wembley Studios

10 Northfield Industrial
Estate
Beresford Avenue
Wembley
Middlesex HA0 1RT
Tel: 081 903 4296
Studios: 3640 sq ft,
production offices,
dressing rooms

Whitelion Facilities

Bradley Close
White Lion Street
London N1 9PN
Tel: 071 837 4836
Fax: 071 833 0013
Location units: Sony
BVP7 cameras recording
onto Betacam SP
Graphics: Quantel
Paintbox with Abekas
A60 digital disc recorder
Editing: main suite
equipped with D2, 1″,
Beta SP, Abekas A53-D,
Abekas A60, Sony 9000,
caption camera and Aston
On-line 2 equipped with
D2, 1″, Beta SP, Abekas
A53-D, Sony 910, caption
camera and Aston
Off-line: 2 and 3 machine
computer controlled U-
Matic suites

Windmill Lane Pictures

4 Windmill Lane
Dublin 2
Tel: 0001 713444
Fax: 0001 718413/718898
Film, video, news,
recording and production
facilities

Wiseman

29-35 Lexington Street
London W1R 3HQ
Tel: 071 439 8901
Fax: 071 437 2481
Editing: 1 – Abekas A84,
A64, A53, A72, caption
camera, 2 x Bosch D1
DVTR, 2 x Betacam
SP, CMX Controller;
2 – GVG 200CV, A72,
ADO, caption camera,
4 x VPR3, 2 x Betacam
SP, ACE controller;
3 – GVG 2000CV, A72,
ADO, Caption camera,
3 x Betacam SP, ACE
controller; 4 – GVG
100CV, 4 x Betacam SP,
ACE controller; 5 – 3 x lo-
band U-Matic. ACE
controller
Off-line: 2 x lo-band U-
Matic off-line with edit
lister
Telecine: 1 – Rank Cintel
4:2:2 XYZoom, digigrade,
Steadigate, secondary
colour correction,
Matchbox, digislate and
Aaton timecode readers;

2 – Rank Cintel Jump-
scan, Amigo grading
Harry: Harry LP, V series
Paintbox, Encore HUD,
D1 DVTR, caption camera
Paintbox: V series
paintbox, Quantel
carousel, colour video
printer, caption camera
Rostrum: IMC computer
controlled camera
Video transfer formats
available: 1″C, 2″ Quad,
Betacam SP and most
cassette formats
Standards conversion: 2 x
ADAC, AVS6500; Fostex
DAT, Nagra T, Aston 3
and Telecom lines

Wolff Productions

6a Noel Street
London W1V 3RB
Tel: 071 439 1838/734
4286
35mm/16mm rostrum
camera work; animation
production

Workhouse

Granville House
St Peter Street
Winchester
Hants SO23 9AF
Tel: 0962 63449
Fax: 0962 841026
Video formats: 1″C,
Betacam SP
Studio: 300 sq metres
Editing: Betacam SP to
1″, VHS off-line
Vision effects:
VistaVision mixer and
ADO 100 digital effects

World Wide Sound

21-25 St Anne's Court
London W1V 3AW
Tel: 071 434 1121
Fax: 071 734 0619
High-speed rock'n'roll
dubbing theatres; effects
recording; post
synchronisation;
translation facilities

Worldwide Television News Corporation

31-36 Foley Street
London W1P 7LB
Tel: 071 323 3255
Fax: 071 631 3750
BVU editing (PAL and
NTSC); multi-machine
editing with digital
effects and colour
captioning; Betacam
record/replay; 1″C editing;
digital standards
conversion; PAL/SECAM
transcoding; duplication;
local and international
feeds, single camera
studio

THE LONDON
•INTERNATIONAL•
FILM SCHOOL

• Training film makers for over 30 years •
• Graduates now working worldwide •
• Located in Covent Garden in the heart of London •
• Recognised by A.C.T.T. •
• 16mm documentary & 35mm studio filming •
• Two year Diploma course in film making
commences three times a year: January, April, September •

London International Film School, Department F20, 24 Shelton Street, London WC2H 9HP
071 - 836 9642

FESTIVALS

Listed below by country of origin are the main international film, TV and video festivals with contact addresses and brief synopses

AUSTRALIA

Australian Video Festival (Sept)
PO Box 316
NSW 2021
Tel: (61) 02 339 9555
Competitive for video – art, graphics, music, documentary and drama/narrative. Also includes a student section

Melbourne Film Festival (June)
41-45 A'Beckett Street
Victoria 300
GOP Box 2760
Melbourne 3001
Tel: (61) 03 663 1395
Fax: (61) 03 662 1218
Non-competitive section for feature films (60 mins and over) and a competitive section for short films (less than 60 mins). Films should not previously have been shown in Melbourne

Sydney Film Festival (June)
Box 25
PO Glebe
NSW 2037
Tel: (61) 02 660 3844
Fax: (61) 02 692 8793
Non-competitive for feature films and shorts not previously shown in Australia

AUSTRIA

Viennale (March)
Turmstiege
Uraniastrasse 1
1010 Vienna
Tel: (43) 1 72 61 910
Fax: (43) 1 75 32 85
Non-competitive for features and documentaries

BELGIUM

Antwerp International Film Festival (March-April)
Antwerpse Film Stichting
Theatercentrum
Theaterplein 1
B-Antwerp
Tel: (32) 03 232 66 77
Fax: (32) 03 219 47 68
Non-competitive for documentary, fiction and animation. Films must have been completed in three years prior to festival and not previously screened in Belgium, the Netherlands and Luxembourg

Brussels International Film Festival (Jan)
288 rue Royale
B-1210 Brussels
Tel: (32) 02 218 12 67/ 218 10 45
Fax: (32) 02 218 79 33
Competitive for feature films

Brussels International Festival of Fantasy and Science Fiction Films (March)
144 avenue de la Reine
B-1210 Brussels
Tel: (32) 2 242 17 13
Fax: (32) 2 216 21 69
Competitive for features and shorts (less than 50 mins), including animation, produced in the previous two-and-a-half years

International Flanders Film Festival (Oct)
1104 Kortrijksesteenweg
B-9820 Ghent
Fax: (32) 9 121 90 74
Competitive film festival of musical films and films on music

BRAZIL

FESTRIO (Rio de Janeiro International Festival of Film, TV and Video) (+Market) (Nov)
Rua Paissandu 362
2210 Laranjeiras
Rio de Janeiro
Tel: (55) 21 285 6642/ 285 7968
Competitive for films – features and shorts, TV and video – including music, educational, drama and news programmes, experimental video, produced in previous year. Owing to political upheaval surrounding the elections, the festival was held in Fortaleza in 1989

BULGARIA

Varna World Animated Film Festival (Oct odd years)
1 Bulgaria Square
Sofia 1414
Tel: (359) 2 586 014/ 589 159/586 167
Competitive for animated films produced in previous two years, including children's animation, animation for TV, student films, first films. (NB Films awarded prizes at Annecy or Zagreb not accepted)

BURKINA FASO

Panafrican Film Festival (Fespaco) (Feb/March alternate years)
BP 2505 Ouagadougou
Tel: (266) 307 538

CANADA

Atlantic Film Festival (Oct-Nov)
Suite 24
5211 Blowers Street
Halifax
Nova Scotia
Tel: (1) 902 422 3429
Competitive for feature films, animation, experimental, documentary, educational and industrial. Also includes student section, first film/video, short drama, news/current affairs, TV variety and commercials. All work must have been made during two years preceding festival

Banff Television Festival (May-June)
St Julien Road
PO Box 1020
Banff
Alberta T0L 0C0
Tel: (1) 403 762 3060
Fax: (1) 403 762 5357
Competitive for films
made for television,
including features, drama
special, limited series,
continuing series,
documentary, children's
programmes and comedy
which were broadcast for
the first time in the
previous year

Canadian International Animation Festival
(Sept-Oct even years)
217 George Street
Toronto
Ontario
Tel: (1) 416 367 0088
Competitive for
animation

International Animation Festival
(Oct)
Canadian Film Institute
150 Rideau Street
Ottawa
Ontario K1N 5X6
Fax: (1) 613 232 6315

International Festival of New Cinema and Video
(Oct)
3724 Boulevard Saint-
Laurent
Montreal
Quebec H2X 2V8
Tel: (1) 514 843 4725
Non-competitive for
innovative films produced
during previous two years
which have not been
screened in Canada

Montreal World Film Festival (+Market) (Aug)
1455 de Maisonneuve
Blvd West
Montreal
Quebec H3G IM8
Tel: (1) 514 848 3883
Fax: (1) 514 848 3886
Competitive for feature
films and shorts (up to
30 mins), produced in
previous year, which have
not been screened outside
country of origin or been
entered in other
competitive festivals

Toronto Annual International Festival of Festivals
(Sept)
69 Yorkville Avenue
Suite 205
Toronto
Ontario M5R 1B8
Tel: (1) 416 967 7371
Non-competitive for
feature films and shorts
not previously shown in
Canada. Also includes
some American
premieres, retrospectives
and national cinema
programmes. Films must
have been completed
within the year prior to
the festival to be eligible

Vancouver International Film Festival (Sept-Oct)
303-788 Beatty Street
Suite 303
Vancouver BC V6B 2M1
Tel: (1) 604 685 0260
Fax: (1) 604 688 8221

COLOMBIA

Cartagena International Film Festival (April)
Apartado Aereo 1834
Cartagena
Tel: (1) 53 653 952
Competitive for films
produced in Colombia and
Latin America. Also non-
competitive section for
feature films, shorts and
documentaries. Films
must be subtitled in
Spanish and not
previously screened
in Colombia

CUBA

Havana International Film Festival (Dec)
ICAIC, Calle 23
No 1155 Plaza de la
Revolucion
Havana 4
Tel: (53) 7 400 4711

International Festival of New Latin American Cinema
(Dec)
Calle 23, No 1155 Vedado
Havana

CZECHOSLOVAKIA

Golden Prague International TV Festival (June)
Czechoslovakia
Television
Gorkeho nam 29
111 50 Prague 1
Tel: (42) 2 220158

Karlovy Vary International Film Festival (+ Market)
(June-July even years,
alternates with Moscow)
Jindrisska 34
Prague 1
Tel: 2365385 9
Competitive for feature
films and shorts,
including first films and
documentaries, produced
in previous 14 months
and not shown in
competition at other
festivals

DENMARK

Odense Film Festival
Vindegade 18
DK-5000 Odense C
Tel: (45) 913 1372 x4294
Fax: (45) 991 4318
Competitive film festival
held alternate years

EGYPT

Cairo International Film Festival (Dec)
Kasr El Nil Street
Cairo
Tel: (20) 2 392 3562/
392 3962
Fax: (20) 2 393 8979
Non-competitive film
festival and market

EIRE

Cork Film Festival
(Sept-Oct)
5 Tuckey Street
Cork
Tel: (353) 21 271 711
Fax: (353) 21 273 704
Non-competitive for
features, documentaries,
animation, video, and
student films. Also
competitive for short films
(up to 35 mins) produced
in the previous year

Dublin Film Festival
(Oct)
1 Suffolk Street
Dublin 2
Tel: (0001) 792 937

Festival of Irish films

FINLAND

Midnight Sun Film Festival (June)
Vainämoïsenkatu 19A
SF-00100 Helsinki
Tel: (358) 0 498 366
Fax: (358) 0 498 661
Held in Sodankyla,
Finnish Lapland, in 1990

Tampere International Short Film Festival (March)
PO Box 305
SF-33101 Tampere 10
Tel: (358) 31 35681
Fax: (358) 31 196756
Competitive for short
films (up to 35 mins),
including fiction,
animation, documentary,
experimental and
children's fiction,
produced in the previous
year

FRANCE

Annecy International Festival of Animation (+Market) (June)
Jica/ifa
BP 399
74013 Annecy Cedex
Tel: (33) 50 57 41 72
Fax: (33) 50 67 81 95
Competitive for animated
short films, non-
competitive for animated
feature-length films,
produced in the previous
26 months

Avoriaz International Fantasy Film Festival (Jan)
33 Avenue MacMahon
75017 Paris
Tel: (331) 42 67 71 40
Fax: (331) 46 22 88 51
Competitive for science
fiction, horror,
supernatural and fantasy
feature films, which have
not been commercially
shown in France or
participated in festivals
in Europe

Cannes International Film Festival (May)
71 rue du Faubourg
St Honoré
75008 Paris
Tel: (331) 42 66 92 20
Fax: (331) 42 66 68 85

Directors Fortnight
215 rue du Faubourg
St Honoré
75008 Paris
Tel: (331) 45 61 01 66
Semaine de la Critique
90 rue d'Amsterdam
75009 Paris
Tel: (331) 40 16 98 30/
(331) 45 74 53 53
Competitive section for
feature films and shorts
(up to 15 mins) produced
in the previous year,
which have not screened
outside country of origin
nor been entered in other
competitive festivals.
Plus non-competitive
events – Director's
Fortnight, Critic's Week
and programme of French
cinema

**Cognac
International Film
Festival of the
Thriller** (March-April)
33 avenue MacMahon
75017 Paris

**Creteil
International
Festival of
Women's Films
(+Market)**
(March-April)
Maison des Arts
Place Salvador Allende
94000 Creteil
Tel: (331) 48 99 90 50/
(331) 42 07 38 98
Competitive for feature
films, shorts,
retrospectives directed by
women and produced in
the previous 23 months
and not previously shown
in France

**Deauville European
Festival of
American Film** (Sept)
33 avenue MacMahon
75017 Paris
Tel: (33) 17 55 71 40
Non-competitive festival
of American feature films,
not yet released in Europe
(except UK), or shown in
other French film
festivals

**European
Environmental Film
Festival** (April)
55 rue de Varenne
75341 Paris Cedex
Festival of environmental
films

**French-American
Film Workshop**
(July)
23 rue de la Republique
84000 Avignon
Also held in New York
in November

**International
Festival of Film and
Television in Celtic
Countries** (March)
29 rue du Rosmeur
BP 6
29172 Douarnenez Cedex
Tel: (33) 98 92 97 23
Fax: (33) 98 92 09 21
10th festival was held in
Roscoff, Brittany

MIPCOM (Oct)
179 avenue Victor Hugo
75116 Paris
Tel: (331) 45 05 14 03
Fax: (331) 47 55 91 22

**MIP-TV
International TV
Programme Market**
(April)
179 avenue Victor Hugo
75116 Paris
Tel: (331) 45 05 14 03
Fax: (331) 47 55 91 22
Market for television
programmes, TV films
and video. Non-
competitive

**Montbéliard
International Video
and TV Festival**
(May)
Centre d'Action
Culturelle
12 rue du College
25204 Montbéliard
Tel: (33) 81 91 37 11/
81 91 49 67/81 91 09 23
Competitive for
documentaries, news,
fiction, art, animation,
music, computer graphics
produced during 18
months preceding festival

**Nantes Festival of
Three Continents**
(Nov-Dec)
BP 3306
44033 Nantes Cedex
Competitive film festival

**Paris Festival of
Science Fiction and
Fantasy Films
(+Market)** (Nov)
9 rue du Midi
92200 Neuilly
Tel: (33) 624 04 71/
745 62 31

Competitive for features
and shorts

**Rouen Festival du
Cinéma Nordique**
(March)
91 rue Crevier
76000 Rouen
Tel: (331) 35 98 28 46
Competitive festival of
Scandinavian films

GERMANY

**Berlin International
Film Festival** (Feb)
Budapester Strasse 50
D-1000 Berlin 30
Tel: (49) 30 254 89 0
Competitive for feature
films and shorts (up to
15 mins), plus a separate
competition for children's
films – feature length
and shorts – produced in
the previous year and not
entered for other
festivals. Also has non-
competitive programme
consisting of forum of
young cinema, film
market and an
information show

**European Low
Budget Film Forum**
(June)
Friedensallee 7
D-2000 Hamburg 50
Tel: (49) 40 390 4040
Fax: (49) 40 390 0142

Filmfest Dresden
Ermeler – Haus
Maerkisches Ufer 10
D-1020 Berlin
Tel: (37) 2 275 5103
Festival of independent
films

**Leipzig
International
Documentary,
Short Film and TV
Festival** (Nov)
D-1055 Berlin
Chodowieckistrasse 32
Leipzig
Tel: (37) 2 430 0617

**Lubeck Nordic Film
Days** (Nov)
Postfach 1889
D-2400 Lubeck
Tel: (49) 451 122 4105
Fax: (49) 451 122 1331
Festival of Scandinavian
films

**Mannheim
International
Filmweek** (Oct)
Stadt Mannheim
Rathaus E5
D-6800 Mannheim 1
Tel: (49) 621 192 2745
Competitive for first
features, documentaries,
short films, animation
and TV films, released in
the previous year not
previously shown in
W Germany

**Munich Film
Festival** (June-July)
München Filmwochen
Turkenstrasse 93
8000 München 40
Tel: (49) 89 39 3011/12
Non-competitive for
feature films, shorts and
documentaries which
have not previously been
shown in W Germany

**Oberhausen
International Short
Film Festival** (April)
Christian-Steger Strasse
10
4200 Oberhausen 1
Tel: (49) 208 825 2652
Competitive for social
documentaries (up to
60 mins), animation,
experimental and short
features (up to 35 mins),
student films, which have
been produced in the
previous 16 months and
not previously shown in
W Germany

**Prix Futura
International Radio
and TV Contest**
(April odd years)
Sender Freies Berlin
Masurenallee 8-14
D-1000 Berlin 19
Tel: (49) 30 308 2302
Competition for TV
programmes
(documentary and drama)
and radio (documentary
and drama) which were
first broadcast in the
preceding two years. Only
two entries per
organisation are accepted

**Prix Jeunesse
International
Television
Competition**
(May-June even
years only)
Bayerischer Rundfunk
Rundfunkplatz 1

D-8000 Munich 2
Tel: (49) 89 5900 2058
Competitive for TV drama, documentaries and music programmes, produced in the previous two years. Only two entries per organisation are accepted

Stuttgart International Animated Film Festival (Jan-Feb even years only)
Stuttgarter Trickfilmtage
Kernerstrasse 65
D-7000 Stuttgart 1
Competitive for animated short films of an artistic and experimental nature, which have been produced in the previous five years

HONG KONG
Hong Kong International Film Festival (April)
Level 7, Admin Building
Hong Kong Cultural Center
10 Salisbury Road
Tsim Sha Tsui
Hong Kong
Tel: (852) 734 29006
Fax: (852) 366 5206
Non-competitive for feature films, documentaries and invited short films, which have been produced in the previous two years

INDIA
Bombay International Film Festival for Documentary and Short Films (March)
c/o Films Division
Ministry of Information & Broadcasting
24 Dr Gopalrao Deshmuky Marg
Bombay 400 026
Tel: (91) 22 361461
Fax: (91) 22 4949751
Non-competitive festival devoted to the promotion of the Indian documentary film

International Film Festival of India (+Market)/ Filmotsav (Jan)
Directorate of Film Festivals
Lok Nayak Bhawan

Fourth Floor
Khan Market
New Delhi 110 003
Tel: (91) 11 697167
National Film Development Corporation
601-602 The Linen Hall
162 Regent Street
London W1R 5TB
Tel: 071 287 3723
Subi Lakshmanan
Held in New Delhi in odd years when it is competitive for feature films and shorts which have not been shown in competition elsewhere. In even numbered years it is non-competitive and held at various other locations. In 1990 it was held in Calcutta

ISRAEL
Jerusalem Film Festival (June)
PO Box 8561
Jerusalem 91083

ITALY
Cattolica International Mystery Festival – Mystfest (June-July)
Direzione Mystfest
Via dei Coronari 44
00186 Rome
Tel: (39) 6 656 7902
Competitive for television thrillers between 30-180 mins length, which have been produced in the previous year and not broadcast in Italy

Florence International Festival of Independent Cinema (May)
Via Martiri del Popolo 27
50122 Florence
Tel: (39) 55 24 58 69/ 24 36 51
Non-competitive for recent quality feature-length fiction films

Florence International Festival of Social Documentary Films – Festival dei Popoli (Nov-Dec)
Via Fiume 14
14-50123 Florence
Tel: (39) 55 21 27 71
Fax: (39) 55 21 36 98

Competitive for documentaries on sociological, political, anthropological, economic, folklore and ethnographic subjects. Plus a non-competitive information section. Entries must not have been released previously in Italy

MIFED (Milan) (April)
Largo Domodossola 1
CP 1270
20145 Milan
Tel: (39) 24 99 72 67
Fax: (39) 24 99 72 74
Competitive for films and television programmes on aspects of maritime activities, including technical, scientific, tourism, sports, energy research subjects. Entries must have been produced during three years preceding festival

Pesaro International Festival of New Cinema (+ Market) (June)
Via Yser 8
00198 Rome
Tel: (39) 6 36 95 24
Fax: (39) 6 62 45 96
Non-competitive for films from new directors, film groups and national cinemas

Pordenone Le Giornate del Cinema Muto (Sept-Oct)
Segretaria
Viale Grigoletti 20
33170 Pordenone
Tel: (39) 34038
Fax: (39) 98 04 58
Non-competitive silent film festival. Annual award for restoration and preservation of the silent film heritage

Prix Italia (Sept)
RAI Radiotelevisione Italiana
Via del Babuino 9
00187 Rome
Tel: (39) 6 86 27 97
Fax: (39) 6 05 27 97
Competitive for television and radio productions (up to 90 mins) from national broadcasting organisations. Only two productions per country accepted

Salerno International Film Festival (Oct)
Casella Postale 137
Salerno 84100
Tel: (39) 89 2 23 19 53
Fax: (39) 89 23 72 88
Competitive for scientific, medical, educational, animation, sponsored feature and documentary films

Taormina International Film Festival (July)
Via PS Mancini 12
00196 Rome
Tel: (39) 6 67 91 97
Competitive for directors of first and second feature films. Emphasis on new directors and cinema from developing countries

Turin International Youth Film Festival (Oct)
Via Cavour 19
10123 Turin
Tel: (39) 11 54 00 37/ 53 17 33
Non-competitive for films by and for young people made during the preceding 21 months and not screened commercially in Italy

La Biennale di Venezia (Aug-Sept)
Settore Cinema and Spettacolo Televisivo
Ca' Giustinian
San Marco
30124 Venice
Tel: (39) 45 20 03 11
Competitive for feature films which have not been shown at other festivals or released outside the country of origin. By invitation only

JAPAN
Hiroshima International Animation Festival (Aug)
11-1 Nakajima-cho
Naka-ku
Hiroshima 730
Tel: (81) 82 245 0145/46
Non-competitive for promotional material (up to 5 mins), student debut and work by independent filmmakers intended for public exhibition. Also includes works for

children and educational purposes

Tokyo International Film Festival
(Sept odd years only)
Organizing Committee
Asano Building No 3
2-14-19 Ginza Chuo-Ku
Tokyo 104
Tel: (81) 3 563 6305
Fax: (81) 3 536 310
Competitive international festival. Young cinema section for first films by young directors born in or after 1952. Films must have been produced during the 18 months prior to the festival, and not have won any award at events recognised by the IFFPA

Tokyo Video Festival (Sept)
c/o Victor Co of Japan
1 Nihombashi-Honcho
4 Chome
Chuo-ku
Tokyo 103
Michael Whyman
Video Information Centre
82 Piccadilly
London W1
Tel: 071 491 3909
Competitive for videos up to 20 mins in length

MALAYSIA
Asia-Pacific Film Festival (Oct-Nov)
c/o Malaysian Film Producers Association
9th Floor
Syed Kecik Foundation Building
Bangsar
Kuala Lumpur
Tel: (60) 3 947 066

MALTA
Golden Knight International Amateur Film & Video Festival (Nov)
Malta Amateur Cine Circle
PO Box 450
Valletta
Tel: (356) 442803/331095
Held in San Anton

MONACO
Monte Carlo International TV Festival (+ market)
(Feb)

CCAM Boulevard Louis II
98000 Monte Carlo
Tel: (3393) 304944
Fax: (3393) 250600

THE NETHERLANDS
Dutch Film Days
(Sept)
1990 Stichting Nederlandse Film-Tagen Hoogt
4 3512GW Utrecht
Tel: (31) 30 322 684
Fax: (31) 30 312 940

Stichting Film Festival Rotterdam
(Jan-Feb)
Kruishofkade 36b
3012 EJ Rotterdam
Tel: (31) 10 411 80 80
Non-competitive for feature films. Retrospective programmes

NEW ZEALAND
Auckland International Film Festival (July)
PO Box 1411
Auckland
Tel: (64) 933 629
Non-competitive for shorts (up to 45 mins) and feature films (up to 180 mins)

Wellington Film Festival (July)
PO Box 9544
Courtenay Place
Wellington
Tel: (64) 485 0162
Non-competitive for feature and short films not screened at festivals outside New Zealand. By invitation only

NORWAY
Nordic Film Festival
(March-April)
PO Box 356
4601 Kristiansand
Tel: (47) 421629
Fax: (47) 420390
Festival of feature films

Norwegian Film Festival (August)
PO Box 145
5501 Haugesund
Tel: (47) 428422
Competitive film festival

POLAND
Cracow International Festival of Short Films (May-June)
Pl Zwyciestwa 9
PO Box 127
00950 Warsaw
Tel: (48) 22 26 40 51
Competitive for short films (up to 30 mins), including documentaries, fiction, animation, popular science and experimental subjects, produced in the previous 15 months and not awarded prizes in other international festivals

PORTUGAL
Algarve International Film Festival (May)
Festival de Amigos
PO Box 8091
1801 Lisboa Codex
Held at Praia da Rocha in the Algarve

Cinanima (International Animated Film Festival) (Nov)
Organizing Committee 'Cinanima'
Apartado 43
4501 Espinho Codex
Portugal
Tel: (351) 2 72 16 21/ 72 46 11
Fax: (351) 2 72 60 15
Competitive for features, advertising, children, youth and experimental films. Also includes work by student directors. Entries must have been completed in the two years preceding festival

Figueira da Foz
(Sept)
Rua Luis de Camoes 106
2600 Vila Franca de Zira
Competitive film festival

Oporto Fantasporto (Feb)
Rua Diogo Brandao 87
4000 Oporto
Tel: (351) 2 32 07 59
Fax: (351) 2 38 36 79
Competitive section for feature films and shorts, produced in the previous three years. Also holds retrospectives, an information section and a

programme of Portuguese cinema

Troia International Film Festival (June)
2902 Setúbal Codex
Troia
Tel: 44121/44124
Fax: 44162
Film/TV/video festival and market

SINGAPORE
International Film Festival (Jan, biennial)
11 Keppel Hill
Singapore 0409
Fax: (65) 2722069

SPAIN
Barcelona Film Festival
Passefg de Garcia 47 3er 2a
08007 Barcelona
Tel: (34) 3 215 2424

Bilbao International Festival of Documentary and Short Films (Nov-Dec)
Colón de Larreátegui 37-40
48009 Bilbao
Tel: (34) 4 24 8698/ 16 5429/24 7860
Fax: (34) 4 42 3045
Competitive for documentary, animation, drama and experimental short films (up to 60 mins, except documentaries), produced in the previous two years, which have not won awards at other European festivals

Huesca International Short Film Festival (Nov)
Cortos – Ciudad de Huesca
Ricado de Arco 6
22003 Huesca
Tel: (34) 7 422 70 58
Competitive for short films (up to 30 mins) on any theme except tourism and promotion. Films which have won awards at other festivals are not eligible. Entries must have been produced in the previous two years

Madrid International Film Festival – Imagfic
(March-April)
Gran Via 62-8

Madrid 28013
Tel: (34) 1 241 3721/
241 5545
Fax: (34) 1 542 5495
Competitive for science
fiction and fantasy films

Murcia International Festival of Short Films (March)
Centro Cultural
Salzillo 7
30001 Murcia
Tel: (34) 6 821 7752/
6 871 2302
Competitive for fiction,
animation and
documentaries

Oviedo International Video-Film Festival
(July)
Nueve de Mayo 2-1 A
Oviedo 1
Tel: (34) 8 522 2096/7/
8 x30
Competitive for
programmes made on
video (up to 30 mins),
defence of nature
programmes (up to 45
mins) and feature films
recorded on video. Non-
competitive information
section

San Sebastián International Film and Video Festival
(Sept)
Apartado Correos 397
Reina Regenta s/n
20080 San Sebastian
Tel: (34) 4 342 96 25
Fax: (34) 4 328 59 79
Competitive for feature
films and shorts (up to
15 mins), produced in the
previous year and not
released in Spain or
shown in any other
festivals. Also section for
new directors

Seville International Film Festival (Oct)
Paseo de Colón II
Seville
Non-competitive for
features and shorts (up to
35 mins). Also holds
information and official
screenings and an
Andalusian film
competition

Sitges International Festival of Fantastic Cinema
(Oct)
Rambla Catalunya 81
Barcelona 08008
Tel: (34) 3 215 7491/
3 215 7317
Competitive for fantasy
and horror films and
shorts. Plus information
section and retrospective
programmes

Valencia Mediterranean Cinema Exhibition
(Oct)
Pl del Arzobispo 2acc
46003 Valencia
Tel: (34) 6 332 1506
Fax: (34) 6 331 5156
Competitive film festival
and market

SWEDEN

Gothenburg Film Festival (Jan-Feb)
Box 7079
S-402 32 Gothenburg
Tel: (46) 31 410546/
410547
Fax: (46) 31 410063/2
Non-competitive for
independent feature films
which have not been
released in Sweden

Uppsala International Film Festival (Oct)
Kulturforeningen for
Filmfestival i
Uppsala
Box 1746
75147 Uppsala
Tel: (46) 18 10 18 30
Fax: (46) 18 10 15 10
Competitive for shorts,
features and children's
films, fiction,
documentaries,
animation and
experimental (up to 60
mins). No advertising or
tourist films

SWITZERLAND

Festival of Third World Cinema (Jan)
Rue de l'Industrie 8
CH-1700 Fribourg
Tel: (41) 37 249 337
Fax: (41) 37 240 909

Geneva International Video Week (Nov)
Maison des Jeunes et de
la Culture
5 rue du Temple
CH-1201 Geneva
Competitive for original
work displaying an
individual approach (up
to 13 mins in length) and
made less than a year
before festival

Golden Rose of Montreux TV Festival (May)
Case Postale 97
CH-1820 Montreux
Secretariat de la Rose
d'Or de Montreux
Direction Generale de la
SSR
Giacomettistrasse 1-3
CH-3000 Berne 15
Tel: (41) 31 43 92 11
Fax: (41) 31 43 94 74
Competitive for TV
productions (24-60 mins)
of light entertainment,
music and variety, first
broadcast in the previous
14 months

Locarno International Film Festival (+ market)
(Aug)
Via della Posta G
CP 465
CH-6600 Locarno
Tel: (41) 93 32 02 32
Fax: (41) 93 31 74 65
Competitive for fiction
films by new directors and
TV movies, produced in
the previous year, which
have not won prizes at
other festivals. Plus
information and
retrospective programmes

Nyon International Documentary Film Festival (Oct)
PO Box 98
CH-1260 Nyon
Tel: (41) 22 61 60 60
Fax: (41) 22 61 071
Competitive documentary
film festival

Stars of Tomorrow
(June)
PO Box 418
CH-1211 Geneva
Tel: (41) 22 21 54 66
Fax: (41) 22 21 98 62
Competitive

Vevey International Comedy Film Festival (August)
44 avenue de Lausanne
CH-1201 Geneva
Tel: (41) 921 4825
Fax: (41) 731 0429

TAIWAN

Taipei International Film Exhibition (Oct)
Film Library
4/F 7 Ch'ingato East Road
Taipei

TUNISIA

International Film Festival of Carthage (Oct even years only)
The JCC Managing
Committee
PO Box 1029-1045
Tunis RP
Tel: (216) 1 262 034
Competitive for short and
full-length films by, or
concerned with, African
and Arab societies. Also
children's film section and
international film
market. Entries must
have been made within
two years before festival
and not have been
awarded a prize at any
previous festival in an
African or Arab country

TURKEY

Istanbul International Film Festival (March-April)
Istanbul Foundation for
Culture and Arts
Yildiz Kultur ve Sanat
Merkezi Beskitas
Istanbul
Tel: (90) 1 160 45 33
Fax: (90) 1 161 88 23
Annual competitive event
for features on the theme
of 'Cinema and the Arts'.
Entry by invitation

UNITED KINGDOM

Birmingham Film and Television Festival (Oct-Nov)
The Bond
180-182 Fazeley Street
Digbeth
Birmingham B5 5SE
Tel: 021 766 6707

Brighton Festival Media Programme

Duke of York's Cinema
Preston Circus
Brighton BN1 4AA
Tel: 0273 602503
Non-competitive thematic film festival with seminars/discussions with visiting directors and other professionals, screening retrospectives, previews, new releases and films directly from production companies abroad. Special interest in political and cultural issues

Cambridge Film Festival (July)

Arts Cinema
Market Passage
Cambridge CB2 3PF
Tel: 0223 462666
Non-competitive for feature films; some selected from other festivals, original choices, short retrospectives and revived classics

Edinburgh International Film Festival (Aug-Sept)

Filmhouse
88 Lothian Road
Edinburgh EH3 9BZ
Scotland
Tel: 031 228 6382/3
Fax: 031 229 5501
Non-competitive for feature films and shorts produced in the previous year. Plus retrospective programmes

Edinburgh International Television Festival

(Aug-Sept)
c/o EITF
5 Betterton Street
London WC2H 9BU
Conference discussing current issues in television, accompanied by screenings of television programmes grouped according to the themes/topics under discussion

Guildford Independent Video Festival (March-April)

13 Litchfield Way
Onslow Village
Guildford
Surrey
Non-competitive for video (max 20 mins) produced in and around West

Surrey. Work originated on other media is accepted, but final product must be on video

IVCA Film and Video Festival (June)

International Visual Communications Association (incorporating BISFA and ITVA)
Bolsover House
5-6 Clipstone Street
London W1P 7EB
Tel: 071 580 0962
Competitive for industrial/training films and videos, covering all aspects of the manufacturing and commercial world, plus categories for educational, environmental, leisure and communications subjects. Entries to have been produced or sponsored by a British company in the preceding 18 months

The International Animation Festival, Brighton (formerly the Bristol Animation Festival)

(Oct-Nov odd years only)
79 Wardour Street
London W1V 3PH
Tel: 071 287 1194
Fax: 071 287 2112
Non-competitive thematic festival. Entry by invitation only

International Festival of Film and TV in the Celtic Countries (Scotland, Wales, Ireland, Brittany – March peripatetic)

The Library
Farraline Park
Inverness IV1 1LS
Scotland
Tel: 0463 226189
Competitive for films whose subject matter has particular relevance to the Celtic nations

Leeds International Film Festival (Oct)

19 Wellington Street
Leeds LS1 4DG
Tel: 0532 463349
Fax: 0532 426761
Non-competitive for feature films and shorts, plus thematic retrospective programme

Leicester Super 8 Festival (Nov)

Leicester Film and Video Association
11 Newark Street
Leicester LE1 5SS
Tel: 0533 559711 x294
Non-competitive for Super 8 films, includes international retrospective and programmes of new work

London International Film Festival (Nov-Dec)

National Film Theatre
South Bank
London SE1 8XT
Tel: 071 928 0536
Non-competitive festival for feature films and shorts, by invitation only, which have not previously been released in Great Britain. Films are selected from other festivals, plus some original choices

National Festival of Independent Video

(Oct-Nov)
The Media Centre
South Hill Park
Bracknell
Berkshire RG12 4PA
Tel: 0344 427272
Non-competitive for educational, political, community and arts video. Entries must have been produced during previous 12 months

Piccadilly Film and Video Festival (June)

79 Wardour Street
London W1V 3PH
Fax: 071 497 8062

Southampton Film Festival (Feb-March)

Room 342
Civic Centre
Southampton SO9 4XF
Tel: 0703 223855
Non-competitive festival open to all categories

Tyneside Film Festival (Oct)

Tyneside Cinema
10-12 Pilgrim Street
Newcastle upon Tyne
Tel: 091 232 8289
Fax: 091 221 0535
Competitive for independent cinema from around the world, covering feature films, shorts and documentary

productions which have not had general cinema distribution

UK Horror Film Festival (biannual)

51 Thatch Leach Lane
Whitefield
Manchester M25 6EN
Tel: 061 766 2566
Non-competitive for horror and horror-related pre-release features with some shorts, produced in the previous year. Special guests. Plus retrospective programmes

USA

American Film Festival (May-June)

Educational Film Library Association
45 John Street
New York NY 10038
Competitive for films on all subjects, intended for non-theatrical use in educational institutions. Films must have been produced in the previous two years and be available for hire or sale in USA

American Film Institute Film Festival (Oct)

2021 N Western Avenue
Los Angeles CA 90027
Fax: (1) 213 462 4049

American Film Market – AFM

(Feb-March)
9000 Sunset Boulevard
Suite 516
Los Angeles CA 90069
Tel: (1) 213 275 3400
Fax: (1) 213 447 1666
Market for international film, TV and video

Asian American International Film Festival (July)

c/o Asian Cinevision
82 East Broadway
New York NY 10002
Tel: (1) 212 925 8685
Fax: (1) 212 925 8157

Athens Video Festival (Nov)

PO Box 388
Athens OH 45701
Tel: (1) 614 594 6888/
593 1330
Competitive for video including art, narrative, documentary, education

and video record. Entries must have been produced in two years preceding festival

Chicago International Film Festival (Oct-Nov)
415 North Dearborn Street
Chicago IL 60610
Tel: (1) 312 644 3400
Fax: (1) 312 644 0784
Competitive for feature films, shorts, animation, TV productions, student films and commercials

Cleveland International Film Festival (March-April)
6200 Som Center Road C20
Cleveland OH 44139
Tel: (1) 216 349 0270
Fax: (1) 216 349 0210
Non-competitive for feature, narrative, documentary, animation and experimental films

Denver International Film Festival (Oct)
999 Eighteenth Street
Suite 247
PO Box 17508
Denver CO 80217
Tel: (1) 303 298 8223
Fax: (1) 303 297 8326
Non-competitive mainly for independent material – features, shorts, documentary, animation and children's films. Entry by invitation only

Hawaii International Film Festival (Nov)
1777 East-West Road
Honolulu HA 96848
Tel: (1) 808 944 7666
Fax: (1) 808 944 7970

Houston International Film Festival (April)
PO Box 56566
Houston TX 77256
Tel: (1) 713 965 9955
Fax: (1) 713 965 9960
Competitive film festival

Los Angeles International Film Exposition – Filmex (April)
Berwin Entertainment Complex
6525 Sunset Boulevard
Hollywood CA 90028

7275
Tel: (1) 213 856 7707
Non-competitive for feature films, shorts, animation, documentary and experimental films – mostly by invitation

Miami Film Festival (Feb)
Film Society of Miami
7600 Red Road
Suite 307
Miami FL 33143
Tel: (1) 305 377 3456
Fax: (1) 305 577 9768
Non-competitive film festival

New York Film Festival (Sept-Oct)
140 West 65th Street
New York NY 10023
Tel: (1) 212 877 1800
Non-competitive for feature films, shorts (up to 30 mins), including drama, documentary, animation and experimental films. Films must have been produced in the 15 months prior to festival

New York International Film and TV Festival (Nov)
IFTF of New York Inc
5 West 37th Street
New York NY 10018
Tel: (1) 914 238 4481
Fax: (1) 914 238 5040
Competitive for industrial and educational films, filmstrips, shorts and commercials which have been produced in the previous year

Philadelphia International Film Festival (July)
121 North Broad Street
Suite 618
Philadelphia PA 10101
Tel: (1) 215 977 2831

San Francisco International Film Festival (March)
1560 Fillmore
San Fransicso CA 94115
Tel: (1) 415 567 4641
Fax: (1) 415 921 5032
Primarily non-competitive for features by invitation only. Also includes a competitive section for shorts, documentaries, animation, experimental

works, and TV productions

San Francisco Lesbian and Gay Film Festival (June)
Frameline
PO Box 14792
San Francisco CA 94114
Tel: (1) 415 861 5245
Features, documentary, short film and video

Seattle International Film Festival (May)
801 East Pine Street
Seattle WA 98122
Film and animation

US Film and Video Festival (April)
841 North Addison Avenue
Elmhurst IL 60126
Tel: (1) 312 834 7773
Competitive for films and videos produced during previous year

USSR

Moscow International Film Festival
(July odd years)
Sovinfest
State Committee for Cinematography of the USSR
10 Khokhlovsky Pereulok
Moscow 109028
Tel: (7) 95 297 7645
Competitive for feature films (up to 150 mins), shorts, children's films (up to 35 mins), produced in the previous two years. Plus a non-competitive section and an information programme

Tashkent International Film Festival of Asian, African and Latin American Countries (May)
1990 10 Khokhlovsky Pereulok
Moscow 109028
Tel: (7) 95 297 7645

YUGOSLAVIA

Belgrade International Film Festival (Jan-Feb)
Sava Centar
Milentija Popovica 9

11070 Belgrade
Tel: (38) 11 222 4961
Fax: (38) 11 222 1156

Pula Film Festival (July)
Festival Jugoslavenskog Igranog Filma Marka
Lagirije 5
52000 Pula

Zagreb World Festival of Animated Films
(June even years)
Nova Ves 18
41000 Zagreb
Tel: (38) 41 271 355
Fax: (38) 41 275 994
Competitive for animated films (up to 30 mins), educational children's films and first films categories. Films must have been completed in two years prior to festival and not have been awarded prizes at Annecy or Varna in the previous year

FILM SOCIETIES

Listed below are UK film societies which are open to the public, and those based in educational establishments and private companies and organisations (included in these listings for the first time). Addresses are grouped in broad geographical areas, along with the regional officers who can offer specific local information. There is a constant turnover of society officers, so if you are not certain whom to contact or your enquiry goes astray, you should contact the Film Society Unit at the BFI (see p 7)

BFFS CONSTITUENT GROUPS

The Film Society Unit exists to service the British Federation of Film Societies. The BFFS is divided into Constituent Groups which usually follow the borders of Regional Arts Associations, but sometimes include more than one RAA area

Eastern
Bedfordshire, Cambridgeshire, Ely, Essex, Hertfordshire, Huntingdon, Norfolk, Peterborough, Suffolk

Lincolnshire and Humberside
East Riding, Lincolnshire

London
Greater London Arts Association area

Midlands
Derby, Herefordshire, Leicestershire, Northamptonshire, Nottinghamshire, Shropshire, Staffordshire, Warwickshire, Worcestershire

North West
Cheshire, Lancashire, Northern Ireland

Northern
Cumberland, Durham, Northumberland, Westmoreland

Scotland

South West
Channel Islands, Cornwall, Devon, Dorset, Gloucestershire, Somerset, Wiltshire

Southern
Berkshire, Buckinghamshire, Hampshire, Isle of Wight, Kent, Oxfordshire, Surrey, Sussex

Wales

Yorkshire
North and West Ridings

EASTERN

BFFS Eastern Group
Mr Alan Barker
74 Paddock Drive
Springfield
Chelmsford
Essex

Bedford Film Society
Mr Derek Ebden
59 Greenshield Road
Bedford
Beds MK40 3TU

Berkhamsted Film Society
Dr C J S Davies
Seasons
Gardenfield Lane
Berkhamsted
Herts HP4 2NN

British Telecom Film Society
Mr A P Martin
Dept R181.1.1
BT Research Labs
Ipswich
Suffolk
IP5 7RE

Bury St Edmunds Film Society
Mr J W Garbutt
Sharon Livermere Road
Conyers Green
Bury St Edmunds
Suffolk IP31 2QG

CCAT Film Society
Ms Katharine Russell
CCAT Student Union
East Road
Cambridge CB1 1PT

Cambridge Union Film Society
Chairman
Film Committee
Bridge Street
Cambridge
CB2 1DB

Chelmsford Film Club
Mr Lawrence Islip
11 Sunningdale Road
Chelmsford
Essex CM1 2NH

Coopers' Company & Coborn School Film Society
Mr David Wynne-Jones
Coopers' Company &
Coborn School
St Mary's Lane
Upminster
Essex

University of East Anglia SU Film Society
Mr N Rayns
University of East Anglia

The Plain
Norwich
Norfolk NR4 7TJ

Ely Film Society
Mrs Jessica Keeley
28 Dovehouse Close
Ely
Cambs CB7 4BY

Epping Film Society
Mr A R Carr
58 Centre Drive
Epping
Essex CM16 4JE

University of Essex Film Society
Kitty Kahan/Peter Reyland
Students' Union Building
Wivenhoe Park
Colchester CO4 3SQ

Fermoy Centre Film Society
Mr A Wilkinson
27 King Street
Kings Lynn
Norfolk PE30 1HA

Great Yarmouth Film Society
Mr E C Hunt
21 Park Lane
Norwich
Norfolk NR2 3EE

Hatfield Polytechnic Film Society
Mr David Cowan, Drama Tutor
Wall Hall Campus
Aldenham
Watford
Hertfordshire

International University Film Society
Mr D B Rogalski
The Avenue
Bushey
Herts WD2 2LN

Ipswich Film Society
Mr Terry Cloke
4 Burlington Road
Ipswich
Suffolk IP1 2EU

Letchworth Film Society
Sean Boughton
29 Norton Road
Letchworth
Herts SG6 1AA

Malden Cinema Club
Administrator
Oakwood Arts Centre
Market Place
Malden
Essex CM9 6UA

Old Town Hall Film Society
Jackie Alexander
Old Town Hall Arts Centre
High Street
Hemel Hempstead
Herts HP1 3AE

Peterborough Film Society
Mr A J Bunch
196 Lincoln Road
Peterborough
Cambs PE1 2NQ

Playhouse Co-operative Film Society (Harlow)
Mrs S Herbert
72 Broadfields
Harlow
Essex CM20 3PT

Redtec Film Society
Mr Alan Barker
Redbridge Technical College
Little Heath
Romford
Essex

Towngate Theatre
Paul Steeples
Pagel Mead
Basildon
Essex

UDT Film Society
Mr T N Carolan
1 Lyonsdown Road
New Barnet
Herts EN5 1HU

Welwyn Garden City Film Society
Mr Michael Massey
3 Walden Place
Welwyn Garden City
Herts AL8 7PG

LINCOLNSHIRE AND HUMBERSIDE

BFFS Lincolnshire and Humberside Group
Mr G Dobson
Kennel Cottage
Burton

Nr Lincoln
Lincs

Lincoln Film Society
Mr M Bingham
27 Breedon Drive
Lincoln LN1 3XA

Stamford Schools' Film Society
Dr J P Slater
St Paul's Street
Stamford
Lincs PE9 2BS

LONDON

BFFS London Group
Mr M Sullivan
7 Contour House
663 London Road
North Cheam
Surrey SM3 9DF

Aquila Film Society
Mr M A Lever
Block 4, DGDQA
'Aquila' Golf Road
Bromley
Kent BR1 2JB

Australian Film Society
Mr S Hughes
'Eagle'
33 Delius Way
Stanford-le-Hope
Essex SS17 8RG

Avant-Garde Film Society
Mr C White
9 Elmbridge Drive
Ruislip
Middlesex HA4 7XD

BBC Film Club
Mr D Charlton
Room 2504
BBC TV Centre
Wood Lane
London W12 7RJ

BCC Sport and Social Club Film Society
Miss Janice Bullen
CIN Management
PO Box 10
London SW1X 7AD

BP Film Society
Mrs J Ireson
Britannic House
Moor Lane
London EC2Y 9BU

Barclays Bank Film Society
The Secretary
Fleetway House
25 Farringdon Street
London EC4A 4LP

Bowring Film Society
Ms D Woods
58 Beehive Lane
Redbridge
Ilford
Essex IG1 3RS

Brunel Film Society
The President
Brunel University
Uxbridge
Middlesex UB8 3PH

Channel 4 Film Society
Ms D Thorpe
Channel 4 Television
60 Charlotte Street
London W1P 2AX

Devotees of Hammer Video Unit
Mr Thomas Maylott
50 Dighton Court
John Ruskin Street
London

Durning Hall Film Society
Nim Njuguna
Durning Hall
Earlham Grove
Forest Gate
London E7 9AB

Gothique Film Society
Mr R James
75 Burns Avenue
Feltham
Middlesex TW14 9LX

Greenwich Film Society
Mr Stan Slaughter
11 Campana Road
Fulham
London SW6 4AS

Holborn Film Society
Mr Ray Mills
217c West End Lane
London NW6 1XJ

Hounslow Film Society
Mr B Walkinshaw
Civic Centre
Lampton Road
Hounslow
Middx TW3 4DN

ICRF Film Club
Ms Marie Fleetwood
Tis.Ant.Lab.
ICRF
PO Box 123
Lincoln's Inn Fields
London WC2A 3PX

Imperial College Union Film Society
Mr Martin Gans
c/o Dept of Civil
Engineering
Imperial College
Exhibition Road
South Kensington
London

Institut Français Film Society
The Secretary (Cinema
Dept)
17 Queensberry Place
London SW7 2DT

John Lewis Partnership Film Society
Mr P Allen
Social Secretary
4th Floor
4 Old Cavendish Street
London W1A 1EX

Kino Club
Katia Rossini
Fine Art, Film and Video
Dept
Central St Martin's
School of Art
Long Acre
London WC2

Lensbury Film Society
Mrs A Catto
Shell Centre
Room Y1085, York Road
Waterloo
London SE1 7NA

London Film Makers' Co-operative
Ms Moira Sweeney
The Cinema
42 Gloucester Avenue
London NW1

Middlesex Polytechnic SU Film Society
Ms Clare Squire
104w Gubbay Hall
Trent Park
Cockfosters Road
Barnet
Herts EN4 0PT

Mullard House Film Society
Ms L S Denny
Chairman
Mullard House
Torrington Place
London WC1E 7HD

NPL Film Society
Mr R Townsend
National Physical
Laboratory
Queens Road
Teddington
Middlesex TW11 0LW

North London Film Theatre
Miss B Underwood
7 Hillary Rise
Barnet
Herts
EN5 5AZ

Polish Social and Cultural Association
Mr A Ostaszewski
238-246 King Street
London W6 0RF

Polytechnic of Central London SU Film Society
Mr J Ronson
104-108 Bolsover Street
London W1P 7HF

Richmond Film Society
Mr N Wilson
94 Fifth Cross Road
Twickenham
Middx TW2 5LB

School of Oriental and African Studies Film Society
Mr Nigel Boyd
Thornhaugh Street
Russell Square
London WC1H 0XG

South London Film Society
Dr M Essex-Lopresti
14 Oakwood Park Road
Southgate
London N14 6QG

Southwark Arts Film Club
Ms Valerie Chang
Southwark Arts
186 Walworth Road
London SE17 1JJ

St George's Hospital Medical School
Mr Matthew Clarke
Cranmer Terrace
Tooting
London SW17

John Stanley Media Management
John Stanley
28 Nottingham Place
London W1M 3FD

Thames Polytechnic Film Society
Ms Sally Baldry
Students Union
Thomas Street
London SE18 6HU

Town and Country Club Film Society
Ms Joss Bates
9-17 Highgate Road
Kentish Town
London NW5

University College Union Film Society
Mr N McAlpine
University College
London
25 Gordon Street
London WC1H 0AH

Waltham Forest (Libs) Film Society
Mrs V Bates
William Morris Gallery
Lloyd Park
Forest Road
Walthamstow E17 4PP

Woolwich and District Co-op Film Society
Mr P Graham
10 Harden Court
Tamar Street
Charlton
London SE7 8DQ

MIDLANDS

BFFS Midlands Group
Mr P Collins
Beech Haven
Cobden Street
Wollaston
Stourbridge
Worcs

BGS Film Society
Dr D Savage
Fluid Processes Research
Group
British Geological Survey
Nottingham NG12 5GG

Bablake School Film Society
Mr J R Lawrence
Coventry School, Bablake
Coundon Road
Coventry CV1 4AU

Bishops Castle Film Society
Ms J Parker
4 Lavender Bank
Bishops Castle
Shropshire SY9 5BD

Central Television SSC Film Society
Mr G Lee
Central House
Broad Street
Birmingham B1 2JP

University of Keele Film Society
Mrs D Steele
Accounts Office
Students Union
Keele
Staffs ST5 5BJ

Kinver Film Society
Ms Pat Adams
38 Vicarage Road
Amblecote
Stourbridge
W Midlands DY8 4JD

Lion Street Cultural Centre Film Society
Richard Seabury
Lion Street
Oakengates
Telford
Shropshire TF2 6AQ

Loughborough Students Union Film Society
Union Building
Ashby Road
Loughborough
Leics

Ludlow and District Film Society
Mrs K Taylor
7 Castle View Terrace
Ludlow
Shropshire SY8 2NG

Malvern Film Society
Bob Fromer
Birchwood Hall
Storridge
Malvern
Worcestershire

New Kettering Film Society
Mr C J E Owen
4 Church Street
Cottingham
Market Harborough
Leics

Northampton Arts Centre Film Society
Mr Alan A Smith
College of F/E
Booth Lane South
Northampton NN3 4JR

Open Film Society
Gaynor Arrowsmith
c/o Maths Department
Open University
Walton Hall
Milton Keynes
Bucks MK7 6AA

Oundle School Snr Film Society
Mr Michael Aubrey
North Street
Oundle
Northants

Ross Film Society
Mrs B Laws
Meadow Cottage
Broad Oak
Hereford HR2 8QX

Shrewsbury Film Society
Mr B Mason
Pulley Lodge
Lower Pulley Lane
Bayston Hill
Shrewsbury
Shropshire

Solihull Film Society
Mr S Sharam
2 Coppice Road
Solihull
W Midlands B92 9JY

Stafford Film Society
Mrs A Paterson
22 Peel Street
Stafford
Staffs ST16 2DZ

Stourbridge Film Society
Mr G Holt
6 Bernwall Close
Stourbridge
West Midlands DY8 1SD

University of Warwick Film Society
Mr W Ingram
Secretary
Students Union
University of Warwick
Coventry CV4 7AL

Weston Coyney and Caverswall Film Society
Ms D Brassington
13 Green Lane
Blythe Bridge
Stoke-on-Trent ST11 9LZ

NORTH WEST

BFFS North West Group
Mr A Payne
18 Cecil Street
Lytham St Annes
Lancs FY8 5NN

Birkenhead Library Film Society
Mr H G Mortimer
Music Dept
Borough Road
Birkenhead
Merseyside L41 2XB

Black Sunday Horror Film Society
Mr David Bryan
51 Thatch Leach Lane
Whitefield
Manchester M25 6EN

Blackburn and District Film Society
Mr I Ibbotson
15 Gorse Road
Blackburn
Lancs BB2 6LY

Cheshire NALGO Film Society
Management Audit
Treasury
County Hall
Chester
Cheshire CH1 1SG

Chester Film Society
Mr G Mayled
19 Crofters Way
Saughall
Chester
Cheshire CH1 6AA

Chorley Film Society
Mr C Collison
21 Weldbank Lane
Chorley
Lancs PR7 3NG

Citadel Arts Centre Film Society
Paul Hogan/Robert Cave
Citadel Arts Centre
Waterloo Street
St Helens WA10 1PX

Daneside Film Society
Mr Mike Hales
Biddulph Old Hall
Biddulph
Staffs ST8 7SQ

Deeside Film Society
Mr C Ramsey Hewson
44 Albion Street
Wallasey
Merseyside L45 9JG

Ellesmere Port Library Film Society
Mr J G Fisher
Ellesmere Port Library
Civic Way
Ellesmere Port

Forum Film Society
Mrs M Holleran
Central Library
Wythenshawe
Manchester M22 5RT

Frodsham Film Society
Mr M F Donovan
58 The Willows
Frodsham
Cheshire WA6 7QS

Heswall Film Society
Mr P Reed
Stanton
90 Irby Road
Heswall
Wirral
Merseyside L61 6XG

Lancashire Polytechnic Film Society
Mr A Payne
18 Cecil Street
Lytham St Annes
Lancashire FY8 5NN

University of Lancaster Film Society
The President
Bowland Annexe
Bailrigg
Lancs LA1 4GT

Lytham St Annes Film Society
Mr A Payne
18 Cecil Street
Lytham St Annes
Lancs FY8 5NN

The MGS Film Society
Mr S V Leeming
The Manchester
Grammar School
Manchester
M13 0XT

Manchester and Salford Film Society
Mr H T Ainsworth
64 Egerton Road
Fallowfield
Manchester M14 6RA

Manchester University Film Society
Hon Secretary
Union Building
Oxford Road
Manchester M13 9PR

Manchester Women's Film Group
Ms E Gent
27 Thorpe Street
Old Trafford
Manchester M16 9PR

The Media Centre Film Society
Ms C Dahl
Leigh College
Railway Road
Leigh WN7 7AH

Merseyside Film Institute
Mr G Donaldson
45 Bluecoat Chambers
School Lane
Liverpool L1 3BX

Preston Film Society
Mr M Lockwood
14 Croftgate
Highgate Park
Fulwood
Preston
Lancs PR2 4LS

Runcorn Library Film Society
Mrs S Davies
Runcorn Library
Shopping City
Runcorn
Cheshire WA7 2PF

Saddleworth Film Society
Ms Sheila Watts
45 Oldham Road
Delph

Oldham
O13 5EB

The Society of Fantastic Films
Mr H Nadler
5 South Mesnesfield Road
Salford 7
Lancashire
M7 0QP

Southport Film Guild
Mike Ratcliffe
Rydings Farm
North Road
Bretherton
Southport
Merseyside

UMIST Union Film Society
Hon Secretary
PO Box 88
Sackville Street
Manchester M60 1QD

University of Ulster Film Society
Mrs J Rushton
c/o Estates Dept
Cromore Road
Coleraine
County Londonderry
N Ireland
BT52 1SA

Winnington Hall Club Film Society
Mr C Riemer
15 Hadrian Way
Sandiway
Northwich
Cheshire CW8 2JR

Workers' Film Association Film Society
Mr F Coker
WFA
9 Lucy Street
Old Trafford
Hulme
Manchester M15 4BX

NORTHERN

BFFS Northern Group

Centre Film Club
Mr R A Smith
20 Stanhope Grove
Acklam
Middlesbrough
Cleveland TS5 9SG

Cleveland Film Group
Mr Steven D Moses
45 Oxford Road

Linthorpe
Middlesbrough
Cleveland

Durham University Film Unit
The President
Dunelm House
New Elvet
Durham City

Elvet Film Society
Mrs Bryden
Durham University
Durham House
New Elvet
Durham DH1 3AN

Film Club at the Roxy
Ms Sue De Gryther
4 Three Bridges
Ulverston
Cumbria

Hartlepool Film Society
Mr A Gowing
6 Warkworth Drive
Hartlepool
Cleveland TS26 0EW

Newcastle Polytechnic SU Film Society
Mr Graham Ramsey
Union Building
2 Sandyford Road
Newcastle upon Tyne
NE1 8SB

Penrith Film Club
Mr B R Jimack
1 Beacon Edge
Penrith
Cumbria

201 Society (Durham)
Mr Michael Kkais
St Aidan's College
Windmill Hill
Durham DH1 3LJ

Wansbeck Film Theatre
Paul Maddison
17 Stead Lane
Bedlington
Northumberland

SCOTLAND

BFFS Scottish Group
Ms Helene Telford
6 Dickson Street
Edinburgh
EH6 8RL

Aberdeen University Film Society
The Film Society
Aberdeen University
Union
Broad Street
Aberdeen

Alternative Screen Film Society
Gale H Chrisman
Flat 4
10 Culduthel Road
Inverness IV2 4AG

Avondale Film Society
Mr Tom Goodwillie
3 Kirkhill Road
Strathaven
Lanarkshire ML10 6HN

Ayr & Craigie Film Society
Mr R J Currie
15A Carrick Road
Ayr KA7 2RA

Bank of Scotland Film Society
Mr H Boyd
Tax Department
PO Box 41
101 George Street
Edinburgh EH2 3JH

The Barony Film Society
Ms M Macivor
Top Flat
1 Lower Granton Road
Edinburgh EH5 3RS

Berwickshire Film Society
Mr E B Sykes
64 Castle Street
Duns
Berwickshire TD11 3DE

Broughton High School Film Society
Mr R Armstrong
Broughton High School
Carrington Road
Edinburgh EH4 1EG

Broughton High School Junior Film Society
Mr L Timson
Broughton High School
Carrington Road
Edinburgh EH4 1EG

Crieff Film Society
Ms M Thomson
Glenshira
Drummond Terrace

Crieff
Perthshire PH7 4AF

University of Dundee Film Society
Films Convener
Students Association
Airlie Place
Dundee DD1 4HN

East Kilbride Film Society
Mrs Barbara Perry
67 Cantieslaw Drive
Calderwood
East Kilbride G74 3AH

Edinburgh Film Guild
Mr Jim Dunningham
Secretary
The Filmhouse
88 Lothian Road
Edinburgh EH3 9BZ

Edinburgh University Film Society
Societies' Centre
60 The Pleasance
Edinburgh EH8 9TJ

Haldane Film Society
Mr A S Davis
12 Wylie Avenue
Burnbrae
Alexandria
Dumbartonshire G83 0AX

Lanarkshire Schools Film Society
Robert Stewart
Brannock High School
Loanhead Road
Newarthill
Motherwell
Strathclyde

Lewis Film Society
Mr D Ledbitter
14 Builnacraig Street
Stornoway
Isle of Lewis PA87 2RY

Linlithgow Film Society
Mr G Shinwell
90 Deanfield Road
Bo'ness
West Lothian EH51 0ER

Lloyds Bowmaker Film Club
Helen Watson
Finance House
Orchard Brae
Edinburgh

North Ayrshire Arts Centre
Mrs N Yuill
Sannox
Ardrossan Road
Seamill
W Kilbride
Ayrshire KA23 9LX

Robert Burns Centre Film Theatre
Kenneth Eggo
Dumfries Museum
The Observatory
Dumfries DG2 7SW

St Andrews University Film Society
Film/Theatre Convenor
Students Union Building
3 St Mary's Place
St Andrews
Fife KY16 9UZ

Scottish Office Film Society
Mrs L Cook
Room 6/118
Andrew's House
New Street
Edinburgh EH15 2EX

Shetland Film Club
Mr R Tait
Flat 3
The Old School
Cunningsburgh
Shetland Isles ZE2 9HB

Standard Life Film Society
Mrs Nancy Moore
5 North Lorimer Place
Cockenzie
East Lothian

University of Stirling Film Circle
The Secretary
Film/Media Department
Stirling
Scotland FK9 4LA

Strathclyde University Students Association Film Society
Michael Daly
Strathclyde University
SA
90 John Street
Glasgow

Trinity Academy Film Society
Mr T Ablett
c/o Trinity Academy
Craighall Avenue
Edinburgh EH6 4RT

Tweeddale Film Club
Mrs Jeanette Carlyle
23 Marchmont Road
Edinburgh EH9 1HX

SOUTH WEST

BFFS South West Group
Mr B Clay
1 Arbutus Close
Dorchester
Dorset DT1 1PZ

Bath Film Society
Ms Carole Sartain
c/o Royal Photographic Society
Milsom Street
Bath
Avon BA1 1DN

Bath Schools' Film Society
Mrs J Wheals
Oldfield Girls School
Kelston Road
Bath
Avon BA1 9AB

Bideford Film Club
Mr A Whittaker
Factory Cottage
Rope Walk
Bideford
Devon EX39 2NA

Blandford Forum Film Society
Mr J E England
6 Kings Road
Blandford Forum
Dorset DT11 7LD

Bournemouth and Poole College of Further Education Film Society
Mr T Baber
Learning Resources
The Lansdowne
Bournemouth BH1 3JJ

Bournemouth and Poole Film Society
Mrs C Stevenson
15 Milestone Road
Oakdale
Poole
Dorset BH15 3DR

Bridport Film Society
Mrs M Wood
Greenways
9 Bowhayes
Bridport
Dorset DT6 4EB

Bristol Student Films
The Chairman
University of Bristol
Students Union
Queens Road
Clifton
Bristol BS8 1LN

Cheltenham Film Society
Mrs G Sage
35 Bookway Road
Charlton Kings
Cheltenham
Glos

The Cinema at the Warehouse
Malcolm Young
33 East Street
Ilminster
Somerset

Dartington Arts Film Society
The Arts Officer
College of Arts
Dartington Hall
Totnes
Devon TQ9 6EJ

Dorchester Film Society
Catherine Dyer
12 Victoria Road
Dorchester
Dorset DT1

Exeter Film Society
Ms H James
16 Pavilion Place
Exeter
Devon EX2 4HR

Exeter University CinSoc
The President
Devonshire Houses
Stocker Road
Exeter
Devon EX4 4PZ

Falmouth School of Art/Design Student Union Film Club
Mr A Villalon
President
Woodlane
Falmouth TR11 4RA

Gloucester Film Society
Mr C Toomey
8 Garden Way
Longlevens
Gloucester GL2 9JL

Holsworthy Film Society
Ms C Wade

Belmont
Trewyn Road
Holsworthy
Devon

Lyme Regis Film Society
Ms Selina Hill
Chairperson
Sundial House
Marine Parade
Lyme Regis
Dorset DT7 3JQ

Merlin Theatre Film Society
Mr M Golder
c/o Merlin Theatre
Bath Road
Frome
Somerset BA11 2HQ

Mirage Film Society
Robert Lethbridge
King Alfred School
Burnham-on-Sea
Somerset

Real to Reel Film Society
Athos Pittordou
The Beaford Arts Centre
Beaford
Nr Winkleigh
Devon EX19 8LU

Rolle College Community Arts Group Film Society
Mr J Collins
Rolle College
2 Douglas Avenue
Exmouth
Devon EX8 2AT

Shaftesbury Arts Centre Film Society
Mr P Schilling
Sheepwash Cottage
Barton Mere
Warminster
Wilts BA12 6BR

Sherborne School Film Society
Mr A Swift
Abbey Road
Sherborne
Dorset DT9 3AP

Stroud and District Film Society
Mrs M G Allington
'Camelot'
East Drive
Ebley
Stroud
Glos GL5 4QF

Thornbury Film Society
Mr A J Gullick
9 Meadowside
Thornbury
Bristol BS12 2EN

Yeovil Cinematheque
Ms Nina Gilman
42 Bowden Road
Templecombe
Somerset

SOUTHERN

BFFS Southern Group
Mr D Smithers
1 Vanstone Cottages
Bagshot Road
Englefield Green
Egham
Surrey TW20 0RS

Abingdon College and District Film Society
Mr M Bloom
Abingdon College of FE
Northcourt Road
Abingdon
Oxon OX14 1NN

Amersham and Chesham Film Society
Mr D Goddard
9 Hospital Hill
Chesham
Bucks HP5 1PJ

Arundel Festival Film Society
Mrs Margaret Frankcom
Queens House
34A Tarrant Street
Arundel
West Sussex BN18 9DJ

The Ashcroft Arts Centre
Mr Richard Finch
Fareham and Gosport
Drama Centre
Osborn Road
Fareham
Hants PO16 7DX

Aylesbury Vale Film Society
Mr A Brockington
3 Kings Road
Aylesbury
Bucks HP21 7RR

Banbury Film Club
Matthew Holder
Laurel Cottage
North Newington
Nr Banbury

Barton Peveril College 6th Form Film Society
Mr T C Meaker
Cedar Road
Eastleigh
Hants SO5 5ZA

Bracknell Film Society
Mrs Shelagh Barnett
35 Spinis
Roman Wood
Bracknell
Berks RG12 4XA

Bradford on Avon Film Society
Neil McDougall
4 Wine Street
Bradford on Avon
Wiltshire

Charterhouse Film Society
Mr Christopher O'Neill
Brooke Hall
Charterhouse
Godalming
Surrey

Chertsey Film Society
Mr H Lawes
29 Sayes Court
Addlestone
Surrey KT15 1NA

Chichester City Film Society
Mr R Gibson
Westlands
Main Road
Hunston
Chichester
West Sussex PO20 6AL

Cranbrook Film Society
Mrs C Williams
1 Aurania Villas
Cranbrook Road
Hawkhurst
Kent

Cranleigh Film Society
Mr H B Hemingway
9 Hitherwood
Cranleigh
Surrey GU6 8BN

Ditchling Film Society
Mr G Hinckley
11 The Fieldway
Lewes Road
Ditchling
Hassocks
West Sussex BN6 8UA

Dover Film Society
Mr J Roy
68 Valley Road
Dover
Kent CT17 0QW

Eastbourne Film Society
Miss B Wilson
2 Chalk Farm Close
Willingdon
Eastbourne
East Sussex BN20 9HY

Eton College Film Society
Mr Adam Pettitt
2 Common Lane
Eton College
Windsor
Berks

Farnham Film Society at the Maltings
Mrs P M Woodroffe
c/o The Maltings
Bridge Square
Farnham
Surrey GU9 7QR

Faversham Film Society
Mrs V Cackett
15 South Road
Faversham
Kent ME13 7LR

Harwell Film Society
Ms J Allan
B150 AERE
Harwell
Didcot
Oxon OX11 0RA

Havant College Film Society
Mr P Turner
New Road
Havant
Hants PO9 1QL

Havant Film Society
Mrs P Stallworthy
The Old Town Hall
East Street
Havant
Hants PO9 1BS

Henley-on-Thames Film Society
Mr P Whitaker
10 St Andrews Road
Henley-on-Thames
Oxon RG9 1HP

Heythrop Park Film Society
Ms Trisha Clarke
National Westminster
Bank plc
Heythrop Park Staff
College
Chipping Norton
Oxon OX7 5UE

Horsham Film Society
Mr Norman Chapman
Farthings
King James Lane
Henfield
Sussex BN5 9ER

Intimate Cinema Film Society
Mr A J Henk
10 Aston Way
Epsom
Surrey

Isle of Wight Film Society
Mr D Havis
52 Victoria Avenue
Shanklin
Isle of Wight PO37 6LY

Jersey Film Society
Ms Fiona Emmett
7 Grouvill Park
Grouvill
Jersey
Channel Islands

Lancing College Film Society
Mr G Jones
Lancing College
Lancing
West Sussex BN15 0RW

Lewes Film Society
Ms Mary Burke
6 Friars Walk
Lewes
E Sussex BN7 2LE

Maidstone Film Society
Libby Bernard
2 Wjote Rock Court
Maidstone
Kent

Newbury Film Society
Mrs J Markham
19 Gloucester Road
Newbury
Berks RG14 5JF

Radley College Film Society
Mr C R Barker
Radley College
Abingdon

Oxon OX14 2HR

Reigate and Redhill Film Society
Mrs A Spice
17 Parkgate Road
Reigate
Surrey RH2 7JL

Rewley House Film Theatre Club
M J Shallis
Rewley House (Dept Ext Studies)
1 Wellington Square
Oxford OX1 2JA

Richmond College Film Society
Mr B Nevitt
Richmond College
Queen's Road
Richmond
Surrey

Royal Holloway and Bedford New College Student Union Film Society
Laura Corkell
70 Hythe Park Road
Egham
Surrey TW20 8DA

Salisbury Film Society
Mrs S Collier
45 St Ann Street
Salisbury
Wiltshire

Slough Co-Operative Film Society
Mr Simon Bishop
45 Ruscombe Gardens
Datchet
Slough
Berks

Southampton Film Theatre – The Phoenix
Dr Peter Street
24 The Parkway
Bassett
Southampton SO2 3PQ

Union Films, Southampton University
Martin Freeman
Southampton University Students' Union
Highfield
Southampton SO9 5NH

Stables Film Society
Stuart Rosen
23 Glebe Close
Little Common
Bexhill-on-Sea

Steyning Film Society
Mr W Martin
6 Elm Terrace
Elm Grove Lane
Steyning
West Sussex BN4 3RB

Oscar Film Unit, Surrey University
Mr A Noyce
University of Surrey (SU)
Guildford
Surrey GU2 5XH

Swindon Film Society
Mrs S Suchopar
The Limes
22 Oxford Street
Ramsbury
Marlborough
Wilts SN8 2PS

Trowbridge College Film Society
Ms Antoinette Midgley
Dept of General and

Social Studies
Trowbridge College
College Road
Trowbridge
Wiltshire BA14 0ES

Walton and Weybridge Film Society
Joan Westbrook
28 Eastwick Road
Walton on Thames
Surrey

West End Centre (Aldershot) Film Society
Ms J Bowden
West End Centre
Queens Road
Aldershot
Hants GU11 3JD

West Hoathly Film Society
Mrs W Cole
2 Fern Cottage
Sandy Lane
West Hoathly

West Kent College Film Society
Mr D B Davies
West Kent College of Further Education

Brook Street
Tonbridge
Kent TN9 2PN

**Winchester College
Film Society**
Mr P J M Roberty
Winchester College
Winchester SO23 9NA

**Winchester Film
Society**
Ms A Rushworth
1 Lower Farm Cottages
Owslebury
Winchester
Hants SO21 1JJ

**Windsor Arts
Centre Film Society**
Mr C Brooker
61 Sheet Street
Windsor
Berks SL4 1BY

**Woking's New
Cinema Club**
Mr A E Rozelaar
67 Lansdown Close
St Johns
Woking
Surrey GU21 1TG

**Wolfson College
Film Society**
Ms J C Denyer
Wolfson College
Oxford OX2 6UD

WALES

BFFS Welsh Group
Peter Richards
49 Coity Road
Bridgend
CF31 1LT

**Abergavenny Film
Society**
Mrs C Philips
Ty-Bryn
Tal-y-Doed
Monmouth
Gwent

**Canton Film
Appreciation Group**
Mr F Sharpe
c/o 235 Cowbridge Road
East
Canton
Cardiff CF1 9AL

**Fishguard Film
Society**
Ms J Worsley
Church Hill House
Treffgarne
Haverfordwest
Dyfed

**Gweithdy Fidio
Cymunedol Scrin**
Robin Williams
Gweithdy Scrin
Safle ATS
Ffordd Bangor
Caernarfon
Wales

**Haverfordwest Film
Society**
Mrs J Evans
Dyfed County Library
Dew Street
Haverfordwest
Dyfed SA16 1SU

**Monmouth Film
Society**
Mrs J M Waters
The Mount
83 Hereford Road
Monmouth
Gwent NP5 4JZ

Phoenix Film Club
Ms S Hallam
48 Barrack Hill
Newport
Gwent NP9 5FY

**Presteigne Film
Society**
Mr R Scadding
Llugw Farm
Llanbister Road
Llandrindod Wells
Powys

**Swansea Film
Society**
Mrs K Burrell
Cilhendre Cottage
Wernddu
Alltwen
Pontardawe
Swansea SA8 3HY

**Swansea
University College
Film Society**
The Secretary
Union House
University College
Singleton Park
Swansea

**Theatr Mwldan
Film Society**
Ms Helen Steel
Theatr Mwldan
Cardigan
Dyfed
Wales

YORKSHIRE

**BFFS Yorkshire
Group**
Mr Richard Fort

Yorkshire Group
8 Bradley Grove
Silsden
Keighley
West Yorkshire BD20
9LX

**Ampleforth Film
Society**
Rev S P Wright
Junior House
Ampleforth College
York YO6 4EN

Anvil Civic Cinema
Dr D Godin
Senior Film Officer
21 Charter Square
Sheffield S1 4HS

**University of
Bradford Union
Film Society**
The Secretary
Richmond Road
Bradford
West Yorkshire BD7 1DP

**Castle Hall Middle
School Film Society**
Mr J H C Cohen
Crowless Road
Mirfield
West Yorks

**Friends of the
Grange
Film Society for the
Disabled**
Mrs K A Ransome
50 Manor Park Road
Rawcliffe
York YO3 6UL

**Giggleswick School
Film Society**
Mr J R Pennell
Giggleswick School
Settle
N Yorkshire BD24 0DE

**Halifax Playhouse
Film Club**
Mr Paul S Cairns
23 Plane Tree Nest
Halifax
West Yorks HX2 7PR

**Harrogate Film
Society**
Mr P Caunt
19 Keats Walk
Harrogate
North Yorks HG1 3LN

**Hebden Bridge Film
Society**
Ms Sue Bower
Windyroyd

3 Stile Road
Todmorden
Lancs OL14 5NU

**Huddersfield and
District Film
Society**
Mr J E Cooper
43 St Helen's Gate
Almondbury
Huddersfield HD4 6SD

Ilkley Film Society
Mr R J Fort
8 Bradley Grove
Silsden
Keighley
West Yorks BD20 9LX

**Scarborough Film
Society**
Mr A E Davison
29 Peasholm Drive
Scarborough
North Yorks YO12 7NA

**Sheffield University
SU Film Unit**
Ms Yvonne Rippeth
Student Union
Sheffield University
Western Bank
Sheffield S10 2TG

**York University
Film Society**
Mr David Lowe
Students' Union
Goodricke College
Heslington
York HY01 5DD

Look what's on HTV

HTV has enjoyed over 22 years of awards and recognition since the day it won its first award, the ITV programme contract for Wales and the West of England on 10th June 1967.

At HTV, programme quality has always gone hand in hand with programme quantity and as well as building a close relationship with its viewers and serving its franchise area

with distinction, HTV has earned an international reputation.

Major films and drama featuring the biggest names from stage and screen have established HTV's reputation far beyond Wales and the West and have

led to the attainment of a Queen's Award for Export Achievement, the first ITV company to gain this accolade.

All in all it's an enviable record. From this firm foundation, HTV means to go on expanding and improving and to maintain its unique high standards in the increasingly competitive 1990's.

Attainment for Entertainment.

INTERNATIONAL SALES

These companies acquire the rights to audiovisual product for sale to foreign distributors in all media (see also Distributors Theatrical and Non-Theatrical p 126)

All American Leisure Group
6 Woodland Way
Petts Wood
Kent BR5 1ND
Tel: 0689 71535/71519
Fax: 0689 71519

Allied Vision
Avon House
360 Oxford Street
London W1N 9HA
Tel: 071 409 1984
Fax: 071 493 4286
Peter McRae

Arts Council of Great Britain
14 Great Peter Street
London SW1P 3NQ
Tel: 071 333 0100
Fax: 071 973 6590
Distributes Arts Council funded films such as *Science and Light: Joseph Wright of Derby, Hidden Heritage* and *Word of Mouth*. Also distributes films by independent producers including *Haydn's Creation, Hoppla* and *Brian Eno: Imaginary Landscapes.*
See also under Organisations

August Entertainment
Apt 10, Seven Dials Court
Shorts Gardens
London WC2H 9AP
Tel: 071 836 4412
Fax: 071 240 0249
Eleanor Powell
Emma Crawford
International sales agent for independent producers. Films include *Naked Tango, Glengarry Glen Ross, The Cotton Club, Babette's Feast*

Australian Film Commission
2nd Floor
Victory House
99-101 Regent Street
London W1R 7HB
Tel: 071 734 9383
Fax: 071 434 0170

BBC Enterprises
Woodlands
80 Wood Lane
London W12 0TT
Tel: 081 743 5588/576 2000
Fax: 081 749 0538
Commercial exploitation and export of BBC product, including books, records and programmes edited as videograms for consumer and educational markets. Also responsible for BBC television co-productions and BBC magazines ('Radio Times', 'BBC Wildlife', 'Fast Forward', 'BBC Good Food' and 'World')

BFI Production
29 Rathbone Street
London W1P 1AG
Tel: 071 636 5587
Fax: 071 580 9456
Sue Bruce-Smith
Sales and distribution of own BFI Production films *Silent Scream, Melancholia, Distant Voices, Still Lives, On the Black Hill, New Directors Shorts*

Jane Balfour Films
Burghley House
35 Fortess Road
London NW5 1AD
Tel: 071 267 5392
Fax: 071 267 4241
Jane Balfour
Mary Barlow
Ashley Luke
Distribution agent for Channel 4 and independent producers, handling drama, documentaries and specialised feature films

The Box Office
3 Market Mews
London W1Y 7HH
Tel: 071 499 3968
Fax: 071 491 0008
Paul Shields
TV product. London representatives for Channel 9, Australia and Hong Kong TVB

CBC Enterprises
43-51 Great Titchfield Street
London W1P 8DD
Tel: 071 580 0336
Fax: 071 323 5658
Susan Jolley
Sabine Kanngiesser
Yvonne Body
Véronique Vergès
The marketing division of Canadian Broadcasting Corporation and Société Radio-Canada

CBS Broadcast International Europe
1 Red Place
London W1Y 3RE
Tel: 071 355 4422
Fax: 071 355 4429
Sonja Mendes
Anne Hirsch
Wide range of US TV product

CTVC
Beeson's Yard
Bury Lane
Rickmansworth
Herts WD3 1DS
Tel: 0923 777933
Fax: 0923 896368
Peter Leeming
Programmes that explore areas of social concern, including dramas, documentaries and children's programming

Castle Target International
Avon House
360 Oxford Street
London W1N 9HA
Tel: 071 493 0440
Fax: 071 491 9049
Ric Phillips
An international distributor of quality feature films. Currently involved with *Buddy's Song, The Monk, That Summer of White Roses* and *Conspiracy*

Central Television Enterprises
35-38 Portman Square
London W1A 2HZ
Tel: 071 486 6688
Fax: 071 486 1707
Philip Jones
Anthony Utley
Evi Nicoupolis
Sale of all Central TV-produced films and TV

programmes, amounting currently to a 2,000-hour catalogue

Channel 4 International
60 Charlotte Street
London W1P 2AX
Tel: 071 631 4444
Fax: 071 580 2622
Jane Small
Where Channel 4 retains sales rights in its programmes, they are handled either through this in-house programme sales operation or through its approved distributors and sales agents. For film sales, see Film Four International

Chatsworth Television
97-99 Dean Street
London W1V 5RA
Tel: 071 734 4302
Fax: 071 437 3301
Halina Stratton
Extensive library of documentary and special interest films. Also Chatsworth-produced light entertainment, drama and adventure series

Colstar Communications and Entertainment
11 Wythburn Place
London W1H 5WL
Tel: 071 437 5725
Fax: 071 706 1704
International distributors of broadcast programming for all media; documentaries, short films, drama, programme specials and series. Library includes films and series on art, the sciences, history, sport and nature. Titles include *The National Gallery – A Private View* series, *Kenneth Clark's Romantic Classic Art* series, *The Wandering Company* (50 mins), *The Life and Times of Lord Mountbatten* series, *The Monkey's Paw* (30 mins), *The Man Who Loves Giants* (70 mins), *Journey to Australia's Inland Sea* (50 mins) and *The Most Dangerous Animal* (50 mins)

Columbia Pictures Television
19 Wells Street
London W1P 3FP
Tel: 071 637 8444
Fax: 071 528 8849
Nick Bingham
Production and co-production of TV product and international distribution of Columbia's and Tri-Star's feature films and TV product

Consolidated Distribution
5 Jubilee Place
London SW3 3TD
Tel: 071 376 5151/8
Fax: 071 225 2890
Worldwide distributor of films and television programming

CORI Distribution Group
19 Albemarle Street
London W1X 3HA
Tel: 071 493 7920
Fax: 071 493 8088
Marie Hoy
Fiona Mitchell
Bob Jenkins
Involved in international sales and co-production funding, with offices in London, Los Angeles, Tokyo and Vancouver. Recent acquisitions include the features *Dr. M*, *Torn Apart*, *Two Brothers Running*, and *The Boneyard*, the television drama special *Separation*, the children's special *Klondike Christmas* and the cartoon series *Wicked Willie*

Dee and Co
Suite 204
Canalot
222 Kensal Road
London W10 5BN
Tel: 081 960 2712
Fax: 081 960 2728
Drew Ellicott
Distributes film and television programmes. Catalogue contains selected award-winning titles under the headings wildlife, documentary and animation

The Walt Disney Company
31-32 Soho Square
London W1V 6AP
Tel: 071 734 8111

Fax: 071 734 5619
Etienne de Villiers
Ed Borgering
Worldwide television distribution arm of a major US production company

English Film Co (Exports)
6 Woodland Way
Petts Wood
Kent BR5 1ND
Tel: 0689 71535/71519
Fax: 0689 71519

Film Four International
60 Charlotte Street
London W1P 2AX
Tel: 071 631 4444
Fax: 071 580 2622
Bill Stephens
Heather Playford-Denman
Film sales arm of Channel 4, set up in 1984 to sell feature films which it finances or part-finances. Recent titles include *Paper Mask*, *December Bride*, *Bearskin*, *1871*, *The Fool* and *Ladder of Swords*

Gavin Film
120 Wardour Street
London W1V 3LA
Tel: 071 439 6655
Fax: 071 439 0472
Bill Gavin
International sales of feature films such as *Metropolitan*, *The Children*, *Strapless*, *Venus Peter* and *Prick Up Your Ears*

Glinwood Films
Swan House
52 Poland Street
London W1V 3DF
Tel: 071 437 1181
Fax: 071 494 0634
Terry Glinwood
Marie Vine
Sale of feature films such as *Insignificance*, *Merry Christmas Mr Lawrence*, *The Last Emperor*, *When The Wind Blows*, *Erik the Viking*, *Everybody Wins* and *The Sheltering Sky*

Global Television Services
1 Duke of York Street
St James's
London SW1Y 6JE
Tel: 071 839 5644
Fax: 071 839 4330
Tom Donald
Long-established TV and

video distribution company

Goldcrest Films and Television
36-44 Brewer Street
London W1R 3HP
Tel: 071 437 8696
Fax: 071 437 4448
John Quested
Thierry Wase-Bailey
Tony Murphy
Acquisition, sales, distribution and marketing of Goldcrest's film productions in all media worldwide

Golden Communications (Overseas)
47 Greek Street
London W1V 5LQ
Tel: 071 439 1431
David Shepperd
Part of the Golden Harvest Group responsible for selling the company's features: *High Road to China*, *Cannonball Run II*, *Teenage Mutant Hero Turtles*, *Lassiter*, *The Protector*, *Flying* and other projects

The Samuel Goldwyn Co
St George's House
14-17 Wells Street
London W1P 3FP
Tel: 071 436 5105
Fax: 071 580 6520
Diana Hawkins
Liz Elton
Gary Phillips
Offices in Los Angeles, London, New York. Acquisition, sales, distribution and marketing of films and television product worldwide. Recent film titles include *Longtime Companion*, *Object of Beauty* and *Stella*. Television product includes Goldwyn Classics Library and the Rodgers and Hammerstein Film Library

Grampian Television
Queen's Cross
Aberdeen AB9 2XJ
Tel: 0224 646464
Fax: 0224 635127
Michael J McLintock
North Scotland ITV station producing a wide

range of product including documentaries *The Energy Alternative*, *Too Many Widows* (on heart disease) and *Storm on the Mountain*. Children's animation *James the Cat* is available, as is extensive footage on the world's oil industry with large library of offshore material. Represented by ITEL

Granada Television International
36 Golden Square
London W1R 4AH
Tel: 071 734 8080
Fax: 071 494 6280
Vivien Wallace

HIT Communications
The Pump House
13-16 Jacob's Well Mews
London W1H 5PD
Tel: 071 224 1717
Fax: 071 224 1719
Peter Orton
Sophie Turner Laing
Jane Smith
Charles Cominada
Distributors of *Spitting Image's Winjin' Pom*, Harvey library of classic cartoons, *The Adventures of the Black Stallion*, *Mother Goose Rock 'n' Rhyme*, *Dream Patrol*, *RARG*, *Postman Pat*, *Metronome HIT Collection*, and *Bush Beat*

Hemdale
21 Albion Street
London W2 2AS
Tel: 071 724 1010
Fax: 071 724 9168
UK sales office of US production company. Titles include *Terminator*, *Platoon*, *The Last Emperor* and *Return of the Living Dead*

ITC Entertainment
24 Nutford Place
London W1H 4YN
Tel: 071 262 3262
Fax: 071 724 0160
Lynden Parry
Vickie Gubby
Distributors of *Night of the Fox*, *People Like Us*, *Fear Stalk*, *True Betrayal*, *Lethal Charm*, *Stepfather II*, *Poor Little Rich Girl* – The Barbara Hutton story, *Billionaire Boys Club*, *Windmills of the Gods*, *Without a Clue*, and

many other titles

Ideal Communications Films and Television
26 Soho Square
London W1V 5FJ
Tel: 071 494 0011
Fax: 071 287 8337
Kevin Christie
Co-production and sales company. For list of product, see under Production Companies

Ideal-Opix Sales
26 Soho Square
London W1V 5FJ
Tel: 071 494 0011
Fax: 071 287 8337
Aideen A Leonard
Distributes television programmes internationally, covering areas such as TV drama, feature films, music, light entertainment, arts and sport. Recent programmes include *Jensen's Canada*, *Calvi-God's Banker*, and *Champions – Where Are They Now?*

International Television Enterprises (ITEL)
48 Leicester Square
London WC2H 7FB
Tel: 071 491 1441
Fax: 071 493 7677
Andrew Macbean
Distribution and production development company representing Anglia TV, Anglia Films, ITN, Home Box Office, and Little Bird among others. Interested in co-production and the acquisition of programming for distribution. Representation in US through two full-time offices, and worldwide through a network of representatives. Works closely with producers at all stages of production and subsequent distribution

J & M Entertainment
2 Dorset Square
London NW1 6PU
Tel: 071 723 6544
Fax: 071 724 7541
Julia Palau
Michael Ryan
Michael Brawley

Anthony Miller
Specialise in sales of all media, distribution and marketing of independent feature films. Recent films are *Ironweed*, *Major League*, *Tales from the Dark Side*, *King's Whore*, and Clive Barker's *Nightbreed*

Liberty Films
The Forum
74-80 Camden Street
London NW1 0JL
Tel: 071 387 5733
Fax: 071 383 5368
John Kelleher
Distribution of films, video and television programmes to all media worldwide

Link Licensing
United Newspapers Building
23-27 Tudor Street
London EC4Y 0HR
Tel: 071 353 7305
Fax: 071 583 3479
Claire Derry
David Hamilton
Gillian Akester
Peter Woodhead
Specialists in children's programmes for worldwide distribution and character licensing. New properties include: *Barney*, *Count Duckula*, *What-a-Mess*, *Dogtanian*, *Penny Crayon*, *The Good Thing About . . .*

London Film Productions
44a Floral Street
London WC2E 9DA
Tel: 071 379 3366
Fax: 071 240 7065
Mark Shelmerdine
Rosie Bunting
Sheila Berry
Independent production and distribution company, with offices in London and LA. London Films offers a distribution and sales service to independent producers as well as selling its own productions

London Television Service
Hercules Road
London SE1 7DU
Tel: 071 261 8592
Fax: 071 928 5037
Sally Barrett
Distributors and producers of

documentaries worldwide including science and technology series *Perspective*

London Weekend Television International
South Bank Television Centre
London SE1 9LT
Tel: 071 620 1620
Fax: 071 928 8476
Sydney Perry
Sue Lytle
Colin Jarvis
Programme sales and distribution arm of London Weekend Television. Best-selling programmes include *Upstairs, Downstairs*, *Agatha Christie's Poirot*, *The Professionals*, *Bouquet of Barbed Wire* and *The Charmer*

MCA TV
1 Hamilton Mews
London W1V 9FF
Tel: 071 491 4666
Fax: 071 493 4702
Roger Cordjohn
Gabrielle Foy
Penny Craig
UK operation for the major US corporation which owns Universal Pictures

MGM/UA Television
see **Turner International**

McCann International Programme Marketing
68 Gloucester Place
London W1H 3HL
Tel: 071 224 4748
Fax: 071 487 5071
Andrew Luff
Jean Thompson
International distributors of drama series, TV movies, music, light entertainment, documentaries and children's programmes to broadcasters, cable and satellite operators and home-video distributors worldwide

Majestic Films International
Gloucester Mansions
Cambridge Circus
London WC2H 8HD

Tel: 071 836 8630
Fax: 071 836 5819
Guy East
Organises finance, sales, distribution and marketing of feature films throughout the world. Recent titles include *Driving Miss Daisy, Henry V, Last Exit to Brooklyn, Dances with Wolves, Until the End of the World* and *Once . . .*

Manifesto Film Sales
10 Livonia Street
London W1V 3PH
Tel: 071 287 4362
Fax: 071 437 9964
Wendy Palmer
Formed by Polygram International, Working Title and Propaganda Films to handle the sales and marketing of their films. Also some other acquisitions. Titles include *Chicago Joe and the Showgirl, Fools of Fortune, Daddy's Dyin' – Who's Got the Will?, Wild at Heart, Banton Fink*

NBD Pictures
Remo House
310-312 Regent Street
London W1R 5AJ
Tel: 071 499 9701
Nicky Davies
Ian Morris
Company specialising in music and entertainment programming, but broadening into features and drama. Clients include The Elvis Presley Estate, Warner Bros records, Lightyear, CBS Records International and Island Visual Arts

NVC Arts
The Forum
74-80 Camden Street
London NW1 0JL
Tel: 071 388 3833
Fax: 071 383 5332
Helen Asquith
Hazel Wright
Barbara Bellini-Witkowski
Producers and distributors of opera, ballet, dance, music specials and documentaries for television broadcast. Recent productions include Kenneth MacMillan's *The Prince of the Pagodas* and Werner

Herzog's *Giovanna D'Arco*

National Film Board of Canada
1 Grosvenor Square
London W1X 0AB
Tel: 071 629 9492 x3482
Fax: 071 495 8085
Jane Taylor
European agent for documentary, drama and animation productions from Canada's National Film Board

Nelson Entertainment International
8 Queen Street
London W1X 7PH
Tel: 071 493 3362
Fax: 071 409 0503
International sales for *When Harry Met Sally, Far North, Winter People, The Moderns, Destiny,* and *Queen of Hearts*

Orbit Films
14 Campden Hill Gardens
London W8 7AY
Tel: 071 221 5548
Fax: 071 727 0515
Chris Ranger
Gordon Pilkington
Specialises in vintage product from the first decade of American TV: *The Golden Years of Television*

Paramount Television
23 Berkeley House
Hay Hill
London W1X 8JB
Tel: 071 629 1150
Fax: 071 491 2086
Peter Cary

Perfect Features
78a Santos Road
London SW18 1NS
Tel: 081 877 9563
Fax: 081 877 0690
Grace Carley
Financing and sales of low-budget cult-type movies, including *Meet the Feebles, Deadline* and *Brain Dead*

Picture Music International
20 Manchester Square
London W1A 1ES
Tel: 071 486 4488
Fax: 071 465 0748
Dawn M Stevenson
Nigel Kennedy's performance of Vivaldi's Four Seasons – 1990's

Golden Rose of Montreux winner

Playpont Films
1-2 Ramillies Street
London W1V 1DF
Tel: 071 734 7792
Fax: 071 734 9288
Don Getz
Ellen Trost
International sales representatives for feature films and TV series. Titles include *Enemy, Tigers on Ice, Man Eaters, Five Card Stud, Flying Dutchman* and *Death Masque*

Richard Price Television Associates (RPTA)
Seymour Mews House
Seymour Mews
Wigmore Street
London W1H 9PE
Tel: 071 935 9000
Fax: 071 487 3975
Richard Price
RPTA distributes for over 100 producers

The Production Line Sales Co
Regal Chambers

51 Bancroft
Hitchin
Herts SG5 1LL
Tel: 0462 421818
Fax: 0462 420393
Film sales division of Medusa Communications. For list of product, see Medusa Pictures in Distributors

Radio Vision International
Avon House
360 Oxford Street
London W1N 9HA
Tel: 071 493 0439
Fax: 071 493 0421
Leading contemporary music distributors, specialising in live and recorded concerts including: *Nelson Mandela, Knebworth 1990 The Television Event, The Wall/Berlin 1990, Billy Joel – Live* and many others

Rank Film Distributors
127 Wardour Street
London W1V 4AD
Tel: 071 437 9020
Fax: 071 434 3689
Nicole Mackey

A library of 500 feature films plus TV series. Also 200 hours of colour programming from the Children's Film and Television Foundation. New product includes *Dead Ringers, Dealers, Scenes from the Class Struggle in Beverly Hills, Wilt, The Fabulous Baker Boys, Mannequin on the Move, Porky's Reunion,* and *Weekend at Bernie's*

Red Rooster Films
11-13 Macklin Street
London WC2B 5NH
Tel: 071 405 8147
Fax: 071 831 0679
Linda James
Feature film production and producers and distributors of quality television fiction and documentaries: *Joni Jones, And Pigs Might Fly, The Works, The Flea and the Giant, Hazel's Children, Coming Up Roses, Equinox: Earthquake Country, Just Ask for Diamond, Travelling Hopefully* and *The Gift*

S4C Enterprises
Sophia Close
Cardiff CF1 9XY
Tel: 0222 343421
Fax: 0222 341643
Christopher Grace
Teleri Roberts
Distributing programmes commissioned by S4C from independent producers and from HTV Cymru/Wales. Also distributes programming from the National and English Regions of the BBC, acting on behalf of BBC Enterprises

Safir Films
22 Soho Square
London W1V 5FJ
Tel: 071 734 5085
Fax: 071 734 1329
Lawrence Safir
Sidney Safir
Holds rights to a number of Australian, US and British pictures, including Sam Spiegel's *Betrayal*, Steve Jodrell's *Shame*, and the Romulus Classics comprising more than 30 titles such as *The African Queen, Moulin Rouge, Room at the Top* and *Beat the Devil*

The Sales Company
62 Shaftesbury Avenue
London W1V 7AA
Tel: 071 434 9061
Fax: 071 494 3293
Carole Myer
Alison Thompson
Penny Rigby
Formed October 1986 by British Screen, Palace and Zenith to represent their theatrical productions worldwide in all media. Recent films include *Dancin' Thru the Dark, Hardware, The Reflecting Skin, Harbour Beat, She's Been Away, American Friends, Miracle* and *The Big Man.* Also represent outside product such as *La captive du desert*

Scottish Television International
Cowcaddens
Glasgow G2 3PR
Tel: 041 332 9999
Fax: 041 332 6982
Jeffrey Henry
Sales of all programmes from Scottish Television

Screen Ventures
49 Goodge Street
London W1P 1FB
Tel: 071 580 7448
Fax: 071 631 1265
Dominic Saville
Christopher Mould
Specialise in international TV and video licensing of music specials with artists such as John Lennon, Jimi Hendrix, Chuck Berry, Jerry Lee Lewis, Otis Redding, B B King and Lou Reed. Sales agents for international independent producers, handling documentaries, current affairs and drama programmes.

Silverbach-Lazarus
South Bank Television Centre
Upper Ground
London SE1 9LT
Tel: 071 261 1284
Fax: 071 633 0412
George Blaug
UK base of SLG, Los Angeles. Properties include six TV movies and six mini-series from PBL Australia, *The Littlest Hobo* (114 half hours), and *The March of Time* (60 half hours) plus

wildlife documentaries

Smart Egg Pictures
62 Brompton Road
London SW3 1BW
Tel: 071 581 1841
Fax: 071 581 8998
Tom Sjoberg
Independent foreign sales company. Titles include *Spaced Invaders, Cameron's Closet, Double Revenge, Montenegro, The Coca-Cola Kid,* and *Operation Paratrooper*

D L Taffner (UK)
10 Bedford Square
London WC1B 3RA
Tel: 071 631 1184
Fax: 071 636 4571
Don Taffner
UK base of D L Taffner, New York (US representative of Thames TV International). International distributors of all types of TV material

Talbot Television
Greendon House
7c/d Bayham Street
London NW1 0EY
Tel: 071 380 1189
Fax: 071 383 5369
Anthony S Gruner
London arm of NY-based Fremantle Int. Produces and distributes game shows and light entertainment

Televentures
19-23 Wells Street
London W1P 3FP
Tel: 071 436 5720/5729
Fax: 071 409 3148
Ray Lewis
Representing: Stephen J Cannell Productions, Witt/Thomas/Harris Productions, Tri-Star Pictures

Television Entertainment
65 Blandford Street
London W1H 3AJ
Tel: 071 486 6626
Fax: 071 224 5385
Rod Allen
Noel Copley
Lynn James
Represents HTV, RTE, Channel Television, Partridge Films, Brook Productions, The Vision Group, Leo Dickinson and a number of independent producers worldwide

Telso International
84 Buckingham Gate
London SW1E 6PD
Tel: 071 976 7188
Fax: 071 976 7113/4
Ann Harris
Bernard Macleod
Properties include: *Granpa*, an enchanting half-hour animation from the producers of the legendary *The Snowman*, and *Perfect Scoundrels*, a comic drama series about two confidence tricksters

Thames Television International
149 Tottenham Court Road
London W1P 9LL
Tel: 071 387 9494
Fax: 071 388 6073
Mike Phillips
Roger Miron
Represents largest programme producer in ITV network and its subsidiaries Euston Films and Cosgrove Hall Productions in programme sales, co-productions, the non-theatrical and home video markets, publishing and merchandising. Also represents major UK independent, Tyburn Productions

Trans World International
TWI House
23 Eyot Gardens
London W6 9TN
Tel: 081 846 8070
Fax: 081 746 5334
Buzz Hornett
UK wing of the Mark McCormack Organisation, specialising in sport programming

Turner International
25 Old Burlington Street
London W1X 1LB
Tel: 071 434 4341
Fax: 071 434 9727
Howard Karshan
US production amd distribution company. Distributor of MGM, pre-1950 Warner Bros features and Turner series

Twentieth Century Fox Television
31-32 Soho Square
London W1

Tel: 071 437 7766
Fax: 071 439 1806/437 1625
Malcolm Vaughan
Sales of all Twentieth Century Fox product to TV worldwide

Tyne Tees Enterprises
15 Bloomsbury Square
London WC1A 2LJ
Tel: 071 405 8474
Fax: 071 242 2442
Ann Gillham
International sales division of Tyne Tees TV. Also represents the catalogues of TSW, Border TV and other independent producers

United Media Film Sales
14-17 Wells Mews
London W1A 1ET
Tel: 071 580 5586
Fax: 071 323 0464
John Wolstenholme
Acquisition, sales and marketing worldwide of quality feature films, including *The Krays* and *Cold Justice*

VATV
60-62 Margaret Street
London W1N 7FJ
Tel: 071 636 9421
Fax: 071 436 7426
David Llewellyn-Jones
As well as distributing its own product, the company represents other independent companies in the international market. Approved distributor for Channel 4 documentary and factual programmes

VCI Programme Sales
Strand VCI House
Caxton Way
Watford
Herts WD1 8UF
Tel: 0923 55558
Fax: 0923 816744
Kevin J Lagden
Lisa Gamble
A wholly owned subsidiary of the Video Collection International, responsible for all overseas activities. Distributes a wide variety of product from music, sport, educational, fitness, documentary and features. Has a joint venture partnership with ITN and distributes its product for video internationally

Viacom International
40 Conduit Street
London W1R 9FB
Tel: 071 434 4483
Fax: 071 439 0858
Peter Press
UK-based distribution operation for the US independent company. Current product includes *The Cosby Show* (sixth year), *Different World* (third year), *Roseanne* (second year), *Garry Shandling* (fourth year), *Jake and the Fatman* (third year), Perry Mason TV movie specials, plus an extensive library of theatrical and made-for-TV movies

Virgin Vision
5 Great Chapel Street
London W1V 3AG
Tel: 071 494 3756
Fax: 071 494 1235
Isabel Hughes

Visnews
Cumberland Avenue
London NW10 7EH
Tel: 081 965 7733
Fax: 081 965 0620
Syndication of international TV news sport, library footage and complete programmes

Warner Bros Television
(a division of Warner Bros Distributors)
135 Wardour Street
London W1V 4AP
Tel: 071 494 3710
Fax: 071 287 9086
Stuart B Graber
Includes Lorimar Telepictures product

Weintraub Screen Entertainment
167-169 Wardour Street
London W1V 3TA
Tel: 071 439 1790
Fax: 071 734 1509
Richard Milnes
A library of over 1500 titles from classic to contemporary: *Highlander*, *The Hitcher*, *Link*, *Clockwise*, *Sweet Dreams* and *Deadly Game*

Worldwide Television News Corporation
WTN House
31-36 Foley Street
London W1P 7LB
Tel: 071 323 3255
Fax: 071 580 1437
Keith Reynolds
Gerry O'Reilly
International TV news, features, sport, documentary programmes, *Earthfile* (an environmental programme series), *Healthfile*, weather, archive resources. Camera crews in major global locations, plus in-house broadcasting and production facilities

LABORATORIES

Bucks Motion Picture Laboratories
714 Banbury Avenue
Slough
Berks SL1 4LH
Tel: 0753 76611
Fax: 0753 691762
Full motion picture laboratory services, 35mm, 16mm, 8mm, filmstrips, photogard protective coating, Chromascan (tape to film). Specialist archive/ nitrate stock restoration services. Colour dubbing prints

Colour Film Services Group
10 Wadsworth Road
Perivale
Greenford
Middx
Tel: 081 998 2731
Fax: 081 997 8738
Full 35mm, 16mm and Super 16mm 24-hour laboratory services, handling all aspects of film work from feature films and TV programming to industrial shorts and commercials. In-house sound transfer and telecine mastering. Tape to film transfer to 35mm and 16mm. Bulk cassette duplication. Conference centre, equipment hire

Colour Tone Film Laboratories
PO Box 1098
Gerrards Cross
Bucks SL9 8DY
Tel: 02407 71513/4
Fax: 02407 71086
Film duplication for specialised distributors

Film and Photo Design
Motion Picture Laboratory
13 Colville Road
South Acton Industrial Estate
London W3 8BL
Tel: 081 992 0037
Fax: 081 993 2409
Specialists in shrunken nitrate preservation and 35mm and 16mm colour reversal printing and processing

Filmatic Laboratories/ Filmatic Television
16 Colville Road
London W11 2BS
Tel: 071 221 6081
Fax: 071 229 2718
Complete film processing laboratory and sound transfer service with full video post production facility including Digital Telecines, 1″ VTRs, Betacam SP and other video formats. On-line editing, duplication and standard conversion. Electronic Film Conforming (EFC), the system that produces the highest quality video masters from any original source, with frame accurate editing

Henderson Film Laboratories
18-20 St Dunstan's Road
South Norwood
London SE25 6EU
Tel: 081 653 2255
Fax: 081 653 9773
Full b/w laboratory service in 35mm and 16mm including b/w reversal processing in 16mm and Super 8. Blow-up to 16mm from 9.5mm and Std 8mm. Specialists in the handling of archive material, especially shrunken and nitrate film

London Film Makers' Co-operative
42 Gloucester Avenue
London NW1 8JD
Tel: 071 722 1728
16mm b/w processing

Metrocolor London
91-95 Gillespie Road
London N5 1LS
Tel: 071 226 4422
Fax: 071 359 2353
Full 16mm, Super 16mm and 35mm processing services, handling a range from 16mm short films through pop promos, commercials, BBC and ITV programmes to feature films, video mastering, sound transfer and stereo-optical camera

Rank Film Laboratories
North Orbital Road
Denham
Uxbridge
Middx UB9 5HQ
Tel: 0895 832323
Fax: 0895 833617
Principal laboratories at Denham in the UK and Film House in Toronto, Canada, with Satellite Laboratories at Manchester, Leeds and Glasgow. Full optical facilities available from General Screen Enterprises at Uxbridge. Large experienced sales and servicing personnel able to advise on and handle work in the theatrical, television, commercials and documentary markets. Recipient of two American Academy Awards for Technological Achievements

Studio Film and Video Group
8-14 Meard Street
London W1V 3HR
Tel: 071 437 0831
Fax: 071 734 9471
Full film processing facilities plus telecine transfer, mastering and video duplication. Film restoration and preservation (Film Clinic)

Technicolor
PO Box 7
Bath Road
West Drayton
Middx UB7 0DB
Tel: 081 759 5432
Fax: 081 759 6270
24-hour laboratory service, adjacent to London Heathrow Airport. Modern high speed plant caters for all formats: 16mm, 35mm, 70mm. Laboratories in Rome, Hollywood and New York

Universal Film and Video
Braintree Road
Ruislip
Middx HA4 0XP
Tel: 081 841 5101
Fax: 081 841 1406
Specialist 16mm film laboratory with overnight rushes service. Unitab: Video mastering directly from 16mm A & B roll cut negative and reversal masters in one generation. Facilities include four Rank Cintel 4:2:2 Digital Telecines with wet gates; two Rank Cintel III C Telecines; Beta SP, MII, 1″, D2; cassette duplication

LEGISLATION

The principal acts affecting the operation of the film and television industries in the UK are listed chronologically below with a brief explanation of their provisions. The list does not include statutory instruments by which the measures may be modified or implemented. All the items listed are published by HMSO and available in public reference libraries or through BFI Library Services. The more important measures are marked by ✳

CINEMA LEGISLATION

✳ Cinematograph Act, 1909
Provisions for licensing of exhibition premises and the safety of audiences. (The first Act of Parliament relating to cinema)

Celluloid and Cinematograph Film Act, 1922
Provisions for the prevention of fire in premises where raw celluloid or cinematograph film is stored or used

✳ Cinematograph Films Act, 1927
(repealed by Cinematograph Films Act, 1948)
Restrictions on blind booking and advance booking of films. Registration of films exhibited to the public. Provisions for securing a 'quota' of British films for renting by exhibitors

Sunday Entertainment Act, 1932
(amended by Sunday Cinema Act 1972)
Permits and regulates the opening and use of premises on Sundays for certain entertainments. Establishment of the Sunday Cinematograph Fund for 'encouraging the use and development of the cinematograph as a means of entertainment and instruction'. (This is the means by which the BFI was originally funded)

The Cinematograph Films (Animals) Act, 1937
Designed to prevent exhibition or distribution of films in which suffering may have been caused to animals

Cinematograph Films Act, 1938
(repealed by and consolidated in Films Act, 1960)
Renters' and exhibitors' quotas. Restrictions on blind and advance booking. Registration of films for public exhibition. Wages and conditions of people employed in production

Cinematograph Films Act, 1948
(repealed and consolidated in Films Act, 1960)
Provisions on quotas. Composition of Cinematograph Films Council

✳ Cinematograph Film Production (Special Loans) Act, 1949
Establishment of the National Film Finance Corporation

✳ British Film Institute Act, 1949
Provides for payment of grants to BFI from the Treasury as well as from the (Sunday) Cinematograph Fund (see also Sunday Cinema Act, 1972)

Cinematograph Film Production (Special Loans) Act, 1950
(repealed by Films Act, 1970)
Amends the 1949 Act

Cinematograph Film Production (Special Loans) Act, 1952
(repealed by Films Act, 1980)
Empowers the NFFC to borrow otherwise than from the Board of Trade

✳ Cinematograph Act, 1952
Extends the 1909 Act to cover exhibition premises using non-flam film and television. Control of cinema exhibition for children. Exemptions for non-commercial exhibition. Music and dancing licences not required for cinematograph exhibitions

Cinematograph Film Production (Special Loans) Act, 1954
Extended the period during which loans and advances may be made under The Cinematograph Film Productions (Special Loans) Acts, 1949 and 1952 and authorised the NFFC to enter into special arrangements on certain loans

✳ Cinematograph Films Act, 1957
(amended by Films Act, 1960)
Provides for a statutory levy on exhibitors to be collected by Customs and Excise and paid to the British Film Fund

Agency (to be established by Statutory Instrument). The BFFA to pay the resulting funds to makers of British films and to the Children's Film Foundation. This put the formerly voluntary levy, known as 'Eady Money' on a statutory footing. Amends law relating to National Film Finance Corporation, laying down its duty to pay its way and providing for its eventual dissolution under certain specified conditions

Cinematograph Films Act, 1960
(repealed by and consolidated in Films Act, 1960)
Extension of existing legislation with minor variations

✱ Films Act, 1960
(consolidates The Cinematograph Film Acts, 1938-1960. Repealed by Films Act, 1985)
Includes the up-to-date legislation on: quota;

registration: conditions for registration as British or foreign, renters' and exhibitors' licences; restrictions on blind and advance booking; registration of newsreels; wages and conditions of employment; powers of Board of Trade; constitution of The Cinematograph Films Council, amends the Copyright Act, 1956 as it relates to film; amends references to previous legislation in Cinematograph Films Act, 1957

Films Act, 1964
(repealed by Films Act, 1985)
Amends the Films Act, 1960 in its relation to newsreels

Films Act, 1966
(repealed by Films Act, 1985)
Extends and adjusts provisions of previous measures. Much of it subsequently repealed by Films Act, 1970

Films Act, 1970
(repealed by Films Act, 1985)
Extends functions of the National Film Finance Corporation. Imposes time limit of 1980 on all loan arrangements. Repeals various provisions of previous Acts

Sunday Cinema Act, 1972
Repeals certain sections of The Sunday Entertainments Act, 1932 and The British Film Institute Act, 1949. Winds up the Cinematograph Fund. Ends restrictions on Sunday opening of cinemas

European Communities Act, 1972
Community films not to be classed as foreign but as quota films under The Films Acts, 1960-1970

Cinematograph Films Act, 1975
(repealed by Films Act, 1980)

Films Act, 1979
(repealed by Films Act, 1985)
Amends Films Act, 1960 in relation to foreign films shown for at least eight weeks

✱ Films Act, 1980
(repealed by Films Act, 1985)
Extends functions of NFFC. Provides for Government grant of £1 million and write-off of accumulated outstanding capital and interest repayments. NFFC may borrow up to £5 million at any time. Extends levy and quota periods. Provides for aggregation of screen time for quota when more than one cinema in a building. Provides power to suspend quota by Statutory Instrument. (Note: Quota ended 1982)

National Film Finance Corporation Act, 1981

Consolidates The Cinematograph Film Production (Special Loans) Acts, 1949-1980 and makes certain changes in the operation of the NFFC

Film Levy Finance Act, 1981

Consolidates The Cinematograph Films Acts, 1957-1980. Contains provisions for a certain proportion of Eady Levy to be paid to the NFFC

Cinematograph (Amendment) Acts 1982

Extends the provisions of the 1909 Act to 'all exhibitions of moving pictures for private gain'. This brings pornographic cinema and video 'clubs' within the licensing requirements. Bona fide film societies and 'demonstrations' such as those used in video shops are excluded. Also excluded are exhibitions to provide information, education or instruction

Cinema Act, 1985

This consolidates the Cinematograph Acts 1909 to 1982. Licences are required for exhibition, and the Act lays down the procedure for application for and renewal of licences. Exempted exhibition includes exhibition in private dwelling houses, non-commercial shows and premises used only occasionally. The Act also specifies the conditions for Sunday opening

✱ Films Act, 1985

This Act repeals the Films Acts 1960 to 1980, abolishes the Cinematograph Films Council, ends Eady Levy and dissolves the National Film Finance Corporation. It makes provision for future Government financial assistance to the film industry – should Government decide

to provide such assistance. (In fact, the Government has agreed to provide £1.5 million for five years – extended for a further three years in 1990 – to the loan fund of the British Screen Finance Consortium which takes over from the NFFC and whose members include Screen Entertainment, Rank and Channel 4). The Register of Films, started by the Board of Trade in 1928, is to be discontinued

TELEVISION LEGISLATION

The rapid development of the new medium was foreseen in the Wireless Telegraphy Act, 1904 which reserved wide powers to the State for the regulation of wireless telegraphy. It was the first Wireless Act in the world and gave the Postmaster General the duty to license all wireless-telegraphy apparatus. The BBC was originally registered as a company (The British Broadcasting Co Ltd) in 1922 and received a licence from the Post Office in 1923. The present Corporation has never been a statutory body but has operated under a Royal Charter since 1926. The present Charter came into force on 1 August 1981 for 15 years. Subsequently developments in television have been covered by statutory measures and the principal ones are listed below

Television Act, 1954

Provides for a commercial television service from companies supervised by the Independent Television Authority (the ITA, later the IBA). Advertising was to be separated from programming, and requirements were laid down on the content of programmes

Copyright Act, 1956

Provides for copyright protection of broadcasting for the first time

Television Act, 1963

Extends the period for which the ITA should provide services until 1976

Television Act, 1964

Consolidates the 1954 and 1963 Acts

Sound Broadcasting Act, 1972

Extends the functions of the Independent Television Authority (ITA) to cover provision of local sound broadcasting services and renames it the Independent Broadcasting Authority (IBA)

Independent Broadcasting Authority Act, 1973

Consolidates the Television and Sound Broadcasting Acts, 1964 and 1972. Its provisions are essentially the same as those two Acts

Independent Broadcasting Authority Act, 1974

Makes further provision on payments to be made to the IBA by television programme contractors. The 'Exchequer Levy' payments are changed to a tax on profits instead of advertising revenue only

Independent Broadcasting Authority (No 2) Act, 1974

Extends the date until which IBA provides television and sound broadcasting services to 31 July 1979

Independent Broadcasting Authority Act, 1978

Extends the above functions to 31 December 1981. Removes prohibition on certain specified people from broadcasting opinions where opinion is expressed in proceedings of parliament or local authorities

Independent Broadcasting Authority Act, 1979

Confers power on IBA to transmit a fourth channel

Broadcasting Act, 1980

Extends IBA's functions to provision of programmes, but not advertisements, for the fourth channel. Extends IBA's function to 31 December 1996. Establishes a Broadcasting Complaints Commission

Broadcasting Act, 1981

Consolidates the Independent Broadcasting Authority Acts, 1973, 1974 and 1978 and the Broadcasting Act, 1980

Copyright (Amendment) Act, 1983

This act increases significantly the penalties for trading in and making pirate videocassettes, with heavier fines and possible prison sentences

Video Recordings Act, 1984

This Act requires the certification of all new video releases. In view of the large number of titles to be classified, the work was to be done in six phases, beginning on 1 September 1985 – from which date any new release on video has to have a certificate – and finishing on 1 September 1988, by which time the backlog of titles should have been classified

Cable and Broadcasting Act, 1984

This Act set up the new Cable Authority, following a second reading of the Cable and Broadcasting Bill, introduced in 1983. The Cable Authority has the job of selecting operators for particular areas on the basis of the range of services which they intend to offer, and of seeing that they then live up to their promises

ORGANISATIONS

Listed below are the main trade/government organisations and bodies relevant to the film and television industry. A separate list of the Regional Arts Associations is included at the end of this section

APRS – The Professional Recording Association
163a High Street
Rickmansworth
Herts WD3 1AY
Tel: 0923 772907
Fax: 0923 773079
Represents the interests of the professional recording industry, including radio, TV and video studios and companies providing equipment and services in the field. It runs the international APRS Exhibition held at Olympia, London each year

Advertising Association
Abford House
15 Wilton Road
London SW1V 1NJ
Tel: 071 828 2771
Fax: 071 931 0376
Contact: Information Officer
The Advertising Association is a federation of 29 trade associations and professional bodies representing advertisers, agencies, the advertising media and support services. It is the lobbying organisation for the UK advertising business, on British and European legislative proposals and other issues of common concern, both at national and international levels, and as such campaigns actively to maintain the freedom to advertise and to improve public attitudes to advertising. It publishes UK and European statistics on advertising expenditure, instigates research on advertising issues and organises seminars and courses for people in the communications business. Its Information Centre is one of the country's leading sources for advertising and associated subjects

Advertising Film and Videotape Producers' Association (AFVPA)
26 Noel Street
London W1V 3RD
Tel: 071 434 2651
Fax: 071 434 9002
Contact: Cecilia Garnett
The Association represents most producers of TV commercials. It negotiates with recognised trade unions, with the advertisers and agencies and also supplies a range of member services

Advertising Film Rights Society (AFRS)
26 Noel Street
London W1V 3RD
Tel: 071 434 2651
Fax: 071 434 2651
Contact: Wayne Fitzgerald
Negotiates on behalf of producer members to collect royalties for further uses of members' material, such as overseas cable and satellite usage, and any other media

Arts Council of Great Britain
Film, Video and Broadcasting
14 Great Peter Street
London SW1P 3NQ
Tel: 071 333 0100
Fax: 071 973 6590
Director: Rodney Wilson
Film and Video Officer: David Curtis
Film Education Services Officer: Will Bell
Film Sales Executive: Richard Gooderick
The Arts Council is funded by the Office of Arts and Libraries to encourage and support the arts. One of the means of achieving its objectives is the funding of documentary films on the arts intended for broad public use, particularly television and education. As an extension of its support for the visual arts, funds are available for the production, distribution and exhibition of artists' film and video

Arts Council of Northern Ireland
181a Stranmillis Road
Belfast BT9 5DU
Tel: 0232 381591
Fax: 0232 661715
Contact: Brian Ferran
The Northern Irish Arts Council is funded from the Department of Education for Northern Ireland and promotes film culture in the region by supporting the Queen's Film Theatre, assisting film societies and occasionally commissioning films on arts subjects

Association of Black Film and Video Workshops
Unit 215
22 Highbury Grove
London N5 2EA
Tel: 071 359 0302
The Association aims to represent and advance the interests of the black grant-aided sector in all areas of film and video production, distribution, training and exhibition, to initiate discussion and where relevant, policies on film culture, training and matters related to the grant-aided sector

Association of Cinematograph, Television and allied Technicians (ACTT)
111 Wardour Street
London W1V 4AY
Tel: 071 437 8506
Fax: 071 437 8268
General Secretary: Alan Sapper
The Association of Cine

Technicians was formed in 1933 and in 1956 TV and allied technicians were included. ACTT is a union which represents the interests of people employed in many aspects of film and TV. It negotiates agreements with bodies such as the Producers Association, ITCA, IPPA, AFVPA and MFVPA on behalf of its members, and is involved in lobbying for the film and broadcasting industries. Membership of the ACTT in either the freelance or the fully-employed sector is a useful credential for employment within the film and TV industries. See also Crews Employment Agency under Specialised Goods and Services

Association of Independent Cinemas (AIC)

Theatre One
Ford Street
Coventry
Tel: 0203 220446
Fax: 0203 550328
AIC was formed in 1953 to safeguard the interests of independent cinema owners against those exhibitors who are also involved in production or distribution. It is active on behalf of its 200 members on questions of barring and product allocation and, with the Producers Association, on copyright issues

Association of Professional Composers

34 Hanway Street
London W1P 9DE
Tel: 071 436 0919
Contact: Rosemary Dixson
APC represents composers from all sides of the profession – concert music, film, television, radio, theatre, electronic media, library music, jazz and so on. Its aims are to further the collective interests of its members and to inform and advise them on professional and artistic matters

Association of Professional Video Distributors

PO Box 25
Godalming
Surrey GU7 1PL
Tel: 04868 23429
Contact: Charles Potter MBE
Formed to improve the standards of the video industry with regard to the hardware by imposing professional discipline and controlling quality

Audio Visual Association

46 Manor View
London N3 2SR
Tel: 081 349 2429
Sandy Boyle
The Audio Visual Association is the only professional body which protects and enhances the interests of all parties involved in non-broadcast visual and audio media and communications within the UK, whether creative, technical, admin or supply

Australian Film Commission (AFC)

European Marketing Branch
2nd Floor, Victory House
99-101 Regent Street
London W1
Tel: 071 734 9383
Fax: 071 434 0170
The AFC is a statutory authority established in 1975 to assist the development, production and distribution of Australian films. The European marketing branch services producers and buyers, advises on co-productions and financing, and promotes the industry at markets and through festivals

British Academy of Film and Television Arts (BAFTA)

195 Piccadilly
London W1V 9LG
Tel: 071 734 0022
Fax: 071 734 1792
BAFTA was formed in 1946 by Britain's most eminent filmmakers as a non-profit making company. It aims to advance the art and technique of film and

television and encourage experiment and research. Membership is restricted to those who have made a creative contribution to the industry. BAFTA has facilities for screenings and discussion meetings, and makes representations to parliamentary committees. Its awards to the industries (Craft Awards and Production and Performance Awards) are annual televised events. The Academy has branches in Manchester, Glasgow, Cardiff and Los Angeles. See also under Awards and Preview Theatres

British Academy of Songwriters, Composers and Authors (BASCA)

34 Hanway Street
London W1P 9DE
Tel: 071 436 2261/2
Aims to assist both established and aspiring British songwriters with advice, guidance and encouragement. It issues standard contracts between publisher and songwriter

British Amateur Television Club (BATC)

Grenehurst
Pinewood Road
High Wycombe
Bucks HP12 4DD
BATC publish a quarterly technical publication 'CQV', which is only available via subscription, and covers television engineering at a constructional and practical level. The BATC also produce printed circuit boards for their projects which range from a simple fade to black to electronic test cards, SPGs and vision switchers

British Board of Film Classification (BBFC)

3 Soho Square
London W1V 5DE
Tel: 071 439 7961
Fax: 071 287 0141
The 1909 Cinematograph Films Act forced public

cinemas to be licensed by their local authority. Originally this was a safety precaution against fire risk but was soon interpreted by the local authorities as a way of censoring cinema owners' choice of films. In 1912, the British Board of Film Classification was established to impose a conformity of viewpoint: films cannot be shown in public in Britain unless they have the BBFC's certificate or the relevant local authorisation. The Board finances itself by charging a fee for the films it views. When viewing a film, the Board attempts to judge whether a film is liable to break the law, for example by depraving and corrupting a significant proportion of its likely audience. It then assesses whether there is material greatly and gratuitously offensive to a large number of people. The Board seeks to reflect contemporary public attitudes. There are no written rules but films are considered in the light of the above criteria, previous decisions and the examiners' personal judgement. It is the policy of the Board not to censor anything on political grounds. Five film categories came into effect in 1982, with the introduction of a '12' category in August 1989:

Universal:
Suitable for all

Parental Guidance:
Some scenes may be unsuitable for young children

Passed only for persons of 12 years and over

Passed only for persons of 15 years and over

Passed only for persons of 18 years and over

For Restricted Distribution only, through segregated premises to which no one under 18 years is admitted

The final decision, however, still lies with the local authority. In 1986 the GLC ceased to be the licensing authority for London cinemas, and these powers devolved to the Borough Councils. Sometimes films are passed by the BBFC and then banned by local authorities (*Straw Dogs*, *Caligula*). Others may have their categories altered (*Monty Python's Life of Brian*, *9½ Weeks*). Current newsreels are exempt from censorship. In 1985 the BBFC was designated by the Home Secretary as the authority responsible for classifying video works under the Video Recordings Act 1984. The film categories listed above are the basis for video classification

British Broadcasting Corporation (BBC)
Portland Place
London W1A 1AA
Tel: 071 580 4468
Fax: 071 636 9786
The BBC provides its radio and TV services under the auspices of the Home Office, which deals with legislative and constitutional aspects of broadcasting. See also under Television Companies

British Copyright Council
29-33 Berners Street
London W1P 4AA
Provides liaison between societies which represent the interest of those who own copyright in literature, music, drama and works of art, making representation to Government on behalf of its member societies

British Council
10 Spring Gardens
London SW1A 2BN

Tel: 071 930 8466
Contact: Brian Humphreys
11 Portland Place
London W1N 4EJ
Tel: 071 389 3065
Fax: 071 389 3199
As part of its work of promoting understanding of Britain in other countries, the British Council purchases films for showing by its offices in around 80 countries. It also selects the films for British film weeks and film festivals overseas. The British Council has a Film, TV and Video Advisory Committee chaired by Lord Brabourne. The British Council receives funds from the Foreign and Commonwealth Office and from the Overseas Development Administration

British Equity
8 Harley Street
London W1N 2AB
Tel: 071 636 6367/
637 9311
Fax: 071 580 0970
Equity was formed in 1930 by professional performers to achieve solutions to the problems of casual employment and short-term engagements. Equity has over 45,000 members, an increase by 35,000 since the 1950s. It represents performers (other than musicians), stage managers, stage directors, stage designers and choreographers in all spheres of work from variety and circus to television. It negotiates agreements on behalf of its members with producers' associations and other employers. In certain areas of work it has agreements with employers which regulate entry into the profession. In some fields of work only artists with previous professional experience are normally eligible for work. Membership of Equity is treated as evidence of professional experience under these agreements. It publishes a quarterly Equity Journal

British Federation of Film Societies (BFFS)
British Film Institute
21 Stephen Street
London W1P 1PL
Tel: 071 255 1444
Fax: 071 436 7950
The BFFS exists to promote the work of some 300 film societies in the UK. In 1982 the BFI set up the Film Society Unit to service the BFFS. See also p7

British Film Institute (BFI)
21 Stephen Street
London W1P 1PL
Tel: 071 255 1444
Fax: 071 436 7950
Founded in 1933, the BFI was incorporated by Royal Charter in 1983; its aim is to encourage the development of the art of film and TV. It is funded largely by a grant from the OAL. The BFI is involved in almost every aspect of film and television in Britain, through the Regional Film Theatre network including the National Film Theatre, a Distribution library, funding of film and video workshops, the preservation work of the National Film Archive, and a Production arm which makes both feature-length and short low-budget films. The BFI also publishes books and periodicals and acts as a centre for original research. The BFI Library and Stills, Posters and Designs Collection are unparalleled sources for the documentation of film and television history; highlights of these collections are on display in the prize-winning Museum of the Moving Image where the development of film and television is displayed from its earliest beginnings. For a full description of BFI activities, see pages 5-10

British Kinematograph, Sound and Television Society (BKSTS)
547-549 Victoria House

Vernon Place
London WC1B 4DJ
Tel: 071 242 8400
Fax: 071 405 3560
Contact: Ray Mobsby
British technicians formed this society in 1931 to keep in touch with major technical developments. The Society arranges regular meetings, where new equipment and techniques are demonstrated and discussions held. It also provides training courses and seminars for the industry and organises a biennial International Conference and Exhibition attended by delegates from all over the world. The monthly BKSTS journal, 'Image Technology', includes technical articles and reviews. Corporate members must hold responsible positions in film or TV. There is also an associate membership and a third membership for students

British Radio and Electronic Equipment Manufacturers' Association
Landseer House
19 Charing Cross Road
London WC2H 0ES
Tel: 071 930 3206
Fax: 071 839 4613
Trade association for British consumer electronics industry

British Screen Advisory Council
13 Bateman Street
London W1V 6EB
Tel: 071 437 9617/8
The BSAC is a non-statutory advisory body set up to replace the statutory-based Cinematograph Films Council and the non-statutory Interim Action Committee which were respectively abolished and wound up on the passing of the Films Act 1985. The Council is a broadly based industry body embracing film, television and video, meeting every month under the Chairmanship of Sir Richard

Attenborough to consider a number of industry questions

British Screen Finance (British Screen)

37-39 Oxford Street
London W1R 1RE
Tel: 071 434 0291
Fax: 071 434 9933
Since January 1986, British Screen, a private company aided by Government grant, has taken over the role and the business of the National Film Finance Corporation which was dissolved following the Films Act 1985. The Department of Trade and Industry has pledged support until the end of 1993. British Screen aims to support new talent in commercially viable productions which might find difficulty in attracting mainstream commercial funding. Between 1986 and 1990 i supported 44 productions and hopes to support a further 10 in 1990

British Tape Industry Association

Carolyn House
22-26 Dingwall Road
Croydon CR0 9XF
Tel: 081 681 1680
Trade association for the manufacturers of audio and videotape

British Universities Film and Video Council (BUFVC)

55 Greek Street
London W1V 5LR
Tel: 071 734 3687
Fax: 071 287 3914
Contact: Murray Weston
The BUFVC is an organisation with members in many institutions of higher education. It provides a number of services in the general area of production and use of film, television and other audiovisual materials for teaching and research and receives a grant from the Department of Education and Science for its work in the higher education sector. It operates a comprehensive

Information Service, produces a regular magazine 'Viewfinder', catalogues and other publications, such as the 'Researchers' Guide to British Film and Television Collections', organises conferences and seminars and distributes specialised film and video material. It maintains a preview service called the Audiovisual Reference Centre where visitors may see a wide range of items, mainly on videocassette.
Researchers in history come to the Council's offices to use the Slade Film History Register, with its information on British newsreels

British Videogram Association (BVA)

22 Poland Street
London W1V 3DD
Tel: 071 437 5722
Fax: 071 437 0477
Contact: N C B Abbott
The BVA represents the interests – with particular regard to copyright – of British producers and distributors of pre-recorded videocassettes and videodiscs

Broadcasters' Audience Research Board (BARB)

5th Floor, North Wing
Glenthorne House
Hammersmith Grove
London W6 0ND
Tel: 081 741 9110
Fax: 081 741 1943
Succeeding the Joint Industries' Committee on Television Audience Research (JICTAR), BARB commissions audience research on behalf of the BBC and ITV

Broadcasting and Entertainment Trades Alliance (BETA)

181-185 Wardour Street
London W1V 4BE
Tel: 071 439 7585
Fax: 071 434 3974
Contact: D A Hearn
BETA is the general trade union for the broadcasting and entertainment industry.

It was formed in early 1984 by the merger of the Association of Broadcasting Staff (ABS), and the National Association of Theatrical Television and Kine Employees (NATTKE). The origins of the latter go back to 1890. BETA's 31,000 members include staff in the BBC, independent broadcasting, film and video production (craft and general grades), cinema exhibition and theatre

Broadcasting Complaints Commission (BCC)

Grosvenor Gardens House
35-37 Grosvenor Gardens
London SW1W 0BS
Tel: 071 630 1966
A statutory body set up by the Home Secretary under the Broadcasting Act 1981 to consider complaints of unjust or unfair treatment or unwarranted infringement of privacy in television or radio programmes broadcast by the BBC, IBA or included in a licensed cable programme service

Broadcasting Press Guild

c/o Harvey Lee
25 Courthouse Gardens
Finchley
London N3 1PU
Tel: 081 346 0643
An association of journalists who write about TV and radio in national, regional and trade press. Membership by invitation

Broadcasting Research Unit

City University
Northampton Square
London EC1V 0HB
Tel: 071 253 4399 x3228/9
Fax: 071 250 0837
The Broadcasting Research Unit was set up in 1980 to initiate and implement research into issues related to broadcasting policy. The aim of BRU is to clarify complex issues and inform the decisions of broadcasters and policy-makers. In February 1988 BRU became an

independent company with charitable status, and then in April 1990 moved to City University. BRU is funded by a combination of core grants and individual project funding. BRU has developed a tradition of large-scale empirical investigation, particularly in the field of attitudinal surveys and cross-cultural studies. Recent and current topics of study include: methods of audience measurement, Channel 4, radio usage in the UK, images of disability on television, the use of schools' broadcasting, funding structures for broadcasters in several countries, standards of taste and decency on television, and the effects of deregulation on European broadcasting. A list of publications is available from the above address. Articles by BRU researchers appear regularly in newspapers and specialist press

Broadcasting Standards Council

5-8 The Sanctuary
London SW1P 3JS
Tel: 071 233 0544
Fax: 071 233 0397
In May 1988, the Home Secretary announced the establishment of the BSC to consider the portrayal of violence, of sex and matters of taste and decency in any television or radio programme or advertisement. Chaired by Lord Rees-Mogg, the Council has four main tasks: to draw up a Code of Practice, consider complaints, monitor programmes and undertake relevant research

CFL Vision

PO Box 35
Wetherby
Yorkshire LS23 7EX
Tel: 0937 541010
Fax: 0937 541083
CFL Vision began in 1927 as part of the Imperial Institute and is reputedly the oldest non-theatrical film library in the world. It is part of the COI and is the UK distributor for

their audiovisual productions as well as for a large number of programmes acquired from both public and private sectors. Over 2,000 titles are available for hire or purchase by schools, film societies and by industry

Cable Authority

Gillingham House
38-44 Gillingham Street
London SW1V 1HU
Tel: 071 821 6161
Fax: 071 821 5835
The Cable Authority was established under the Cable and Broadcasting Act 1984 to license and regulate the UK cable industry. The Authority awards franchises for the operation of large wide-band cable systems and shorter licences for smaller systems. It also draws up a number of codes of practice, dealing with programming issues and the conduct of advertising and sponsorship

The Cable Television Association

50 Frith Street
London W1V 5TE
Tel: 071 437 0549
Represents the interests of cable operators, installers, programme providers and equipment suppliers. For further information on cable, see under Cable and Satellite

Campaign for Press and Broadcasting Freedom

9 Poland Street
London W1V 3DG
Tel: 071 437 2795
A broad-based membership organisation campaigning for more diverse, accessible and accountable media in Britain, backed by the media unions. Established in 1979, it now incorporates the Campaign Against Racism in the Media (CARM), the Television Users Group (TUG) and is developing regional structures. Specialist groups deal with women's issues and media studies. CPBF publications cover

all aspects of the media from broadcasting policy to sexism; its bi-monthly journal 'Free Press' watches ethical, industrial and political developments, with regular supplements on topical issues; its video library includes Open Door films It Ain't Half Racist, Mum, Why Their News is Bad News, Making News and Wapping Lies. CPBF organises conferences, offering the public assistance in obtaining a right of reply against media bias or misrepresentation. It helped set up the educational project, Media Research Trust, and is promoting a Media Manifesto

Celtic Film and Television Association

The Library
Farrlaine Park
Inverness IV1 1LS
Tel: 0463 226189
Fax: 0463 237001
Development of film, TV and video production relevant to the languages of the Celtic nations and regions. Organises an annual competitive festival/conference, itinerant Scotland/Ireland/Wales/Brittany in March/April

Central Office of Information (COI)

Films and Television Division
Hercules Road
London SE1 7DU
Tel: 071 261 8500
Fax: 071 928 5037
Contact: Charles Skinner
COI Films and Television Division is responsible for government filmmaking on informational themes as well as the projection of Britain overseas. The COI organises the production of a wide range of documentary films, television programmes, video programmes and audiovisual presentations including videodisc production. It uses staff producers and draws on the film and video industry for production facilities. It provides help

to visiting overseas television teams

Centre for the Study of Communication and Culture

221 Goldhurst Terrace
London NW6 3EP
Tel: 071 328 2868
Fax: 071 372 1193
A Jesuit-founded centre which promotes inter-disciplinary applied research on the problems of modern communication. Particular attention is paid to issues affecting the Third World and to the field of religious communication

Children's Film and Television Foundation

Goldcrest Elstree Studios
Borehamwood
Herts WD6 1JG
Tel: 081 953 0844
Fax: 081 207 0860
In 1944 Lord Rank founded the Children's Entertainment Film Division to make films specifically for children. In 1951 this resulted in the setting up of the Children's Film Foundation (now CFTF), a non-profit making organisation which, up to 1981, was funded by an annual grant from the BFFA (Eady money). The CFTF no longer makes films from its own resources but, for suitable children's/family cinema/television projects, is prepared to consider financing script development for eventual production by commercial companies. Films from the Foundation's library are available for hiring at nominal charge in 35mm, 16mm and video format from Glenbuck Films, with overseas sales handled by Rank Film Distributors (see under Distributors and International Sales)

Church of England Broadcasting Department

Church House
Great Smith Street
London SW1P 3NZ

Tel: 071 222 9011 x356/7
(Out of office hours: 071 222 6672)
Contact: Rev Ronald Farrow
Responsible for liaison between the Church of England and the broadcasting and film industries. Advises the C of E on all matters relating to broadcasting

Cinema and Television Benevolent Fund (CTBF)

Royalty House
72 Dean Street
London W1V 6LT
Tel: 071 437 6567
Fax: 071 437 7186
The CTBF helps those in need who have worked in cinema and/or ITV industries

Cinema and Television Veterans

Pinewood Studios
Iver
Bucks SL0 0NH
Tel: 0753 651700
An association open to anyone with 30 years or more service in cinema and/or television

Cinema Exhibitors' Association of Great Britain and Ireland (CEA)

1st Floor
Royalty House
72-73 Dean Street
London W1V 5HB
Tel: 071 734 9551
The first branch of the industry to organise itself was the cinema owners, who formed the CEA in 1912. CEA members account for the vast majority of all UK commercial cinemas, including independents, Regional Film Theatres and a growing number of cinemas in local authority ownership. The Association represents members' interests both within the industry, and to Government – European, national and local. It has been closely involved with all recent and proposed legislation affecting exhibition coming from both the UK Government and the European Commission

Cinema Theatre Association

40 Winchester Street
London SW1V 4NF
Tel: 071 834 0549
Contact: Richard Gray
The Cinema Theatre Association was formed in 1967 to promote interest in Britain's cinema building legacy, in particular the magnificent movie palaces of the 1920s and 1930s. It is the only major organisation committed to cinema preservation in the UK. It campaigns for the protection of architecturally important cinemas and runs a comprehensive archive. The CTA publishes a bi-monthly bulletin and the magazine 'Picture House'

Commonwealth Broadcasting Association

Broadcasting House
London W1A 1AA
Tel: 071 927 5022
An association of 58 public service broadcasting organisations in 51 Commonwealth countries

Composers' Guild of Great Britain

34 Hanway Street
London W1P 9DE
Tel: 071 436 0007
The Guild represents composers of serious music, covering the stylistic spectrum from jazz to electronics. Although its main function is to safeguard and assist the professional interests of its members, it also provides information for those wishing to commission music and will put performers or societies in touch with composers

Confederation of Entertainment Unions (CEU)

Contact: John Morton via Musicians' Union
A confederation made up of the Federation of Broadcasting Unions (FBU), Federation of Film Unions (FFU) and Federation of Theatre Unions

Critics' Circle

Film Section
31 Hampstead Lane
London N6
Tel: 081 340 7862
Fax: 081 340 0003
Chairman: William Hall
Vice-Chairman: George Perry
Honorary Sec: Alan Frank
Honorary Treasurer: Peter Cargin
The film section of the Critics' Circle brings together most national and regional critics for meetings, functions and the presentation of annual awards

Deaf Broadcasting Council (DBC)

592 Kenilworth Road
Balsall Common
Coventry CV7 7DQ
Tel: 0203 832076
Fax: 0203 832150
Contact: Austin Reeves
An umbrella voluntary group working as a link between deaf people/organisations working for the deaf and the TV broadcasters – aiming for increased access to TV programmes

Defence Press and Broadcasting Committee

Room 2235
Ministry of Defence
Main Building
Whitehall
London SW1A 2HB
Tel: 071 218 2206
This committee is responsible for D notices. These give guidance on the publication of information which it regards as sensitive for reasons of national security

Department of Education and Science (DES)

Elizabeth House
York Road
London SE1 7PH
Tel: 071 934 9000
Fax: 071 934 9082
The DES is responsible for: policies for education in England; the Government's relations with universities in England, Scotland and Wales; fostering civil science

Department of Trade and Industry (DTI)

Kingsgate House
66-74 Victoria Street
London SW1E 6SW
Tel: 071 215 7877
Fax: 071 931 0397
The DTI is responsible for carrying out Government policy concerning the commercial and business aspects of the film, video and cinema industries including the film facilities sector; UK and EEC films legislation; OECD (Organisation for Economic Co-operation and Development) and GATT (General Agreement on Tariff and Trade) films interest. It is also responsible for the administration of co-production agreements and the certification of British films

Designers and Art Directors' Association

Nash House
12 Carlton House Terrace
London SW1Y 5AH
Tel: 071 839 2964
A professional association, registered as a charity, which publishes an annual of the best of British design, advertising, television commercials, pop promos/videos and organises travelling exhibitions. Membership is selected and only those who have had work accepted are eligible

Directors' Guild of Great Britain

1st Floor
Suffolk House
1-8 Whitfield Place
London W1P 5SF
Tel: 071 383 3858
Fax: 071 383 5175
Contact: Kevin Horlock
Represents interests and concerns of directors in all media

Educational Broadcasting Services, BBC

Villiers House
The Broadway
Ealing
London W5 2PA
Tel: 081 991 8037
Fax: 081 567 9356

Contact: Brian Wright
EBS supports the work of BBC Education radio and television production departments. It services the Educational Broadcasting Council representing professional users

Educational Television Association

The King's Manor
Exhibition Square
York Y01 2EP
Tel: 0904 433929
Contact: Josie Key
An umbrella organisation of institutions and individuals using TV for education and training. Award scheme and conference held annually. Membership enquiries welcome

Electrical Electronic Telecommunication and Plumbing Union (EETPU)

Hayes Court
West Common Road
Bromley BR2 7AU
Tel: 081 462 7755
Fax: 081 462 4959
A trade union representing – among others – people employed in film and TV lighting/electrical/electronic work

European Film Awards Permanent

Secretariat
Lietzenburger Strasse 44
D-1000 Berlin 30
Germany
Tel: (49) 30 261 1888/89
Fax: (49) 30 243 545

European Script Fund

39c Highbury Place
London N5 1QP
Tel: 071 226 9903
Fax: 071 354 2706
Contact: Renee Goddard
MEDIA 92 Script Development Fund based in London and supported by the BFI

The Federation Against Copyright Theft (FACT)

7 Victory Business Centre
Worton Road
Isleworth
Middlesex TW7 6ER
Tel: 081 568 6646
Fax: 081 560 6364

An organisation founded in 1982 by the legitimate film and video industry, dedicated to stamping out copyright piracy in the UK

Federation of Broadcasting Unions (FBU)
Contact: Paddy Leech, BETA
The FBU comprises Broadcasting and Entertainment Trades Alliance (BETA), Association of Cinematograph, Television and allied Technicians (ACTT), Musicians' Union (MU), British Actors' Equity, Electrical Electronic Telecommunication and Plumbing Union (EETPU), the NUJ and the Writers' Guild

Federation of Commercial Audio-Visual Libraries (FOCAL)
PO Box 422
Harrow
Middx HA1 3YN
Tel: 081 423 5833
Fax: 081 423 5833
Administrator: Anne Johnson
An international, non-profit making professional trade association representing commercial film/audiovisual libraries and interested individuals. Among other activities, it organises regular meetings, maximises copyright information, and produces a directory of libraries

Federation of Film Unions (FFU)
111 Wardour Street
London W1V 4AY
Tel: 071 437 8506
Secretary: Alan Sapper
Represents a group of unions in the entertainment industry devoted to film production. Each union is an independent and autonomous body coming together under the Federation. The unions are: ACTT, BETA, British Actors' Equity, Electrical, Electronics Telecommunication and

Plumbing Union, Film Artistes' Association, Musicians' Union and Writers' Guild of Great Britain

Feminist Library and Information Centre (formerly WRRC)
5 Westminster Bridge Road
London SE1 7XW
Tel: 071 928 7789
Has a large collection of fiction and non-fiction (books, pamphlets, papers etc) by and for all women. It also keeps an index of research by and on women and women's issues and information on women's studies courses. It holds a wide selection of journals and newsletters from all over the world and publishes its own newsletter. Open Tuesday (11.00-20.00) and Saturday and Sunday (14.00-17.00)

Ffilm Cymru
33 Castle Arcade
Cardiff CF1 2BW
Tel: 0222 340868
Fax: 0222 342235
Artistic Director: John Hefin
Director, Business Affairs: Richard J Staniforth
An organisation founded in 1988 by S4C and BBC Cymru to fund low budget feature films in Welsh, English and other European languages. Films completed: two 90-minute features *White Hall* and *Un Nos Ola Leuad (One Moonlit Night)*. Three further theatrical feature films in production

Film and Television Lighting Contractors Association
20 Darwin Close
New Southgate
London N11 1TA
Tel: 081 361 2122
Contact: A W Jacques
Set up in 1983 to negotiate with the EETPU on behalf of individual lighting contractors

Film Artistes' Association (FAA)
61 Marloes Road
London W8 6LF
Tel: 071 937 4567
The FAA represents extras, doubles, stand-ins and small part artistes. Under an agreement with the Producers Association and IPPA, supplies all background artistes in the major film studios and within a 40 mile radius of Charing Cross on all locations

Film Education
37-39 Oxford Street
London W1R 1RE
Tel: 071 434 9932
Fax: 071 434 9933
Ian Wall
Film Education is a film industry sponsored body. Its aims are to promote the use of film across the school curriculum and to further the use of cinemas by schools. To this end it publishes a variety of teaching materials – including study guides on individual films – and organises visits, lectures and seminars

Film Industry Council
c/o TPA
Paramount House
162-170 Wardour Street
London W1V 4LA
Tel: 071 434 7700
Fax: 071 734 4564
Contact: Andrew Patrick
Membership of FIC is open to recognised industry bodies only. Its purpose is to create a forum for industry discussion, to explore common interests, to achieve wherever possible a collective policy on key issues and problems and to represent the film industry with an effective political voice

First Film Foundation
Canalot Studios
222 Kensal Road
London W10 5BN
Tel: 071 969 5195
Fax: 071 960 6302
Contact: Deborah Burton
Set up to work with first time filmmakers in film and TV

German Film Board
Century House
4th Floor
100 Oxford Street
London W1N 9FB
Tel: 071 580 4422
Fax: 071 631 3049
Contact: Dina Lom
UK representative of the German film board, the official government organisation, and the German film export union, concerned with distribution and to a growing extent co-production

Guild of Animation
26 Noel Street
London W1V 3RD
Tel: 071 434 2651
Contact: Cecilia Garnett
Represents interests of producers of animated films. The AFVPA acts as secretariat for this association

Guild of British Camera Technicians
5-11 Taunton Road
Metropolitan Centre
Greenford
Middlesex UB6 8UQ
Tel: 081 578 9243
Fax: 081 575 5972
Contact: Julie Curran
ADUTG Consultant: Ron Bowyer (Eyepiece)
The Guild exists to further the professional interests of technicians working with motion picture cameras. Membership is restricted to those whose work brings them into direct contact with motion picture cameras and who can demonstrate competence in their particular field of work. They must also be members of the appropriate union. By setting certain minimum standards of skill for membership, the Guild seeks to encourage its members, especially newer entrants, to strive to improve their art. Through its publication, 'Eyepiece', GBCT disseminates information about latest developments in equipment and techniques

Guild of British Film Editors

c/o Alfred E Cox
Travair
Spurlands End Road
Great Kingshill
High Wycombe
Bucks HP15 6HY
Tel: 0494 712313
To ensure that the true value of film and sound editing is recognised as an important part of the creative and artistic aspects of film production

Guild of Television Cameramen

1 Churchill Road
Whitchurch
Tavistock
Devon PL19 9BU
The Guild was formed in 1972 'to ensure and preserve the professional status of the television cameramen and to establish, uphold and advance the standards of qualification and competence of cameramen'. The Guild is not a union and seeks to avoid political involvement

Home Office

50 Queen Anne's Gate
London SW1H 9AT
Tel: 071 273 3000
The Home Office deals with questions of policy on broadcasting, classification of videos, cinema licensing and obscenity, and issues exemption certificates under the Cinemas Act 1985. It also sponsors publicity and training films

Imperial War Museum

Department of Film
Lambeth Road
London SE1 6HZ
Tel: 071 416 5000
Fax: 071 416 5379
The Imperial War Museum illustrates and records all aspects of the two World Wars and other military operations involving Britain and the Commonwealth since 1914. It maintains an extensive archive of film and video material on a broad range of topics. The Museum offers research and viewing facilities which are extensively

used by film and television companies. It also promotes activities to do with film history and holds special seminars and conferences

Incorporated Society of British Advertisers (ISBA)

44 Hertford Street
London W1Y 8AE
Tel: 071 499 7502
Fax: 071 629 5355
Contact: Deborah Morris
The ISBA was founded in 1900 as an association for advertisers, both regional and national. Subscriptions are based on advertisers' expenditure and the main objective is the protection and advancement of the advertising interests of member firms. This involves organised representation, co-operation, action and exchange of information and experience, together with conferences, workshops and publications

Incorporated Society of Musicians

10 Stratford Place
London W1N 9AE
Tel: 071 629 4413/4302
Fax: 071 408 1538
Contact: Neil T E Hoyle
A professional association for all musicians: teachers, performers and conductors. The ISM produces various publications, including the monthly 'Music Journal', and gives advice to members on professional issues

Independent Broadcasting Authority (IBA)

70 Brompton Road
London SW3 1EY
Tel: 071 584 7011
Fax: 071 589 5533
The IBA operates under the Broadcasting Act 1981 and is the controlling body for Independent Local Radio, ITV and Channel 4. Its four main functions are to select and appoint the programme companies, supervise the programme planning, control the

advertising and to own and operate the transmitters

Independent Film Distributors' Association (IFDA)

c/o Glenbuck Films
Glenbuck Road
Surbiton
Surrey
Tel: 081 339 0022
Contact: Sid Brooks
The IFDA was formed in 1973, and its 18 members are mainly specialised film distributors who deal in both 16mm and 35mm from 'art' to 'popular music' films. They supply to many sources including schools

Independent Programme Producers' Association (IPPA)

50-51 Berwick Street
London W1A 4RD
Tel: 071 439 7034
Fax: 071 494 2700
IPPA is the trade association for British independent television producers, representing over 700 production companies based throughout the UK. Services to members include a specialist industrial relations unit and advice on all matters relating to independent production for television. Having led the successful campaign for 25% of all new British TV programmes to be made by independents, IPPA maintains an active lobby to ensure that the needs of the sector are heard and understood by Government in Britain and Europe

Independent Television Association (ITVA)

Knighton House
56 Mortimer Street
London W1N 8AN
Tel: 071 636 6866
Fax: 071 580 7892
Contact: Margaret Bassett
Incorporated as a company limited by guarantee, the ITVA is the organisation which provides a Central Secretariat to service the

needs of the industry requiring a co-ordinated and centralised approach. The governing body is the Council, comprising all the Managing Directors, and its main task is to determine the joint policy of the companies over a wide range of industry matters. Several committees – Network Programme, Industrial Relations, Marketing, Finance and General Purposes, Rights and Technical, supported by specialised sub-committees and working groups – undertake the detailed work

Indian Videogram Association

PO Box 230
London W2 1BN
Represents concerns of producers and distributors of Indian videos

Institute of Practitioners in Advertising (IPA)

44 Belgrave Square
London SW1X 8QS
Tel: 071 235 7020
Fax: 071 245 9904
The IPA is the representative body for UK advertising agencies and the people who work in them. It represents the collective views of its member agencies in liaison with Government departments, the media and industry and consumer organisations

International Association of Broadcasting Manufacturers (IABM)

4b High Street
Burnham
Slough SL1 7JH
Tel: 0628 667633
Fax: 0628 665882
Administrator: Alan Hirst
IABM aims to foster the interests of manufacturers of broadcast equipment from all countries. Areas of interest include liaison with broadcasters, standardisation and exhibitions. All companies active in the

field of broadcast equipment manufacturing are welcome to join

International Federation of the Phonographic Industry (IFPI)
IFPI Secretariat
54 Regent Street
London W1R 5PJ
Tel: 071 434 3521
Fax: 071 439 9166
An international association of over 900 members in 61 countries, representing the copyright interests of the sound recording and music video industries

International Institute of Communications
Tavistock House South
Tavistock Square
London WC1H 9LF
Tel: 071 388 0671
Fax: 071 380 0623
Contact: Victoria Rubensohn
The IIC provides a centre for the analysis of social, economic, political, cultural and legal issues related to media and electronic communication. It carries out research projects and consultancy, holds conferences and seminars and publishes books. UK members include BBC, IBA, C4 and many individuals. Its journal is 'InterMedia' which appears bi-monthly

International Visual Communications Association (IVCA)
Bolsover House
5-6 Clipstone Street
London W1P 7EB
Tel: 071 580 0962
Fax: 071 436 2606
Contact: Stuart Appleton
IVCA is the professional association providing a voice and a network for the promotion and use of screen communications. Among its membership services IVCA publishes a monthly magazine and runs the industry's premier festival

London Screenwriters' Workshop
1 Greek Street
London W1V 6NQ
Tel: 081 989 5199
Christina Jarvis
Promotes contact between screenwriters and producers, agents, development executives and other film and TV professionals through a wide range of seminars. Practical workshops provide training in all aspects of the screenwriting process. Membership is open to anyone interested in writing for film and TV, and to anyone in these and related media

Mechanical Copyright Protection Society (MCPS)
Elgar House
41 Streatham High Road
London SW16 1ER
Tel: 081 769 4400
Fax: 081 769 8792
Contact: Chéo Rhodes
Music copyright society whose functions include the clearance of music and record copyrights for film, video, and TV programme-makers. Production companies who want to use music in their films should contact the Licensing Department

Media Team of the Volunteer Centre UK
29 Lower Kings Road
Berkhamsted
Herts HP4 2AB
Tel: 0442 873311
Contact: James Ford Smith, Liz Schofield
The Media Team provides information, training and support for volunteers and voluntary organisations using broadcast media

Mental Health Film Council
380 Harrow Road
London W9 2HU
Tel: 071 286 2346
Contact: Sylvia Hines
An independent charity founded in 1965, the MHFC provides information, advice and

consultancy on film/video use and production relevant to mental health education. Newsletter, bi-monthly screenings, resource lists, videography available on annual subscription

Music Film and Video Producers' Association (MFVPA)
26 Noel Street
London W1V 3RD
Tel: 071 434 2651
Contact: Cecilia Garnett
The MFVPA was formed in 1985 to represent the interests of pop/music promo production companies. It negotiates agreements with bodies such as the BPI and ACTT on behalf of its members. Secretariat support is run through AFVPA

Music Publishers' Association
7th Floor
Kingsway House
103 Kingsway
London WC2B 6QX
Tel: 071 831 7591
Fax: 071 242 0612
The only trade association representing UK music publishers. List of members available at £3.00

Musicians' Union (MU)
60-62 Clapham Road
London SW9 0JJ
Tel: 071 582 5566
Fax: 071 582 9805
Contact: Don Smith
The MU represents the interests of performing musicians in all areas

National Association for Higher Education in Film and Video
c/o London International Film School
24 Shelton Street
London WC2H 9HP
Tel: 071 836 9642/240 0168
Contact: Martin Amstell
The Association's main aims are to act as a forum for debate on all aspects of film, video and TV education and to foster links with industry, the professions and Government bodies. It

was established in 1983 to represent all courses in the UK which offer a major practical study in film, video or TV at the higher educational level. Some 40 courses are currently in membership

National Audiovisual Aids Centre and Library (NAVAC)
The George Building
Normal College
Bangor
Gwynedd LL57 2PZ
Tel: 0248 370144
Fax: 0248 351415
NAVAC gives advice and information on the application of audiovisual resources, mainly in education. Offers films and videos for sale and hire

National Campaign for the Arts
Francis House
Francis Street
London SW1P 1DE
Tel: 071 828 4448
Fax: 071 828 5504
Director: Simon Mundy
Administrator: Kathryn Farrell
Research officer: Graham Hitchen
The NCA specialises in lobbying, campaigning (eg running the 'I Vote for the Arts' events at the last election, or the National Arts Advocacy Day), research and information. It provides up-to-the-minute facts and figures for politicians, journalists and any other interested parties. The NCA is independent of any political party or government agency and is funded solely by membership subscriptions and donations from arts organisations and individuals

National Council for Educational Technology (NCET)
Sir William Lyons Road
Science Park
University of Warwick
Coventry CV4 7EZ
Tel: 0203 416994
Fax: 0203 411418
A government-funded development agency for

Telefilm Canada; Your contact with the Canadian Film and Television Industry

The London Office can put you in touch with the key professionals in Canada's rapidly expanding film and television industry.

Telefilm Canada in London
55/59 Oxford Street
Fourth Floor
London W1R 1RD
Telephone : 071 437-8308
Fax : 071 734 8586

Head Office :
Montreal, Canada
Other offices in
Toronto, Vancouver,
Halifax, Los Angeles
and Paris.

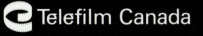

Telefilm Canada

promoting the application of educational technology (including new information technology) in all sectors of education and training. Merged in 1988 with the Microelectronics Education Support Unit

National Film and Television School
Beaconsfield Studios
Station Road
Beaconsfield
Bucks HP9 1LG
Tel: 0494 671234
Fax: 0494 674042
Director: Colin Young
The National Film and Television School provides advanced training and retraining in all major disciplines to professional standards. Graduates are entitled to ACTT membership on gaining employment. It is an autonomous non-profit making organisation funded by the Office of Arts and Libraries and the film and television industries. See also under Courses

National Film Development Fund (NFDF)
37-39 Oxford Street
London W1R 1RE
Tel: 071 434 0291
Fax: 071 434 9933
Administrator: Tessa Ross
The NFDF was set up in 1976 to make loans for the development of British cinema feature films. Funded originally from the Eady Levy, it has helped to develop such films as *Defence of the Realm, Dance with a Stranger, A Room with a View, Tree of Hands, Joyriders, A Very British Coup* and *Soursweet*. Under the 1985 Films Act, the fund receives £500,000 annually from the Department of Trade and Industry – £350,000 for the development of scripts and £150,000 for the production of short films. The NFDF is managed by British Screen Finance (the semi-privatised successor of the NFFC), but has a separate administrator

and panel of independent consultants

National Union of Journalists
314 Grays Inn Road
London WC1X 8DP
Tel: 071 278 7916
Fax: 071 837 8143
Contact: John Fray
NUJ represents all journalists working in broadcasting in the areas of news, sport, current affairs and features. It has agreements with all of the broadcasting companies and the BBC. It also has agreements with the main broadcasting agencies, WTN and Visnews with approximately 5,000 members in broadcasting

National Viewers' and Listeners' Association (NVALA)
Ardleigh
Colchester
Essex C07 7RH
Tel: 0206 230123
Contact: Mary Whitehouse
General Sec: John Beyer
Concerned with moral standards in the media, particularly the role of TV in the creation of social and cultural values

Network of Workshops
79 Wardour Street
London W1V 3TH
Tel: 071 494 1819
Contact: Cahal MacLaughlin
Network of independent film and video workshops franchised under the ACTT workshop declaration

Office of Arts and Libraries (OAL)
Horse Guards Road
London SW1P 3AL
Tel: 071 270 5865/6326
Within its wider concern with matters affecting the arts, museums and libraries, the OAL is the major source of government finance for film. It funds – among other bodies – the BFI and the Arts Council

Office of Fair Trading
Field House
Bream's Buildings
London EC4A 1PR
Tel: 071 242 2858
Fax: 071 269 8800
The Office of Fair Trading has an interest in the film industry following two reports on the supply of films for exhibition in cinemas – by the Monopolies Commission in October 1966 and by the Monopolies and Mergers Commission in 1983

Performers' Alliance
Consists of British Equity, Musicians' Union, Writers' Guild of Great Britain. Contact through member organisations above

Performing Right Society (PRS)
29-33 Berners Street
London W1P 4AA
Tel: 071 580 5544
Fax: 071 631 4138
The PRS is a non-profit making association of composers, authors and publishers of musical works. It collects and distributes royalties for the use, in public performances, broadcasts and cable programmes, of its members' copyright music and has links with other performing right societies throughout the world. Explanatory literature and/or a film explaining the Society's operations is available from the Public Relations Department

Phonographic Performance
Ganton House
14-22 Ganton Street
London W1V ILB
Tel: 071 437 0311
Fax: 071 734 9797
Formed by the British recording industry for the collection and distribution of revenue in respect of the UK public performance and broadcasting of sound recordings

The Producers Association
162-170 Wardour Street
London W1V 4LA
Tel: 071 437 7700
Fax: 071 734 4564
Contact: John Woodward
The Producers Association was formed out of a merger between the British Film and Television Producers' Association (BFTPA) and the Association of Independent Producers (AIP) in 1990. The Producers Association is the leading British trade association representing UK-based feature film and television producers in Britain and abroad. It works to secure the future for film and TV production in the UK ensuring liaison with BBC, ITV and Channel 4. It runs an industrial relations service with IPPA which negotiates and maintains trade union agreements and provides detailed information to producers on the interpretation of agreements etc. It provides a wide range of information services, publishes handbooks and the magazine 'Producer', and offers international marketing advice, British Overseas Trade Board subvention schemes and acts as the UK contact for the EEC-backed Euro-Aim distribution network

Radio, Electrical and Television Retailers' Association (RETRA)
Retra House
St John's Terrace
1 Ampthill Street
Bedford MK42 9EY
Tel: 0234 269110
Fax: 0234 269609
Contact: Anthony Gallagher
The Association was founded in 1942 to represent the interests of independent electrical dealers to all those who make decisions likely to affect the selling and servicing of electrical and electronic products

Royal Television Society (RTS)

Tavistock House East
Tavistock Square
London WC1H 9HR
Tel: 071 387 1970
Fax: 071 387 0358
Contact: Tracey Dyer
The Royal Television
Society, founded in 1927,
has over 3,000 members
in the UK and overseas,
half of which are serviced
by the Society's 14
regional centres. The
Society aims to bring
together all the
disciplines of television by
providing a forum for
debate on the technical,
cultural and social
implications of the
medium. This is achieved
through the many
lectures, conferences,
symposia and training
courses organised each
year. A monthly journal
'Television' is published
by the RTS as well as
monographs, television
engineering textbooks,
career broadsheets and a
number of topical papers
relating to Society events.
The RTS Television
Journalism Awards are
presented every year in
February and the
Programme Awards in
May. There are also
Design and Educational
Television Awards. See
also under Awards

Scottish Film Council

Dowanhill
74 Victoria Crescent Road
Glasgow G12 9JN
Tel: 041 334 4445
Fax: 041 334 8132
Sisterbody to the BFI, the
SFC receives funds from
the Scottish Education
Department for the
promotion of film culture
in Scotland

Scottish Film Production Fund

74 Victoria Crescent Road
Glasgow G12 9JN
Tel: 041 337 2526
Fax: 041 334 8132
Director: Penny Thomson
The Fund was set up in
1982 with a brief to foster
and promote film and
video production in
Scotland. The Production
Fund committee meets

quarterly to consider
applications for finance
for projects which must
have a particular
connection with and
relevance to Scotland.
The Fund's annual budget
now stands at £200,000

Scottish Film Training Trust

74 Victoria Crescent Road
Glasgow G12 9JN
Tel: 041 337 2526
Fax: 041 334 8132
Contact: Penny Thomson
A charitable trust set up
in 1982 and financed by
the Scottish Film Council,
the European Social
Fund, Scottish Television
plc and BAFTA/Shell. It
aims to assist in the
training of young Scots
entering the film and TV
industries

Society of Authors' Broadcasting Committee

84 Drayton Gardens
London SW10 9SB
Tel: 071 373 6642
Fax: 071 373 5768
Specialities: Radio,
television and film
scriptwriters

Society of Cable Television Engineers (SCTE)

10 Avenue Road
Dorridge
Solihull
West Midlands B93 8LD
Tel: 0564 774058
Fax: 0564 779032
Contact: T H Hall
Aims to raise the
standard of cable TV
engineering to the
highest technical level
and to elevate and
improve the status and
efficiency of those
engaged in cable TV
engineering

Society of Film Distributors (SFD)

Royalty House
72-73 Dean Street
London W1V 5HB
Tel: 071 437 4383
Fax: 071 734 0912
SFD was founded in 1915
and membership includes
all the major distribution
companies and several
independent companies.
It promotes and protects
its members' interests
and co-operates with all

other film organisations
and Government agencies
where distribution
interests are involved

Society of Television Lighting Directors

46 Batchworth Lane
Northwood
Middlesex HA6 3HG
The Society provides a
forum for the exchange of
ideas in all aspects of the
TV profession including
techniques and
equipment. Meetings are
organised throughout the
UK and abroad. Technical
information and news of
members' activities are
published in the Society's
magazine. The Society
has no union or political
affiliations

Sovexport Film

60 Hillway
Highgate
London N6 6DP
Tel: 081 340 8684
Fax: 081 348 1390
Contact: Yevgeny
Beginin
Exports Soviet films to
different countries and

imports films to Soviet
Union. Provides facilities
to foreign companies
wishing to film in Soviet
Union. Co-production
information for producers

Telefilm Canada

4th Floor
55-59 Oxford Street
London W1R 1RD
Tel: 071 437 8308
Fax: 071 734 8586
Contact: Robert Linnell,
Director
Canadian government
organisation financing
film and television
productions. The London
office advises on co-
productions between
Canada and the UK

Variety Artistes Ladies and Children's Guild

Bon Marche House
Unit 131
44 Brixton Road
London SW9 8EJ
Tel: 071 978 8776
Contact: June Groves
Founded in 1906 for the
purpose of assisting
members of the
entertainment

professions and their children. Funds are raised by the organisation of an annual dinner and dance, stars bazaar, theatre collections and contributions

Variety Club of Great Britain
32 Welbeck Street
London W1M 7PG
Tel: 071 935 4466
The greatest children's charity in the world

Video Trade Association
54d High Street
Northwood
Middlesex HA6 1BL
Tel: 0927 429122
Fax: 0923 835980
Trade association set up to improve trading standards and customer service offered by the video software retailer

Voice of the Listener
101 King's Drive
Gravesend
Kent DA12 5BQ
Tel: 0474 564676
An independent non-profit making association working to ensure high standards in broad-casting. Membership is open to all concerned for the future quality and range of British radio and television

Welsh Arts Council
9 Museum Place
Cardiff CF1 3NX
Tel: 0222 394711
Fax: 0222 221447
Director: T A Owen
Film Director: Martyn Howells
Advises the Arts Council on matters in Wales. Like the English Regional Arts Associations, it is eligible to receive funds from the BFI

Wider Television Access (WTVA)
c/o Flashbacks
6 Silver Place
London W1R 3LJ
A pressure group and publisher of 'Primetime' magazine, seeking to stimulate interest in old UK and US TV programmes and promote greater use of TV archives

Women's Media Action Group
c/o London Women's Centre
Wesley House
4 Wild Court
London WC2B 5AU
Feminist group campaigning to promote positive and representative images of women and to eliminate sexist stereotyping in all areas of the media. With Women's Monitoring Network, it has published seven reports on various aspects of sexism in the media. Publishes bi-monthly bulletin

Writers' Guild of Great Britain
430 Edgware Road
London W2 1EH
Tel: 071 723 8074
Fax: 071 706 2413
The Writers' Guild is the recognised TUC-affiliated trade union for writers working in film, television, radio, theatre and publishing. It has negotiated industrial agreements in all the areas mentioned above. These agreements set the minimum rates and conditions for each field of writing

REGIONAL ARTS ASSOCIATIONS

Council of Regional Arts Associations
13a Clifton Road
Winchester SO22 5BP
Tel: 0962 851063
Fax: 0962 842033
Executive Officer: Christopher Gordon
Administrator: Nicola Gunn

East Midlands Arts
Mountfields House
Forest Road
Loughborough
Leicestershire LE11 3HU
Tel: 0509 218292
Fax: 0509 262214
Director: John Buston
Film Officer: Caroline Pick
Derbyshire (excluding High Peak District), Leicestershire, Northamptonshire, Nottinghamshire, Buckinghamshire

Eastern Arts
Cherry Hinton Hall
Cherry Hinton Road
Cambridge CB1 4DW
Tel: 0223 215355
Director: Jeremy Newton
Media Officer: Martin Ayres
Bedfordshire, Cambridgeshire, Essex, Hertfordshire, Norfolk and Suffolk

Greater London Arts
Coriander Building
20 Gainsford Street
London SE1 2NE
Tel: 071 403 9013
Fax: 071 403 9072
Director: Trevor Vibert
Film Officer: Felicity Sparrow
The area of the 32 London Boroughs and the City of London

Lincolnshire and Humberside Arts
St Hugh's
23 Newport
Lincoln LN1 3DN
Tel: 0522 533555
Fax: 0522 545867
Director: Clive Fox
Principal Officer, Media: David Baker

Merseyside Arts
Graphic House
Duke Street
Liverpool L1 4JR
Tel: 051 709 0671
Fax: 051 708 9034
Director: Peter Booth
Liverpool, Sefton, Knowsley, St Helens, Wirral, West Lancashire, Ellesmere Port and Neston, Halton

Northern Arts
9-10 Osborne Terrace
Jesmond
Newcastle upon Tyne
NE2 1NZ
Tel: 091 281 6334
Fax: 091 281 3276
Director: Peter Stark
Film Officer: John Bradshaw
Cleveland, Cumbria, Durham, Northumberland, Tyne and Wear

North West Arts
12 Harter Street
Manchester M1 6HY
Tel: 061 228 3062
Fax: 061 236 5361
Director: Josephine Burns
Film Officer: Sue Todd
Greater Manchester,

Lancashire (except West Lancashire DC), High Peak DC, Cheshire (except Ellesmere Port and Neston, Halton DCs)

South East Arts
10 Mount Ephraim
Tunbridge Wells
Kent TN4 8AS
Tel: 0892 515210
Fax: 0892 549383
Director: Chris Cooper
Film Officer: Tim Cornish
East Sussex, Kent and Surrey (West Sussex from April 1991)

South West Arts
Bradninch Place
Gandy Street
Exeter EX4 3LS
Tel: 0392 218188
Fax: 0392 413554
Director: Martin Rewcastle
Film and TV Officer: Judith Higginbottom
Avon, Cornwall, Devon, Dorset (except Bournemouth, Christchurch and Poole DCs), Gloucestershire and Somerset

Southern Arts
19 Southgate Street
Winchester
Hampshire SO23 9DQ
Tel: 0962 55099
Director: Bill Dufton
Film Officer: David Browne
Berkshire, Hampshire, Isle of Wight, Oxfordshire, West Sussex, Wiltshire; Bournemouth, Christchurch and Poole DCs

West Midlands Arts
82 Granville Street
Birmingham B1 2LH
Tel: 021 631 3121
Fax: 021 643 7239
Director: Mick Elliot
Film Officer: Helen Doherty
Hereford and Worcester, Shropshire, Staffordshire, Warwickshire, West Midlands

Yorkshire Arts
Glyde House
Glydegate
Bradford BD5 0BQ
Tel: 0274 723051
Fax: 0274 394919
Director: Roger Lancaster
Film Officers: Paul Brookes, Soo Ostler
North, South and West Yorkshire

FILM FINANCES

Since 1950, Film Finances has been the world leader in the provision of completion guarantees for the film and television industry.

Richard Soames
Chief Executive

LONDON
Film Finances Ltd
1/11 Hay Hill
Berkeley Square
London W1X 7LF
Tel: (071) 629 6557
Fax: (071) 491 7530
Graham Easton

LOS ANGELES
Film Finances Inc
9000 Sunset Blvd
Los Angeles, CA 90069
Tel: (213) 275 7323
Fax: (213) 275 1706
Lindsley Parsons, Sr
Kurt Woolner
Steve Ransohoff

MONTREAL
Film Finances Canada Ltd
1001 de Maisonneuve Blvd West
Montreal, Quebec H3A 3CB
Tel: (514) 288 6763
Fax: (514) 288 1324
Michael Spencer

PARIS
Film Garantie Finance
20 Rue de la Tremoille
75008 Paris
Tel: (331) 47233846
Fax: (331) 47233844
Patrice Dutru
Francois Garcon

ROME
Film Finances Italia Sri
124 Via Panama
00198 Rome
Tel: (396) 853 385
Fax: (396) 474 0123
Umberto Sambuco

SYDNEY
c/o Samson Productions Pty Ltd
119 Pyrmont Street
Pyrmont, NSW 2009
Tel: (612) 660 3244
Fax: (612) 692 8926
Sue Milliken

TORONTO
Film Finances Canada Ltd
Cinevillage
65 Heward Avenue
Toronto, Ontario M4M 2TY
Tel: (416) 446 2760
Fax: (416) 446 0876
John Ross

PR COMPANIES

These are companies which handle all aspects of promotion and publicity for film and video production companies and/or individual productions

Tony Brainsby Publicity
16b Edith Grove
London SW10 0NL
Tel: 071 834 8341
Fax: 071 352 9451
Tony Brainsby

Byron Advertising, Marketing and PR
Byron House
Wallingford Road
Uxbridge
Middx UB8 2RW
Tel: 0895 52131
Fax: 0895 52137
Les Barnes

Jacquie Capri Enterprises
c/o Floreat Productions
46 St James's Place
London SW1A 1MS
Tel: 071 499 1996
Fax: 071 499 6727

Max Clifford Associates
109 New Bond Street
London W1Y 9AA
Tel: 071 408 2350
Fax: 071 409 2294
Max Clifford

Corbett and Keene
122 Wardour Street
London W1V 3LA
Tel: 071 494 3478
Fax: 071 734 2024
Ginger Corbett
Sara Keene

Derek Coyte
116 Old Park Ridings
London N21 2EP
Tel: 081 360 0550
Fax: 081 360 1132
Derek Coyte
Liz Ihre

Dennis Davidson Associates
Royalty House
72-74 Dean Street
London W1V 5HB
Tel: 071 439 6391
Fax: 071 437 6358
Dennis Davidson
Dennis Michael

Daniel J Edelman
Kingsgate House

536 King's Road
London SW10 0TE
Tel: 071 835 1222
Fax: 071 351 7676
Rosemary Brook

Clifford Elson (Publicity)
1 Richmond Mews
Off Dean Street
London W1V 5AG
Tel: 071 437 4822
Fax: 071 287 6314
Clifford Elson
Patricia Lake-Smith
Howard Elson

FEREF Associates
14-17 Wells Mews
London W1A 1ET
Tel: 071 580 6546
Fax: 071 631 3156
Peter Andrews
Ken Paul
Robin Behling
Phil Howard-Jones
Frank Hillary

Soren Fischer Associates
37 Ollgar Close
London W12 0NF
Tel: 081 740 9059/0202 393033
Soren Fischer

Foresight Communications
48 Lexington Street
London W1R 3LH
Tel: 071 734 6691
Fax: 071 734 2359
Sara Munds

Lynne Franks PR
6-10 Frederick Close
Stanhope Place
London W2 2HD
Tel: 071 724 6777
Fax: 071 724 8484

Frontline Public Relations
26-27 D'Arblay Street
London W1V 3FH
Tel: 071 439 0808
Fax: 071 287 9722

Good Relations
59 Russell Square
London WC1B 4HJ
Tel: 071 631 3434

Fax: 071 631 1399
Jeffrey Lyes

Gruber Public Relations
5 Dryden Street
Covent Garden
London WC2E 9NW
Tel: 071 829 8498/9
Fax: 071 240 5600
Christiana Gruber
Michael Bee Slade

HPR Publicity
22 Mount View Road
London N4 4HX
Tel: 071 263 7736
Fax: 081 341 0748
Gwyn Headley

Ray Hodges Associates
Unit 6 Kings Grove
Maidenhead
Berks SL6 4DX
Tel: 0628 75171
Fax: 0628 781301
Maureen Ward

Sue Hyman Associates
70 Chalk Farm Road
London NW1 8AN
Tel: 071 485 8489/5842
Fax: 071 267 4715
Sue Hyman

JAC Publicity
Hammer House
113 Wardour Street
London W1
Tel: 071 734 6965
Fax: 071 439 1400
Claire Forbes

Carolyn Jardine Publicity
2nd Floor
3 Richmond Buildings
Off Dean Street
London W1V 5EA
Tel: 071 287 6661
Fax: 071 437 0499

Richard Laver Publicity
3 Troy Court
Kensington High Street
London W8
Tel: 071 937 7322
Fax: 071 937 8670
Richard Laver

Lay & Partners
Citybridge House
235-245 Goswell Road
London EC1V 7JD
Tel: 071 837 1475
Fax: 071 833 4615
Philip Lay

Media Relations
125 Old Brompton Road
London SW7 3RP
Tel: 071 835 1000
Fax: 071 373 0265
Judy Tarlo

Namara Cowan Associates
45 Poland Street
London W1V 3DF
Tel: 071 434 3871
Fax: 071 439 6489
Theo Cowan
Laurie Bellew
Jane Harker

Optimum Communications
30 Eastbourne Terrace
London W2 6LF
Tel: 071 402 3408
Fax: 071 724 8829
Nigel Passingham

PSA Public Relations
3 Grosvenor Gardens

London SW1W 0BD
Tel: 071 630 9082
Fax: 071 630 9998
Philip Symes
Terry Pritchard

Premier Relations
18 Exeter Street
Covent Garden
London WC2E 7DU
Tel: 071 497 2055
Fax: 071 497 2117
Victoria Franklin

Productions Associates (UK)
The Stable Cottage
Pinewood Studios
Iver Heath
Bucks SL0 0NH
Tel: 071 486 9921
Fax: 0753 656844
Michael Baumohl

Rogers and Cowan International
29 Gainsford Street
London SE1
Tel: 071 522 2200
Fax: 071 522 2201
Tony Fitzpatrick
Richard Dennise
Brian Daly
Alan Edwards

Sue Rolfe Associates
Lyric Theatre
King Street
London W6 0QL
Tel: 081 748 9133
Fax: 081 741 7694
Sue Rolfe

Taylor and New
11 Uxbridge Street
London W8 7TQ
Tel: 071 727 7682/0734
Annie Taylor
Janie New

Peter Thompson Associates
134 Great Portland Street
London W1N 5PH
Tel: 071 436 5991/2
Fax: 071 436 0509
Peter Thompson
Amanda Malpass

Town House Publicity
45 Islington Park Street
London N1 1QB
Tel: 071 226 7450
Fax: 071 359 6026
Mary Fulton

Tristan Whalley Publicity
46C Handforth Road

London SW9 0LP
Tel: 071 582 8767
Tristan Whalley

Alan Wheatley Associates
12 Poland Street
London W1V 3DE
Tel: 071 734 1290
Fax: 071 734 1289
Alan Wheatley

Stella Wilson Publicity
130 Calabria Road
London N5 1HT
Tel: 071 354 5672
Fax: 071 354 2242
Stella Wilson

Winsor Beck Public Relations
Network House
29-39 Stirling Road
London W3 8DJ
Tel: 081 993 7506
Fax: 081 993 8276
Geri Winsor

Zakiya and Associates
13 Tottenham Mews
London W1P 9PJ
Tel: 071 323 4050
Fax: 071 580 0397
Zakiya Powell

Ernst & Young
British Film Institute Awards

"A celebration of film and television at its best"

Vanessa Redgrave

Gérard Depardieu

Orson Welles

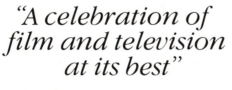

Deborah Kerr   *Dirk Bogarde*

Bette Davis

Below are magazine and newspaper critics and journalists who write about film, TV and video. Also listed are the news and photo agencies which handle media news syndication, and TV and radio programmes concerned with the visual media

African Times
(weekly)
139-149 Fonthill Road
London N4 3HF
Tel: 071 281 1191
Fax: 071 263 9656
Editor: Arif Ali
Tabloid dealing with issues pertinent to community it serves. Also at this address are 'Caribbean Times' and 'Asian Times'
Press day: Sat
Circulation: 30,000

Arena (bi-monthly)
The Old Laundry
Ossington Buildings
London W1M 3JD
Tel: 071 935 8232
Fax: 071 935 2237
Editor: Dylan Jones
Magazine for men covering general interest, avant-garde, film, music and fashion
Lead time: 4-5 weeks
Circulation: 66,000

Art Monthly
36 Great Russell Street
London WC1B 3PP
Tel: 071 580 4168
Fax: 071 240 5958
Editors: Jack Wendler, Peter Townsend
Aimed at artists, arts administrators, teachers, collectors, amateurs directly connected with the visual arts
Lead time: 4 weeks
Circulation: 4,000

Blitz Magazine
(monthly)
40-42 Newman Street
London W1P 3TP
Tel: 071 436 5211
Fax: 071 436 5290
Editor: Simon Tesler
Publisher: Carey Labovitch
Essential coverage in film, photography, fashion, print and the arts
Lead time: 6 weeks
Circulation: 50,000

Broadcast (weekly, Fri)
7 Swallow Place
London W1R 7AA
Tel: 071 491 9484
Fax: 071 355 3177
Publisher: Martin Jackson
Editor: Marta Worhle
Broadcasting industry news magazine with coverage of TV, radio, cable and satellite, corporate production and international programming and distribution in a monthly section 'Worldwatch'.
Press day: Wed
Lead time: 2 weeks
Circulation: 10,000

The Business of Film (monthly)
24 Charlotte Street
London W1P 1HJ
Tel: 071 580 0141
Fax: 071 225 1264
Publisher/executive editor: Elspeth Tavares
Editor: Judith Gracie
Aimed at film industry professionals – producers, distributors, exhibitors, investors, financiers
Lead time: 2 weeks

City Limits (weekly, Thur)
102 Curtain Road
London EC2A 3AA
Tel: 071 729 6222
Fax: 071 729 0929
Film: Jonathan Romney
TV: John Lyttle
Video: Mark Currah
London listings magazine with cinema and TV sections
Press day: Mon
Lead time: 8-11 days
Circulation: 31,000

Company (monthly)
National Magazine House
72 Broadwick Street
London W1V 2BP
Tel: 071 439 5372
Arts/style editor: Dee Pilgrim
Glossy magazine for women aged 18-30
Lead time: 10 weeks
Circulation: 185,136

Cosmopolitan
(monthly)
National Magazine House
72 Broadwick Street
London W1V 2BP
Tel: 071 439 7144
Fax: 071 437 6886
Film: Derek Malcolm
TV: Sue Summers
Arts/General: Vanessa Raphaely
Aimed at women aged 18-35
Lead time: 12 weeks
Circulation: 400,135

Creative Review
(monthly)
50 Poland Street
London W1V 4AX
Tel: 071 439 4222
Fax: 071 734 6748
Editor: Lewis Blackwell
Deputy editor: Lyndy Stout
Publisher: Annie Swift
Trade paper for creative people covering film, advertising and design. Film reviews, profiles and technical features
Lead time: 4 weeks
Circulation: 20,000

Daily Express
245 Blackfriars Road
London SE1 9UX
Tel: 071 928 8000
Fax: 071 922 7970
Showbusiness: David Wigg
Ian Christie, Peter Tory, Richard Compton-Miller
National daily newspaper
Circulation: 1,700,000

Daily Mail
2 Derry Street
London W8 5EE
Tel: 071 938 6000
Fax: 071 937 3745
Showbusiness: Corinna Honan
Film: Shaun Usher
TV: Peter Paterson
National daily newspaper
Circulation: 1,676,423

Daily Mirror
Holborn Circus
London EC1P 1DQ
Tel: 071 353 0246

Film: Pauline McLeod
TV: Hilary Bonner
National daily newspaper
Circulation: 3,150,000

Daily Telegraph
Peterborough Court
at South Quay
181 Marsh Wall
London E14 9SR
Tel: 071 538 5000
Fax: 071 538 6242
Arts: Miriam Gross
TV: Edna Pottersman
National daily newspaper
Circulation: 1,075,000

The Economist
(weekly)
25 St James's Street
London SW1A 1HG
Tel: 071 839 7000
Film/video: Ann Wroe
TV (cultural): Anthony
Gottlieb
Film/video/TV (business):
John Micklethwaite
International coverage of
major political, social and
business developments
with arts section
Press day: Wed
Circulation: 390,000

Elle (monthly)
Rex House
4-12 Lower Regent Street
London SW1Y 4PE
Tel: 071 930 9050
Fax: 071 839 2762
Editor: Maggie Alderson
Features editor: Carl
Hindmarch
Glossy magazine aimed at
18-35 year old working
women
Lead time: 8 weeks

Empire (monthly)
42 Great Portland Street
London W1N 5AH
Tel: 071 436 5430
Fax: 071 631 0781
Editor: Barry McIlheney
Quality film monthly
incorporating features,
interviews and movie
news as well as reviews of
all new movies and videos
Lead time: 6 weeks
Circulation: 50,000

The European
(weekly)
Holborn Circus
London EC1P 1DQ
Tel: 071 353 0246
Fax: 071 377 4773
Arts editor: Derwent May
In-depth coverage of
European politics and
culture

European Cable and Pay TV/ European Television Investor
(monthly)
Shackleton House
4 Battle Bridge Lane
London SE1 2HR
Tel: 071 403 8786
Managing editor: Jay
Stuart
Business and financial
information on companies
and markets broadcasting
television and producing
television programming
and film
Lead time: 10 days

Evening Standard
(Mon-Fri)
New Northcliffe House
2 Derry Street
London W8 5EE
Tel: 071 938 6000
Fax: 071 937 3745
Arts: Brian Sewell
Film: Alexander Walker
TV: Jacquie Stephen
London weekday evening
newspaper

Everywoman
(monthly)
34a Islington Green
London N1 8DU
Tel: 071 359 5496
Editor: Barbara Rogers
Arts editor: Barbara
Norden
A current affairs
magazine for women
Lead time: 6 weeks
Circulation: 15,000

The Face (monthly)
The Old Laundry
Ossington Buildings
Moxon Street
London W1
Tel: 071 935 8232
Fax: 071 935 2237
Film/TV: Sheryl Garratt,
Lindsay Baker
Visual-orientated youth
culture magazine:
emphasis on music,
fashion and films
Lead time: 4 weeks
Circulation: 60,000

Film (10 issues a year)
Film Society Unit
BFI, 21 Stephen Street
London W1P 1PL
Tel: 071 255 1444
Editor: Peter Cargin
Non-commercial aspects
of film
Lead time: 2 weeks

Film and Television Technician
(10 issues a year)
111 Wardour Street
London W1
Tel: 071 437 8506
Fax: 071 437 8268
Editor: Janice Turner
ACTT members' journal
Circulation: 28,000

Film Review
(monthly)
4th Floor Century House
Mandela Street
London NW1 0DU
Tel: 071 387 3848
Fax: 071 388 8532
Editor: David Aldridge
Reviews of films on
cinema screen and video;
articles; star interviews
and profiles; book reviews
Incorporates Films and
Filming
Lead time: 8 weeks
Circulation: 34,000

Financial Times
1 Southwark Bridge
London SE1 9HL
Tel: 071 873 3000
Fax: 071 873 3076
Arts: J D F Jones
Film: Nigel Andrews
TV: Victoria Cooper
National daily newspaper
Circulation: 300,000

The Glasgow Herald
1 Jerome Street
London E1 6NJ
Tel: 071 377 0890
Fax: 071 375 2001
London editor/film critic:
William Russell
Scottish daily newspaper
Circulation: 124,715

The Guardian
119 Farringdon Road
London EC1R 3ER
Tel: 071 278 2332
Fax: 071 837 2114
Arts: Helen Oldfield
Film: Derek Malcolm
TV: Nancy Banks-Smith
Media editor: Georgina
Henry
National daily newspaper
Circulation: 429,000

Harpers & Queen
(monthly)
National Magazine House
72 Broadwick Street
London W1V 2BP
Tel: 071 439 7144
Fax: 071 439 5506
Art/reviews: Rupert
Christiansen
Glossy magazine for

women
Lead time: 10 weeks
Circulation: 86,000

The Hollywood Reporter
(daily; weekly
international, Tues)
23 Ridgmount Street
London WC1E 7AH
Tel: 071 323 6686
Fax: 071 323 2314/16
European bureau chief:
Neil Watson
European television
editor: Adam Dawtrey
Showbusiness trade paper

i-D Magazine
(monthly)
3rd Floor
134-146 Curtain Road
London EC2A 3AR
Tel: 071 729 7305
Fax: 071 729 7266
Film: Laurence Earle
Fashion/style magazine
with items on film
Lead time: 8 weeks
Circulation: 40,000

Illustrated London News
(6 issues per year)
Lawrence House
91-93 Southwark Street
London SE1 0HX
Tel: 071 928 2111
Fax: 071 620 1594
Editor: James Bishop
Film listings: Roger Sabin
News, pictorial record and
commentary, and a guide
to coming events
Lead time: 8-10 weeks
Circulation: 61,500

The Independent
40 City Road
London EC1Y 2DB
Tel: 071 253 1222
Fax: 071 956 1435
Arts: Thomas Sutcliffe
Film: Sheila Johnston
Media: Maggie Brown
Circulation: 415,000

The Independent on Sunday
40 City Road
London EC1Y 2DB
Tel: 071 253 1222
Fax: 071 415 1333
Arts: Michael Church

The Jewish Chronicle (weekly)
25 Furnival Street
London EC4A 1JT
Tel: 071 405 9252
Fax: 071 405 9040
Editor: Edward J Temko
Film critic: Pamela

Melnikoff
Press day: Fri
Circulation: 50,000

The List (fortnightly, Thur)
14 High Street
Edinburgh EH1 1TE
Tel: 031 558 1191
Editor: Alan Taylor
Film/video: Trevor Johnston
TV: Alastair Mabbott
Glasgow and Edinburgh events guide
Lead time: 1 week
Circulation: 12,000

The Listener (weekly, Thur)
Listener Publications Ltd
199 Old Marylebone Road
London NW1 5QS
Tel: 071 258 3581
Fax: 071 724 8071
Editor: Peter Fiddick
Broadcasting weekly with current affairs and arts slant. Covers the whole broadcasting spectrum. Extensive programme preview section
Lead time: 3 weeks
Circulation: 22,000

London Weekly Diary of Social Events
(weekly, Sun)
25 Park Row
Greenwich
London SE10 9NL
Tel: 081 305 1274/1419
Fax: 081 853 2355
Editor/film critic: Denise Silvester-Carr
Arts-oriented subscription magazine with weekly film column
Lead time: 8 days
Circulation: 18,000

Mail on Sunday
(weekly, Sun)
2 Derry Street
London W8 5EE
Tel: 071 938 6000
Fax: 071 937 3745
Film: Tom Hutchinson
TV: Alan Coren
TV/video: Liz Cowley
Press day: Wed
Circulation: 2,030,000

Marie Claire
(monthly)
2 Hatfields
London SE1 9PG
Tel: 071 261 6939
Fax: 071 261 5277
Film/TV: Sean French
Features: Marianne Thomas

Lead time: 2-3 months
Circulation: 156,000

Marxism Today
(monthly)
16 St John Street
London EC1M 4AY
Tel: 071 608 0265
Fax: 071 250 3654
Arts: Chris Granlund
Lively current affairs and cultural magazine
Lead time: 8 weeks
Circulation: 17,500

Media Week (weekly, Thur)
City Cloisters
188-196 Old Street
London EC1V 9BP
Tel: 071 490 5500
Fax: 071 490 0957
Editor: Steven Buckley
News Editor: Liz Roberts
Broadcast Editor: Richard Gold
News magazine aimed at the advertising and media industries
Press day: Wed
Circulation: 17,766

Melody Maker
(weekly, Tues)
King's Reach Tower
Stamford Street
London SE1 9LF
Tel: 071 261 6228
Fax: 071 261 6706
Film: Steve Sutherland
Rock music newspaper
Press day: Thur
Circulation: 70,000

Midweek (weekly, Thur)
7-9 Rathbone Street
London W1P 1AF
Tel: 071 636 6651
Fax: 071 872 0806
Arts/Film: Bill Williamson
Free magazine with film section
Press day: Tues
Circulation: 124,000

Morning Star
74 Luke Street
London EC2A 4PY
Tel: 071 739 6166
Fax: 071 739 5463
Film: Jeff Sawtell
TV: Jeffrey James
The only national daily owned by its readers as a co-operative. Weekly film and TV reviews
Circulation: 28,000

Ms London (weekly, Mon)
7-9 Rathbone Street

London W1P 1AF
Tel: 071 636 6651
Fax: 071 872 0806
Arts editor: Juliet Rieden
Free magazine with film section
Press day: Fri
Circulation: 138,238

New Musical Express
(weekly, Wed)
25th Floor
King's Reach Tower
Stamford Street
London SE1 9LS
Tel: 071 261 5000
Fax: 071 261 5185
Film/TV: Gavin Martin
Rock music newspaper
Press day: Mon
Circulation: 106,000

New Scientist
(weekly, Thur)
King's Reach Tower
Stamford Street
London SE1 9LS
Tel: 071 261 5000
Fax: 071 261 6162
Editor: David Dickson
Audio-visual: Barry Fox
Contains articles and reports on the progress of science and technology in terms which the non-specialist can understand
Press day: Mon
Circulation: 97,000

New Socialist
(monthly)
11 Dartmouth Street
London SW1H 9BN
Tel: 071 976 7129
Fax: 071 976 7153
Editor: Gordon Marsden
Arts: Lois Sparling
Political magazine with coverage of a wide range of cultural activities
Lead time: 4 weeks
Circulation: 10,000

New Statesman and Society (weekly, Fri)
Foundation House
Perseverance Works
38 Kingsland Road
London E2 8DQ
Tel: 071 739 3211
Fax: 071 739 93307
Editor: Stuart Weir
Arts editor: Sally Townsend
Independent radical journal of investigation, revelation and comment
Press day: Mon
Circulation: 40,000

News of the World
(weekly, Sun)
News International
1 Pennington Street
London E1 9BD
Tel: 071 782 4000
Editor: Patsy Chapman
Film: Greg Miskiew
TV: Charles Catchpole
National Sunday newspaper
Press day: Sat
Circulation: 5,100,000

Nine to Five (weekly)
9a Margaret Street
London W1
Tel: 071 637 1377
Fax: 071 636 4694
Editor: John Symes
Film/entertainments editor: Linda Hancock
Free magazine
Press day: Wed
Circulation: 325,000

19 (monthly)
IPC Magazines
King's Reach Tower
London SE1 9LS
Tel: 071 261 6360
Fax: 071 261 6032
Film: Maureen Rice
Arts: Maureen Rice
Magazine for young women

The Observer
(weekly, Sun)
Chelsea Bridge House
Queenstown Road
London SW8 4NN
Tel: 071 627 0700
Fax: 071 627 5570
Arts editor: Gillian Widdicombe
Film: Philip French
TV: John Naughton
National Sunday newspaper
Press day: Fri
Circulation: 675,000

Observer Magazine
(Sun)
Editor: Angela Palmer
Supplement to 'The Observer'

Options (monthly)
IPC
King's Reach Tower
Stamford Street
London SE1 9LS
Tel: 071 261 5000
Fax: 071 261 6023
Film: Dave Pirie
TV: Jennifer Selway
Magazine for women
Lead time: 12 weeks
Circulation: 240,000

The People
Orbit House
9 New Fetter Lane
London EC4A 1AR
Tel: 071 353 0246
Fax: 071 822 3864
Film/TV: Peter Bishop
National Sunday
newspaper
Press day: Fri
Circulation: 2,617,000

Producer (quarterly)
The Producers
Association
Paramount House
162-170 Wardour Street
London W1V 4LA
Tel: 071 437 7700
Fax: 071 734 4564
Editor: John Murray
The magazine of The
Producers Association

Punch (weekly, Wed)
Ludgate House
245 Blackfriars Road
London SE1 9UZ
Tel: 071 583 9199
Features editor: Sean
Macaulay
Film: Dilys Powell
TV: Sean Macaulay
A combination of topical
satire, comment and
wide-ranging arts
coverage
Lead time: 10 days
Circulation: 58,250

Q (monthly)
42 Great Portland Street
London W1N 5AH
Tel: 071 436 5430
Fax: 071 631 0781
Editor: Mark Ellen
Specialist music
magazine for 18-45 year
olds. Includes reviews of
new albums, films and
books
Lead time: 14 days
Circulation: 160,000

Sanity (monthly)
22-24 Underwood Street
London N1 7JG
Tel: 071 250 4010
Fax: 071 490 0554
Editor: Ben Webb
Film: Adam Gee
CND's magazine,
covering film, TV and
video. Reviews cover a
wide range of political/
environmental topics as
well as general interest
Lead time: 3 weeks
Circulation: 24,000

The Scotsman
20 North Bridge
Edinburgh EH1 1YT
Tel: 031 225 2468
Fax: 031 226 7420
Arts/film/TV: Allen
Wright
National daily newspaper

Screen Digest
(monthly)
37 Gower Street
London WC1E 6HH
Tel: 071 580 2842
Editorial chairman:
John Chittock
Editor: David Fisher
News editor: Ben Keen
An industry news digest
and research report
covering film, TV, cable,
satellite, video and other
multimedia information.
Has a centre page
reference system every
month on subjects like
law, statistics or sales.
Now also available on a
computer data base via
fax at 071 580 0060 under
the name Screenfax
Lead time: 10 days

Screenfax (database)
see entry under Screen
Digest

**Screen
International**
(weekly, Fri)
7 Swallow Place
249-259 Regent Street
London W1R 7AA
Tel: 071 491 9484
Fax: 071 355 3337
Editor: Paul Mungo
Deputy editor/features:
Oscar Moore
International trade
magazine for the film, TV,
video, cable and satellite
industries. Regular news,
features, production
information from around
the world
Press day: Thur
Circulation: 15,000

Spare Rib (monthly)
27 Clerkenwell Close
London EC1R 0AT
Tel: 071 253 9792
Film: Esther Bailey
TV: Jennifer Mourin
Women's liberation
magazine produced by an
editorial collective
Lead time: 3-6 weeks
Circulation: 25,000

The Spectator
(weekly, Thur)
56 Doughty Street
London WC1N 2LL
Tel: 071 405 1706
Fax: 071 242 0603
Arts editor: Jenny
Naipaul
Film: Hilary Mantel
TV: Wendy Cope
Independent review of
politics, current affairs,
literature and the arts
Press day: Wed
Circulation: 40,000

The Star
Ludgate House
245 Blackfriars Road
London SE1 9UX
Tel: 071 928 8000
Film: Pat Codd, Alec Lom
TV: Michael Burke,
Ollie Wilson
National daily newspaper

The Sun
PO Box 481
1 Virginia Street
London E1 9BD
Tel: 071 782 4000
Fax: 071 488 3253
Film: Garry Bushell
TV: Jim Taylor
National daily newspaper
Circulation: 4,002,021

**Sunday
Correspondent**
21 Clerkenwell Close
London EC1R 0AA
Tel: 071 251 1000
Fax: 071 608 0858
Film: Chris Peachment
Film/video: Anne Billson
TV: Howard Jacobson,
Martin James
National Sunday
newspaper
Press day: Wed/Thu
Circulation: 210,000

Sunday Express
Ludgate House
245 Blackfriars Road
London SE1 9UX
Tel: 071 928 8000
Fax: 071 620 1656
Film/TV: Clive
Hirschhorn
National Sunday
newspaper
Circulation: 1,880,000

**Sunday Express
Magazine**
Ludgate House
245 Blackfriars Road
London SE1 9UX
Tel: 071 928 8000
Editor: Sue Peart
Deputy editor: Hilary
Smith
Film/TV: Gill Morgan
Supplement to 'Sunday
Express' newspaper
Lead time: 6 weeks

Sunday Magazine
214 Gray's Inn Road
London WC1X 8EZ
Tel: 071 782 7000
Fax: 071 782 7474
Editor: Colin Jenkins
Features editor: Pete
Picton
Supplement to 'News of
the World'
Lead time: 8 weeks

Sunday Mirror
33 Holborn Circus
London EC1P 1DQ
Tel: 071 353 0246
Fax: 071 822 3405
Film: Madeleine
Harmsworth
TV: Keith Richmond
National Sunday
newspaper
Circulation: 2,999,000

Sunday Telegraph
Peterborough Court
at South Quay
181 Marsh Wall
London E14 9SR
Tel: 071 538 5000
Fax: 071 538 1330
Arts: Michael Shepherd
Film: Richard Mayne
TV: Christopher Tookey
National Sunday
newspaper
Circulation: 648,000

Sunday Times
News International
1 Pennington Street
London E1 9BD
Tel: 071 782 5000
Screen Media
Correspondent: Steve
Clarke
Film Reviews: Iain
Johnstone
TV Reviews: Patrick
Stoddart
National Sunday
newspaper
Press day: Fri

**Sunday Times
Magazine**
214 Gray's Inn Road
London WC1X 8EZ
Tel: 01 782 7000
Editor: Philip Clarke
Films editor: George
Perry
Supplement to 'Sunday
Times'
Lead time: 6 weeks
Circulation: 1,310,000
Tel: 071 323 3222
Guide to ITV and
Channel 4 TV
programmes
Circulation: c 3,000,000

TV Times (weekly, Tues)
ITV Publications
247 Tottenham Court Road
London W1P 0AU

TV World (monthly)
7 Swallow Place
249-259 Regent Street
London W1R 7AA
Tel: 071 491 9484
Fax: 071 355 3176
Editor: Marta Wohrle
International monthly for executives in programming industry – buyers, distributors, producers
Lead time: 5 days
Circulation: 12,000

The Tatler (10 issues a year)
Vogue House
1-2 Hanover Square
London W1R 0AD
Tel: 071 499 9080
Fax: 071 409 0451
Arts: Jessamy Calkin
Smart society magazine favouring profiles, fashion and the arts
Lead time: 12 weeks
Circulation: 51,000

The Teacher (3 times per school term)
National Union of Teachers
Hamilton House
Mabledon Place
London WC1H 9BD
Tel: 071 388 6191
Fax: 071 387 8458
Editor: Mitch Howard
Circulation: 250,000
Mailed direct to all NUT members and to educational instutions

Telegraph Weekend Magazine
Editor: Nigel Horne
Supplement to Saturday edition of the 'Daily Telegraph'
Lead time: 6 weeks

Television (bi-monthly)
Royal Television Society
Tavistock House East
Tavistock Square
London WC1H 9HR
Tel: 071 387 1970
Fax: 071 387 0358
Editor: Harvey Lee
The magazine of the Royal Television Society, now incorporating 'Talkback'

Television Today
(weekly, Thur)

47 Bermondsey Street
London SE1 3XT
Tel: 071 403 1818
Fax: 071 403 1418
Editor: Peter Hepple
'Television Today' constitutes the middle section of 'The Stage' and is a weekly trade paper

Television Week
Meed House
21 John Street
London WC1N 2BP
Tel: 071 404 5513
Fax: 071 831 4607
Editor: Charles Brown
Press day: Monday
Published Wednesday
Circulation: 15,000

Televisual (monthly)
50 Poland Street
London W1V 4AX
Tel: 071 439 4222
Fax: 071 439 8065
Editor: Mundy Ellis
Monthly business magazine for production professionals in the business of moving pictures
Circulation: 8,900

Time Out (weekly, Wed)
Tower House
Southampton Street
London WC2E 7HD
Tel: 071 836 4411
Fax: 071 836 7118
Film: Geoff Andrew
Film listings: Wally Hammond
Films on TV: Adrian Turner
TV: Alkarim Jivani
London listings magazine with cinema and TV sections
Listings lead time: 8 days
Features lead time: 1 week
Circulation: 89,000

The Times
News International
1 Pennington Street
London E1 9BD
Tel: 071 782 5000
Fax: 071 488 3242
Film: David Robinson
Video: Peter Waymark
Arts (TV): Richard Morrison
Saturday editor: Andrew Harvey
National daily newspaper
Circulation: 429,000

The Times Educational Supplement (weekly, Fri)
Priory House
St John's Lane

London EC1M 4BX
Tel: 071 253 3000
Fax: 071 608 1599
Arts: Heather Neill
Film critic: Robin Buss
Broadcasting: Gillian Macdonald
Video: Sean Coughlan
Press day: Wed
Circulation: 116,833

The Times Higher Education Supplement (weekly, Fri)
Priory House
St John's Lane
London EC1M 4BX
Tel: 071 253 3000
Arts: Anne-Marie Conway
Features: Peter Aspden
Press day: Wed
Lead time for reviews: copy 10 days before publication
Circulation: 16,500

The Times Literary Supplement (weekly, Fri)
Priory House
St John's Lane
London EC1M 4BX
Tel: 071 253 3000
Fax: 071 251 3424
Commentary editor: Lindsay Duguid
Press day: Tues
Circulation: 30,000

The Times Scottish Education Supplement
(weekly, Fri)
37 George Street
Edinburgh EH2 2HN
Tel: 031 220 1100
Fax: 031 220 1616
Editor: Willis Pickard
Press day: Wed

Today
70 Vauxhall Bridge Road
London SW1V 2RP
Tel: 071 630 1300
Fax: 071 630 6839
Film: Sue Heal
TV: Kate Battersby
Showbusiness editor: Lester Middlehurst
National daily newspaper (Sundays inclusive)

Tribune (weekly, Fri)
308 Gray's Inn Road
London WC1X 8DY
Tel: 071 278 0911
Reviews editor: Paul Anderson
Political, literary newspaper with socialist and feminist approach

20/20 (monthly)
Tower House
Southampton Street
London WC2E 7HD
Tel: 071 836 4411
Fax: 071 836 7118
Film: Adrian Turner
Film listings: Geoff Andrew, Colette Maude
National arts and entertainment magazine with extensive film coverage
Listings lead time: 1 month
Features lead time: 5 weeks
Circulation: 41,260

Variety (weekly, Wed)
34-35 Newman Street
London W1P 3PD
Tel: 071 637 3663
Fax: 071 580 5559
London editor: Jack Pitman
International showbusiness newspaper
Press day: Tues

Videographic
monthly
7 Swallow Place
London W1R 7AA
Tel: 071 491 9484
Fax: 071 355 3177
Editor: Marta Wohrle
For those interested in creative applications of the latest post production special effects technology
Circulation: 12,000

Vogue (monthly)
Vogue House
Hanover Square
London W1R 0AD
Tel: 071 499 9080
Editor: Elizabeth Tiberis
Features: Eve MacSweeny, Kathy O'Shaughnessy, Lisa Armstrong
Glossy magazine for women
Lead time: 12 weeks

The Voice (weekly)
370 Coldharbour Lane
London SW9 8PL
Tel: 071 737 7377
Fax: 071 274 8994
Editor: Steve Pope
Film: Lorraine Griffiths
Britain's leading black newspaper with mainly 18-35 age group readership. Regular film, TV and video coverage
Press day: Fri
Circulation: 50,000

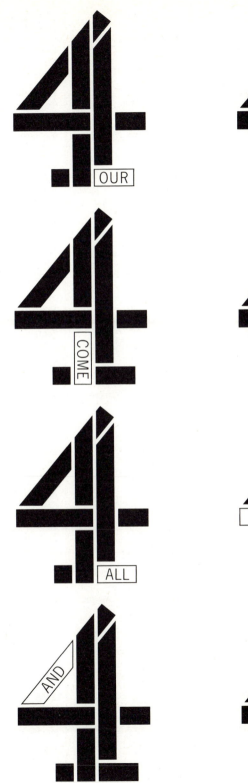

Western Mail
Thomson House
Cardiff CF1 1WR
Tel: 0222 233022
Features editor:
Gareth Jenkins
Film: Mario Basini
TV: Gethyn Stoodley
Thomas, Brinley
Haymer Jones
Previews: Terry Herbs
National daily of Wales

What's On in
London (weekly, Tues)
182 Pentonville Road
London N1 9LB
Tel: 071 278 4393
Fax: 071 837 5838
Editor: David Parkes-
Bristow
Film editor: Michael
Darvell
Film correspondent:
Phillip Bergson
London based weekly
covering cinema, theatre,
music, arts, entertain-
ment, books and fashion
Press day: Mon
Lead time: 10 days
Circulation: 50,000

Yorkshire Post
Wellington Street
Leeds
West Yorkshire LS1 1RF
Tel: 0532 432701
Fax: 0532 443430
Regional daily morning
newspaper
Deadline: 10.00 pm
Circulation: 94,000

NEWS AND PHOTO AGENCIES

Associated Press
12 Norwich Street
London EC4
Tel: 071 353 1515

Central Office of Information
Hercules Road SE1
Tel: 071 928 2345

Central Press Features
20 Spectrum House
32-34 Gordon House
Street
London NW5 1LP
Tel: 071 284 1433

Fleet Street News Agency
68 Exmouth Market
London EC1R 4RA

Tel: 071 278 5661
Fax: 071 278 8480

Knights Ridder Unicom News Service
72 Fleet Street
London EC4Y 1HY
Tel: 071 353 4861

London News Service
68 Exmouth Market
London EC1R 4RA
Tel: 071 278 5661/1223
Fax: 071 278 8480

More News
Dalling House
132 Dalling Road
London W6 0EP
Tel: 081 741 7000

Press Association
85 Fleet Street
London EC4P 4BE
Tel: 071 353 7440

Reuters
85 Fleet Street
London EC4P 4AJ
Tel: 071 250 1122

United Press International
Meridian House
2 Greenwich View
Millharbour
London E14 9NN
Tel: 071 538 5310

BBC TELEVISION

BBC
Television Centre
Wood Lane
London W12 7RJ
Tel: 081 743 8000
BBC1
*Omnibus; Film '90;
Breakfast Time*
BBC2
Arena; The Late Show

INDEPENDENT TELEVISION

Anglia Television
Anglia House
Norwich NR1 3JG
Tel: 0603 615151
*Anglia News East; Anglia
News West; Anglia
Reports*

Border Television
Television Centre

Carlisle CA1 3NT
Tel: 0228 25101
Lookaround

Central Independent Television
Central House
Broad Street
Birmingham B1 2JP
Tel: 021 643 9898
East Midlands Television
Centre
Nottingham NG7 2NA
Tel: 0602 863322
Unit 9, Windrush Court
Abingdon Business Park
Abingdon
Oxon OX14 1SA
Tel: 0235 554123
Central News (separate
bulletins prepared for
east, south and west);
*Central Lobby; Central
Weekend; First Night*

Channel 4 Television
60 Charlotte Street
London W1P 2AX
Tel: 071 631 4444
Channel 4 News c/o ITN;
Right to Reply

Channel Television
The Television Centre
La Pouquelaye
St Helier
Jersey
Channel Islands
Tel: 0534 68999
Television Centre
St George's Place
St Peter Port
Guernsey
Channel Islands
Tel: 0481 23451
Channel Report

Grampian Television
Queen's Cross
Aberdeen AB9 2XJ
Tel: 0224 646464
*North Tonight; Crossfire;
Crann Tara*

Granada Television
Quay Street
Manchester M60 9EA
Tel: 061 832 7211
Bridgegate House
5 Bridge Place
Lower Bridge Street
Chester CH1 1SA
Tel: 0244 313966
White Cross
Lancaster LA1 4XQ
Tel: 0524 60688
Albert Dock
Liverpool L3 4BA
Tel: 051 709 9393
Granada Tonight

HTV Wales
Television Centre
Culverhouse Cross
Cardiff CF5 6XJ
Tel: 0222 590590
Scene at Six

HTV West
Television Centre
Bath Road
Bristol BS4 3HG
Tel: 0272 778366
Press Officer: 0272
722214
Fax: 0272 722400
*Your Say; What's On;
Scene; The Time The
Place; Problems;
Newsweek*

Independent Television News
ITN House
48 Wells Street
London W1P 4DE
Tel: 071 637 2424

London Weekend Television
South Bank Television
Centre
London SE1 9LT
Tel: 071 261 3434
South Bank Show

S4C
Sophia Close
Cardiff CF1 9XY
Tel: 0222 343421
Fax: 0222 341643
Head of Press, Publicity
and International Affairs:
Ann Benyon

Scottish Television
Cowcaddens
Glasgow G2 3PR
Tel: 041 332 9999
The Gateway
Edinburgh EH7 4AH
Tel: 031 557 4554
Scotland Today

TV-am
Hawley Crescent
London NW1 8EF
Tel: 071 267 4300/4377
*Good Morning Britain;
After Nine; Anne
Diamond on Sunday;
WAC 90; David Frost on
Sunday*

TVS Television
Television Centre
Vinters Park
Maidstone
Kent ME14 5NZ
Tel: 0622 691111
Television Centre
Northam
Southampton SO9 5HZ
Tel: 0703 634211

Television South West
Derry's Cross
Plymouth
Devon PL1 2SP
Tel: 0752 663322
Compass; Consumer File; Business South West

Thames Television
306-316 Euston Road
London NW1 3BB
Tel: 071 387 9494
01; Video View

Tyne Tees Television
The Television Centre
City Road
Newcastle upon Tyne
NE1 2AL
Tel: 091 261 0181
Fax: 091 261 2302

Ulster Television
Havelock House
Ormeau Road
Belfast BT7 1EB
Tel: 0232 328122
Six Tonight; Spectrum; Preview

Yorkshire Television
The Television Centre
Leeds LS3 1JS
Tel: 0532 438283
Calendar

BBC RADIO

BBC
Broadcasting House
London W1A lAA
Tel: 071 580 4468
Fax: 071 636 9786
RADIO 1
Steve Wright, Mark Goodier
RADIO 2
Cinema 2; Round Midnight; Gloria Hunniford Show
RADIO 3
Critics' Forum; Third Ear
RADIO 4
Kaleidoscope
WORLD SERVICE
Bush House
Strand
London WC2B 4PH
Tel: 071 257 2244
Meridian

BBC LOCAL RADIO STATIONS

Greater London Radio (BBC)
35c Marylebone High Street
London W1A 4LG
Tel: 071 224 2424
Fax: 071 487 2908

Greater Manchester Radio (GMR)
PO Box 90
New Broadcasting House
Oxford Road
Manchester M60 1SJ
Tel: 061 200 2000
What's On; Russell Harris

Radio Bedfordshire
PO Box 476
Hastings Street
Luton
Bedfordshire LU1 5BA
Tel: 0582 459111
Fax: 0582 401467
Programme organiser:
Ann Jones

Radio Bristol
PO Box 194
Bristol BS99 7QT
Tel: 0272 741111
Fax: 0272 732549
What's On; Events West; Tea-Time Show

Radio Cambridgeshire
104 Hills Road
Cambridge CB2 1LD
Tel: 0223 315970
Rowland Myers

Radio Cleveland
PO Box 1548
Broadcasting House
Newport Road
Middlesbrough TS1 5DG
Tel: 0642 225211
Ann Davies

Radio Cornwall
Phoenix Wharf
Truro TR1 1UA
Tel: 0872 75421
Fax: 0872 40679
Seen and Heard; Cornwall Daily; Saturday Breakfast Show

Radio Cumbria
Hilltop Heights
London Road
Carlisle CA1 2NA
Tel: 0228 31661
Fax: 0228 511195
What's On; Cumbria Today

Radio CWR
25 Warwick Road
Coventry CV1 2WR
Tel: 0203 559911
Fax: 0203 520080
Manager: Mike Marsh
Programme organiser:
Charles Hodkinson

Radio Derby
PO Box 269
Derby DE1 3HL
Tel: 0332 361111
Fax: 0332 290794
Sound and Vision; Chris Baird Show; Peter Gore

Radio Devon
PO Box 100
Exeter EX4 4DB
Tel: 0392 215651
Arts: Howard Turner
PO Box 5
Catherine Street
Plymouth PL1 2AD
Tel: 0752 260323
The Arts Programme

Radio Essex
198 New London Road
Chelmsford
Essex
Tel: 0245 262393
Fax: 0245 490703

Radio Foyle
PO Box 927
8 Northland Road
Londonderry BT48 7NE
Tel: 0504 262244
Fax: 0504 260067
The Afternoon Show; AM on Foyle

Radio Hereford & Worcester
Hylton Road
Worcester WR2 5WW
Tel: 0905 748485
Fax: 0905 748006
Manager: John Pickles
Programme Organiser:
Denzil Dudley

Radio Humberside
63 Jameson Street
Hull HU1 3NU
Tel: 0482 23232
Fax: 0482 226409
Steve Massam

Radio Guernsey
Commerce House
Les Banques
St Peter Port
Guernsey
Tel: 0481 28977
Manager: Bob Bufton

Radio Kent
Sun Pier
Chatham
Kent ME4 4EZ
Tel: 0634 830505
Soundtrack

Radio Jersey
Broadcasting House
Rouge Bouillon
St Helier
Jersey
Tel: 0534 70000
Fax: 0534 32569
Manager: Bob Bufton

Radio Lancashire
Darwin Street
Blackburn
Lancs BB2 2EA
Tel: 0254 62411
Fax: 0254 680821
Arts producer: Joe Wilson
Film specialist: Wendy Howard

Radio Leeds
Broadcasting House
Woodhouse Lane
Leeds LS2 9PN
Tel: 0532 442131
Fax: 0532 420652
Tony Fisher

Radio Leicester
Epic House
Charles Street
Leicester LE1 3SH
Tel: 0533 516688
Fax: 0533 511463
The Light Programme; Prime Time; Listening In

Radio Lincolnshire
PO Box 219
Newport
Lincoln LN1 3XY
Tel: 0522 511411
Fax: 0522 511058
Arts producer: Alan Stennett
What's On Diary; Gallery

Radio Merseyside
55 Paradise Street
Liverpool L1 3BP
Tel: 051 708 5500
Fax: 051 709 2394
Film critic: Ramsey Campbell

Radio Newcastle
Broadcasting Centre
Fenham
Newcastle upon Tyne
NE99 1RN
Tel: 091 232 4141
Fax: 091 232 5082
Arts producer: Simon Pattern

Radio Norfolk
Norfolk Tower
Surrey Street
Norwich NR1 3PA
Tel: 0603 617411
Fax: 0603 633692
Arts producer: Stewart
Orr

Radio Northampton
PO Box 1107
Northampton NN1 2BE
Tel: 0604 239100
Fax: 0604 230709
Arts producers: David
Saint, Laurence Culhane

Radio Nottingham
PO Box 222
Nottingham NG1 3NZ
Tel: 0602 415161
Fax: 0602 481482
Programme organiser:
Nick Brunger

Radio Oxford
269 Banbury Road
Oxford OX2 7DW
Tel: 0865 311444
Fax: 0865 311996
Phil Rapps

Peterborough FM
Broadway Court
Broadway
Peterborough PE1 1RP
Tel: 0733 312832
Fax: 0733 43768
Senior producer: Steve
Somers

Radio Sheffield
Ashdell Grove
60 Westbourne Road
Sheffield S10 2QU
Tel: 0742 686185
Fax: 0742 686185
Programme organiser:
Frank Mansfield

Radio Solent
South Western House
Canute Road
Southampton SO9 4PJ
Tel: 0703 631311
Fax: 0703 339648
Programme organiser:
John Smith

Somerset Sound
14-16 Paul Street
Taunton
Somerset
Tel: 0823 251641
Fax: 0823 332539
Senior Producer: Richard
Austin

Radio Stoke
Cheapside
Hanley
Stoke-on-Trent ST1 1JJ
Tel: 0782 208080
Fax: 0782 289115
First Edition

Radio Sussex
Marlborough Place
Brighton BN1 1TU
Tel: 0273 680231
Fax: 0273 601241
Arts producer: Jim
Beaman

Radio WM
PO Box 206
Birmingham B5 7SD
Tel: 021 414 8484
Entertainment WM

INDEPENDENT LOCAL RADIO

Radio Aire
PO Box 362
Leeds LS3 1LR
Tel: 0532 452299
Fax: 0532 421830
Programme controller:
Paul Faiburn

BRMB Radio
Radio House
PO Box 555
Aston Road North
Birmingham B6 4BX
Tel: 021 359 4481
Fax: 021 359 1117
Features producer: Nick
Meanwell

Beacon Radio
267 Tettenhall Road
Wolverhampton WV6
0DQ
Tel: 0902 757211
Fax: 0902 745456
Programme manager:
Pete Wagstaff

Beacon Shropshire
Thorn's Hall
28 Castle Street
Shrewsbury SY1 2BQ
Tel: 0743 232271
Fax: 0742 232271

Breeze AM
PO Box 3000
Southend-on-Sea
Essex SS1 1SY
Tel: 0702 430966
Fax: 0702 345224
Programme Controller:
Keith Rogers

Brunel Radio
Watershed Studios
Canons Road
Bristol BS99 7SN
Station Director: Mike
Henfield

CN.FM 103
PO Box 1000
The Vision Park
Chivers Way
Histon
Cambridge CB4 4WW
Tel: 0223 235255
Fax: 0223 235161
Programme controller:
Adrian Crookes

Capital Radio
Euston Tower
Euston Road
London NW1 3DR
Tel: 071 388 1288
Fax: 071 387 2345
David Castell
*The Richard Allinson
Show; The Way It Is; The
David Jensen Show*

Chiltern Radio
Chiltern Road
Dunstable LU6 1HQ
Tel: 0582 666001
Fax: 0582 661725
Programme controller:
Paul Robinson

City Talk
PO Box 1548
Liverpool L69 7DQ
Tel: 051 227 5100
Fax: 051 255 1143
Senior producer

County Sound
93 Chertsey Road
Woking
Surrey GU21 5XY
Tel: 0483 740066
Fax: 0483 740753
Paul Owens

DevonAir Radio
35-37 St David's Hill
Exeter EX4 4DA
Tel: 0392 430703
Fax: 0392 411893

Downtown Radio
Newtownards BT23 4ES
Tel: 0247 815555
Fax: 0247 817878
Film/video: John Daly

Essex Radio
Radio House
Clifftown Road
Southend-on-Sea SS1 1SX
Tel: 0702 333711
Programme manager

GWR
Lime Kiln Studios
Wootton Bassett
Swindon
Wilts SN4 7EX
Tel: 0793 853222
Station Director: Simon
Cooper

Great North Radio
Swalwell
Newcastle upon Tyne
NE99 1BB
Tel: 091 496 0377
Fax: 091 488 9222
Programme Controller:
Roy Leonard

Hallam FM
PO Box 194
Hartshead
Sheffield S1 1GP
Tel: 0742 766766
Presentation controller:
Dean Pepall

Hereward Radio
PO Box 225
Queensgate Centre
Peterborough PE1 1XJ
Tel: 0733 4622
Fax: 0733 427145
Programme controller:
Adrian Crookes

IRN
Crown House
72 Hammersmith Road
London W14 8YE
Tel: 071 603 2400
Editor: John Perkins

Invicta Radio
15 Station Road East
Canterbury
Kent CT1 2RB
Tel: 0227 767661
Fax: 0227 451312
News editor: Sue Slipping

LBC News Talk
Crown House
72 Hammersmith Road
London W14 8YE
Tel: 071 603 2400
Fax: 071 371 2155
Film/TV: Carol Allen;
Rebecca Nicholson

Leicester Sound
Granville House
Granville Road
Leicester LE1 7RW
Tel: 0533 551616
Fax: 0533 550869
Programme controller:
David Lloyd
Film and media
programmes: Mark
Hayman

London Talkback Radio
Crown House
72 Hammersmith Road
London W14 8YE
Tel: 071 603 2400
Fax: 071 371 2155

MAX AM
PO Box 4000
Forth House
Forth Street
Edinburgh EH1 3LF
Tel: 031 556 9255
Fax: 031 558 3277
Programme Controller:
Ken Haynes

Marcher Sound
The Studios
Mold Road
Gwersyllt
Wrexham
Clwyd LL1 4AF
Tel: 0978 752202
Fax: 0978 759701
Programme Controller:
Paul Mewies

Mercia Sound
Hertford Place
Coventry CV1 3TT
Tel: 0203 633933
Fax: 0203 258206
Managing director/
programme controller:
Stuart Linnell
Head of news: Colin
Palmer

Metro FM
Newcastle upon Tyne
NE99 1BB
Tel: 091 488 3131
Fax: 091 488 8611
Programme controller:
Giles Squire

Moray Firth Radio
PO Box 271
Inverness IV3 6SF
Tel: 0463 224433
Fax: 0463 243224
Music Box

Northsound Radio
45 King's Gate
Aberdeen AB2 6BL
Tel: 0224 632234
Fax: 0224 637289
Head of news: Barry
Young

Ocean Sound
Whittle Avenue
Segensworth-West
Fareham
Hants PO15 5PA
Tel: 04895 89911
Fax: 04895 589453
Film reviews: Cheryl
Phillips

Orwell FM
Electric House
Lloyds Avenue
Ipswich IP1 3HZ
Tel: 0473 216971
Fax: 0473 230350
Stephen Foster

Pennine Radio
PO Box 235
Pennine House
Forster Square
Bradford
W Yorks BD1 5NP
Tel: 0274 731521
Fax: 0274 392031
News Editor: Charles
Lees

Piccadilly Radio
127-131 The Piazza
Piccadilly Plaza
Manchester M1 4AW
Tel: 061 236 9913
Fax: 061 228 1503
Programme controller:
John Clayton

Plymouth Sound
Earl's Acre
Alma Road
Plymouth PL3 4HX
Tel: 0752 227272
Fax: 0752 670730
Head of News and
Current Affairs: Malcolm
Carroll

Radio Broadland
47-49 St Georges Plain
Colegate
Norwich NR3 1DB
Tel: 0603 630621
Fax: 0603 666353
Programme Controller:
Mike Stewart

Radio Clyde
Clydebank Business Park
Glasgow G81 2RX
Tel: 041 941 1111
Fax: 041 952 0080
Mike Riddoch, Andy
Dougan

Radio Forth RFM
PO Box 4000
Forth House
Forth Street
Edinburgh EH1 3LF
Tel: 031 556 9255
Fax: 031 558 3277
Films: Colin Somerville

Radio Tay
PO Box 123
Dundee DD1 9UF
Tel: 0382 200800
Fax: 0382 24549
Station manager: A J
Wilkie

Radio Wyvern
5-6 Barbourne Terrace
Worcester WR1 3JZ
Tel: 0905 612212
Fax: 0905 29595
Programme controller:
Stephanie Denham/
Norman Bilton

Red Dragon Radio
Radio House
West Canal Wharf
Cardiff CF1 5XJ
Tel: 0222 384041
Fax: 0222 384014
Programme controller:
Peter Milburn
Film/video: John Dash

Red Rose Radio
PO Box 301
St Paul's Square
Preston PR1 1YE
Tel: 0772 556301
Fax: 0772 201917
Programme controller:
Mark Matthews

Saxon Radio
Long Brackland
Bury St Edmunds
Suffolk IP33 1JY
Tel: 0284 701511
Fax: 0284 706446
Nigel Rennie

Severn Sound
PO Box 388
67 Southgate Street
Gloucester GL1 2DQ
Tel: 0452 423791
Fax: 0452 29446
Arts producer: Tony
Wickham

Signal Radio
Stoke-on-Trent ST4 2SR
Tel: 0782 747047
Fax: 0782 744110
Programme Controller:
John Evington

Southern Sound FM
PO Box 2000
Brighton BN4 2SS
Tel: 0273 43011
Fax: 0273 424783
Richard Gwynn, Simon
Blaxland
PO Box 2000
Eastbourne BN21 4ZZ
Tel: 0323 430111
Fax: 0323 412241
Jackie Skinner

Swansea Sound
Victoria Road
Gowerton
Swansea SA4 3AB
Tel: 0792 893751
Fax: 0792 898841

Programme controller:
David Thomas

TCR FM
5-7 Southcote Road
Bournemouth BH1 3LR
Tel: 0202 294881
Fax: 0202 299314
Programme controller:
Stan Horobin
News editor: Chris Kelly

TFM 96.60
74 Dovecot Street
Stockton-on-Tees
Cleveland TS18 1HB
Tel: 0642 615111
Fax: 0642 674402
Heather Raw

Trent FM
29-31 Castle Gate
Nottingham NG1 7AP
Tel: 0602 581731
Fax: 0602 585087
Market Place
Derby DE1 3AA
Tel: 0332 292945
Fax: 0332 292229
Programme controller:
Chris Hughes

210fm
PO Box 210
Reading RG3 5RZ
Tel: 0734 413131
Fax: 0734 431215
Programme controller:
Phil Coope

WABC
267 Tettenhall Road
Wolverhampton WV6
0DQ
Tel: 0902 757211
Fax: 0902 745456
Programme Manager:
Pete Wagstaff

West Sound
Radio House
54 Holmston Road
Ayr KA7 3BE
Tel: 0292 283662
Fax: 0292 283665
Programme controller:
John McCauley
*Kenny Campbell Show;
John McCauley's Show*

Xtra-AM
PO Box 555
Ashton Road North
Birmingham B6 4BX
Tel: 021 359 4481
Fax: 021 359 1117
Programme Manager:
Alan Carruthers

Alva Films
16 Brook Street
Alva
Clackmannanshire FK12 5JL
Tel: 0259 60936
Fax: 0259 69436
Formats: 16mm double-head, U-Matic, VHS
Seats: 24

BAFTA
195 Piccadilly
London W1V 9LG
Tel: 071 734 0022
Fax: 071 734 1792
Formats: Twin 16mm and Super 16mm double-head stereo, 35mm double-head Dolby stereo at all aspect ratios, U-Matic and VHS stereo
Seats: Princess Anne:213, Run Run Shaw:30

BFI
21 Stephen Street
London W1P 1PL
Tel: 071 255 1444
Fax: 071 436 7950
Formats: 35mm double-head/Dolby stereo optical, 16mm double-head/optical, U-Matic hi/lo-band/triple standard, VHS triple standard.
Seats: 1 (film):36, 2 (video):12, 3 (film):36

Baronet Theatre
84 Wardour Street
London W1V 3LF
Tel: 071 437 2233
Fax: 071 434 9990
Formats: 16mm and 35mm double-head, U-Matic, VHS
Seats: 25

Bijou Theatre
113 Wardour Street
London W1V 3LF
Tel: 071 437 2233
Fax: 071 434 9990
Formats: 16mm and 35mm double-head, Dolby stereo
Seats: 88

British Universities Film and Video Council (BUFVC)
55 Greek Street
London W1V 5LR
Tel: 071 734 3687
Fax: 071 728 3914
Formats: 16mm double-head, VHS, U-Matic
Seats: 15–20

CFS Conference Centre
22 Portman Close
London W1A 4BE
Tel: 071 486 2881

Fax: 071 486 4152
Formats: 16mm and 35mm film projection. Full in-house and outside catering
Seats: 110

Cannon Cinemas
Preview Theatre
Ground Floor
Pathé House
76 Hammersmith Road
London W14 9YR
Tel: 071 603 4555
Fax: 071 603 4277
Formats: 16mm and 35mm double-head, U-Matic, VHS triple standard
Seats: 36

Century Preview Theatres
31-32 Soho Square
London W1V 6AP
Tel: 071 437 7766
Fax: 071 437 1625
Formats: Century Theatre: 35mm Dolby optical and magnetic stereo, Dolby A & SR noise reduction, 2000′ double-head capacity; Executive Theatre: Dolby stereo optical and magnetic, A type noise reduction, 2000′ double-head capacity
Seats: Century:61, Executive:38

Chapter Cinema
Market Road
Canton
Cardiff CF5 1QE
Tel: 0222 396061
Formats: 35mm optical, 16mm double-head, high quality video projection, U-Matic/VHS. Reception space and restaurant
Seats: 78

Columbia Tri-Star Films UK
19-23 Wells Street
London W1P 3FP
Tel: 071 580 2090
Fax: 071 580 8980
Formats: 16mm, 35mm double-head Dolby SR stereo and full video projection, induction loop system. Catering and reception facilities
Seats: 68

Coronet Theatre
84 Wardour Street
London W1V 3LF
Tel: 071 437 2233
Fax: 071 434 9990
Formats: 35mm double-head, U-Matic, VHS
Seats: 15

Crawford Preview Theatre
15-17 Old Compton Street
London W1V 6JR
Tel: 071 734 5298
Fax: 071 287 0370
Formats: 16mm, 35mm. Triple standard U-Matic, VHS, Beta
Seats: 1 (film):15, 2 (video):15

Crown Theatre
86 Wardour Street
London W1V 3LF
Tel: 071 437 2233
Fax: 071 434 9990
Formats: 16mm, 35mm double-head, Dolby stereo
Seats: 45

De Lane Lea Sound Centre
75 Dean Street
London W1V 5HA
Tel: 071 439 1721
Fax: 071 437 0913
Formats: 35mm and 16mm, Dolby stereo SR & A with double-head capacity. ¾″ hi- and lo-band video and VHS
Seats: 30

Edinburgh Film Studios
Nine Mile Burn
Penicuik EH26 9LT
Tel: 0968 72131
Fax: 0968 72685
Formats: 16mm and 35mm double-head, U-Matic, VHS
Seats: 100

Goldcrest Elstree Studios
Shenley Road
Borehamwood
Herts WD6 1JG
Tel: 081 953 1600
Fax: 081 207 0860
Formats: 16mm, 35mm
Seats: 1:102, 2:17, 3:18

Grip House Preview Theatre
5-11 Taunton Road
Metropolitan Centre
Greenford
Middx UB6 8UQ
Tel: 081 578 2382
Fax: 081 578 1536
Formats: 16mm and 35mm, optical and magnetic double-head projection
Seats: 40

King's Lynn Arts Centre
27 King Street
King's Lynn
Norfolk PE30 1HA

Tel: 0553 774725
Formats: 16mm, 35mm
Seats: 359

The Metro
11 Rupert Street
London W1V 7FS
Tel: 071 434 3357/734
1506
Fax: 071 287 2112
Formats: 16mm and
35mm double-head. Two
screens available until
2pm only
Seats: 195, 86

The Minema
45 Knightsbridge
London SW1X 7NL
Tel: 071 235 4225
Fax: 071 235 4330
Formats: 35mm and
16mm, full AV systems
Seats: 68

Mr Young's
First Floor
1–6 Falconberg Court
London W1V 5FG
Tel: 071 437 1771
Fax: 071 734 4520
Formats: 16mm, Super
16mm, 35mm, Super
35mm, U-Matic, VHS,
Betamax, Dolby stereo
double-head optical and
magnetic Dolby SR.
Catering by request
Seats: 35 (extended to 40
on request)

Pinewood Studios
Iver
Bucks SL0 0NH
Tel: 0753 656296
Fax: 0753 656844
Formats: 16mm, 35mm,
70mm, U-Matic
Seats: Five theatres with
12 to 115 seats

**Prominent Studios
THX Preview
Theatre**
68a Delancey Street
London NW1 7RY
Tel: 071 284 0242
Fax: 071 284 1020
Formats: 35mm Dolby
optical and magnetic,
2,000' double-head, rock
'n' roll. All aspect ratios,
24-25-30 fps, triple-
track, interlock, Dolby A
& SR. Fully air
conditioned, kitchen and
reception area.
Wheelchair access
Seats: 26

**Rank Preview
Theatre**
127 Wardour Street
London W1V 4AD
Tel: 071 437 9020 x257
Fax: 071 434 3689
Formats: U-Matic, 16mm,
35mm double-head, Dolby
stereo, VHS, U-Matic,
slides
Seats: 58

**Royal Society of
Arts**
8 John Adam Street
London WC2N 6EZ
Tel: 071 930 5115
Fax: 071 839 5805
Formats: VHS triple
standard, Super VHS,
Sony Video 8, data
projection. Catering
available
Seats: 60

**Scottish Council for
Educational
Technology**
Dowanhill
74 Victoria Crescent Road
Glasgow G12 9JN
Tel: 041 334 9314
Fax: 041 334 6519
Formats: 16mm, 35mm
double-head and 8mm
Seats: 173

**Shepperton
Studios**
Shepperton
Middx TW17 0QD
Tel: 0932 862611
Fax: 0932 568989
Formats: 35mm, 16mm
Seats: 1 (35mm):40,
2 (16mm):20

Sherman Theatre
Senghenydd Road
Cardiff CF2 4YE
Tel: 0222 396844
Formats: 16mm, 35mm,
Dolby stereo, U-Matic
Seats: 474

**Twickenham
Studios**
St Margaret's
Twickenham
Middx TW1 2LT
Tel: 081 892 4477
Fax: 081 981 0168
Formats: 16mm, 35mm
Seats: 31

**Warner Bros
Preview Theatre**
135 Wardour Street
London W1V 3TD
Tel: 071 734 8400
Fax: 071 437 9544
Formats: 16mm, 35mm
double-head, Dolby stereo
Seats: 32

**Watershed Media
Centre**
1 Canons Road
Bristol BS1 5TX
Tel: 0272 276444
Fax: 0272 213958
Formats: Super 8mm,
16mm double-head,
35mm, U-Matic, VHS
Seats: 1:200, 2:50

**Weintraub House
Preview Theatre**
167–169 Wardour Street
London W1V 3TA
Tel: 071 439 1790
Fax: 071 734 1509
Formats: 35mm Dolby
stereo, U-Matic, VHS
Seats: 35–40

These are UK companies which are currently active in financing and/or making audiovisual product for UK and international media markets. Also making audiovisual product are film and video workshops (see p290). Not listed below are the numerous companies making TV commercials, educational and other non-broadcast material, nor those companies set up to facilitate the production of particular films (see Facilities p136)

Aardman Animations
14 Wetherell Place
Clifton
Bristol BS8 1AR
Tel: 0272 744802
Fax: 0272 736281
Peter Lord
David Sproxton
Made 'Lip Synch', a series of films for Channel 4. A full-length model animation feature is in development. Aardman is committed to adult animation with the emphasis on character and movement

Acacia Productions
80 Weston Park
London N8 9TB
Tel: 081 340 2619/
341 9392
Fax: 081 341 4879
J Edward Milner
Nikki Nagasiri
In 1989 productions included *Storm on the Mountain* and *The Greening of Thailand*, both programmes shown on the Channel Four series *Fragile Earth*. Also produced *Vietnam: After the Fire*

After Image
32 Acre Lane
London SW2 5SG
Tel: 071 733 7300
Fax: 071 326 1850
Jane Thorburn
Mark Lucas
After Image is best known for the long-running arts series *Alter Image* featuring artists and performers. Recent productions include *The Greatest Show on Earth*, two short operas jointly called *Tales of Faith and Foxes* and *Gran Gran Fiesta!* a celebration of Latin American music

and dance. Currently working on music and drama projects

Allied Stars
55 Park Lane
London W1Y 3DH
Tel: 071 493 1050
Fax: 071 499 5889
Dodi Fayed
Luke Randolph
Made *Breaking Glass*, co-financed *Chariots of Fire* and produced *F/X* for Orion

Allied Vision
Avon House
360 Oxford Street
London W1N 9HA
Tel: 071 409 1984
Fax: 071 493 4286
Edward Simons
Peter McRae
Completed *Howling V – The Rebirth* in 1989. Producing the next two films in the series in 1990

Amy International Productions
Lee Shepperton Studios
Shepperton
Middlesex TW17 0QD
Tel: 0932 562611
Fax: 0932 568989
Susan George
Simon MacCorkindale
Hunted, Odds End

Andor Films
8 Ilchester Place
London W14 8AA
Tel: 071 602 2382
Fax: 071 602 1047
Production of theatrical motion pictures

Anglia Films
48 Leicester Square
London WC2H 7FB
Tel: 071 321 0101
Graeme McDonald
Brenda Reid
John Rosenberg
David FitzGerald

The filmmaking and drama production arm of Anglia TV. Current projects include *The Chief Series 2, Chimera* (in association with Zenith Productions), *Devices and Desires, Frankie's House, Growing Rich, Riders* and *Sea Ghosts*

Anglo/Fortunato Films
170 Popes Lane
London W5 4NJ
Tel: 081 840 4196
Fax: 081 840 0279
Luciano Celentino
Feature film production company

Anglo International Films
Twickenham Film Studios
St Margarets
Twickenham
Middlesex TW1 2AW
Tel: 081 892 4477
Don Boyd
Robert McCrum
Mary Davies
Continuing in the tradition established with such films as *The Tempest, The Great Rock 'n' Roll Swindle, An Unsuitable Job for a Woman, Scum, Honky Tonk Freeway, Captive, The Last of England* and the multi-directional *Aria*, in 1988 Boyd produced *War Requiem* starring Laurence Olivier. In 1989 he returned to his directorial career with *Goldeneye* and in 1990 *Twenty-One*

Animation City
69 Well Street
London W1P 3RB
Tel: 071 494 3084
Fax: 071 436 8934
Sue Oakley

Company currently producing animated and live action commercials, pop promos, designs and TV and film titles and optical effects

Antelope Films
3 Fitzroy Square
London W1P 5AH
Tel: 071 387 4454
Fax: 071 388 9935
Clive Syddall
Peter Montagnon
Productions undertaken for various broadcast television companies including BBC, ITV and Channel 4 in 1990: *Testament, Global Rivals, Margot Fonteyn Story, The Midas Touch, Childhood, Terror* and *Pasternak*. In development: *Great Women Explorers, Nureyev – Story of a Dancer*, drama: *The Russian Album* from a book by Michael Ignatieff, and *True Blue*, a film based on the book by Daniel Topolski and Patrick Robinson

Antonine Productions
Blackcat Studios
830 Springfield Road
Glasgow G31 4HG
Tel: 041 554 4667/2742
Fax: 041 554 0939
Paddy Higson
Most recent credit *Silent Scream*, a Channel 4/BFI co-production

Arena Films
Twickenham Film Studios
St Margarets
Twickenham
Middlesex TW1 2AW
Tel: 081 892 4477
Fax: 081 891 0168
Made *Vincent and Theo* - for theatrical release and television. In production *Coup de Foudre*, 27 half hour films for television. Also made *Magic Moments* for Yorkshire Television

Ariel Productions
93 Wardour Street
London W1V 3TE
Tel: 071 494 2169
Fax: 071 494 2695
Otto Plaschkes
Produced *Shadey*, written by Snoo Wilson, directed by Philip Saville and starring Anthony Sher,

for Film Four International. In development are *Changing Places*, scripted by Peter Nichols, and *The Double Helix*, by James Watson

Artifax
17 Clifford Street
London W1X 1RG
Tel: 071 734 4584
Elizabeth Queenan
Documentaries, arts, music, drama and light entertainment. Recent productions: the 1987 Prix Italia prize-winning *Behind the Mask – Perspectives on the Music of Harrison Birtwistle. Big, Big Country*, a six-part series on country music with Hank Wangford. In production: a second series of *The Secret Life of Machines*, with Tim Hunkin

Aspect Film and Television Production
36 Percy Street
London W1P 9FG
Tel: 071 636 5303
Fax: 071 436 0666
Mark Chapman
Producers of documentaries, comedies and drama

Associates Film Productions (AFP)
60 Farringdon Road
London EC1R 3BP
Tel: 071 251 3885
Fax: 071 253 2045
Christian Wangler
Mike Dodds
Offshoot of the AKA film facility company

Avatar Film Corporation World Sales
Unit 5
Imperial Studios
Imperial Road
London SW6 2AG
Tel: 071 384 1366
Jon Brewer
Robert Patterson

BFI Production
29 Rathbone Street
London W1P 1AG
Tel: 071 636 5587
Fax: 071 580 9456
Young Soul Rebels, Silent Scream, Fellow Traveller, Melancholia, New Directors Shorts, Play Me Something, La Deuda Interna, Distant Voices

Still Lives, On the Black Hill, Caravaggio, The Draughtsman's Contract

BJE
Home Farm
Church Hill
High Littleton
Bristol BS18 5HF
Tel: 0761 71055
John King
Laurie Lee's *As I Walked Out One Midsummer Morning* and *A Rose For Winter, Telly Addicts*
Animal dramas include: *Priddy The Hedgehog, Carna The Otter, Drift the Mute Swan, The Lion* and *A Walk on the Wild Side*

Banner Film and TV
11 Swaledale Road
Sheffield S7 2BY
Tel: 0742 556875
David Rea
Broadcast documentaries and drama

Peter Batty Productions
Claremont House
Renfrew Road
Kingston
Surrey KT2 7NT
Tel: 081 942 6304
Fax: 081 336 1661
Peter Batty
Recent Channel 4 productions include *Swastika Over British Soil, A Time for Remembrance, The Divided Union, Fonteyn and Nureyev, The Algerian War, Swindle* and *Il Poverello*. Previous independent productions include *The Story of Wine, Battle for Warsaw, Battle for Dien Bien Phu, Birth of the Bomb, Search for the Super, Battle for Cassino, Operation Barbarossa* and *Farouk: Last of the Pharaohs*

Bedford Productions
6th Floor
6 Vigo Street
London W1X 1AH
Tel: 071 437 5452
Fax: 071 287 9870
Mike Dineen
Francis Megahy
Television, documentary, drama production, and business to business programming

Bevanfield Films
22 Soho Square
London W1V 5FJ

Tel: 071 287 0628
Fax: 071 439 0138
Producers of animated and feature films

Bordeaux Films International
22 Soho Square
London W1V 5FJ
Tel: 081 959 8556
Recent projects include *Caravans, Double Jeopardy, Giselle, Guns and the Fury, Laura, Mr Wrong* and *The Witch*

Britannia Entertainment
Pinewood Studios
Iver
Bucks SL0 0NH
Tel: 0753 651700
Fax: 0753 656844
David Nicholas Wilkinson
Gary Tuck
Long established independent production company specialising in international co-production. Also raises finance for and acts as consultant to other independent producers

British Lion
Pinewood Studios
Iver Heath
Bucks SL0 0NH
Tel: 0753 651700
Peter Snell
As Britannic Films, first project was the telemovie *Squaring the Circle*, co-financed with TVS and Metromedia Producers Associates. *Lady Jane* for Paramount Pictures and *Turtle Diary*, in association with United British Artists. *A Man for All Seasons* for Turner Network Television and *Treasure Island* also for TNT. Most recent production is *A Prayer for the Dying* for Samuel Goldwyn Co

Broadcast Communications (Corporate)
14 King Street
London WC2E 8HN
Tel: 071 240 6941
Fax: 071 379 5808
Michael Braham
Michael Braham is currently executive producer of the Channel 4 *Business Programme* and *Business Daily*

Brook Productions

21-24 Bruges Place
Randolph Street
London NW1 0TF
Tel: 071 482 6111
Fax: 071 284 0626
Udi Eichler
Philip Whitehead
Produced *Three of a Kind* (discussion series) and *The Session* for the BBC and the following for Channel 4: *The Thatcher Factor, Reagan on Reagan* (documentary series), *Prisoners of Childhood* (psychological drama), *Goodbye Russia, Brewing Trouble, Under the Influence*. Works in progress for the BBC include *Museums of Madness*

Buena Vista Productions

31-32 Soho Square
London W1V 6AP
Tel: 071 734 8111
Fax: 071 287 6338
David Simon
European television production arm of The Walt Disney Co

Burrill Productions

19 Cranbury Road
London SW6 2NS
Tel: 071 736 8673
Fax: 071 731 3921
Timothy Burrill
Burrill Productions co-produced *Return of the Musketeers* and *Valmark*. Produced *The Rainbow Thief. Princess of Siberia* in development with Enigma

Cabachon Films

16a Brechin Place
London SW7 4QA
Tel: 071 373 6453
Celestino Coronado
Productions include: *Smoking Mirror, The Lindsey Kemp Circus, Miroirs, Le Belle Indifferent, Hamlet, A Midsummer Night's Dream*

Camden Productions

20 Jeffreys Street
London NW1 9PR
Tel: 071 482 0527
Theresa FitzGerald
Small company consisting of two writers who develop their own work for film and TV

Cartwn Cymru

Model House
Bull Ring
Llantrisant
Mid Glamorgan
Tel: 0443 222316
Naomi Jones
Animation production

Celador Productions

39 Long Acre
London WC2E 9JT
Tel: 071 240 8101
Fax: 071 836 1117
Paul Smith
Television: primarily entertainment programming for all broadcast channels. Includes game shows, variety, with selected factual and drama output

Celtic Films

1-2 Bromley Place
London W1
Tel: 071 637 7651
Fax: 071 436 5387
Muir Sutherland
The Monk

Centre Films

118 Cleveland Street
London W1P 5DN
Tel: 071 387 4045
Fax: 071 388 0408
Jeffrey Taylor
Derek Granger
Kent Walwin

Chain Production

11 Hornton Street
London W8 4ND
Tel: 071 937 1981
Fax: 071 376 0556
Garwin Davison
Roberta Licurgo
Distribution/production specialist in Italian films.Theatrical release of *Mignon Has Left* through Metro cinema

Champion Television

TWI House
23 Eyot Gardens
London W6
Tel: 081 846 8088
Fax: 081 746 5381
Alan Bushell
Champion Television, a wholly owned subsidiary of Trans World International, the British subsidiary of Mark McCormack's International Management Group, has been contracted to produce The Sports Channel for British Satellite Broadcasting.

Launched in March 1990 Champion TV produces up to 16 hours a day of British and international sports programming every day of the year

Charisma Films

4th Floor
Russell Chambers
London WC2E 8AA
Tel: 071 379 4267
James Atherton

Chatsworth Television

97-99 Dean Street
London W1V 5RA
Tel: 071 734 4302
Fax: 071 437 3301
Malcolm Heyworth
Sister company to Chatsworth distribution and merchandising companies. Producers of light entertainment and drama. *Operation Julie* for Tyne Tees. *Interceptor* for Thames TV and *The Crystal Maze* for Channel 4

Cheerleader Productions

The Trocadero
19 Rupert Street
London W1V 7FS
Tel: 071 287 3333
Fax: 071 287 5908
Charles Balchin
Producers of sports programmes (American football, sumo wrestling, motor racing, three day eventing, karting, arena ball etc) for Channel 4, BBC, Sky, BSB

Children's Film and Television Foundation

Goldcrest Elstree Studios
Borehamwood
Herts WD6 1JG
Tel: 081 953 0844
Fax: 081 207 0860
The CFTF does not make films from its own resources but, for suitable children's/family cinema/television projects, is prepared to consider financing script development for eventual production by commercial companies. For further information, see under Organisations

The Children's Film Unit

Unit 4
Berrytime Studios
192 Queenstown Road

London SW8 3NR
Tel: 071 622 7793
A registered Educational Charity, the CFU makes low-budget films for television and PR on subjects of concern to children and young people. Crews and actors are trained at regular weekly workshops in Battersea. Work is in 16mm and video and membership is open to children from 8-16. Latest films for Channel 4 *Hard Road, Doombeach* for the Samaritans *Time to Talk*

Chrysalis Visual Programming

4th Floor
Threeways House
40-44 Clipstone Street
London W1P 7EA
Tel: 071 436 3933
Fax: 071 436 3523
Shelley Miller
Producers of *The Max Headroom Show*

Cinema Verity

The Mill House
Millers Way
1a Shepherds Bush Road
London W6 7NA
Tel: 081 749 8485
Fax: 081 743 5062
Verity Lambert
Ann Weir
In 1988, Verity Lambert produced *A Cry in the Dark* in Australia, starring Meryl Streep, Sam Neill and directed by Fred Schepisi. She also recently executive produced the sitcom *May to December* for the BBC

Colstar Communications and Entertainment

11 Wythburn Place
London W1H 5WL
Tel: 071 437 5725
Fax: 071 706 1704
Producers of art, history, sport, biography and wildlife documentaries for video sale

Columbia Pictures

19-23 Wells Street
London W1P 3FP
Tel: 071 580 2090
Arthur Leese

The Comic Strip

43a Berwick Street
London W1V 3RE
Tel: 071 439 9509
fax: 071 494 3133
Peter Richardson

Compact Yellowbill Group
118 Cleveland Street
London W1P 5DN
Tel: 071 387 4045
fax: 071 388 0408
Kent Walwin
Pom Oliver
Eddie Leahy

Compass Film Productions
3rd Floor
18-19 Warwick Street
London W1R 5RB
Tel: 071 439 6456
Fax: 071 439 1865
Simon Heaven
Involved since 1974 in cultural, educational and sponsored programmes for television. 1990 work includes *Violence*, a series of three programmes for Channel 4

Consolidated Productions (UK)
5 Jubilee Place
London SW3 3TD
Tel: 071 376 5151
Stephen Smallwood
Producer of television films, mini-series and comedy programmes

Cosgrove Hall Productions
Albany House
8 Albany Road
Chorlton-cum-Hardy
Manchester M21 1BL
Tel: 061 881 9211
A subsidiary of Thames Television

Creative Law
Media Legal Services
Burbank House
75 Clarendon Road
Sevenoaks
Kent TN13 1ET
Tel: 0732 460592
John Wheller
Production arm of Media Legal Services developing legal projects for film and TV, including series centred on The Inns of Court

Cue Film and Video Productions
2/32 Finchley Road
London NW8
Tel: 071 722 2012
Maureen McCue
Television and low-budget features; training films

DBA Television
21 Ormeau Avenue
Belfast BT2 8HD

Tel: 0232 231197
Fax: 0232 333302
David Barker
Northern Ireland's leading production company. Wide range of documentary programmes for Channel 4 and BBC. Just completed: *Heart on the Line* Channel 4, *Two Villages* BBC2, *Dust on the Bible* Channel 4/RTE. In production/development: *Hobos, The Jeff Healey Band, Drink Talking, Godonall, The Mass*

Debonair Productions
40-44 Clipstone Street
London W1P 7EA
Tel: 071 323 3220
Fax: 071 637 2590
Toni Strasburg
Mike Rossiter
Ivan Strasburg
Productions include *Chain of Tears, The Other Bomb, The Wasted Hand, Fog of War* and *Fragile Earth: South Africa – The Wasted Land*, a documentary about the effects of apartheid on the environment

Deptford Beach Productions
79 Wardour Street
London W1V 3TH
Tel: 071 734 8508
Fax: 071 287 2122
Tony Kirkhope

Distant Horizon
5-6 Portman Mews South
London W1H 9AU
Tel: 071 493 1625
Fax: 071 493 3429
Paul Janssen
Recent productions include *American Kickboxer, Terminal Bliss, Reason to Die*

Diverse Production
6-12 Gorleston Street
London W14 8XS
Tel: 071 603 4567
Fax: 071 603 2148
Philip Clarke
Company with commitment to innovative television. Producers of *Check Out, Europe Express, Uncertainties, 9-II-5* and a number of other broadcast series

Domino Films
8 Stockwell Terrace
Stockwell

London SW9 0QD
Tel: 071 582 0393
Fax: 071 582 0437
Joanne Mack
Steve Humphries
Producers of *Lost Children of the Empire* for Granada, *A Century of Childhood* – eight part documentary series for Channel 4, *Return of the Death Squads* and *Soviet Citizens* also for Channel 4, *West at War* – four part documentary series for HTV West. In production *Secret World of Sex* – six part social history series for BBC, *Breadline Britain in the Nineties* – six part documentary on poverty for LWT and *The Travelling Talkshows* – worldwide discussion series for Channel 4

Dramatis Personae
122 Kennington Road
London SE11 6RE
Tel: 071 735 0831
Maria Aitken
Nathan Silver
Completed production of second TV series on *Acting*, co-produced with the BBC. Series *Boom Architecture* and two others in preparation. This company is concerned primarily with features on artistic skills and human development having broad cultural or social interest

Driftwood Films
40-42 King Street
London WC2E 8TS
Tel: 071 379 5396
Fax: 071 240 7311
Made *Dark River* and *Les Bikes*. In development *Looking On*. Also do corporate/commercials

East End Films
30 Berwick Street
London W1V 3RF
Tel: 071 734 4636
Fax: 071 734 4638
Producers of documentaries, promotional films and feature films

Edinburgh Film and Video Productions
Edinburgh Film and TV Studios
Nine Mile Burn
by Penicuik
Midlothian EH26 9LT
Tel: 0968 72131
fax: 0968 72685
Robin Crichton

Major Scottish production company. Currently in production *The Stamp of Greatness* TV series and *Silent Mouse*, a TV Christmas special

Endboard Productions
Zair Works
111-119 Bishop Street
Birmingham B5 6JL
Tel: 021 622 1325
fax: 021 622 1554
Yugesh Walia
Sunandan Walia
Producers of TV programmes and information videos. In 1989/90 produced a '40 Minutes' for BBC2 called *Many Happy Returns* and an 'Encounter' for Central TV called *Shadows of Caste*. Future plans include a new sports series for Channel 4

Enigma Productions
Pinewood Studios
Pinewood Road
Iver
Bucks SL0 0NH
Tel: 0753 630 555
Fax: 0753 630 393
David Puttnam
Film and television production

Equal Time
Heath Lodge
Heathside
London NW3 1BL
Tel: 071 431 1927
Martin Minns
Produces broadcast documentaries on music, the arts and current affairs

Euston Films
365 Euston Road
London NW1 3AR
Tel: 071 387 0911
John Hambley
Andrew Brown
The filmmaking subsidiary of Thames TV. Recent projects include: *Minder, Dealers, Capital City, The Fear*, and *Shrinks*

Eye Film and Television
The Guildhall
Church Street
Eye
Suffolk IP23 7BD
Tel: 0379 870083
Fax: 0379 870987

Fairwater Films
68 Vista Rise
Llandaff
Cardiff CF5 2SD
Tel: 0222 554416
Fax: 0222 578488
Tony Barnes
Award winning
animation producers.
Recent work includes
Satellite City for S4C,
Billy the Fish for Channel
4 *Transylvania Pet Shop*
and *All Round AL*
in development

Falkman Communications
33 Gresse Street
London W1 1PN
Tel: 071 636 1371
Bernard Falk
Independent television
production company set
up by BBC presenter
Falk. Produced *Travelog*
for Channel 4 and *The
Waltons Meet Mickey
Mouse* for ITV. Corporate
video clients include ICI,
Lucas Industries,
Memorex Telex, dixons
and Lex Service

The Film Company
115 Goldhawk Road
London W12 8EJ
Film and video production

Film Four International
60 Charlotte Street
London W1P 2AX
Tel: 071 631 4444
Fax: 071 580 2622
International film sales
and distribution arm of
Channel 4, often credited
as a co-production partner
for UK and international
productions. Decisions on
programming and finance
relating to these
productions are initiated
by Film on Four, the film
programming strand of
Channel 4's drama
department. See also under
International Sales

FilmFair
1-4 Jacobs Well Mews
London W1
Tel: 071 935 1596
Lewis Rudd
Prolific producers of
cartoon and puppet
animation series for
children, including
*Huxley Pig, Bangers and
Mash, Paddington Bear,*
and *The Wombles*

The Filmworks
65 Brackenbury Road
Hammersmith
London W6 0BG
Tel: 081 741 5631
Fax: 081 748 3198
Recent productions: *On
the Trail of the Chinese
Wildman, Struggle for the
Pole – In the Footsteps of
Scott, A Day in the Life of
a Medical Officer,
Antarctic Challenge* and
Anything's Possible

The First Film Company
38 Great Windmill Street
London W1V7PA
Tel: 071 439 1640
Fax: 071 437 2062
Feature film, television
and commercial
production

Flamingo Pictures
47 Lonsdale Square
London N1 1EW
Tel: 071 607 9958
Christine Oestreicher
James Scott
Produced *Loser Takes All,*
based on Graham
Greene's novel. Future
plans include *Dibs,* based
on a true story by
Virginia M Axlune

Flashback Productions
22 Kildare Terrace
London W2 5LX
Tel: 071 727 9904
Victoria Wegg-Prosser
Producers of *Flashback,*
a 20-part series for
Channel 4 which won a
BFI Award and *The
Games in Question, Fifties
Features, Tales Out of
School* and 60
programmes on *The
March of Time.* Makers
of documentaries for
Channel 4, the BBC and
overseas co-producers.
Commmitted to public
service broadcasting

Flashback Television
2/3 Cowcross Street
London EC1M 6DR
Tel: 071 490 8996
Fax: 071 490 5610
Taylor Downing
Produces documentary
programmes for broadcast
television and corporate
work for non-broadcast.
We specialise in historical
documentaries, *Civil War*
for Channel Four, drama
documentaries *Divorce* for

Thames, sports
documentaries, *Bidding
for '96* for Granada and
business programming

Focus Films
Rotunda Studio
R/O 116-118 Finchley
Road
London NW3 5HT
Tel: 071 435 9004
Fax: 071 431 3562
David Pupkewitz
Marsha Levin
Louise Whitby
Oz Antser
Most recent productions
include Janet Suzman's
critically acclaimed
Othello for Channel Four
and Gad Hollander's film
Diary of a Sane Man
selected for Berlin
International Film
Festival 1990. Now also
financing international
co-productions

Mark Forstater Productions
8A Trebeck Street
London W1Y 7RL
Tel: 071 408 0733
fax: 071 499 8772
Mark Forstater
Produced *Wherever You
Are* by Krzysztof Zanussi,
*The Wolves of Willoughby
Chase* for Zenith
Productions, *Streets of
Yesterday* directed by
Judd Ne'eman and
Painted It Black directed
by Tim Hunter.
Productions for 1990
include *The Touch*
directed by Krzysztof
Zanussi, *Timbuctoo*
directed by Charlotte
Trench and *Paper
Marriage* directed by
Krzysztof Lang

Freeway Films
67 George Street
Edinburgh EH2 2JG
Tel: 031 225 3200
Fax: 031 225 3667
John McGrath
Susie Brown

Frontroom Productions
79 Wardour Street
London W1V 3TH
Tel: 071 734 4603
Fax: 071 287 0849
John Davies
Robert Smith
Chris Harvey
Now involved in the
production of drama and
commercials. Produced
the 1983 feature
Acceptable Levels directed

by John Davies. Short
features include: *Intimate
Strangers* directed by
Robert Smith, and *Ursula
and Glenys* devised and
directed by John Davies
in 1985. 1987 feature *The
Love Child* directed by
Robert Smith. 1989
feature *Wild Flowers*
written by Sharman
Macdonald, directed by
Robert Smith. Planned for
1990: a feature *The Little
Dancer* written by Sue
Townsend, directed by
Robert Smith and a
feature *The Golondrina*
written by Tom Murphy,
directed by John Davies

Fugitive Features
2nd Floor
87 Notting Hill Gate
London W11 3JZ
Tel: 071 727 2060
Fax: 071 792 0804
Makers of *The Krays* and
The Reflecting Skin

David Furnham Films
39 Hove Park Road
Hove
East Sussex BN3 6LH
Tel: 0273 559731
New developments:
*Harriet and Her
Harmonium,* a new
musical; *South Coast
Jazz,* a series; *The David
Heneker Collection,* a
performance
documentary; and *Our
Lady of Good Counsel* for
BBC TV

Gainsborough (Film and TV) Productions
3 Audley Square
London W1Y 5DR
Tel: 071 409 1925
Fax: 071 408 2042
John Hough
Made *Hazard of Hearts,
The Lady and the
Highwayman, A Ghost in
Monte Carlo.* New
production in 1990 *Jewel
of Love*

John Gau Productions
Burston House
1 Burston Road
London SW15 6AR
Tel: 081 788 8811
Fax: 081 789 0903
Ivan Rendall
Anne Munyard
Television documentary
production, including
productions for BSB

Noel Gay Television
143 Charing Cross Road
London WC2H 0EE
Tel: 071 287 0087
Bill Cotton
Paul Jackson
Light entertainment/
documentaries, including:
*Ten Glorious Years, Red
Dwarf, Euro Disney
Christmas special*. Main
contractor to BSB's
Galaxy Channel

General Entertainment Investments
65-67 Ledbury Road
London W11 2AD
Tel: 071 221 3512
Fax: 071 792 9005
John Oakley
Feature film financiers/
producers. Recent work
includes *Tropic of Ice*
Anglo-Finnish co-
production, *Soweto*
African Music Feature,
Olympus Force Anglo-
Greek co-production.
Currently preparing
Extreme Remedies
US-Anglo-Polish
co-production and *Bank
Robber* Anglo-US
co-production

Gibb Rose Organisation (GRO)
Pinewood Studios
Pinewood Road
Iver Heath
Bucks SL0 0HN
Tel: 0753 651700
Fax: 0753 656935
Sydney Rose
Company formed by
Sydney Rose and Bee Gee
Maurice Gibb to make
international film and TV
productions

Nick Gifford
Street Farmhouse
Woodnesborough
Nr Sandwich
Kent CT13 ONF
Tel: 0304 612631
Fax: 0304 614949
Nick Gifford
c/o Hope and Lyne
Made *Sid's Children* for
Channel 4, shot *Not Pots*,
made a documentary on a
French village

Bob Godfrey Films
199 Kings Cross Road
London WC1X 9DB
Tel: 071 278 5711
Fax: 071 278 6809
Bob Godfrey
Mike Hayes

Children's programmes,
entertainments, promos,
audiovisual and
educational films

Goldcrest Films and Television
36-44 Brewer Street
London W1R 3HP
Tel: 071 437 8696
Major feature film, sales
and finance company.
Recent films include *All
Dogs Go To Heaven, Black
Rainbow, Rock-a-Doodle,*
and *Scorchers*

The Grade Company
Embassy House
3 Audley Square
London W1
Tel: 071 409 1925
Fax: 071 408 2042
Lord Grade
Company currently
producing TV films based
on Barbara Cartland
novels and developing
other potential film
projects

Grasshopper Productions
50 Peel Street
London W8 7PD
Tel: 071 229 1181
Fax: 071 229 1181
Joy Whitby
Productions to date: for
children *Grasshopper
Island, Emma and
Grandpa* and *East of the
Moon*, film series based on
the Terry Jones fairy
tales with music by Neil
Innes; *The Angel and the
Soldier Boy* 25 minute
animation by Alison de
Vere and family telefilm
A Pattern of Roses

Greenpoint Films
5a Noel Street
London W1V 3RB
Tel: 071 437 6492
Fax: 071 437 0644
Ann Scott
Patrick Cassavetti
A loose association of
eight filmmakers: Simon
Relph, Christopher
Morahan, Ann Scott,
Richard Eyre, Stephen
Frears, Patrick
Cassavetti, John
Mackenzie and Mike
Newell. Projects have
included Eyre's *The
Ploughman's Lunch* and
Laughterhouse,
Morahan's *In The Secret
State*, David Hare's
Wetherby and *Paris by
Night*, Newell's *The Good*

Father, Giles Foster's
Tree of Hands, Mike
Bradwell's *Chains of Love*
and Peter Barnes' *Nobody
Here But Us Chickens*

Colin Gregg Films
Floor 2
1-6 Falconberg Court
London W1V 5FG
Tel: 071 439 0257
Colin Gregg
Gregg directed *Lamb* for
Flickers-Limehouse
Productions. Completed
third feature *We Think
the World of You* in 1988,
followed by *Genoa* for the
BBC and *Earthly Powers*,
an eight-part drama
series

Griffin Productions
Balfour House
46-54 Great Titchfield
Street
London W1P 7AE
Tel: 071 636 5066
Fax: 071 436 3252
Adam Clapham
Drama and factual
programmes. Produced
Act of Betrayal mini-
series for TVS and ABC
Australia, *Secret Weapon*
for TVS and Turner
Network Television,
Painting with Light for
BBC, *Club X* and *Odyssey*
for Channel 4. Co-
produced *Captain James
Cook* with Revcom for ITV

Hammer Film Productions
Goldcrest Elstree Studios
Borehamwood
Herts WD6 1JG
Tel: 081 953 1600
Fax: 081 905 1127
Roy Skeggs
The company responsible
for many classic British
horror films was revived
under new management
in 1983 to start work on
13 films under the title
*Hammer House of Mystery
and Suspense*, to be
released worldwide by
20th Century Fox. A
second series is in
development. Also
purchased rights in 1985
to six novels with a view
to feature film production

HandMade Films (Productions)
26 Cadogan Square
London SW1X 0JP
Tel: 071 584 8345
Fax: 071 584 7338
George Harrison
Denis O'Brien

Producers of *Monty
Python's Life of Brian,
The Long Good Friday,
Time Bandits, Privates on
Parade, The Missionary,
Scrubbers, A Private
Function, Mona Lisa,
Withnail and I, Five
Corners, Bellman and
True, Track 29, The
Lonely Passion of Judith
Hearne*, and *Raggedy
Rawney*. Current releases
include *Powwow
Highway, Checking Out*
and *How to Get Ahead in
Advertising*. Filming in
1989 *Cold Dog Soup,
Nuns on the Run*. Filming
in 1990 *Land of
Opportunity*

Harcourt Films
77 Camden Mews
London NW1 9BU
Tel: 071 267 0882
Fax: 071 267 1064
Jeremy Marre
Producer and director of
documentaries for
Channel 4, BBC and ITV.
Also many overseas co-
productions. Most recent
productions include:
14-part music series *Beats
of the Heart*; 7-part series
for Channel 4 *Chasing
Rainbows*; 12-part
wildlife series *Ourselves
and Other Animals,
Nature of Music* – three
films produced for
Channel 4 and RM Arts.
Two films for BBC's
'Under the Sun' series and
in production 4 films on
the theme of musical
improvisation for
Channel 4 and RM Arts

Hartswood Films Limited
Shepperton Studios
Studios Road
Shepperton
Middlesex TW17 0QD
Tel: 0932 562611
Fax: 0932 68989
Independent production
company for theatre and
television, owned and run
by producer Beryl Vertue

Hemdale Holdings
21 Albion Street
London W2 2AS
Tel: 071 724 1010
Fax: 071 724 9168
George Miller
Produced *Terminator,
Return of the Living Dead,
Body Slam, River's Edge,
Vampire's Kiss, Shag,
Staying Together,
Chattahoochee,* and

Hidden Agenda. All production activities currently based in US. UK office, sales outfit only

Jim Henson Productions

Goldcrest Elstree Studios
Shenley Road
Borehamwood
Herts WD6 1JG
Tel: 081 435 7121
Fax: 081 905 1324
Messages: 081 905 1412
Duncan Kenworthy
Peter Coogan
Producers with TVS of *The Storyteller*, currently producing a second series *Greek Myths*, starring Michael Gambon in the title role. Producers of Warners' 1990 feature *The Witches*, directed by Nic Roeg from the novel by Roald Dahl. Recently produced series of 13 half-hour episodes of *The Ghost of Fafner Hall* for Tyne Tees and 26 8-minute episodes of *Mother Goose* for TSW

Jim Henson's Creature Shop

1b Downshire Hill
Hampstead
London NW3
Tel: 071 431 2818
Fax: 071 431 3737
John Stephenson
William Plant
John Geraghty
Creators of animatronic, puppet and prosthetic designs for feature films, television and commercials. Outstanding examples can be seen on *Teenage Mutant Ninja Turtles*, *The Witches* and *The Bear*. Previous work includes characters for *Dark Crystal*, *Labyrinth*, *Dreamchild* and fantasy characters in *The Storyteller*

Hightimes Productions

7 Garrick Street
London WC2E 9AR
Tel: 071 240 1128/
240 0943
Fax: 071 497 9242
Tony Humphreys
Al Mitchell
Production and packaging company which set up the Anglia quiz show *The Zodiac Game* and packaged the *Me and My Girl* situation comedy for LWT (five completed

series). Drama series, situation comedy and game shows in development and pre-production for 1990/91

Holmes Associates

10-16 Rathbone Street
London W1P 1AH
Tel: 071 637 8251
Fax: 071 637 9024
Andrew Holmes
Robert Eagle
Adrian Bate
Stephen Taylor
Recent work: *Signals* Channel Four's weekly arts series; *Rock Steady* Channel Four's live rock concert roadshow and *Piece of Cake* major film mini-series for LWT

HTV International

126 Baker Street
London W1M 1FH
Tel: 071 224 4048
Fax: 071 486 0615
A wholly owned subsidiary of the HTV Group, HTV International was set up in 1988 to specialise in theatrical and television production for world markets. First production *King of the Wind* starring Richard Harris and Glenda Jackson. Currently in production are *The Last Butterfly* and *Eminent Domain*

Ideal Communications Films and Television

26 Soho Square
London W1V 5FJ
Tel: 071 494 0011
Fax: 071 287 8337
Productions include *Money Talks* (aka *Loser Takes All*) co-produced with Miramax, BBC and British Screen. *Medium Rare* co-produced with Limelight. Currently in pre-production *Calvi – God's Banker*

Illuminations

19-20 Rheidol Mews
Rheidol Terrace
London N1 8NU
Tel: 071 226 0266
Fax: 071 359 1151
John Wyver
Linda Zuck
Producers of cultural programmes for Channel 4, BBC Television and others. Recent projects include *The A-Z of TV*, an evening of archive

television; *Signs of Life* for *Horizon*, a compilation series of new video; *White Noise* and a special for *The Late Show* about Roland Barthes. Projects in development include *Global Village* exploring satellite television, and a film about the painter Jean-Michel Basquiat

Illustra Communications

13-14 Bateman Street
London W1V 6EB
Tel: 071 437 9611
Douglas Kentish

Independent Film Production Associates (IFPA)

87 Dean Street
London W1V 5AA
Tel: 071 734 3847/
439 3795
Charles Thompson
Aileen McCracken
Film, video, TV production in the areas of documentary, light entertainment, music and the arts. Recent work comprises *Crossing the Line*, *Disciples of Chaos* and *Royal Ellington* for Channel 4

Independent Producers

5 Elm Quay
Nine Elms Lane
London SW8 5DE
Tel: 071 498 6822
Fax: 071 498 6517
Jan Martin
Corporate programmes and live events: the big screen live transmission from The Royal Opera House to the Covent Garden Piazza, now in its fourth year

Infovision

63 White Lion Street
London N1 9PP
Tel: 071 837 0012
Fax: 071 278 1632
Helen McCrorie
Infovision is a corporate and employee communications consultancy providing live event, print, media training and video production services. Clients include British Steel, the Water Companies, Electricity Distribution Companies

Initial Film and Television

22 Golden Square

London W1R 3PA
Tel: 071 439 8994
Fax: 071 439 4326
Eric Fellner
Scott Millaney
Malcolm Gerrie
Mike Bolland

Insight Productions

Gidleigh Studio
Gidleigh
Chagford
Newton Abbot
Devon TQ13 8HP
Tel: 0647 432686
Brian Skilton
TV production in arts, drama, entertainment, environment and documentary. In production: *Camargue* and *Dartmoor the Threatened Wilderness*, environment documentaries. In pre-production *Words in a Landscape* with Ted Hughes

International Broadcasting Trust

2 Ferdinand Place
London NW1 8EE
Tel: 071 482 2847
Fax: 071 284 3374
Paddy Coulter
A consortium of some 80 organisations, including development agencies, churches and trade unions, formed to make programmes about the Third World, development and the environment, both for TV and non-broadcast. Recent productions include *Young, British and Muslim* for Yorkshire TV and programmes for BBC Schools

Interprom

7a Tythings Court
Minehead
Somerset TA24 5NT
Tel: 0643 706774
Fax: 0643 702698
Clive Woods
Producers and distributors of various music programmes, specialising in jazz and blues

Isolde Films

4 Kensington Park Gardens
London W11 3HB
Tel: 071 727 3541
Fax: 071 439 0472
Recent productions include *Testimony*, *The Children*

Jennie & Co
3 Duck Lane
London W1V 1FL
Tel: 071 437 0600
Fax: 071 439 2377
Gower Frost
Terry Bedford
Kate Symington

Kai Productions
1 Ravenslea Road
London SW12 8SA
Tel: 081 673 4550
George Haggerty
Mike Wallington
Channel 4 productions:
Malltime (1987),
Robotopia (1989).
Current: *Fun-a-Thon*
(1990) for Granada

Kestrel Films
11 Landford Road
London SW15 1AQ
Tel: 081 788 6244
Bill Shapter

King Rollo Films
Dolphin Court
High Street
Honiton
Devon EX14 8LS
Tel: 0404 45218
Fax: 0404 45328
Clive Juster
Producers and
distributors of the
animated series:
*Mr Benn, King Rollo,
Victor and Maria, Towser,
Watt the Devil, The
Adventures of Spot, Ric*
and *The Adventures of Ric
and Elton*

Kinmonth
c/o Foxtrot Films
5 Kensington Park
Gardens
London W11
Tel: 071 229 1322
Margy Kinmonth
Drama productions
include *Baker's Dozen* and
To the Western World,
Steven Berkoff

Kohler
16 Marlborough Road
Richmond
Surrey TW10 6JR
Tel: 081 940 3967
Fax: 071 287 3779
Michael Kohler
Cabiri, The Experiencer

Koninck
175 Wardour Street
London W1V 3AB
Tel: 071 734 4943
Fax: 071 494 0405
Keith Griffiths and The
Brothers Quay.
Specialists in puppet

animation. Producers of
arts documentaries and
fiction. Latest projects
include: *Sketch for
Troubled Sleep, De
Artificiali Perspectiva,
Secret Joy, Warhol's
Cinema 1963-68* and *Dogs
Talk, Fish Walk & the
Baron Jumps Over the
Moon.* In development:
*Faust, The Institute
Benjamenta* and *The
Presence*

**Kruger Leisure
Organisation**
PO Box 130
Hove
East Sussex BN3 6QU
Tel: 0273 550088
Fax: 0273 540969
Jeffrey Kruger
A division of the Kruger
Organisation, making
music programmes for
TV, satellite and video
release worldwide as well
as co-producing various
series and full length
feature films. Latest
co-production with
Central TV music
division *21st Anniversary
Tour of Glen Campbell*

**Lambeth
Productions**
Twickenham Studios
St Margaret's
Twickenham TW1 2AW
Tel: 081 892 4477
Fax: 081 891 0168
Sir Richard Attenborough
Terry Clegg
Diana Hawkins
Feature *Charlie* in
preparation for shooting
in 1990/1

**Landseer Film and
Television
Productions**
140 Royal College Street
London NW1 0TA
Tel: 071 485 7333
Fax: 071 485 7573
Documentary, drama,
music and arts.
Productions include:
Sinfonietta Series II, for
Channel Four, two *South
Bank Shows: Two Women
in Three Dimensions,
From the New World; Sex,
Politics and Alan
Ayckbourn* for BBC
Omnibus; a profile of
Kenneth MacMillan *Out
of Line* also for the BBC
and *Not Pots,* a crafts
series for Channel 4

**Helen Langridge
Associates of
London**
75 Kenton Street
London WC1N 1NN
Tel: 071 833 2955
Fax: 071 837 2836
Helen Langridge
Juliet Naylor
Commercials, music
videos, television drama

**Brian Lapping
Associates**
21-24 Bruges Place
Randolph Street
London NW1 0TF
Tel: 071 482 5855
Fax: 071 284 0626
Producers of TV
programming, including
Countdown to War with
Ian McKellan as Hitler;
Hypotheticals, the 1990
series of 3 one-hour
programmes, dealt with
media, government and
the law; *The Second
Russian Revolution* seven
one hour documentaries
on politics inside the
Kremlin

Large Door
41-45 Beak Street
London W1R 3LE
Tel: 071 439 1381
John Ellis
Simon Hartog
Producers of current
affairs and media
documentaries, including
the award-winning *This
Food Business, New
Chinese Cinema, Whisky
Galore* and Channel 4's
Visions series (1982-85).
Projects in development
include series on catering,
Asian cinema and TV in
Brazil

**Lazer
Entertainments
(UK)**
118 Cleveland Street
London W1P 5DN
Tel: 071 388 2323
Feature production
company. Editing and
other post-production
facilities

**Limehouse
Productions**
The Trocadero
19 Rupert Street
London W1V 7FS
Tel: 071 287 3333
Fax: 071 287 5908
Iain Bruce
Richard Key
A wide range of projects
in development

Limelight Films
3 Bromley Place
London W1P 5HB
Tel: 071 255 3939
Fax: 071 436 4334
Steve Barron
Simon Fields
Producers of pop promos,
TV commercials, TV
programming and feature
films, with offices in
London and LA

Little Bird Co
91 Regent Street
London W1R 7TA
Tel: 071 434 1131
Fax: 071 434 1803
James Mitchell
Jeffrey Rosenblatt
Company has made three
series of *The Irish RM,*
two two-hour mini-series
Troubles. Feature films
Joyriders and *December
Bride*

**Living Tape
Productions**
Ramillies House
1-2 Ramillies Street
London W1V 1DF
Tel: 071 439 6301
Fax: 071 439 0731
Nick Freethy
Stephen Bond
Producers of educational
and documentary
programmes for TV and
video distribution.
Currently completed
major new TV series
Oceans of Wealth

**Euan Lloyd
Productions**
Pinewood Studios
Iver Heath
Bucks SL0 0NH
Tel: 0753 651700
Fax: 0753 656844
Euan Lloyd
Chris Chrisafis
Since 1968, Lloyd has
made nine major action
adventures including *The
Wild Geese, Who Dares
Wins* and *The Sea Wolves.*
In development are
Centrifuge and *Okavango*

**London Film
Productions**
44a Floral Street
London WC2E 9DA
Tel: 071 434 3100
Mark Shelmerdine
Rosie Bunting
Founded in 1932 by
Alexander Korda. Many
co-productions with the
BBC, including
I, Claudius, Poldark and
Testament of Youth.
Produced *The Country*

Girls for Channel 4. In receipt of a direct drama commission from a US network for *Scarlet Pimpernel* and *Kim*. Renowned for productions of classics, now developing more contemporary fiction work

Lusia Films
7-9 Earlham Street
London WC2 1HL
Tel: 071 240 2350
Mark Karlin
Karlin made *For Memory*, a BFI/BBC co-production, and a four-part series of documentaries on Nicaragua. Also a two-hour film called *Utopias* for Channel 4. Currently in production: a film on the last ten years of the Nicaraguan revolution

Jo Lustig
PO Box 472
London SW7 4NL
Tel: 071 937 6614
Jo Lustig
Represents Mel Brooks and Managing Director of Brooksfilms (UK). Co-producer *84 Charing Cross Road* (Brooksfilms and Columbia), producer of TV documentaries: *Maria Callas – Life and Art* (Channel 4); *The Unforgettable Nat 'King' Cole* (BBC TV); *John Cassavetes* (BBC TV)

MGMM
22 Golden Square
London W1R 3PA
Tel: 071 439 9527
Scott Millaney
Commercials, pop promos, live concerts and shorts

MGM-UA Communications Co
UIP House
45 Beadon Road
Hammersmith
London W6 OEG
Tel: 081 741 9041 ext 4069/4156
Fax: 081 563 0659

Magic Hour Films and Television Ltd
143 Chatsworth Road
London NW2 5QT
Tel: 081 459 8987
Fax: 081 459 3074
Bianka Ford
Production company making films, dramas, documentaries and series

for TV. Also provides research and packaging for film and television projects

Malachite
East Kirkby House
Spilsby
Lincolnshire PE23 4BX
Tel: 07903 538/
071 487 5451
Charles Mapleston
Hugh Newsam
Nancy Thomas
Ken Baynes
Specialists in arts, music and documentary programming. Recent productions include *A Painter's Paradise*

Malone Gill Productions
Canaletto House
39 Beak Street
London W1R 3LD
Tel: 071 287 3970
Fax: 071 287 8146
Michael Gill
Georgina Denison
Lita Yong
Hugh Newsam
Mandy Field
Recent productions include *Nature Perfected* (1990) for the Japan Association for the International Garden and Greenery Exhibition, WETA and Channel Four; *Monet: Legacy of Light* (1990) for WGBH; and *Vintage: A History of Wine by Hugh Johnson* for WGBH and Channel Four. In production is *The Buried Mirror: Images of Latin America* for the Smithsonian Institute (US), Sociedad General de Television (Spain) and BBC TV (UK); and *Nomads* for ITEL and Channel Four. In development *New World View* for Pacem Productions, Los Angeles, WGBH Boston, and NHK Tokyo; *The Garden* for WETA (US), Channel Four (UK) and a Japanese consortium and *Masters of Art* with Sir Lawrence Gowing and Christie's International

Manhattan Films
217 Brompton Road
London SW3 2EJ
Tel: 071 584 2408
Robert Paget
Directed and wrote *The Choice* in Switzerland. Currently preparing *Persona Non Grata* to be

shot in England and *Mistakes* to be shot in London

Mike Mansfield Television
5-7 Carnaby Street
London W1V 1PG
Tel: 071 494 3061
Fax: 071 494 3057
39 30 minute *Sportsmasters* for ITV; *Comedy Store* for ITV

Marble Arch Productions
Twickenham Studios
St Margaret's
Twickenham TW1 2AW
Tel: 081 892 4477
Fax: 081 891 0168
Sir Richard Attenborough
Terry Clegg
Diana Hawkins
Preparing feature on the life of Thomas Paine

Medialab
Unit 8 Chelsea Wharf
15 Lots Road
London SW10 0QH
Tel: 071 351 5814
Fax: 071 351 7898
John Gaydon
Kevin Godley
Geoff Foulkes
Producers of commercials, music videos, documentaries and videolas. Also run *Exposed Films* and *The Videolabel*

Meditel Productions
Bedford Chambers
The Piazza
Covent Garden
London WC2 8HA
Tel: 071 836 9216/9364
Joan Shenton
Provides medical and science-based documentaries for TV. Made *HRT – Pause for Thought*, *This Week* for Thames TV, *Impotence – One in Ten Men* for Channel Four, and *AIDS – Infectious or Not?* (*Despatches*) Channel Four

Bill Melendez Productions
32-34 Great Marlborough Street
London W1V 1HA
Tel: 071 439 4411
Fax: 071 439 6808
Steve Melendez
Graeme Spurway

Mendoza Productions
22 Soho Square
London W1V 5FJ
Tel: 071 434 9641
Fax: 071 439 1226
Debby Mendoza

Mentorn Films
138-140 Wardour Street
London W1V 3AU
Tel: 071 287 4545
Fax: 071 287 3728
Tom Gutteridge
Arts and entertainment. *Challenge Anneka, 01, Box Office, Early Bird, 1st Night* (with subsidiary Mentorn Midlands), *Wide Angle*. Currently developing drama projects

Merchant Ivory Productions
46 Lexington Street
London W1
Tel: 071 437 1200
Fax: 071 734 1579
Ismail Merchant
Paul Bradley
Producer Ismail Merchant and director James Ivory together made *Heat and Dust*, *The Bostonians, A Room with a View, Maurice, Slaves of New York*, and *Mr and Mrs Bridge. The Ballad of the Sad Cafe* will be completed during 1990, to followed by E M Forster's *Howards End*

Mersey Television
18 Rodney Street
Liverpool L1 2TQ
Tel: 051 250 1602
Fax: 051 708 7750
Phil Redmond
Operates Brookside Productions, which has a Channel 4 contract to produce the twice-weekly drama series *Brookside*. Mersey Music and Mersey Casting are subsidiary companies of Mersey Television

Mersham Productions
41 Montpellier Walk
London SW7 1JH
Tel: 071 589 8829
Fax: 071 584 0024
Lord Brabourne
Lord Brabourne, a Fellow and a Governor of the BFI, is a director of Thames Television. Amongst other films, he has produced in conjunction with Richard Goodwin four films based on stories by Agatha

Christie and *A Passage to India* directed by David Lean. During 1986, co-produced *Little Dorrit*. In 1988/9, co-produced the TV series *Leontyne*

Midnight Films
4th Floor
Ramillies House
1/2 Ramillies Street
London W1V 1DF
Tel: 071 494 0926
Fax: 071 494 2676
Michael Hamlyn
Iain Brown
Features, promos and television (1987/8). Produced the full-length feature film *U2 Rattle and Hum* – part concert film, part cinema verité documentary. Currently developing future feature projects

Milesian Film Productions
10 Selwood Place
London SW7 3QQ
Tel: 071 373 8858
Fax: 071 373 8858
Christopher Miles

Mirus Productions
2nd Floor
9 Carnaby Street
London W1V 1PG
Tel: 071 439 7113/
494 2399
Howard Johnson
Mike Wallington
Produced *Songs of Freedom; CLR James* in 1986. *Colonial Madness; This Joint is Jumpin'* in 1987. *One Love* and *Art Tatum* in 1988. *Family Saga* and *Black Faith* in 1990

Montage Films
21 Noel Street
London W1V 4DB
Tel: 071 439 8113
Fax: 071 287 1983
Revenge of Billy the Kid

Moving Pictures
25 Noel Street
London W1V 3RD
Tel: 071 434 3100
Fax: 071 437 3951
Hazel Hindler
Commercials production, corporate and interactive communications

Multivision Communications
21 Queens Grove
London NW8 6EL
Tel: 071 586 9717
Fax: 071 586 7234
Edward Joffe
Clive Delmain
Film and television

producers/co-producers/consultants. Projects for 1990/91 include 26 part series *Video View* for Thames. Ongoing series of 60 minute programmes *Preview* for UK video stores. 60 minute documentary *The War Games*. Projects in active development include TV comedy series *County Kilburn*

NVC Arts
The Forum
74-80 Camden Street
London NW1 0JL
Tel: 071 388 3833
Fax: 071 383 5332
Produces recordings of live opera and ballet from the world's leading international venues and companies. Recent recordings include *Giovanna d'Arco* from the Teatrodi Bologna, *Paris Dances Diaghilev* with the Paris Opera Ballet and *The Prince of the Pagodas* with the Royal Ballet

Nelson Entertainment International
8 Queen Street
London W1X 7PH
Tel: 071 493 3362
Fax: 071 409 0503
Produced *Destiny, Far North* and *When Harry Met Sally*

Nelson Television
8 Queen Street
London W1X 7PH
Tel: 071 493 3362
Fax: 071 409 0503
A new company, part of the Nelson Entertainment Group

Network Screen Production
Pinewood Film Studios
Iver Heath
Bucks SL0 0NH
Tel: 0753 651700/656592
Fax: 0753 656844
Kevin Moran
Film and TV production company

New Era Productions
First Floor
113 Wardour Street
London W1V 3TD
Tel: 071 439 6889
Fax: 071 287 3711
Marc Samuelson
Joanna Dewar-Gibb

New Media
12 Oval Road
London NW1 7DH
Tel: 071 482 5258

Fax: 071 482 4957
Alison Turner
Multimedia and production company involved in the production of tape/slide, film, interactive videodiscs, CD-Rom and CD-I

New World/Trans Atlantic Pictures (UK)
27 Soho Square
London W1V 5FL
Tel: 071 434 0497
Fax: 071 434 0490
A new company born out of the old New World Pictures company. Trans Atlantic pictures are currently preparing *Hellraiser III – Hell on Earth* for production originally by Clive Barker

Nordfeld Animation
77 Kingshurst Road
Northfield
Birmingham B31 2LJ
Tel: 021 476 3552
Dale Hemenway
Kevan Goode
Produced animation for the BBC TV series *Hartbeat*. Other projects include a pilot for an animated TV series. All forms of cel animation work undertaken

North South Productions
Woburn Buildings
1 Woburn Walk
London WC1H 0JJ
Tel: 071 388 0351
Fax: 071 388 2398
Film and video production company that specialises in programmes on environmental issues, world development and other international themes. Productions include BBC series *Only One Earth*, Channel Four series *Stolen Childhood* and many other documentaries and current affairs programmes for Channel Four

OG Films
Pinewood Studios
Pinewood Road
Iver Heath
Bucks SLO 0NH
Tel: 0753 651700
Fax: 0753 656844
Oliver Gamgee
Production, packaging, and distribution company for feature films and TV

Ocean Pictures
25 Melody Road
London SW18 2QW
Tel: 081 870 5345
Lucinda Sturgis
Roger Brown

Opix Films
Pinewood Studios
Pinewood Road
Iver Heath
Bucks SL0 0NH
Tel: 0753 651700
Fax: 0753 630006
Terry Ryan
Productions include *Owain Prince of Wales*, a TV feature with S4C, a four-part series *Boyce Goes West*, co-produced with Brent Walker for the BBC, *American Carrott*, made for Channel 4 and HBO, and two films for TV, *Going Home* and *Heaven on Earth*, co-produced with Primedia (Canada), BBC and CBC. In production *The Fourth Dimension*, a 13 half-hour fantasy series, feature films *Puckoon* from the novel by Spike Milligan and *The Brylcream Boys*

Orion Pictures Corporation
31-32 Soho Square
London W1V 6AP
Tel: 071 437 8753
Stuart Salter
Productions include *Mississippi Burning, Dirty Rotten Scoundrels* and *Another Woman* in 1988/89 and Woody Allen's *Crimes and Misdemeanours, She Devil* and *The Package* in 1989/90

Oxford Film Company
2 Mountfort Terrace
London N1 1JJ
Tel: 071 607 8200
Fax: 071 607 4037
Andy Paterson
Producers of feature films and television including most recently *Sisters* (MGM) and *Promised Land* (Vestron). Films in development include Greenpeace Chairman David MacTaggart's *Journey into the Bomb* and *Touching the Void* based on Joe Simpson's award-winning book. TV projects include *Under Fire* based on Simon Hayward's book. Currently producing a

6-hour documentary series *Hollywood Now* for BBC TV

Oxford Scientific Films

Long Hanborough
Oxford OX7 2LD
Tel: 0993 881881
Fax: 0993 882808
OSF specialises in natural history and environmental documentaries, corporate and medical videos, sports programmes. See also under Facilities and Distributors (Non-Theatrical)

PAC Video Productions

Rosehill
Erbistock
Bangor on Dee
Wrexham
North Wales
Tel: 0978 780181
Corporate, promotional, training and educational programmes

Pacesetter Enterprises

11 Wythburn Place
London W1H 5WL
Tel: 071 437 5725
Fax: 071 706 1704
Production and co-production of international broadcast programming. A subsidiary of Colstar Communications and Entertainment. Credits include *The Wandering Company*, *In Search of Wildlife* (series), *Defending Wildlife*, *Antarctic Challenge*. In production *In Search of Wildlife* (second and third series), *Smith Island Antarctica* (working title), a series of adventure/environmental programmes. Currently looking at co-production properties in drama, documentary and the arts, sciences and nature

Pacesetter Productions

New Barn House
Leith Hill Lane
Ockley
Surrey RH5 5PH
Tel: 0306 70433
Fax: 0306 881021
Adele Spencer
On-going feature, documentary, TV drama and sponsored production

Palace Productions, Pictures, Video

16-17 Wardour Mews
London W1V 3FF
Tel: 071 734 7060
Fax: 071 437 3248
Nik Powell
Stephen Woolley
Daniel Battsek
Robert Jones
Made *Absolute Beginners*, *Company of Wolves*, *Shag*, *High Spirits*, *Scandal* and *The Big Man*

Panoptic Productions

296a Latimer Road
London W10 6QW
Tel: 081 960 5588
Fax: 081 964 0616
Nicholas Fraser
Michael Jones
Jean Newington
Producer of *Dispatches* (*Hungary*), *Sex on TV*, *Trial of Lady C* (*Sexual Intercourse Began in 1963*) and *Censorship*

Paramount Pictures

UIP House
45 Beadon Road
London W6 0EG
Tel: 081 741 9041
Fax: 081 741 22209
Michael O'Sullivan

Paramount Revcom

Balfour House
46-54 Great Titchfield Street
London W1P 7AE
Tel: 071 636 5066
Fax: 071 436 3252
Michael Deakin
Drama, mini-series and TV movies. Co-produced Jeffrey Archer's *Not a Penny More, Not a Penny Less* with BBC for USA Network. Co-producing Arthur C Clarke's *A Fall of Moondust* with Channel 9 Australia

Paravision (UK)

114 The Chambers
Chelsea Harbour
London SW10 0XF
Tel: 071 351 7070
Fax: 071 352 3645
Linda Agran
Nick Barton
Roy Stevens
Tony Kenber
Paravision (UK) is the international production arm of Paravision International – the major French media group. Projects include *Minder*, *Poirot*, *The Great Moghuls*, *Cry in the Dark*, and *Shirley Valentine*.

The Company is currently developing feature films, telemovies, drama series and documentaries

Partridge Films

38 Mill Lane
London NW6 1NR
Tel: 071 435 8211
Fax: 071 431 1715
Michael Rosenberg
Makers of the wildlife series *Path of the Rain God* for Channel 4; *Okavango: Jewel of the Kalahari* and *Amazon – the Flooded Forest* for the BBC and the National Geographic Society

Partridge TV and Video

Ellerncroft
Wotton-under-Edge
Glos GL12 7AY
Derek Anderson
Makers of wildlife documentaries and videos for television and educational distribution. Extensive natural history stock shot library

Pelicula Films

7 Queen Margaret Road
Glasgow G20 6DP
Tel: 041 945 3333
Fax: 041 946 8345
Mike Alexander
Producer of programmes for TV, including Channel 4 and BBC TV

Pennies from Heaven

83 Eastbourne Mews
London W2
Tel: 071 402 0051/
081 576 1197
Kenith Trodd
Kenith Trodd is a prolific producer of films for the BBC and others. Recent work includes *After Pilkington*, *The Singing Detective*, *She's Been Away* and *Old Flames* all for the BBC. He also produced for PFH the features *Dreamchild* and *A Month in the Country*. Much of this work has been from screenplays by Dennis Potter, the company's other principal director. Currently Kenith Trodd is making *They Never Slept*, *For the Greater Good* and *Common Pursuit* with several others in development

Persistent Vision Productions

133 Ravenslea Road
London SW12 8RT
Tel: 071 639 5596/
081 673 7924
John Stewart
Carol Lemon
Short films completed include the award-winning *Crash* and *The Gaol*. In preparation is a short film *The Break-In* and a feature film *Straker*

Picture Palace Productions

1 Beak Street Studios
65-69 Beak Street
London W1R 3LF
Tel: 071 439 9882
Fax: 071 734 8574
Currently filming *The Orchid House*, 4 x 1 hour drama series set in the Caribbean during 1918 and 1938, for Channel Four. Recently completed *Eurocops* English episodes and *When Love Dies* 4 play for Channel Four. In development Michael Scott's *The Fancy Man*, Po Chi Leong's *Passage to Heaven* and Gillies McKinnon's *French Kisses*

Picture Parade

3 Percy Street
London W1P 9FA
Tel: 071 580 1157
Fax: 071 436 4808
Recently completed *Gentleman Jim Reeves*, a co-production with TVS and SVT 1 Sweden for Channel Four. In pre-production *The Rich Tradition*, a thirteen-part series, with CTE (Central), SVT 1 Sweden and SBS Australia. In development *Hesketh – First Came the Fun*

Picture Partnership Productions

73 Newman Street
London W1
Tel: 071 637 8056
Fax: 071 631 4902
Brian Eastman
Recently completed *Jeeves and Wooster* TV series for Granada. In production with further series of *Agatha Christie's Poirot* and *Forever Green* for LWT. Previously made feature films *Wilt* and *Whoops Apocalypse*; *Traffik* for Channel Four, *Words of Love* (shown in the BBC

Screen 2 slot), *Porterhouse Blue* (Channel Four) and *Blott on the Landscape* (BBC)

Portman Entertainment

Pinewood Studios
Iver Heath
Bucks SL0 0NH
Tel: 0753 630366
Fax: 0753 630332
Victor Glynn
Andrew Warren

Portobello Productions

56 Long Acre
London WC2E 9JL
Tel: 071 379 5566
Fax: 071 379 5599
Eric Abraham
Specialize in drama, documentary, music and arts programming. Completed projects in 1989/90: *Still Life at the Penguin Cafe, Jacqueline du Pre Memorial Concert, Murray Perahia's Mozart.* Projects planned for 1990/91 include *Hobson's Choice, The Maestro and the Diva, My Friend Walter, The Old Curiosity Shop, Darkness at Noon,* and *The Extraordinary Adventures of Private Ivan Chonkin*

Poseidon Productions

1st Floor
Hammer House
113 Wardour Street
London W1V 3TD
Tel: 071 734 4441/5140
Fax: 071 437 0638
Frixos Constantine
Productions include: *Autism – A World Apart* for Channel Four, *Lysistrata* a feature film co-production with the USSR

Praxis Films

14 Manor Drive
Binbrook
Lincoln LN3 6BX
Tel: 0472 83547
Fax: 0472 83683
John Goddard
Film and video production of documentaries and current affairs films world-wide. Recent credits include films for Yorkshire Television and for Channel Four's *Dispatches, Cutting Edge* and *World This Week* series. Moving into drama shortly

Primetime Television

Seymour Mews House
Seymour Mews
Wigmore Street
London W1H 9PE
Tel: 071 935 9000
Fax: 071 487 3975
Richard Price
Independent TV production/packaging company associated with distributors, RPTA. Specialise in international co-productions. Recent projects include: *Jupiter Moon* 150 half hours drama (Primetime / Andromeda BSB), *Othello* RSC, BBC, *Tales of Helpmann* (South Bank Show), *Great Expectations* (6 hours for HTV, Disney, Tesauro), *The Bolshoi at the Bolshoi* (NHK Enterprises, Videofilm/Bolshoi Ballet), *The Great Moguls* (Ecoss Films, Channel four)

Prominent Features

68a Delancey Street
London NW1 7RY
Tel: 071 284 0242
Fax: 071 284 1004
Steve Abbott
Anne James
Company formed by Steve Abbott, John Cleese, Terry Gilliam, Eric Idle, Anne James, Terry Jones and Michael Palin to produce in-house features. Produced *The Adventures of Baron Munchausen, Erik The Viking* and *A Fish Called Wanda.* In pre-production: *American Friends*

Quanta

Old Forge House
Rodbourne Road
Corston
Malmesbury
Wiltshire SN16 0HA
Tel: 0666 825626
Fax: 0666 825626
Glyn Jones
Nicholas Jones
Specialists in TV science programming – commissions include *Equinox* (Channel Four) and *Horizon* (BBC2). Also development of international TV drama series

RM Arts

44 Great Marlborough Street
London W1V 1DB
Tel: 071 439 2637
Fax: 071 439 2316
RM Arts produces music and arts programming and co-produces on an international basis with major broadcasters including BBC, LWT, Channel 4, ARD and ZDF in Germany, NOS-TV in Holland, Danmarks Radio and TV2/Denmark, ORF in Austria, SVT in Sweden, RTVE in Spain and La Sept in France. Recent work includes a 4 part drama series on the life of Van Gogh, *Masterworks* an internationally co-produced series of ten-minute films made in galleries around the world and *A TV Dante* a multi-format video feature by Peter Greenaway and Tom Phillips

RSPB Film and Video Unit

The Lodge
Sandy
Bedfordshire SG19 2DL
Tel: 0767 680551
Fax: 0767 692365
Jeffery Boswall
Producers of *Osprey, Kingfisher, Where Eagles Fly* and most recently *The Year of the Stork.* The unit also acts as an independent producer of environmental films and videos

Ragdoll Productions

34 Harborne Road
Edgbaston
Birmingham B15 3AA
Tel: 021 454 5453/4344
Fax: 021 452 1807
Anne Wood
Specialist children's TV producer of live action and animation. *Pob* for Channel 4, *Playbox* for Central TV, *Story-time* for BBC TV, *Magic Mirror* for ITV, *Boom!* for Channel Four *Rosie & Jim* for Central TV

Recorded Development

8-12 Broadwick Street
London W1V 1FH
Tel: 071 439 0607
Fax: 071 434 1192
A subsidiary of Recorded Picture Co set up to bring projects to pre-production stage. In development are David Cronenberg's *The Naked Lunch* and a project with Nagisa Oshima

Recorded Picture Co

8-12 Broadwick Street
London W1V 1FH
Tel: 071 439 0607
Fax: 071 434 1192
Jeremy Thomas
Thomas produced Nagisa Oshima's *Merry Christmas, Mr Lawrence,* Stephen Frears' *The Hit,* Nicolas Roeg's *Insignificance* and *The Last Emperor,* directed by Bernardo Bertolucci. In production: *Everybody Wins* directed by Karel Reisz, *Sheltering Sky* directed by Bernardo Bertolucci

Red Rooster Films

11-13 Macklin Street
London WC2B 5NH
Tel: 071 405 8147
Fax: 071 831 0679
Linda James
Stephen Bayly
Non Morris
Carolyn Parry-Jones
Jenny Matheson
Mary Ann Simmons
Company formed in 1982 by Linda James and Stephen Bayly, producing quality television and feature films. Produced 18 hours of film including four TV movies and two features. In production in 1990 *Kersplat!* (youth programme for Channel Four), *The Gift* (drama series for TVS). In development: *Keeping Clean* and *Cruikshank, Vanderpump and Styles*

Red Shadow Films

36 Ritherdon Road
London SW17 8QF
Tel: 081 672 0606
Fax: 081 672 6334
David Young
Jonathan Holloway
Red Shadow Films is a young production company founded by Jonathan Holloway and David Young. First film *Eclipsed,* a half hour anti-war drama, was broadcast by ITV on Remembrance Sundays 1988 and 1989. Currently producing *The Hammer,* a feature length super-natural detective story

Rediffusion Films

c/o Buxton Films
5 The Square

Buxton
Derbyshire SK17 6AZ
Tel: 0298 77623
Jette Bonnevie
The production finance
arm of a diversified
communications
company. In the past has
provided finance for TV
productions and feature
films. Most recent
involvements include a
13-part athletic coaching
series financed in
conjunction with the
International Athletic
Federation

Regent Production
Brander House
Broomhill Road
London SW18 4JG
Tel: 081 877 1444
William Stewart
Productions for 1990/91
include two new series of
the Channel Four quiz
series *Fifteen-to-One*
(125 programmes). Two
development deals in
situation comedy and a
four-part drama series

Revere Entertainment Company
24 D'Arblay Street
London W1V 3FH
Tel: 071 437 4551
John Goldstone
Goldstone produced
*Monty Python's The
Meaning of Life* and *Erik
the Viking*

Rite Films
20 Bouverie Road West
Folkestone
Kent CT20 2SZ
Tel: 0303 52335
George Wright
Mainly engaged in
corporate videos,
documentary film
productions, and TV news
gathering

Riverfront Pictures
Dock Cottages
Peartree Lane
Glamis Road
Wapping
London E1 9SR
Tel: 071 481 2939
Fax: 071 480 5520
Jeff Perks
Carole Crouch
Specialise in music, arts
and drama-
documentaries. Jeff Perks'
is currently working on a
major documentary series
for the BBC. In
development, a comedy
series, also for the BBC

Roadshow Productions
c/o 6 Basil Mansions
Basil Street
London SW3 1AP
Tel: 071 584 0542
Fax: 071 584 1549
Kurt Unger
Daniel Unger
Recent productions
include feature film
*Return from the River
Kwai*

SVP Communications
Jordans
Cakeham Road
West Wittering
Chichester
West Sussex PO20 8AA
Tel: 0243 511 256
Fax: 0243 511 373
Jeremy Jacobs
Video programmme
production service

Sandfire Productions
Pinewood Studios
Iver Heath
Bucks SL0 0NH
Tel: 0753 651700
Anthony Williams
Feature film producers.
Projects include *Messiah*
and *The Stranger*

Sands Films
119 Rotherhithe Street
London SE16 4NF
Tel: 071 231 2209
Fax: 071 231 2119
Richard Goodwin
Goodwin produced *Stories
From A Flying Trunk;* the
puppet animation short
The Nightingale; and
features *Biddy* and the
six-hour feature *Little
Dorrit* both directed by
Christine Edzard at the
company's Rotherhithe
Studios base. Latest
production *The Fool*
written and directed by
Christine Edzard, and
produced in the
company's Rotherhithe
studios

Stephen Saunders Films
32 Selwood Road
Addiscombe
Croydon
Surrey CR0 7JJR
Tel: 081 654 4495
TV, corporate,
documentary productions

Scimitar Films
6-8 Sackville Street
London W1X 1DD
Tel: 071 734 8385
Fax: 071 602 9217

Michael Winner
Winner has produced and
directed many films,
including *Death Wish 3,
Appointment with Death,
A Chorus of Disapproval*
and *Bullseye!*

Screen Ventures
49 Goodge Street
London W1P 1FB
Tel: 071 580 7448
Christopher Mould
Dominic Saville
Screen Ventures is a
production company
specialising in
documentaries, current
affairs and music
production. Productions
include: *Afghanistan,
Iran The Revolution,
Refugees in Africa, Desert
Island, Tayarra – A
Racing Legend, Burma –
A Special Report* and
Dhows of the Arabian Sea
for Channel 4, BBC TV,
Central TV, KRO –
Holland, and others

Secker Walker
Suite 101
The Colosseum
Production Centre
Portland Gate
Leeds LS2 3AW
Tel: 0532 461311
David Secker
Stan Walker
Producers of broadcast
programme material and
business television

Seventh Art Productions (UK)
116 Grafton Road
London NW5 4BA
Tel: 071 485 7132
Fax: 071 284 0260
Phil Grabsky
Michael Whiteley
Factual programme-
makers for UK and
international TV. Recent
work includes acclaimed
series for Channel Four
on modern Spain entitled
*Spain – in the Shadow of
the Sun*

Siriol Productions
Phoenix Buildings
3 Mount Stuart Square
Butetown
Cardiff CF1 6RW
Tel: 0222 488400
Fax: 0222 485962
Robin Lyons
Formerly Siriol
Animation. Producers of
high quality animation
for television and the
cinema

Skan Productions International
Vermont
Beech Close
Cobham
Surrey KT11 2EN
Tel: 0932 68255
Fax: 0932 67905
Malcolm Hossick
Shane Selger
Feature film production

Skreba Films
5a Noel Street
London W1V 3RB
Tel: 071 437 6492
Fax: 071 437 0644
Ann Skinner
Simon Relph
Produced *Return of the
Soldier* and *Secret Places*,
directed by Zelda Barron.
Other projects include
*Bad Hats, A Profile of
Arthur J Mason, Honour,
Profit and Pleasure* and
The Gourmet. Relph
produced the Bill
Douglas-directed
Comrades and Skinner
was executive producer on
Heavenly Pursuits and
produced *The Kitchen
Toto* and *A Very British
Coup* for Channel 4

Skyline Film and TV Productions
4 Picardy Place
Edinburgh EH1 3JT
Tel: 031 557 4580
Fax: 031 556 4377
Trevor Davies
24 Scala Street
London W1P 1LU
Tel: 071 631 4649
Fax: 071 436 6209
Steve Clark-Hall
Producers of *Years
Ahead, Senior Service,
Scottish Eye* and *Walkie
Talkie* for Channel Four

Span Pictures
Oxford House
35/36 Oxford Street
Southampton SO1 1DS
Tel: 0703 222429
Fax: 0703 635526
Phillip Goodhand-Tait
Independent production
company for TV and
video. Rock and classical
music, documentaries,
children's programmes.
Productions include:
*An Evening with Placido,
Live from London* – a
series of 69 rock music
concerts, *Live on Stage*
– 12 rock music concerts
from the USA, *The
Worlds Greatest
Cricketers* and *The Story
of Steam*

Spectre Productions
41-45 Beak Street
London W1R 3LE
Tel: 071 439 1381
Simon Hartog
Michael Whyte
Spectre is a co-operative of nine filmmakers which also includes the Large Door production company. Productions include Stephen Dwoskin's *Further and Particular;* Philip Mullay's *The Return;* Vera Neubaver's animation series *World of Children; Mid-Air;* and *End of a Journey.* Other films include: Michael Whyte's *The Gourmet,* and Anna Ambrose's film about Handel *Honour, Profit and Pleasure* – both made in association with Skreba

Speedy Films
8 Royalty Mews
Dean Street
London W1V 5AW
Tel: 071 437 9313/
494 4043
Fax: 071 434 0830
Paul Vester
Barry Baker
Producers of shorts *Sunbeam* and *Picnic*

Spitting Image Productions
17-19 Plumbers Row
Aldgate
London E1 1EQ
Tel: 071 375 1561
Fax: 071 375 2492
Comedy-based production company specialising in international television and film, commercials and corporate video, using puppets, live action, cell and stop-frame animation. Productions include nine series of *Spitting Image* to November 1990, and *The Winjin' Pom*

Stagescreen Productions
118 Cleveland Street
London W1P 5DN
Tel: 071 387 4045
Fax: 071 388 0408
Jeffrey Taylor
Derek Granger
Film, television and theatre company whose work includes *A Handful of Dust,* and *Death of a Son* (for BBC TV)

Robert Stigwood Organisation
118-120 Wardour Street

London W1V 4BT
Tel: 071 437 2512
Fax: 071 437 3674
David Land
David Herring
Theatre and film producer Stigwood is currently involved in the film of *Evita* and several other projects

Swanlind
Stafford House
Fordhouses
Wolverhampton
WV10 7EL
Tel: 0902 784848
Fax: 0902 788840
Film and television programme producers

TV Cartoons
39 Grafton Way
London W1P 5LA
Tel: 071 388 2222
Fax: 071 383 4192
John Coates
Claire Braidley
Gail Wright
TVC produced the Academy Award-nominated film *The Snowman,* and the feature *When The Wind Blows,* both adaptations from books by Raymond Briggs. Production was completed in May 1989 of *Granpa,* a ½-hour television special for Channel 4 and TVS. Currently in pre-production with the feature-length film – *The Adventures of Peter Rabbit* from the Beatrix Potter books

Tartan Television
35 Little Russell Street
London WC1A 2HH
Tel: 071 323 3022
Fax: 071 323 4857
Norrie Maclaren
Christopher Mitchell
Producing for both TV and film

Richard Taylor Cartoon Films
76 Dukes Avenue
London N10 2QA
Tel: 081 444 7547
Richard Taylor
Catherine Taylor

Television History Workshop
42 Queen Square
London WC1N 3AJ
Tel: 071 405 6627
Fax: 071 242 1426
Sharon Goulds
Marilyn Wheatcroft
Greg Lanning
Recent productions

include a documentary for Channel Four about morale in schools (Sep 1990) and a major series for BBC about youth culture since the war – *Almost Grown* (Spring 1990). BMA Silver Award 1990 for *In the Club?* (Birth Control)

Tempest Films
33 Brookfield
Highgate West Hill
London N6 6AT
Tel: 081 340 0877
Fax: 081 340 9309
Jacky Stoller
Produced three two hour television movies filmed in Canada, Germany and Ireland based on the books of Dick Francis. Two drama series in development with Anglia and the BBC. Russian four part series, feature film and 26 half hour films also in development

Third Eye Productions
Unit 210 Canalot Studios
222 Kensal Road
London W10 5BN
Tel: 081 969 8211
Fax: 081 960 8780
Samantha Drummond-

Hay
TV productions covering the worlds of arts, music, ethnography and developing world culture

Time and Light Productions
5 Darling Road
London SE4 1YQ
Tel: 081 692 0145
Fax: 081 691 5270
Roger Elsgood
Works with European commissioning agencies to produce film and television programmes featuring the work of European artists and writers. Made *Time and Light,* with writer John Berger. Current work includes *Between the Dog and the Fox* and *The Wrong Way*

Timeless Films
134 Royal College Street
London NW1 6TA
Tel: 071 267 7625
Ian Emes has directed cinema shorts *French Windows, The Beard, The Oriental Nightfish, The Tent, The Magic Shop,* Paramount's Academy Award-winning *Goody Two Shoes,* his first

feature for Enigma, *Knights and Emeralds*, *The Yob* for Channel 4, *How To Be Cool* for GTV, *Streetwise* for TVS, and, more recently, *Kersplat* for Channel 4

Tiny Epic Video Co
138-140 Wardour Street
London W1V 3AU
Tel: 071 437 2854
Fax: 071 434 0211
Luke Jeans
Roger Thomas

Trans World International
TWI House
23 Eyot Gardens
London W6 9YN
Tel: 081 846 8070
Fax: 081 746 5334
Eric Drossart
Buzz Hornett
Bill Sinrich
Founded in 1968. TV sports production and rights representation branch of Mark McCormack's International Management Group. Product ranges from made-for-TV events – *Superstars, World's Strongest Man, Tennis Legends* and *Conquer the Arctic* and sports documentaries to event highlights and live coverage. The company represents the television rights to over 70 international sports worldwide

Transatlantic Films
100 Blythe Road
London W14 OHE
Tel: 071 727 0132
Revel Guest
10-part documentary series on the legacy of Ancient Greece in the modern world, *Greek Fire*. Recent productions include a 13-part series, *In Search of Paradise;* a four-part series directed by Peter Greenaway, *Four American Composers; Placido – A Year in the Life of Placido Domingo;* and an eight-part series *The Horse in Sport* with Channel 4 and ABC Australia.

Triple Vision
11 Great Russell Street
London WC1B 3NH
Tel: 071 323 2881
Fax: 071 323 0849

Terry Flaxton
Penny Dedman
Producers and off-line edit facility. Producing social documentaries, drama and arts programmes since 1982 for various sponsors including Channel 4 and the BBC and for non-broadcast purposes. Recent productions include: 1989: *Intensive Care* and *Soviet Cinema* for Channel 4. 1990: Programme on female circumcision and infibulation for Channel 4

Try Again
The Production Centre
5th Floor
Threeways House
40-44 Clipstone Street
London W1P 7EA
Tel: 071 323 3220
Fax: 071 637 2590
Michael Darlow
Rod Taylor
Produces documentary, drama, light entertainment, arts, music

Turner Lane Boyle Productions
9-12 St Anne's Court
London W1V 3AX
Tel: 071 439 0489
Fax: 071 434 0353
Ken Turner
David Lane
Bob Boyle
Producers of TV commercials and films

Twentieth Century Fox
31-32 Soho Square
London W1V 6AP
Tel: 071 437 7766
Fax: 071 437 1625

Twentieth Century Vixen
25 Southampton Street
Brighton
East Sussex BN2 2UT
Tel: 0273 692 336
Fax: 081 802 3911
Claire Hunt
Kim Longinotto
Film/video production and distribution. 1990 production for Channel 4 is a documentary about the Egyptian writer, doctor and activist Nawal el Sadaawi. Other programmes include *Fireraiser* (1988) and *Eat the Kimono* (1989). Also made a number of tapes on special needs issues

Twenty Twenty Television
10 Stucley Place
London NW1 8NS
Tel: 071 284 1979
Fax: 071 284 1810
Claudia Milne
Mike Whittaker
The company continues to produce programmes exclusively for broadcast television, specialising in worldwide investigative journalism, current affairs, factually-based drama and science. Recent productions include: a six-part series *Inside The Brotherhood* for Granada TV, *Inside Story* for BBC TV, *Viewpoint '90* for Central TV, *Cutting Edge* for Channel 4 and *Toxic Terror* for Channel 4 and USA

Ty Gwyn Films
Y Ty Gwyn
Llanllyfni
Caernarfon
Gwynedd LL54 6DG
Tel: 0286 881235
Gareth Wynn Jones

Tyburn Productions
Pinewood Studios
Iver Heath
Bucks SL0 0NH
Tel: 0753 651700
Fax: 0753 656844
Kevin Francis
Gillian Garrow
Long-established independent TV production company

UBA
Pinewood Studios
Iver Heath
Bucks SLO 0NH
Tel: 0753 651 700
Fax: 0753 656 844
Peter Shaw
Richard Gregson
Christina Robert
Production company for cinema and TV projects. Past productions include: *Turtle Diary* for the Samuel Goldwyn Company, *Castaway* for Cannon and *The Lonely Passion of Judith Hearne* for HandMade Films, *Taffin* for MGM, and *Windprints* for Virgin Vision

Uden Associates
Chelsea Wharf
Lots Road
London SW10 0QJ
Tel: 071 351 1255
Fax: 071 376 3937
Adam De Wan

Umbrella Entertainment Productions
25 Denmark Street
London WC2H 8NJ
Tel: 071 379 6145
Sandy Lieberson
Formed in 1977. First production was *Performance,* and since then has produced a number of films, including *The Mighty Quinn* starring Denzel Washington for MGM, *Stars and Bars* starring Daniel Day Lewis and directed by Pat O'Connor for Columbia, and *Rita, Sue and Bob Too* for Channel 4. Sandy Lieberson is currently President of international production at Pathe Entertainment

Umbrella Films
c/o Twickenham Film Studios
St Margarets
Twickenham
Middlesex TW1 2AW
Tel: 081 892 4477
Simon Perry
Stacy Bell
Made Michael Radford's *Another Time, Another Place, 1984* and *White Mischief*, Richard Eyre's *Loose Connections*, Conny Templeman's *Nanou* and Jana Bokova's *Hotel du Paradis*. In development are *The Playboys*, written by Kerry Crabbe and Shane Connaughton; Agatha Christie's *Towards Zero*, to be directed by Claude Chabrol and *The Elixir* to be directed by Michael Radford

Unicorn Organisation
Pottery Lane Studios
34a Pottery Lane
Holland Park
London W11 4LZ
Tel: 071 229 5131
Fax: 071 229 4999
Michael Seligman
Julian Roberts

VATV
60-62 Margaret Street
London W1N 7FJ
Tel: 071 636 9421
Jane Lighting
Mike Latham
Most recent productions include a two-part

programme for BBC's *QED* series: *Back to the Drawing Board*, a film report for *Eye Witness* on LWT, and home video *7lbs In 7 Days*. VATV distributes for 22 independent companies, the BBC and is one of Channel 4's approved distributors

VPL
1 Cowcross Street
London EC1
Tel: 071 608 2131/490 1864
Fax: 071 490 1864
Sue Hayes
Sally French
Developing drama and documentary projects for Channel 4, Granada TV and the BBC

Verronmead
30 Swinton Street
London WC1X 9NX
Tel: 071 278 5523
Fax: 071 278 0643
Maureen Harter
David Wood
Produced *Back Home*, a TV film drama with TVS and the Disney Channel, corporate video for PACE on *Neuro Linguistic Programming*

The Video Connection
68-70 Wardour Street
London W1V 3HP
Tel: 071 734 4609
Fax: 071 437 1366
Nicholas de Rothschild
Produced a documentary *Glory of the Gardens*. Most recently has produced a film *A Vision of Paradise*

Videotel Productions
Ramillies House
1/2 Ramillies Street
London W1V 1DF
Tel: 071 439 6301
Fax: 071 437 0731
Nick Freethy
Stephen Bond
Producers of educational and training packages for TV and video distribution including the series *Catering With Care*, *Working With Care*, *Chemical Plant Safety*, *Chemical Spills at Sea*, *Alcohol Beware, Coshh Dead Ahead*

Vivid
1st Floor
Centro House

Mandela Street
London NW1
Tel: 071 388 7489
Fax: 071 388 4559
Luc Roeg
Rob Warr

WKBC-TV
1 St Andrew's Road
London W14 9SX
Tel: 071 385 1907
Fax: 071 385 0328
George Snow
Adam Boome
A video production company. Past productions include drama for the BFI and Channel 4. Offer an integrated audio/video studio facility

WTTV
10 Livonia Street
London W1V 3PH
Tel: 071 439 2424
Fax: 071 437 9964
Anthony Root
Tim Bevan
Sarah Radclyffe
Television programmes, single drama and mini-series. A subsidiary of Working Title

Wall To Wall TV
The Elephant House
35 Hawley Crescent
London NW1 8NP
Tel: 071 485 7424
Fax: 071 267 5292
Alex Graham
Jane Root
Andy Lipman
Producers of *The Media Show* for Channel 4, *Style Trial* for BBC1, and a range of other projects for the BBC, Channel 4 and foreign broadcasters

The Walnut Partnership
Crown House
Armley Road
Leeds LS12 2EJ
Tel: 0532 456913
Fax: 0532 439614
Geoff Penn
Television, film and video production company

Warner Sisters
21 Russell Street
London WC2
Tel: 071 836 0134
Fax: 071 836 6559
Lavinia Warner
Jane Wellesley
Producer of drama and documentary programmes, the company was founded by Warner, following the

success of *Tenko*. Recent productions include *Wish Me Luck* (3 x eight-part drama with LWT), *Tristan da Cunha* (documentary for Granada/WNET), *That's Entertaining* Channel 4. In production 1990: a documentary about *Madagascar* (Granada/WNET), 6 short plays by new women writers (Channel 4), *In Search of the White Rajahs* (BBC/WNET/ABC), *Rides* (6-part drama series for BBC1), *Selling Hitler* (mini-series on the Hitler diaries scandal with Euston Films)

Waterloo Films
Silver House
31-35 Beak Street
London W1R 3LD
Tel: 071 494 4060
Fax: 071 284 6366
Dennis Woolf
Ray Davies
Producer of *Return to Waterloo*, a fantasy film for Channel 4 written and directed by Ray Davies of The Kinks, which was co-financed by Channel 4 and RCA Video Productions. Other projects in development

Watershed Television
53 Queen Square
Bristol BS1 4LH
Tel: 0272 276864
Fax: 0272 252093
Video and film production. Broadcast as well as corporate and commercials

White City Films
79 Sutton Court Road
London W4 3EQ
Tel: 081 994 6795
Fax: 081 995 9379
Aubrey Singer
Current affairs and documentary productions

Michael White Productions
13 Duke Street
St James's
London SW1Y 6DB
Tel: 071 839 3971
Michael White
Trade product. Film and theatre producer. Recent films include *High Season, Eat the Rich, White Mischief*, and *Nuns on the Run*

David Wickes Productions
169 Queen's Gate
London SW7 5HE
Tel: 071 225 1382
Fax: 071 589 8847
David Wickes
Joanna Elferink
Jekyll & Hyde for ABC and LWT starring Michael Caine, Cheryl Ladd and Joss Ackland. Wickes produced, directed, co-wrote *Jack the Ripper* for CBS and Thames, starring Michael Caine and Lewis Collins. Two series of *Marlowe Private Eye*, for HBO and LWT

Winkast Programming
Pinewood Studios
Iver Heath
Bucks SL0 0NH
Tel: 0753 651 700
Fax: 0753 652525
Chantal Ribeiro
Robert Shaw
Elliott Kastner's company, independent producer of over 65 motion pictures in less than two decades, which include: *Where Eagles Dare, The Long Goodbye, Farewell My Lovely, Equus*, and *Angel Heart*. Currently developing *Jericho, Louie's Widow*

Witzend Productions
3 Derby Street
Mayfair
London W1Y 7HD
Tel: 071 355 2868
Fax: 071 495 3310
Tony Charles
Producers of comedy programming and films for US and UK outlets. Projects include *Auf Wiedersehen, Pet; Shine on Harvey Moon; Roll Over Beethoven; Mog* and *Girls on Top* for Central TV, and *Lovejoy* for the BBC

Woodfilm
61a Great Titchfield Street
London W1P 7FL
Tel: 071 631 5429
Elizabeth Wood
Producers of arts, features and TV drama *The Pantomime Game, The Future of Things Past, Stairs, In Praise of Folly, Go For It* two six part documentary series for Channel 4 and *By Herself*

– *Sophie* a half hour drama starring Joan Plowright in co-production with Channel 4 and Italoons Corp, New York

Dennis Woolf Productions
Silver House
31-35 Beak Street
London W1R 3LD
Tel: 071 494 4060
Fax: 071 287 6366
A growing company specialising in current affairs *Dispatches*, documentaries *Cutting Edge*, music *Epitaph: Charles Mingus*, and studio reconstructions of contemporary trials *The Court Report* series for Channel 4, *The Trial of Klaus Barbie* for the BBC

Working Title
10 Livonia Street
London W1V 3PH
Tel: 071 439 2424
Fax: 071 437 9964
Sarah Radclyffe
Tim Bevan
Graham Bradstreet
Films include *My Beautiful Laundrette*, *Personal Services*, *Caravaggio* (in association with the BFI), *Wish You Were Here*, *Sammy and Rosie Get Laid*, *A World Apart*, *Paperhouse*, *For Queen and Country*, *The Tall Guy*, *Chicago Joe and the Showgirl* and *Fools of Fortune*. Productions for Channel 4 include *Tears, Laughter, Fear and Rage*; *Elphida*, *Echoes*, *Smack and Thistle*. See also WTTV

Works On Screen
24 Scala Street
London W1P 1LV
Tel: 071 631 4649
Fax: 071 436 6209
Sue Eatwell-Conte
Alison Joseph
Recent productions include: *Through the Devil's Gateway* (1989) presented by Helen Mirren for Channel 4. Current projects include a series, co-produced with France, on the history of art. In development, a further series on women and religion

World Film Services
Pinewood Studios
Iver Heath
Bucks SL0 0NH
Tel: 0753 651700/ 071 493 3045
Fax: 0753 656475
John Heyman

World Wide International Television
21-25 St Anne's Court
London W1V 3AW
Tel: 071 343 1121
Fax: 071 734 0619
The company's main interest is in family drama and children's programmes, but it also produces light entertainment, documentary and current affairs programmes. Recent productions include Catherine Cookson's *The Fifteen Streets*, TV film for ITV, *Kappatoo*, seven half-hour children's series for ITV, *Not on Sunday* 3 series of religious current affairs magazine for Channel 4, *Kids Court*, (26 half hour children's series for BSB), *Finders Keepers* (13 half hour children's series for ITV), *Black Velvet Gown* (TV film for ITV)

Worldmark Productions
The Old Studio
18 Middle Row
London W10 5AT
Tel: 081 960 3251
Fax: 081 960 6150
Recent productions include: *Olympic Experience* with Charlton Heston, *Greatest Goals*, *Soccer Spectacular*, *In Clipper's Wake*. In Production *Marque of a Legend II* one hour TV special, *Every Day of Your Life* a corporate film for Coca-Cola, *Italia 90* The Official Film of the Soccer World Cup, *American Endeabour* TV mini series, *Redheart* UK based theatrical feature

World's End Productions
60 Berwick Street
London W1V 3PA
Tel: 071 439 7275
Fax: 071 494 1952
Recent productions include *The Forgotten Holocaust* (BBC1) 1989, *Jimi Hendrix, South Bank Show* (LWT) 1989, *Living with Spill* (Channel 4) 1990. Productions planned for 1990 include drama and documentary films for Channel 4 and Granada

Year 2000 Television
3 Benson Road
Blackpool FY3 7HP
Tel: 0253 35403/824057
Fax: 0253 500117
Satellite television programme producers

Yorkshire Film Co
Capital House
Sheepscar Court
Meanwood Road
Leeds LS7 2BB
Tel: 0532 441224
Fax: 0532 441220
Keith Hardy
Producers of satellite/broadcast sports documentaries, news coverage, and corporate and commercial work

ZED
KJP House
11 Great Marlborough Street
London W1V 1BE
Tel: 071 494 3181
Sophie Balhetchet
Glenn Wilhide
Completed productions for transmission in 1990 include a second six-part drama series of *The Manageress*, directed by Christopher King. Starring Cherie Lunghi for Channel 4 and the ECA. Also *The Missing Reel* a drama documentary special about the inventor Augustin Le Prince, written and directed by Christopher Rawlence. ZED's new projects include a new four-part series written by Stan Hey and an adaptation of Mary Wesley's *The Camomile Lawn*

Zenith North
7th floor
Cale Cross House
156 Pilgrim Street
Newcastle Upon Tyne
NE1 6SU
Tel: 091 261 0077
Fax: 091 222 0271
Ian Squires
Subsidiary of Zenith Productions. Producers of *Byker Grove* for BBC1, *Big World* for Channel 4 and co-producers of *Gophers* for Channel 4

Zenith Productions
43-45 Dorset Street
London W1H 4AB
Tel: 071 224 2440
Fax: 071 224 3194
Charles Denton
Scott Meek

Film and TV production subsidiary of Carlton Communications. Recent feature films include *Soursweet, For Queen and Country, The Wolves of Willoughby Chase, Patty Hearst, Trust, Harbour Beat*. Recent TV productions include *Inspector Morse IV, The Paradise Club, Jewish Humour, Chimera*. Recent music specials include *Graceland: The African Concert, Acoustic: Joan Armatrading, Nigel Kennedy: the Four Seasons*

Zero One
44 Newington Green Mansions, Green Lanes
London N16 9BT
10 Martello Street
London E8 3PE
Tel: 071 249 8269
Tel: 071 354 5965
Fax: 071 704 0135
Mark Nash
James Swinson
Producers of documentary and fiction. Most recent production *First Time Tragedy...* (documentary co-production with Australia). Currently developing *Memoirs of a Spacewoman* with Limbo Film AG, Switzerland and support from the European Script Fund

Zooid Pictures
63-67 Hargrave Park
London N19 5JW
Tel: 071 272 9115
Fax: 071 281 1797
Richard Philpott
Jasmine Nancholas
Founded by Philpott in 1984 after producing feature documentary *Road Movie*. Producers of experimental and television documentaries such as *Spirit of Albion* and shorts, including *The Messiah in the Shadow of Death, Dead Pigeon, Stones Off Holland, the Flora, Faddy Furry, Dance Day*. First feature drama *Shaman* and five 10 minutes (or one 50 minutes) landscape comedy set in USA, now in production. Operates 'The Art of Film' scheme, programming and promoting new British experimental cinema internationally (festivals, cinémathèques, TV, etc). Zooid provides specialist technical services to independent filmmakers

VIVID

FILM · TELEVISION · POST PRODUCTION · INFORMATION DESIGN

VIVID PRODUCTIONS LTD

COMPLETE PRODUCTION FACILITIES FOR

FILM · PROMOS · TELEVISION

VIVID POST PRODUCTION LTD

HI-BAND SP ONLINE

MULTIMACHINE OFF-LINE

2 MACHINE LOW-BAND EDITMASTER COMPUTERISED OFF-LINE

VID PRODUCTIONS LTD: CENTRO HOUSE, 23 MANDELA STREET, LONDON NW1 0DY. TELEPHONE: 071 388 4559. FACSIMILIE: 071 388 7489
VIVID WEST: 8221 SANTA MONICA BLVD., LOS ANGELES, CALIFORNIA 90046. TELEPHONE: (213) 654 1422. FACSIMILIE: (213) 654 2201
D POST PRODUCTIONS LTD: 4th. FLOOR, 155-157 OXFORD STREET, LONDON W1 R1TB. TELEPHONE 071 287 4464. FACSIMILIE: 071 434 0724

Below are listed British-made and financed features, USA productions based in Britain and some television films running over 73 minutes which began production during 1989 and the first quarter of 1990

The Accountant
BBC TV/BBC Enterprises
Locations: London/
Manchester/Naples
Producer: Paul Knight
Associate producer: Ralph Wilton
Director: Les Blair
Screenwriter: Geoffrey Case
Camera: John Hooper
Editor: Roy Sharman
Cast: Alfred Molina, Tracie Hart, Clive Panto, Ivano Staccioli, Georgia Mitchell

Act of Will
Portman Entertainment/
Tyne Tees TV
Studio: Pinewood
Locations: Yorkshire
Dales/London/France/
New York
Executive producer: Tom Donald
Producer: Victor Glynn
Associate producer:
Andrew Warren
Director: Don Sharp
Screenwriter: Jill Hyem, from the novel by Barbara Taylor Bradford
Camera: Frank Watts
Editor: Teddy Darvas
Cast: Victoria Tennant,
Peter Coyote, Elizabeth Hurley, Kevin McNally, Lynsey Baxter

Air America
Carolco International –
Daniel Melnick/IndieProd
Locations: Chiang Ming, Thailand/London
Executive producers:
Mario Kassar, Andrew Vajna
Producers: Daniel Melnick, Allen Shapiro, John Eskow
Director: Roger Spottiswoode
Screenwriter: John Eskow
Camera: Roger Deakins
Editors: John Bloom, Lois Freeman-Fox
Cast: Mel Gibson, Robert Downey Jr, Nancy Travis, David Marshall Grant, Lane Smith

Back Home
TVS Films/Verronmead/
Citadel Entertainment/
TVS Television/Disney Channel
Location: south of England ▼

Executive producers:
Graham Benson, David Ginsberg
Producers: J Nigel Pickard, Maureen Harter
Director: Piers Haggard
Screenwriter: David Wood
Camera: Witold Stok
Editor: Peter Coulson
Cast: Hayley Mills, Hayley Carr, Jean Anderson, Rupert Frazer, Brenda Bruce

Ball-Trap on the Côte Sauvage
BBC TV
Locations: Cornwall/
Brittany
Executive producer:
Richard Broke
Producer: Sue Birtwistle
Associate producer:
Christopher Cherry
Director: Jack Gold
Screenwriter: Andrew Davies
Camera: Philip Bonham-Carter
Editor: Sue Wyatt
Cast: Jack Shepherd, Miranda Richardson, Zoë Wanamaker, Michael Kitchen, Peter Howitt

Bearskin – An Urban Fairytale
Film Four International/
British Screen/Instituto Portugues de Cinema/
Radiotelevisao Portuguesa
Locations: London/
Portugal
Producers: Eduardo Guedes, Leontine Ruette
Directors/screenwriters:
Ann Guedes, Eduardo Guedes
Camera: Michael Coulter
Editor: Edward Marnier
Cast: Tom Waits, Damon Turner, Charlotte Coleman, Julia Britton, Isabelle Ruth

Beatrix Potter – The Taylor of Gloucester
Thames Television/
Dreamscape Productions

Studio: Teddington
Executive producer: Ian Martin
Producer: Timothy Woolford
Director: John Michael Phillips
From the tale by Beatrix Potter
Cast: Ian Holm, Barrie Ingham, Thora Hird, Francois Testory, Jude Law

The Big Man ▶

Palace
Location: Glasgow
Executive producers: Nik Powell, Harvey Weinstein, Bob Weinstein
Producer: Stephen Woolley
Associate producer: Redmond Morris
Director: David Leland
Screenwriter: Don MacPherson, based on the book by William McIlvanney
Camera: Ian Wilson
Editor: George Akers
Cast: Liam Neeson, Joanne Whalley-Kilmer, Ian Bannen, Billy Connolly

Blore

BBC Film Production/Snipe Productions
Location: London
Producer: Innes Lloyd
Director: Robert Young
Screenwriter: Robin Chapman, from the novel by A N Wilson
Camera: John McGlashan
Editor: Ken Pearce
Cast: Timothy West, Jill Baker, Stephen Moore, Maggie O'Neill, Ray Winstone

Buddy's Song

Curbishley-Baird Enterprises
Studio: Pinewood
Executive producer: Roy Baird
Producers: Bill Curbishley, Roy Baird, Roger Daltrey
Associate producers: Ron Bareham, Brenda Baird
Director: Claude Whatham
Screenwriter: Nigel Hinton, from his own novel
Camera: John Hooper
Editor: John Grover
Cast: Roger Daltrey, Michael Elphick, Chesney Hawkes, Sharon Duce

Bullseye!

21st Century Film Corporation (UK)
Locations: London/Home Counties/Scotland
Executive producer: Menahem Golan
Producer/director: Michael Winner
Screenwriter: Leslie Bricusse
Camera: Alan Jones
Editor: Terry Rawlings
Cast: Michael Caine, Roger Moore, Sally Kirkland, Deborah Barrymore, Lee Patterson

The Care of Time

Anglia Films
Location: Austria
Producer: John Rosenberg
Director: John Davies
Screenwriter: Alan Seymour, from the novel by Eric Ambler
Cast: Michael Brandon, Christopher Lee, Ian Hogg, Yolanda Vazquez, Ben Masters

Cello

BBC TV Screen Two
Location: Bristol
Producer: Robert Cooper
Associate producer: Simon Mills

Director: Anthony Minghella
Camera: Remi Adefarasin
Editor: John Stothart
Cast: Juliet Stevenson, Alan Rickman, Michael Maloney, Stella Maris, Christopher Rozycki

Centrepoint

Rosso Productions/Channel 4
Locations: London/Folkestone/Boulogne/Paris
Producers: Joanna Smith, Franco Rosso
Director: Piers Haggard
Screenwriter: Nigel Williams
Camera: Richard Greatrex
Editor: David Gladwell
Cast: Jonathan Firth, Murray Head, Cheryl Campbell, John Shrapnel, Derrick O'Connor

Changing Step

BBC Scotland
Location: Ayrshire, Scotland

Producer: Andy Park
Associate producer: Carol Balchin
Director: Richard Wilson
Screenwriter: Antony Sher
Camera: Stuart Wyld
Editor: Dave Harvie
Cast: James Convey, Susan Wooldridge, Eleanor Bron, Antony Sher, Laurence McCann

Chicago Joe and the Showgirl

Polygram/Working Title/BSB
Studio: Pinewood
Location: London
Producer: Tim Bevan
Associate producer: Jane Frazer
Director: Bernard Rose
Screenwriter: David Yallop
Camera: Mike Southon
Editor: Dan Rae
Cast: Kiefer Sutherland, Emily Lloyd, Patsy Kensit, Keith Allen, Liz Fraser

▼

The Children
Isolde Films
Locations: Switzerland/
Venice/Bavaria/Paris
Executive producers:
Maureen Murray, Karin
Bamborough, Harald
Albrecht, Georg Bogner
Producers: Tony Palmer,
Andrew Montgomery,
Monika Aubele
Director: Tony Palmer
Screenwriter: Timberlake
Wertenbaker, from the
novel by Edith Wharton
Camera: Nic Knowland
Cast: Ben Kingsley, Kim
Novak, Geraldine
Chaplin, Joe Don Baker,
Donald Sinden

Circles of Deceit
BBC TV
Location: London
Producer: Louis Marks
Associate producer: Chris
Cherry
Director: Stuart Burge
Screenwriter: Stephen
Wakelam
Camera: John Hooper
Editor: Tariq Anwar
Cast: Edward Fox, Jane
Lapotaire, Brenda
Saunders, Brenda Bruce,
Stefan Schwartz

Cold Dog Soup
HandMade Films
Executive producers:
George Harrison, Denis
O'Brien
Producers: Richard
G Abramson, William
E McEven, Thomas Pope
Director: Alan Metter
Screenwriters: Stephen
Dobyns, Thomas Pope
Camera: Frederick Elmes
Cast: Randy Quaid,
Frank Whaley, Christine
Harnos

Cold Justice ▶
(working title: Father
Jim)
East End Films/United
Media Films
Location: Chicago, USA
Executive producers: Paul
Shakespeare, Carey
Shakespeare
Producers: Ross Cameron,
Dennis Waterman
Associate producer: Steve
Kelly
Director/screenwriter:
Terry Green
Camera: Dusty Miller
Editors: Tom Morrish,
Crispin Green
Cast: Dennis Waterman,

Roger Daltrey, Ron Dean,
Ralph Foody, Penelope
Milford

Cold Light of Day ▶
Creative Artists
Studio: Bray
Producer: Richard
Driscoll
Director/screenwriter:
Fhiona Louise
Camera: Nigel Axworthy
Cast: Bob Flagg, Martin
Byrne-Quinn, Geoffrey
Greenhill, Andrew
Edmans, Jackie Cox

Come Home Charlie and Face Them
LWT
Studio: Lee International,
Shepperton
Locations: Isle of Man/
Wales/London
Executive producer: Nick
Elliot
Producer: Sue
Whatmough
Director: Roger Bamford
Camera: Vernon Layton
Editor: Mike Paterson
Cast: Tom Radcliffe,
Mossie Smith, Jennifer
Calvert, Peter Sallis,
Sylvia Kay

Confessional
Granada TV/Harmony
Gold/Rete Europa
Locations: north Wales/
Lake District/Paris/
Jersey/north west of
England
Executive producer:
David Plowright, Bill
McCutcheon
Producer: Richard Everitt
Director: Gordon
Flemyng

Screenwriter: James
Mitchell, from the novel
by Jack Higgins
Camera: Ray Goode
Editor: Tony Ham
Cast: Keith Carradine,
Anthony Higgins,
Valentina Yakunina, Sir
Anthony Quayle, Robert
Lang

Dancin' thru the Dark
Palace Pictures/British
Screen/BBC Films/
Formost
Location: Liverpool
Executive producers:
Richard Broke, Chris
Brown, Charles Negus-
Fancey, Nik Powell
Producers: Andrée
Molyneux, Annie Russell
Associate producer: Derek
Nelson
Director: Mike Ockrent
Screenwriter: Willy
Russell
Camera: Philip Bonham-
Carter
Editor: John Stothart
Cast: Con O'Neill, Claire
Hackett, Peter Watts,
Andrew Naylor, Mark
Womack

Dark City 7
CSL/Filmafrica/BBC
Elstree
Location: Zimbabwe
Executive producers:
Peter Armstrong, Neil
Dunn
Producer: Celestia Fox
Director: Chris Curling
Screenwriter: David Lan
Camera: Dick Pope
Editor: Neil Thomson
Cast: Sello KaNcube,
Vusi Dibakwane, Thapelo
Mofokeng, Charles Pillai,
Pierre Knoesen

Dark River
Driftwood Films
Locations: London/
Malawi/Kenya/Zimbabwe
Producers: Malcolm
Taylor, Shellie Smith
Director/screenwriter:
Malcolm Taylor
Camera: Colin Clarke,
Graham Latter
Cast: Tom Bell, Kate
Buffery, Sian Phillips,
Tony Haygarth, Michael
Denison

Dead Sleep
Village Roadshow
Pictures
Location: Australia
Executive producers:
Graham Burke, Greg
Coote, Vincent O'Toole
Producer: Stanley O'Toole
Associate producer: David
Munro
Director: Alec Mills
Screenwriter: Michael
Rhymer
Camera: John Stokes
Editor: David Halliday
Cast: Linda Blair, Tony
Bonner, Christine Amor,
Andrew Booth, Sueyan
Cox

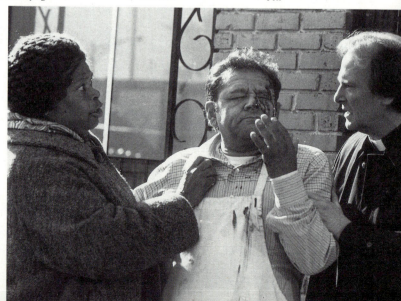

◄ 1871
Looseyard/Film Four International/La Sept/ Palawood Developments/ Animatografo Producao de Filmes LDA
Locations: Portugal (Evora/Lisbon)
Producer: Stewart Richards
Associate producer: Olivia Stewart
Director: Ken McMullen
Screenwriters: Terry James, James Leahy, Ken McMullen
Camera: Elso Roque
Editor: Bill Diver
Cast: Ana Padrao, Roshan Seth, John Lynch, Jack Klaff, Timothy Spall

Eminent Domain
HTV International/ Arama Entertainment

Editor: Mike Cross
Cast: Andrew Kazamia, Monica Vassiliou, Adriani Maleni, Dimitri Andreas, John Burgess

The Field
Noel Pearson/Granada Films
Studio: MTM Ardmore
Location: western Ireland
Executive producer: Steve Morrison
Producer: Noel Pearson
Director/screenwriter: Jim Sheridan, from the play by John B Keane
Camera: Jack Conroy
Editor: J Patrick Duffner
Cast: Richard Harris, John Hurt, Tom Berenger, Sean Bean, Frances Tomelty

The Fifteen Streets
World Wide International Television/Tyne Tees TV
Location: Tyneside
Producer: Ray Marshall
Associate producer: Joanna Collins
Director: David Wheatley
Screenwriters: Rob Bettinson, Rosemary Anne Sisson, from the novel by Catherine Cookson
Camera: Ken Morgan
Editor: Martin Walsh
Cast: Owen Teale, Ian Bannen, Sean Bean, Clare Holman, Billie Whitelaw

The Fishing Trip
CRC Films
Location: London
Producer/screenwriter: Toby Courlander
Director: Christopher Robin Collins
Camera: Joe Dyer
Editor: Tristram Charnley
Cast: Keith Allen, Toby Davies, Rowland Wybenga

Dear Sarah
Bondway/RTE/ Cvitanovich Films
Locations: Dublin/Belfast/ London
Executive producer: Joe Mulholland
Producer: Peter Jacques
Associate producer: Liam Miller
Director: Frank Cvitanovich
Screenwriter: Tom McGurk
Camera: Ronan Lee
Editor: Paul Endicott
Cast: Stella McCusker, Barry McGovern, Patrick F Rocks, Janice McAdam, Bronagh Gallagher

December Bride
Little Bird
Locations: Strangford Lough, Northern Ireland/ Dublin
Executive producer: James Mitchell
Producer: Jonathan Cavendish
Associate producer: Redmond Morris
Director: Thaddeus O'Sullivan
Screenwriter: David Rudkin, from the novel by Sam Hanna Bell
Camera: Bruno De Keyzer
Editor: Rodney Holland
Cast: Donal McCann, Ciaran Hinds, Saskia Reeves, Geoffrey Golden, Brenda Bruce

Doombeach
The Children's Film Unit
Producer: Brianne Perkins
Director: Colin Finbow
Screenwriters: Colin Finbow and children
Cast: Glenda Jackson, Jeremy Coster, Donna Taibe, Alex Mitchell, Emma Freud

Dramarama – Just Wild about Harry
Tyne Tees TV
Location: north-east England
Producer: Lesley Oakden
Director: Mike Connor
Screenwriter: Jenny McDade
Camera: Dave Dixon
Cast: Lisa Clarkson, Rory Gibson, Richard Sands, Roger Showman, Tony Neilson

December Bride

Location: Warsaw/ Gdansk, Poland
Executive producer: Patrick Dromgoole
Producer: Shimon Arama
Director: John Irvin
Camera: Witold Adamek
Editor: Peter Tanner
Cast: Donald Sutherland, Anne Archer, Bernard Hepton, Paul Freeman, Anthony Bate

Family
Jericho/Channel 4
Location: London
Executive producer: Karin Bamborough
Producer: Bernard Krichefski
Director: Mary McMurray
Screenwriter: Andrew Kazamia
Camera: John Shann

The Field

The Fool ▶
Sands Films/Film Four
International/British
Screen/John Tyler
Producer: Richard
Goodwin
Director/screenwriter:
Christine Edzard
Cast: Derek Jacobi, Cyril
Cusack, Maria Aitken,
Michael Hordern

Fools of Fortune
Polygram/Working Title/
Channel 4
Locations: Millingar/
Dublin, Ireland
Executive producers: Tim
Bevan, Graham
Bradstreet
Producer: Sarah Radclyffe
Associate producer:
Caroline Hewitt
Director: Pat O'Connor
Screenwriter: Michael
Hirst, based on the novel
by William Trevor
Camera: Jerzy Zielinski
Editor: Mike Bradsell
Cast: Mary Elizabeth
Mastrantonio, Iain Glen,
Julie Christie, Michael
Kitchen, Niamh Cusack

Fragments of Isabella
MCK Films
Studio: MTM Ardmore
Executive producer: Noel
McKeown
Producers: Ronan
O'Leary, Michael Scott
Director/screenwriter:
Ronan O'Leary, from the
novel by Isabella Leitner
Camera: Walter Lassally
Editor: Stephen Marians
Cast: Gabrielle Reidy

Frankenstein's Baby
BBC TV/BBC Enterprises
Location: London
Executive producer:
Richard Broke
Producer: Ruth
Baumgarten
Associate producer: Ralph
Wilton
Director: Robert Bierman
Screenwriter: Emma
Tennant
Camera: John McGlashan
Editor: Bill Wright
Cast: Nigel Planer, Kate
Buffery, Yvonne
Bryceland, Sian Thomas,
William Armstrong

Get Back
Front Page Films
Executive producer: Jake
Eberts
Producers: Henry
Thomas, Philip
Knatchbull
Director: Richard Lester
Camera: Bob Paynter
With Paul McCartney

A Ghost in Monte Carlo
Lord Grade/Turner
Network TV/
Gainsborough Pictures
Studio: Goldcrest Elstree
Locations: Monte Carlo/
England
Executive producer: Lord
Grade
Producer/director: John
Hough
Associate producer:
Laurie Johnson
Screenwriter: Terence
Feely, from the novel by
Barbara Cartland
Camera: Terry Cole
Editor: Peter Weatherley
Cast: Sarah Miles, Oliver
Reed, Christopher
Plummer, Samantha
Eggar, Fiona Fullerton

Goldeneye ▶
Anglia Films
Studio: Grip House
Locations: London/
Jamaica
Executive producers:
Graeme McDonald, David
FitzGerald
Producer: Brenda Reid
Associate producer:
Anthony Waye
Director: Don Boyd
Screenwriter: Reg
Gadney

Camera: Richard
Greatrex
Editor: David Spears
Cast: Charles Dance,
Lynsey Baxter, Phyllis
Logan, Patrick Ryecart,
Marsha Fitzalan

Harbour Beat
Palm Beach/Zenith
Productions
Locations: Sydney,
Australia/Glasgow
Producers: David Elfick,
Irene Dobson
Director: David Elfick
Screenwriter: Morris
Gleitzman
Camera: Ellery Ryan

Cast: John Hannah,
Steven Vidler

Hard Road
The Children's Film Unit
Producer: Brianne
Perkins
Director: Colin Finbow
Screenwriters: Colin
Finbow and children
Cast: Francesca Camillo,
Max Rennie, John Luis
Mansi, David Savile,
Amanda Murray

Hardware
Palace/Wicked
Executive producers:
Stephen Woolley, Nik
Powell

Producers: Joanne Sellar, Paul Trybits
Director/screenwriter: Richard Stanley
Camera: Steve Chivers
Cast: Stacey Travis, Dylan McDermott, John Lynch

Hidden Agenda
Initial Film and Television
Locations: Belfast/Dublin/London
Executive producers: John Daly, Derek Gibson
Producers: Eric Fellner, Rebecca O'Brien
Director: Ken Loach
Screenwriter: Jim Allen
Camera: Clive Tickner
Cast: Brad Dourif, Frances McDormand, Mai Zetterling, Brian Cox

I Bought a Vampire Motorcycle
Dirk Productions
Producers/screenwriters: Mycal Miller, John Wolskel
Associate producer: Jim Allan
Director: Dirk Campbell
Camera: Tom Ingle
Editor: Mycal Miller
Cast: Neil Morrissey, Amanda Noar, Michael Elphick, Anthony Daniels

I Hired a Contract Killer
Villealfa Filmproductions/First City International Production Services
Location: London
Director: Aki Kaurismäki
Camera: Timo Salminen
Cast: Jean-Pierre Léaud, Margi Clarke, Kenneth Colley

Impromptu
Sovereign Pictures/Governor Productions/Les Films Ariane
Location: France
Executive producer: Jean Nachbaur
Producers: Stuart Oken, Daniel A Sherkow
Director: James Lapine
Screenwriter: Sarah Kernochan
Camera: Bruno De Keyzer
Editor: Michael Ellis
Cast: Judy Davis, Hugh Grant, Mandy Patinkin, Bernadette Peters, Julian Sands

Jekyll and Hyde
(working title: Dr Jekyll and Mr Hyde)
David Wickes Television/King Phoenix Entertainment/LWT/ABC
Location: London
Executive producers: David Wickes, Nick Elliott, Gerry Abrams
Producer: Patricia Carr
Associate producer: Joanna Elferink
Director/screenwriter: David Wickes, from the novel by Robert Louis Stevenson
Camera: Norman Langley
Editor: John Shirley
Cast: Michael Caine, Cheryl Ladd, Joss Ackland, Ronald Pickup, Lionel Jeffries ▼

I Bought a Vampire Motorcycle

Kappatoo
World Wide International Television/Tyne Tees TV
Studio: Tyne Tees TV
Location: north-east of England
Executive producer: Michael Chaplin
Producer: Ray Marshall
Director: Tony Kysh
Screenwriter: Ben Steed

Camera: Dave Dixon, Dave Bowen, Brian Maddison, Chris Bruce, Alistair McKenzie
Editor: Peter Telford
Cast: Simon Nash, Andrew O'Connor, Denise Outen, Gillian Eaton, John Abbot

King of the Wind
HTV International/Davis Panzer Productions
Locations: Turkey/west of England
Executive producers: Patrick Dromgoole, Johnny Goodman, Guy Collins
Producers: Michael Guest, Peter Davis, William Panzer, Paul Sarony
Director: Peter Duffell
Screenwriter: Leslie Sayle, based on the novel by Marguerite Henry
Camera: Brian Morgan
Editor: Lyndon Matthews
Cast: Richard Harris, Frank Finlay, Jenny Agutter, Nigel Hawthorne, Navin Chowdhry

A Kiss before Dying ▶

Initial Film and Television/Robert Lawrence Productions/ Universal Pictures
Studio: Lee International, Shepperton
Locations: USA/UK
Executive producer: Eric Fellner
Producer: Robert Lawrence
Associate producer: Chris Thompson
Director/screenwriter: James Dearden
Camera: Mike Southon
Editor: Mike Bradsell
Cast: Matt Dillon, Sean Young, Max von Sydow, James Russo, Diane Ladd

The Krays

Parkfield Entertainment/ Fugitive Features
Studio: Jacob Street
Location: UK
Executive producers: Jim Beach, Michele Kimche
Producers: Dominic Anciano, Ray Burdis
Associate producer: Paul Cowan
Director: Peter Medak
Screenwriter: Philip Ridley
Camera: Alex Thomson
Editor: Martin Walsh
Cast: Gary Kemp, Martin

▼

Kemp, Billie Whitelaw, Steven Berkoff, Tom Bell

The Kremlin Farewell

BBC TV Screen Two
Producer: David M Thompson
Director: Tristram Powell
Screenwriter: Nigel Williams
Camera: Nigel Walters
Editor: Ardan Fisher
Cast: Daniel Eastland, Freddie Jones, Kenneth

Colley, Polly Walker, Richard Wilson

Madly in Love

Shaker Films/Channel 4
Location: London
Producer: Lynn Horsford
Director: Ross Devenish
Screenwriter: Sandy Welch
Camera: Mick Coulter
Editor: Jon Gregory
Cast: Penelope Wilton, Samantha Bond, Martin Wenner, Caroline

Goodall, Anna Healy

Malevolence

Continental Pictures
Executive producer: Dudley Brown
Producer: Judy Parkinson
Director: Marcus Thompson
Screenwriter: Tony Rooke
Cast: Marian McLoughlin, Niven Boyd, Jonathan Izard, Tim Turnbull

The March

(working title: The March on Europe)
BBC TV
Locations: Morocco/ London
Executive producer: Ritchie Cogan
Producer: Peter Goodchild
Associate producer: Peter Woles
Director: David Wheatley
Screenwriter: William Nicholson
Camera: John Hooper
Editors: Tariq Anwar, Sue Lockerby, Graham Richmond
Cast: Malick Bowens, Juliet Stevenson, Dermot Crowley, Joseph Mydell, Lon Satton

Memphis Belle ▶

Enigma/Warner Bros
Studio: Pinewood
Locations: Lincolnshire/ Duxford, Cambridgeshire
Producers: David Puttnam, Catherine Wyler
Associate producer: Eric Rattray
Director: Michael Caton-Jones
Screenwriter: Monte Merrick
Camera: David Watkin
Editor: Jim Clark
Cast: Matthew Modine, Eric Stoltz, D B Sweeney, Tate Donovan, Billy Zane

Missing Persons

Yorkshire Television
Locations: Worthing/ London/Yorkshire
Executive producer: Keith Richardson
Producer/director: Derek Bennett
Associate producer: Pat Brown
Camera: Peter Jackson
Cast: Patricia Routledge, Jimmy Jewel, Jean Heywood, Gary Waldhorn, Tony Melody

The Monk

Celtic Films/ Mediterranean Films/ Target International Pictures
Location: Madrid/Soria, Spain
Executive producer: Muir Sutherland
Producer: Muir Sutherland, Paco Lara
Director/screenwriter: Paco Lara, based on the story by M G Lewis
Camera: Salvador Gines, Angel Luis Fernandez
Editor: Jose Luis Matesanz
Cast: Paul McGann, Sophie Ward, Isla Blair, ▼ Freda Dowie, Aitana Sanchez Gijon

Morphine and Dolly Mixtures

BBC Wales
Location: Cardiff
Executive producer: Ruth Caleb
Producer: Ruth Kenley-Letts
Director/screenwriter: Karl Francis
Camera: Russ Walker
Editor: Roy Sharman
Cast: Patrick Bergin, Joanna Griffiths, Sue Roderick, Sue Jones ▶ Davies, Gwenllian Davies

Newshounds

BBC TV/Working Title TV
Studio: Ealing
Location: London
Producer: Sarah Curtis
Associate producer: Jacinta Peel
Director: Les Blair
Camera: Remi Adefarasin
Editor: Sue Wyatt
Cast: Alison Steadman, Judith Scott, Adrian Edmondson, Paul Kember, Antony Marsh

The Nightmare Years

Consolidated/Turner Network TV
Location: Budapest ·
Executive producer: Gerald Rafshoon
Producer: Graham Ford
Director: Anthony Page
Screenwriters: Bob Woodward, Christian Williams
Camera: Ernest Vincza
Editor: Keith Palmer
Cast: Sam Waterston, Marthe Keller, Kurtwood Smith, Ronald Pickup, Peter Jeffrey

1996

BBC Wales/BBC TV
Location: Cardiff
Producer: Ruth Caleb
Associate producer: Ruth Kenley
Director: Karl Francis
Screenwriter: G F Newman
Camera: Russ Walker
Editor: Chris Lawrence
Cast: Keith Barron, Alan Armstrong, Tom Marshall, Dudley Sutton, Gillian Eaton

Nuns on the Run ▶

HandMade Films
Studio: Lee International, Shepperton
Location: London
Executive producers: George Harrison, Denis O'Brien
Producers: Michael White, Simon Bosanquet
Director/screenwriter: Jonathan Lynn
Camera: Mike Garfath
Editor: David Martin
Cast: Eric Idle, Robbie Coltrane, Camille Coduri, Janet Suzman, Doris Hare

The Object of Beauty

Avenue Pictures/BBC Films
Location: London
Executive producer: Cary Brokaw
Producer: Jon S Denny, Alex Gohar
Director/screenwriter: Michael Lindsay-Hogg
Camera: David Watkin
Editor: Ken Pearce
Cast: John Malkovich, Andie MacDowell, Peter Riegert, Rudi Davies, Joss Ackland

Old Flames

BBC Drama Plays
Locations: London/Oxford
Producer: Kenith Trodd
Associate producer: Carolyn Montagu
Director: Christopher Morahan
Screenwriter: Simon Gray
Camera: David Feig
Editor: Bill Wright
Cast: Stephen Fry, Simon Callow, Clive Francis, Miriam Margolyes, Graham Seed

One Man's War

TVS/Skreba Films/HBO/Film Four International
Locations: Mexico City/Vera Cruz
Executive producers: Graham Benson, Colin Callender
Producer: Ann Skinner
Associate producer: David Ball
Director: Sergio Toledo
Screenwriters: Mike Carter, Sergio Toledo
Camera: Rodolfo Sanchez
Editor: Laurence Mery Clark
Cast: Anthony Hopkins, Norma Aleandro, Fernando Torres, Reuben Blades

Othello

Primetime/BBC/Royal Shakespeare Company
Studio: Goldcrest Elstree
Executive producer: Michael Darlow
Producer: Greg Smith
Associate producer: Ralph Wilton
Director: Trevor Nunn
From the play by William Shakespeare
Camera: Paul Harding, Jim Day
Editor: St John O'Rorke
Cast: Willard White, Ian McKellen, Imogen Stubbs, Zoë Wanamaker, Sean Baker

Outpost ▲
HTV/Columbia Pictures
TV/Linnea Productions
Studio: Pinewood
Executive producer: Jeff
Melvoin, Patrick
Dromgoole, Johnny
Goodman
Producer/screenwriter:
Jeff Melvoin
Associate producer: Keith
Webber
Director: Tommy Lee
Wallace
Camera: Bob Edwards
Cast: Joanna Going, Ben
Marley, Neil Dickson,
David Robb

Paper Mask ▶
Film Four International/
Granada/British Screen
Location: London
Producers: Christopher
Morahan, Sue Austen
Director: Christopher
Morahan
Screenwriter: John Collee
Camera: Nat Crosby
Editor: Peter Coulson
Cast: Paul McGann,
Amanda Donohoe,
Frederick Treves, Tom
Wilkinson, Barbara
Leigh-Hunt

Pentecost
BBC2 Theatre Night
Locations: London/
Glasgow
Producers: Robert Cooper,
Tim Ironside Wood
Director: Nicolas Kent
Screenwriter: Lesley
Bruce, from the play by
Stewart Parker
Camera: Ian Turner
Editor: St John O'Rorke
Cast: Dearbhla Molloy,
Adrian Dunbar, Barbara
Adair, Michelle Fairley,
Sam Dale

A Perfect Hero
Havahall Pictures/LWT
Location: England
Executive producers:
Michael Whitehall, Nick
Elliott
Producer/director: James
Cellan Jones
Screenwriter: Allan Prior,
from the novel 'The Long
Haired Boy' by
Christopher Matthew
Camera: Ernest Vincze
Cast: Nigel Havers,
James Fox, Bernard
Hepton, Barbara Leigh-
Hunt, Patrick Ryecart

Phoenix Hall
Central TV
Executive producers:
Lewis Rudd, Sandie
Hastie
Producer/director: Geoff
Husson
Associate producer: Terry
Bezant
Camera: Peter Sanderson
Cast: Georgia Allen,
Clare Byam Shaw,
Adrian McLoughlin, Ben
Thomas, Mary Sheen

Pied Piper
Granada TV
Locations: Cumbria/
Lancashire/Cheshire/
Manchester/north
Yorkshire/France
Executive producers: Stan
Margulies, Michael Cox
Director: Norman Stone
Screenwriter: Jerome
Kass, from the novel by
Nevil Shute
Camera: Ken Morgan
Editor: Edward Mansell
Cast: Peter O'Toole, Mare
Winningham, Michael
Kitchen, Susan
Wooldridge, Ron
Donachie

A Private Life
Totem Productions
Executive producer: Innes
Lloyd
Producers: Francis
Gerard, Roland Robinson
Director: Francis Gerard
Screenwriter: Andrew
Davies
Camera: Nat Crosby
Cast: Bill Flynn, Jana
Cilliers, Kevin Smith, Ian
Roberts

Puja Puja
Limelight Films/
Channel 4
Executive producer:
Alison Owen
Producer: Caroline Spack
Director: Indra Bhose
Camera: Chris Morphet
Editor: Graham Whitlock

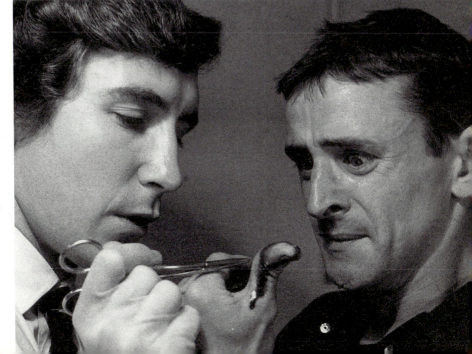

The Rainbow Thief
Timothy Burrill
Productions
Studio: Lee International,
Shepperton
Executive producer:
Johannes Weineck
Producer: Vincent Winter
Director: Alejandro
Jodorowsky
Screenwriter: Berta
Domingues
Camera: Ronnie Taylor
Editor: Les Healey
Cast: Peter O'Toole, Omar
Sharif, Christopher Lee

The Reflecting Skin ▶
Fugitive Features/British
Screen/BBC Films/Zenith
Location: Calgary,
Alberta, Canada
Executive producer: Jim
Beach
Producers: Dominic
Anciano, Ray Burdis, Di
Roberts
Director/screenwriter:
Philip Ridley
Camera: Dick Pope
Cast: Lindsay Duncan,
Vigo Mortensen, Jeremy
Cooper, Evan Hall, Bob
Kooms

Revenge of Billy the Kid
Montage Films
Executive producers: Tim
Dennison, James Groom
Producer: Tim Dennison
Director: James Groom
Screenwriters: Richard
Mathews, James Groom,
Tim Dennison
Camera: David Read
Cast: Samantha Perkins,
Michael Balfour

Rosencrantz and Guildenstern are Dead
Brandenberg Productions
Producers: Michael
Brandman, Iris Merlis,
Patrick Whitley
Director/screenwriter:
Tom Stoppard, from his
own play
Camera: Peter Biziou
Editor: Timothy Gee
Cast: Richard Dreyfuss,
Tim Roth, Gary Oldman,
Iain Glen, Ian Richardson

The Russia House
Pathé Entertainment/
Fred Schepisi
Studio: Pinewood
Locations: Russia/
Portugal/Canada/UK
Producers: Paul

Maslansky, Fred Schepisi
Director: Fred Schepisi
Screenwriter: Tom
Stoppard, from the novel
by John Le Carré
Camera: Ian Baker
Editor: Peter Honess
Cast: Sean Connery,
Michelle Pfeiffer, Roy
Scheider, James Fox,
Klaus Maria Brandauer

Sandy's Day
Location: Glasgow
Producers: Steve
McAteer, Michael
McConnell, Colin Monie
Director/screenwriter:
Steve McAteer
Camera: Stephen
McMillan
Cast: Gerard Kelly,
Francis Burns, Paul
Haggerty, Sheilagh Hind,
Alex McLeod

The Secret Life of Ian Fleming
Saban/Scherick/TNT
Studio: Lee International,
Shepperton
Location: England

Executive producer:
Edgar J Scherick
Producer: Aida Young
Associate producer: Peter
Manley
Director: Ferdinand
Fairfax
Camera: Mike Southon
Editor: Lesley Walker
Cast: Jason Connery,
Kristin Scott Thomas,
Patricia Hodge, Joss
Ackland, David Warner

Secret Weapon
Griffin/TVS/TNT/ABC
Australia
Locations: London/Rome/
Sydney
Executive producers:
Michael Deakin, Graham
Benson, Bob O'Connor,
Michael Apted, Penny
Chapman
Producer/screenwriter:
Nick Evans
Director: Ian Sharp
Camera: Alan Hume
Editor: Keith Palmer
Cast: Griffin Dunne,
Karen Allen, Jeroen
Krabbe, Stuart Wilson,
Joe Petruzzi

bfi – **Produced and/or
distributed by the
British Film Institute**

The Shell Seekers
Central Films/Marian
Rees Associates
Studio: Lee International,
Shepperton
Locations: Ibiza/
Cornwall/Cotswolds
Executive producer:
Marian Rees
Producers: Anne Hopkins,
William Hill
Director: Waris Hussein
Screenwriter: John
Pielmeier, from the novel
by Rosamunde Pilcher
Camera: Brian West
Cast: Angela Lansbury,
Sam Wanamaker,
Patricia Hodge, Anna
Carteret, Christopher
Bowen

The Sheltering Sky
Sahara Company
Locations: Morocco/
Algeria/Niger
Executive producer:
William Aldrich
Producer: Jeremy Thomas
Director: Bernardo
Bertolucci
Screenwriters: Mark
Peploe, Bernardo
Bertolucci, from the novel
by Paul Bowles
Camera: Vittorio Storaro
Editor: Gabriella
Cristiani
Cast: Debra Winger, John
Malkovich, Campbell ▼
Scott,
Jill Bennett,
Timothy Spall

She's Been Away
BBC TV/BBC Enterprises
Producer: Kenith Trodd
Director: Sir Peter Hall
Screenwriter: Stephen Poliakoff
Camera: Philip Bonham-Carter
Cast: Peggy Ashcroft, James Fox, Geraldine James

Shooting Stars
Viva Pictures/Granada/NDR West Germany/Channel 4
Location: Manchester
Executive producer: John Goldschmidt
Producer: David Jones
Associate producer: William Sargent
Director: Chris Bernard
Screenwriter: Barry Hines, from the novel by Dixie Williams
Camera: Witold Stok
Editor: Tony Ham
Cast: Gary McDonald, Sharon Duce, Keith Allen, Helmut Griem

bfi Silent Scream
Antonine/Channel 4/BFI
Studio: Blackcat
Location: Glasgow
Executive producers: Alan Fountain, Colin MacCabe,

Ben Gibson
Producer: Paddy Higson
Associate producer: Alan J Wands
Director: David Hayman
Screenwriter: Bill Beech
Camera: Denis Crossan
Editor: Justin Krish
Cast: Iain Glen, Anne Kristen, Tom Watson, David Mckail

Skulduggery
BBC TV
Location: Slough
Producer: Ann Scott
Associate producer: Elinor Carruthers
Director/screenwriter: Philip Davis
Camera: Barry McCann
Editor: Peter Harris
Cast: Steve Sweeney, Chris Pitt, Paul McKenzie, David Thewlis, Gillian Raine

Smack and Thistle
Working Title
Location: London
Producers: Sarah Cellan-Jones, Alison Jackson
Director/screenwriter: Tunde Ikoli
Camera: Peter Sinclair
Editor: Angus Newton
Cast: Charlie Caine, Rosalind Bennett, Patrick Malahide, Geoffrey Palmer, Connie Booth

Smoking Mirror
Cabachon Films
Executive producer: Tim Milson
Producer: Ingrid Lewis
Director: Celestino Coronado
Screenwriter: Alfredo Cordal
Camera: Martin Jeffrey

Treasure Island
Cast: Edmund Dehn, Paloma Zazoya, Francoise Testory

They Never Slept
BBC TV Screen Two
Locations: London/Cirencester
Producer: Kenith Trodd
Associate producer: Geoffrey Paget
Director: Udayan Prasad
Screenwriter: Simon Gray
Camera: Chris Seager
Editor: Ken Pearce
Cast: Edward Fox, Emily Morgan, James Fleet, Harriet Walter, Patricia Lawrence

Treasure Island
Agamemnon Films/British Lion/Turner Pictures
Studio: Pinewood
Location: Jamaica
Executive producer: Peter Snell
Producer/director/screenwriter: Fraser C Heston, from the novel by Robert Louis Stevenson
Associate producer: Ted Lloyd
Camera: Robert Steadman, Tony Westman
Editor: Eric Boyd-Perkins
Cast: Charlton Heston, Christian Bale, Oliver Reed, Christopher Lee, Julian Glover

PRODUCTION STARTS

Valentine Falls
Landseer Film &
Television Productions/
Channel 4
Location: London
Executive producer: Alan
Shallcross
Producer: Neil Richards
Director: Ian Knox
Screenwriter: Mark
Brennan
Camera: Simon Archer
Editor: Alan Knight
Cast: Gary McDonald,
Michelle Fairley, Ian
McElhinney, Emer
McCourt, Joseph Crilly

The Veiled One
(The Ruth Rendell
Mystery Movie)
TVS
Executive producer:
Graham Benson
Producer: Neil Zeiger
Director: Mary McMurray
Screenwriter: Trevor
Preston, from the novel by

▼

Ruth Rendell
Camera: Michael J Davis
Editor: Chris Wentzell
Cast: George Baker,
Christopher Ravenscroft,
Louie Ramsay, Deborah
Poplett, Ian Fitzgibbon

Wanted: Marjory
and Oliver
Initial Film and
Television/Georgian
Television/Channel 4

Locations: Islington,
London/Georgia
Producer: Jonathan
Hewes
Associate producer: David
Stranks
Director: Georgi
Levashov-Tumanishvili
Camera: Vladimir
Meletin
Cast: Alex Kingston

When Love Dies
Picture Palace/Channel 4

Location: north London
Producer: Malcolm
Craddock
Director: Horace Ové
Screenwriter: Nigel
Moffatt
Camera: Sean Van Hales
Cast: Josette Simon,
Brian Bovell, Norman
Beaton, Stefan Kalipha,
Mona Hammond

Wilt
Picture Partnership
Production/TalkBack/
Rank Film Distributors/
LWT
Location: north London
Executive producers:
Nick Elliott, Peter
Fincham
Producer: Brian Eastman
Associate producer:
Donna Grey
Director: Michael
Tuchner
Screenwriters: Andrew
Marshall, David Renwick,
from the novel by Tom
Sharpe
Camera: Norman Langley
Editor: Chris Blunden
Cast: Griff Rhys Jones,
Mel Smith, Alison
Steadman, Diana Quick

bfi Women in
Tropical Places
Glass Fish Productions/
Channel 4/Tyne Tees/BFI
Location: Newcastle
Executive producer: Ben
Gibson
Producer: Fizzy Oppè
Director: Penny Woolcock
Screenwriters: Candy
Guard, Penny Woolcock
Camera: Cinders
Forshaw, Janet Tovey
Editor: Robert
Hargreaves
Cast: Alison Doody,
Scarlet O'Hara, Huffty
Reah, Cleo Silver, Alan
Igbon

bfi – Produced and/or
distributed by the
British Film Institute

Thaddeus O'Sullivan's
DECEMBER BRIDE

Christopher Morahan's
PAPER MASK

Christine Edzard's
THE FOOL

Sergio Toledo's
ONE MAN'S WAR

Rob Tregenza's
THE ARC

Stephen Poliakoff's
CLOSE MY EYES

Bille August's
BEST INTENTIONS

Terence Davies'
THE LONG DAY CLOSES

Mike Leigh's
NEW PROJECT

FFi
FILM FOUR INTERNATIONAL

BILL STEPHENS
HEATHER PLAYFORD-DENMAN
60 CHARLOTTE STREET
LONDON W1P 2AX
TEL (71) 631 4444
FAX (71) 580 2622
TELEX 892355

PUBLICATIONS

MAJOR REFERENCE BOOKS

The BFI Library (see p7) currently holds some 35,000 books in many languages. Below is a selection of its general cinema and TV reference books in English. The Library produces bibliographies on specific subjects and a list of these is obtainable from the Librarian

CINEMA

ACTT Directory of Members
London: PEAR Books, 1985-86. Ed Peter Avis
Contact information, credits

Academy Awards
New York: Frederick Ungar, 1982. Compiled by Richard Shale. 2nd ed
For 1927-1977, full lists of nominations organised by category and by year. With a supplement containing a chronological listing for 1978-1981. Cross-indexed by name and title

The American Film Institute Catalog of Motion Pictures Produced in the United States Feature Films 1911-1920
Berkeley, Ca: University of California Press, 1988. 2 vols
Feature Films 1921-1930
New York: R R Bowker, 1971. 2 vols
Feature Films 1961-1970
New York: R R Bowker, 1976. 2 vols
Alphabetical listing of US features released during these decades, with credits and plot synopses. Credit and subject indices

A Biographical Dictionary of the Cinema
London: Secker & Warburg, 1975 (revised 1980). By David Thomson
Over 800 entries on directors, actors, producers. Described by its author as 'personal, opinionated and obsessive'

British Film Actors' Credits, 1895-1987
Jefferson, NC: McFarland, 1988. By Scott Palmer
Short career sketches with lists of films

British Film Catalogue, 1895-1985
Newton Abbott: David & Charles, 1986. Ed Denis Gifford. 2nd ed
Basic reference work on British cinema, listing films by month and year of release. Includes footage or r/t, cast, basic technical credits and category

bfi British Films 1927-1939
London: BFI, 1986. Ed Linda Wood
Concise survey of the period followed by annual 'in production' charts, and comprehensive statistics for the British film industry 1927-1939

bfi British Films 1971-1981
London: BFI, 1983. Ed Linda Wood
Concise survey of the period followed by lists, with basic credits, of commercial features made and/or released in Britain between 1971 and 1981

Broadcast Production Guide 1989/90
London: International Thomson, 1989
Comprehensive directory of companies involved in film and broadcasting in Britain

Catalog of Copyright Entries: Motion Pictures, 1894-1981
(various vols)
Washington: Library of Congress

Entries give copyright date and owner, production company, sound, colour, r/t, director, writer, editor and where appropriate, author and title of original story and composer. Indices of series, authors and organisations

Cinema. A Critical Dictionary
London: Secker & Warburg, 1980. Ed Richard Roud. 2 vols
Biographical and critical entries on over 200 major filmmakers in world cinema

Directors Guild of Great Britain Directory of Members 1988/89
London: Directors Guild of Great Britain, 1988
Type of work, credits, contact addresses

bfi Directory of International Film and Video Festivals 1989-90
London: British Council/ BFI, 1989
Film, television and video festivals, contact addresses, coverage and requirements for awards

Encore Directory 1990
Darlinghurst, NSW: Trade News Corporation, 1990
Australian directory of film, video and television companies, technicians and services

The Great Movie Stars: The Golden Years
London: Macdonald, 1989. By David Shipman. Revised ed
Entries for 200 stars, tracing their lives and careers during the peak years of Hollywood and mentioning all their films

The Great Movie Stars: The International Years
London: Macdonald, 1989. By David Shipman. Revised ed
Life and career entries for

over 230 stars who have become known in the post-war years

The Guinness Book of Movie Facts and Feats
Enfield, Middx: Guinness Books, 1988. By Patrick Robertson. 3rd ed
Illustrated compendium of facts and figures on cinema

Halliwell's Film Guide
London: Grafton, 1989. By Leslie Halliwell. 7th ed
Alphabetical listing of over 10,000 film titles with main credits, brief summary of plot and evaluation

Halliwell's Filmgoer's and Video Viewer's Companion
London: Grafton, 1988. By Leslie Halliwell. 9th ed
Biographical dictionary with entries also on subjects and fictional characters

The Illustrated Guide to Film Directors
London: Batsford, 1983. By David Quinlan
Career studies and full filmographies for 550 directors

The Illustrated Who's Who in British Films
London: B T Batsford, 1978. By Denis Gifford
Outline biographical entries with lists of credits for 1,000 British actors and directors

The International Directory of Films and Filmmakers
London: St James Press, 1984-87. 5 vols
Dictionary of world cinema

The International Encyclopedia of Film
London: Michael Joseph, 1972. Ed Roger Manvell and others
Articles on national cinema, technical developments, genre and other topics as well as entries for individuals

The International Film Encyclopedia
London: Macmillan, 1980. By Ephraim Katz
More than 7,000 entries mainly biographical but including industry and technical processes

International Film Guide 1990
London: Cahners Publishing, 1990. Ed Peter Cowie
Regular features include worldwide production surveys, film books and magazines, film schools, and festivals. Also special features and studies of directors

International Motion Picture Almanac 1990
New York: Quigley, 1990
Yearbook of the US industry, including who's who section, running index of releases from 1955, market analyses from some 50 countries, awards and top US box-office films

Kay's Database: video, film, television
London: B L Kay Publishing Co, 1989
Annual UK directory of film, video and television companies and services

Kay's International Production Manual 1987
London: B L Kay Publishing Co
International directory of film, video and television companies and technicians organised by country (and state for USA, Canada and Australia), then by activity

Kemp's International Film and Television Yearbook 1989/90
London: Kemp's Printing and Publishing Co
Information on a wide range of companies and technical services in the UK plus directory entries for the industry abroad

The Knowledge 1989
London: PA Publishing Co, 1989
Annual directory of British film and TV companies and services

The Motion Picture Guide 1927-1989
Evanston, Ill: Cinebooks, 1985 to date. 12 vols plus annual updates
A listing of 50,000 English and notable foreign film titles with credits and synopses

Movies on TV: 1989/90
New York: Bantam Books, 1989. Ed Stephen H Scheuer
Alphabetical listing, with brief notes on films available on TV in USA

New York Times Encyclopedia of Film
New York: Times Books, 1984. Ed Gene Brown. 13 vols
A collection of articles on film from the New York Times 1896-1979, arranged chronologically with an index

The Oxford Companion to Film
London: OUP, 1976. Ed Liz-Anne Bawden
3,000 entries on all aspects of world cinema

Quinlan's Illustrated Directory of Film Stars
London: B T Batsford, 1989. By David Quinlan. Revised ed
1,700 brief career studies of top players and full lists of credits

Reel Facts: The Movie Book of Records
London: Penguin Books, 1981. New York: Vintage Books, 1982 (revised ed). By Cobbett Steinberg
Lists of awards and prize winners, top box office films, most successful stars etc

Researcher's Guide to British Film and Television Collections
London: British Universities Film and Video Council, 1989. Ed Elizabeth Oliver. 3rd ed
Combines guidance for researchers with information about collections of film, video and relevant documentation and how to access them

Researcher's Guide to British Newsreels
London: British Universities Film and Video Council, 1983. Ed James Ballantyne
Full abstracts of writing published between 1901 and 1982 provide a history of British newsreels. Additional information includes lists of newsreel company staff and details of relevant film libraries and documentation centres, their holdings and policies. vol II, 1988

Screen International Film and TV Yearbook 1989/90
London: International Thomson. Ed Peter Noble
A who's who of British film and TV with directory information on cinemas, studios, companies etc, with a foreign section

Screen World 1988
London: Frederick Muller, 1988. Ed John Willis
Pictorial and statistical record of the movie season

60 Years of the Oscar
New York: Abbeville Press, 1989. By Robert Osborne
The official history of the Academy Awards, with full lists of nominations and awards. Index by name and title

The Studio Blu-Book: 1989 Directory
Hollywood: Hollywood

Reporter, 1989
Directory of California film and TV specialist services

Variety Film Reviews 1907-1986
New York, London: R R Bowker, 1983-86. 19 vols
Chronologically arranged collection of 'Variety' film reviews, with a title index

Variety International Show Business Reference
New York, London: Garland Publications, 1983. Ed Mike Kaplan
Includes career biographies, credits for films and TV programmes released 1976-1980, major awards

Who Played Who on the Screen
London: B T Batsford, 1988. By Roy Pickard
An A-Z guide to film portrayals of famous figures of fact and fiction

Who Was Who on the Screen
New York: R R Bowker, 1983. By Evelyn Mack Truitt. 3rd ed
Biographical dictionary of over 9,000 screen personalities who died between 1905 and 1975

Who Wrote the Movie, and What Else Did He Write?
Los Angeles: Academy of Motion Picture Arts and Sciences, 1970
An index of American screenwriters and their works, 1936-1969, compiled from Academy publications

Who's Who in the Motion Picture Industry 1986/87
Hollywood: RG Publishing, 1986. Ed Rodman Gregg
A-Z of directors, producers, writers and executives with credits, addresses, agents

The World Encyclopedia of the Film
London: Studio Vista, 1972. Ed John M Smith

and Tim Cawkwell
Biographical entries with filmographies and a film index of 22,000 titles

TV/VIDEO

Actors' Television Credits 1950-1972
Metuchen, NJ: Scarecrow Press, 1973. Supplement 1 (1973-1976), 1978. Supplement 2 (1977-1981), 1982. Supplement 3 (1982-1985), 1986. By James Robert Parish
Each name is followed by a list of titles with transmission date and US TV company

The American Vein; Directors and Directions in Television
London: Talisman Books, 1979. By Christopher Wicking and Tise Vahimagi
Critical evaluation and credits for American TV directors

BBC Annual Report and Accounts 1988/89
London: BBC, 1988
The Corporation's annual report and accounts

BBC Annual Report and Handbook 1987
London: BBC, 1987
The Corporation's annual report and accounts with details of organisation, programmes, etc

Broadcast Yearbook and Diary 1990
London: International Thomson, 1990. Ed Nick Radlo
Diary containing information on British television industry and services

The Complete Directory of Prime Time Network TV Shows
New York: Ballantine Books, 1988. By Tim Brooks and Earle Marsh. 4th ed
The detailed information,

from 1946 to the present, includes broadcasting history, front of camera credits and descriptive and evaluative comment

Halliwell's Television Companion
London: Granada, 1986. By Leslie Halliwell with Philip Purser. 3rd ed
Revision of Halliwell's Teleguide. An A-Z of programmes and personalities in UK television with critical comment

International TV and Video Guide 1987
London: Tantivy Press, 1986. Ed Richard Paterson
The TV and video companion volume to the International Film Guide

International Television and Video Almanac 1990
New York: Quigley, 1990
Record of US television industry and its personalities. UK and World Market sections

Leonard Maltin's TV Movies and Video Guide, 1990
New York: New American Library, 1990. Ed Leonard Maltin
Brief credits and plot synopses for 15,000 films appearing on US television

Les Brown's Encyclopedia of Television
New York: Zoetrope, 1982. By Les Brown
A-Z guide to programmes, people, history, and business of American television

Professional Video International Yearbook 1987-88
Croydon: Link House, 1985
Directory of technical information for the TV and video industries

TV Facts
New York: Facts on File,

1980. By Cobbett S Steinberg
'50,000 facts about American TV.' Ratings, awards, revenues, prime-time schedules, etc

TV Guide Almanac
New York: Ballantine Books, 1980. Ed Craig T and Peter G Norback
Encyclopedia of information on television in the US

Television and Radio 1988
London: IBA, 1987
Annual IBA guide to independent broadcasting

Television Drama Series Programming: Comprehensive Chronicle 1959-1975
Metuchen, NJ: Scarecrow Press, 1978. Supplements (1975-1980), 1981. (1980-1982), 1983. (1982-1984), 1987. By Larry James Gianakos
Provides a season by season breakdown of American TV drama series. Gives title of each episode, date of first transmission, series stars and guest stars

Television Programming Source Books
New York: Broadcast Information Bureau, 1989
Annual listing with supplements including all feature films and TV series currently available to American TV companies or which have already been televised. Includes brief technical and credit information with a plot synopsis and names of export and domestic sales agents

Who's Who on Television
London: Independent Television Publications, 1988
Alphabetical listing of information on over 1,000 personalities in British television

PUBLICATIONS AVAILABLE FROM THE INTERNATIONAL FEDERATION OF FILM ARCHIVES

The International Federation of Film Archives (FIAF) was founded in 1938 to encourage the establishment of film archives throughout the world. Its specialist publications are often the only detailed research works available in this field.
The titles below can be ordered from: FIAF, Room 113, Canalot Studios, 222 Kensal Road, London W10 5BN. (Prices include p & p)

International Index to Film Periodicals
Published since 1972, this indexes literature on film in over 100 of the world's most important film magazines under general subjects, film and personalities
Available as: microfiches cumulating 15 years, 1972-86, including directors index at £280. 1987-89 cumulation at £35. 1990 cumulating microfiche service (6 despatches per year) £465
Annual published volumes from 1974-88 (£56.00), 1989 (£60.00)

International Index to Television Periodicals
Published since 1979, this indexes literature on television in over 40 media journals under general subjects, television programmes and personalities.
Available as: microfiches cumulating 1979-86, including directors index at £75, 1987-89 cumulation at £15. 1990 cumulating microfiche service (6 despatches per year) at £215
Published volumes cumulated as 1979-80, 1981-82 (£25.00 each),

1983-86 (£56.00), 1987-88 (£35.00)

FIAF Classification Scheme for Literature on Film and Television
By Karen Jones and Michael Moulds, 1990. 52nd ed
120pp, £30

The following FIAF publications are available from the FIAF Secretariat, Coudenberg 70, 1000 Brussels, Belgium. (Prices, in Belgian francs, include p & p)

FIAF Bulletin
Published twice a year by FIAF Brussels. Annual subscription BF400 + bank costs

Annual Bibliography of FIAF Members' Publications
Prepared by the National Film & TV Archives, Ottawa from 1979. BF300 + bank costs

Bibliography of National Filmographies
Compiled by Dorothea Gebauer. Edited by Harriet W Harrison, 1985 Annotated list of filmographies, journals and other publications
80pp, BF800

Cinema 1900-1906: An Analytical Study
Proceedings of the FIAF Symposium at Brighton 1978. Vol I contains transcriptions of the papers, Vol II contains an analytical filmography of 550 films of the period. Prepared by the National Film Archive, London, 1982
372pp and 391pp, BF1500

Evaluating Computer Cataloguing Systems – A Guide for Film Archivists
By Roger Smither for the Cataloguing Commission, 1989
35pp BF900
(Available with 'Study on

the Usage of Computers for Film Cataloguing' for BF1500)

50 Years of Film Archives 1938-1988
FIAF yearbook published for the 50th anniversary, containing descriptions of its 78 members and observers and a historical account of its development. 1988
203pp, BF950

Glossary of Filmographic Terms
Compiled by Jon Gartenberg, 1985. Lists and defines English, French, German, Spanish and Russian terms
141pp, BF1000

Glossary of Filmographic Terms, Version II
Compiled by Jon Gartenberg, 1989. Includes terms and indexes in English, French, German, Spanish, Russian, Swedish, Portuguese, Dutch, Italian, Czech, Hungarian, Bulgarian
149pp, BF1300

Manuel des Archives du Film
Edited by Eileen Bowser and John Kuiper, 1980. Basic manual on the functioning of a film archive. French version
151pp, BF1000

Preservation and Restoration of Moving Images and Sound
A report by the FIAF Preservation Commission, covering the physical properties of film and sound tape, their handling and storage, and the equipment used by film archives to ensure permanent restoration, 1986
268pp, BF1300

The Slapstick Symposium
Edited by Eileen Bowser, 1988. Dealings and proceedings of the Early American Slapstick Symposium held at the

Museum of Modern Art, New York, May 1985
121pp, BF800

Study on the Usage of Computers for Film Cataloguing
Edited by Roger Smither, 1985. A survey and analysis on the usage of computers for the cataloguing of material in film and television archives
275pp, BF900
(Available with 'Evaluating Computer Cataloguing Systems – A Guide for Film Archivists' for BF1500)

Technical Manual of the FIAF Preservation Committee
A user's manual on practical film and video preservation procedures. Ongoing loose leaf publication in A4 + folder. 1987-
150pp (by end 1989), BF1500

ENGLISH LANGUAGE FILM, TV, VIDEO AND CABLE PERIODICALS

A select list of film, television, video and cable journals, most of which can be studied in the BFI Library (see p7)

£ Afterimage
(irregular)
20 Landrock Road
London N9 7HL
Each issue deals with a specific area of film and/or critical theory

American Cinematographer
(monthly)
1782 N Orange Drive
Hollywood CA 90028
USA
International journal of film and video production techniques. Published by the American Society of Cinematographers

American Film
(10 pa)
BPI Communications Inc
1515 Broadway
39th Floor
New York NY 10036
USA
Journal of the AFI.
A magazine of the Film
and Television Arts

Animator
(quarterly)
13 Ringway Road
Park Street
St Albans
Herts AL2 2RE
Intended for all levels of
animators and animation
fans

Ariel (weekly)
BBC
Room G1
12 Cavendish Place
London W1A 1AA
The BBC staff magazine.
Contains articles of
general interest about the
BBC

Audio Visual
(monthly)
PO Box 109
Maclaren House
Scarbrook Road
Croydon
Surrey CR9 1QH
Tel: 081 760 9690
Aimed at management
and businesses which use
audiovisual materials

**Audiovisual
Librarian** (quarterly)
Library Association
Publishing
7 Ridgmount Street
London WC1E 7AE
Tel: 071 636 7543
The official organ of the
audiovisual groups Aslib
and the LA. Includes
articles, book reviews and
a bibliographic update

BETA News
(irregular)
Broadcasting and
Entertainment Trades
Alliance
181-185 Wardour Street
London W1V 3AA
Tel: 071 439 7585
The official journal of the
Broadcasting and
Entertainment Trades
Alliance

**bfi British
National Film
and Video
Catalogue**
(quarterly)
British Film Institute
21 Stephen Street
London W1P 1PL
Tel: 071 255 1444
Details of films and
videocassettes made
available for non-
theatrical use in the UK,
classified by subject.
Cumulates annually

Broadcast (weekly)
International Thomson
Publishing
2nd Floor
7 Swallow Place
London W1R 7AA
Tel: 071 491 9484
Television industry news
magazine. Regular
sections devoted to video,
cable and industry news.
Now incorporates
Television Weekly

Broadcasting
(weekly)
Broadcasting
Publications Inc
1705 De Sales Street
NW Washington DC
20036
USA
America's main
broadcasting trade
weekly

Bulgarian Films
(8 pa)
Bulgarian
Cinematography State
Corporation
135-a Rakovski Street
Sofia
Bulgaria
News of the Bulgarian
cinema in English

**The Business of
Film** (monthly)
24 Charlotte Street
London W1P 1HJ
Tel: 071 580 0141
Aimed at film industry
professionals –
producers, distributors,
exhibitors, investors,
financiers

**Cable and Satellite
Europe** (monthly)
531-533 Kings Road
London SW10 0TZ
Journal covering the
European cable and
satellite industry

Cineaste (quarterly)
200 Park Avenue South
New York NY 10003
USA
Reviews, interviews,
articles on the art and
politics of cinema.
International in scope

Cinema Papers (6 pa)
MTV Publishing
43 Charles Street
Abbotsford
Victoria
Australia 3067
Australia's leading film
journal

Combroad (quarterly)
Commonwealth
Broadcasting Association
Broadcasting House
London W1A 1AA
Tel: 071 580 4468
Articles on
Commonwealth
television, radio and
broadcasting in general

Commercials
(monthly)
EMAP Commercials
12-13 Kingly Street
London W1V 5LP
Tel: 071 494 2035
Articles and news from
the commercials industry

**Communication
Research Trends**
(quarterly)
Centre for the Study of
Communication and
Culture
221 Goldhurst Terrace
London NW6 3EP
Tel: 071 328 2868
Information on
international
communications research

Czechoslovak Film
(quarterly)
Czechoslovak Filmexport
Press Department
Praha 1
Vaclavske Namesti '28
Czechoslovakia
News from the Czech
cinema in English

Direct (8 pa)
Directors' Guild of Great
Britain
125 Tottenham Court
Road
London W1P 9HN
Tel: 071 387 7131
Journal of Directors'
Guild of Great Britain

EMMY (6 pa)
Academy of Television

Arts and Sciences
3500 West Olive Avenue
Suite 700
Burbank CA 91505
USA
Published by the
Academy of Television
Arts and Sciences

Empire (monthly)
42 Great Portland Street
London W1N 5AH
Tel: 071 436 5430
Articles, news and
reviews of films, videos
and books

Encore (fortnightly)
PO Box 1377
Darlinghurst
NSW 2010
Australia
Entertainments
magazine now
incorporating The
Australian Film Review

bfi Film (monthly)
British Federation
of Film Societies
Film Society Unit
BFI
21 Stephen Street
London W1P 1PL
Tel: 071 255 1444
Non-commercial aspects
of film. See also p156

**Film and Television
Technician** (monthly)
ACTT
111 Wardour Street
London W1V 4AY
Tel: 071 437 8506
ACTT members' journal

Film Comment
(bi-monthly)
140 West 65th Street
New York NY 10023
USA
Published by the Film
Society of Lincoln Center.
Aimed at intelligent
American filmgoers

£ Film Dope
(irregular)
88 Port Arthur Road
Nottingham NG2 4GE
Mainly an A-Z of
international film
personalities but also
includes some long
interviews

Film Monthly
Argus House
Boundary Way
Hemel Hempstead
H12 7ST
Film-fan magazine
incorporating 'Photoplay'

Film Quarterly
University of California
Berkeley CA 94720
USA
International critical
journal with particular
emphasis on film
literature and book
reviews

Film Review
(monthly)
Punch Publications
Ludgate House
245 Blackfriars Road
London SE1 9UZ
Tel: 071 921 5900
All English-speaking
films on release and
in production covered in
reviews, interviews,
articles and pictures, book
and record reviews. Now
incorporating 'Films and
Filming'

Films in Review
(10 pa)
PO Box 589
Lennox Hill Station
New York NY 10021
USA
Popular magazine aimed
at 'film buffs'. Notable for
career articles and
historical information

 Framework
(irregular)
17 Cheriton
Queens Crescent
London NW5 1LP

Historical Journal of Film, Radio and Television
(bi-annual)
Carfax Publishing
PO Box 25
Abingdon
Oxfordshire OX14 3UE
Academic journal founded
by IAMHIST in 1981.
Articles, book reviews,
archival reports and
reviews of film, television
and radio programmes of
historical or educational
importance

The Hollywood Reporter
(daily)
6715 Sunset Boulevard
Hollywood CA 90028
USA
International
showbusiness trade paper

IPPA Bulletin
(irregular)
Independent Programme
Producers Association
50-51 Berwick Street

London W1A 4RD
Tel: 071 439 7034
The journal of the
Independent Programme
Producers Association

Independent Media
(monthly)
7 Campbell Court
Bramley
Basingstoke
Hants RG26 5EG
Tel: 0256 882032
A broadsheet designed for
makers and consumers of
independent film and
video productions. Covers
television and radio
media, with items on
international, education
and art topics, news,
interviews and reviews.
Sponsored by the Arts
Council of Great Britain
and Channel 4

Intermedia
(bi-monthly)
International Institute of
Communications
Tavistock House South
Tavistock Square
London WC1H 9LF
Tel: 071 388 0671
Articles on international
communications and
broadcasting

International Broadcasting
(monthly)
7 Swallow Place
London WC1R 7AA
Tel: 071 491 9484
Articles, news and other
information on mainly
technical and engineering
topics

International Media Law
(monthly)
21-27 Lamb's Conduit
Street
London WC1N 3NJ
A monthly bulletin on
rights clearances and
legal practice. Includes
a regular update section

Journal of Broadcasting and Electronic Media
(quarterly)
Broadcast Education
Association
1771 N Street
NW Washington DC
20036
USA
Articles on current
research mainly in the
US; book reviews

Journal of Communication
(quarterly)
Oxford University Press
200 Madison Avenue
New York NY 10016
USA
Theoretical and research
articles and book reviews

Journal of Film and Video
(quarterly)
Division of Mass
Communication
Emerson College
100 Beacon Street
Boston MA 02116
USA
Articles on current
academic research in film
and television, as well as
film and video practices,
book reviews, video and
film reviews

The Journal of Media Law and Practice
(3 pa)
Frank Cass
11 Gainsborough Road
London E11 1RS
Tel: 071 530 4226
Covers media law
relating to copyright and
video recording. Includes
articles, news and book
reviews

The Journal of Popular Film and Television
(quarterly)
Heldref Publications
4000 Albemarle Street
NW
Washington DC 20016
USA
Dedicated to popular film
and television in the
broadest sense.
Concentration on
commercial cinema and
TV

Jump Cut
(quarterly)
PO Box 865
Berkeley CA 94701
USA
Radical critical journal
with a special interest in
politics of cinema

Kino
(irregular)
Dina Lom
Century House
4th Floor
100 Oxford Street
London W1N 9FB
Tel: 071 580 4422
Official publication in
English on German
cinema published by the
German Film Board and

the German Film Export
Union

The Listener
(weekly)
BBC Publications
199 Old Marylebone Road
London NW1 5QS
Tel: 071 258 3581
Reviews, discussion and
transcripts of BBC
television and radio
programmes

£ Media, Culture and Society
(quarterly)
Sage Publications
28 Banner Street
London EC1Y 8QE
Articles on the mass
media in their political,
cultural and historical
contexts

Media Report to Women
(bi-monthly)
3306 Ross Place
NW Washington DC
20008
USA
Published by the
Women's Institute for
Freedom of the Press, this
journal deals with what
women are thinking and
doing to change the
communications media

bfi Monthly Film Bulletin
British Film Institute
21 Stephen Street
London W1P 1PL
Tel: 071 255 1444
Full credits, synopses and
reviews of all UK
theatrical releases, and
some video releases, along
with articles and
interviews. See also p8

£ Movie
(irregular)
2a Roman Way
London N7 8XG
Tel: 071 609 4019/4010
Journal of theory and
criticism with special
emphasis on American
cinema

On Air/Off Air
(bi-monthly)
The Volunteer Centre
29 Lower King's Road
Berkhamsted
Herts HP4 2AB
Tel: 04427 73311
The magazine of the
Media Project at the
Volunteer Centre, giving
news about nationwide

projects, for example, community broadcasting

Onfilm (bi-monthly)
PO Box 6374
Wellington
New Zealand
The magazine of the NZ picture industry

£ **Picture House**
(irregular)
44 Warlingham Road
Thornton Heath
Surrey CR4 7DE
The magazine of the Cinema Theatre Association, presenting historical articles on cinema buildings, circuits, architects, etc

Postscript (3 pa)
Jacksonville University
Jacksonville FL 32211
USA
Journal of essays in film and the humanities

Premiere (monthly)
Murdoch Magazines
2 Park Avenue
New York NY 10016
USA
News, reviews and interviews

£ **Primetime**
(quarterly)
Wider TV Access
c/o Flashbacks
6 Silver Place
London W1R 3LJ
Primetime is published by WTVA, a society devoted to the wider circulation of, and discussion about, old TV programmes, with reviews of TV material available on video

Producer (monthly)
The Producers Association
Paramount House
162-170 Wardour Street
London W1V 4LA
Tel: 071 437 7700

Quarterly Review of Film and Video
University of Southern California
School of Cinema-Television
University Park
Los Angeles CA 90089-2211
USA
Academic journal dealing with cinema in context of larger aesthetic or sociopolitical issues

Radio Times (weekly)
BBC
35 Marylebone High Street
London W1M 4AA
Tel: 071 580 5577
Guide to BBC programmes

£ **Screen**
(quarterly)
(incorporating Screen Education)
Department of Theatre, Film and Television Studies
University of Glasgow
Glasgow G12 8QF
Aimed at teachers/lecturers in film theory

Screen Digest
(monthly)
37 Gower Street
London WC1E 6HH
Tel: 071 580 2842
An industry news digest covering film, TV, cable, satellite, video and other multimedia presentations. Has a centre page reference section every month on subjects like law, statistics or sales

Screen Finance
(fortnightly)
Financial Times Business Information
Tower House
Southampton Street
London WC2E 7HA
Tel: 071 240 9391
International financial news for the film and television industry

Screen International
(weekly)
7 Swallow Place
249-259 Regent Street
London W1R 7AA
Tel: 071 734 9452
Cinema industry magazine mainly focussed on the cinema, with a regular section which has industry news and information about upcoming productions for TV and video

 Sight and Sound
(quarterly)
British Film Institute
21 Stephen Street
London W1P 1PL
Tel: 071 255 1444
International critical journal of film and

television now in its 60th year. See also p8

Soviet Film (monthly)
9b Gnezdnikovsky Pereulok
Moscow 103009
USSR
News in English of Soviet films and filmmakers

The Stage and Television Today
(weekly)
47 Bermondsey Street
London SE1 3XT
Tel: 071 403 1818
'Television Today' constitutes the middle section of 'The Stage' and is a weekly trade paper

TV Times (weekly)
Independent Television Publications
247 Tottenham Court Road
London W1P 0AU
Tel: 071 636 3666
Guide to ITV and Channel 4 TV programmes

Talkback (monthly)
Royal Television Society
Tavistock House East
Tavistock Square
London WC1H 9HR
Tel: 071 387 1970
Bulletin of RTS events and members, with relevant television industry news items

Television
(bi-monthly)
The Royal Television Society
Tavistock House East
Tavistock Square
London WC1H 9HR
Tel: 071 387 1970
Articles on the television industry, technical and general

Television Week
MEED House
21 John Street
London WC1N 2BP
Tel: 071 404 5513
News magazine for the television industry

Televisual (monthly)
Centaur Publications
St Giles House
50 Poland Street
London W1V 4AX
Tel: 071 437 4377
Glossy publication aimed at the industrial and business user of video. Features, details of shows

and exhibitions, a hardware catalogue and new programmes of interest to the industrial user

Trade Guide (weekly)
Manek Chambers
Lamington Road
Bombay 400 004
India
Trade journal

Variety (weekly)
475 Park Avenue South
New York NY 10016
USA
The American showbiz journal including worldwide coverage of cinema and other media

The Velvet Light Trap (irregular)
PO Box 9240
Madison
Wisconsin 53715
USA
Critical journal in which each issue addresses a particular aspect of film theory or culture

Video Maker
(monthly)
Oasis Publishing
Media House
Boxwell Road
Berkhamsted
Herts HP4 3ET
Tel: 0442 876191
Amateur cine and video monthly. Incorporates 'Making Better Movies'

Video Today
(monthly)
Argus Specialist Publications
Argus House
Boundary Way
Hemel Hempstead
Herts
Consumer-orientated magazine with short reviews of new releases. It also includes readers' problems, hardware tests, articles, with information on London and regional dealers

Video Trade Weekly
20 Bowling Green Lane
London EC1R 0BD
Weekly newspaper aimed at the retail trade, with news about the distribution industry, new products, festivals, awards and so on

Viewfinder (3 pa)
British Universities Film
and Video Council
55 Greek Street
London W1V 5LR
Tel: 071 734 3687
News and reviews of new
productions available to
workers in higher
education, articles on, for
example, storing and
handling videotape.
Includes some book
reviews

Wide Angle
(irregular)
Johns Hopkins
University Press
701 W 40th Street
Baltimore MD 21211
USA
Academic journal with
each issue concentrating
on a single aspect of film
culture

FOREIGN LANGUAGE FILM PERIODICALS

**L'Avant-Scène
Cinéma** (monthly)
16 rue des Quatre Vents
75006 Paris
France
Articles, reviews,
interviews, often
complete scripts

Bianco e Nero
(quarterly)
Via Tuscolana 1524
00173 Roma
Italy
The leading Italian
critical journal. Film and
book reviews. articles

**Cahiers de la
Cinémathèque**
(irregular)
Palais des Congrés
66000 Perpignan
France
Published with the
Cinémathèque de
Toulouse. Each issue
treats one subject

Cahiers du Cinéma
(monthly)
9 Passage de la Boule
Blanche
75012 Paris
France
Leading critical journal
with a special interest in
US cinema

Chaplin (bi-monthly)
Filmhuset
Box 27 126
102 52 Stockholm
Sweden
Journal of the Swedish
Film Institute

Cine Cubano
(irregular)
Calle 23 no 1155
Havana
Cuba
Critical journal mainly
concerned with the Latin-
American cinema

Cineinforme
(bi-monthly)
Gran Via 64
28013 Madrid
Spain
Trade magazine on
Spanish and Latin-
American cinema

Cinema e Cinema
(quarterly)
Editrice Clueb Bologna
Via Marsala 24
Italy
Critical journal with a
special interest in Italian
cinema

Cinema Nuovo
(bi-monthly)
Casello Postale 362
70100 Bari
Italy
Serious critical journal –
features many book
reviews

Cinéma 88/89
(weekly)
49 rue Faubourg
Poissonniere
75009 Paris
France
This journal, previously
monthly, is now published
weekly and in tabloid
form. Reviews of current
releases in France,
articles, interviews, book
reviews are included plus
a section on films on
television

Film (monthly)
Westerbachstrasse 33-35
6000 Frankfurt 90
West Germany
Authoritative film journal
featuring articles and
criticism

Film a Doba (monthly)
Halkova 1, 120 72
Praha 2

Czechoslovakia International film journal with emphasis on eastern European cinema

Film Echange
(quarterly)
16 rue des Quatre-Vents
75006 Paris
France
Substantial journal of information on international law, economics and sociology of the audiovisual media

Film Echo/Film Woche (72 pa)
Wilhelmstrasse 42
6200 Wiesbaden
West Germany
West German trade magazine

Film Français
(weekly)
90 rue de Flandre
75943 Paris
France
Trade paper for French cinema professionals. Includes video information

Filmowy Serwis Prasowy (2 per month)
ul Mazawiecka 6/8
00-950 Warszawa
Poland
Official journal of Polish film contains information on films and filmmakers

Frauen und Film
(irregular)
Verlag Stoemfeld/Roter Stern
Postfach 180147
6000 Frankfurt am Main
West Germany
Concentrates on German and foreign issues concerning women and film

Iskusstvo Kino
(monthly)
Moscou Smalenskaja –
Sennaja
32/34 V/O
Mezadunarodnaja Kniga
USSR
Leading Soviet journal concentrating on national cinema with credits

Kosmorama
(quarterly)
Det Danske Filmmuseum
Store Søndervoldstraede
1419 København K
Denmark

Leading Danish periodical containing essays, credits and film and book reviews

Positif (monthly)
Nouvelles Editions Opta
1 Quai Conti
75006 Paris
France
International critical journal with wide festival coverage

Revue du Cinéma/ Image et Son
(monthly)
3 rue Recamier
75007 Paris
France
Reviews of films, television and video. Aimed at cine-club audience

Skoop (10 pa)
Postbus 871
2300 AW Leiden
Netherlands

INDEXES TO FILM AND TV PERIODICALS

*For many years BFI Library Services (see p7) has been indexing periodicals from around the world for information and articles about film and TV programme titles, personalities, organisations, festivals, awards and other subjects. All of this information is keyed into the department's database SIFT (Summary of Information on Film and TV).
As the number of periodicals published has grown, so the proportion which the department can index has diminished. Happily there has been a corresponding increase in the number of published indexes which complement the service provided by the department. A selection of such publications is listed below*

The Critical Index: A Bibliography of Articles on Film in English, 1946-1973
By John C Gerlach and

Lana Gerlach. New York;
London: Teachers College Press, 1974

The Film Index: A Bibliography
Vol 1 The Film as Art: compiled by Workers of the Writers' Program of the Work Projects Administration in the City of New York. New York: Museum of Modern Art Film Library; HW Wilson, 1941. Vol 2 The Film as Industry. White Plains, NY: Kraus, 1985. Vol 3 The Film in Society. White Plains, NY: Kraus, 1985

The Film Literature Index
Quarterly Author-Subject Periodical Index to the International Literature of Film 1973 to date. Albany, NY: Film & Television Documentation Center, 1975 to date. Quarterly issues with annual cumulations

Index to Critical Film Reviews in British and American Film Periodicals
Compiled by Stephen E Bowles. New York: Burt Franklin, 1974

Index to Motion Pictures Reviewed by Variety, 1907-1980
By Max Joseph Alvarez. Metuchen, NJ; London: Scarecrow Press, 1982

International Index to Film Periodicals 1972 to date International Index to Television Periodicals 1979 to date
These annotated guides are published as monthly cumulative microfiche and annual volumes. Over 100 journals from over 20 countries are indexed to include general subjects, reviews and personalities together with author and director indexes. London: International Federation of Film Archives

Motion Picture Directors: A Bibliography of Magazine and Periodical Articles, 1900-1972
Compiled by Mel Schuster. Metuchen, NJ: Scarecrow Press, 1973

Motion Picture Performers: A Bibliography of Magazine and Periodical Articles, 1900-1969
Compiled by Mel Schuster. Metuchen, NJ: Scarecrow Press, 1973. Supplement 1 (1970-74), 1976

The New Film Index: A Bibliography of Magazine Articles in English, 1930-1970
By Richard Dyer MacCann and Edward S Perry. New York: EP Dutton, 1975

Performing Arts Biography Master Index
Ed Barbara McNeil and Miranda C Herbert. 2nd ed Detroit: Gale Research Co, 1981

Retrospective Index to Film Periodicals 1930-1971
By Linda Batty. New York; London: RR Bowker, 1975

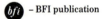

bfi – BFI publication

£ – BFI-supported

We make television worth watching.

GRANADA

TELEVISION

GRANADA TELEVISION LTD · MANCHESTER · LIVERPOOL · LANCASTER · CHESTER · LONDON

RELEASES

Listed here are films of 40 minutes and over, both British and foreign, which had a theatrical release in the UK during 1989 and the first quarter of 1990. (For early 1989 releases, see the 1990 edition of the Handbook.) Entries quote the title, country of origin, director/s, leading players, distributor, release date, duration, gauge if other than 35mm, and the Monthly Film Bulletin reference. A list of distributors' addresses and telephone numbers can be found on p 132 . Back issues of MFB are available for reference from BFI Library Services

The Abyss (12)
USA Dir James Cameron with Ed Harris, Mary Elizabeth Mastrantonio, Michael Biehn. 20th Century Fox, 13 Oct 1989. 139 mins. MFB Nov 1989 p328

The Accidental Tourist (PG) USA Dir Lawrence Kasdan with William Hurt, Kathleen Turner, Geena Davis. Warner Bros, 24 Feb 1989. 121 mins. MFB Apr 1989 p103

Alien Nation (18) ▶
USA Dir Graham Baker with James Caan, Mandy Patinkin, Terence Stamp. 20th Century Fox, 7 Apr 1989. 90 mins. MFB Apr 1989 p104

Always (PG) USA Dir Steven Spielberg with Richard Dreyfuss, Holly Hunter, Brad Johnson. UIP, 20 Mar 1990. 123 mins. 70mm/35mm. MFB Apr 1990 p94

American Stories see **Histoires d'Amérique: Food, Family and Philosophy**

The American Way
UK Dir Maurice Phillips with Dennis Hopper, Michael J Pollard, Eugene Lipinski. Paul Cowan, 15 Sept 1989. 104 mins

Amsterdamned (18)
Netherlands Dir Dick Maas with Huub Stapel, Monique Van de Ven, Serge-Henri Valcke. Vestron, 21 July 1989. 113 mins. Subtitles. MFB July 1989 p200

Another Woman (PG) USA Dir Woody Allen with Gena Rowlands, Mia Farrow, Ian Holm. Rank, 28 July 1989. 81 mins. MFB Aug 1989 p232

Apartment Zero (15) ▶
UK Dir Martin Donovan with Colin Firth, Hart Bochner, Dora Bryan. Mainline, 15 Sept 1989. 125 mins. MFB Sept 1989 p265

Ariel (15) Finland Dir Aki Kaurismäki with Turo Pajala, Susanna Haavisto, Matti Pellonpää. Electric Pictures/Contemporary, 6 Oct 1989. 72 mins. Subtitles. MFB Oct 1989 p295

Ashik Kerib USSR
Dirs Dodo Abashidze,
Sergei Paradjanov with
Yuri Mgoyan, Veronika
Metonidze, Levan
Natroshvili. Poseidon, 22
Sept 1989. 78 mins.
Subtitles. MFB Sept 1989
p265

***Asterix and the Big
Fight*** see ***Le coup de
menhir***

Asya's Happiness
see ***Istoriya Asi
Klyachinoi,
kotoraya lyubila, da
nie vshla zamuzh***

***Back to the Future
Part II*** (PG) USA Dir
Robert Zemeckis with
Michael J Fox,
Christopher Lloyd, Lea
Thompson. UIP, 24 Nov
1989. 108 mins. 70mm/
35mm. MFB Jan 1990 p7

Bad Taste (18) New
Zealand Dir Peter
Jackson with Terry
Potter, Pete O'Herne,
Craig Smith. Blue
Dolphin, 15 Sept 1989. 91
mins. MFB Sept 1989
p267

Batman (12) USA Dir
Tim Burton with Michael
Keaton, Jack Nicholson,
Kim Basinger. Warner
Bros, 11 Aug 1989. 126
mins. 70mm/35mm. MFB
Sept 1989 p268

Beaches (15) USA Dir
Garry Marshall with
Bette Midler, Barbara
Hershey, John Heard.
Warner Bros, 26 May
1989. 123 mins. MFB
June 1989 p169

The Bear (PG) France
Dir Jean-Jacques Annaud
with Tcheky Karyo, Jack
Wallace, André Lacombe.
Columbia Tri-Star, 22
Sept 1989. 98 mins.
English dialogue. MFB
Oct 1989 p295

***Beiqing Chengshi
(A City of Sadness)***
(15) Taiwan Dir Hou
Hsiao-Hsien with Tony
Leung, Xin Shufen, Li
Tianlu. Artificial Eye, 23
Mar 1990. 160 mins.
Subtitles. MFB June 1990
p152

***Bert Rigby, You're a
Fool*** (15) USA Dir Carl
Reiner with Robert

Lindsay, Anne Bancroft,
Corbin Bernsen. Warner
Bros, 10 Nov 1989. 94
mins. MFB Dec 1989 p358

Best of the Best (15)
USA Dir Bob Radler with
Eric Roberts, James Earl
Jones, Louise Fletcher.
Entertainment, 9 Feb
1990. 100 mins

Betrayed (18) USA Dir
Costa-Gavras with Debra
Winger, Tom Berenger,
John Heard. UIP, 28 Apr
▼

1989. 127 mins. MFB Apr
1989 p105

Black Rain (18) USA
Dir Ridley Scott with
Michael Douglas, Andy
Garcia, Ken Takakura.
UIP, 26 Jan 1990. 125
mins. MFB Jan 1990 p8

Blaze (15) USA Dir Ron
Shelton with Paul
Newman, Lolita
Davidovich, Jerry
Hardin. Warner Bros, 23
Feb 1990. 117 mins. MFB
Feb 1990 p37

The Blob (18) USA Dir Chuck Russell with Shawnee Smith, Donovan Leitch, Ricky Paull. Braveworld, 26 May 1989. 95 mins. MFB June 1989 p170

La Boca del Lobo (The Lion's Den) (15) Peru/Spain Dir Francisco J Lombardi with Gustavo Bueno, Toña Vega, José Tejada. New People's Cinema-Twinray, 9 June 1989. 116 mins. Subtitles. MFB June 1989 p171

Born on the Fourth of July (18) USA Dir Oliver Stone with Tom Cruise, Raymond J Barry, Kyra Sedgwick. UIP, 2 Mar 1990. 144 mins. 70mm/35mm. MFB Apr 1990 p97

Broken Noses (15) USA Dir Bruce Weber. Documentary. Mainline, 9 June 1989. 77 mins. MFB June 1989 p172

Bull Durham (15) USA Dir Ron Shelton with Kevin Costner, Susan Sarandon, Tim Robbins. Rank, 25 Aug 1989. 108 mins. MFB Sept 1989 p269

The 'burbs (PG) USA Dir Joe Dante with Tom Hanks, Bruce Dern, Carrie Fisher. UIP, 28 July 1989. 102 mins. MFB Aug 1989 p233

Burning Secret (PG) UK/USA Dir Andrew Birkin with David Eberts, Faye Dunaway, Klaus Maria Brandauer. Vestron, 13 Apr 1989. 105 mins. MFB Apr 1989 p106

Camille Claudel (PG) France Dir Bruno Nuytten with Isabelle Adjani, Gérard Depardieu, Laurent Grevill. Pathé Releasing (Cannon), 7 Apr 1989. 174 mins. Subtitles. MFB Apr 1989 p108

Camp de Thiaroye (Camp Thiaroye) (15) Sénégal/Algeria/Tunisia Dirs Ousmane Sembène, Thierno Faty Sow with Ibrahima Sane, Sigiri Bakara, Hamed Camara. Metro Pictures, 25 Aug 1989. 152 mins. Subtitles. MFB Sept 1989 p270

Candy Mountain (15) Switzerland/France/Canada Dirs Robert Frank, Rudy Wurlitzer with Kevin J O'Connor, Harris Yulin, Tom Waits. Oasis, 29 Dec 1989. 92 mins. English dialogue. MFB Jan 1990 p10

La Casa de Bernarda Alba (The House of Bernarda Alba) (15) Spain Dir Mario Camus with Irene Gutierrez Caba, Ana Belén, Florinda Chico. Gala, 2 Mar 1990. 103 mins. Subtitles. MFB Mar 1990 p63 ▼

Casualties of War (18) USA Dir Brian De Palma with Michael J Fox, Sean Penn, Don Harvey. Columbia Tri-Star, 26 Jan 1990. 113 mins. MFB Feb 1990 p38

Cat Chaser (18) USA Dir Abel Ferrara with Peter Weller, Kelly McGillis, Charles Durning. Entertainment, 8 Dec 1989. 90 mins. MFB Dec 1989 p358

Celia (15) Australia Dir Ann Turner with Rebecca Smart, Nicholas Ede, Mary-Anne Fahey. Electric Pictures/Contemporary, 16 Mar 1990. 103 mins. MFB Mar 1990 p63 ▶

Checking Out (15) UK Dir David Leland with Jeff Daniels, Melanie Mayron, Michael Tucker. Virgin Vision, 29 Sept 1989. 95 mins. MFB Oct 1989 p296

Child's Play (15) USA
Dir Tom Holland with
Catherine Hicks, Chris
Sarandon, Alex Vincent.
UIP, 2 June 1989. 87
mins. MFB June 1989
p173

Chocolat (15) France
Dir Claire Denis with
Isaach de Bankolé, Giúlia
Boschi, François Cluzet.
Electric Pictures, 21 Apr
1989. 105 mins. Subtitles.
MFB Apr 1989 p109

**A Chorus of
Disapproval** (PG) UK
Dir Michael Winner with
Anthony Hopkins,
Jeremy Irons, Richard
Briers. Hobo, 3 Nov 1989.
99 mins. MFB Nov 1989
p329

Cinema Paradiso see
**Nuovo Cinema
Paradiso**

The Citadel see **El
Kalaa**

A City of Sadness
see **Beiqing
Chengshi**

Clara's Heart (15)
USA Dir Robert Mulligan
with Whoopi Goldberg,
Michael Ontkean,
Kathleen Quinlan.
Warner Bros, 2 June
1989. 108 mins. MFB
June 1989 p174

**Cocoon: The
Return** (PG) USA Dir

Daniel Petrie with Don
Ameche, Wilford Brimley,
Courteney Cox. 20th
Century Fox, 26 May
1989. 115 mins. MFB
June 1989 p175

Cohen and Tate (18)
USA Dir Eric Red with
Roy Scheider, Adam
Baldwin, Harley Cross.
Guild, 30 Apr 1989. 86
mins. MFB June 1989
p176

Comic Book Confidential (15) Canada Dir Ron Mann. Documentary. ICA Projects, 8 Dec 1989. 90 mins. MFB Dec 1989 p360

The Commissar see **Komissar**

 **Conquest of the South Pole** (12) UK Dir Gillies MacKinnon with Steven Rimkus, Ewen Bremner, Leonard O'Malley. BFI, 16 Mar 1990. 95 mins. 16mm. MFB June 1990 p162

The Cook, the Thief, His Wife and Her Lover (18) UK/ France Dir Peter Greenaway with Richard

Bohringer, Michael Gambon, Helen Mirren. Palace Pictures, 13 Oct 1989. 124 mins. MFB Nov 1989 p323

Cookie (15) USA Dir Susan Seidelman with Peter Falk, Dianne Wiest, Emily Lloyd. Warner Bros, 6 Oct 1989. 93 mins. MFB Nov 1989 p330

Le coup de menhir (Asterix and the Big Fight) (U) France/West Germany Dir Philippe Grimond with the voices of Bill Oddie, Bernard Bresslaw, Ron Moody. Palace Pictures, 13 Oct 1989. 81 mins. English version. MFB Dec 1989 p361

Cousins (15) USA Dir Joel Schumacher with Ted Danson, Isabella Rossellini, Sean Young. UIP, 25 Aug 1989. 113 mins. MFB Aug 1989 p235

Crack in the Mirror (18) USA Dir Robby Benson with Robby Benson, Tawny Kitaen, Danny Aiello. Blue Dolphin, 26 May 1989. 93 mins. MFB July 1989 p201

Crossing Delancey

Critters 2: The Main Course (15) USA Dir Mick Garris with Terrence Mann, Don Opper, Cynthia Garris. Palace Pictures, 14 Apr 1989. 86 mins. MFB Nov 1989 p331

Crossing Delancey (PG) USA Dir Joan Micklin Silver with Amy Irving, Peter Riegert, Jeroen Krabbe. Warner Bros, 7 Apr 1989. 97 mins. MFB Apr 1989 p109

Crusoe (15) USA Dir Caleb Deschanel with Aidan Quinn, Elvis Payne, Richard Sharp. Virgin Vision, 18 Aug 1989. 94 mins. MFB Aug 1989 p230

A Cry in the Dark (Evil Angels) (15) Australia Dir Fred Schepisi with Meryl Streep, Sam Neill, Jim Holt. Pathé Releasing (Cannon), 26 May 1989. 121 mins. MFB June 1989 p176

Da (PG) USA Dir Matt Clark with Barnard Hughes, Martin Sheen, William Hickey. Premier

Comic Book Confidential

bfi – *Produced and/or distributed by the British Film Institute*

Releasing, 21 Apr 1989. 102 mins. MFB Apr 1989 p110

Dad (PG) USA Dir Gary David Goldberg with Jack Lemmon, Ted Danson, Olympia Dukakis. UIP, 23 Feb 1990. 118 mins. MFB Apr 1990 p101

Dancin' thru the Dark (15) UK Dir Mike Ockrent with Con O'Neill, Ben Murphy, Peter Beckett. Palace Pictures, 2 Mar 1990. 95 mins. MFB Mar 1990 p64

Danny the Champion of the World (U) UK Dir Gavin Millar with Jeremy Irons, Robbie Coltrane, Samuel Irons. Portobello Productions, 28 July 1989. 99 mins. MFB Aug 1989 p236

Daughter of the Nile see **Niluohe Nüer**

Dead Bang (18) USA Dir John Frankenheimer with Don Johnson, Penelope Ann Miller, William Forsythe. Warner Bros, 23 June 1989. 102 mins. MFB June 1989 p178

Dead Calm (15) ▶
Australia Dir Phillip Noyce with Nicole Kidman, Sam Neill, Billy

Zane. Warner Bros, 3 Nov 1989. 96 mins. MFB Nov 1989 p332

Dead Heat (18) USA Dir Mark Goldblatt with Treat Williams, Joe Piscopo, Lindsay Frost. Entertainment, 9 Sept 1988. 83 mins. MFB Jan 1990 p11

Dead Poets Society (PG) USA Dir Peter Weir with Robin Williams, Robert Sean Leonard, Ethan Hawke. Warner Bros, 22 Sept 1989. 129 mins. MFB Sept 1989 p272

The Dead Pool (18) USA Dir Buddy Van Horn with Clint Eastwood, Patricia Clarkson, Liam Neeson. Warner Bros, 14 Apr 1989. 91 mins. MFB Apr 1989 p111

Dealers (15) UK Dir Colin Bucksey with Paul McGann, Rebecca De Mornay, Derrick O'Connor. Rank, 25 Aug 1989. 91 mins. MFB Aug 1989 p237

The Decline of Western Civilization Part II: The Metal Years (15) USA Dir Penelope Spheeris. Documentary with Aerosmith, Alice Cooper, Kiss. Palace Pictures, 11 Aug 1989. 93 mins. MFB Aug 1989 p238

DeepStar Six (15) USA Dir Sean S Cunningham with Taurean Blacque, Nancy Everhard, Greg Evigan. Guild, 1 Dec 1989. 99 mins. MFB Aug 1989 p238

The Delinquents (12) Australia Dir Chris Thomson with Kylie Minogue, Charlie Schlatter, Angela Punch McGregor. Warner Bros, 26 Dec 1989. 105 mins. MFB Mar 1990 p65

Directed by Andrei Tarkovsky see **Regi – Andrej Tarkovskij**

Dirty Rotten Scoundrels (PG) USA Dir Frank Oz with Steve Martin, Michael Caine, Glenne Headly. Rank, 27 June 1989. 110 mins. MFB July 1989 p202

Do the Right Thing (18) USA Dir Spike Lee with Danny Aiello, Ossie Davis, Ruby Dee. UIP, 23 June 1989. 120 mins. MFB July 1989 p202

Dominick and Eugene see **Nicky and Gino**

Dorado, El (15) Spain/ France Dir Carlos Saura with Omero Antonutti, Eusebio Poncela, Lambert Wilson. Palace Pictures, 4 Aug 1989. 123 mins. Subtitles. MFB Oct 1989 p298

The Dream Team (15) USA Dir Howard Zieff with Michael Keaton, Christopher Lloyd, Peter Boyle. UIP, 15 Dec 1989. 113 mins. MFB June 1989 p179

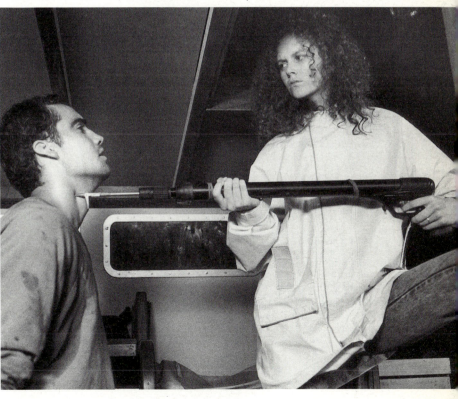

Driving Me Crazy
(15) UK Dir Nick
Broomfield. Documentary
with André Heller, Clent
Bowers, Victor Cook.
Virgin Vision, 13 Oct
1989. 81 mins. 16mm.
MFB Nov 1989 p333

Driving Miss Daisy
(U) USA Dir Bruce
Beresford with Morgan
Freeman, Jessica Tandy,
Dan Aykroyd. Warner
Bros, 23 Feb 1990. 99
mins. MFB Mar 1990 p66

Drôle d'endroit ▶
**pour une rencontre
(A Strange Place to
Meet)** (15) France Dir
François Dupeyron with
Catherine Deneuve,
Gérard Depardieu, André
Wilms. Artificial Eye, 8
Sept 1989. 98 mins.
Subtitles. MFB Oct 1989
p297

Drugstore Cowboy
(18) USA Dir Gus Van
Sant with Matt Dillon,
Kelly Lynch, James Le
Gros. Virgin Vision, 8 Dec
1989. 101 mins. MFB Dec
1989 p362

**A Dry White
Season** (15) USA Dir
Euzhan Palcy with
Donald Sutherland, Janet
Suzman, Zakes Mokae.
UIP, 19 Jan 1990. 107
mins. MFB Jan 1990 p12

Dust in the Wind see
Lianlian Feng Chen

Earth Girls are Easy
(PG) USA Dir Julien
Temple with Geena
Davis, Jeff Goldblum, Jim
Carrey. Braveworld/20th
Century Fox, 22 Dec
1989. 100 mins. MFB Dec
1989 p363

Eat a Bowl of Tea
(12) USA Dir Wayne
Wang with Victor Wong,
Russell Wong, Cora Miao.
Artificial Eye, 8 Dec 1989.
103 mins. Some subtitles.
MFB Dec 1989 p364

Edge of Sanity USA
Dir Gerard Kikoine with
Anthony Hopkins, Glynis
Barber, Sarah Maur-
Thorp. Palace Pictures, 21
Apr 1989

Eight Men Out (PG)
USA Dir John Sayles
with John Cusack, John
Mahoney, Charlie Sheen.
Rank, 21 July 1989. 120
mins. MFB July 1989
p204

**Encounter at
Raven's Gate** (15)
Australia Dir Rolf de
Heer with Steven Vidler,
Celin Griffin, Ritchie
Singer. Castle Premier
Releasing, 16 Mar 1990.
89 mins. MFB Apr 1990
p103

**An Enemy of the
People** see
Ganashatru

Erik the Viking (12)
UK Dir Terry Jones with
Tim Robbins, Mickey
Rooney, Eartha Kitt. UIP,
29 Sept 1989. 107 mins.
MFB Oct 1989 p299

**Ernest Saves
Christmas** (U) USA
Dir John Cherry with Jim
Varney, Douglas Seale,
Oliver Clark. Warner
Bros, 17 Nov 1989. 91
mins. MFB Dec 1989 p365

**Everybody's All-
American** see **When
I Fall in Love**

Evil Angels see **A Cry
in the Dark**

Erik the Viking

**The Fabulous Baker
Boys** (15) USA Dir
Steve Kloves with Jeff
Bridges, Michelle Pfeiffer,
Beau Bridges. Rank, 9
Mar 1990. 113 mins. MFB
Mar 1990 p67

Fair Game see
Mamba

Family Business (15)
USA Dir Sidney Lumet
with Sean Connery,
Dustin Hoffman,
Matthew Broderick.
Palace Pictures, 9 Feb
1990. 113 mins. MFB Mar
1990 p59

Far North (12) USA
Dir Sam Shepard with
Jessica Lange, Charles
Durning, Tess Harper.
Rank, 2 Feb 1990. 89
mins. MFB Mar 1990 p69

**Farewell to the
King** (PG) USA Dir John
Milius with Nick Nolte,
Nigel Havers, Frank
McRae. Vestron, 7 July
1989. 117 mins. MFB July
1989 p197

**Fat Man and Little
Boy** see **Shadow
Makers**

bfi **Fellow
Traveller** (15)
UK/USA Dir Philip
Saville with Ron Silver,
Imogen Stubbs, Hart
Bochner. BFI, 5 Jan 1990.
97 mins. MFB Jan 1990
p13

Field of Dreams (PG)
USA Dir Phil Alden
Robinson with Kevin
Costner, Amy Madigan,
James Earl Jones. Guild,
24 Nov 1989. 106 mins.
MFB Dec 1989 p365

Fletch Lives (PG) USA
Dir Michael Ritchie with
Chevy Chase, Hal
Holbrook, Julianne
Phillips. UIP, 19 May
1989. 95 mins. MFB May
1989 p135

The Fly II (18) USA Dir
Chris Walas with Eric
Stoltz, Daphne Zuniga,
Lee Richardson. 20th
Century Fox, 8 Sept 1989.
104 mins. MFB Oct 1989
p300

bfi – *Produced and/or
distributed by the
British Film Institute*

Fright Night Part 2
(18) USA Dir Tommy Lee Wallace with Roddy McDowall, William Ragsdale, Traci Lin. Columbia Tri-Star, 7 Apr 1989. 104 mins. MFB Apr 1989 p113

Full Moon in Blue Water (15) USA Dir Peter Masterson with Gene Hackman, Teri Garr, Burgess Meredith. Entertainment, 7 July 1989. 95 mins. MFB July 1989 p205

Fun Down There (18) USA Dir Roger Stigliano with Michael Waite, Nickolas Nagurney, Martin Goldin. Metro Pictures, 2

Peter Cook. Medusa, 20 Oct 1989. 102 mins. MFB Oct 1989 p301

Ghostbusters II (PG) USA Dir Ivan Reitman with Bill Murray, Dan Aykroyd, Sigourney Weaver. Columbia Tri-Star, 1 Dec 1989. 108 mins. MFB Dec 1989 p366

Ghosts... of the Civil Dead (18) Australia Dir John Hillcoat with Dave Field, Mike Bishop, Chris De Rose. Electric Pictures, 12 May 1989. 93 mins. MFB June 1989 p180

Gleaming the Cube (PG) USA Dir Graeme Clifford with Christian

Field of Dreams

Hakayitz shel Aviya (The Summer of Aviya) (PG) Israel Dir Eli Cohen with Gila Almagor, Kaipo Cohen, Eli Cohen. Mutual, 6 Sept 1989. 96 mins. Subtitles. MFB Apr 1990 p107

Halloween 4: The Return of Michael Myers (18) USA Dir Dwight H Little with Donald Pleasence, Ellie Cornell, Danielle Harris. 20th Century Fox, 3 Nov 1989. 88 mins. MFB Dec 1989 p369

Hamlet Liikemaailmassa (Hamlet Goes Business) Finland Dir Aki Kaurismäki with Pirkka-Pekka Petelius, Esko Salminen, Kati Outinen. Electric Pictures, 23 Feb 1990. 86 mins. Subtitles. MFB Feb 1990 p39

Hanussen (15) Hungary/West Germany Dir István Szabó with Klaus Maria Brandauer, Erland Josephson, Ildikó Bánsági. Columbia Tri-Star, 21 Apr 1989. 117 mins. Subtitles. MFB June 1989 p181

The Fabulous Baker Boys

June 1989. 88 mins. 16mm. MFB Apr 1990 p105

Ganashatru (An Enemy of the People) (U) India Dir Satyajit Ray with Soumitra Chatterjee, Ruma Guhathakurta, Dhritiman Chatterjee. Electric Pictures/Contemporary, 29 Dec 1989. 100 mins. Subtitles. MFB Jan 1990 p14

Getting It Right (15) USA Dir Randal Kleiser with Jesse Birdsall, Helena Bonham Carter,

Slater, Steven Bauer, Richard Herd. Rank, 20 Oct 1989. 104 mins. MFB Nov 1989 p333

Glory (15) USA Dir Edward Zwick with Matthew Broderick, Denzel Washington, Cary Elwes. Columbia Tri-Star, 2 Mar 1990. 133 mins. MFB Apr 1990 p105

Great Balls of Fire! (15) USA Dir Jim McBride with Dennis Quaid, Winona Ryder, John Doe. Rank, 10 Nov 1989. 107 mins. MFB Dec 1989 p368

Ganashatru (An Enemy of the People)

Heathers

Hard Road UK Dir
Colin Finbow with
Francesca Camillo, Max
Rennie, John Louis
Mansi. ICA Projects, 2
Sept 1989. 90 mins. MFB
Oct 1989 p302

Hard Times see
**Tempos difíceis,
este tempo**

Haunted Summer
(18) USA Dir Ivan Passer
with Philip Anglim,
Laura Dern, Alice Krige.
Pathé Releasing
(Cannon), 7 Apr 1989. 106
mins. MFB May 1989
p136

Heathers (18) USA Dir
Michael Lehmann with
Winona Ryder, Christian
Slater, Shannen Doherty.
Premier Releasing, 17
Nov 1989. 103 mins. MFB
Jan 1990 p15

**Hellbound:
Hellraiser II** (18) UK
Dir Tony Randel with
Clare Higgins, Ashley
Laurence, Kenneth
Cranham. Premier
Releasing, 16 June 1989.
93 mins. MFB July 1989
p206

Henry V (PG) UK Dir ▶
Kenneth Branagh with
Kenneth Branagh, Derek
Jacobi, Simon Shepherd.
Curzon, 6 Oct 1989. 137
mins. MFB Oct 1989 p302

Her Alibi (PG) USA Dir
Bruce Beresford with Tom
Selleck, Paulina
Porizkova, William
Daniels. Warner Bros, 12
May 1989. 94 mins. MFB
May 1989 p137

Hider in the House
(18) USA Dir Matthew
Patrick with Gary Busey,
Mimi Rogers, Michael
McKean. Vestron, 1 Dec
1989. 108 mins. MFB Dec
1989 p370

**Histoires
d'Amérique: Food,
Family and
Philosophy
(American Stories)**
(PG) France/Belgium Dir
Chantal Akerman.
Documentary with Mark
Amitin, Eszter Balint,
Stefan Balint. Metro
Pictures, 12 Jan 1990. 95

mins. English dialogue.
MFB Feb 1990 p40

**Hol Volt, Hol Nem
Volt (A Hungarian
Fairy Tale)** (PG)
Hungary Dir Gyula
Gazdag with David
Vermes, Hušák
František, Pál Hetényi.
Pathé Releasing
(Cannon), 30 June 1989.
97 mins. Subtitles. MFB
Aug 1989 p239

Homeboy (15) USA
Dir Michael Seresin with
Mickey Rourke,
Christopher Walken,
Debra Feuer. Braveworld/
20th Century Fox, 14 July
1989. 116 mins. MFB July
1989 p206

**Honey, I Shrunk the
Kids** (U) USA Dir Joe
Johnston with Rick
Moranis, Matt Frewer,
Marcia Strassman.
Warner Bros, 9 Feb 1990.
93 mins. MFB Feb 1990
p41

Hotel du Paradis (15)
UK/France Dir Jana
Bokóva with Fernando
Rey, Fabrice Luchini,
Berangère Bonvoisin.
Umbrella Films, 19 May

1989. 113 mins. Subtitles.
MFB June 1989 p182

**The House of
Bernarda Alba** see
**La Casa de
Bernarda Alba**

**How to Get Ahead
in Advertising** (15)
UK Dir Bruce Robinson
with Richard E Grant,
Rachel Ward, Richard
Wilson. Virgin Vision, 28
July 1989. 94 mins. MFB
Aug 1989 p227

**A Hungarian Fairy
Tale** see **Hol Volt,
Hol Nem Volt**

**I Miei Primi 40 Anni
(My First 40 Years)**
(18) Italy Dir Carlo
Vanzina with Carol Alt,
Elliott Gould, Jean
Rochefort. Columbia Tri-
Star, 8 Sept 1989. 107
mins. Dubbed. MFB Nov
1989 p339

**I'm Gonna Git You
Sucka** (15) USA Dir
Keenen Ivory Wayans
with Keenen Ivory
Wayans, Bernie Casey,
Antonio Fargas. UIP, 10
Nov 1989. 89 mins. MFB
Nov 1989 p334

I'm Gonna Git You Sucka

In Country (15) USA Dir Norman Jewison with Bruce Willis, Emily Lloyd, Joan Allen. Warner Bros, 12 Jan 1990. 115 mins. MFB Jan 1990 p17

In Fading Light (15) UK Dirs Murray Martin, Amber Films with Joe Caffrey, Maureen Harold, Dave Hill. Side Distribution, 12 Feb 1990. 107 mins. 16mm. MFB Mar 1990 p70

Indiana Jones and the Last Crusade (PG) USA Dir Steven Spielberg with Harrison Ford, Sean Connery, Denholm Elliott. UIP, 28 June 1989. 127 mins. 70mm/35mm. MFB July 1989 p198

Iron Eagle II (PG) Canada Dir Sidney J Furie with Louis Gossett Jnr, Mark Humphrey, Stuart Margolin. Guild, 24 Mar 1989. 100 mins. MFB Apr 1989 p114

The Iron Triangle (18) USA Dir Eric Weston with Beau Bridges, Haing S Ngor, Liem Whatley. Medusa, 29 Sept 1989. 91 mins. MFB Oct 1989 p303

Istoriya Asi Klyachinoi, kotoraya lyubila, da nie vshla zamuzh (Asya's Happiness) (PG) USSR Dir Andrei Mikhalkov-Konchalovsky with Iya Savvina, Lyubov Sokolova, Alexander Surin. Artificial Eye, 10 Nov 1989. 98 mins. Subtitles. MFB Oct 1989 p291

Jacknife (15) USA Dir David Jones with Robert De Niro, Ed Harris, Kathy Baker. Vestron, 8 Sept 1989. 103 mins. MFB Sept 1989 p273

Jakarta (18) Indonesia/ USA Dir Charles Kaufman with Christopher Noth, Sue Francis Pai, Franz Tumbuan. Medusa, 27 Oct 1989. 94 mins. MFB Nov 1989 p336

The January Man (15) USA Dir Pat O'Connor with Kevin Kline, Susan Sarandon, Mary Elizabeth Mastrantonio. UIP, 5 May 1989. 97 mins. MFB May 1989 p138

Jésus de Montréal (Jesus of Montreal) (18) Canada/France Dir Denys Arcand with Lothaire Bluteau, Catherine Wilkening, Johanne-Marie Tremblay. Artificial Eye, 19 Jan 1990. 119 mins. Subtitles. MFB Jan 1990 p3

Joyriders (15) UK Dir Aisling Walsh with Patricia Kerrigan, Andrew Connolly, Billie Whitelaw. Pathé Releasing (Cannon), 28 Apr 1989. 96 mins. MFB May 1989 p139

Judgement in Berlin (PG) USA Dir Leo Penn with Martin Sheen, Sam Wanamaker, Max Gail. Hobo, 23 Mar 1990. 96 mins. MFB Apr 1990 p109

K-9 (12) USA Dir Rod Daniel with James Belushi, Mel Harris, Kevin Tighe. UIP, 6 Oct 1989. 101 mins. MFB Oct 1989 p304

El Kalaa (The Citadel) (PG) Algeria Dir Mohamed Chouikh with Khaled Barkat, Djillali Ain Tedelles, Fettouma Ousliha. Metro Pictures, 30 Mar 1990. 98 mins. Subtitles. MFB Apr 1990 p109

Kamikaze (15) France Dir Didier Grousset with Richard Bohringer, Michel Galabru, Dominique Lavanant. Blue Dolphin, 14 Apr 1989. 89 mins. Subtitles. MFB Apr 1989 p114

The Karate Kid part III (PG) USA Dir John G Avildsen with Ralph Macchio, Noriyuki "Pat" Morita, Robyn Lively. Columbia Tri-Star, 28 July 1989. 112 mins. MFB Sept 1989 p274

Kickboxer (18) USA Dirs Mark DiSalle, David Worth with Jean Claude Van Damme, Dennis Alexio, Dennis Chan. Entertainment, 18 Aug 1989. 102 mins. MFB Sept 1989 p274

The Kill-Off (18) USA Dir Maggie Greenwald with Loretta Gross, Andrew Lee Barrett, Jackson Sims. Palace Pictures, 9 Feb 1990. 97 mins. MFB Feb 1990 p34

Killing Dad (PG) UK Dir Michael Austin with Denholm Elliott, Julie Walters, Richard E Grant. Palace Pictures, 1 Sept 1989. 93 mins. MFB Sept 1989 p275

Indiana Jones and the Last Crusade

The Kiss (18) USA Dir Pen Densham with Pamela Collyer, Peter Dvorsky, Joanna Pacula. Columbia Tri-Star, 21 July 1989. 98 mins. MFB Aug 1989 p240

Komissar (The Commissar) (PG) USSR Dir Alexander Askoldov with Nonna Mordyukova, Rolan Bykov, Raisa Niedashkovskaya. Artificial Eye, 12 May 1989. 108 mins. Subtitles. MFB May 1989 p140

Krótki Film o Miłości (A Short Film about Love) ▲
(18) Poland Dir Krzysztof Kieślowski with Grazyna Szapolowska, Olaf Lubaszenko, Stefania Iwińska. Gala, 30 Mar 1990. 87 mins. Subtitles. MFB May 1990 p131

Krótki Film o Zabijaniu (A Short Film about Killing)
(18) Poland Dir Krzysztof Kieślowski with Miroslaw Baka, Krzysztof Globisz, Jan Tesarz. Gala, 17 Nov 1989. 84 mins. Subtitles. MFB Dec 1989 p371

Ladder of Swords
(15) UK Dir Norman Hull with Martin Shaw, Eleanor David, Juliet Stevenson. Hobo, 12 Jan 1990. 98 mins. MFB Jan 1990 p18

Lady in White (15)
USA Dir Frank LaLoggia with Lukas Haas, Len Cariou, Alex Rocco. Virgin Vision, 16 June 1989. 113 mins. MFB June 1989 p183

The Lair of the White Worm (18) UK Dir Ken Russell with Amanda Donohoe, Hugh Grant, Catherine Oxenberg. Vestron, 10 Mar 1989. 93 mins. MFB Apr 1989 p115

The Land before Time (U) USA Dir Don Bluth with the voices of Gabriel Damon, Helen Shaver, Bill Erwin. UIP, 4 Aug 1989. 69 mins. MFB Sept 1989 p276

Landscape in the Mist see **Topio stin omichli**

Last Exit to Brooklyn see **Letzte Ausfahrt Brooklyn**

Leave to Remain
(15) UK Dir Les Blair with Jonathan Phillips, Meda Kidem, Kazuko Hohki. Spellbound, 2 May 1989. 107 mins

La leggenda del santo bevitore (The Legend of the Holy Drinker) (PG) Italy Dir Ermanno Olmi with Rutger Hauer, Anthony Quayle, Sandrine Dumas. Artificial Eye, 1 Sept 1989. 128 mins. English version. MFB Sept 1989 p277

Leningrad Cowboys Go America (12) Finland/Sweden Dir Aki Kaurismäki with Matti Pellonpää, Nicky Tesco, Kari Väänänen. Artificial Eye, 16 Feb 1990. 79 mins. English dialogue. MFB Mar 1990 p71

Lenny Live and Unleashed (15) UK Dir Andy Harries. Documentary with Lenny Henry, Robbie Coltrane, Jeff Beck. Palace Pictures, 28 July 1989. 97 mins. MFB Aug 1989 p241

Lethal Weapon 2 (15) USA Dir Richard Donner with Mel Gibson, Danny Glover, Joe Pesci. Warner Bros, 15 Sept 1989. 113 mins. MFB Oct 1989 p305

Let's Get Lost (15) USA Dir Bruce Weber. Documentary with Chet Baker. Mainline, 2 Feb 1990. 120 mins. MFB Feb 1990 p42

The Land before Time

Letzte Ausfahrt Brooklyn (Last Exit to Brooklyn) (18) ▶ West Germany Dir Ulrich Edel with Stephen Lang, Jennifer Jason Leigh, Burt Young. Guild, 5 Jan 1990. 98 mins. English dialogue. MFB Jan 1990 p18

Lianlian Feng Chen (Dust in the Wind) (15) Taiwan Dir Hou Hsiao-Hsien with Wang Jingwen, Xin Shufen, Li Tianlu. ICA Projects, 30 Mar 1990. 110 mins. Subtitles. MFB Apr 1990 p111

Licence to Kill (15) USA Dir John Glen with Timothy Dalton, Carey Lowell, Robert Davi. UIP, 14 June 1989. 132 mins. MFB July 1989 p207

Life and Nothing But see **La vie et rien d'autre**

Life is a Long Quiet River see **La vie est un long fleuve tranquille**

The Lion's Den see **La Boca del Lobo**

Little Vera see **Malenkaya Vera**

Lock Up (18) USA Dir John Flynn with Sylvester Stallone, Donald Sutherland, John Amos. Guild, 2 Feb 1990. 109 mins. MFB Feb 1990 p44

Melancholia

Looking for Langston (15)
UK Dir Isaac Julien with Ben Ellison, Matthew Baidoo, Akim Mogaji. BFI, 2 June 1989. 46 mins. 16mm. MFB Feb 1990 p45

Mac and Me (U) USA Dir Stewart Raffill with Christine Ebersole, Jonathan Ward, Tina Caspary. Guild, 21 July 1989. 99 mins. MFB Aug 1989 p242

Major League (15) USA Dir David S Ward with Tom Berenger, Charlie Sheen, Corbin Bernsen. Braveworld/20th Century Fox, 22 Sept 1989. 106 mins. MFB Nov 1989 p336

Malenkaya Vera (Little Vera) (15) USSR Dir Vasili Pichul with Natalya Negoda, Liudmila Zaitseva, Andrei Sokolov. Mainline, 9 June 1989. 134 mins. Subtitles. MFB July 1989 p195

Mamba (Fair Game) (15) Italy Dir Mario Orfini with Trudie Styler, Gregg Henry, Bill Moseley. Medusa, 23 June 1989. 81 mins. English dialogue. MFB July 1989 p208

Married to the Mob (15) USA Dir Jonathan Demme with Michelle Pfeiffer, Matthew Modine, Dean Stockwell. Rank, 23 June 1989. 104 mins. MFB July 1989 p209

Matewan (15) USA Dir John Sayles with Chris Cooper, Mary McDonnell, Will Oldham. Enterprise Pictures, 14 Apr 1989. 133 mins. Subtitles, some Italian dialogue. MFB May 1989 p141

Melancholia (15) UK Dir Andi Engel with Jeroen Krabbé, Susannah York, Ulrich Wildgruber. BFI, 20 Oct 1989. 87 mins. MFB Oct 1989 p306

The Mighty Quinn (15) USA Dir Carl Schenkel with Denzel Washington, James Fox, Mimi Rogers. UIP, 16 June 1989. 98 mins. MFB July 1989 p210

Miles from Home (15) USA Dir Gary Sinise with Richard Gere, Kevin Anderson, Brian Dennehy. Braveworld/20th Century Fox, 30 June 1989. 108 mins. MFB Aug 1989 p243

Millennium (PG) USA Dir Michael Anderson with Kris Kristofferson, Cheryl Ladd, Daniel J Travanti. Rank, 20 Oct 1989. 105 mins. MFB Nov 1989 p338

Mississippi Burning (18) USA Dir Alan Parker with Gene Hackman, Willem Dafoe, Frances McDormand. Rank, 5 May 1989. 127 mins. MFB May 1989 p142

Monkey Shines (18) ▶ USA Dir George A Romero with Jason Beghe, John Pankow, Kate McNeil. Rank, 23 Feb 1990. 113 mins. MFB Feb 1990 p45

Moon over Parador (15) USA Dir Paul Mazursky with Richard Dreyfuss, Raul Julia, Sonia Braga. UIP, 2 June 1989. 104 mins. MFB June 1989 p184

Mujeres al borde de un ataque de nervios (Women on the Verge of a Nervous Breakdown) (15) Spain Dir Pedro Almodóvar with Carmen Maura, Antonio Banderas, Julieta Serrano. Rank, 16 June 1989. 89 mins. Subtitles. MFB June 1989 p185

My First 40 Years see *I Miei Primi 40 Anni*

My Left Foot (15) Eire Dir Jim Sheridan with Daniel Day Lewis, Ray McAnally, Brenda Fricker. Palace Pictures, 18 Aug 1989. 103 mins. MFB Sept 1989 p278

My Stepmother is an Alien (15) USA Dir Richard Benjamin with Dan Aykroyd, Kim Basinger, Jon Lovitz. Columbia Tri-Star, 28 Apr 1989. 108 mins. MFB May 1989 p143

Mystery Train (15) USA Dir Jim Jarmusch with Masatoshi Nagase, Youki Kudoh, Screamin' Jay Hawkins. Palace Pictures, 8 Dec 1989. 110 mins. MFB Dec 1989 p372

Mystic Pizza (15) USA Dir Donald Petrie with Annabeth Gish, Julia Roberts, Lili Taylor. Virgin Vision, 5 Jan 1990. 104 mins. MFB Jan 1990 p19

The Navigator: A Medieval Odyssey (PG) Australia Dir Vincent Ward with Bruce Lyons, Chris Haywood, Hamish McFarlane. Recorded Releasing, 12 May 1989. 91 mins. MFB May 1989 p144

New York Stories (15) USA Dirs Martin Scorsese (Life Lessons), Francis Coppola (Life Without Zoe), Woody Allen (Oedipus Wrecks) with Nick Nolte, Rosanna Arquette, Heather McComb, Talia Shire, Woody Allen, Mia Farrow. Warner Bros, 10 Nov 1989. 124 mins. MFB Nov 1989 p339

Nicky and Gino (Dominick and Eugene) (15) USA Dir Robert M Young with Tom Hulce, Ray Liotta, Jamie Lee Curtis. Rank, 31 Mar 1989. 109 mins. MFB Apr 1989 p116

bfi – Produced and/or distributed by the British Film Institute

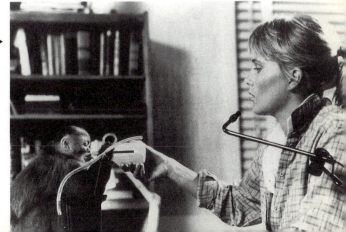

A Nightmare on Elm Street 4: The Dream Master (18) USA Dir Renny Harlin with Robert Englund, Rodney Eastman, Danny Hassel. Palace Pictures, 5 May 1989. 92 mins. MFB May 1989 p145

Niluohe Nüer (Daughter of the Nile) (PG) Taiwan Dir Hou Hsiao-Hsien with Yang Lin, Gao Jie, Yang Fan. Artificial Eye, 21 Apr 1989. 84 mins. Subtitles. MFB Apr 1989 p117

1969 (15) USA Dir Ernest Thompson with Robert Downey Jnr, Kiefer Sutherland, Bruce Dern. Entertainment, 26 May 1989. 95 mins. MFB Aug 1989 p244

Noi Vivi (We the Living) (PG) Italy 1942 Dir Goffredo Alessandrini with Alida Valli, Rossano Brazzi, Fosco Giachetti. Everyman/Mutual, 21 July 1989. 174 mins. Subtitles

La nuit de Varennes (That Night in Varennes) (15) France/Italy Dir Ettore Scola with Jean-Louis Barrault, Marcello Mastroianni, Hanna Schygulla. Contemporary/Electric Pictures, 14 Apr 1989. 128 mins. Subtitles. MFB May 1989 p147

Parents

Nuovo Cinema Paradiso (Cinema Paradiso) (PG) Italy/France Dir Giuseppe Tornatore with Philippe Noiret, Jacques Perrin, Salvatore Cascio. Palace Pictures, 23 Feb 1990. 123 mins. (Original running time: 155 mins.) Subtitles. MFB Mar 1990 p72

Old Gringo (15) USA Dir Luis Puenzo with Jane Fonda, Gregory Peck, Jimmy Smits. Columbia Tri-Star, 20 Oct 1989. 120 mins. MFB Oct 1989 p307

Oliver & Company (U) USA Dir George Scribner with the voices of Joey Lawrence, Billy Joel, Cheech Marin. Warner Bros, 15 Dec 1989. 74 mins. MFB Jan 1990 p20

Out of the Dark (18) USA Dir Michael Schroeder with Cameron Dye, Karen Black, Lynn Danielson. Medusa, 19 May 1989. 87 mins. MFB May 1989 p148

Paperhouse (15) UK Dir Bernard Rose with Charlotte Burke, Jane Bertish, Samantha Cahill. Vestron, 2 June 1989. 92 mins. MFB June 1989 p186

Parenthood (15) USA Dir Ron Howard with Steve Martin, Mary Steenburgen, Dianne Wiest. UIP, 12 Jan 1990. 124 mins. MFB Jan 1990 p21

Parents (18) USA Dir Bob Balaban with Randy Quaid, Mary Beth Hurt, Sandy Dennis. Vestron, 7 Apr 1989. 82 mins. MFB June 1989 p187

Paris by Night (15) UK Dir David Hare with Charlotte Rampling, Michael Gambon, Robert Hardy. Virgin Vision, 2 June 1989. 103 mins. MFB July 1989 p211

Patti Rocks (18) USA Dir David Burton Morris with Chris Mulkey, John Jenkins, Karen Landry. Premier Releasing, 15 Sept 1989. 87 mins. MFB Oct 1989 p308

Patty Hearst (18) USA/UK Dir Paul Schrader with Natasha Richardson, William Forsythe, Ving Rhames. Entertainment, 7 Apr 1989. 104 mins. MFB Apr 1989 p119

Pelle Erobreren (Pelle the Conqueror) (15) ▶ Denmark/Sweden Dir Bille August with Max von Sydow, Pelle Hvenegaard, Erik Paaske. Curzon, 23 June 1989. 150 mins. Subtitles. MFB Aug 1989 p245

Pet Sematary (18) USA Dir Mary Lambert with Dale Midkiff, Fred Gwynne, Denise Crosby. UIP, 17 Nov 1989. 103 mins. MFB Nov 1989 p341

La Petite Voleuse (15) France Dir Claude Miller with Charlotte Gainsbourg, Didier Bezace, Simon de la Brosse. Pathé Releasing, 23 June 1989. 109 mins. Subtitles. MFB Aug 1989 p246

Parenthood

Physical Evidence
(18) USA Dir Michael
Crichton with Burt
Reynolds, Theresa
Russell, Ned Beatty.
Rank, 18 Aug 1989. 99
mins. MFB Sept 1989
p279

Piravi (The Birth)
India Dir Shaji with
Premji, S V Raman,
Chandran Nair.
Contemporary, 26 Jan
1990. 110 mins. Subtitles.
MFB Feb 1990 p47

**Plaff! or Too Afraid
of Life** Cuba Dir Juan
Carlos Tabio with Daisy
Granados, Thais Valdes,
Luis Alberto Garcia.
Metro Pictures, 9 Mar
1990. 95 mins. Subtitles

 **Play Me
Something** (15)
UK Dir Timothy Neat
with Lucia Lanzarini,
John Berger, Tilda
Swinton. BFI, 6 Oct 1989.
72 mins. MFB Nov 1989
p342

**Police Academy 6:
City under Siege**
(PG) USA Dir Peter
Bonerz with Bubba
Smith, David Graf,
Michael Winslow. Warner
Bros, 21 July 1989. 84
mins. MFB Sept 1989
p280

**Les portes
tournantes (The
Revolving Doors)**
(U) Canada/France Dir
Francis Mankiewicz with
Monique Spaziani,
Gabriel Arcand, Miou-

Miou. Gala, 16 Feb 1990.
102 mins. Subtitles. MFB
Mar 1990 p73

A Private Life (15) UK
Dir Francis Gerard with
Bill Flynn, Jana Cilliers,
Kevin Smith. Hobo, 24
Nov 1989. 93 mins. MFB
Jan 1990 p5

Punchline (15) USA
Dir David Seltzer with
Sally Field, Tom Hanks,
John Goodman. Columbia
Tri-Star, 7 Apr 1989. 122
mins. MFB Apr 1989 p120

**¿Que he hecho YO
para merecer esto!!
(What Have I Done
to Deserve This?)**
(18) Spain Dir Pedro
Almodóvar with Carmen
Maura, Luis Hostalot,
Angel De Andres-López.
Metro Pictures, 4 Aug
1989. 101 mins. Subtitles.
MFB Sept 1989 p281

Queen of Hearts
(PG) UK Dir Jon Amiel
with Vittorio Duse,
Joseph Long, Anita
Zagaria. Enterprise
Pictures, 29 Sept 1989.
112 mins. MFB Oct 1989
p309

The Rachel Papers
(18) UK Dir Damian
Harris with Dexter
Fletcher, Ione Skye,
Jonathan Pryce. Virgin
Vision, 27 Oct 1989. 95
mins. MFB Nov 1989
p343

**The Raggedy
Rawney** (15) UK Dir
Bob Hoskins with Bob
Hoskins, Dexter Fletcher,
Zoë Nathenson. Virgin
Vision, 30 June 1989. 103
mins. MFB July 1989
p212

The Rainbow (15) UK
Dir Ken Russell with
Sammi Davis, Paul
McGann, Amanda
Donohoe. Vestron, 3 Nov
1989. 111 mins. MFB Jan
1990 p22

**Reefer and the
Model** (15) Eire Dir Joe
Comerford with Ian
McElhinney, Eve
Watkinson, Carol
Scanlan. Metro Pictures,
24 Nov 1989. 93 mins.
MFB Dec 1989 p373

**Regi – Andrej
Tarkovskij
(Directed by
Andrei
Tarkovsky)**
(15)
Sweden Dir
Michal
Leszczylowski.

Documentary. Artificial
Eye, 14 July 1989. 101
mins. English narration,
subtitles. MFB Apr 1989
p121

Renegades (15) USA
Dir Jack Sholder with
Kiefer Sutherland, Lou
Diamond Phillips, Clark
Johnson. Virgin Vision, 9
Mar 1990. 105 mins. MFB
Mar 1990 p73

Resurrected (15) UK
Dir Paul Greengrass with
David Thewlis, Tom Bell,
Rita Tushingham. Hobo,
29 Sept 1989. 92 mins.
MFB Oct 1989 p310

**Return from the
River Kwai** (15) UK
Dir Andrew V McLaglen
with Edward Fox,
Denholm Elliott,
Christopher Penn. Rank,
7 Apr 1989. 101 mins.
MFB Apr 1989 p122

bfi – *Produced and/or
distributed by the
British Film Institute*

Plaff! or Too Afraid of Life

The Return of Swamp Thing (12) ▶
USA Dir Jim Wynorski with Louis Jourdan, Heather Locklear, Sarah Douglas. Medusa, 22 Dec 1989. 85 mins. MFB Feb 1990 p48

The Return of the Musketeers (PG) UK/France/Spain Dir Richard Lester with Michael York, Oliver Reed, Frank Finlay. Entertainment, 4 Aug 1989. 101 mins. MFB Aug 1989 p248

The Revolving Doors see **Les portes tournantes**

Road House (18) USA Dir Rowdy Herrington with Patrick Swayze, Kelly Lynch, Sam Elliott. UIP, 10 Nov 1989. 114 mins. MFB Nov 1989 p344

Romero (15) USA Dir John Duigan with Raul Julia, Richard Jordan, Ana Alicia. Warner Bros, 23 Feb 1990. 105 mins. MFB Feb 1990 p49

Rooftops (15) USA Dir Robert Wise with Jason Gedrick, Troy Beyer, Eddie Vélez. 20th Century Fox, 9 Feb 1990. 95 mins. MFB Feb 1990 p50

Rosalie Goes Shopping (15) West Germany Dir Percy Adlon with Marianne Sägebrecht, Brad Davis, Judge Reinhold. Mainline, 12 Jan 1990. 94 mins. English dialogue. MFB Mar 1990 p74

The Return of the Musketeers

Roselyne et les lions (Roselyne and the Lions) (12) France Dir Jean-Jacques Beineix with Isabelle Pasco, Gérard Sandoz, Philippe Clevenot. Palace Pictures, 15 Dec 1989. 137 mins. Subtitles. MFB Dec 1989 p373

Rouge see **Yanzhi Kou**

Rude Awakening (15) USA Dirs Aaron Russo, David Greenwalt with Cheech Marin, Eric Roberts, Robert Carradine. Rank, 23 Mar 1990. 100 mins. MFB Mar 1990 p75

Running on Empty (15) USA Dir Sidney Lumet with Christine Lahti, River Phoenix, Judd Hirsch. Warner Bros, 28 July 1989. 116 mins. MFB Aug 1989 p249

Russicum (15) Italy Dir Pasquale Squitieri with F Murray Abraham, Treat Williams, Danny Aiello. Columbia Tri-Star, 8 Dec 1989. 112 mins. English version. MFB Feb 1990 p51

Scenes from the Class Struggle in Beverly Hills (18) USA Dir Paul Bartel with Jacqueline Bisset, Ray Sharkey, Mary Woronov. Rank, 19 Jan 1990. 103 mins. MFB Jan 1990 p23

Sea of Love (18) USA Dir Harold Becker with Al Pacino, Ellen Barkin, John Goodman. UIP, 16 Mar 1990. 113 mins. MFB Mar 1990 p76

See No Evil, Hear No Evil (15) USA Dir Arthur Hiller with Richard Pryor, Gene Wilder, Joan Severance. Columbia Tri-Star, 1 Sept 1989. 102 mins. MFB Sept 1989 p282

Sen-Kyuhyaku-Kyuju-Kyu-Nen no Natsu Yasumi (Summer Vacation 1999) (15) Japan Dir Shusuke Kaneko with Eri Miyajima, Tomoko Otakara, Miyuki Nakano. ICA Projects, 16 Feb 1990. 90 mins. Subtitles. MFB Mar 1990 p60

La Senyora (18) Spain Dir Jordi Cadena with Silvia Tortosa, Hermann

Bonnin, Luis Merlo. ICA Projects, 21 Apr 1989. 103 mins. Subtitles. MFB May 1989 p150

The Serpent and the Rainbow (18) USA Dir Wes Craven with Bill Pullman, Cathy Tyson, Zakes Mokae. UIP, 21 Apr 1989. 98 mins. MFB May 1989 p131

sex, lies, and videotape (18) USA Dir Steven Soderbergh with James Spader, Andie MacDowell, Peter Gallagher. Virgin Vision, 8 Sept 1989. 100 mins. MFB Sept 1989 p282

Shadow Makers (Fat Man and Little Boy) (PG) USA Dir Roland Joffé with Paul Newman, Dwight Schultz, Bonnie Bedelia. UIP, 9 Mar 1990. 127 mins. MFB Mar 1990 p77

Shame (15) Australia Dir Steve Jodrell with Deborra-Lee Furness, Tony Barry, Simone Buchanan. Metro Pictures, 5 May 1989. 94 mins. MFB June 1989 p188

She's Been Away (PG) UK Dir Peter Hall with Peggy Ashcroft, Geraldine James, James Fox. BBC Enterprises, 22 Sept 1989. 103 mins

Shirley Valentine (15) USA Dir Lewis Gilbert with Pauline Collins, Tom Conti, Julia McKenzie. UIP, 13 Oct 1989. 108 mins. MFB Nov 1989 p345

A Short Film about Killing see **Krótki Film o Zabijaniu**

A Short Film about Love see **Krótki Film o Miłości**

Sing (PG) USA Dir Richard Baskin with Lorraine Bracco, Peter Dobson, Jessica Steen. Columbia Tri-Star, 9 June 1989. 97 mins. MFB July 1989 p213

Sisters (Some Girls) (15) USA Dir Michael Hoffman with Patrick Dempsey, Jennifer Connelly, Sheila Kelley. UIP, 19 Jan 1990. 93 mins. MFB Jan 1990 p24

Skin Deep (18) USA Dir Blake Edwards with John Ritter, Vincent Gardenia, Alyson Reed. Braveworld/20th Century Fox, 7 July 1989. 101 mins. MFB July 1989 p214

Arsinée Khanjian, Gabrielle Rose. Recorded Releasing, 15 Sept 1989. 92 mins. MFB Sept 1989 p283

Splendor (PG) Italy/France Dir Ettore Scola with Marcello Mastroianni, Massimo Troisi, Marina Vlady. Warner Bros, 4 Aug 1989. 99 mins. Subtitles. MFB Aug 1989 p251

Sea of Love

Star, 9 Feb 1990. 117 mins. MFB Feb 1990 p51

A Strange Place to Meet see **Drôle d'endroit pour une rencontre**

Strapless (15) UK Dir David Hare with Blair Brown, Bruno Ganz, Bridget Fonda. Virgin Vision, 23 Mar 1990. 100 mins. MFB Apr 1990 p118

The Summer of Aviya see **Hakayitz shel Aviya**

Summer Vacation 1999 see **Sen-Kyuhyaku-Kyuju-Kyu-Nen no Natsu Yasumi**

Sur (15) Argentina/France Dir Fernando E Solanas with Miguel Angel Sola, Susu Pecoraro, Philippe Léotard. Gala, 2 Feb 1990. 119 mins. MFB Mar 1990 p79

Talk Radio (18) USA Dir Oliver Stone with Eric Bogosian, Alec Baldwin, Ellen Greene. 20th Century Fox, 22 Sept 1989. 109 mins. MFB Sept 1989 p284

The Tall Guy (15) UK Dir Mel Smith with Jeff Goldblum, Emma Thompson, Rowan Atkinson. Virgin Vision,

14 Apr 1989. 92 mins. MFB May 1989 p152

Tango & Cash (15) USA Dir Andrei Konchalovsky with Sylvester Stallone, Kurt Russell, Jack Palance. Warner Bros, 23 Mar 1990. 101 mins. MFB May 1990 p143

Tank Malling (18) UK Dir James Marcus with Ray Winstone, Jason Connery, Amanda Donohoe. Cineplex/Parkfield Pictures, 24 Nov 1989. 109 mins. MFB Dec 1989 p375

Tap (PG) USA Dir Nick Castle with Gregory Hines, Suzzanne Douglas, Sammy Davis Jnr. Columbia Tri-Star, 16 June 1989. 111 mins. MFB July 1989 p215

Tempos difíceis, este tempo (Hard Times) (PG) Portugal/UK Dir João Botelho with Luís Estrela, Julia Britton, Isabel de Castro. Artificial Eye, 2 June 1989. 96 mins. Subtitles. MFB July 1989 p216

Tequila Sunrise (15) USA Dir Robert Towne with Mel Gibson, Michelle Pfeiffer, Kurt Russell. Warner Bros, 31 Mar 1989. 115 mins. MFB May 1989 p152

Shadow Makers

Slaves of New York (15) USA Dir James Ivory with Bernadette Peters, Madeleine Potter, Adam Coleman Howard. Columbia Tri-Star, 18 Aug 1989. 125 mins. MFB Aug 1989 p250

Some Girls see **Sisters**

Soursweet (15) UK Dir Mike Newell with Sylvia Chang, Danny An-Ning Dun, Jodi Long. Curzon, 17 Feb 1989. 111 mins. MFB Apr 1989 p123

Speaking Parts (18) Canada Dir Atom Egoyan with Michael McManus,

Star Trek V: The Final Frontier (PG) USA Dir William Shatner with William Shatner, Leonard Nimoy, DeForest Kelley. UIP, 20 Oct 1989. 107 mins. MFB Nov 1989 p346

Stealing Heaven (15) UK/Yugoslavia Dir Clive Donner with Derek de Lint, Kim Thomson, Denholm Elliott. Rank, 28 Apr 1989. 115 mins. MFB May 1989 p151

Steel Magnolias (PG) USA Dir Herbert Ross with Sally Field, Dolly Parton, Shirley MacLaine. Columbia Tri-

Testament (PG) UK ▶
Dir John Akomfrah with
Tania Rogers, Evans
Hunter, Emma Francis
Wilson. Black Audio Film
Collective, 1 Sept 1989. 80
mins. MFB Sept 1989
p259

**That Night in
Varennes** see *La nuit
de Varennes*

**That Summer of
White Roses** (15) UK/
Yugoslavia Dir Rajko
Grlic with Tom Conti,
Susan George, Rod
Steiger. Premier
Releasing, 16 Feb 1990.
103 mins. MFB Mar 1990
p80

**Thelonius Monk:
Straight No Chaser**
(PG) USA Dir Charlotte
Zwerin. Documentary.
Warner Bros, 29 Sept
1989

They Live (18) USA
Dir John Carpenter with
Roddy Piper, Keith
David, Meg Foster. Guild,
23 June 1989. 94 mins.
MFB June 1989 p163

**That Summer of White
Roses**

**The Thin Blue
Line** (15) USA Dir
Errol Morris.
Documentary. BFI, 17
Mar 1989. 101 mins. MFB
Apr 1989 p124

Three Fugitives (15)
USA Dir Francis Veber
with Nick Nolte, Martin
Short, Sarah Rowland

Doroff. Warner Bros, 25
Aug 1989. 96 mins. MFB
Aug 1989 p252

**Time and
Judgement** UK Dir
Menelik Shabazz with
Doris Harper-Wills,
Thomas Pinnock, Anita
Breveld. Ceddo Film and
Video Workshop, 17 Mar

1989. 80 mins. MFB Apr
1989 p100

A Time of Destiny
(15) USA Dir Gregory
Nava with William Hurt,
Timothy Hutton, Melissa
Leo. Rank, 12 May 1989.
118 mins. MFB June 1989
p189

The Thin Blue Line

Topio stin omichli (Landscape in the Mist) (15) Greece/France/Italy Dir Thodoros Angelopoulos with Michalis Zeke, Tania Palaiologou, Stratos Tzortzoglou. Artificial Eye, 16 June 1989. 124 mins. Subtitles. MFB Aug 1989 p253

Torch Song Trilogy ▶ (18) USA Dir Paul Bogart with Harvey Fierstein, Anne Bancroft, Matthew Broderick. Palace Pictures, 19 May 1989. 119 mins. MFB May 1989 p154

Tree of Hands (18) UK Dir Giles Foster with Helen Shaver, Lauren Bacall, Malcolm Stoddard. Pathé Releasing (Cannon), 12 May 1989. 89 mins. MFB May 1989 p155

Trop belle pour toi! (18) France Dir Bertrand Blier with Gérard Depardieu, Josiane Balasko, Carole Bouquet. Artificial Eye, 2 Mar 1990. 91 mins. Subtitles. MFB Mar 1990 p81

Turner & Hooch (PG) USA Dir Roger Spottiswoode with Tom Hanks, Mare Winningham, Craig T Nelson. Warner Bros, 12 Jan 1990. 99 mins. MFB Jan 1990 p25

Twilight City UK Dir Reece Auguiste. Documentary. Black Audio Film Collective, 23 Oct 1989. 52 mins. 16mm. MFB Dec 1989 p375

Two Moon Junction (18) USA Dir Zalman King with Sherilyn Fenn, Richard Tyson, Louise Fletcher. Recorded Releasing, 3 Nov 1989. 105 mins. MFB Dec 1989 p376

The Unholy (18) USA Dir Camilo Vilo with Ben Cross, Ned Beatty, William Russ. Vestron, 3 Mar 1989. 102 mins. MFB Apr 1989 p125

bfi **Venus Peter** (12) UK Dir Ian Sellar with Ray McAnally, David Hayman, Sinead Cusack. Oasis, 1 Dec 1989. 94 mins. MFB Dec 1989 p355 ▼

La vie est belle (PG) Belgium/France/Zaire Dirs Benoit Lamy, Ngangura Mweze with Papa Wemba, Bibi Krubwa, Landu Nzunzimbu Matshia.

Blue Dolphin, 14 July 1989. 72 mins. Subtitles. MFB Aug 1989 p255

La vie est un long fleuve tranquille (Life is a Long Quiet River) (15) France Dir Etienne Chatiliez with Benoît Magimel, Valerie Lalande, Tara Romer. Electric Pictures/Contemporary, 27 Oct 1989. 91 mins. Subtitles. MFB Dec 1989 p377

La vie et rien d'autre (Life and Nothing But) (PG) France Dir Bertrand Tavernier with Philippe Noiret, Sabine Azéma, Pascale Vignal. Artificial Eye, 27 Oct 1989. 134 mins. Subtitles. MFB Nov 1989 p347

Walker (18) USA Dir Alex Cox with Ed Harris, Richard Masur, René Auberjonois. Recorded Releasing, 31 Mar 1989. 94 mins. MFB May 1989 p156

bfi *– Produced and/or distributed by the British Film Institute*

The War of the Roses (15) USA Dir Danny DeVito with Michael Douglas, Kathleen Turner, Danny DeVito. 20th Century Fox, 9 Mar 1990. 116 mins. MFB Mar 1990 p81

Warlock (15) USA Dir Steve Miner with Richard E Grant, Julian Sands, Lori Singer. Medusa, 2 June 1989. 102 mins. MFB June 1989 p190

Watchers (18) Canada Dir Jon Hess with Michael Ironside, Christopher Carey, Graeme Campbell. Guild, 9 June 1989. 91 mins. MFB July 1989 p218

Waxwork (18) USA Dir Anthony Hickox with Zach Galligan, Deborah Foreman, Michelle Johnson. Vestron, 9 June 1989. 96 mins. MFB July 1989 p219

We the Living see **Noi Vivi**

We Think the World of You (PG) UK Dir Colin Gregg with Alan Bates, Max Wall, Liz Smith. Recorded Releasing, 22 Sept 1989. 94 mins. MFB Oct 1989 p311

When Harry Met Sally...

Weekend at Bernie's (12) USA Dir Ted Kotcheff with Andrew McCarthy, Jonathan Silverman, Catherine Mary Stewart. Rank, 16 Mar 1990. 92 mins. MFB Mar 1990 p83

Welcome Home (15) USA Dir Franklin J Schaffner with Kris Kristofferson, JoBeth Williams, Sam Waterston. Rank, 19 Jan 1990. 92 mins. MFB Mar 1990 p83

What Have I Done to Deserve This? see **¿Que he hecho YO para merecer esto!!**

When Harry Met Sally... (15) USA Dir Rob Reiner with Billy Crystal, Meg Ryan, Carrie Fisher. Palace Pictures, 1 Dec 1989. 95 mins. MFB Dec 1989 p377

When I Fall in Love (Everybody's All-American) (15) USA Dir Taylor Hackford with Jessica Lange, Dennis Quaid, Timothy Hutton. Warner Bros, 16 Feb 1990. 127 mins. MFB Mar 1990 p84

When the Whales Came (U) UK Dir Clive Rees with Helen Mirren, Paul Scofield, David Suchet. 20th Century Fox, 8 Sept 1989. 100 mins. MFB Oct 1989 p312

Who's Harry Crumb? (PG) USA Dir Paul Flaherty with John Candy, Jeffrey Jones, Annie Potts. Columbia Tri-Star, 7 July 1989. 90 mins. MFB July 1989 p219

Wilt (15) UK Dir Michael Tuchner with Griff Rhys Jones, Mel Smith, Alison Steadman. Rank, 3 Nov 1989. 93 mins. MFB Nov 1989 p349

Winter People (15) USA Dir Ted Kotcheff with Kurt Russell, Kelly McGillis, Lloyd Bridges. Rank, 23 Feb 1990. 111 mins. MFB Feb 1990 p53

A Winter Tan Canada Dirs Jackie Burroughs, Louise Clarke, John Frizzell, John Walker, Aerlyn Weissman with Jackie Burroughs, Erando Gonzalez, Javier Torres. Films Transit/ Canada, 24 Nov 1989. 91 mins

Wired (18) USA Dir Larry Peerce with Michael Chiklis, Patti D'Arbanville, J T Walsh. Entertainment, 6 Oct

1989. 109 mins. MFB Oct 1989 p312

Without a Clue (PG) USA Dir Thom Eberhardt with Michael Caine, Ben Kingsley, Jeffrey Jones. Rank, 28 Apr 1989. 107 mins. MFB May 1989 p157

The Wolves of Willoughby Chase (PG) UK Dir Stuart Orme with Stephanie Beacham, Mel Smith, Geraldine James. Entertainment, 15 Dec 1989. 93 mins. MFB Dec 1989 p378

Women on the Verge of a Nervous Breakdown see **Mujeres al borde de un ataque de nervios**

Working Girl (15) USA Dir Mike Nichols with Melanie Griffith, Harrison Ford, Sigourney Weaver. 20th Century Fox, 31 Mar 1989. 113 mins. MFB Apr 1989 p99

Yaaba (PG) Burkino Faso/France/Switzerland Dir Idrissa Ouedraogo with Fatima Sanga, Noufou Ouedraogo, Barry Roukietou. Oasis, 26 Jan 1990. 90 mins. Subtitles. MFB Jan 1990 p25

Yanzhi Kou (Rouge) (15) Hong Kong Dir Stanley Kwan with Anita Mui, Leslie Cheung, Alex Man. ICA Projects, 20 Oct 1989. 96 mins. Subtitles. MFB Feb 1990 p31

The Year My Voice Broke (15) Australia Dir John Duigan with Noah Taylor, Loene Carmen, Ben Mendelsohn. Palace Pictures, 28 Apr 1989. 105 mins. MFB May 1989 p158

Young Einstein (PG) Australia Dir Yahoo Serious with Yahoo Serious, Odile Le Clezio, John Howard. Warner Bros, 13 Oct 1989. 91 mins. MFB Oct 1989 p313

SPECIALISED GOODS AND SERVICES

Agfa-Gevaert
Motion Picture Division
27 Great West Road
Brentford
Middx TW8 9AY
Tel: 081 560 2131
Fax: 081 847 5803
Film stock

Any Effects
43 Farlton Road
London SW18 3BJ
Tel: 081 874 0927
Fax: 081 877 1372
Mechanical (front of
camera) special effects
Pyrotechnics: simulated
explosions, bullet hits
Weather: rain, wind, fog,
snow
Breakaways: shatterglass
windows, bottles, glasses,
collapsing furniture,
walls, floors
Mechanical effects and
prop-making service

Boulton-Hawker Films
Hadleigh
Ipswich
Suffolk IP7 5BG
Tel: 0473 822235
Fax: 0473 823187
Time-lapse,
cinemicrography and
other specialised scientific
filming techniques

Crews Employment Agency
111 Wardour Street
London W1V 4AY
Tel: 071 437 0721/0810/
0350
Fax: 071 494 4644
A licensed employment
agency set up by ACTT
(see under Organisations)
in 1989. Operating a
computerised database,
they are able to scan for
ACTT freelancers by
grade, geographical
location, foreign
languages, specialist
skills and experience, etc.
This is a free service to
the film and television
industry

De Wolfe
80-88 Wardour Street
London W1V 3LF
Tel: 071 439 8481
Fax: 071 437 2744
Major production music
library of tapes and CDs,
controlling 26,000 titles
as publisher. Offices in
New York, Tokyo, Paris,
Holland, Italy and

Brussels. Specially
composed film and TV
scores; 24-track studio;
film cutting rooms; sound
effects CDs

ETH Screen Music
York Lane
22 Broughton Street
Edinburgh EH1 3RH
Tel: 031 557 2721
Music, musicians,
arrangers, composers for
film, TV and video. Work
for drama, comedy,
documentary; specialists
for live accompaniment
with restored silent films

Eureka Location and Production Management
16 Broadwick Street
London W1V 1FH
Tel: 071 734 4100
Fax: 071 734 0150
Finds locations, clears
permissions, manages
location shooting,
production manages.
Offices in London and
Toronto

FTS (Freight Forwarders)
Unit 2b
Northumberland Close
Stanwell
Staines
Middx TW19 7LN
Tel: 0784 243901
Fax: 0784 247249
International air-freight
with full bonded
warehouse and freight
forwarding

Film Finances
1-11 Hay Hill
Berkeley Square
London W1X 7LF
Tel: 071 629 6557
Fax: 071 491 7530
Graham Easton
Provide completion
guarantees for the film
and television industry

The Film Stock Centre
68-70 Wardour Street
London W1V 3HP
Tel: 071 734 0038
Fax: 071 494 2645
Film stock supplies:
Kodak, Agfa, Ilford and
Fuji 16mm, 35mm
Videotape supplies

Harkness Screens
The Gate Studio
Station Road

Borehamwood
Herts WD6 1DQ
Tel: 081 953 3611
Fax: 081 207 3657
Projection screens and
complete screen systems

Jim Henson's Creature Shop
1b Downshire Hill
Hampstead
London NW3 1NR
Tel: 071 431 2818
Fax: 071 431 3737
Animatronics, puppets
and prosthetics

Hirearchy Classic and Contemporary Costume
45 Palmerston Road
Boscombe
Bournemouth
Dorset BH1 4HW
Tel: 0202 394465
Fax: 0202 309660
Specialise in twentieth
century costume hire

Image Diggers Picture and Tape Library
618b Finchley Road
London NW11 7RR
Tel: 081 455 4564
35mm slides, stills,
postcards, sheet music,
magazine and book
material for hire (NB no
film footage)
Audiovisual tape
resources in performing
arts and other areas, plus
theme research

Kodak
Motion Picture and
Television Products
PO Box 66
Hemel Hempstead
Herts HP1 1LV
Tel: 0442 62333
Fax: 0442 232505
Film stock

Lip Service Casting
Unit 131 Canalot Studios
222 Kensal Road
London W10 5BN
Tel: 081 969 8535
Fax: 081 968 6911
Voiceover agency for
actors, and voiceover
casting agency. Produce
'The Voice Analysis' – a
breakdown of actors' vocal
abilities

Location Works
8 Greek Street
London W1V 5LE
Tel: 071 434 4211

Fax: 071 437 3097
Locations library,
location finding and
management
(London, UK and world)

Ocean Film and Research

Production Centre
Threeways House
40-44 Clipstone Street
London W1P 7EA
Tel: 071 323 3220
Fax: 071 637 2590
Floating production
company, facility and
exploration charter
organisation, based on the
North Sea cutter,
'O-Lucia'
Equipment: broadcast
video production unit
with Betacam SP and sub-
aqua cameras; 8-track
sound facilities; 2
inflatable dinghies,
1 flying boat; sub-aqua
equipment
Communications and
computer systems: 100
watt Kenwood amateur
radio; computer link for
weather/fax and inter-
computer communica-
tions; Samsung 640

kilobyte IBM compatible
with hard disk and
printer, protable ICOM
IC725, walkie-talkie and
mobile phone

Oxford Scientific Films (OSF)

Long Hanborough
Oxford OX7 2LD
Tel: 0993 881881
Fax: 0993 882808
10 Poland Street
London W1V 3DE
Tel: 071 494 0720
Fax: 071 287 9125
Specialists in macro,
micro, time-lapse, high-
speed and snorkel optic
photography for natural
history programmes,
commercials, corporate
videos and videodiscs

Security Archives

Saref House
135 Shepherdess Walk
London W1 7PZ
Tel: 071 253 0027
Fax: 071 608 0640
Film and video storage
and retrieval services

Stanley Productions

147 Wardour Street
London W1V 3TB
Tel: 071 439 0311
Fax: 071 437 2126
Ronnie Arlen, Sales
Director
Distributors worldwide of
videotape, video
equipment, audiotape,
film stock, and accessories

Ten Tenths

106 Gifford Street
London N1 0DF
Tel: 071 607 4887
Fax: 071 609 8124
Props service specialising
in vehicles (cars, bikes,
boats and planes) ranging
from 1901 to present day
– veteran, vintage,
classic, modern – with
additional wardrobe
facilities

STUDIOS

Bray Studios
Down Place
Windsor Road
Water Oakley
Windsor
Berks SL4 5UG
Tel: 0628 22111
Fax: 0628 770381
STAGES
1(sound)	955 sq metres
2(sound)	948 sq metres
3(sound)	235 sq metres
4(sound)	173 sq metres
5(silent)	65 x 30 ft
6 accoustic rehearsal	30 x 20ft

FILMS/PROGRAMMES
Hope and Glory for John Boorman
The Manageress for Zed
Saracen for Central TV
Tecx for Central TV
The Witches for Henson Organisation

Goldcrest Elstree Studios
Borehamwood
Herts WD6 1JG
Tel: 081 953 1600
Fax: 081 207 0860
STAGES
1	1350 sq metres
2	1350 sq metres
3	1350 sq metres
4	1350 sq metres
5	1470 sq metres
6	2787 sq metres
7	480 sq metres
8	720 sq metres
9	720 sq metres
10	720 sq metres

FILMS/PROGRAMMES
Capital City for Euston Films
Countdown to War for Brian Lapping Associates
A Ghost in Monte Carlo for Gainsborough (Film and TV) Pictures, director John Hough
Greek Myths for Jim Henson Organisation

Halliford Studios
Manygate Lane
Shepperton
Middx TW17 9EG
Tel: 0932 226341
Fax: 0932 246336
STAGES
A	334 sq metres
B	223 sq metres

Isleworth Studios
Studio Parade
484 London Road
Isleworth
Middx TW7 4DE
Tel: 081 568 3511
Fax: 081 568 4863

STAGES
A	292 sq metres
B	152 sq metres
C	152 sq metres
D	152 sq metres
Packshot stage	141 sq metres

Jacob Street Studios
9-19 Mill Street
London SE1 2DA
Tel: 071 232 1066
Fax: 071 252 0118
STAGES
A	1250 sq metres
B	600 sq metres
C	170 sq metres
D	235 sq metres
E	185 sq metres
F	185 sq metres
G	170 sq metres

FILMS/PROGRAMMES
The Krays
London's Burning
The Paradise Club

Lee International Studios Shepperton
Studios Road
Shepperton
Middx TW17 0QD
Tel: 0932 562611
Fax: 0932 568989
STAGES
A	1674 sq metres
B	1116 sq metres
C	1674 sq metres
D	1116 sq metres
E	294 sq metres
F	294 sq metres
G	629 sq metres
H	2790 sq metres
I	657 sq metres
J	284 sq metres
K	120 sq metres
L	604 sq metres
M	260 sq metres
T	261 sq metres

FILMS/PROGRAMMES
Cry Freedom starring Kevin Kline, Denzel Washington and Penelope Wilton; producer/director Sir Richard Attenborough
Gorillas in the Mist starring Sigourney Weaver, Brian Brown and Julie Harris; director Michael Apted; producer Terry Clegg
A Handful of Dust starring James Wilby and Kristin Scott Thomas; director Charles Sturridge; producer Derek Granger
The Lonely Passion of Judith Hearne, for HandMade, starring Maggie Smith and Bob Hoskins; director Jack

Clayton
The Raggedy Rawney for HandMade, starring Bob Hoskins; director Bob Hoskins
You Bet series for LWT, starring Bruce Forsyth

Pinewood Studios
Pinewood Road
Iver
Bucks SL0 0NH
Tel: 0753 651700
Fax: 0753 656844
STAGES
A	1685 sq metres
B	827 sq metres
C	827 sq metres
D	1685 sq metres
E	1685 sq metres
F	700 sq metres
G	247 sq metres
H	300 sq metres
J	825 sq metres
K	825 sq metres
L	880 sq metres
M	880 sq metres
007 (silent)	4350 sq metres
South Dock (silent)	1548 sq metres
North Dock (silent)	628 sq metres
Large Process	439 sq metres
Small Process	226 sq metres

FILMS
Act of Will
Chicago Joe and the Showgirl
The Gravy Train
Memphis Belle
Nightbreed
Outpost
Press Gang
The Russia House
Treasure Island

Twickenham Film Studios
St Margaret's
Twickenham
Middx TW1 2AW
Tel: 081 892 4477
Fax: 081 891 0168
STAGES
1	701 sq metres
2	186 sq metres
3	516 sq metres

Westway Studios
8 Olaf Street
London W11 4BE
Tel: 071 221 9041
Fax: 071 221 9399
STAGES
1	602 sq metres
2	520 sq metres
3	169 sq metres
4	242 sq metres
5	70 sq metres

The team LWT put together for Evelyn Waugh's **A Handful Of Dust** created a Bafta Award winning drama.

The drama Gryff Rhys Jones had with an inflatable doll in LWT's **Wilt** was an hilarious handful for Mel Smith.

And Mel had already

WHEN YOU'RE PRODUCING FILMS THE BEST SHOWS.

enjoyed a big hand for his film directing debut **The Tall Guy**, another LWT production.

They all produced resounding box office successes for LWT and with a similar variety of films in the pipeline you can be sure you're in safe hands for the future.

TELEVISION COMPANIES

Below are listed all British television companies, with a selection of their key personnel and programmes. The titles listed are a cross-section of productions initiated (but not necessarily broadcast) during 1988 and the first quarter of 1989. 'F' and 'V' indicate whether productions were shot on film or video. For details of feature films made for TV, see Production Starts (p224)

INDEPENDENT TELEVISION

ANGLIA
Television Limited

Anglia Television
Anglia House
Norwich NR1 3JG
Tel: 0603 615151
Chairman: Sir Peter Gibbings
Chief Executive: David McCall
Managing Director, Broadcasting Division: Philip Garner

A Brief History of Time
Production companies: Anglia Television/Gordon Freedman Productions/Amblin Entertainment
Producers: Gordon Freedman, David Hickman
Director: Errol Morris
1 x 90 mins V
A documentary special, based on the life and work of brilliant Cambridge physicist Professor Stephen Hawking, taking a stunning visual journey into his conception of the fundamental mysteries of the universe

The Chief
Production company: Anglia Films
Producer: Ruth Boswell
Director: Brian Farnham
Writer: Jeffrey Caine
Cast: Tim Piggott-Smith, Karen Archer, Judy Loe
6 x 1 hour V
Power and politics at the top of a provincial police force with a new Chief Constable trying to put his principles into practice. He comes under pressure from the Home Office and politicians –

but stays determined to do what he thinks is right and remain accountable to the individual citizen

Chimera
Production company: Zenith Productions
Producer: Nick Gillott
Director: Lawrence Gordon Clark
Writer: Stephen Gallagher
Cast: John Lynch, Christine Kavanagh, Kenneth Cranham
4 x 1 hour V
A prophetic video set in the chilling world of genetic engineering where science fact has overtaken science fiction. A journalist's investigations into a mass murder lead to the discovery of a secret so terrible the highest authorities want him silenced

Devices and Desires
Production company: Anglia Films
Producer: John Rosenberg
Director: John Davies
Dramatist: Thomas Ellice
Cast: Roy Marsden, Susannah York, Gemma Jones, James Faulkner
6 x 1 hour V
Detective thriller serial based on the novel by PD James and revolving around the passions aroused by the presence of a nuclear power station in East Anglia where a psychopathic killer is on the loose

Knightmare
Production company: Broadsword Productions
Producer: Tim Child
Director: Jimmy McKinney
Writer: Tim Child
Cast: Hugo Myatt, John Woodnutt
16 x 25 mins V

Children's fantasy adventure game using computer graphics and animations
Other programmes include:
Anything Goes
Anything to Declare
Castle's in Europe
Cross Question
Farming Diary
Folio
Go Fishing
Heirloom Lucky
Ladders
A Place in the Sun
Survival
WideAngle

Border Television
The Television Centre
Carlisle CA1 3NT
Tel: 0228 25101
Fax: 0228 41384
Chairman: Melvyn Bragg
Managing Director: James Graham
Programmes Director: Paul Corley

Enterprize Challenge
Producer: Tony Nicholson
7 x 30 mins
A yearly competition for small businesses in the Border Television region

KTV Krankies Television
Executive Producer: Paul Corley
Producer/Director: Harry King
7 x 30 mins
The Krankies set up their own satellite station

That's History
Producer: Jane Hambly
6 x 30 mins
Andy Craig presents a new format for a history quiz shot in various stately homes

Union and the League
Producer: Jack Johnstone
10 x 30 mins
A monthly series which
proves that rugby union
and rugby league can be
covered in one
programme

Vive la Difference
Producer: Liz Bloor
6 × 30 mins V
Vive la Difference takes
six women and swaps
their lives for a day with
their European
equivalent

Word of Mouth
Producer: John Gwyn
10 x 30 mins
John Hegley is resident
poet with various guests
in this Arts Council
assisted project

CENTRAL

Central Independent Television

Central House
Broad Street
Birmingham B1 2JP
Tel: 021 643 9898
East Midlands Television
Centre
Nottingham NG7 2NA
Tel: 0602 863322
35-38 Portman Square
London W1A 2HZ
Tel: 071 486 6688
Hesketh House
43-45 Portman Square
London W1A 2HZ
Tel: 071 486 6688
Central South:
Unit 9 Windrush Court
Abingdon Business Park
Abingdon
Oxon OX14 1SA
Tel: 0235 554123
Television House
23-25 Commercial Road
Gloucester GL1 2ED
Chairman: David
Justham
Managing Director:
Leslie Hill
Managing Director,
Central Broadcasting:
Andy Allan
General Manager,
Central Productions:
Philip Gilbert
Controller of Drama &
Managing Director of
Central Films: Ted Childs
Controller of Features
Group: Richard Creasey
Controller of

Entertainment: Tony
Wolfe
Controller of Young
People's Programmes &
Managing Director of
FilmFair: Lewis Rudd

Chancer
Producer: Sarah D Wilson
Director: Alan Grint,
Laurence Moody
Writer: Guy Andrews
Camera: Colin Munn,
Peter Greenhalgh
Cast: Lynsey Baxter,
Susannah Harker,
Caroline Langrishe,
Matthew Marsh, Clive
Owen, Sean Pertwee,
Leslie Phillips, Peter
Vaughan, Benjamin
Whitrow
13 x 1 hour
City business analyst
Steven Crane is used to
taking risks but he takes
the biggest gamble of his
life to help save the
elegant but ailing sports
car business, Douglas
Motors, from financial
ruin. As he leaves the city
behind and heads for the
unknown world of
prestige sports cars in the
Midlands, he inspires
everything from passion
to hatred in the various
members of the Douglas
family

The Cook Report
Producer/Director: Clive
Entwistle, Peter Salkeld
Camera: Peter Salkend,
Graham Wickings
Editor: Mike Townson
Cast: Roger Cook
8 x 30 mins
Roger Cook returns to
expose more crime and
injustice in the fourth
series of the no holds
barred investigative
programme

Inspector Morse
Production company:
Zenith Productions
Producer: David Lascelles
Directors: John Madden,
Peter Hammond, Sandy
Johnston, Danny Boyle
Writers: Alma Cullen,
Jeremy Burnham,
Anthony Minghella,
Julian Mitchell
Camera: Paul Wheeler
Editors: Bob Dearberg,
Alan Jones
4 x 2 hours
John Thaw returns as
Britain's most popular
detective, Inspector

Morse, in a series of
complex and perplexing
murder mysteries set in
Oxford. The enigmatic
Morse joins forces again
with Kevin Whateley,
who plays his partner,
Sergeant Lewis, to
investigate the tangles
web of evidence
surrounding each of the
two hour mysteries

Press Gang
Production company:
Richmond Film and
Television Productions
Producer: Sandra Hastie
Directors: Bob Spiers,
Bren Simson, John Hall,
Lorne Magory
Writer: Steven Moffat
Editors: Geoff Hogg,
Chris Ridsdale, Michael
John Bateman
Cast: Julia Sawalaha,
Dexter Fletcher
13 x 30 mins
The Junior Gazette
return with a second
series of Press Gang.
Single minded editor
Lynda Day not only has
tough working decisions
to make – her 'will they
won't they' relationship
with rebel reporter Spike
reaches its peak

**Viewpoint '89:
Cambodia – Year Ten**
Producer/Director: David
Munro
Writer: John Pilger
Camera: Ivan Strasburg
Editor: McDonald Brown
Cast: John Pilger
1 hour
John Pilger and David
Munro return to
Cambodia. Cambodia –
Year Ten warns that now
the Vietnamese have
withdrawn from
Cambodia, Pol Pot and
the Khmer Rouge are
poised to return and bring
about another holocaust
in Asia

Vincent and Theo
Producers: Ludi Boeker
and David Conroy
Director: Robert Altman
Writer: Julian Mitchell
Cast: Tim Roth, Paul
Rhys
2 x 2 hours
Vincent and Theo tells
the moving story of the
unique relationship
between Vincent Van
Gogh and his brother
Theo

Other programmes
include:
About Face
Boon
**Cliff Richard – The
Event**
Democracy
Find a Family
A King of Magic
$64,000 Question
Spitting Image
Upper Hand
**Viewpoint '90: Struggle
for Democracy**
What-a-Mess
The Winjin' Pom
The Wombles

Channel Television

Television Centre
La Pouquelaye
St Helier
Jersey JE2 3ZD
Tel: 0534 68999
Fax: 0534 59446
Television Centre
St George's Place
St Peter Port
Guernsey
Tel: 0481 23451
Fax: 0481 710739
Chairman: Major J R
Riley
Managing Director:
John Henwood

Bertie the Bat
Producer: Jane Bayer
Animator: Julia
Coutanche
Scriptwriter: Lisa
Beresford
Editor: John Le Signe
10 x 5 mins V
A new character to
children's ITV, Bertie the
Bat longs to be different
and with the help of his
friend the Skypainter, he
achieves his dream

Channel Report
Director: Paul Brown
News Editor: Martyn
Farley
Presenter: Russell Labey
30 mins V
News magazine broadcast
Monday to Friday jointly
presented from Channel's
Jersey and Guernsey
news studios – also
featuring live or taped
inserts from the smaller
islands Sark and
Alderney

The Last RoundUp
Producer: Bob Evans
Director: Frank
Cvitanovich

Camera: Tim Ringsdore
Editor: John Le Signe
With Gerald Durrell, Lee Durrell
1 x 1 hour V
Gerald Durrell in Madagascar on potentially his last expedition capturing endangered animals in a long and distinguished career

Swastika over British Soil
Producer: Jane Bayer
Director/writer: Peter Batty
Camera: Tim Ringsdore
Editor: Garry Knight
1 x 1 hour V
The Channel Islands were the only British soil occupied by the Germans in the Second World War. Swastika over British Soil tells the story of both the Occupiers and the Occupied marking the 50th anniversary of the beginning of the Occupation June/July 1940

The Time, The Place
Producer: Jane Bayer
Director: Paul Brown
Cast: Mike Scott
40 mins

Valued Opinion
Producer/Director: Jane Bayer
Writer: Max Robertson
Cameras: Kevin Banner, Richard Hall
With Max Robertson, Sotheby's experts
6 x 30 mins V
A series about collecting and collectables. Porcelain, Channel Islands silver, Old Masters, Miniatures, Art Deco, Victoriana are among the subjects covered

Other programmes include:
Highway
Link Up

Channel Four Television
60 Charlotte Street
London W1P 2AX
Tel: 071 631 4444
Chairman: Sir Richard Attenborough

Chief Executive: Michael Grade
Director of Programmes: Liz Forgan
Deputy Director of Programmes & Controller of Factual Programmes: John Willis
Director of Programme Acquisitions & Sales: Colin Leventhal
Controller, Arts & Entertainment: Andrea Wonfor
Head of Drama: David Aukin
Commissioning Editors: David Lloyd (Senior Commissioning Editor, News & Current Affairs); Gwynn Pritchard (Senior Commissioning Editor, Education); Seamus Cassidy (Entertainment); Farrukh Dhondy (Multicultural Programmes); Alan Fountain (Independent Film and Video); Stephen Garrett (Youth); Waldemar Januszczak (Arts); Caroline Thomson (Finance, Industry and Science); Bob Towler (Education and Religion); Avril MacRory (Music); Mike Miller (Sport); Peter Moore (Documentaries); Michael Attwell (Talk & Features); Karin Bamborough (Single Drama)
Chief Film Buyer: Mairi Macdonald

The Orchid House
Production company: Picture Palace Productions
Producer: Malcolm Craddock
Director: Horace Ove
Writer: Jim Hawkins
4 x 60 mins
Adaptation of Phyllis Shand Allfrey's novel. 'The Orchid House' tells the story of 3 white creole sisters who grow up on the Island of Dominica and then leave their Caribbean island for the cold northern lands of England and America

Rock Steady
Production company: Holmes Associates
Executive producer: Andrew Holmes
16 x 60 mins
A 16 week live rock series for 'grown ups' with performances based in association with ILR to provide a stereo simulcast

Spaceship Earth
Production company: Network Television
Executive producer: Nicholas Barton
Producer/Director: John Selwyn Gilbert
Writer: Nigel Calder
10 x 26 mins
A major series covering various aspects of geography from around the world

Things to Come
Production company: Inca
Producer: Chris Haws
13 x 30 mins
Youth magazine programme with international possibilities about the future

GRAMPIAN TELEVISION

Grampian Television
Queen's Cross
Aberdeen AB9 2XJ
Tel: 0224 646464
Fax: 0224 635127
Chairman: Sir Douglas Hardie CBE
Chief Executive: Donald H Waters
Director of Television: Robert L Christie
Director of Finance: Graham Good
Director of Programmes: George W Mitchell

The Energy Alternative
Grampian Producer: Ted Brocklebank
Grampian Director: Michael Steele
InCA Producer: William Woollard
InCA Director: John Shepherd
3 x 60 mins V
This series asks what steps can be taken to reduce western energy consumption by over 50% during the next 40 years to allow the third world to reach current western standards without creating the worst effects of the first industrial revolution

Grundig UK Mountain Bike Championship
Production company: TSL
Commissioning editor: George Mitchell
1 x 60 mins V
The world's top mountain

bikers compete for the honours, from the spectacular setting of the Scottish highlands, in this British round of the World Cup series

Hot Property
Executive Producer: George Mitchell
Director: John Pluck
6 x 30 mins V
A magazine series, presented by Judith Chalmers, on all aspects of running and owning a home, with each programme having a housing-related story. The programme also visits the stars at home for a peep into the private world of public faces

Portrait of the Wild
Production company: Shearwater Productions
Producer/Director: Mike Herd
Commissioning Editor: Ted Brocklebank
4 x 30 mins V
The magic of the wild is captured on canvas by top Scottish wildlife artists as the programmes follow the flora and fauna of the country through the seasons

Shooting Stars
Production company: TSL
Executive Producer: George Mitchell
1 x 60 mins V
From luxurious Gleneagles Hotel in Perthshire, a glittering galaxy of stars, including film and television stars, sporting personalities and even Royalty gather to shoot clay pigeons for charity in an event organised and presented by Jackie Stewart

Too Many Widows
Producer: Ted Brocklebank
Director: Berndt Schulze
1 x 60 mins V
Scotland has the worst record for heart disease in the world and this documentary asks what are the underlying reasons and what can be done to reduce the level of fatalities

Other programmes include:
Abair!
The Art Sutter Show
Fionnan-Feoir

Grampian Sheepdog Trials
Highland Cross
No Mean Town
The Old Grey Ladies of Lossiemouth
Patter Merchants
Scotland the What?
Top Club
You'd Better Believe It

Granada Television

Granada Television Centre
Quay Street
Manchester M60 9EA
Tel: 061 832 7211
Fax: 061 832 7211 x 3405
Granada News Centre
Albert Dock
Liverpool L3 4BA
Tel: 051 709 9393
Fax: 051 709 3389
Granada News Centre
White Cross
South Road
Lancaster LA1 4XH
Tel: 0524 60688
Fax: 0524 67607
Granada News Centre
Bridgegate House
5 Bridge Place
Lower Bridge Street
Chester CH1 1SA
Tel: 0244 313966
Fax: 0244 320599
Chairman: David Plowright
Managing Director: Andrew Quinn
Director of Programmes: Steve Morrison
Programme Board: Rod Caird, Paul Doherty, Ray Fitzwalter, Stuart Prebble, David Liddiment, Sally Head

El Cid
Producer: Matthew Bird
Director: Robert Gabriel, Tom Clegg, Brian Parker, Tim Sullivan, Robert Tronson
Scriptwriters: Chris Kelly, Iain Roy, Paul Anderson, Terry Hodgkinson, Jimmy McGovern
Camera: Mike Popley, Howard Summers
Editor: Chris Gill
Cast: Simon Andrew, John Bird, Alfred Molina, Viviane Vives
6 x 1 hour F
El Cid is the story of two Scotland Yard detectives who throw in their lot in London, and escape from the murky gloom of Metropolitan routine to a new life on the Costa Del Sol

Josie Smith
Producer/Director: Barbara Roddam
Scriptwriter: Magdalen Nabb
Cast: Vicky Graham, Josef Minta, Katy Stamp, Adam Woods
15 x 5 mins F
There are everyday adventures for five year-old Josie Smith and her gang of friends. There's her best friend Eileen, who has a squeaky pram, and two boys Gary Grimes and Rawley Baxter. Rawley wears his anorak tied around his neck and thinks he's Batman

Pied Piper
Executive Producers: Stan Margulies, Michael Cox
Director: Norman Stone
Scriptwriter: Nevil Shute
Camera: Ken Morgan, Andy Stephen
Editor: Edward Mansell
Cast: Clare Drummond, Alastair Hayley, Peter O'Toole, Mare Winningham
1 x 2 hour F
John Sidney Howard is on holiday in France in the summer of 1940. In the peace of the Jura mountains, near the Swiss border, he hopes to recover from both a deep tragedy and a personal illness. But northern France – even Paris – is threatened by the German advance

Who Bombed Birmingham?
Producer: Michael Beckham, Leslee Udwin
Director: Michael Beckham
Scriptwriter: Rob Ritchie
Cast: Roger Allam, John Hurt, Martin Shaw, Niall Toibin
1 x 2 hour F
Unravels the inter-twining political, judicial stories behind the case of the Birmingham Six, reconstructing events stretching from 1974 to the present day

Other programmes include:
But Can You Do It on TV?
Children's Ward
Coded Hostile
Coronation Street
(Friday edition)
Inside the Brotherhood
Jeeves & Wooster
Tristan da Cunha – No Place Like Home

HTV

Television Centre
Culverhouse Cross
Cardiff CF5 6XJ
Tel: 0222 590590
HTV Ltd
126 Baker St
London W1M 2AJ
Tel: 071 224 4048
Fax: 071 224 3750
HTV Group
Chairman: Sir Melvyn Rosser
Chief Executive: Patrick Dromgoole
Director Television Group: H H Davies
Director Finance and Administration: Alan Burton
HTV Cymru/Wales Ltd
Chairman: I E Symonds
Managing Director: H H Davies
Director of Programmes: Emyr Daniel

Emlyn's Moon
Producer/Director: Pennant Roberts
Scriptwriter: Julia Jones from a story by Jenny Nimmo
Cast: Sian Phillips, Steffan Morris, Osian Roberts, Lucy Donovan, Sharon Morgan, Robert Blythe, Gareth Thomas
5 x 30 mins
Set in the present, a story of magic and friendship – a sequel to the award-winning 'The Snow Spider'

Other programmes include:
And All That Jazz
Better Late
Day Return
Farming Wales
Missing
The Owen Money Show
Rugby Round-Up
Stopwatch
Wales at Six
Wales at Westminster
Wales on Sunday
Wales this Week

HTV West

Television Centre
Bath Road
Bristol BS4 3HG
Tel: 0272 778366
Fax: 0272 722400
Chairman: Colin Atkinson
Managing Director: Ron Evans
Director of Programmes: Derek Clark
Head of News: Steve Matthews

Blue Revolution
Crimestoppers
Gallery
HTV News
Keynotes
Loads More Muck and Magic
Police 5
Rolf's Cartoon Club
Scene
Sportsmasters
West at War
The West This Week

Independent Television News

ITN House
48 Wells Street
London W1P 4DE
Tel: 071 637 2424
Chairman and Chief Executive: David Nicholas
Editor: Stewart Purvis
Independent Television News provides programmes of national and international news for the independent television network. It also produces the award-winning Channel Four News each weekday evening and since March 1989 has produced the World News for the Channel Four Daily. ITN also operates the first international English language news programme. ITN World News is a daily programme specifically designed for a worldwide audience and is now seen on four continents.

Other programmes for the other ITV companies include *The World This Week* and *The Parliament Programme* for Channel Four; elections at home and abroad, the budget, royal tours, state visits, overseas events and special celebrations. ITN also provides general, sport and business news for Oracle

**Channel Four News
Eurodiario
5am Morning News
ITN Radio News
ITN Telephone News
ITN World News
Morning Bulletins
News at One
News at 5.40
News at Ten
Night Time Bulletins
Oracle
The Parliament
Programme
Special Programmes
The World This Week
World News on
Channel Four Daily**

London Weekend Television

South Bank Television Centre
London SE1 9LT
Tel: 071 620 1620
Chairman: Brian Tesler
Managing Director and Director of Programmes: Greg Dyke
Director of Corporate Affairs:
Barry Cox
Controller of Arts:
Melvyn Bragg
Controller of Drama: Nick Elliott
Controller of Entertainment:
Marcus Plantin
Controller of Features and Current Affairs:
Robin Paxton
Controller of Sport:
Stuart McConachie

Agatha Christie's Poirot
Executive Producer: Nick Elliott
Producer: Brian Eastman
1 x 120 mins and 8 x 60 mins F
Winner of four awards at the 1990 BAFTA ceremonies. David Suchet is now established as the definitive Hercule Poirot and will reappear both in a new series and in a 'special' linked to the Agatha Christie centenary

Forever Green
Production Company:

Picture Partnership Production
Executive Producer: Nick Elliott
Director: David Giles
6 x 60 mins F
Ratings-topping drama starring John Alderton and Pauline Collins as a city couple who move to the country. New series planned for 1991

Hale & Pace
Executive Producer:
Marcus Plantin
Producer: Alan Nixon
Director: David G Hillier
7 x 30 mins V
Sketch series starring Gareth Hale and Norman Pace, television's anarchic comedy duo who won the Golden Rose of Montreux

The Piglet Files
Executive Producer:
Marcus Plantin
Producer/Director: Robin Carr
14 x 30 mins V
New vehicle for comedy actor Nicholas Lyndhurst, poking fun at the world of espionage. He plays an electronics engineer who becomes involved in MI5

The South Bank Show
Producer: Melvyn Bragg
Executive Producer:
Nigel Wattis
1 x 120 mins, 1 x 105 mins, 22 x 60 mins, 1 x 40 mins F & V
ITV's flagship arts strand, covering subjects as diverse as Peter Brook and Paul Hindemith, Dustin Hoffman and Robert Altman, George Michael and August Wilson, John Updike and Willard White

The Walden Interview
Executive Producer:
David Cox
Editor: John Wakefield
10 x 60 mins live
Brian Walden's series of major one-to-one interviews with leading political figures, expanded to 25 annually from Autumn 1990

Other programmes include:
**Aspel & Company
Blind Date
Brave New Wilderness
Brian Conley – This Way Up**

**Come Home Charlie and Face Them
The Dame Edna Experience
Frederick Forsyth presents
London's Burning
The London Programme
A Perfect Hero
Stolen
Wish Me Luck**

S4C

S4C
Sophia Close
Cardiff CF1 9XY
Tel: 0222 43421
Chairman: John Howard Davies CBE DL
Chief Executive: Geraint Stanley Jones
Programme Controller: Euryn Ogwen Williams
Controller of Planning and Marketing:
Christopher Grace

Chwedl Nadolig Richard Burton
Production company:
Teliesyn
Producer: Richard Meyrick
Director: Alan Clayton
Scriptwriter: Michael Povey, from a short story by Richard Burton
Cast: Alun Horan, Catherine Tregenna, Sue Jones Davies, Dafydd Hywel
1 x 60 mins
Mainly autobiographical recollections of a childhood Christmas in a South Wales valley during the Depression

Hapus Dyrfa
Production company:
Matinee
Producers: Carys Hall Evans, Elin Hefin
Director: Huw Eirug
Scriptwriters: Caryl Parry Jones, Tony Llewellyn
Cast: Caryl Parry Jones, Dewi Morris, Arwel Davies, Aled Pugh, Claire Williams
8 x 30 mins
Situation comedy centred on a rural vet and his lively young family

Mwy Na Phafur Newydd
Production company:
Lluniau Lliw
Producer: Peter Edwards

Directors: Peter Edwards, Emlyn Williams, Hugh Thomas
Scriptwriters: Menna Cravos, Sion Eirian, Geraint Lewis, Gareth Miles, Gwenlyn Parry, Ed Thomas, Jeff Thomas
Cast: Bryn Fon, William Thomas, Nicola Beddoe, Richard Lynch
12 x 45 mins
Ambitious drama series centred on the offices of an imaginary West Wales weekly paper and set during the early 60s

Tydi Bywyd Yn Boen
Production Company:
Ffilmiau Eryri
Producer: Norman Williams
Director: Gwennan Sage
Scriptwriter: Gwenno Hywyn
Cast: Mirain Llwyd Owen, Gwen Ellis, Dafydd Aeron, Steven Owen
6 x 30 mins
Comedy drama about the growing pains of a teenage girl

Other programmes include:
**Dihirod Dyfed
Dressed to Thrill
Grym yn Eu Dwylo
The Little Engine That Could
Y Llyffant
Princess and the Goblins**

SCOTTISH TELEVISION
Scottish Television

Cowcaddens
Glasgow G2 3PR
Tel: 041 332 9999
Fax: 041 332 6982
114 St Martin's Lane
London WC2N 4AZ
Tel: 071 836 1500
Fax: 071 528 9390
The Gateway
Edinburgh EH7 4AH
Tel: 031 557 4554
Fax: 031 557 4554 x 239
Chairman: Sir Campbell Fraser LLD DUniv
Deputy Chairman:
William Brown CBE
Managing Director: Gus Macdonald
Director of Programmes:
Alistair Moffat

Head of Programmes –
Scotland: David Scott
Controller of Drama:
Robert Love
Controller of
Entertainment:
Sandy Ross

The Disney Club
Executive Producer:
Sandy Ross
Sunday morning
children's entertainment

NB
Executive Producer:
Alistair Moffat
Weekly Scottish arts
programme

Rescue
Producer: Paul Berriff
Network documentary
series on the RAF Air Sea
Rescue services

Scotsport
Executive Producer:
David Scott
60 mins
Weekly sports magazine

Taggart
Executive Producer:
Robert Love
Glasgow detective series

Take the High Road
Producer: Brian Mahoney
Drama serial set on Loch
Lomond

Other programmes
include:
**The Base Line
Glen Michael's
Cavalcade
Scotland's War
Scotland Today
Scotsport Extra Time
Scottish Action
Scottish Frontiers on
Medicine
Scottish Questions
Scottish Women
Selling Scotland
Wheel of Fortune
Win, Lose or Draw**

**TSW – Television
South West**
Derry's Cross
Plymouth
Devon PL1 2SP
Tel: 0752 663322
Fax: 0752 671970
Chairman: Sir Brian
Bailey OBE

Managing Director:
Harry Turner
Controller of
Programmes: Paul
Stewart Laing
Head of News: Jon
Williams
Head of Current Affairs:
Tom Keene
Head of Education and
Religion: Tom Goodison
Head of Documentaries:
Frank Wintle
Head of Programme
Planning: Elizabeth
Mahoney

**The TSW Documentary
'A Grin of Bitterness'**
A documentary unlocking
the secret behind Thomas
Hardy's marital
relationships

**The Man Who Went
Mad On Paper**
This programme
counterpoints the hilarity
of the work that won
cartoonist H M Bateman
fame with the sombre
obsessions which
destroyed his marriage
and turned him into a
dour recluse

Mitchin'
An episode for the
Dramarama series on
Children's ITV about two
boys from opposite ends of
the social ladder who
cause chaos when they
take a forbidden day off
school because of family
problems

Sonia's Report
Producer: Frank Wintle
Director: Chris Watson
Scriptwriter: Frank
Wintle
Camera: Mike Ford
Editor: Jim de Wan
1 hour
Ruth Werner, the spy who
successfully passed Klaus
Fuchs' nuclear secrets to
Moscow from 1940s
Britain, revealed her
amazing story to the West
for the first time in this
remarkable documentary

Sounds Like Music
Bobby Crush returns to
the small screen to
compere a musical quiz
testing knowledge of film
and musicals

**Stranger in a Strange
Land**
Production company:
Cheriton Enterprises

Producer: John Pett
Executive Producer:
Frank Wintle
Director: John Pett
Scriptwriter: Vicky Pett
Camera: Mike Ford
Editor: David Taylor
1 hour
About Karen Gershon,
a Jewish daughter robbed
of her parents by Riga
concentration camp – a
mother who lost the
confidence to fully love
even her own children –
a grandmother whose
scattered grandchildren
lack even a common
language

TV-am
Breakfast Television
Centre
Hawley Crescent
London NW1 8EF
Tel: 071 267 4300
Fax: 071 267 4332
Chairman: Ian Irvine
Managing Director: Bruce
Gyngell
Director of Programmes:
Bill Ludford
Director of Regions and
Training: Dave
Davidovitz
Director of Sales: Tony
Vickers
Director of Finance:
Stratis Zographos
Controller, News and
Current Affairs: Jeff
Berliner

**Good Morning Britain/
After Nine**
Presenters: Mike Morris,
Lorraine Kelly, Kathy
Tayler, Lisa Aziz, Lizzie
Webb, Geoff Clark,
Ulrika Jonsson, Maya
Even, Anne Diamond,
David Frost
News, current affairs,
weather, sport and
features on a wide range
of topics

TVS
Television Centre
Vinters Park
Maidstone
Kent ME14 5NZ
Tel: 0622 691111
Television Centre
Southampton SO9 5HZ
Tel: 0703 634211
60 Buckingham Gate

London SW1 6PD
Tel: 071 828 9898
Chairman: Lord Boston of
Faversham
Chief Executive: James
Gatward
Director of Programmes:
Alan Boyd
Deputy Director of
Programmes: Clive Jones
Controller of Factual
Programmes: Peter
Williams
Controller of Drama:
Graham Benson
Controller of Children's
Programmes: Nigel
Pickard
Controller of
Entertainment: Gill
Stribling-Wright
Head of Sport: Gary
Lovejoy
Head of News: David
Morris Jones

**The Castle of
Adventure**
Production Company:
TVS Films
Executive Producer:
Nigel J Pickard
Producer: Edward Francis
Co-producer: John Price
Director: Terry Marcel
Scriptwriter: Lionel
Augustus, Edward
Francis
Camera: Ken Brinsley
Editors: Mike Hunt,
Belinda Cottrell
Cast: Isobel Black, Brian
Blessed, Susan George,
Gareth Hunt, Corrinne
Ransom
8 x 30 mins F
Enid Blyton's famous
action story about five
children, a cockatoo and a
fox cub is brought up to
date with an all-star cast.
Four children on holiday
team up with a gypsy girl
only to stumble on a web
of spies hiding in the
ruins of a mysterious
castle

Catchphrase
Producer: Graham C
Williams
Director: Liddy Oldroyd
Scriptwriters: Jimmy
Nairn, Colin Edmunds
Camera: David Hutton
Editors: Simon Cruise,
Doug Collopy
Host: Roy Walker
22 x 30 mins V
Roy Walker hosts this
hi-tech game show where
contestants have to solve
animated word puzzles as
they appear on a giant
computer screen before

them. An exotic holiday of a lifetime awaits the lucky contestant

Perfect Scoundrels
Producer: Tim Aspinall
Director: Jan Toynton, Barry Davis
Scriptwriter: Ray Connolly (5 episodes), Tim Aspinall
Camera: Michael Smith
Editors: Nick McPhee, Michael Hunt
Cast: Peter Bowles, Bryan Murray (with special guest appearances by) Sir Michael Hordern, Oliver Tobias, Lulu, Brian Cox
6 x 1 hour F
Peter Bowles and Bryan Murray are con men Guy Buchanan and Harry Cassidy. They love the good things in life and have plenty of ideas on how to get their hands on other people's money. They'll bend the law, tell lies and mislead people. When it comes to charm and persuasion, there's no one better than these

Posh Frocks and New Trousers
Production Company: The Barrass Company
Producer: Vicky Barrass
Presenters: Sarah Greene, Annabel Giles
10 x 30 mins V
A programme for anyone who has ever got up in the morning and wondered what to wear. The second series of the magazine show helps viewers sort out the latest looks and how to wear – or avoid them

The Ruth Rendell Mysteries
Producer: Neil Zeiger
Director: Sandy Johnson
Scriptwriter: Matthew Jacobs
Camera: Mike Smith
Editor: Chris Wentzell
Cast: George Baker, Christopher Ravenscroft, Louie Ramsay
3 x 1 hour F
A new series of Rendell Mysteries for 1990. They are: Some Lie and Some Die, Best Man to Die, An Unkindness of Ravens, A Rendell Mystery Movie

The War Within
Producer/Director: Graham Hurley
Camera: John Mills, Ray Brislin

Editor: Jim Hubbard
Presenter: Dr Richard Holmes
1 x 1 hour V
A one-hour documentary about the relationship between Field Marshal Montgomery and General Eisenhower during the period after D-Day in June 1944, to the end of the war in May 1945. The programme examines the tensions between the two men in particular, and the American and British armies in general

Other programmes include:
Art of the Western World
Davro
Facing South
The Human Factor
It's a Dog's Life
Moneywise
Mr Majeika
Rules of Engagement
The Storyteller
TV Weekly
Tell the Truth

Thames Television
Thames Television House
306-316 Euston Road
London NW1 3BB
Tel: 071 387 9494
149 Tottenham Court Road
London W1P 9LL
Tel: 071 387 9494
Teddington Lock
Teddington
Middlesex TW11 9NT
Tel: 081 977 3252
Mobile Division
Twickenham Road
Hanworth
Middlesex
Tel: 081 898 0011
Regional Sales
Norfolk House
Smallbrook Queensway
Birmingham B5 4LJ
Tel: 021 643 9151
Chairman: Sir Ian Trethowan
Deputy Chairmen: John Davey, Mrs Mary Baker, Timothy Gold Blyth, Lord Brabourne
Chief Executive: Richard

Dunn
Director of Finance: Derek Hunt
Company Secretary & Director of Personnel: Ben Marr
Director of Sales & Marketing: Jonathan Shier
Director of Production: Ewart Needham
Directors of Programmes: David Elstein, Colin Wills, Michael Metcalf, Harold Mourgue
Press and Publicity Director: Roy Addison
Controller of Network Factual Programmes: Roger Bolton
Controller of Sport and Outside Broadcasts: Bob Burrows
Controller of Programme Administration: James Corsan
Controller of Light Entertainment: John Howard Davies
Co-ordinator of Independent Productions: Roy English
Head of Variety: John Fisher
Executive Producer: James Gilbert
Controller, Children's & Education Department: Allan Horrox
Head of Purchased Programmes: Pat Mahoney
Controller, Sales & Marketing: David Mansfield
Head of Music & Arts: Ian Martin
Head of Features: Mary McAnally
Deputy Director of Programmes: Barrie Sales
Director of Drama: Lloyd Shirley

The BFG
Production company: Cosgrove Hall Productions
Producers: Mark Hall, Brian Cosgrove
Director: Brian Cosgrove
Scriptwriter: John Hambley
Editor: Nigel Rutter
Voice-over: David Jason, Amanda Root, Angela Thorne
1 x 90 mins F
An animated version of Roald Dahl's best-seller, the BFG tells the tale of little Sophie who is snatched from her orphanage bed one night by an awesome giant. It is

the start of thrilling, funny and scary adventures with the quirky old Big Friendly Giant, who blows dreams to sleeping children

Capital City
Production company: Euston Films
Producer: Irving Teitelbaum
Directors: Mike Vardy, Diarmuid Lawrence, Clive Fleury
Scriptwriter: Andrew Maclear
Camera: Peter Bartlett, Simon Kossoff
Editor: Roger Wilson, Brian Freemantle
Cast: William Armstrong, Emily Bolton, John Bowe, Denys Hawthorne, Douglas Hodge, Jason Isaacs, Joanna Kanska, Trevyn McDowell, Anna Nygh
10 x 1 hour F
A new series which follows the loves and lives of eight high-flying dealers hired by Shane Longman, a merchant bank, for their particular blend of style, genius and energy; Capital City follows the frenetic atmosphere of the dealing room, but above all, the people themselves and their daily lives

French Fields
Producer: James Gilbert
Director: Mark Stuart
Scriptwriter: John Chapman, Ian Davidson
Cast: Anton Rodgers, Julia McKenzie
6 x 25 mins V
A second series continuing Hester and William's adaptation to their new way of life in France

Lorna Doone
Production company: Thames Television/ Working Title
Producers: Alan Horrox, Antony Root
Director: Andrew Grieve
Scriptwriter: Matthew Jacobs
Cast: Sean Bean, Clive Owen, Polly Walker, Billie Whitelaw
100 mins F
Based on RD Blackmore's novel, this vivid production tells the story of John Ridd, a young West Country yeoman during the lawless times

of King Charles II. Ridd's father has been killed by the aristocratic and murderous Doones. John's search for vengeance is complicated by his love for Lorna, a daughter of the Doone clan. Their passionate love for one another drives the story towards a thrilling and romantic climax

Stalin
Executive producer: Phillip Whitehead
Producers: Jonathan Lewis, Tony Cash
Directors: Jonathan Lewis, Tony Lewis
Research: Adrian Wood, Raye Farr
Picture editor: Alan Ritchie
Voice-over: Ian Holm
3 x 1 hour F & V
A three part documentary series, featuring previously unseen archive material and unique interviews, charting Joseph Stalin's route from impoverished childhood to undisputed leadership of a massive empire. A definitive study of Stalin's impact on his country and on the world

Van der Valk
Production company: Elmgate Productions
Producer: Chris Burt
Director: Anthony Simmons
Scriptwriter: Jonathan Hales
Script Executive: Kenneth Ware
Director of Photography: Colin Munn
Editor: Ralph Sheldon
Cast: Tom Bell, Amanda Burton, Judy Cornwell, Donald Churchill, Meg Davies, Barry Foster, Ronald Hines, Richard Huw, Philip Locke
4 x 2 hours F
A return of the highly-acclaimed detective series based on the character created by Nicholas Freeling. Shot in and around Amsterdam

Tyne Tees Television
Television Centre
City Road

Newcastle upon Tyne
NE1 2AL
Tel: 091 261 0181
Fax: 091 261 2302
Chairman: Sir Ralph Carr-Ellison TD
Deputy Chairman: R H Dickinson
Managing Director: David Reay
Director of Programmes: Geraint Davies
Controller Drama, Arts & Entertainment: Michael Chaplin
Controller, Factual Programmes: Jim Manson
Controller of Public Affairs: Peter Moth
Head of Programme Organisation: Paul Black
Head of Education: Sheila Browne

And a Nightingale Sang
Production company: Portman Entertainment/Tyne Tees
Producer: Philip Hinchcliffe
Director: Robert Knights
Scriptwriter: Jack Rosenthal
Camera: Dave Dixon
Editor: Chris Wimble
Cast: Pippa Hinchley, Phyllis Logan, Joan Plowright, Stephen Tompkinson, Tom Watt, John Woodvine, Des Young
1 x 100 mins F
Adapted from C P Taylor's drama of wartime romance. The story of two sisters – Helen who is resigned to being left on the shelf and Joyce who has a pair of nylons from every Yank in town

Born Lucky
Producer: Liddy Oldroyd
Directors: Jim Brown, Mike Esthop
Camera: Mike Parker
Editor: Kevin Tait
Presenter: Jeremy Beadle
10 x 30 mins V
The only game show to go on the road with the game played on a huge 19ft high board. Six contestants are plucked from obscurity to find out if they are 'Born Lucky' and the winner can walk off with £500

The Fifteen Streets
Production company: World Wide International/Tyne Tees

Producer: Ray Marshall
Director: David Wheatley
Scriptwriter: Rob Bettinson
Camera: Dave Dixon
Editor: Martin Walsh
Cast: Ian Bannen, Sean Bean, Clare Holman, Jane Horrocks, Owen Teale, Billie Whitelaw, Frank Windsor
1 x 110 mins F
Adapted from Catherine Cookson's best selling novel, the powerful and moving drama of one man's battle for survival against the harsh and turbulent background of poverty and class distinction on Tyneside at the turn of the century

Kappatoo
Production company: Tyne Tees, World Wide International Television
Producer: Ray Marshall
Director: Tony Kysh
Scriptwriter: Ben Stead
Camera: Dave Dixon, Dave Bowen, Brian Maddison, Chris Bruce, Alistair McKenzie
Editor: Peter Telford
Cast: John Abbott, Gillian Eaton, Filipe Izquierdo, Simon Nash, Andrew O'Connor, Denise Outen
7 x 25 mins F & V
An off-beat comedy science fiction series in which Kappatoo, a street-wise teenager from the 23rd century does a time-swap with hi 20th century double with hilarious results for both as they struggle to adapt to their strange and bewildering new lifestyles

McNally
Producer: Trevor Hearing
Associate Producer: Ed Skelding
Research: Sue Kennett
Presenter: Michael McNally
7 x 30 mins V
Off-beat and frequently hilarious documentary series in which actor Michael McNally as special investigator extraordinary unveils his many and varied talents as the streetwise Geordie boy getting to grips with the world around him

Tell Them in Gdansk
Producer: Trevor Hearing
Director: Tom Pickard
1 x 60 mins V

Focuses on the controversial chain of events following the close of Sunderland shipyards – and the fight to re-open them. The documentary uses the Flying Pickets' music and Mike Elliott's humour – entertaining the redundant workforce at a party to illustrate the poignant imagery

Other programmes include:
The Back Page
Celebration '89
Chain Letters
Commercial Break
Cross Wits
55 North
Northern Edge
Northern Life
On the Edge
Point of Order
Up Country
Women in Tropical Places

Ulster Television
Havelock House
Ormeau Road
Belfast BT7 1EB
Tel: 0232 328122
Fax: 0232 246695
6 York Street
London W1H 1FA
Tel: 071 485 5211
Chairman: R B Henderson CBE
Managing Director: J D Smyth
Assistant Managing Director: J A Creagh
General Manager: J McCann
Controller of Programmes: M Smyth
Commissioning Editor (Documentaries, Music): A Crockart
Commissioning Editor (News and Current Affairs): M Beattie

All God's Children
Producer: John Anderson
A musical odyssey with the African Children's Choir in Ireland, Germany, America and back to the realities of their homes in Uganda

A Grief Observed
Producer: Michael Beattie
Award-winning documentary about a young mother who is told

the baby she is carrying will be stillborn or die quickly because of a brain abnormality

Kelly
Producer: David Donaghy
Director: Will Armstrong
36 x 90 mins
A music and chat show hosted by Gerry Kelly. The series features top names and faces from today and yesterday in sport, entertainment and music

No Poor Parish
Producer: Ruth Johnston
The inhabitants of towns across Ulster tell their own story of how their community has evolved over their lifetime

Opera House Shows
A series of shows featuring top groups and singers to mark Ulster Televisions's 30th anniversary providing the 'best view' for Northern Ireland

A Tale of Two Visits
Producer: David Donaghy
A party of 25 Irish musicians take Estonia by storm – and the Russians decide they will spread some of their own glasnost on a return trip

YORKSHIRE TELEVISION

Yorkshire Television
The Television Centre
Leeds LS3 1JS
Tel: 0532 438283
Fax: 0532 445107
Television House
32 Bedford Row
London WC1R 4HE
Tel: 071 242 1666
Fax: 071 405 8062
Chairman: Sir Derek Palmar
Managing Director: Clive Leach
Director of Programmes: John Fairley
Controller of Drama: Keith Richardson
Controller of Entertainment: Vernon Lawrence
Head of Documentaries and Current Affairs: Grant McKee
Head of Science and Features:

Duncan Dallas
Head of Education, Children's Programmes and Religion: Chris Jelley
Head of Local Programme: Graham Ironside
Head of Sport: Robert Charles
Controller Corporate Affairs: Geoff Brownlee

The Darling Buds of May
Executive producers: Vernon Lawrence, Richard Bates, Philip Burley
Producers: Robert Banks Stewart, Richard Bates
Adapted by: Bab Larbey, Robert Banks Stewart
Director: Rodney Bennett, Robert Tronson, David Giles
Director of Photography: Peter Jackson
Editor: Robin McDonnell
Cast: David Jason, Pam Ferris, Philip Franks, Catherine Zeta Jones
6 x 1 hour
The Larkins, created by H E Bates, are one big happy loving family. Ma and Pop and their six children radiate happiness and have hardly a care in the world. The world is 'perfick', even with the arrival of the Inland Revenue!

First Tuesday
Executive Producer: Grant McKee
Producers: Various, including Jill Turton, Mark Halliley, Jill Nichols
Directors: Various, including Chris Bryer, Ian McFarlane, Kevin Sim
Camera: Mike Shrimpton, Alan Wilson
Editors: Terry Warwick, Clive Trist, Barry Spink, David Aspinall
12 x 1 hour (monthly)
Yorkshire's award winning documentary showcase which brings home and international issues to the screen. Recipient recently of an international Emmy, a BAFTA award and the Grand Award at the International Film and TV Festival of New York for its film 'Four Hours in Mai Lai'

Jimmy's
Executive Producer:

Grant McKee
Producer/Director: Irene Cockcroft
Camera: Alan Wilson
Editors: Steve Fairholme, Tim Dawson, Don MacMillan
14 x 30 mins
Set in Britain's largest general hospital, tells the everyday stories of joy and anguish, pain and sorrow of the staff and patients, and behind the scenes workers at St James's University Hospital in Leeds

Shoot to Kill
Production company: Zenith Productions
Executive producer: Keith Richardson
Producer: Nigel Stafford-Clark
Scriptwriter: Michael Eaton
Director: Peter Kosminsky
Director of Photography: Allan Pyrah
Editor: David Aspinall
Cast: Jack Shepherd, David Calder, T P McKenna, George Shane
1 x 4 hours
The explosive story of six killings in Northern Ireland which triggered a chain of events culminating in John Stalker's removal from the inquiry which followed

Stay Lucky
Executive Producer: David Reynolds
Producer: Andrew Benson
Directors: David Reynolds, John Glenister, Graeme Harper
Director of Photography: Peter Jackson, Allan Pyrah
Writers: Geoff McQueen, Michael Aitkens, Steven Moffatt
Editors: Clive Trist, David Aspinall, David Stocks
Cast: Dennis Waterman, Jan Francis, Niall Toibin, Emma Wray
7 x 1 hour
Thomas Gynn (Dennis Waterman), the refugee Cockney up North, and Sally Hardcastle (Jan Francis), the tough young businesswoman with a soft centre, get together again for further hair-raising hilarious adventures

The World of Eddie Weary
Production company: Fingertip Film Productions
Executive Producer: Keith Richardson
Producer: Terry Mellis, Steve Lanning
Scriptwriter: Roy Clarke
Director: Alan Grint
Director of Photography: Allan Pyrah
Editor: Mike Eustace
Cast: Ray Brooks, Celia Imrie
1 x 2 hours
When top actor Alex Conway discovers his TV creation, private eye Eddie Weary, is getting more mail than himself - mainly from people asking for help – he dons Eddie's persona and becomes involved in a fan's personal problems

Other programmes include:
Emmerdale
Fiddlers Three
Haggard
Hurray for Today
The James Whale Radio Show
The New Statesman
The Raggy Dolls
Round the Bend
Science Fiction
Through the Keyhole

BBC TELEVISION

British Broadcasting Corporation
Television Centre
Wood Lane
London W12 7RJ
Tel: 081 743 8000
Broadcasting House
Portland Place
London W1A 1AA
Tel: 071 580 4468
Chairman: Marmaduke Hussey
Director-General: Michael Checkland
Deputy Director-General: John Birt
Managing Director Network Television and Chairman BBC Enterprises: Paul Fox CBE
Managing Director, Regional Broadcasting: Ronald Neil

Assistant Managing Director, Network Television: Will Wyatt
Controller of BBC1: Jonathan Powell
Controller of BBC2: Alan Yentob

BBC TV Children's Programmes

Television Centre
Wood Lane
London W12 7RJ
Head: Anna Home
Tel: 081 743 8000

Blue Peter

Programme editor: Lewis Bronze
Presenters: Yvette Fielding, John Leslie, Diane-Louise Jordan
Continuing x 25 mins F and live V
Blue Peter began in October 1958. The programme is named after the blue and white flag which is raised within 24 hours of a ship leaving harbour: the idea is that the programme is like a ship setting out on a voyage, having new adventures and discovering new things

Going Live!

Programme editor: Chris Bellinger
Cast: Sarah Greene, Phillip Schofield
Continuing x 3 hrs F and live V
A mixture of cartoons, live music, videos, competitions and the chance to speak to famous guests on the telephone

Grange Hill

Producer: Albert Barber
Script Editor: Leigh Jackson
Writers: Barry Purchese, David Angus, Margaret Simpson, Chris Ellis, Kay Trainor
20 x 25 mins V
Fictional characters face true-to-life situations at a large comprehensive school

Other programmes include:
Hart Beat
The Really Wild Show
Take Two

BBC Community Programme Unit

39 Wales Farm Road
North Acton
London W3 6XP
Tel: 081 743 8000
Editor: Tony Laryea
This Unit is responsible for programmes made by and with the general public, usually as a direct response to public request. A voice is given to those who feel that the media distorts or ignores their point of view, and so offers viewers new perspectives on issues of social concern they would not expect to find aired elswhere on television. Currently the Unit's output is presented under three main titles, *Open Space, Video Diaries* and *Inside Out*

Inside Out

A series of occasional documentaries consisting of a pair of films exploring two sides of an institution. Covered so far: Swansea jail and an infantry battalion

Open Space

Contributors make their own programme on their chosen subjects with production help from the Unit but keeping full editorial control, or in 'partnership' with the Unit if they prefer. Alternatively members of the public can simply suggest programme ideas

Video Diaries

A unique series of programmes giving people self-operated video cameras to record the unfolding events of their lives

BBC TV Continuing Education

Villiers House
The Broadway
London W5 2PA
Tel: 081 743 8000
Fax: 081 567 9356

The Big E

Series producer: Ron Bloomfield
Presenter: Chris Baines
6 x 10 mins, 6 x 25 mins
Examination of how each individual's actions affect the environment. The topics of food, leisure, water, waste, energy and transport are covered in two programmes, a 10-minute introduction followed by a 25-minute analysis of the topic

Hindi Urdu Bol Chaal

Producer: Jeremy Orlebar
Presenters: Sneh Gupta, Omar Salimi
10 × 25 mins
Conversational Hindi and Urdu for beginners introducing the language needed in everyday situations starting with greetings and progressing to colloquial conversation. Filmed on location in Bradford, Manchester, Birmingham, Glasgow and London, the series is BBC Education's first venture into the 'community languages' of the United Kingdom

It Doesn't Have to Hurt!

Producers: Peter Ramsden, Alan Russell
Presenter: June Whitfield
7 × 10 mins
How to get healthy by increasing everyday activity such as walking, climbing the stairs, gardening, dancing, DIY, rather than through strenuous exercise. There are strategies and advice on improving health through activity for all age groups from 14 year olds to octogenarians

Mosaic

Series producer: John Twitchin
6 x 30 mins
In its first year, BBC Education's 5 year initiative concerned with discrimination against 'visible' minority groups, what is needed to establish equal opportunities, and the cultural and attitudinal responses to Britain's cultural diversity, looked at discrimination and how it is being tackled in the areas of housing provision, immigration, education, mental health and industrial tribunals

Through the Looking Glass

Producers: Suzanne Davies, Robert Albury
6 x 30 mins
The social history of fashion from 1870 to the present day looking at street wear rather than haute couture, underwear as well as outerwear, and examining the influences of social and artistic movements and political events on the clothes men

and women have worn over the past 100 years

Who Cares?

Producer: Tony Matthews
Presenter: Jonathan Miller
6 x 30 mins
Ideas and information to help and encourage those who care for someone at home, aiming to reduce the isolation and stress of caring. Carers coping; what happens when they can no longer cope; the help available from health and social services, voluntary or self-help groups; and where help is inadequate or non-existent how things could be improved

Other programmes include:
Advice Shop
Bazaar
Business Matters
Clean Slate
Electric Avenue
Europeans
Facing up to AIDS
Quit and Win
See Hear! and **Sign Extra**
The Software Show
Stepping up and **Step Up to Wordpower**
When in Italy

BBC TV Documentary Features

Kensington House
Richmond Way
London W14 0AX
Tel: 081 895 6611
Head: Colin Cameron

40 Minutes

Series Editor: Caroline Pick
26 × 40 mins F
A series of documentary films about the way we live now

Holiday 90

Series Producer: Patricia Houlihan
Presenters: Anne Gregg, Kathy Tayler, Eamonn Holmes

Inside Story

Executive producer: Paul Hamann

Saturday Night Clive

Producer: Beatrice Ballard
Executive producer: Richard Drewett
Presenter: Clive James
Clive James attempts to

make some sense of the new and de-regulated universe of ever expanding media

Taking Liberties
Series producer: Elizabeth Clough
Presenter: David Jessel

BBC TV Drama Films
Television Centre
Wood Lane
London W12 7RJ
Tel: 081 743 8000
Head of Drama Group, BBC Television: Mark Shivas

Screen One
Executive Producer, BBC1 Films: Richard Broke
An annual series of popular feature-length films for television on BBC1. Highlights from the 1989 autumn season include *The Accountant, She's Been Away, One Way Out* and *First and Last*

Screen Two
Executive Producer, BBC2 Films: Mark Shivas
BBC Television's original feature-length film strand. Highlights of the 1990 season include *Kremlin Farewell, Close Relations, Circles of Deceit, Impossible Spy, Old Flames, Children Crossing, Drowning in the Shallow End*

BBC TV Light Entertainment Comedy Programmes
Television Centre
Wood Lane
London W12 7RJ
Tel: 081 743 8000
Head: Robin Nash

'Allo 'Allo
Producer: David Croft
Scriptwriters: David Croft, Jeremy Lloyd
Cast: Gorden Kaye, Carmen Silver

Blackadder Goes Forth
Producer: John Lloyd
Director: Richard Boden
Scriptwriters: Richard Curtis, Ben Elton
Cast: Rowan Atkinson, Tony Robinson, Stephen Fry, Hugh Laurie

Bread
Producer/Director: Robin Nash
Scriptwriter: Carla Lane
Cast: Graham Bickley, Jean Boht, Nick Conway, Hilary Crowson, Ronald Forfar, Melanie Hill, Victor McGuire, Jonathan Morris, Bryan Murray, Eileen Pollock, Pamela Power, Kenneth Waller, Giles Watling

Brush Strokes
Producer/Director: John B Hobbs
Scriptwriters: John Esmonde, Bob Larbey
Cast: Karl Howman, Elizabeth Counsell

Last of the Summer Wine
Producer/Director: Alan Bell
Scriptwriter: Roy Clarke
Cast: Bill Owen, Peter Sallis, Michael Aldridge

Only Fools and Horses
Producer: Gareth Gwenlan
Director: Tony Dow
Scriptwriter: John Sullivan
Cast: David Jason, Nicholas Lyndhurst, Buster Merryfield

BBC TV Light Entertainment Variety Programmes
Television Centre
Wood Lane
London W12 7RJ
Tel: 081 743 8000
Head: Jim Moir

Bob Says Opportunity Knocks
Producer: Stewart Morris
Programme Associate: Gary Chambers
Musical Director: John Coleman
Presenter: Les Dawson
13 x 50 mins

French and Saunders
Producer: Jon Plowman
Scriptwriters: Dawn French, Jennifer Saunders
Cast: Jennifer Saunders, Dawn French, with Raw Sex
7 x 30 mins

The Paul Daniels Magic Show
Producer/director: Geoff Miles
Cast: Paul Daniels and

guests
9 x 45 mins
Magician Paul Daniels and speciality act guests

The Rory Bremner Show
Script Editors: Barry Cryer, John Langdon
Cast: Rory Bremner, Steve Nallon, John Bird, Enn Reitel
6 x 30 mins

The Russ Abbot Show
Producer/Director: John Bishop
Script Associate: Barry Cryer, Peter Vincent
Cast: Russ Abbott, Les Dennis, Bella Emberg, Sherrie Hewson, Tom Bright, Lisa Maxwell
12 x 30 mins
Zany comedy and music show

Takeover Bid
Producer/Director: David Taylor
Programme Associates: Colin Edmonds, Wally Malston
Cryptic Questions: Norman Beedle
Host: Bruce Forsyth with Claire Sutton
14 x 30 mins
A unique game show in which the contestants begin with all the prizes and try to keep them

Wogan
Executive Producer: Peter Estall
Producers: Jane O'Brien, Graham Owens
Assistant Producers: Natalie Elsey, Tom Webber
3 x 30/45 mins per week
Talk show hosted by Terry Wogan

BBC TV Music and Arts
Kensington House
Richmond Way
London W14 0AX
Tel: 081 743 1272
Head: Leslie Megahey

Arena
Editors: Anthony Wall, Nigel Finch

Homelands
Executive Producer: Diana Lashmore

The Late Show
Editor: Roly Keating

Music on Two
Executive Producer: Dennis Marks

Omnibus
Editor: Andrew Snell

BBC TV News and Current Affairs
Television Centre
Wood Lane
London W12 7RJ
Tel: 081 743 8000
Fax: 081 740 7766
Editor, News and Current Affairs, Television: Tony Hall
Deputy editor, News and Current Affairs, Television: Samir Shah
Main news programmes: BBC1 1.00pm, 6.00pm, 9.00pm; hourly summaries
Breakfast News 6.30am – 9.00am
BBC2 10.30pm
Newsnight (Saturdays)

Other programmes include:
The Money Programme
On The Record
Panorama
Public Eye
Question Time
Westminster This Week

BBC TV Programme Acquisition
Centre House
56 Wood Lane
London W12 7RJ
Tel: 081 743 8000
General Manager: Alan Howden
Purchased Programmes Head: June Morrow
Selects and presents BBC TV's output of feature films and series on both channels

Business Unit
Business Manager: Felicity Irlam
Contact for commissioned material and acquisition of completed programmes, film material and sequences for all other programme departments

BBC TV Religious Programmes
Television Centre
Wood Lane
London W12 7RJ
Tel: 081 743 8000
Head: Stephen Whittle

Everyman
Editor: Jane Drabble
26 x 40 mins F
Reflective religious documentary series

Heart of the Matter
Producer: Olga Edridge
18 x 35 mins F
Immediate and topical
religious documentary
series

Songs of Praise
Editor: Roger Hutchings
39 x 35 mins V
Community hymn-
singing

This is the Day
Editor: Helen Alexander
34 x 30 mins live and V
Morning worship from a
viewer's home, with the
viewing audience itself
making up the
congregation

When I Get to Heaven
Editor: Helen Alexander
6 x 30 mins V
Interviews on ultimate
belief

Other programmes
include:
Articles of Faith
Five to Eleven
Home on Sunday
Praise Be!

BBC TV Schools Broadcasting
Villiers House
The Broadway
London W5 2PA
Tel: 081 743 8000
Head: Alan Rogers

Language File
Producer/Director/Writer:
Paul Ashton
Editors: Paul Willey,
Brenda Phillips
10 x 30 mins V
Accent, dialect, talking
posh, talking common,
how humans learn to
speak, language
repertoire, register, taboo
language, English as a
world language, scripted
speech and the language
of feelings – for 14-16
year olds

Look and Read: Through the Dragon's Eye
Producer/Director: Sue
Weeks
Scriptwriters:
Christopher and
Christine Russell
Camera: William
Dudman
Editor: Steve Knattress
Video Effects: Dave Jervis
Design: Kathy Atty,
Magie Carroll
Cast: Sean Barrett, David

Collings, Charles
Collingwood, Simon
Fenton, Marlaine Gordon,
Katie Hebb, Michael
Heath, Timothy Lynn,
Carolyn Pickles, Nicky
Stewart
10 x 20 mins V
A new fantasy adventure
story for the **Look and
Read** series told in 10
episodes. It features 3
school children and their
adventures in the race
against time to help fix
the exploded Veetacore
and save the land of
Pelamar

Scene: Sweet Seventeen
Producer/Director: Roger
Tonge
Scriptwriter: Grazyna
Monvid
Camera: Graham Veevers
Editor: Kate Evans
Cast: Emma Bolton,
Lyndon Davies, Jenny
Jay, Andrew Laycock,
Cherith Mellor, Anya
Phillips, Will Tacey
2 x 30 mins V
Bridget's father suddenly
returns for her 17th
birthday, after a year
away. Instead of sharing
her family's happiness,
she is edgy, rude and
angry. Only through her
friend does she reveal
that her father had been
abusing her sexually
since the age of 9 – her
younger sister's age now

Search Out Science
Producers: Lambros
Atteshlis, Neil Ryder
Director: Tina Fletcher
Presenters: Elin Rhys,
Carmen Pryce, Paul
Viragh
20 x 20 mins
A television series for
9–11 year olds reflecting
the National Curriculum,
designed for use with a
variety of teaching styles
whether science is taught
in isolation or part of a
cross-curricular scheme

Soviet Union
Producer/Director/Writer:
Bruce Jameson
Camera: Dave Swan,
Eugene Carr, Chris
Sadler
Editors: Luis Espana,
Rick Spurway
5 x 20 mins F,
transmitted on V
A five-part series, aimed
at GCSE students,
provides a unique

opportunity to hear
people from many
different regions of the
Soviet Union describing
their lives and
commentary on some of
the issues which affect
them. The films were shot
in Georgia, Uzbeckistan,
Siberia and Moscow

Techno
Producer: Robin Mudge
Assistant Producer:
Derek Butler
Editor: Adele Reuben
Presenters: Dilly
Bellingham, Mat Irvine
10 x 20 mins V
From London's Design
Museum to the industries
of Japan Techno, a lively
magazine series for 11-14
year olds, takes a new and
different look at the world
of design and technology

Other programmes
include:
English Time
Issues
Landmarks
Lernexpress
Lifeschool
Music Time
Questions
Science Challenge
Storytime
Watch
Who-Me?
Words and Pictures

BBC TV Science and Features
Kensington House
Richmond Way
London W14 0AX
Tel: 081 895 6611
Head: Graham Massey
Manager: Maggie
Bebbington

Antenna
BBC2
50 mins
Monthly science series
exploring the unexpected
in science, medicine and
technology

Horizon
BBC2
Editor: Jana Bennett
24 x 50 mins
Single subject
documentaries presenting
science to the general
public and analysing the
implications of new
discoveries

QED
Executive producer:
David Filkin
14 x 30 mins F

Documentary films, each
on a single subject. Topics
vary enormously, using a
very broad interpretation
of science

Tomorrow's World
BBC1
Executive producer:
Richard Reisz
Presenters: Judith Hann,
Peter Macann, Howard
Stableford, Kate
Bellingham
Continuing x 30 mins live
Studio-based programme
which includes filmed
items investigating and
demonstrating the latest
in science and technology

Your Life In Their Hands
BBC2
Executive producer:
David Paterson
5 x 40 mins
Series about medicine

BBC TV Serials
Television Centre
Wood Lane
London W12 7RJ
Tel: 081 743 8000
Head of Drama Group,
BBC Television: Mark
Shivas
Head of Serials: Michael
Wearing

Bloodrights
BBC2
Producer: Caroline
Oulton
Director: Lesley Manning
Scriptwriter: Mike
Phillips
Camera: Rex Maidment
Editor: Chris Swanton
Cast: Brian Bovell,
Struan Roger, Maggie
Steed
3 x 50 mins F
A gritty thriller set in
London which follows
Sammy Dean, a black
freelance reporter
struggling to make ends
meet. Then an old friend
who works for a
government minister
employs Sammy to find a
missing person

Children of the North
BBC2
Producer: Chris Parr
Director: David Drury
Scriptwriter: John Hale
from a trilogy of novels by
M S Power
Camera: Alec Curtis
Editor: Iain Farr
Cast: Paul Brooke, Tony
Doyle, Adrian Dunbar,

Michael Gough, Jonathan Hyde, John Kavanagh, Ian McElhinney, Patrick Malahide, Derrick O'Connor
4 x 60 mins F
The recruitment of an eccentric diplomat to run a Belfast betting shop which launders Provo funds triggers a fast-moving story of undercover activity, complex treacheries and unexpected alliances involving army, RUC and IRA personnel and their nearest and dearest

Die Kinder
BBC2
Producer: Michael Wearing
Director: Robert Walker
Scriptwriter: Paula Milne
Camera: Kevin Rowley
Editor: Ardan Fisher
Cast: Tina Engel, Frederick Forrest, Ulrich Pleitgen, Miranda Richardson, Hans Zischler
6 x 55 mins F
Set against the contemporary climate of fast-moving political change in both Germanies. The ex-wife of a West German is searching for her abducted children. When the British police show more interest in her husband's political past than in the disappearance of her children, she begins her own search

The Green Man
BBC1
Producer: David Snodin
Director: Elijah Moshinsky
Scriptwriter: Malcolm Bradbury from the novel by Kingsley Amis
Camera: John McGlashan
Editor: Masahiro Hirakubo
Cast: Sarah Berger, Albert Finney, Nicky Henson, Sir Michael Hordern, Josie Lawrence, Linda Marlowe
3 x 50 mins F
A sophisticated comedy based on the Kingsley Amis ghost story about an alcoholic restaurateur

Parnell and the Englishwoman
BBC2
Producer: Terry Coles

Director: John Bruce
Scriptwriter: Hugh Leonard
Camera: John Kenway
Editor: Christopher Rowlands
Cast: Francesca Annis, Trevor Eve, David Robb
4 x 54 mins F
In 1880 Charles Stewart Parnell became leader of the Irish Party and he met Katharine O'Shea, two events which were to change his life and career

Screenplay
BBC2
Executive Producer: George Faber
A mixture of plays on tape or film between 60' and 90', presenting a season of challenging and contemporary drama, risking innovation in form or content. Titles from the 1990 season include *Romania, Needle, Amongst Barbarians, Antonia and Jane: The Definitive Mid-life Report*

BBC TV Series
Television Centre
Wood Lane
London W12 7RJ
Tel: 081 743 8000
Head of Drama Group, BBC Television: Mark Shivas
Head of Series: Peter Cregeen

All Creatures Great and Small
Producer: Bill Sellars
Directors: Michael Brayshaw, Steve Goldie, Richard Martin
Scriptwriters: Johnny Byrne, Joan Salter, Michael Russell, Christopher Penfold, Rodger Davenport, Sam Snape
Cast: Peter Davison, Robert Hardy, Christopher Timothy
12 x 50 mins F & V
Based on the hugely popular James Herriot books, a Yorkshire veterinary practice in the 50s is brought wittily to life

Bergerac
Producer: George Gallaccio
Directors: Tony Dow, Michael Rolfe, Tristen de Vere Cole, Colm Villa, Ken Grieve

Scriptwriters: John Milne, John Brown, Graham Hurley, Christopher Russell, Douglas Watkinson, John Fletcher, Tony McNabb, Desmond Lowden
Cast: John Nettles
10 x 50 mins F
The popular series featuring Jersey detective Jim Bergerac with a clutch of action-packed mysteries in France and Jersey

Casualty
Producer: Peter Norris
Directors: Jim Hill, Andrew Morgan, Michael Morris, Alan Wareing, Michael Brayshaw
Scriptwriters: Rona Munro, Tony Etchell, Robin Mukherjee, Ben Aaronovitch, Jim Hill, Ian Briggs, Ginnie Hole
Cast: Brenda Fricker, Derek Thompson
13 x 50 mins V
Oscar winner Brenda Fricker leads the cast with Derek Thompson in this highly realistic and much-praised drama from the front-line of medicine

Lovejoy
Producer: Richard Everitt (BBC), Tony Charles (Witzend)
Directors: Bill Brayne, Baz Taylor, John Woods, Don Leaver
Scriptwriters: Dick Clement, Ian La Frenais, Geoff Lowe, Alan Clews, Roger Marshall, Terry Hodgkinson, Steve Coomes, Dave Robinson
Cast: Ian Mcshane
10 x 50 mins F
The infamous East Anglian antiques dealer returns for a second series with Ian McShane in the title role

Making Out
Producer: John Chapman
Scriptwriter: Debbie Horsfield
Cast: Tracie Bennett, Moya Brady, Margi Clarke, Rachel Davies, Melanie Kilburn, Shirley Stelfox
10 x 50 mins V
A sharp modern comedy set in a northern electronics factory with a group of women destined for trouble

Spender
Producer: Martin McKeand
Directors: Mary McMurray, Richard Standeven
Scriptwriters: Ian La Frenais, Jimmy Nail, John Harvey
Cast: Jimmy Nail
8 x 50 mins F
New series about a Geordie detective sent back from the Met. to take on undercover work in his native Tyneside

Other programmes include:
Bingo
Iphigenia at Aulis
Othello
Pentecost
Roughest Way (working title)
Sharpend

BBC TV Sport and Events
Kensington House
Richmond Way
London W14 0AX
Tel: 081 895 6611
Fax: 081 749 7886
Head: Jonathan Martin
Deputy Head: John Rowlinson
Assistant Head, Events: Tim Marshall

Football
Editor: Brian Barwick
Producer: John Shrewsbury
Director: Vivien Kent
Presenter: Desmond Lynam/Jimmy Hill

Grandstand
Editor: John Philips
Producer/director: Martin Hopkins
Presenter: Desmond Lynam

One Man and His Dog
Producer: Ian Smith
Presenter: Phil Drabble

Royal Tournament
Producer/director: Peter Hylton Cleaver

Sportsnight
Editor: Brian Barwick
Producer: Vivien Kent
Presenter: Steve Rider

VIDEO LABELS

These companies acquire the UK rights to all forms of audiovisual product and arrange for its distribution on videodisc or cassette at a retail level (see also under Distributors). Listed is a selection of titles released on each label

A & M Sound Pictures
136-144 New King's Road
London SW6 4LZ
Tel: 071 736 3311
Fax: 071 731 4606
Chris de Burgh: High on Emotion – Live from Dublin
Gun: Taking on the World
Joe Jackson: Stepping Out
This is Sam Brown

Albany Video Distribution
Battersea Studios
Television Centre
Thackeray Road
London SW8 3TW
Tel: 071 498 6811
Fax: 071 498 1494
Coffee Coloured Children
Framed Youth
Jean Genet is Dead
Looking for Langston
Ostia
The Passion of Remembrance
Perfect Image
Territories
Two in Twenty

BBC Video
Woodlands
80 Wood Lane
London W12 0TT
Tel: 081 576 2236
Fax: 081 743 0393
Distributed by CBS Distribution and Pickwick International
The Boys From Brazil - Official History of Brazilian World Cup Team
The Black Adder
Black Adder II: Parts 1 & 2
Black Adder III: Parts 1 & 2
Doctor Who: Various
The Lion, the Witch and the Wardrobe
Liverpool – Team of Decade
Play Better Golf
Supersense
Victoria Wood as Seen on TV
More Victoria Wood

Buena Vista Home Video
3 Centaurs Business Park
Grant Way
Off Syon Lane
Isleworth
Middx TW7 5QD
Tel: 081 569 8080
Distribute Walt Disney and Touchstone product
Cocktail
Dead Poets Society
Dumbo
Good Morning Vietnam
Robin Hood
Sleeping Beauty
Who Framed Roger Rabbit?

CBS/Fox Video UK
Unit 1
Perivale Industrial Park
Greenford
Middx UB6 7RU
Tel: 081 997 2552
Abyss
Aliens
Die Hard
Leviathan
Monty Python's Life of Brian
A Nightmare on Elm Street 1, 4, 5
9½ Weeks
Nuns on the Run
The Seven Year Itch

CIC Video
4th Floor
Glenthorne House
5-17 Hammersmith Grove
London W6 0ND
Tel: 081 846 9433
Fax: 081 741 9773
Back to the Future Parts I-III
ET
Indiana Jones and the Last Crusade
Sea of Love
Shirley Valentine
Star Trek

Castle Communications
15-16 Northfields
Prospect
Putney Bridge Road
London SW18 1PE
Tel: 081 877 0922
Fax: 081 871 0470
Major video distribution company in UK, Europe, and Australasia, with catalogue of programmes licensed from UK TV companies (Granada, Yorkshire, Central, LWT, Channel 4) and from national and international independents (TWI, Worldvision, NBC, King Features, Filmfair, NVC Arts, RAI, Hanna-Barbera). Sell-through labels specialising in feature films, children's programmes, sport, documentaries, comedy and rock, pop and classical music
An Audience with Victoria Wood
The Augusta Masters Golf Tournament 1990
Disappearing World
The Doors in Europe
Hale and Pace
Kenny Dalglish – Portrait of a Natural Footballer
Paddington Bear
Popeye
Rising Damp
Tugs

Castle Home Video
(trading as Castle Pictures)
A29 Barwell Business Park
Leatherhead Road
Chessington
Surrey KT9 2NY
Tel: 081 974 1021
Fax: 081 974 2674
Bill & Ted's Excellent Adventure
Cartouche
Fistfighter
Girl on a Motorcycle
A Handful of Dust

Magic
Night Porter
The Slipper and the Rose
True Blood
Witchfinder General

Channel 5 Video Distribution

3 Castle Row
Horticultural Place
London W4 4JQ
Tel: 081 994 9899
Fax: 081 994 9906
A joint venture between
Heron International and
Polygram International.
Video titles include
feature films, music
videos, special interest
and children's
programmes. New titles
available through retail/
sell-through outlets
*The Carpenters: Greatest
Hits*
Labyrinth
Noddy
The Prisoner
Tears for Fears
Thunderbirds

Chrysalis Records

12 Stratford Place
London W1N 9AF
Tel: 071 408 2355
Distributed by
Pickwick Video
*Billy Connolly: Bites Yer
Bum*
*Billy Connolly: Hand
Picked*
Billy Idol: More Vital Idol
Blondie: Best of
Dance Craze
*Housemartins: Now
That's What I Call Quite
Good*
Huey Lewis: Video Hits
Pat Benatar: Best Shots
The Proclaimers
*Spandau Ballet: Over
Britain*

Colstar Home Video

11 Wythburn Place
London W1H 5WL
Tel: 071 437 5725
Fax: 071 706 1704
Distributed through
Odyssey Video, Start
Records and others
*Daley Thompson's Body
Shop*
*In Search of Wildlife with
David Shepherd*
*Kenneth Clark's Romantic
versus Classic Art*
*The Life and Times of
Lord Mountbatten*
*The Man Who Loves
Giants*

*The Most Dangerous
Animal*
*The National Gallery – A
Private View*

Connoisseur Video

Glenbuck House
Glenbuck Road
Surbiton
Surrey KT6 6BT
Tel: 081 399 0022
*Confidential Report (aka
Mr Arkadin)*
Kings of the Road
Monsieur Hulot's Holiday
Playtime
Orphée
Wings of Desire

Walt Disney Co

See under Buena Vista
Home Video

Elephant Video

Tivoli Cinema
Station Street
Birmingham B5 4DY
Tel: 021 616 1021
Fax: 021 616 1019
Video distribution of
feature films

Entertainment in Video

27 Soho Square
London W1V 5FL
Tel: 071 439 1979
Fax: 071 734 2483
Arena
The Caine Mutiny
Cat Chaser
Kickboxer
Nightgame
1969
Patty Hearst
*The Return of the
Musketeers*
Slipstream
*The Wolves of Willoughby
Chase*

Guild Home Video

Crown House
2 Church Street
Walton-on-Thames
Surrey KT12 2QS
Tel: 081 546 3377
Fax: 081 546 4568
Cookie
DeepStar Six
Field of Dreams
Johnny Handsome
Last Exit to Brooklyn
Lock Up
Mac & Me
Mountains of the Moon
Next of Kin
Wilt

Hendring

8 Northfields Prospect
Putney Bridge Road

London SW18 1PE
Tel: 081 877 0922
Fax: 081 877 0416
Russian classics,
including the Eisenstein
Catalogue and the Gorky
Trilogy
The Sherlock Holmes
Collection
A Bigger Splash
Comic Book Confidential
*Dizzy Gillespie: A Night
in Havana*
Jazz at Ronnie's including
Nina Simone and Chet
Baker
Jazz on a Summer's Day
Marlene

Island Visual Arts

22 St Peter's Square
London W6 9NW
Tel: 081 741 1511
Fax: 081 748 0841
Distributed by PolyGram
Record Operations

Jettisoundz

28-30 The Square
St Annes-on-Sea
Lancashire FY8 1RF
Tel: 0253 712453
Fax: 0253 712362
Cud
Killdozer
The Man from Delmonte
Psychic TV
Ska Explosion
Throbbing Gristle
Kenneth Anger's *Magick
Lantern Cycle*
William Burroughs' *Thee
Films*
Derek Jarman's *Time
Zones*
Klaus Maeck's *Decoder*

Jubilee Film and Video

Egret Mill
162 Old Street
Ashton-under-Lyne
Manchester
Lancashire OL6 7ST
Tel: 061 330 9555

London Weekend Television

South Bank Television
Centre
London SE1 9LT
Tel: 071 620 1620
Agatha Christie's Poirot
*Frederick Forsyth
Presents . . .*
Jekyll and Hyde
London's Burning
*The Robbie Coltrane
Special*
Scoop
*Torvill and Dean in Fire
and Ice*

*21 Years of London
Football*
*Watch Out: It's the Best of
Beadle's About*
Distributed through The
Video Collection (qv)

MCEG Virgin Vision

Atlantic House
1 Rockley Road
London W14 0DL
Tel: 081 740 5500
Fax: 081 967 1360
Robocop
Roxy Music: Total Recall
Simple Minds: Verona
UB40: Labour of Love II
The Y Plan

MGM/UA

Hammer House
113-117 Wardour Street
London W1V 3TD
Tel: 071 439 9932
Fax: 071 287 3553
The Fabulous Baker Boys
First Power
A Fish Called Wanda
The Garbo Collection
*Tom and Jerry's 50th
Anniversary*

Media Releasing Distributors

27 Soho Square
London W1V 5FL
Tel: 071 437 2341
Fax: 071 734 2483
Day of the Dead
Eddie and the Cruisers
Kentucky Fried Movie
*Return of Captain
Invincible*
Distributed through
Entertainment in Video
(qv)

Medusa Communications

Home Video Division
Regal Chambers
51 Bancroft
Hitchin
Herts SG5 1LL
Tel: 0462 421818
Fax: 0462 420393
Dark Side of the Moon
Moon 44
976-EVIL II
Re-animator II
Two Evil Eyes
For further product, see
Medusa Pictures in
Distributors

Mogul

35-37 Wardour Street
London W1A 4BT
Tel: 071 734 7195
Devil in the Flesh
No Sweat
Shout

New World Video
27 Soho Square
London W1V 5FL
Tel: 071 434 0497
Fax: 071 434 0490
Dead Trouble
18 Again
Elvira – Mistress of the
  Dark
The Gunrunner
Hellgate
Midnight Cop
Reason to Die
ShadowMan
Slugs

Odyssey Video
15 Dufours Place
London W1V 1FE
Tel: 071 437 8251
Fax: 071 734 6941
The First of the Few
Marla
The Naked and the Dead
The Seventh Veil

Palace Video
16-17 Wardour Mews
London W1V 3FF
Tel: 071 734 7060
Fax: 071 437 3248
Asterix and the Big Fight
The Cook, the Thief, His
  Wife and Her Lover
Jean de Florette
Killing Dad
Manon des Sources
My Left Foot
Rosalyne and the Lions
Shag

Parkfield Entertainment
103 Bashley Road
London NW10 6SD
Tel: 081 965 5555
Fax: 081 961 8040
B.O.R.N.
Best of Times
Billy the Kid
Breaking Point
The Lady and the
  Highwayman
Life on the Edge
A Man for All Seasons
Moontrap
Tank Malling
That Summer of White
  Roses

Pathé Video
76 Hammersmith Road
London W14 8YR
Tel: 071 603 4555
Fax: 071 603 4277
Berlin Blues
A Cry in the Dark
The Dead Can't Lie
Five Corners
Hanna's War
Kinjite
Joyriders

The Lonely Passion of
  Judith Hearne
The Raggedy Rawney
Tree of Hands
Distributed through
Warner Home Video

Pickwick Video
Hyde Industrial Estate
The Hyde
London NW9 6JU
Tel: 081 200 7000
Fax: 081 200 8995
Blackadder
The Blues Brothers
Nursery Rhymes
Peter Pan
Sleeping Beauty
Thomas, Percy and
  Harold
Watch with Mother
Water Babies

Picture Music International
20 Manchester Square
London W1A 1ES
Tel: 081 486 4488
Fax: 081 465 0748
Cliff Richard: From a
  Distance – The Event
Duran Duran: Decade
Hard 'n' Heavy
Iron Maiden: Maiden
  England
Kate Bush: The Whole
  Story
Nat King Cole: The
  Unforgettable Nat
  King Cole
Now That's What I Call
  Music
Pink Floyd: Delicate
  Sound of Thunder
Queen: Real Lives
Tina Turner: Foreign
  Affair

Polygram Music Video International
6 Castle Row
Horticultural Place
Chiswick
London W4 4JQ
Tel: 081 994 9199
Fax: 081 994 6840
A subsidiary of Polygram
International making
music programming for
video release with such
bands as Bananarama,
Bon Jovi, Def Leppard,
Dire Straits, Tears for
Fears

Quadrant Video
37a High Street
Carshalton
Surrey SM5 3BB
Tel: 081 669 1114
Fax: 081 669 8831
Sports video cassettes

RCA/Columbia Pictures Video (UK)
Horatio House
77-85 Fulham Palace
Road
London W6 8JA
Tel: 081 748 6000
Fax: 081 748 4546
The Last Emperor
Little Nikita
Monster Squad
My Demon Lover
Running Man
Suspect
Vice Versa

Shiva Video
Unit 3 Pop In Building
South Way
Wembley
Middx HA9 0AJ
Tel: 081 903 6957
Indian videos

Thames Video Collection
149 Tottenham Court
Road
London W1P 9LL
Tel: 071 387 9494
Fax: 071 388 9604/6073
The Bill
Button Moon
Dangermouse
Kenny Everett
Learn with Sooty
Minder
Rainbow
Rod, Jane & Freddy
Rumpole of the Bailey

Touchstone
See under Buena Vista
Home Video

Vestron (UK)
69 New Oxford Street
London WC1A 1DG
Tel: 071 379 0221
Fax: 071 528 7771
Backtrack
Blue Steel
Cannonball Fever
Communion
Far North
Fear
Little Monsters
Sundown
Upworld
Winter People

The Video Collection
Strand VCI House
Caxton Way
Watford
Herts WD1 8UF
Tel: 0923 55558
Fax: 0923 816744
The Bobby Charlton Story

Count Duckula
Help
Jane Fonda's Workouts
Kylie – On the Go
Lizzie Webb
Magical Mystery Tour
The Quiet Man
Start to Read with Sooty
Thomas The Tank Engine

Video Gems
1st Floor
Acorn House
Victoria Road
London W3 6UL
Tel: 081 993 7705
Fax: 081 993 0209
Cardio-Funk
Defenders of the Earth
Denver the Last Dinosaur
Robin of Sherwood I-III
Rosemary Conley: Hip
  and Thigh Diet
Rosemary Conley: Inch
  Loss Plan

Video Programme Distributors (VPD)
Building No 1
GEC Estate
East Lane
Wembley
Middx HA9 7FF
Tel: 081 904 0921
Fax: 081 908 6785
Distributors for VPD,
American Imperial and
Rogue
Above the Law
Dragons Forever
No Holds Barred
Police Story 2
Simple Justice

Virgin Vision
See MCEG Virgin Vision

Warner Home Video
135 Wardour Street
London W1
Tel: 071 437 5600
Fax: 071 494 3297/
287 8535
Warner markets and
distributes certain UIP,
Pathé and Weintraub
Entertainment products
as well as films from
Warner subsidiaries
Beetlejuice
Cyborg
The Dead Pool
Empire of the Sun
Gorillas in the Mist
Her Alibi
Lethal Weapon 2
Police Academy VI
Rain Man
Tequila Sunrise

MESURES POUR ENCOURAGER LE DEVELOPPEMENT DE L'INDUSTRIE AUDIOVISUELLE
MEASURES TO ENCOURAGE THE DEVELOPMENT OF THE INDUSTRY OF AUDIOVISUAL PRODUCTION

PROGRAMME MEDIA
COMMISSION DES COMMUNAUTES EUROPEENNES
200, RUE DE LA LOI B-1049 BRUXELLES TEL: 02 236.07.18

MEDIA PROGRAMME
COMMISSION OF THE EUROPEAN COMMUNITIES
200, RUE DE LA LOI B-1049 BRUSSELS TEL: 02 236.07.18

WORKSHOPS

The film and video workshops listed below are non-profit-distributing and subsidised organisations. Some workshops are also active in making audiovisual product for UK and international media markets

A19 Film and Video
21 Foyle Street
Sunderland SR1 1LE
Tel: 091 565 5709
Mick Catmull
Nick Oldham
Alan Carter
Video production, distribution and exhibition. A19 makes films and videotapes which reflect the needs, concerns and aspirations of people on Wearside. Also offers production facilities, training and advice to schools, community groups and institutions

APHRA Workshops for Women
99 Leighton Road
London NW5 2RB
Tel: 071 485 2105
Carmelita Kadeena-Whyte
Scriptwriting and pre-production workshops for women – in particular, black and ethnic minorities – through which skills for employment in the film, television and satellite broadcasting industries can be developed. Basic introductory workshops, intermediate and specialised theme based workshops and seminars. Access includes community and commercial hire of VHS off-line edit suite and U-Matic CCD camera kit

AVA (Audio Visual Arts)
110 Mansfield Road
Nottingham NG1 3HL
Tel: 0602 483684
Chris Ledger
Madeline Holmes
Women's film/video production co-operative, specialising in art and education work. Commissioned tapes for galleries, museums, arts and education organisations including a 'Video Showcase' series on contemporary craftspeople. Grant-aided production of *Wedding Album/Great*

Expectations, a video installation funded by East Midlands Arts

Activision Irish Project
Roger Casement Centre
131 St John's Way
London N19 3QR
Tel: 071 281 5087
Fax: 071 281 4973
AIP collects, and makes available for individual viewing, Irish films and videos. The archive is accessible on U-Matic and VHS, and booking must be made in advance. Also supplies a catalogue of titles held, as well as providing information relating to Irish film and video

Alva Films
Island House
16 Brook Street
Alva
Clackmannanshire FK12 5JP
Tel: 0259 60936
Fax: 0259 69436
Russell Fenton
Bill Borrows
Film/video production, distribution and exhibition. Offers production, post-production and exhibition facilities to others. Scottish Working Class History Unit

bfi Amber Side Workshop
5 Side
Newcastle upon Tyne
NE1 3JE
Tel: 091 232 2000
Fax: 091 261 5509
Murray Martin
Film/video production, distribution and exhibition. Most recent production *In Fading Light*

Avid Productions
Keswick House
30 Peacock Lane
Leicester LE1 5NY
Tel: 0533 539733
Laura McGregor
Video production mainly for local authorities and the voluntary sector. Training, promo, education, public

information, with back-up publications where required.
Training in video/photography within the community, particularly gay groups, women's and special needs groups

Barnet Arts Workshop
1 Thomas More Way
East Finchley
London N2 0UL
Tel: 081 346 7120
Ann Latimer
Alan Everatt
Regular training in video at beginners and intermediate levels. Video production with local community organisations. Hire of production and post-production equipment (2-machine VHS edit)

Bath Community Television
7 Barton Buildings
Bath
Avon BA1 2JR
Tel: 0225 314480
Ray Brooking
Naomi Bolser
Community video resource. VHS and lo-band U-Matic equipment for hire at reasonable prices. Reduced rates for community projects. Training courses for all levels, free advice, productions including a regular video programme for local elderly people. Flexible opening hours to suit clients. Recent productions for British Gas, Bath City Council

Belfast Film Workshop
37 Queen Street
Belfast BT1 6EA
Tel: 0232 326661
Fax: 0232 246657
Alastair Herron
Kate McManus
Only film co-operative in Northern Ireland offering film/video/animation production and exhibition. Offers both these facilities to others. Made *Acceptable Levels* (with Frontroom), *Thunder Without Rain*

and various youth animation pieces

 Belfast Independent Video

4-8 Donegall Street Place
Belfast BT1 2FN
Tel: 0232 245495
Fax: 0232 324448
Co-operative providing video production, distribution and exhibition. Offers Beta and hi-/lo-band recording, editing and 16 track sound recording. Productions include 1988 *Our Words Jump to Life*, 1989 *Moving Myths*, 1990 *Schizophrenic City* and *The Write Off*. Facilities biased towards community, women's and campaign groups

 **Birmingham Film and Video Workshop**

2nd Floor
Pitman Buildings
161 Corporation Street
Birmingham B4 6PT
Tel: 021 233 3423
Rob Burkitt
Film/video production, distribution and exhibition. Offers production facilities with reduced rates for grant-aided work. Recent productions include *The Black and White Pirate Show*, *Out of Order* and *Paradise Circus*. Catalogue of productions and accompanying education packs available on request

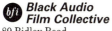 **Black Audio Film Collective**

89 Ridley Road
London E8 2NH
Tel: 071 254 9527/9536
Lina Gopaul
Avril Johnson
Film/video production, distribution, exhibition and consultancy in the field of black filmmaking. Produced *Handsworth Songs*, *Testament*, and *Twilight City*

Black Film and Video Workshop in Wales

1 West Close
Butetown
Cardiff CF1 5LD
Anthony Blenman

Black Vision

649 High Road
London N17 8AA
Tel: 081 801 8896

Lo-band U-Matic and VHS recording and editing facilities. Productions include *Taste of Carnival*, *Reggae Starwars*, *Beach Bash*, *Sister Angela*, *Tiger Spectacular*, *Drug Video*, *Alan Boesak Speaks* and many others

Bristol Asian Video Association

75 Coldharbour Road
Bristol BS6 7LU
Tel: 0272 245859
Gurmit Singh
Developing projects to assist the Asian community in gaining video skills

CREU COF (of the Ceredigion Media Association)

Blwch Post 86
Aberystwyth
Dyfed
Wales SY23 1LN
Tel: 0970 624001
Catrin M S Davies
Media education for all ages and interests with specific reference to Welsh speakers and to rural themes and issues. Comprises training, teaching and development of photography, audio work, basic S8 film and VHS video. Runs longer term practical projects

Cambridge Video Unit

The Enterprise Centre
Haggis Gap
Fulbourn
Cambridge
Tel: 0223 881688
Fax: 0223 881678
Anna Kronschnabl
Andy Lomas
Stewart Dempster
Video production co-operative. Production of experimental, community and commercial videos. Workshops in video production using lo-band U-Matic and VHS equipment

Cambridge Women's Resource Centre

Hooper Street
Cambridge CB1 2NZ
Tel: 0223 321148
Ila Chandavarkar
Mary Knox
Video classes for women include scriptwriting, basic camera techniques, lighting, production and

editing using U-Matic equipment

 **Ceddo Film and Video Enterprises**

Entrance B
South Tottenham Education and Training Centre
Braemar Road
London N15 5EU
Tel: 081 802 9034
Fax: 081 800 6949
Film/video production, distribution and exhibition. Offers all these facilities to others. Provides training workshops in film and video, organises screenings and discussions and is currently establishing an archive. Productions include *Street Warriors*, *The People's Account*, *Time and Judgement – A Diary of a 400 Year Exile*, *Omega Rising: Woman of Rastafari*, *We Are the Elephant*, and *Flame of the Soul*

Chapter Film and Animation Workshop

Chapter Arts Centre
Market Road
Canton
Cardiff CF5 1QE
Tel: 0222 396061
Fax: 0222 225901
Christine Wilks
Dane Gould
Film and animation production, training and distribution. Offers production equipment and post-production and exhibition facilities to others. Provides training courses in animation and 16mm and Super 8 film. Projects include *Off the Peg – Independent Animation Review* June '89 and animation productions *Whale Song*, *Not Waving but Drowning*, *Ozone Alert*

The Children's Film Unit

Unit 4
Berrytime Studios
192 Queenstown Road
London SW8 3NR
Tel: 071 622 7793
A registered educational charity, the CFU makes low-budget films for television and PR on subjects of concern to children and young people. Crews and actors

are trained at regular weekly workshops in Battersea. Work is in 16mm and video and membership is open to children from 8-16. Latest films for Channel 4 *Hard Road*, *Doombeach*. For the Samaritans *Time to Talk*

 **Cinema Action**

27 Winchester Road
London NW3
Tel: 071 586 2762
Fax: 071 722 5781
Gustav Lamche
Film/video production, distribution and exhibition. Offers all these facilities to others. Productions include *Rocking the Boat*, *So That You Can Live*, *The Miners' Film*, *People of Ireland*, *Film from the Clyde* and *Rocinante*

Cinestra Pictures

The Co-op Centre
11 Mowll Street
London SW9 6BG
Tel: 071 793 0157
Women's video production and training company. Aim to promote an alternative women's cinema and TV culture through production and training. U-Matic video courses from beginners to specialist advanced

Clapham-Battersea Film Workshop

Wandsworth Adult College
Latchmere Road
London SW11 2DS
Tel: 071 223 5876
Offers a range of 16mm filmmaking courses including a one year part-time course in film, video and photography. 16mm production facilities are available to those completing courses. Weekly screenings of experimental and avant-garde films

Clio Co-op

91c Mildmay Road
London N1
Tel: 071 249 2551
Ros Pearson
Produce documentaries about women's history. Latest documentary for Channel 4 *Women Like Us* (49 minutes), about the lives of older lesbians from the 1920s to their present day philosophies. Shown on Channel 4 in April 1990

Colchester Film and Video Workshop
21 St Peters Street
Colchester CO1 1EW
Tel: 0206 560255
Film/video resource for
community. U-Matic, S-
VHS and VHS production
and post production,
Super 8 and 16mm film.
Services in training,
media education,
equipment hire and
production

Community Productions Merseyside
Merseyside Innovation
Centre
131 Mount Pleasant
Liverpool L3 5TF
Tel: 051 708 5767/0123
x225
Offers production,
training, distribution and
exhibition to enable
voluntary groups and
organisations in the
Merseyside area to
undertake video projects
of specific benefit to their
local communities and
also to enable
traditionally
disadvantaged groups and
individuals to represent
themselves, primarily
through the medium of
video

Connections
Palingswick House
241 King Street
London W6 9LP
Tel: 071 741 1766/7
Paul Jones
Shabnam Grewal
Video project providing
short and long term
training in production
and post production.
Undertakes
commissioned
productions and training
programmes. Editing
facilities in U-Matic, hi-
band, lo-band and VHS.
Due to expand into
interactive media.
Editing facilities are
wheelchair accessible

Counter Image
Swan Building
Swan Street
Manchester
Tel: 061 228 3551
Ivor Frankell
Janet Shaw
Independent media
charity. Film/video
production, distribution
and exhibition. Offers
production and exhibition
facilities to independent
film and video makers

and photographers.
Productions include *Fever
House* and *Land of
Colagne*

Despite TV
178 Whitechapel Road
London E1
Tel: 071 377 0737
Mark Saunders

Doncaster Film Group
Basement Flat
6 Regent Square
Doncaster
South Yorks
Tel: 0427 342982
Rodney Challis
Film/video production.
Offers production/editing
facilities on U-Matic/VHS
suite. Emphasis on
productions of a
collaborative nature and
on training

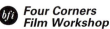 Edinburgh Film Workshop Trust
29 Albany Street
Edinburgh EH1 3QN
Tel: 031 557 5242
David Halliday
Cassandra McGrogan
Robin MacPherson
Edward O'Donnelly
Scotland's only franchised
Workshop. Broadcast,
non-broadcast and
community integrated
production.
Facilities include lo-band
U-Matic production; VHS
and lo-band edit suites;
Neilson Hordell 16mm
Rostrum camera; 8mm
and 16mm cameras; film
cutting room. Women's
unit. Projects 89-90
include *Silicon Fever* and
*Your Health's Your
Wealth* for Channel 4

Edinburgh Film Workshop Trust Animation Workshop
address as above
Edward O'Donnelly

Exeter Film and Video Workshop
c/o Exeter and Devon Arts
Centre
Gandy Street
Exeter EX4 3LS
Tel: 0392 218928
Mark Jeffs
Film/video production,
distribution and
exhibition. Offers all
these facilities to others.
Holds training courses in
film and video production
as well as teaching in
schools

Eye to Eye (Film and Video Co-Operative)
Ylyn Dowr
6 Fore Street
Gold Sithney
Penzance TR20 9HD
Tel: 0736 710797/63677
Fax: 0736 64278
Lynn Aubrey
Douglas Cook
Robin Hewell
Alan Burton
Lee Fletcher
Eye to Eye has ACTT
members living in West
Penwith, Cornwall, and
working freelance on
their own ideas for
productions

Faction Films
28-29 Great Sutton Street
London EC1
Tel: 071 608 0654/3
Fax: 071 608 2157
Dave Fox
Sylvia Stevens
Group of independent
filmmakers. Production
facilities include 6-plate
Steenbeck, 16mm edit
suite, VHS off-line edit
suite, 16mm sound
transfer, sound recording.
Titles include *Irish News:
British Stories, Year of the
Beaver, Picturing Derry*
and *Trouble the Calm*

Film Form Productions
64 Fitzjohn's Avenue
London NW3 5LT
Tel: 071 794 6967
Fax: 071 794 6967
Susi Oldroyd
Tony Harrild
Film/video production,
drama and documentary
for television and video
distribution. We offer full
crewing, writers,
producers and directors

Film Work Group
Top Floor
79-89 Lots Road
London SW10 0RN
Tel: 071 352 0538
Fax: 071 351 6479
Michael Tomkins
Video post-production
facilities. Offers three-
machine hi-band SP suite,
lo-band offline telecine
and transfer facilities to
others with special rates
for grant-aided and non-
profit groups

Filmshed
9 Mill Lane
Harbledown
Canterbury
Kent CT2 8NE

Tel: 0227 769415
Tim Reed
Open-access collective for
the promotion and
production of independent
film. Film production and
exhibition. Offers
exhibition facilities to
others; filmmakers on
tour and regular
screenings of political/
workshop films

Forum Television
11 Regent Street
Bristol BS8 4HW
Tel: 0272 741490
David Parker
Co-operative with
emphasis on South West
film and video production,
distribution and
exhibition. Offers film/
video editing suites and
Beta SP Camera kit.
Recent work has involved
social and political issues
around work,
unemployment, the police
and judiciary, racism and
community education.
Titles for Channel 4
include: *Lands at the
Margin, A Question of
Cornwall, A Gilded
Cage?, Like Mothers,
Like Daughters.* For the
BBC: *The School Belongs
to All of Us, Dying for a
Job.* For HTV: *Hurried
Orders, Songs of the
Forest, Time Goes on
Quick, Harry Brown,
Trotting* and *Women
Farmers*

Four Corners Film Workshop
113 Roman Road
London E2 0HU
Tel: 081 981 4243/6111
James Van der Pool
Provides access to film
production courses,
technical theory classes
and film theory courses. A
full programme runs all
year round. Provides
subsidised film equipment
for the low budget
independent film maker
and has a 40 seat cinema.
16mm and Super 8
production and post-
production facilities
available

Fradharc Ur
11 Scotland Street
Stornoway
Isle of Lewis PA87
Tel: 0851 5766
Mairead Nicdhomhnuill
The first Gaelic film and
video workshop, offering
VHS and hi-band editing
and shooting facilities.

Production and training in Gaelic for community groups. Productions include *Under the Surface, Na Deilbh Bheo, The Weaver* and *As an Fhearran*

Free Focus
The Old Co Op
38-42 Chelsea Road
Easton
Bristol BS5 6AF
Tel: 0272 558973
Free Focus promotes community development in Avon through the use of video. We help community groups make their own videos and to develop their video making skills through training, consultancy, information and cheap equipment hire

Glasgow Film and Video Workshop
Dolphin Arts Centre
7 James Street
Glasgow G40 1BZ
Tel: 041 554 6502
GFVW is a film/video resource for independent producers in Scotland. Runs basic video familiarisation courses and provides advanced specialist courses in lo- and hi-band video, 16mm and Super 8. Occasionally offers bursaries to artist filmmakers and continues to programme showings of independent film and video work in the city

Gog Theatre Co
Ostia
Overleigh
Street
Somerset BA16 0TJ
Tel: 0458 47353
Stephen Clarke

Grapevine Television
Hebron House
Sion Road
Bedminster
Bristol BS3 3BD
Tel: 0272 637973/637634
Fax: 0272 631770
Jayne Cotton
Lynne Harwood
Adrian Mack
Video production, distribution and exhibition. Specialising in programmes for community, voluntary and statutory organisations nationally. Offers production and editing facilities to others along with training courses

Guildford Video Workshop
c/o The Guildford Institute
Ward Street
Guildford
Surrey
Michael Aslin
Video production and training facilities

(bfi) Gweithdy Fidio Cydweithredol Scrin Cyf (Community Screen Film and Video Workshop)
12 Palace Street
Caernarvon
Gwynedd LL55 1RR
Tel: 0286 4545
Mair Jones

Hall Place Studios
4 Hall Place
Leeds LS9 8JD
Tel: 0532 405553
Alf Bower
Jacqui Maurice
Sara Worrall
Anna Zaluczkowska
Facility and training centre offering film/video/sound production facilities on site and for hire on sliding scale. Also offers programme of training and events, some for women or black peoples only, membership scheme, community video development programme, and in-service training for youth/community workers

Hull Community Artworks
(formerly Outreach Community Arts)
Northumberland Avenue
Hull HU2 0LN
Tel: 0482 226420
Tony Hales
Film/video production, distribution and exhibition. Offers production and exhibition facilities to others. Holds regular training workshops

Hull Time Based Arts
8 Posterngate
Hull HU1 2JN
Tel: 0482 216446
Fax: 0482 218103
Mike Stubbs
Film/video production, exhibition and education. Also promotes, produces and commissions experimental film, video, performance and music. Provides annual summer

school and *Junk Music/Found Film* workshop. Equipment for hire includes video projector and U-Matic production facilities

'I Can' 1st Chance Project
The Masbro Centre
87 Masbro Road
London W14 0LR
Tel: 071 603 7481/602 5739
Basic training in video for people with disabilities. VHS camera and edit suite for hire. Remote control for camera/recorder. Other adaptions for disabled people soon to be available

Intermedia Film and Video (Nottingham)
110 Mansfield Road
Nottingham NG1 3HL
Tel: 0602 505434
Pat Silburn
Malcolm Leick
Roger Suckling
Offers training, facilities, production, information and advice. Training based on established short course programme in 16mm film, video and related areas

Ipswich Media Project
202 Brunswick Road
Ipswich
Suffolk
Tel: 0473 716609
Mike O'Sullivan
Super 8 film and VHS video production equipment. Familiarisation training and media work

Island Art Centre
The Tiller Center
Tiller Road
Millwall
London E14 8PX
Tel: 071 987 7925
Namita Chakrabarty
Facilities for local groups and individuals; video workshops and productions

Jackdaw Media
96a Duke Street
Liverpool L1 5AG
Tel: 051 709 5858
Fax: 051 709 0759
Laura Knight
Animated film making for school children and adults with or without the use of film. Daytime and evening sessions.

Specialising in educational consultancy. Production commissions accepted. 16mm rostrums, 6-plate Steenbeck, Bolex H16 title cameras and projectors available for hire

Jubilee Arts
84 High Street
West Bromwich
West Midlands
Tel: 021 553 6862
Fax: 021 525 0640
Multi-media arts development based in the West Midlands, using video, film, photography, music, performance and visual art. Working in partnership with community groups and local authorities

Lambeth Video
Unit F7
245a Coldharbour Lane
London SW9 8RR
Tel: 071 737 5903
Lambeth Video is a part-funded video workshop. Run production-based training and hire equipment (hi-band production kit, 3-machine edit suite and VHS edit). A one year training course is run with Brixton College, open only to women and black applicants, who must be unemployed

Latin American Independent Film/Video Association
Latin American House
Kingsgate Place
London NW6 4TA
Tel: 071 372 6442
Offers 16mm film and VHS equipment (production and post-production) for hire. Film and video courses, workshops and exhibitions

(bfi) Leeds Animation Workshop
45 Bayswater Row
Leeds LS8 5LF
Tel: 0532 484997
Jane Bradshaw
A women's collective working in animated film, distribution and exhibition. Offers production, distribution, training. Productions include *Risky Business, Pretend You'll Survive, Give Us a Smile, Council*

Matters, Crops and Robbers, Home and Dry? and *Out to Lunch.* Free catalogue available on request

Light House Media Centre
Art Gallery
Lichfield Street
Wolverhampton WV1 1DU
Tel: 0902 312033
Fax: 0902 26644
Frank Challenger
Krysia Rozanska
Raj Chahal
Isaiah Ferguson
Video production with 3-machine edit, computer graphics/animation; cinema and galleries. Training includes a two-year full-time course. Films, conferences, events, courses and exhibitions. Joint Wolverhampton Borough Council/Wolverhampton Polytechnic development with Arts Council and West Midlands Arts support

Lighthouse Film and Video
19 Regent Street
Brighton
BN1 1UL
Tel: 0273 686479
Tim O'Riordan
A charity established to provide facilities, training, education, exhibition and production services in South East Arts region. S-VHS, U-Matic and 16mm production and post production facilities. Productions include *Who Was Harry Cowley? Rural Views, Education for Life, Another Working Day*

Line Out
138 Charles Street
Leicester
Tel: 0533 621265
Nick Hunt
Film and video production facilities, training and programmes

London Deaf Video Project
Room 303
South Bank House
Black Prince Road
London SE1
Tel: 071 735 8171 ext 115
Translates information from English into British Sign Language for London's deaf community.

Recent productions include videos about solicitors, electricity, women's health, and the history of LDVP (all available for sale to others). Offers occasional courses and use of lo-band/VHS equipment to deaf people. Exhibitions to deaf community. Interested to liaise with any other video projects who feel they should use sign language to make their own material accessible to deaf people

London Fields Film and Video
10 Martello Street
London E8 3PE
Tel: 071 241 2997
Catherine Johnson
Sophie Outram
James Swinson
Lo-band video and 16mm production and editing facilities. Computer graphics for logos, music videos. Productions; Arts Council/11th Hour *Five Steps Backwards, Four Steps Forwards*

London Film Makers' Co-op
42 Gloucester Avenue
London NW1
Tel: 071 586 4806
Sandra Weiland
Film workshop, distribution library and cinema enables filmmakers to control the production, distribution and exhibition of their films. Workshop runs regular practical and theoretical film courses. Distribution has 2,000 films for hire, from 20s to current work. Cinema screenings twice weekly. Work with cultural aesthetic/political aims which differ from the industry

London Media Workshops
101 King's Drive
Gravesend
Kent DA12 5BQ
Tel: 0474 564676
Twelve year old training agency specialising in short intensive courses in writing for radio, television, video and press, and in directing and producing television and video programmes. Regular one and two day courses in London, specially tailored in-

house courses by commission. Mail order booklist. Top working tutors. Small numbers allow individual attention

London Screenwriters Workshop
1 Greek Street
London W1V 6NQ
Tel: 081 989 5199
Christina Jarvis
Screenwriting workshops range from discussion of short TV scripts and film treatments to the development of full-length screenplays and analysis of deep structure. A range of seminars bring screenwriters together with producers, agents, development executives and other film and television professionals

London Video Access (LVA)
23 Frith Street
London W1A 4XD
Tel: 071 437 2786/734 7410
Doug Foot
Clive Gillman
Offers facilities and training for independent video/filmmakers and distributes and exhibits video art

London Women's Centre
Wesley House
4 Wild Court
London WC2B 5AU
Tel: 071 831 6946
A women's resource providing facilities for women and women's organisations to hire with a sliding scale of charges. Facilities include lo-band U-Matic video filming and editing equipment and 16mm, lo-band and VHS playback facilities including screening space. All equipment for use on the premises only. Rooms available for hire range from the 'Theatre Space' with a PA and lighting rig (capacity 150), to a variety of seminar/meeting rooms. Planned extension of audio-visual facilities and training

Media Arts
Town Hall Studios
Regents Circus
Swindon SN1 1QF
Tel: 0793 493451
Fax: 0793 490420

Carol Comly
Steve Chapman
Production, distribution, exhibition, education and training. Well-equipped studios in film, video, photography and sound. Small media library, viewing facilities, multimedia events, archive. Productions include *View from the Sink, Stories from the First Estate, When I Was a Girl* and *Today is a Good Day*

The Media Centre
South Hill Park
Bracknell
Berks RG12 4PA
Tel: 0344 427272
Fax: 0344 411427
Bob Gibbs
Kim Clancy
John Bradshaw
Training, video production, distribution, exhibition and media education. Offers all these facilities to others. Runs national video courses for independent videomakers and general training in arts administration

Media Education Centre
Leigh College
Railway Road
Leigh WN7 4AH
Tel: 0942 675830
Steve Brennan
Paul Grimshaw
Provides video production and exhibition facilities for schools, colleges and local community groups. Facilities include community cinema/small TV studio, teachers resource material and advisor team with technical support

The Media Workshop
Peterborough Arts Centre
Media Department
Orton Goldhay
Peterborough PE2 OJQ
Tel: 0733 237073
Clifton Stewart
Roger Knott-Fayle
Video and photography productions, workshops and exhibitions. Offers U-Matic and VHS production/edit facilities, dark room and gallery space. Committed to equal access for all sections of the community

Migrant Film and Video Collective
90 De Beauvoir Road
London N1 4EN
Tel: 071 254 9701/241 0893
Ken Fero
Dipak Mistry
Esther Springer
Savi Hensman
Production, exhibition, advice, training and support for migrant, immigrant and refugee communities in film and video. Networks with similar organisations across Europe and in Arab countries. Produced *Integration* about the Turkish community in Berlin

Moonshine Community Arts Workshop
(workshop) 1050 Harrow Road
London NW10 5XQ
Tel: 081 969 7969
(office) 1090 Harrow Road
London NW10 5XQ
Tel: 081 960 0055
Jeff Lee
Offers video production facilities to others. Provides training in production and post-production with U-Matic and VHS edit suites and special effects. Also has 16 track recording studio with effects, and silk screen and offset litho printing facilities. Works with Brent-based groups and individuals with emphasis on young people and black community groups producing work including documentaries, music videos and video art

Outline Arts Trust
69 Rothbury Terrace
Heaton
Newcastle upon Tyne
NE6 5XJ
Tel: 091 276 3207
Kate Hancock
A community arts trust using video mostly for very specific and local use

Oxford Film and Video Makers
The Stables
North Place
Headington
Oxford OX3 9HY
Tel: 0865 60074
Offer specialised courses to meet the particular needs of various groups, open access courses

covering the entire production process in film and video, equipment hire, distribution and exhibition, and productions which give voice to people normally denied one, such as *Women in Rock, Journeys, Stopping the Press* and *Give Us a Chance*

Oxford Independent Video
Pegasus Theatre
Magdalen Road
Oxford OX4 1RE
Tel: 0865 250150
Maddie Shepherd
Arts and issue-based video project working with under-represented groups in Oxfordshire to produce tapes for national distribution. Work includes tapes about women in film noir, Eisenstein, integrated dance residencies with people of differing abilities, arts in schools projects, etc

Picture 5 Women
3 Lescudjack Road
Penzance TR18 3AD
Tel: 0736 67164
Elaine Hawkins

Pimlico Arts and Media Scheme
St James the Less School
Moreton Street
London SW1 2PT
Tel: 071 630 6409
Fax: 071 976 6133
Carolyn Shrivers
One of the biggest media training centres in London, running courses in video, photography and graphic design exclusively for unemployed people to give them a grounding in these three areas and prepare them for employment.
Offers graphics studio, VHS, U-Matic equipment, fully-equipped darkroom and exhibition space, and can accommodate 165 trainees

Platform Films
13 Tankerton House
Tankerton Street
London WC1H 8HP
Tel: 071 278 8394
Chris Reeves
Film/video production and distribution. Also VHS Hi-Fi sound off-line edit suite and 16mm cutting room available for

hire. Special rates for non-commercial and student productions

Plymouth Arts Centre
38 Looe Street
Plymouth PL4 0EB
Tel: 0752 660060

Projects UK
1 Black Swan Court
Westgate Road
Newcastle upon Tyne
NE1 1SG
Tel: 091 232 2410
Fax: 091 221 0492
Caroline Taylor
Promotes new and innovative arts and media. Offers education, training, product work, production and distribution in a wide range of art and media products. The main areas of activity are: photography, visual art, performance, site specific work, public events audio and sound

Real Time Video
Newtown Community House
117 Cumberland Road
Reading RG1 3JY
Tel: 0734 351023
Jackie Shaw
Clive Robertson
Julie Scott
Process-based community access video workshop. Video production, distribution and exhibition. Offers exhibition facilities to others. Runs courses and workshops, organises screenings and projects

bfi Red Flannel Films
Maritime Offices
Woodland Terrace
Maesycoed
Pontypridd
Mid Glamorgan
Tel: 0443 401743/480564
Fax: 0443 485667
Red Flannel is a women's collective working on film and video production, distribution, exhibition, education, training, archive and video library. Productions for hire and purchase are *Mam* (16mm and video), *If We Were Asked* (video) and *Midwives* (working title, 16mm and video, to be completed July 1990). Offers lo-band U-Matic editing and VHS production facilities for hire. Basic training courses available

bfi Retake Film and Video Collective
19 Liddell Road
London NW6 2EW
Tel: 071 328 4676
Fax: 071 372 1231
Mahmood Jamal
Seema Gill
Sebastian Shah
Ahmed Jamal
Film/video production, distribution and training. Organising screenings and discussions around the history of Indian cinema. Productions include two feature dramas, *Majdhar* and *Hotel London* and documentaries *Living in Danger, Environment of Dignity, Who Will Cast the First Stone?*, and *Sanctuary Challenge*. Hire of 16mm/lo-band U-Matic editing

bfi Sankofa Film and Video
Unit K
32-34 Gordon House Road
London NW5 1LP
Tel: 071 485 0848
Fax: 071 485 2869
Maureen Blackwood
Robert Crusz
Isaac Julien
Nadine Marsh-Edwards
Film/video production and distribution. Offers production facilities to others, runs training workshops in film and video. Organises screenings and discussions. Productions include *The Passion of Remembrance, Perfect Image, Dreaming Rivers* and *Looking for Langston*

Screenworks – Portsmouth Media Trust
The Hornpipe
143 Kingston Road
Portsmouth PO2 7EB
Tel: 0705 861851
Steve Jackman
Peter Taylor
Margaret O'Connor
Film/video production, training workshops and projects. Regular exhibition of independent film and video in Rendezvous cinema

Second Sight
Zair Works
111 Bishop Street
Birmingham B5 6JL
Tel: 021 622 4223
(productions), 021 622

5750 (training)
Fax: 021 622 1554 (mark attn Second Sight)
Dylis Pugh
Glynis Powell
Pauline Bailey
Video production company specialising in arts, social issues and training programmes. Runs practical training courses for women from beginners level to lo-band production. Provides an information resource on all aspects of AV media

 ### Sheffield Film Co-op

Brown Street
Sheffield S1 2BS
Tel: 0742 727170
Chrissie Stansfield
Women's film and video production workshop reflecting women's views on a wide range of issues. Distribute work on film/tape including *Red Skirts on Clydeside, Changing Our Lives, Women of Steel, Let Our Children Grow Tall!, Bringing It All Back Home, Diamonds in Brown Paper,* and *Thank You, That's All I Knew*

Sheffield Independent Film

Avec
Brown Street
Sheffield S1 2BS
Tel: 0742 720304
Alan Robinson
Lucy Rumney
Gloria Ward
Jo Cammack
Carol Sidney
A resource base for independent film and videomakers in the Sheffield region. Regular training workshops; access to a range of film and video equipment; technical and administrative backup; and regular screenings of independent film and video

Sheffield Media Unit

Central Library
Surrey Street
Sheffield S1 1XZ
Tel: 0742 734746
Georgia Stone
Andy Stamp
Gaining international recognition for developing practical media techniques, particularly for educationalists. Offers

communication skills. Produced 'The Television Programme' workbook in 1987 and 'How to Read Television' in 1990

Siren Film and Video Co-op

6 Harris Street
Middlesbrough
Cleveland
Tel: 0642 221298
Dave Eadington
Wendy Critchley
Sarah Shaw
Film/video production, distribution and exhibition. Offers production facilities to others. Workers' co-operative producing for community groups and television. Recent titles include *All Things Being Equal, A Very Special Place* and *Excuse Me, Are You Afraid of the Russians?*

Sprockettes (York Film Workshop/Women's Group)

156b Haxby Road
York YO3 7JN
Tel: 0904 641394
Nicky Edmonds
Film/video production. Basic training and education courses. Films and videos (mainly short fiction and documentary) for hire

Star Productions

1 Cornthwaite Road
London E5
Tel: 081 986 4470/5766
Fax: 081 533 6597
Raj Patel
Film/video production company working from an Asian perspective. Multilingual productions. Offers studio for hire, video editing suite, 16mm cutting room. Production and exhibition facilities. Output includes community documentaries, video films of stage plays and feature films

 ### Steel Bank Film Co-op

Brown Street
Sheffield S1 2BS
Tel: 0742 721235
Susie Field
Jessica York
Simon Reynell
Dinah Ward
Noemie Mendelle
Film/video production

and distribution. Channel 4 funded. Work includes documentaries, art programmes, campaign tapes and fiction films. Productions include *Winnie, Security, Clocks of the Midnight Hours, Great Noises that Fill the Air, For Your Own Good, Tales from Two New Towns, Spinster* and *Crimestrike*

Studio Nine, The Video Producers

Monyhull Hall Road
Kings Norton
Birmingham B30 3QB
Tel: 021 444 4750/0831 307728
Fax: 021 444 5674
Alison Richards
Gary Liszewski
Michael Smyth
An independent Birmingham based video production house. Documentary/promotional/training films undertaken – from script to screen. Studio 9's in house team of creative professionals provide expertise in all areas of video production, offer a freelancer service for broadcast and non-broadcast

Swingbridge Video

Norden House
41 Stowell Street
Newcastle upon Tyne
NE1 4YB
Tel: 091 232 3762
Hugh Kelly
Sarah McCarthy
A community video project making tapes with and on behalf of community and campaign groups in the North East. Film and video production, distribution and training

TURC Video

7 Frederick Street
Birmingham B1 3HE
Tel: 021 233 4061
Marian Hall
Video production, distribution and exhibition. 3 machine editing. Offers all these facilities to others. Works mainly on trade union and campaign issues, locally and nationally. Productions include *Rights Wot Rights, P & O... Profit before People* and *The Journalist's Tale*

The Television Co-operative

100 Fawnbrake Avenue
London SE24 OBZ
Tel: 071 738 7789
John Underwood
Ron Stoneman
Provide broadcast and non-broadcast factual programmes

33 Video Co-operative

33-35 Guildford Street
Luton
Beds
Tel: 0582 21448
Gary Whiteley
Three machine lo-band, time-code. 2 machine VHS. Computer graphics, Chromakey, lo-band shooting kit

 ### Trade Films

36 Bottle Bank
Gateshead
Tyne and Wear NE8 2AR
Tel: 091 477 5532
Fax: 091 478 3681
Derek Stubbs
Film/video production, distribution and exhibition. Offers production and post-production (hi-/lo-band, 16mm) facilities to others. Workshop comprises Trade Films (fiction/documentary) and Northern Newsreel (current affairs), together with the Northern Film and Television Archive

Trilith Video

Corner Cottage
Brickyard Lane
Bourton
Gillingham
Dorset SP8 5PJ
Tel: 0747 840750/840727
Trevor Bailey
John Holman
Sue Holman
Specialises in rural video on community action, rural issues and the outlook and experience of country-born people. Produces own series of tapes, undertakes broadcast and tape commissions and gathers archive film in order to make it publicly available on video. Distributes own work nationally. Current work includes TSW feature

Valley and Vale Community Arts

Blaengarw Workmen's Hall

Blaengarw
Mid Glamorgan
Tel: 0656 871911
Justine Ennion
The Holm View Centre
Skomer Road
Gibbonsdown
Barry
South Glamorgan
Tel: 0446 742289
Richard McLaughlin
Video production,
distribution and
exhibition. Open-access
workshop offering
training to community
groups in VHS and lo-
band U-Matic

Vera Productions

30-38 Dock Street
Leeds LS10 1JF
Tel: 0532 428646
Fax: 0532 426937
Alison Garthwaite
Catherine Mitchell
Film/video production
(broadcast/non-broad-
cast), training, exhibition
and distribution. Teach
women and mixed groups.
Speak on representation
of women in film and TV.
Information resource and
networking newsletter

Video in Pilton

30 Ferry Road Avenue
West Pilton
Edinburgh EH4 4BA
Tel: 031 343 1151
Joel Venet
Hugh Farrell
Community-based
training facilities;
broadcast productions;
production work for
national campaigning
groups, trade unions and
local authority; exhibition
at the Edinburgh Film
Festival

The Video Workshop/Y Gweithdy Fideo

Chapter Arts Centre
Market Road
Canton
Cardiff CF5 1QE
Tel: 0222 396061
George Auchterlonie
Video production,
distribution and
exhibition in English and
Welsh. Offers production
facilities to others.
Working with community
organisations and trades
unions on social, political
and cultural issues

Vokani

Unit 15
Devonshire House
Digbeth

Birmingham B12 0LP
Tony Small
Black and Third World
film and video exhibition
circuit based in the West
Midlands. Also do some
distribution of new titles
by new black film makers,
offer education packages
around films by or about
Black and Third World
people

WITCH (Women's Independent Cinema House) Black Section

c/o Merseyside Arts
Graphic House
Duke Street
Liverpool L1 4AJ
Tel: 051 709 0671 ext 200
Ann Carney
Barbara Phillips
Video production,
distribution and
exhibition. Workshops in
video and photography.
Also screenings

Watershed Media Centre

1 Canons Road
Bristol BS1 5TX
Tel: 0272 276444
Shafeeq Vellani
Lulu Quinn
Film/video production,
distribution, exhibition,
training and media
education. Offers all these
facilities to others,
primarily grant-aided and
independent producers,
community groups and
educational institutions.
Centre also has cinemas
and darkrooms. Recent
productions include
*Walking Away with the
Music* and *Celebration*

Welfare State International

The Ellers
Ulverston
Cumbria LA12 1AA
Tel: 0229 581127/57146
Fax: 0229 581232
A consortium of artists,
musicians, technicians
and performers. Film/
video production,
distribution and
exhibition. Output
includes community
feature films and work for
television

West Glamorgan Video and Film Workshop

F6-7-10, Burrows
Chambers
East Burrows Road

Swansea SA1 1RQ
Tel: 0792 476441
Lynfa Protheroe
Rob Watling
Community co-operative
dedicated to increasing
the use and
understanding of video,
film and photography
amongst all sections of
the local community in
England and Wales. VHS,
lo-band, 8mm, darkroom
and sound facilities.
Regular training courses,
production groups and
screenings (brochure and
rate card available).
Supported by Welsh Arts
Council

West London Media Workshop

118 Talbot Road
London W11
Tel: 071 221 1859
Tricia King
John Goff
Claire Caragannis
Video production,
distribution and
exhibition. Offers
production facilities to
others. WLMW runs a
bursary scheme aimed to
encourage new makers to
debate various cultural/
social issues

Wide Angle Film Video and Photography Workshop

c/o Birmingham
Community Association
Jenkins Street
Small Heath
Birmingham B10 0HQ
Tel: 021 772 2889
Tracy Symonds
Pauline Walton
Wide Angle works in the
production, exhibition,
and tuition of video, film
and photography. Has
training courses in all
these areas across a range
of levels. Also produces
films and videos and
shows rarely seen or
unusual works

Women's Media Resource Project (WMRP)

85 Kingsland High Street
London E8 2PB
Tel: 071 254 6536
Offers sound engineering
courses, video exhibition
equipment, hire of
equipment and studio,
women only screenings
and discussion

Workers' Film Association

Media and Cultural
Centre
9 Lucy Street
Manchester M15 4BX
Tel: 061 848 9785
Wowo Wauters
Rosemary Orr
Main areas of work
include media access and
training with a full range
of production, post-
production and exhibition
equipment and facilities
for community, semi-
professional and
professional standards.
Video production unit
(ACTT). Distribution and
sale of 16mm films and
videos, booking and
advice service, video
access library. Cultural
work, mixed media
events. Bookshop/
outreach work

Wrexham Community Video

The Place in the Park
Bellevue Road
Wrexham
Clwyd
Tel: 0978 358522
Eddie Meek
Video production,
distribution and
exhibition. Offers
production and exhibition
facilities to others. Runs
short training courses in
video production and
studio sound recording

York Film Workshop

The Old Dairy Studios
156b Haxby Road
York YO3 7JN
Tel: 0904 641394
William Lawrence
Film/video production,
distribution and
exhibition, 8-track sound
recording studio and a
darkroom equipped for
full disabled access.
Courses are held in
production, sound
recording and
photography

 – Supported by the
BFI through finance

LIST OF ABBREVIATIONS

ABW Association of Black Film and Video Workshops

ACGB Arts Council of Great Britain

ACTT Association of Cinematograph, Television and allied Technicians

AFI American Film Institute/Australian Film Institute

AFRS Advertising Film Rights Society

AFVPA Advertising Film and Videotape Producers' Association

AIC Association of Independent Cinemas

AMPAS Academy of Motion Picture Arts and Sciences (USA)

BABA British Advertising Broadcast Awards

BABEL Broadcasting Across the Barriers of European Language

BAFTA British Academy of Film and Television Arts

BARB Broadcasters' Audience Research Board

BASCA British Academy of Songwriters, Composers and Authors

BATC British Amateur Television Club

BBC British Broadcasting Corporation

BBFC British Board of Film Classification

BCC Broadcasting Complaints Commission

BCS British Cable Services

BETA Broadcasting and Entertainment Trades Alliance

BFFA British Film Fund Agency

BFFS British Federation of Film Societies

BFI British Film Institute

BFIC British Film Industry in Cannes

BISFA British Industrial and Scientific Film Association (now part of IVCA)

BKSTS British Kinematograph Sound and Television Society

BNFVC British National Film and Video Catalogue

BPI British Phonographic Industry

BRU Broadcasting Research Unit

BSAC British Screen Advisory Council

BSB British Satellite Broadcasting

BSC Broadcasting Standards Council

BUFVC British Universities Film and Video Council

BVA British Videogram Association

CA Cable Authority

CARM Campaign Against Racism in the Media

CAVIAR Cinema and Video Industry Audience Research

CC Children's Channel

CD Compact Disc

CDI Compact Disc Interactive

CD-Rom Compact Disc – Read Only Memory

CEA Cinematograph Exhibitors' Association of Great Britain and Ireland

CEPI Co-ordination Européenne des Producteurs Independantes

CET Council for Educational Technology

CEU Confederation of Entertainment Unions

CFC Cinematograph Films Council

CFTF Children's Film and Television Foundation

CFU Children's Film Unit

C4 Channel Four

CNN Cable News Network

COI Central Office of Information

COMEX Consortium of Media Exhibitors

CORAA Council of Regional Arts Associations

CPBF Campaign for Press and Broadcasting Freedom

CTA Cinema Theatre Association

CTBF Cinema and Television Benevolent Fund

DADA Designers and Art Directors' Association

DBC Deaf Broadcasting Campaign

DBS Direct Broadcasting by Satellite

DELTA Development of European Learning through Technological Advance

DES Department of Education and Science

DGGB Directors' Guild of Great Britain

DTI Department of Trade and Industry

DVI Digital Video Interactive

EATC European Alliance for Television and Culture

EAVE European Audio-Visual Entrepreneurs

EBU European Broadcasting Union

EEC European Economic Community

EETPU Electrical, Electronic, Telecommunications and Plumbing Union

EFDO European Film Distribution Office

EITF Edinburgh International Television Festival

ESPRIT European Strategic Programme for Information Technology

ETA Entertainment Trades Alliance

EVE Espace Vidéo Européen

EURO-AIM European Organisation for Audiovisual Production

Equity British Actors' Equity Association

European SCRIPT Fund Support for CReative Independent Production Talent (aka SCRIPT)

FAA Film Artistes' Association

FACT Federation Against Copyright Theft

FBU Federation of Broadcasting Unions

FEPACI Federation Pan-African des Cinéastes

FESPACO Festivale Pan-African des Cinémas de Ouagadougou

FFU Federation of Film Unions

FIAF Fédération Internationale des Archives du Film (International Federation of Film Archives)

FIAT Fédération Internationale des Archives de Télévision (International Federation of Television Archives)

FICC International Federation of Film Societies

FOCAL Federation of Commercial Audio-Visual Libraries

FSU Film Society Unit

FTT Film and Television Technicians

FTVLCA Film and Television Lighting Contractors Association

FVL Film and Video Library

FX Effects/special effects

GLA Greater London Arts

HBO Home Box Office

HDTV High Definition Television

HP Homes Passed by Cable

HTV Harlech Television

HVC Home Video Channel

IABM International Association of Broadcasting Manufacturers

IAC Interim Action Committee

IBA Independent Broadcasting Authority

IBT International Broadcasting Trust

ICA Institute of Contemporary Arts

IFDA Independent Film Distributors' Association

IFPA Independent Film Production Associates

IFPI International Federation of Producers of Phonograms and Videograms

IFTA International Federation of Television Archives (aka FIAT)

IIC International Institute of Communications

IPA Institute of Practitioners in Advertising

IPPA Independent Programme Producers' Association

ISA International Songwriters Association

ISBA Incorporated Society of British Advertising

ITC Independent Television Commission

ITCA Independent Television Companies Association

ITEL International Television Enterprises

ITN Independent Television News

ITSC International Television Studies Conference

ITV Independent Television

IVCA International Visual Communications Association

IVLA International Visual Literacy Association

LAIFA Latin American Independent Film/Video Association

LFF London Film Festival

LFMC London Film Makers' Co-Op

LSW London Screenwriters' Workshop

LVA London Video Access

LWT London Weekend Television

MAP-TV Memories – Archives – Programmes

MCPS Mechanical Copyright Protection Society

MEDIA Measures to Encourage the Development of the Industry of Audiovisual Production

MFB Monthly Film Bulletin

MGM Metro Goldwyn Mayer

MFVPA Music, Film and Video Producers Association

MHFC Mental Health Film Council

MIDEM Marché International du Disque et de l'Edition Musicale

MIFED Mercato Internazionale del TV, Film e del Documentario

MIPCOM Marché International des Films et des Programmes pour la TV, la Vidéo, le Câble et le Satellite

MIP-TV Marché International de Programmes de Television

MoMA Museum of Modern Art (New York)

MOMI Museum of the Moving Image

MPA Motion Picture Association of America

MPEA Motion Picture Export Association of America

MU Musicians' Union

NAAS News Afro Asian Service

NATPE National Association of Television Programme Executives (now formally NATPE International)

NAVAL National Audio Visual Aids Library

NCET National Council for Educational Technology

NCVQ National Council for Vocational Qualifications

NFA National Film Archive

NFDF National Film Development Fund

NFFC National Film Finance Corporation

NFT National Film Theatre

NFTS National Film and Television School

NHMF National Heritage Memorial Fund

NUJ National Union of Journalists

NUT National Union of Teachers

NVALA National Viewers' and Listeners' Association

OAL Office of Arts and Libraries

PRS Performing Right Society

RAA Regional Arts Association

RACE Research and Development in Advanced Communication Technologies in Europe

RETRA Radio, Electrical and Television Retailers' Association

RFT Regional Film Theatre

RTS Royal Television Society

SCET Scottish Council for Educational Technology

SCFVL Scottish Central Film and Video Library

SCRIPT Support for CReative Independent Production Talent (aka European SCRIPT Fund)

SCTE Society of Cable Television Engineers

SFC Scottish Film Council

SFD Society of Film Distributors

SFX Special Effects

S4C Sianel Pedwar Cymru

SIFT Summary of Information on Film and Television

SMATV Satellite Master Antenna Television

TSW Television South West

TUG Television Users Group

TVRO Television receive-only

TVS Television South

UA United Artists

UIP United International Pictures

VCPS Video Copyright Protection Society

VCR Video Cassette Recorder

WGGB Writers' Guild of Great Britain

WTN Worldwide Television News

WTVA Wider Television Access

YTV Yorkshire Television

INDEX

A

APRS – The Professional
    Recording Association
    178
Abbreviations 298
Accountant, The 224
Act of Will 224
Advertising Association 178
Advertising Film and
    Videotape Producers'
    Association 178
Advertising Film Rights
    Society 178
After You've Gone 14
Air America 224
Alien Nation 248, *248*
Aliens 60
Amber 49
American Multi-Cinema 38
American Stories 34, 35, **248**
Amiel, Jon 47
Amis, Martin 47
Amundsen, Roald 48
Anglia Television 16, **272**
Apartment Zero 248, 249
Apollo Cinemas 41, 94
Archives/Libraries 68
Ariel 77, **248**
Artificial Eye 31, **132**
Arts Council of Great Britain
    178
Arts Council of Northern
    Ireland 178
Ashcroft, Peggy 72, *72*
Aspel, Michael 63
Association of Black Film and
    Video Workshops 178
Association of
    Cinematograph,
    Television and Allied
    Technicians 178
Association of Independent
    Cinemas 179
Association of Independent
    Producers (now
    Producers Association)
    21
Association of Professional
    Composers 179
Association of Professional
    Video Distributors 179
Astra 50, 60, 61
Atlantic Releasing 16
Attenborough, Sir Richard 4,
    4, 53, 72
Audio Visual Association 179
Australian Broadcasting
    Tribunal 51
Australian Film Commission
    179
Awards 70
  BAFTA 70
  BFI 72
  Berlin 72
  Broadcasting Press Guild 73
  Cannes 13, **73**
  Cesars 72
  Emmy 74
  European Film Awards 74
  Golden Globe 75
  Locarno 76
  Monte Carlo 76
  Montreux 77
  Moscow 77
  Oscars 22, 47, **77**
  Royal Television Society 78
  Venice 79

B

BBC see British Broadcasting
    Corporation
BET 54

BSB 33, 17, 20, 50, 51, 65, **92**
Back Home 224, 224
Ball-Trap on the Cote Sauvage
    224
Bamborough, Karin 17
Barnes, Carol 62
Barra, Francesca 20, 21
Batman 30, 31, *32*, 39, 48, *78*,
    249
Bear, The 30, *33*, **249**
Bearskin – An Urban Fairytale
    13, *224*
*Beatrix Potter – The Taylor of
    Gloucester* 224
Berlin Jerusalem 35
Bertolucci, Bernardo 17
Best of Blind Date, The 62
Betrayed 249, 249
Bevan, Tim 17
Beyond the Groove 25
Big Man, The 20, **225**
Black Audio 49, **132**
Blackadder 63
Blackadder Goes Forth 71
Blackeyes 13, 55, 64, 65
Bleasdale, Alan 62
Blore 225
Blue Dolphin 33, **132**
Blunkett, David 65
Bokóva, Jana 48
Bold and the Beautiful, The 65
Bond, Alan 51
Books, reference
  cinema 238
  television/video 240
Bookshops 80
Border Television 272
Botelho, João 48
Box Office 62
Box office, UK 25, 30
Box office – 10 top films in UK
    1989 34
Boys from the Blackstuff, The
    62
Branagh, Kenneth 48
Breakfast Time 62
Brideshead Revisited 61
British Academy of Film and
    Television Arts 179
British Academy of
    Songwriters,
    Composers and Authors
    179
British Amateur Television
    Club 179
British Board of Film
    Classification 30, 31,
    32, **179**
British Broadcasting
    Corporation 13, 17, 26,
    28, 32, 33, 50, 53, 55,
    56, 57, 61, 62, 63, 64,
    65, 180, **280**
BBC2 25th anniversary 50,
    62
BBC TV
  Children's Programmes
    281
  Community Programme
    Unit 281
  Continuing Education
    281
  Documentary Features
    281
  Drama Films 282
  Light Entertainment
    Comedy Programmes
    282
  Light Entertainment
    Variety 282
  Music and Arts 282
  News and Current Affairs
    61, **282**

  Programme Acquisition
    282
  Religious Programmes
    282
  Schools Broadcasting 283
  Science and Features 283
  Serials 283
  Series 284
  Sports and Events Group
    284
British Copyright Council 180
British Council 180
British Equity 180
British Federation of Film
    Societies 156, 180
  Constituent Groups 156
  Members of the BFFS 156
    Eastern 156
    Lincoln and Humberside
      157
    London 157
    Midlands 158
    North West 159
    Northern 160
    Scotland 160
    South West 161
    Southern 162
    Wales 164
    Yorkshire 164
British Film and Television
    Producers' Association
    (now Producers
    Association) 21
British Film Institute 4, 5, 20,
    30, 32, 180
  BFI Awards 72
  BFI Contacts 9
  BFI Distribution 7
  BFI Education 8
  BFI Facilities for People with
    Disabilities 10
  BFI Film Society Unit 6 (also
    see British Federation
    of Film Societies)
  BFI Library and Information
    Services 7
  BFI Museum of the Moving
    Image see BFI South
    Bank
  BFI National Film Archive **7**,
    68
  BFI National Film Theatre
    see BFI South Bank
  BFI New Directors
    Programme 49
  BFI Planning Unit 8
  BFI Production Board 9
  BFI Publishing Services 8
  BFI Regional Theatres 5, 7, 8,
    43
  BFI Research Division 8
    Education 8
    Periodicals 9
    Production 9
    Publishing Services 8
    TV and Projects Unit 8
  BFI South Bank 5
    Museum of the Moving
      Image 5, 6, *6*, 8, *8*
    National Film Theatre 5
  BFI Stills, Posters and
    Designs 6
British Film Partnership 21,
    22
British Kinematograph Sound
    and Television Society
    180
British Radio and Electronic
    Equipment
    Manufacturers'
    Association 180
British Satellite Broadcasting
    13, 17, 20, 50, 51, 65, **92**

British Screen Advisory Council 16, **180**
British Screen Finance (British Screen) 13, 16, 17, 20, 46, **181,**
British Tape Industry Association 181
British Universities Film and Video Council 181
British Videogram Association 181
Broadcasters' Audience Research Board 181
Broadcasting and Entertainment Trades Alliance 181
Broadcasting Bill 16, 20, 26, 28, 51, 53, 56, 61, 63
Broadcasting Complaints Commission 181
Broadcasting Press Guild 181
Broadcasting Research Unit 181
Broadcasting Standards Council 57, 63, **181**
Brown, Christy 48
Bryant, Michael 62
Buddy's Song 225
Building Sights 62
Bullseye! 225
Burnett, Sir Alastair 52, 53
Burrill, Tim 17
Business Daily 62

C

CAVIAR 36, 37
CBS/Fox Video 20, **286**
CFL Vision 181
CIA 53
Cable, UK franchise areas 82
Cable and satellite 82
Cable Authority 16, **182**
Cable companies 82
Cable Systems, Upgrade 87
Cable Television Association 182
Caine Mutiny Court Martial, The 32
Camden Town Boy 47
Camp de Thiaroye 32, **250**
Campaign for Press and Broadcasting Freedom 182
Campaign for Quality Television 51
Cannon 13, 36, 39, 41, **94**
Capital City 63
Care of Time, The 225
Carlton 53
Casa de Bernarda Alba, La 250, 250
Celia 250, *251*
Cello 225
Celtic Film and Television Authority 182
Central Independent Television 14, 16, **273**
Central Office of Information 182
Centre for the Study of Communication and Culture 182
Centrepoint 225
Changing Step 225
Channel 4 Daily 62
Channel 4 Television 7, 9, 13, 17, 26, 28, 32, 33, 53, 58, 61, 62, **274**
Channel 5 26, 50
Channel Television 273
Charities advertising on tv 57
Checkland, Michael 53, 55, 56, *56*

Chicago Joe and the Showgirl 17, *17,* **225**
Children, The 226
Children's Film and Television Foundation 182
Church of England Broadcasting Department 182
Cinema admissions 1984–88 37
Cinema and Television Benevolent Fund 182
Cinema and Television Veterans 182
Cinema and Video Industry Audience Research 36, 37
Cinema circuits 94
Cinema Exhibitors' Association of Great Britain and Ireland 182
Cinema going in the UK by age group 37
Cinema legislation 174
Cinema Paradiso 75, *75,* **251**
Cinema reference books 238
Cinema Theatre Association 44, **183**
Cinemas in the UK 94
  Channel Islands 107
  England 97
  London, West End – Premiere Run 94
  London, Outer 95
  Northern Ireland 109
  Scotland 107
  Wales 108
Circles of Deceit 226
Circuits, cinema 94
City of Sadness 79, 251
Club X 62, 64
Cohen, Larry 32
Cold Dog Soup 226
Cold Justice 226, *226*
Cold Light of Day 226, *226*
Collins, Pauline 47
Columbia 20, 31, 32, **133**
Come Home Charlie and Face Them 226
Comic Book Confidential 252, *252*
Commission of the European Communities 33
Commonwealth Broadcasting Association 183
Composers' Guild of Great Britain 183
Confederation of Entertainment Unions 183
Confessional 226
Conquest of the South Pole 48, **252**
Contacts at the BFI 9
Contemporary Films 31, **133**
Cook, The Thief, His Wife and Her Lover, The 13, 20, 48, 252
Coronet 44
Council of Regional Arts Associations 190
Courses, film and video 110
Critics' Circle 183
Crossing Delancey 252, *252*
Cry in the Dark, A 30, *30,* **252**
Crystal Maze 26
Curzon 17, 31, **133**

D

Daily Express 55
Dakota Road 22

Dancin' thru the Dark 47, **226,** 253
Dangerous Liaisons 31
Dark City 7 226
Dark River 226
Davies, Terence 49
Day Lewis, Daniel 48
Day·Lewis, Sean 8
De Mornay, Rebecca 47
Dead Calm 253, *253*
Dead Poets Society 30, 31, 70, **253**
Dead Sleep 226
Deaf Broadcasting Council 183
Dealers 47, **253**
Dear Sarah 227
December Bride 13, **227,** 227
Defence Press and Broadcasting Committee 183
Dench, Judi 62
Denham, Maurice 62
Denton, Charles 14, 20, *20*
Depardieu, Gérard 72
Department of Education and Science 183
Department of Trade and Industry 17, 30, 50, **183**
Designer and Arts Directors' Association 183
Dickens, Charles 48
Did You See...? 65
Directors' Guild of Great Britain 183
Disabilities, facilities at the BFI for people with 10
Distant Voices, Still Lives 9, 35
Distributors, film non-theatrical 126 theatrical 132
  UK market share of the 5 majors 35
Distributors, video 286
d'Morais, Joe 33
Doombeach 227
Douglas, Bill 49
Dramarama – Just Wild about Harry 227
Dressmaker, The 35
Driving Miss Daisy 77, **254**
Drôle d'endroit 254, *254*
Drowning by Numbers 35
DV8 64, *64*

E

Eady Levy 25
East Midland Arts 190
Eastern Arts 190
Edge of Darkness, The 61
Education – film and television 110
Educational Broadcasting Services, BBC 183
Educational Television Association 183
8½ 32
1871 13, **227,** *227*
Electric Cinema 44
Electric Pictures 31, 35, **133**
Electrical Electronic Telecommunications and Plumbing Union 183
Elliott, Denholm 13
Elstree 16, 20, **270**
Eminent Domain 227
Enemy of the People, An 254, *255*
Engel, Andi 47
English-language film and TV periodicals 241

English-language satellite channels in Europe 92
Entertainment 31, **133**
Erik the Viking 46, **254,** *254*
European Broadcasting Union 61
European co-productions 48
European Film Awards 183
European Film Distribution Office 33, 34, 35
European Script Fund 14, **183**
European Year of Film and Television 17
Eurosport 60, 61, **92**
Euston 16
Everybody Wins 13
Exile 14
Eyles, Allen 36

F

FIAF 68
FIAF Publications 241
FIAT 68
Fabulous Baker Boys, The 254, *255*
Facilities, film and video *136*
Family 227
Feature film production, average costs of 13
Feature film production – total investment in national product 22
Feature films produced 1984–9, number of 21
Feature films started in the UK in 1989–90 224
Feature films theatrically released in the UK 1989–90 248
Feature films theatrically released in the UK 1989/90, country of origin of 33
Federation Against Copyright Theft 183
Federation of Broadcasting Unions 184
Federation of Commercial Audio-visual Libraries 184
Federation of Film Unions 184
Fellow Traveller 47, **254**
Feminist Library and Information Centre 184
Festival awards, see awards
Festivals, film and video 148
Ffilm Cymru 17, **184**
Field, The 20, **227,** *227*
Field of Dreams 254, *255*
Fifteen Streets, The 227
Film and television courses 110
Film and Television Lighting Contractors Association 184
Film archives 68
Film Artistes' Association 184
Film awards see Awards
Film courses 110
Film distributors non-theatrical 126 theatrical 132
Film Education 184
Film festivals 184
Film Industry Council 184
Film laboratories 173
Film Network 43
Film production companies 206
Film schools 110
Film societies 156
Film studios 270
Film workshops 290

Films Act 1985 30
Films (features) started in the UK in 1989–90 224
Films (features) theatrically released in the UK 1989–90 248
Financial Times 51
First Film Foundation 16, **184**
Fish Called Wanda, A 30, 46, 47
Fishing Trip, The 227
Fly, The 60
Fool, The 228, *228*
Fools of Fortune 14, 17, 228
For Queen and Country 14
Foreword 4
Fragments of Isabella 228
Francis, Freddie 48
Frankenstein's Baby 228
French Revolution 62
Fricker, Brenda 48
Fugitive Films 16
Fujisankei 20
Furst, Anton 48

G

Gala 32, **133**
Gallery 43
Ganashatru 255, *255*
Georgette Meunier 35
German Film Board 184
Get Back 228
Ghost in Monte Carlo, A 228
Glencross, David 52
Glory 48, **255**
Goldblum, Jeff 47
Goldeneye 228, *228*
Government film and television policy 25
Grade, Michael 61
Grampian Television 274
Granada Television 13, 16, 17, 20, 48, 51, 53, 57, **275**
Grant, Richard E 13, 46
Greater London Arts 190
Greenaway, Peter 13, 48
Guardian Lectures 6
Guild 31, **134**
Guild of Animation 184
Guild of British Camera Technicians 184
Guild of British Film Editors 185
Guild of Television Cameramen 185

H

HTV 16, **275**
Hale & Pace 77
HandMade 14, **134**
Hanussen 32, **255**
Harbour Beat 228
Hard News 61, *61*
Hard Road 256
Hard Times 48, **256**
Hardware 228
Hare, David 14, 48
Heathers 256, *256*
Henry V 20, *22*, 48, **256**, *256*
Hidden Agenda 229
High Hopes 75
Histoires d'Amérique 35, **256**
Home Office 51, 63, **185**
Hopkins, John 62
Hotel du Paradis 48, **256**
House Committee on Un-American Activities 47
House of Bernarda Alba, The 250, 256
Houses of Commons and Lords 58, *58*, 63

How to Get Ahead in Advertising 47, **256**
Hypotheticals 57

I

ICA 31, **134**
ITN 53, 55, 61, 62, **275**
ITV 7, 13, 16, 20, 26, 47, 51, 52, 53, 57, 58, 62, 63
I Bought a Vampire Motorcycle 229, *229*
I Hired a Contract Killer 229
I Miei Primi 40 Anni 32, **256**
I'm Gonna Get You Sucka 256, 257
Imperial War Museum *68*, **185**
Impromptu 229
In Fading Light 49, **257**
Incorporated Society of British Advertisers 185
Incorporated Society of Musicians 185
Independent Broadcasting Authority 50, 52, 57, **185**
Independent Film Distributors' Association 185
Independent Programme Producers' Assocation 185
Independent Television Association 9, **185**
Independent Television Commission 52, 53
Independent television companies 272
Independent Television News 53, 55, 61, 62, **275**
Indexes to film and television periodicals 246
Indian Video Association 185
Indiana Jones and the Last Crusade 32, **257**, *257*
Institute of Manpower Studies 21
Institute of Practitioners in Advertising 185
International Association of Broadcasting Manufacturers 185
International Federation of Film Archives (FIAF) 68
FIAF Publications 241
International Federation of Television Archives 68
International Federation of the Phonographic Industry 186
International Institute of Communications 186
International sales agents 166
International Video Enterprise 14
International Visual Communications Association 186
Island Pictures 16

J

J Paul Getty Jnr Conservation Centre 7
Jekyll and Hyde 229, *229*
Jivani, Alkarim 60
JOBFIT 26
Jones, Terry 46
Johnston, Sheila 46
Jupiter Moon 65

K

Kappatoo 229
Kaurismaki, Aki 32
Kennedy, Ludovic 65
Killing Dad 13, *19, 19, 46*, **257**
King of the Wind 229
Kiss Before Dying, A 230, *230*
Korff, Ira 39
Krays, The 17, **230**, *230*
Kremlin Farewell, The 230
Krótki Film o Milósci 258, *258*

L

LA Law 74
Laboratories 173
Ladder of Swords 258
Land before Time, The 258, *258*
Landscape in the Mist 78, 258
Last Emperor, The 17
Last Exit to Brooklyn 258, 259
Late Show, The 62, 64
Lawley, Sue 63
Lawrence, D. H. 49
Lawrence of Arabia 32, 33
Legislation 174
cinema 174
television 176
Lethal Weapon 2 32, **258**
Letze Ausfahrt Brooklyn 258, 259
Lhoest, Holde 35
Libraries, film and television 68
Licence to Kill 30, 31, **258**
Life is a Long Quiet River 35, **258**
Lifestyle 61, **92**
Lincolnshire and Humberside Arts 190
Lodge, David 63
London Film Festival 6, 154
London Screenwriters' Workshop 186
London Weekend Television 16, 62, 64, **276**
Lynch, David 32

M

MCA 38
MGM/UA 31
MIP-TV 35
MTV 61
MacKinnon, Gillies 48
Madly in Love 230
Magazines 241
Mainline 31, **134**
Maisel, Ileen 21
Malcolm, Derek 33
Malevolence 230
Manifesto Film Sales 14
March, The 231
Marie Curie Cancer Care 57, *57*
Mason, Margery 62
Matheson, Margaret 20
Maxwell, Robert 61
Mechanical Copyright Protection Society 186
Media Monitoring Unit 55
MEDIA 92 14, 25, 35
MEDIA 95 26
Media Show, The 46
Media Team of the Volunteer Centre UK 186
Medusa 31, **287**
Meek, Scott 20, *20*
Megahey, Leslie 63
Melancholia 13, 35, 47, **259**, 259
Mellor, David 51, 52

Memphis Belle 16, *16*, **231**, *231*
Mental Health Film Council 186
Merseyside Arts 190
Metro Pictures 31, **134**
Miramax 14
Missing Persons 231
Monk, The 231, *231*
Monkey Shines 259, *259*
Monopolies and Mergers Commission Report on Restrictive Practices in the Entertainment Industry 55
Monthly Film Bulletin 9, 30, 32, 50
Moon over Parador 259
Morahan, Christopher 17
Morphine and Dolly Mixtures 231, *231*
Moulin 41
Mujeres al Borde de un Ataque de Nervios 32, **259**
Multiplexes 25, 36, 37, 38, 39, 41, 43
Multiplexes Opened in the UK 1989–90 38
Murdoch, Rupert 50, 51, 60
Museum of the Moving Image 5, 6, *6*, 8, 8
Music, Film and Video Producers' Association 186
Music Publishers' Association 186
Musicians' Union 186
My Beautiful Laundrette 14
My First 40 Years 32, **259**
My Left Foot 17, 48, **259**

N

National Amusements 38, 39, **94**
National Association for Higher Education in Film and Video 186
National Audiovisual Aids Centre and Library 186
National Campaign for the Arts 196
National Council for Educational Technology 186
National Film and Television School 26, **188**
National Film Archive **6**, 68
National Film Development Fund 188
National Film Theatre 5, 188
National Union of Journalists 188
National Viewers' and Listeners' Association 188
Network of Workshops 188
New Line Cinema 14
Newman, Andrea 65
News and photo agencies 200
News International 50, 60
News '39 63
Newshounds 231
Newsnight 62
Newsreel, production and stockshot libraries 68
Nice Work 63
Nicholas, David 53, *53*
Nightbreed 13, *14*
Nightmare Years 232
Nilsen, Dennis 65
Nina Against the Rest 65
1996 232
Northern Arts 190

North West Arts
Not the Nine O'Clock News 62
Nuns on the Run 12, 13, **232**, 232

O

Oasis 31, **134**
Object of Beauty, The 232
Odeon 41, 43, 44
Office of Arts and Libraries 188
Office of Fair Trading 57, **188**
Old Flames 232
Omnibus 63
One Day in the Life of Television 8, 63
One Man's War 232
Oranges are not the only Fruit 64
Organisations 178
Oscars 22, 48, **77**
Othello 232
Other Cinema, The (now Metro) 31
Outpost 233, 233

P

Palace 13, 14, 20, 26, 30, 31, **134**, 216
Paper Mask 17, **233**, 233
Paradise Club, The 28
Paramount 20, 30, 31, 38
Parenthood 260, 260
Parents 260, 260
Paris By Night 48, **260**
Parkfield Entertainment 16, **134**
Parliament, televising of 63
Pat Garrett and Billy the Kid 32
Pathé 31,
Peacock Report 26
Peat Marwick McLintock 55
Pelle the Conqueror 260, *261*
Pennies from Heaven 65
Pentecost 233
Perfect Hero, A 233
Performers' Alliance 188
Performing Rights Society 188
Periodicals
    English language film, tv, video and cable 241
    Foreign language film 245
    Indexes to film and television periodicals 246
Personal Services 14
Petley, Julian 30
Philosoph, Der 35
Phoenix Hall 233
Phonographic Performance 188
Pick Up Artist 32
Pied Piper 233
Pinewood 16, 20, **270**
Piravi 76, **261**
Plaff! or Too Afraid of Life 261, *261*
Play Me Something 9, 13, 261
Policy Studies Institute 36
PolyGram 17
Potter, Dennis 55, 64, 65
Powell, Jonathan 63
Powergen *56*, 57
Premier Releasing (now Castle Premier Releasing) 31, 132
Press contacts for film, tv, video and broadcasting 194
    News and photo agencies 200

Newspapers and journals 194
Preview theatres 204
    Radio 200
    Television 200
Price is Right, The 60, *61*
Prime Minister's Seminar on the Film Industry 25
Private Life, A **233**, 260
Producers Association 21, **188**
Production companies 206
Production facilities, film and video 136
Proms, The 57
Publications 238
Puja, Puja 233
Puttnam, David 20, 26

Q

Queen of Hearts 35, **261**
Question Time 62

R

Rachel Papers, The 47, **261**
Radio, Electrical and Television Retailers' Association 188
Radio 4 55, 56
Radio Tele Veronique 63
Radio Telefis Eirann 21
Radio Times 56
Rainbow, The 49, **261**
Rainbow Thief, The 234
Rainman 32
Rank Organisation 13, 17, 52, 31, 39, 41, 43, 94, 134
Read, Sir John 17
Recorded Releasing (now Oasis) 31
Reefer and the Model 34, 35, 261
Rees-Mogg, Lord 57
Reference books
    cinema 238
    television/video 240
Reflecting Skin, The 16, 17, **234**, 234
Regional Arts Associations 190
Regional film collections 68
Regional Film Theatres 5, 7, 8, 43
Reisz, Karel 13
Releases 248
Relph, Simon 13, 14, 16, 17
Renaissance Films 21
Renton, Timothy 51
Resurrected 34, 35, **261**
Return of Swamp Thing, The 262, *262*
Return of the Musketeers, The 13, **262**, 262
Return to Salem's Lot 32
Revenge of Billy the Kid 234
Riches, Ian 38
Ridley, Philip 17
Rive, Kenneth 32
Robin Hood 47
Robinson, Bruce 47
Roland Rat 62
Rosencrantz and Guildenstern are Dead 234
Rouge 262, *266*
Royal Television Society 189
Rush, Christopher 49
Russell, Ken 49
Russell, Willy 47
Russia House, The 234
Russicum 32, **262**

S

S4C 276

Sale of the Century 60
Sales agencies, film 166
Sandy's Day 234
Saracen 58
Satellite and cable companies 82
Satellite and cable television 50, 51, 53, 63
Satellite-delivered television channels in Europe 92
Saville, Philip 47
Scandal 13, 14, 31
Scott, Selina 65
Scottish Film Council 189
Scottish Film Production Fund 189
Scottish Film Training Trust 189
Scottish Television 16, **276**
Screen International 22, 30, 31
Screen Sport 61
Sea of Love 262, *263*
Second World War 63
Secret Life of Ian Fleming, The 234
Secret Weapon 234
Sense of Guilt, A 62, 65
Senyora, La 35, 262
Serious Money 47
sex, lies and videotape 31, **262**
Shadow Makers 262, *263*
Sharpe, Tom 46
Shell Seekers, The 76, 234
Sheltering Sky, The 17, 22, **234**, 235
Shepperton 16, 20, **270**
Sheridan, Jim 48
She's Been Away 79, 235
Shirley Valentine 20, 21, 30, 47, **262**
Shivas, Mark 13
Shochiku-Fuji 20
Shooting Stars 235
Short Film about Love, A 258, 262
Showcase 38, 39
Sight and Sound 9
Silent Scream 9, *9*, 72, **235**
Silver, Ron 47
Singin' in the Rain 7
Singing Detective, The 47
Sissons, Peter 55, *55*
Skulduggery 234
Sky Channel 47, 50, 53, 60, 65, **93**
Skye, Ione 47
Smack and Thistle 235
Smith, Mel 47
Smith, W. H. 61
Smoking Mirror 235
Society of Authors' Broadcasting Committee 189
Society of Cable Television Engineers 189
Society of Film Distributors 189
Society of Television Lighting Directors 189
Sony 20
South Bank Show, The 65
South East Arts 190
South West Arts 190
Southern Arts 190
Sovexport Film 189
Sparrow, The 14
Specialised goods and services 268
Splendor 32, **263**
Sponsorship and tv 57
Stock shot libraries 68
Stevenson, Wilf 5

Strange Place to Meet, A 254, 263
Strapless 16, 48, **263**
Studios, film 270
Summary of Information on Film and Television 7
Summer Lease 63
Sun, The 50, 60
Sunday Times 57

T

TECX 58
TSW – Television South West 277
TV Times 56
TV-am 62, **277**
TVS 277
Talking to a Stranger 62
Tall Guy, The 47, 263
Telefilm Canada 189
Television audiences 50
Television awards see Awards
Television companies 272
Television franchise auction 12, 51, 52, 53
Television legislation 176
Television schools 110
Television, top 20 programmes 1989 65
Tempos difíceis este tempo 35, 48, **263**
Testament 49, **264**, 264
Thames Television 53, **278**
That Summer of White Roses 264, 264
Thatcher, Margaret 25, 62, 64
They Never Slept 235
Thin Blue Line, The 264, 264
Thomas, Jeremy 13, 17, 20
Times, The 50, 58
Toback, James 32
Today 50
Torch Song Trilogy 265, 265
Touchstone 31
Trade organisations 178
Traviata, La 65
Treasure Island 235, 235
Trop belle pour toi! 73, **265**
Tumbledown 78
Twentieth Century-Fox 20, 30, **135**
Twickenham 16, 20, **270**
Twin Peaks 32
Tyne Tees Television 17, **279**
Tyson, Mike *52*, 53

U

UIP 31, 32, **135**
Ulster Television 279
United International Pictures 31, 32, **135**
Universal 31
Upgrade Cable Systems 87

V

Valentine Falls 236
Variety Artistes Ladies and Children's Guild 188
Variety Club of Great Britain 190
Veiled One, The 235, 235
Venus Peter 13, 49, **265**, 265
Verotique 63
Vestron 31, 135
Video, films released on 32
Video labels 286
Video Trade Association 190
Video workshops 290
Vie est belle, La 32, **265**
Vie est un long fleuve tranquille, La 35, 35, **265**

Vierny, Sacha 12
Virgin Vision 31, **135**
Voice of the Listener 190

W

Wall Street 47
Walsh, Steve 17
Walt Disney 51
Walters, Julie 13
Wanted: Margery and Oliver 236
Warner Bros 31, 39, 94, **135**
Washington, Denzil 14
Welsh Arts Council 190
Welsh Channel 4 see S4C
West Midlands Arts 190
What the Papers Say 57, *57*, 61
When Harry Met Sally... 31, 31, **266**, *266*
When Love Dies 236
Who Framed Roger Rabbit? 31
Wider Television Access 190
Wilt 13, 31, 47, 236, **266**
Winterson, Jeanette 64
Wish You Were Here 14
Withnail and I 47
Woffinden, Bob 50
Women in Tropical Places 236, 236
Women on the Verge of a Nervous Breakdown 32, *32* **266**
Women's Media Action Group 190
Woodward, John 25
Work Experience 49
Working Title 14, 17, **222**
Workshops, film and video 290
Writers' Guild of Great Britain 190

Y

Yanzhi Kou 266, *266*
Yellowthread Street 58, *58*
Yes Minister 62
Yorkshire Arts 190
Yorkshire Television 280
Young Einstein 30, **266**
Young Musician of the Year 57

Z

Zenith 14, 20, 28, **222**